China among Equals

China among Equals

THE MIDDLE KINGDOM
AND ITS NEIGHBORS,
10TH–14TH CENTURIES

EDITED BY MORRIS ROSSABI

University of California Press—Berkeley · Los Angeles · London

University of California Press
Berkeley and Los Angeles, California
University of California Press, Ltd.
London, England
© 1983 by
The Regents of the University of California
Composition in Hong Kong by
Asco Trade Typesetting Ltd.
Printed in the United States of America
1   2   3   4   5   6   7   8   9

Library of Congress Cataloging in Publication Data
Main entry under title:
China among equals
   Revised papers from a conference held in
Issaquah, Wash., July 1978.
   Bibliography: p.
   Includes index.
   1. China—Foreign relations—To 1644.   2. China—
History—960–1644.   I. Rossabi, Morris.
DS750.82.C46   951′.02   81-11486
ISBN 0-520-04383-9   AACR2
ISBN 0-520-04562-9 (pbk.)

Contents

PART III
Institutions for Foreign Relations in the Multi-State System

PART IV
Foreign Lands and the Sung

PART V
The Mongol Hegemony

Maps

Contributors

Thomas Allsen (Ph.D., University of Minnesota) teaches Asian history at Trenton State College. He specializes in the history of the Mongol empire and has written articles in *Ming Studies*, *Sung Studies*, and other journals.

Herbert Franke received his doctorate from the University of Cologne and is Professor Emeritus of Far Eastern Studies at the University of Munich, and President of the Bavarian Academy of Sciences. He has written extensively on the history and culture of the dynasties of conquest in China. Among his numerous publications is *Geld und Wirtschaft in China unter der Mongolenherrschaft*.

Gari Ledyard (Ph.D., Berkeley) teaches Korean history and East Asian studies and is Chairman of the Department of East Asian Languages and Cultures at Columbia University. He is the author of *The Dutch Come to Korea* and other studies on East Asian history.

Luciano Petech (Ph.D., Rome) teaches Tibetan and East Asian history at the University of Rome. The author of *China and Tibet in the Early 18th Century*, he has written numerous specialized works on Tibet.

Charles Peterson (Ph.D., University of Washington) is an Associate Professor of History at Cornell University. He has contributed to the *Cambridge History of China: Sui and T'ang* and *Perspectives on the T'ang*.

Igor de Rachewiltz (Ph.D., Australian National University) is Senior Research Fellow at the Australian National University. He has published works on the Mongol era, including *Papal Envoys to the Great Khans*, and is translating *The Secret History of the Mongols* in the *Papers on Far Eastern History* (1971–80).

Michael Rogers (Ph.D., Berkeley) teaches Korean history at the University of California, Berkeley. He has written extensively on Koryŏ's relations with the Chin, Liao, and Sung dynasties.

Morris Rossabi (Ph.D., Columbia) teaches East Asian and Central Asian history at Case Western Reserve University. Author of *China and Inner Asia* and specialized publications on Chinese, Muslims, and Central Asian history, he is preparing a book-length biography of Khubilai Khan.

Shiba Yoshinobu studied Chinese economic history at the University of Tokyo and is now Professor of History at Osaka University and a Research Fellow of the Toyo Bunko. One of his influential works has been translated into English as *Commerce and Society in Sung China*.

Tao Jing-shen (Ph.D., Indiana University) teaches Chinese history at the University of Arizona. His latest book is *The Jurchen in Twelfth-Century China*.

Wang Gungwu (Ph.D., University of London) is Professor of Far Eastern history and Director of the Research School of Pacific Studies at the Australian National University. He is serving as President of the Australian Academy of the Humanities. His numerous publications include *The Structure of Power in North China during the Five Dynasties*.

Edmund Worthy (Ph.D., Princeton University) was formerly Assistant Director of the American Historical Association and is Assistant Director of the National Council on the Aging. He has pursued research on the Five Dynasties Period.

Note on Transliteration

The transliteration of Mongol follows the system developed by A. Mostaert in his *Dictionnaire Ordos* (Peking, 1941) as modified by Francis W. Cleaves in his articles in the *Harvard Journal of Asiatic Studies*. The only deviations for this volume are these:

> č is ch
> š is sh
> γ is gh
> q is kh
> ǰ is j

The Wade-Giles system is used to romanize Chinese except for such commonly accepted romanizations as Peking and Sian.

The contributors to this volume have used different editions of the dynastic histories. Each edition is cited in the footnotes and the bibliography.

Preface

This book is a product of a conference on "Multi-State Relations in East Asia, 10th—14th Centuries" held in Issaquah, Washington, in July 1978. Under a grant from the Committee on the Study of Chinese Civilization of the American Council of Learned Societies, seventeen scholars from the United States, Japan, Australia, Great Britain, Italy, and Germany met at the Providence Heights Conference Center to present preliminary papers and to discuss and criticize these essays. The papers were subsequently revised in light of the discussions and critiques offered during the conference. The editor, with the approval of the writers, then made emendations in the papers. They are presented here in their revised forms.

Many individuals contributed to the success of the conference. Professors Herbert Franke, Gari Ledyard, and Charles Peterson helped the editor to plan the conference, to define the themes to be addressed at our sessions, and to work out the list of participants. They offered countless invaluable suggestions during the two years that elapsed between the planning sessions and the actual meetings. Each of them also wrote a paper for the conference. The editor and the other participants are grateful for all their efforts. Professors Hok-lam Chan of the University of Washington, Keith Pratt of the University of Durham, and Klaus Tietze of the University of Munich attended most of the sessions and made use of their extraordinary knowledge of the sources and the history of the period to foster discussion. S. Bills and Thomas Allsen served as rapporteurs for the conference. Their summaries of the discussions proved invaluable in the revision and editing of the papers. Mrs. Mary Jevnikar and Ms. Doris Tomburello retyped many of the papers and helped the editor to complete the myriad chores needed to produce the final manuscript.

Professor E. I. Kychanov of Leningrad, who had intended to participate in the conference, was unable, at the last moment, to attend. His paper reached me after the conference was concluded and proved extremely useful in the revision of the papers.

The planners convened the conference to bring together a group of scholars who had recently begun to study the foreign relations of traditional China. The last major collaborative study of Chinese foreign relations, which was published as *The Chinese World Order* edited by John K. Fairbank (Harvard University Press, 1968), dealt primarily with Ming and Ch'ing China. It provided invaluable insights into the aims and operation of Chinese foreign relations in late imperial times. Some of the contributors to the volume subsequently pursued their research and eventually issued important monographs in this field. Thus the work has stimulated and will continue to stimulate studies of Chinese foreign relations. We hope that the present volume will promote similar such studies of the period for which we have done some preliminary research.

I should say a word about the editing. I have tried to make the volume of use to both the scholar and the general educated reader. I have eschewed documentary overkill. With the consent of the authors, I have deleted portions of the papers which served simply as additional confirmation of a point or a theme already illustrated. The size of a few of the essays has thus been considerably reduced. Scholars who wish to consult the original unedited versions of the texts will find them in the East Asiatic libraries at the University of California (Berkeley), the University of Chicago, and Columbia, Harvard, Princeton, Stanford, and Yale Universities, and other major research centers.

Introduction

MORRIS ROSSABI

China's views of foreigners and of foreign relations have intrigued Westerners from the onset of Sino-Western relations. Imperial China's treatment of foreigners was unique, so that this interest is understandable. Westerners in the nineteenth and twentieth centuries were fascinated by the conduct of traditional Chinese foreign relations. They found Chinese attitudes bizarre, and in their writings they occasionally exaggerated the peculiarity of the Chinese system. They also assumed that the Chinese dynasties had uniformly and rigidly applied this system of foreign relations from the Han dynasty (206 B.C – A.D. 220) on, an assumption that is challenged by the essays in this book.

The Chinese originally developed this structure of foreign relations partly as a defense mechanism. By the time of the Han dynasty, if not earlier, the peoples and tribes to the north raided Chinese territory. They attacked not because they were naturally bellicose or unnaturally aggressive but because they needed Chinese products. Most of them depended on animals for their livelihood: they were hunters, fishermen, or, most important, pastoral nomads. Insufficient grass, caused by drought or early frost, or disease among their animals precipitated a crisis. In order to survive in such times, the pastoral nomads required goods from China. They needed grain, craft or manufactured articles, and textiles. In later times, they also developed a craving for Chinese tea, medicines, salt, and other commodities. When China attempted to limit trade, its northern neighbors attacked Chinese border settlements to obtain by force goods they could not secure peacefully. Trade or raid seemed to be the only options in their relations with China.

China could not easily counter these attacks. After such raids, the nomads simply fled to the northern steppelands, and Chinese troops, lacking adequate supply lines, often could not pursue the elusive enemy

1

cavalry, which also had the advantage of knowledge of the terrain. Moreover, "long wars damaged the Chinese [agrarian] economy, but did not exhaust the nomadic or oasis economies of most Inner Asian peoples." [1] A few Chinese dynasties, such as the Han and the T'ang (618–906), sought to and sometimes did conquer the adjacent nomadic peoples, but their gains were short-lived. As they declined, they were forced to retreat from the steppes. Most of the weaker dynasties could not impose their own rule on the inhabitants of the steppe and forest lands and had to find a different way of dealing with these potentially powerful and dangerous adversaries.

They developed a unique system of foreign relations. Starting with the assumption that their civilization was the most advanced in the world, they devised a scheme which demanded acknowledgement of their superiority. The Chinese asserted that they had a sophisticated culture and written language and had built magnificent cities and palaces, all of which their neighbors lacked. Thus it appeared to the Chinese that their neighbors to the north were uncivilized, crude, intractable, and occasionally treacherous; in short, they were "barbarians." As good Confucians, the Chinese ought, through their own example of creating an orderly society, to encourage foreigners to "come and be transformed" (lai-hua).

The Chinese emperor, who had a Mandate of Heaven to rule his own people, was a vital link to the "barbarians." His conduct inspired them to seek the benefits of Chinese culture. His "virtuous action was believed to attract irresistibly the barbarians who were outside the pale of Chinese civilization proper." [2] His benevolence, compassion, and generosity would serve as a model for foreign rulers and would draw them and their people closer to China. They would naturally accept the superiority of the Chinese.

The ideal vehicle for relations with foreigners was the tribute system. In order to deal with the Chinese, foreign rulers were required to send tribute embassies periodically to the Chinese emperor. When an embassy reached the Chinese border, Chinese officials immediately took charge and accompanied the foreign envoys to the capital. The Chinese government bore all the expenses of the embassy during its stay in China. Its officials taught the envoys the proper etiquette for their appearance at court. After the envoys had been properly coached, they had an audience with the emperor. They performed the rituals, including the kotow, a symbolic recognition of their inferiority and, more important, of their acknowledgment of their status as envoys of a "vassal" state or tribe. Their conduct at court implied that their ruler was subordinate to the emperor. Once they concluded this ritual, the emperor summoned them closer to the throne for a brief conversation. [3] Then they offered their tribute of native goods to him, and he, in turn, bestowed valuable gifts upon them and their ruler. The audience ended, and the envoys then had three to five days to trade with Chinese merchants.

The Chinese, in theory, controlled this relationship. They determined the frequency with which embassies could be admitted into China, the number of men in each embassy, and the length of its stay in the Middle Kingdom. Court officials supervised the foreigners' trade with merchants, regulating the prices and profits and ensuring that neither side exploited the other.

The court contended that it did not gain from such tribute and trade relations. China was self-sufficient. The gifts from the foreigners to the court and the goods they offered to Chinese merchants were superfluous. Nothing essential to China was obtained from the foreigners. On the other hand, the Chinese products granted to the foreigners were vital and valuable.[4] Though the court appeared to be bribing the foreigners, Chinese officials hesitated to describe the relationship in these terms. They could use the threat of a suspension of trade and tribute to bring obstreperous foreigners in line.[5] The court willingly suspended trade and tribute, since pecuniary gain was not its principal objective. Profit did not, in this view, motivate Chinese officialdom. Defense and maintenance of the traditional Chinese system were the paramount considerations.

As additional reinforcements for this system of foreign relations, the Chinese court imposed other demands. It required foreign vassals to accept the Chinese calendar and to use a seal from China in missives to the court. New rulers in neighboring regions were expected to travel to China to be enfeoffed by the emperor. Only then would the Chinese consider the ruler properly invested. Foreign monarchs, even the grandest potentates, would need to address the emperor as their superior and themselves as his subordinates. The emperor would, in turn, reward them for their loyalty with generous gifts, honors, and titles.

Other than this perfunctory relationship, the Chinese court was, according to traditional theory, uninterested in foreign lands. The leading officials knew very little about conditions in neighboring countries, not to mention far-off regions. They appeared to be proud of their ignorance of foreign customs and institutions. Only unusual or bizarre foreign practices attracted their attention. Strange bathing customs or tattooing of the body by foreigners were, on occasion, mentioned in the Chinese accounts, but the native beliefs and politics were scarcely noticed. The Chinese court lacked expertise in foreign affairs and showed scant concern for developing such proficiency.

It seems surprising that foreigners, some of whom were China's military equals, should accept an inferior status in dealings with the Middle Kingdom. One likely explanation is that they profited enormously from tribute and trade with China. The lavish gifts they received from the emperor and the essential goods they obtained in trade with Chinese merchants compensated for the less than exalted position they occupied in their relations with China. The peoples on China's periphery acquiesced to the Chinese system as long as they secured the products they needed. Only when China sought to limit or eliminate trade did they renounce the system and use their armies to challenge the Chinese hegemony. Another explanation for the acquiescence of foreign rulers is that investiture by the Chinese emperor "doubtless enhanced the prestige of the tribal ruler among his own and neighboring tribes."[6] Such Chinese support could be extremely useful to a new ruler, particularly one who faced rivals or opposition within his own land.

In sum, the tribute system enabled China to devise its own world order. The Chinese court dealt with foreigners on its own terms. Equality with China was ruled out. The court could not conceive of international relations. It could not accept other states or tribes as equals. Foreign rulers and their envoys were treated as subordinates or inferiors. The court would not tolerate rulers who did not abide by its world order. It refused entry into China to those who rejected its system of foreign relations. The Chinese emperor was not merely *primus inter pares*. He was the Son of Heaven, the undisputed leader of the peoples of East Asia, if not the world.

The conventional wisdom is that China preserved this system from the second century B.C. until the middle of the nineteenth century. Westerners were, however, unwilling to accept the system. Like China's immediate neighbors, they sought trade with the Chinese. Unlike the peoples of East Asia, they rejected a relationship in which they and their rulers appeared subservient to the Chinese. The opposing views of the Chinese and the Westerners led to misunderstandings and clashes, culminating in the Opium War of 1839–1842. After winning the war, the British dictated a peace treaty which undermined traditional Chinese foreign relations. China was no longer to be the center of the world and to demand that other states recognize it as superior. It could not impose its own view of foreign relations. The Chinese court was forced to concede that all states were to be treated as equals.

The papers in this volume suggest that the so-called Chinese world order, which has just been briefly described, did not persist for the entire period from the second century B.C. to the Opium War. From the tenth to the thirteenth centuries, China did not dogmatically enforce its system of foreign relations. The Sung (960–1279), the principal dynasty during that era, was flexible in its dealing with foreigners. Its officials, recognizing the military weakness of the dynasty, generally adopted a realistic foreign policy. They could not demand that foreigners adhere to a Chinese-imposed scheme of conducting foreign relations. Some of the "barbarian" rulers had already seized Chinese territory and could threaten more land if a new agreeable settlement between them and the Sung was not reached.

China's weakness was apparent much before the Sung. As early as the middle of the eighth century, Chinese military power had waned. In 751 an Arab army had routed a Chinese force at the Talas River in Central Asia, leading shortly thereafter to the Islamization of the region and to the diminution of Chinese influence there. In the same year, the state of Nan-chao, located in the modern province of Yunnan, compelled the Chinese to withdraw from the southwest. These defeats at the hands of foreigners presaged a much more serious domestic revolt against the ruling T'ang dynasty. In 755 An Lu-shan, a general in the T'ang army, rebelled. The T'ang, after some embarrassing defeats, finally crushed the revolt, but the dynasty's success was based upon the support of foreign armies, notably those of a Turkic-speaking group centered in Mongolia and known as the Uighurs.[7] T'ang emperors from this time on relied on foreign troops to maintain their rule. Their own forces had deteriorated drastically since the glorious days of Emperors T'ai-tsung (r. 626–649) and Kao-tsung (r. 649–683), whose armies had routed the opposition as far east as Korea and as far west as Central Asia. Regional Commanders (*chieh-tu shih*) also challenged the authority of the late T'ang rulers. By the ninth century, these local military governors, who were often foreigners, dominated their regions and did not permit interference from the central government.[8] Lacking the power to enforce its will even on its own officials, the T'ang gradually declined. While the early T'ang could have demanded that "barbarians" entering China abide by its distinctive system of foreign relations, the later T'ang, which depended on foreign troops for its survival, could not. Rebellions erupted in the middle of the ninth century, and the dynasty finally collapsed in 907.

China had no true central government for the ensuing half century. Ten Kingdoms, whose monarchs were generally Chinese, ruled South China, and Five Dynasties, whose potentates were usually of foreign origin, governed North China.[9] Farther north, a new and powerful nomadic pastoral group from southern Manchuria known as the Khitans had set up a few agricultural settlements, had established a Chinese-style dynasty, the Liao, and had occupied sixteen prefectures which had previously been part of China, including the area of modern Peking. They had their own emperor, who challenged the supremacy of the emperors and kings in China proper. There were, in short, numerous rulers who claimed to be the Son of Heaven. No single claimant gained the allegiance of the Chinese people, not to mention the respect of foreign potentates.

The attendant confusion doubtless disrupted the traditional system of foreign relations. There was no emperor who had the clearcut support of the rulers of the smaller states. Each pursued his own interest with little concern for loyalty to anyone else's Mandate of Heaven. Allegiances were constantly changing. Chu Wen, who actually deposed the T'ang and founded the Later Liang dynasty, at first had garnered the support of a considerable number of the lesser rulers, but their allegiance was based on self-interest and profit. As soon as he was assassinated in 912, his "vassals" quickly renounced their allegiance to the Later Liang.

Such continual shifts in loyalty diminished the prestige of the imperial institution. It appeared that an emperor attracted a following among lesser rulers because of his military prowess and commercial policies that ensured profit for his less than unswervingly loyal subordinates. The emperor's virtue and position as Son of Heaven were beside the point. Chinese and foreign rulers decided whether to support him purely on the basis of self-interest. The emperor, the key intermediary between his own people and the "barbarians," did not represent a higher civilization to which foreigners might be attracted. He was merely another contender for power. There was no reason to proffer tribute to him or to perform any of the other duties required by the seemingly defunct Chinese world order. The various foreign states, which had occupied territory in China, were concerned with their own profit rather than with the niceties of Chinese rituals for foreigners or with the necessity of absorbing elements of Chinese culture. Similarly, the claimants to the Chinese throne were too busy fending off rivals to be overly concerned with imposing the Chinese system of foreign relations on the "barbarians." The rulers in South China generally did not lay claim to the title of "emperor." Since the Chinese capital had always been in the North, their reluctance is understandable. Only the Northern states competed for control of the whole Chinese empire.

The Khitans capitalized on these difficulties to impose their own system on some of the Chinese states. They demanded and received tribute of silk and silver. Their merchants traded with their Chinese counterparts. The earlier Chinese restraints on trade were not respected. Commerce between the Khitans and both the Northern and Southern states flourished. The trade in tea, silk, salt, horses, and other products persisted despite disputes and wars among the Khitans and the various Chinese and foreign states. The traditional Chinese disdain for trade did not prevent merchants and officials from economic dealings, on a basis of equality, with the Khitans. The Chinese states apparently accepted the diplomatic equality of the foreigners, including the Khitans.

Edmund Worthy offers a detailed view of one of the kingdoms in this multi-state system. Wu Yüeh, a state along the eastern coast which comprised prosperous cities and seaports, conducted relations with other states in South China as diplomatic equals. Its rulers, on occasion, declared themselves to be subordinates of one or another of the Northern dynasties, but in their own land they acted as and took on the prerogatives of emperors. They submitted to the emperors in the North because they sought the latter's support in disputes with their neighboring states. Their motives were purely pragmatic and unrelated to feelings of loyalty to and veneration for the emperor. As soon as they detected signs of weakness or decline in the Northern dynasty, they became more independent. Toward the end of this chaotic period, however, two Northern dynasties, the Chou and the Sung, became dominant. Wu Yüeh's rulers were forced to act as true subordinates. They presented enormous quantities of silk, silver, and ships, which proved invaluable to the Sung. Finally, in 978, they submitted to Sung control.

Before its submission, Wu Yüeh acted as an autonomous state. Its location along the east coast facilitated transport to other lands, but its dealings with non-Chinese states were not defined by the traditional concepts of foreign relations. It traded and maintained diplomatic relations with the Korean states and Japan without demanding any show of submission on their part. Abandoning the traditional Chinese restraint on commerce, Wu Yüeh benefited enormously from foreign trade. It also prospered from trade with the Khitans. The rulers of Wu Yüeh were so eager for foreign trade and for an ally against their Chinese enemies that they accepted a position as tributaries of the Khitans. Here was the strange situation of a Chinese state offering tribute to a "barbarian" dynasty. Wu Yüeh's relations with the Khitans certainly subvert the view that the Chinese state considered itself superior to foreigners and did not tolerate foreign lands that demanded treatment as equals (and occasionally as political superiors). The rulers of Wü Yueh realistically assessed their position in East Asia and acknowledged their weakness vis-à-vis the Khitans. The myths of the traditional Chinese system did not characterize their actions. Realism and pragmatism shaped their foreign policy.

The same realism and pragmatism determined Sung policy toward its neighbors. When the Sung came to power in 960, it was, in Wang Gung-wu's apt phrase, a "lesser empire." Its rulers controlled less territory than had the T'ang. It still faced challenges from other Chinese states and, more important, from the Khitans. By the late tenth century, the Sung emperors had pacified the Chinese states and were virtually the uncontested masters of South and much of North China. They could now lay claim to the Mandate of Heaven, but they still had to contend with the Khitans. After a futile effort to dislodge the Khitans from Chinese territory, the Sung emperors realized that they had to work out an accommodation with the Khitans to prevent the latter from threatening China's borderlands. In 1005 they negotiated the Treaty of Shan-yüan by which the Sung promised payments of 200,000 bolts of silk and 100,000 taels of silver in return for peace along the frontiers. By the very act of signing the treaty, the Sung acknowledged that the Khitans had achieved diplomatic parity with them.

Wang Gungwu's essay shows the realism of the Chinese officials who

devised the agreement with the Khitans. Flexibility was the dominant note
in their foreign policy, as it is reflected in the important contemporary
work, the *Ts'e-fu yuan-kuei*. In this text, they emphasized that different
policies were required in dealing with the different "barbarians." The
lesser foreign states could still be treated as tributaries, but the more
powerful of China's neighbors, such as the Khitans, had to be treated as
equals. Yet the rhetoric of tribute is frequently used in the text. It seems
clear, however, that this rhetoric was for domestic consumption. In actual
dealings with powerful adversaries, they did accept foreigners as equals.
The rhetoric of superiority was comforting, but many Chinese officials
were realistic, even in their writings, in their assessments of the strengths
of the "barbarians" and in their policy recommendations. As Tao Jing-
shen writes in his analysis of the views of Sung officials toward the Khitans,
"on the one hand, they [i.e., scholars and officials] might believe in China's
cultural and even military superiority; on the other hand, they were also
able to make fairly reasonable appraisals of foreign affairs."

Like the myth which emphasized that China conducted foreign relations
on its own terms, the myth of China's lack of interest in foreign commerce is
challenged in this volume. Shiba Yoshinobu describes in some detail the
expansion of Chinese trade during the Sung period. He asserts that Chinese
officials facilitated and promoted commerce with the "barbarians." They
recognized that the government could profit from an increase in foreign
trade. As a result, the government improved transportation facilities,
expanded the currency, made greater use of copper money in its own
transactions, and imposed a monopoly on certain goods which it traded
with foreigners. Foreign trade developed rapidly, partly because of the
Sung's need for horses, furs, and other goods, and partly because of the rise
in the cities of an upper class which coveted foreign luxuries. The Sung
established markets along its northern border for trade with the Khitans,
the Tanguts (a people related to the Tibetans), and the Jurchens (who
founded the Chin dynasty and eventually expelled the Sung from North
China). Shiba believes that China maintained a favorable balance of trade
with its northern neighbors and that the Sung regained much of the silver it
was forced to present as tribute to the Khitans and the Jurchens. In the
south as well, the Sung engaged in foreign commerce. Maritime trade with
Southeast Asia, India, Persia, and the Middle East increased dramatically
during this period. The government encouraged the establishment of fairs
and markets for trade with the merchants who arrived by ship. It is
difficult to determine whether the Sung had a favorable balance of trade in
maritime commerce. The trade in the south, nonetheless, persisted throughout the dynasty, and its continuance disputes the view that China and its
officials were uninterested in commerce.

The myth of China's ignorance of foreign lands is also subject to review.

In his study of Sung embassies to neighboring states, Herbert Franke reveals the wealth of written sources on foreign regions which was available to the government. Chinese envoys often returned to China with valuable accounts of their travels, which occasionally included useful military intelligence. Court officials thus had access to information about China's neighbors. Using this information as a guide, they differentiated among the various "barbarians," treating each one according to its presumed power and wealth. Some foreign rulers and envoys were addressed as equals, whereas others were clearly dealt with as subordinates. In order to gather the information it needed, the Sung court sought to select knowledgeable, well-educated, and capable envoys, and Franke tells us that it generally succeeded. The court also provided supplies, built postal stations, and in general did as much as possible to ensure that the embassies reached their destinations and completed their tasks. The "barbarian" Khitans and Jurchens accorded the Chinese envoys a fine reception, and there was apparently a carefully planned system of ceremonies and rituals at these foreign courts. The Chinese envoys exchanged gifts and often traded illegally in the foreign lands they visited. They had countless opportunities to turn a profit as a result of their position. Despite the hazards and inconveniences of the journey, there was apparently no dearth of envoys.

Similarly, there was no shortage of foreign envoys arriving in Sung China. They came from most of China's neighboring lands both by land and by sea. What is striking is the similarity of the standards set forth by a Chinese dynasty and by the "barbarian" dynasties. Both the Sung and the "barbarians" imposed limits on the private trade conducted by the envoys, but they did not disapprove of "official commerce." They both seemed to employ envoys to gather intelligence while they demanded that their representatives refrain from revealing information about their own military forces or defenses. In sum, the "barbarians," like the Sung, sought trade and intelligence in dealings with foreigners.

The Sung was one of a number of important states in East Asia. Unlike the T'ang, it did not dominate the area and could not impose a Chinese world order. Until the early twelfth century, the Sung had its capital in K'ai-feng and controlled much of North China and all of South China. To the north and northwest, however, were two "barbarian" peoples who founded Chinese-style dynasties. The Khitans established the Liao dynasty, and the Tanguts formed the Hsi Hsia dynasty. In 1126 the Sung was forced to abandon North China and to relocate its capital in Hang-chou in the south. The Sung court, seeking to undermine the power of the Khitans, had helped the Jurchens of Manchuria to oust the Liao from China. Chinese officials quickly regretted this policy. They had assisted a "barbarian" group which became a dangerous adversary rather than a close ally. The

Jurchens founded their own dynasty, the Chin, turned against the Sung, and in 1126 compelled the Chinese court to withdraw from North China.

All of these "barbarian" dynasties requested and received diplomatic parity with the Sung. The Liao and the Chin also demanded tribute, which signified their military superiority, from the Chinese court. They insisted on the same prerogatives as their Chinese counterparts. Lesser states were required to treat them as superiors. In his essay for this volume, Michael Rogers shows that Korea acquiesced to the demands of the Liao and the Chin. The threat of a Khitan invasion prompted Koryŏ to agree to offer tribute to those "barbarian" inhabitants of Manchuria and parts of North China. Koryŏ's officials apparently viewed the Khitans as "barbarians" and still hoped for a resurgence of Chinese military power which would lead to the collapse of the illegitimate Liao dynasty. They implied that their allegiance to the Liao was a temporary expedient. The Jurchen drive into North China, however, undermined Koryŏ's faith in a renewal of Sung power. Koryŏ was compelled to come to terms with the Chin. Its officials accepted this "barbarian" dynasty as superior. They regarded the Jurchens as legitimate inheritors of Chinese authority. The Sung could not, in the end, prevent such traditional tributary states as Korea from paying allegiance to a "barbarian" power.

Once the Sung was expelled from North China, the age-old heartland of the Middle Kingdom, in 1126, several other countries either severed their connections with or no longer offered tribute to the Chinese dynasty. Tibet, as Luciano Petech shows in his essay, suspended tribute missions to the Sung after 1136, within a decade of the Sung expulsion from North China. Earlier, Tibet had traded horses for Chinese tea with Sung officials and merchants and had dispatched periodic embassies to K'ai-feng. Having lost North China, the Sung could not count on official tribute missions from the land of Tibet. Almost a century elapsed before China reestablished relations with and asserted its supremacy over Tibet. Only with the arrival of the Mongols did China actually control its southwestern neighbor. The Mongol armies intimidated the Tibetans and made Tibet into a subordinate state, taking a census, demanding taxes and military service, and establishing postal stations. A special agency in the Mongol government (the *hsüan-cheng-yüan*) was founded to direct Tibetan affairs, and Tibet truly became part of the Mongol empire. The Mongol dynasty differed from the Sung in seeking total control over its neighbors.

The Sung clearly did not perceive this essential difference. The distinctions between the Mongols and the other "barbarian" dynasties eluded Sung policy-makers in the thirteenth century. These officials were primarily interested in avenging themselves on the Chin dynasty, which had ousted the Sung from North China a century earlier. Their passionate desire for revenge caused them to ignore or at least to minimize the Mongol threat.

As Charles Peterson notes in his contribution, they "continued to focus on immediate issues and dangers despite the menacing specter of the Mongols." Instead of joining in common cause with Chinese rebels in the North against the Mongols, they maintained their preoccupation with the Jurchens. In fact, the Sung collaborated with the Mongols in crushing the Chin in 1234. Attempting to capitalize on the defeat of the Jurchens, Sung forces launched a campaign to recover territories in the North that the Chin had seized in 1126. Some Sung officials opposed this campaign. They feared that it would alienate the Mongols. Their objections were overruled, and Sung troops headed north toward the province of Honan. The Mongols trounced them there, forcing them to withdraw from North China. Sung officials had miscalculated and had, not for the last time, underestimated their Mongol adversaries.

With the arrival of the Mongols in China, the period of multi-state relations in East Asia came to an end. The Sung's military weakness compelled its officials to treat the foreign dynasties in China as equals. Thus a true multi-state system operated during Sung times. The Mongols, however, laid claim to universal rule and would not tolerate other sovereign states. They were not as flexible as the Sung in dealings with foreigners. All other peoples were viewed as subordinates.

The Mongols demanded that their subjects contribute to the growth and prosperity of their empire. The Sung had been content with a show of obeisance by their subordinates. But the Mongols required tangible support and assistance. Those states that were ruled directly by the Mongols and those that were subordinates were compelled to pay taxes, to maintain postal stations, and to perform other tasks for the khan's court. In effect, the Mongols simply implemented, albeit more forcefully, the theory of traditional Chinese foreign policy. They dismantled the multi-state system in East Asia and sought universal domination. They recognized, however, at an early stage of their conquests, that they needed the help and the skills of the subject populations.

The Uighurs, a Turkic people residing in East Turkestan, were the first of the subject peoples to assist the Mongols. As Thomas Allsen notes, their assistance was invaluable. Since they submitted peacefully to Chinggis Khan, they were accorded an important position among the Mongol's subjects. Chinggis even referred to the Uighur ruler as his fifth son. The Uighurs benefited enormously from their close ties with the Mongols, but the Mongols also gained from this relationship. Their Uighur subjects not only paid taxes, offered tribute, manned postal stations, and helped to conduct censuses, but also served in the Mongol armies and contributed vital administrative and managerial skills. The Mongols adopted the Uighur script for their written language, and the Mongol khans and nobility employed Uighur learned men to tutor their sons. The Uighurs were, in sum, extremely useful to the early Mongols.

Similarly, the other Turkic peoples performed valuable tasks for the Mongols. Igor de Rachewiltz identifies some of the specific contributions of the Turks. He notes that even in the early stages of Mongol expansion Turks served as advisers and tutors and several headed the Mongol Secretariat. They also became tax collectors, military men, local administrators, and translators in the Mongol service. Khubilai Khan, in particular, employed Turks extensively throughout his domains. The Uighurs were undoubtedly the most significant of the Turks. Their cultural influence on the Mongols cannot be underestimated. Nevertheless, the Mongols were dominant and would not permit any other sovereign state.

The volume concludes with a more general view of China's foreign relations, but it is an essay that fits in with some of the other interpretations offered here. In examining China's relations with Manchuria and Korea from the Ch'in dynasty (3rd century B.C.) until 1911, Gari Ledyard observes two major trends in China's foreign policy. He identifies one as a Yang phase and the other as a Yin phase. During the Yang phase, the Chinese were powerful enough to enforce their system of foreign relations. They were assertive and expansive and demanded that foreigners recognize China's superiority. In the Yin phase, China was weak and surrounded by more powerful and sometimes hostile neighbors. Chinese officials were frequently compelled to accept foreign states as equals. Accommodation characterized their foreign policy during this time.

In sum, the essays in this volume challenge the traditional view of Chinese foreign relations. The Chinese dynasties from the tenth to the thirteenth century adopted a realistic policy toward foreign states. They did not impose their own system on foreigners. Diplomatic parity defined the relations between China and other states during these three centuries. The tribute system did not, by itself, govern China's contacts with foreigners. Throughout its long history, China has often changed the course of its foreign policy. It did not maintain a monolithic policy toward foreigners.

In this volume, we have concentrated on China's northern neighbors. We have not dealt with China's relations with Southeast Asia or Japan from the tenth to the thirteenth century. Whether the same patterns prevail in China's contacts with those regions during that time ought to be the focus of another volume.

NOTES

1. Morris Rossabi, *China and Inner Asia From 1368 to the Present Day* (London, 1975), p. 18.

2. John King Fairbank, *Trade and Diplomacy on the China Coast: The Opening of the Treaty Ports, 1842–1854* (Cambridge, Mass., 1953), p. 27.

3. For a valuable first-hand account of the treatment accorded a foreign embassy in traditional times, see K. M. Maitra (trans.), *A Persian Embassy to China* (New York, 1970 reprint).

4. T. C. Lin, "Manchuria Trade and Tribute in the Ming Dynasty: A Study of Chinese Theories and Methods of Control Over Border Peoples," *Nankai Social and Economic Quarterly* 9 (1937): 857.

5. As late as the nineteenth century, the Chinese attempted to use this tactic. See Lin Tse-hsü's letter to Queen Victoria in 1839 as translated in *China's Response to the West: A Documentary Survey, 1839–1923*, by Ssu-yü Teng and John K. Fairbank (Cambridge, Mass., 1954), pp. 24–27.

6. Rossabi, *China and Inner Asia*, p. 21.

7. On the Uighur involvement in T'ang politics, see Colin Mackerras, *The Uighur Empire (744–840) According to the T'ang Dynastic Histories* (Canberra, 1968).

8. Charles A. Peterson, "The Restoration Completed: Emperor Hsien-tsung and the Provinces," In Arthur F. Wright and Denis Twitchett (eds.), *Perspectives on the T'ang* (New Haven, 1973), pp. 151–191.

9. The standard source on this period is Wang Gungwu, *The Structure of Power in North China during the Five Dynasties* (Kuala Lumpur, 1963).

10. The standard source on the Liao is Karl Wittfogel and Feng Chia-sheng, *History of Chinese Society: The Liao* (Philadelphia, 1949).

PART I

China in Disarray

ONE

Diplomacy for Survival:
Domestic and Foreign Relations of Wu Yüeh, 907–978

EDMUND H. WORTHY, JR.

The tenth century marks a critical and turbulent transition period in the history of East Asia. The internal political order of China, Korea, and Japan either disintegrated or was transformed, and on the Asian mainland the threat of vigorous foreign forces emerged north of the Great Wall. As a consequence of this political flux, the Sinocentric pattern of foreign relations predominant during the T'ang was disrupted. Pressures intensified on rival states and mini-kingdoms to form both foreign and domestic alliances for the sake of self-preservation, political stability, and economic advantage.

The expression "internal disorder and external calamity" (nei-luan wai-huan) characterizes the national and international situation of the era, particularly in mainland Asia. In Korea dramatic changes resulted from the breakdown of the Silla kingdom during the late ninth and early tenth centuries. The ensuing struggle among several competitors to fill the vacuum climaxed with the supremacy of the state of Koryŏ in 936. Consolidation and expansion of Koryŏ's newly acquired power required several more decades.[1] During the same period, beyond the Great Wall the might of the Khitans, transformed into the Liao dynasty, impinged first upon North China and later on Korea. The Jurchens in northern Manchuria and the Tangut Hsi Hsia tribes on China's northwestern frontier also began to grow in power and influence. Meanwhile in Japan, the Fujiwara clan, overcoming some initial challenges, gained ascendancy as imperial regents and thereby altered the nature of Japanese imperial rule. Outside the court and capital, centralized control of the provinces deteriorated, and Japanese-initiated official diplomatic contact with China was discontinued in the face of China's ebbing power and attraction.[2]

Tenth-century China was beset with disunion that was longer lasting and more pervasive than that in other East Asian states of the time. While the successive Five Dynasties in the North and the Sung during its initial

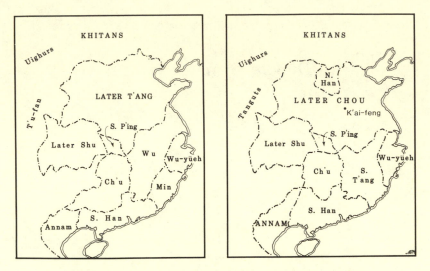

Map 1. The Five Dynasties Period in China, 923–936 A.D.
and The Five Dynasties Period in China, 951–960 A.D.
Based on Albert Herrmann, *An Historical Atlas of China*, p. 33.

two decades pretended sole claim to legitimacy, not all other states in the South, the so-called Ten Kingdoms, recognized this claim. To one degree or another, all acted autonomously, and some openly declared their independence and established an imperial form of government. Thus, in effect, a multi-state system existed internally within China just as it had during such earlier eras of national disintegration as the Spring and Autumn period (722 B.C. – 481 B.C.).[3]

The various states of tenth-century China treated each other like "foreign" lands and conducted diplomacy accordingly. Among themselves they exchanged envoys and diplomatic notes, offered gifts, paid tribute, conducted warfare, and entered into treaties just as a unified China had done and later did with non-Chinese states. This system of domestic multi-state relations lasted until 979 when Sung T'ai-tsung conquered the stubborn Northern Han state.

An international multi-state system in East Asia coexisted and interacted with the domestic system in China. Without a single, universally acknowledged central Chinese state, however, the Sinocentric structure of foreign relations lost much of its compelling logic. Although China continued to exert a strong cultural attraction on other East and Southeast Asian states, they could, during this period of Chinese political division, afford to develop simultaneous relations with one or more of the Chinese states for their own advantage. Or, as in the case of the Japanese court which stopped sending official envoys to China, East Asian states could drift away from the Chinese political orbit.

Until the balance of military power gradually shifted to the Chou (950–959) and Sung after the middle of the tenth century, a political vacuum existed in East Asia that permitted the various domestic and foreign states to deal with each other more or less as diplomatic equals. This situation made for an ever-changing mosaic of relationships. Just as foreign states manipulated their relations with Chinese domestic states for their own advantage, so the Chinese states used their connections with foreign powers, particularly the Khitans, to bolster their own domestic positions.

By focusing on the domestic and foreign relations of one Chinese state, Wu Yüeh, this essay will analyze in microcosm the dual domestic and international multi-state systems of the tenth century. The course of Wu Yüeh's relations with other Chinese states, and their perceptions of Wu Yüeh, will be examined through the year 956, when Chou launched its invasion of the Southern T'ang and dramatically altered the military and diplomatic equation. The next section of the essay will examine Wu Yüeh's domestic relations for the final twenty-two years preceding its capitulation to the Sung in 978. Wu Yüeh's relations with foreign states and its place within the international multi-state system will be considered separately. Finally, in the concluding section, the interaction of the two multi-state systems, especially during the half century before 956, will be examined in the context of a specific international relations theory explaining a balance of power system.

Wu Yüeh consisted of thirteen prefectures (*chou*) and eighty-six sub-prefectures (*hsien*). Its territory roughly corresponded to today's Chekiang Province, that portion of Kiangsu Province south of the mouth of the Yangtze and east of Lake T'ai, and the northeastern quadrant of Fukien Province, including Fu-chou. The territory in Fukien was not appended until 947. Although Wu Yüeh ranked geographically among the smaller states of the tenth century, it certainly was one of the wealthiest. Its population totaled approximately 550,700 households (*hu*),[4] many of whom lived in active commercial centers and major seaports. The rulers of Wu Yüeh promoted land reclamation and waterworks projects that increased agricultural production. While we possess little explicit information about Wu Yüeh's commercial and agricultural development, its tremendous wealth will be obvious when the extent of its tribute is discussed in the next section.

Ch'ien Liu (852–932) was the founder of Wu Yüeh, which for purposes of this study is considered to have begun in 907 when Chu Wen, who destroyed the T'ang and founded the Later Liang dynasty, invested him as Prince (*wang*) of Wu Yüeh.[5] Initially, he gained fame as a defender of Hang-chou against the rebel bands of Huang Ch'ao in 878. Thereafter, his military power increased steadily until he reached the position of regional military governor (*chieh-tu shih*). After he quelled a revolt in 897 against the T'ang by his one-time superior, his fortunes and rank rose even higher. In 902 he was named Prince of Yüeh, and in 904, Prince of Wu.

During the two decades prior to 907, Ch'ien Liu, Yang Hsing-mi, who was the progenitor of the Wu Kingdom (later transformed into the Southern T'ang), Sun Ju, who simply was a military opportunist, and Chu Wen conducted a seesaw struggle for control of the Chiang-Huai and Chekiang regions where the prosperous southern ports of the Grand Canal were located. The contest ultimately came down to a rivalry between Ch'ien (Wu Yüeh) and Yang (Wu/Southern T'ang, which was the largest and most powerful Southern state). This rivalry smoldered and sometimes erupted into open warfare during the next ninety years until the demise of the two states.[6]

Ch'ien Liu's reign until his death in 932 extended through much of the span of two Northern states, Later Liang (907–922) and Later T'ang (923–937). Ch'ien charted a delicately balanced diplomatic course for Wu Yüeh and came closer than any of his successors to making an outright declaration of independence as a separate imperial state. His fifth son, Ch'ien Yüan-kuan (887–941), enjoyed a nine-year reign into the middle of the Later Chin (937–946). Upon his death he was succeeded by his son Ch'ien Tso (928–947), who ruled for six years until the beginning of the Later Han (947–950). Ch'ien Tso's brother Tsung inherited the throne, but only for the last half of 947. A military man named Hu Chin-ssu staged a palace coup and replaced Tsung with his younger brother Ch'ien Shu (929–988), who reigned for the final thirty years of Wu Yüeh's history. During his reign he was faced with the growing problem of preserving the existence of his state in the face of inexorable pressure from Chou and Sung.[7]

Wu Yüeh was the longest lived of all states, North or South, during the T'ang–Sung interregnum. It also suffered the least from external attack, despite the attraction of its riches. The skillful diplomacy of its rulers best explains its survival during these difficult times.

Domestic Multi-State Relations, 907–956

Chu Wen's usurpation of the T'ang throne and his founding of the Later Liang dynasty in 907 shattered the Chinese myth of a legitimate, unified empire.[8] His act of rebellion freed and indeed encouraged other competing regional military governors either to consider an attack on the Later Liang in the name of restoring the T'ang or to establish in some formal fashion their own kingdoms.[9]

Ch'ien Liu was faced with these same options, but characteristically elected to follow a course of action that was to become the guiding diplomatic policy for Wu Yüeh. At the time of the T'ang downfall, several of his advisers urged him to launch an attack against the Later Liang and not submit to a usurper. Even if he were unsuccessful, their reasoning went, Ch'ien could at least retain Hang-chou and Yüeh-chou (present-day Shao-hsing in Chekiang Province) and declare himself the Eastern Emperor (*tung-ti*). He rejected this advice and acknowledged Chu Wen's imperial pretensions. His justification was that an ancient strategy called for nominal submissiveness to the emperor, but his unstated implication was that he would remain free to do as he wished within his own territory.[10] Ch'ien opted not to assert his independence and autonomy openly. The reasons for this will become apparent.

Chu Wen's position at the outset of his reign was by no means completely secure. Confronted with threats from the Sha-t'o Turks in the North under Li K'o-yung, the Later T'ang progenitor, and from Huai-nan or Wu in the South, Chu Wen needed pledges of loyalty, even if nominal, from other states. Ch'ien Liu served as a potential counterbalance to the might of Huai-nan. Consequently, Chu Wen conferred special favors on him. Only one month after the creation of the Liang dynasty, Chu Wen named Ch'ien the Prince of Wu Yüeh, a rank that he had unsuccessfully requested from the T'ang in 904.[11] Almost a year later, Chu Wen discovered from a Wu Yüeh envoy the personal likes of Ch'ien Liu and presented him with ten polo ponies and one jade belt, the first of several such belts to be given to Wu Yüeh rulers.[12] Other titles and honors were granted to Ch'ien and various members of his family during this period.[13] One title in particular reveals Chu Wen's intentions. In 907 Ch'ien received the concurrent title of regional military governor of Huai-nan and the military rank of pacification officer of Huai-nan.[14]

For his part, Ch'ien Liu valued ties with Liang in order to help neutralize the threat from Wu, which was vigorously attempting to expand its influence and territory. In 908 Ch'ien sent an envoy to the Liang court to present a strategy for taking over Wu.[15] This gesture demonstrated his good faith to Liang and also helped enlist Liang's continued support against the incursions of Wu.[16] Hostilities between Wu and Wu Yüeh continued intermittently until 919, with each side staging attacks and counterattacks across the other's northern and southern borders.[17] Fighting on both land and rivers centered primarily around Ch'ang-chou (present-day Wu-chin in the province of Kiangsu) in Wu and Su-chou in Wu Yüeh, two cities which confronted each other across the northern tip of the border.[18]

Wu's most important success was the capture in 918 of Ch'ien-chou (present-day Kan-chou in the province of Kiangsi), a key point in overland transportation between north and south.[19] Wu already controlled the southern terminals of the Grand Canal and closed it as the primary north–south communication artery. Only one other land route to the north lay open to Wu Yüeh and its neighboring state Min, whose territory roughly corresponded to today's Fukien Province. This route led through Ch'ien-chou at the confluence of the Kung River (*Kung-shui*) winding into Min territory and the Kan river (*Kan-chiang*) leading northward into P'o-yang Lake and the Liang border at the Yangtze. Through another river system Ch'ien-chou also connected with the Nan Han kingdom in modern Kwangtung Province. This route from southwestern Wu Yüeh to the Liang border was approximately 5,000 *li* long (roughly 1,500 miles) and traversed the states of Min, Ch'u, and Nan P'ing.[20] Despite its circuitousness, it was preferable to the more direct sea passage to the north, which exposed travelers and cargoes to greater danger.[21]

Until its takeover by Wu in 918, Ch'ien-chou remained under the control of an independent warlord. Trade among the various Southern kingdoms and tribute to the North, especially from Wu Yüeh, brought in transit taxes that helped sustain Ch'ien-chou's defenses. Given its strategic importance as the single link connecting all the states surrounding Wu, including Wu Yüeh, Min, Ch'u, Nan P'ing, and Liang, it was imperative that Wu capture the city and impede communications among its rivals. In 918 Wu attacked Ch'ien-chou, which enlisted the aid of Ch'u, Min, and Wu Yüeh, but their assistance did not prevent a Wu victory.[22] Thereafter until 958, Wu Yüeh's and Min's tribute missions to the North followed the sea route whose terminus was at Teng-chou (modern P'eng-lai in the province of Shantung) and Lai-chou (modern Yeh in the province of Shantung).[23]

The tribute missions that Wu Yüeh sent had a noticeable impact on the Liang economy. According to extant records, Ch'ien Liu first presented tribute to Liang in 909.[24] It is conceivable, though, that he offered tribute or gifts before then, especially in view of the honors he and his family had received. In 916, after Ch'ien had sent another tribute mission and received a prestigious military rank, some court officials expressed concern. They acknowledged the benefit of Wu Yüeh's tribute to commerce in Liang, but felt that Ch'ien should not be granted an excessively high rank in return.[25] The Liang ruler overruled these objections, probably for a combination of diplomatic and economic reasons.

Throughout the Liang dynasty, the honors bestowed on Ch'ien Liu and his family and officials increased. When Chu Yu-kuei briefly usurped the Liang throne in 912, and also in the following year when Liang Mo-ti took the throne, Ch'ien was given the elevated title of "esteemed [imperial] patriarch" (*shang-fu*).[26] This title, which had its origin in the Chou dynasty (1027 B.C.–256 B.C.), was reserved for the few officials most revered by the emperor and was not granted to the ruler of any other kingdom in the Five Dynasties period. Ch'ien also received several battlefield promotions during the campaign against Wu. The most significant was "commander-in-chief of all infantry and cavalry in the empire" (*t'ien-hsia ping-ma tu-yüan-shuai*), which entitled him to a special staff of adjutants.[27]

Since the titles given to Ch'ien Liu and his family were only nominal, and since Wu Yüeh for all intents and purposes was an autonomous state, one may wonder why Liang emperors granted the honors and why Ch'ien accepted and even sought them. The answers to both questions are, in short, legitimacy and diplomacy. Liang, and the other successor Northern states as well, enhanced their legitimacy by bestowing the honors and ranks only a "dynasty" could bestow and at the same time strengthened ties with allies. By accepting the honors, Wu Yüeh demonstrated its nominal loyalty to Liang and, more important, gained legitimacy vis-à-vis the other contending states of the time.

Several incidents testify to the diplomatic value of the titles Wu Yüeh received. In 915 Liu Yen, the ruler of Nan Han, petitioned the Liang emperor to be granted the title Prince of Nan Yüeh (*Nan Yüeh wang*). His incumbent title *Nan P'ing wang* connoted the prince of a commandery (*chün-wang*), but he felt that he deserved the equivalent of Ch'ien Liu's *Wu Yüeh wang*, which implied the prince of a kingdom, because Wu and Yüeh, in name at least, encompassed a region of many prefectures. This request was not granted, and Liu Yen broke off tribute relations with Liang.[28] Ten years later in 925 Ch'ien Liu sent a communiqué to the Wu ruler informing him that he had received from Later T'ang an investiture document made out of jade (*yü-ts'e*) and the title *Wu Yüeh kuo-wang*. The Wu ruler refused to accept the note on the pretext that Wu Yüeh was misusing the name "Wu," which represented a territory that he and not Ch'ien actually occupied.[29] Although there may have been other reasons for Wu's snub of Wu Yüeh, it seems that envy was paramount. The third incident demonstrating the potential diplomatic advantage of the titles given by Liang occurred in 932. Shortly after the death of Ch'ien Liu, the Min ruler unsuccessfully requested that he be given the title *Wu Yüeh wang*, which evidently carried more prestige than his own title of *Min wang*.[30]

During the first half of his reign, Ch'ien Liu established formal ties with three states bordering Wu—Nan Han, Ch'u, and Min. In 914 Liu Yen sent an emissary from Nan Han to present gifts and to request the start of fraternal relations with Ch'ien, who accepted the overture.[31] Five years later when Liu Yen declared his independence and created his own imperial state, the Liang court ordered Ch'ien to launch a punitive expedition against Nan Han. This decree reveals Liang's frustration at not being able to extend and maintain its sphere of influence, a blatant lack of appreciation of the relations between Wu Yüeh and Nan Han, and the limited extent of Liang's own influence over Wu Yüeh. Not wishing to alienate Liang, Ch'ien Liu accepted the imperial order but never acted on it. He reported that the terrain separating the two states was difficult to traverse and requested that the order be rescinded.[32]

Friendly relations with Min and Ch'u were initially cemented through marriage alliances. In 916 one of Ch'ien's sons took a bride from Min. From this point on, the sources say, relations between the two states were cordial.[33] Since Min was its closest friendly neighbor, Wu Yüeh took a keen interest in preserving ties with the kingdom and, as we shall see, twenty years later intervened to save it from destruction. In 921 Wu Yüeh initiated relations with Ch'u when one of Ch'ien's sons married a daughter of the Ch'u ruler.[34]

In 919, at the height of the hostilities between Wu Yüeh and Wu, their relations took an unexpected turn toward peace. In that year, Hsü Chih-kao, who was destined to become the founder of the Southern T'ang, urged that Wu, having gained a decisive victory at Ch'ang-chou, destroy Wu Yüeh. The power behind the Wu ruler, Hsü Wen, rejected this advice, noting that the fighting had already caused a heavy burden on the people and that Ch'ien's strength should not be underestimated. He returned some Wu Yüeh prisoners, whereupon Ch'ien dispatched an envoy proposing peace.[35] An uneasy peace between the two states lasted for the next twenty years.

The extent to which Wu Yüeh actually functioned and was perceived to function as an independent, autonomous state is an intriguing problem about which historians have expressed differing views throughout the centuries. Ch'ien Liu's rule and actions offer much telling evidence that deserves close analysis.

The Mo-ti emperor of the Liang state granted Ch'ien a special prerogative and a title that broke down the barrier between Son of Heaven and official and that elevated Ch'ien to a rank equivalent to an independent sovereign. In 921 Ch'ien was permitted to sign memorials and documents with his official title and not his personal name.[36] The ritual gap and the difference in political status between Ch'ien Liu and the Liang emperor were significantly narrowed. In earlier periods this privilege had been accorded only to men who had already attained a high degree of independence from the throne and potentially could overthrow it.[37]

In 923, two months before the Later T'ang dynasty displaced the Liang, Ch'ien Liu was granted the title of *Wu Yüeh kuo-wang*.[38] Previously he was known as Prince of Wu Yüeh (*Wu Yüeh wang*), but now he was clearly elevated to the status of king of a state (*kuo-wang*). He could hold no higher rank without becoming emperor in name. None of the rulers of other states were awarded this rank. As soon as Ch'ien received it, he established the apparatus of an imperial state. The ceremonies, insignia, and titles were changed to reflect those of the imperial system. His residence was named a palace, the provincial-level offices collectively became known as the court, his commands were termed imperial decrees, and his staff members were all called officials (*ch'en*). One of his first acts was to confer on a favored son his former title of regional military governor. Such an award would previously have been made only by the Liang emperor.[39]

Ch'ien Liu had all the trappings of an emperor except the actual title.[40] He did, according to several stelae, adopt his own reign title (*nien-hao*), one manifestation of an independent political entity.[41] In 908, when it became apparent that the Liang could not reunite China, he adopted the reign title *t'ien-pao*, which was used until approximately 913. Then, for the remainder of the Liang dynasty, he reverted to the use of its reign titles.[42] He adopted the reign titles *pao-ta* in 923 and *pao-cheng* in 926. One other reign title, *kuang-ch'u*, apparently was used, but exactly when is not clear.[43] The use of independent reign titles ceased in 932 when Ch'ien died.

Ch'ien Liu could only afford to enjoy the pleasures of his imperial status within his own state. Beyond his borders, he needed to maintain the fiction of his submission to the Liang and Later T'ang dynasties in order to counteract the ever-present threat from the state of Wu. The escalation of the conflict between Wu and Wu Yüeh after 913 may have been one reason he reverted to use of the Liang reign title. Even after the 919 truce between Wu and Wu Yüeh, he could not admit his de facto independent status, despite the repeated urgings of the Wu ruler and Hsü Wen for him to declare an independent state.[44]

Ch'ien Liu obtained from the Later T'ang tangible recognition that his position was tantamount to that of an emperor. After sending gifts to the new dynasty in 924, he requested a jade patent of investiture (*yü-ts'e*) as *Wu Yüeh kuo-wang*. He also wanted a gold seal. Many T'ang officials argued vehemently that his request ought to be denied. The jade patent and gold seal, they said, were symbols belonging solely to the emperor of China or conferred on a ruler of a foreign state. Only bamboo patents and brass seals could be granted to anyone within China. The emperor overruled these objections and complied with Ch'ien's request in 925.[45] With these new privileges, Ch'ien evidently felt emboldened enough to act overtly in the capacity of an emperor. He sent emissaries to Silla and Po-hai in Korea to grant titles to their rulers.[46]

Ch'ien's imperial style of government and imperious attitude toward the Later T'ang finally provoked a reaction leading to a break in relations between the two states. The spark that ignited this reaction was a disagreement between two T'ang envoys to Wu Yüeh. Upon their return to the capital, one accused the other of a serious breach of protocol that made the Later T'ang seem subservient to Wu Yüeh. The guilty diplomat referred to himself as "your humble servant" (*ch'en*) and to Ch'ien as "your highness" (*t'ien-hsia*), a term of address normally reserved for the imperial crown prince or empress.[47] Ch'ien had always been sensitive to the manner in which envoys treated him, and encouraged their special deference by presenting lavish gifts as a reward. Such diplomatic expressions of respect, appropriate or not, enhanced his status domestically and internationally.

The tensions between the two states were exacerbated by the discourteous way in which Ch'ien addressed An Ch'ung-hui, the most powerful Later T'ang minister. In sending communiqués to An, Ch'ien referred to him as "such and such factotum" (mou-kuan chih-shih), not using his proper title or name and clearly placing him in an inferior position.[48] Ch'ien treated An like one of his own subordinates.

As a result of such behavior, the Later T'ang emperor, at An Ch'ung-hui's insistence, stripped Ch'ien of all his titles and honors in 929.[49] Diplomatic relations between the two states were severed, and the Wu Yüeh envoys and staff in T'ang territory charged with facilitating the transportation of goods were detained and confined.[50] A year later Ch'ien had an opportunity to turn the tables and hold some T'ang envoys hostage. They were bound for the state of Min but were blown off course into Wu Yüeh territory.[51]

This was the first and only rupture in relations between Wu Yüeh and a Northern state. The hiatus of eighteen months disrupted the diplomatic equilibrium and gave both sides cause for concern. Wu Yüeh became more isolated and vulnerable to encroachments by Wu, and the Later T'ang feared a possible alliance between Wu and Wu Yüeh. Shortly after Ch'ien Liu lost his titles, he had his son submit an apologetic letter to the T'ang court, but it apparently was not delivered, either because of the break in communications or because it was ignored.[52]

In 930 circumstances changed so that the Later T'ang began to worry about its lack of ties with Wu Yüeh. At that time Wu was attacking the small kingdom of Ch'u in central China. The Later T'ang emperor, suspecting that Ch'ien may have supported Wu in the invasion, wrote to him seeking to verify the situation.[53] This suspicion, justified or not, jeopardized Wu Yüeh and directly implicated it as hostile to T'ang. To repair the diplomatic rupture, the Wu Yüeh heir apparent, Ch'ien Yüan-kuan, wrote another memorial to Later T'ang in 930, which he sent by one of its envoys who had been detained.[54] Ch'ien Yüan-kuan made a strong case for his father's loyalty to the T'ang, maintaining the pretense that unlike other rulers who had declared independence, only Ch'ien Liu remained faithful to the Northern states. Ch'ien Yüan-kuan also vigorously denied that there was or even could be any alliance between Wu and Wu Yüeh, which, he explained, were bitter enemies. He even offered to be in the vanguard if Later T'ang decided to attack Wu. This memorial produced the desired effect, for in 931, after An Ch'ung-hui had died, Later T'ang restored all of Ch'ien's titles and privileges.[55] A year later Ch'ien died.

None of Ch'ien Liu's successors acted with quite the same degree of imperial pretension, received the same combination of high honors from the northern dynasties, or exercised the same full range of privileges. On his deathbed in 932, Ch'ien urged his sons not to establish a new dynasty.[56] Accordingly, when Ch'ien Yüan-kuan assumed power he followed the ceremonial practices appropriate for a regional military governor and not a ruler of a state. The Later T'ang initially referred to him as Prince of Wu (*Wu wang*),[57] and in 934 the Later T'ang usurper Li Ts'ung-k'o made him Prince of Wu Yüeh, perhaps as a gesture to retain his loyalty during a critical transition period.[58] When the politically weak Chin dynasty replaced the Later T'ang in 936, Ch'ien Yüan-kuan was sufficiently secure to abandon the provincial form of governmental operations. Apparently on his own initiative and authority, he adopted the institutions and ceremonies appropriate for an imperial regime. In Chinese terms he created a state (*chien-kuo*), just as his father had done more than fifteen years before.[59] The Chin dynasty belatedly recognized his self-appointed reign by granting him the title King of Wu Yüeh (*Wu Yüeh kuo-wang*).[60] Although succeeding rulers were offered the same title, sources do not specifically indicate that they also adopted a national form of government.

During the very period when Ch'ien Liu's position vis-à-vis the Later T'ang was improving and his autonomy increasing, the state of Wu became more cautious of and respectful toward the T'ang than it ever had been toward the Liang. The power demonstrated by the T'ang in its conquest of Liang in 923 and of the Shu kingdom in Szechwan in 925 impressed Wu and gave it a reason to fear for its own existence. Plans for an invasion of Wu were even drawn up at one point.[61] Consequently, Wu began to act deferentially toward the T'ang and to present gifts annually. Whether the goods presented were tribute or simply gifts—interpretations naturally differ about this depending on the political perspective of the sources— Wu's intent was clear: to gain the favor of T'ang.[62] Relations broke off in early 928 when An Ch'ung-hui asserted that the Wu ruler, by calling himself an emperor and not declaring himself a subordinate, did not show the proper respect to the Northern dynasty.

The contrast between Wu and Wu Yüeh reactions to the Later T'ang is instructive, for it reveals the benefits and liberties Wu Yüeh enjoyed as a result of its diplomatic policy of recognizing the suzerainty of the Northern dynasties. Simply put, Wu Yüeh did not feel any threat from the North. It was able, in practice, to preserve its internal autonomy and quasi-imperial status, function as the equal of other Southern states, and profit from the prestige conferred by the Northern states.

After Wu and Wu Yüeh declared a truce in 919, they developed diplomatic ties. A latent rivalry still continued between them and periodically erupted into conflicts over control of Min. Records show that until at least 942 Wu Yüeh and Wu and its successor, the Southern T'ang, intermittently exchanged envoys. These diplomatic exchanges typify relations among all Chinese states of that time and therefore deserve a brief description. In 920 Ch'ien Liu sent a mission to Wu for unspecified purposes.[63] Envoys from Wu traveled to Hang-chou in 933 to make a sacrificial offering upon the death of Ch'ien. The Southern T'ang sent an envoy in 937 to announce its establishment,[65] and Wu Yüeh was the first state to offer congratulations to the ruler of the new state.[66] In 939, on the solemn occasion of the Southern sacrifice (*nan-chiao*) in Southern T'ang Wu Yüeh sent an emissary bearing congratulations.[67] In 940 and again in 942, envoys from Wu Yüeh participated in the Southern T'ang ceremonies celebrating the ruler's ascension to the throne.[68] Finally, in 941, Southern T'ang sent a mission to Wu Yüeh to offer a sacrifice for the recently deceased second ruler.[69]

In 941 a serious disaster in Wu Yüeh presented the Southern T'ang with an unusual opportunity to launch an invasion. A major fire in the capital and palace destroyed many buildings and valuable supplies. This calamity evidently precipitated the nervous breakdown of the Wu Yüeh ruler. Officials at the Southern T'ang court strongly urged an attack against their now weakened enemies, but their ruler rejected the plan because he reputedly did not want to inflict further misery on his people or his neighbor's. Instead, he sent aid and condolences.[70] He is also reported to have sent relief supplies that year after a poor harvest in Wu Yüeh, but it is not clear whether this was in response to a separate misfortune.[71] The reasons for the Southern T'ang ruler's restraint and generosity are not readily apparent. No internal political circumstances prevented an attack. The Southern T'ang, moreover, did not as a rule follow a strictly pacifist policy; as will be noted later, it pressed and attacked Min for several years.

Beneath the surface of the routine diplomatic intercourse between Wu/Southern T'ang and Wu Yüeh lay a fairly constant tension. The last half of the 920s was a period when this underlying conflict heightened and came into the open. During this time Wu was feeling pressure from the Later T'ang, and Ch'ien Liu's political status was ascending to even greater heights. In 925 the ruler of Wu rebuffed a Wu Yüeh envoy bringing an announcement of the special honors and title Ch'ien had received from the Later T'ang. The Wu ruler was so angry that he closed his border to envoys and merchants from Wu Yüeh.[72] Exactly how long this prohibition lasted is not known, but a Wu envoy did cross into Wu Yüeh in 926. His ostensible purpose was to ask after the health of Ch'ien Liu, who was ill at the time, but his true mission was to discover whether Ch'ien's condition was serious enough to warrant mounting an attack. Ch'ien's appearance convinced the diplomat from Wu that the Wu Yüeh ruler was sufficiently vigorous to resist any invasion.[73]

While neither Wu/Southern T'ang nor Wu Yüeh violated each other's territory from 919 to 956, the arena of their intense diplomatic and military rivalry merely shifted to a neighbor, the state of Min. Both sides sought to gain influence, if not sovereignty, over Min, or at least to keep the other from doing so. Chien-chou (modern Chien-ou in the province of Fukien) was the scene of the first engagements pitting Wu/Southern T'ang and Wu Yüeh against each other. In late 933 and early 934 a local Wu official, without prior authorization from the Wu ruler, joined forces with a renegade Min official and laid siege to the prefecture. The Min ruler requested military support from Wu Yüeh, but before the relief troops arrived the Wu ruler recalled his forces.[74]

Internecine struggles during the mid-940s among a changing cast of Min competitors invited the intervention of Southern T'ang and Wu Yüeh and hastened the demise of the Min state. The various Min rivals frequently requested aid from either Southern T'ang or Wu Yüeh. Toward the end of 945 the Southern T'ang, by capitalizing on these internal struggles, had gained control of most of Min except Fu-chou. If this prefecture fell into Southern T'ang hands, Wu Yüeh would then be surrounded on all three landward sides by its enemy. In 946 Li Jen-ta at Fu-chou declared himself a vassal of Wu Yüeh and requested aid to resist a Southern T'ang onslaught. Wu Yüeh sent an expedition late that very year. Another amphibious assault in 947 conclusively defeated the Southern T'ang forces and saved Fu-chou and the northeastern section of what was formerly Min territory as a buffer for Wu Yüeh.[75] All that remained of Min were two southern coastal prefectures, which maintained independence until surrendering to the Sung thirty years later.

Diplomatic communications between Southern T'ang and Wu Yüeh apparently ceased after 942. An exchange of prisoners in 950 is the only record of friendly relations between the two states.[76] The break in relations was precipitated by the two rivals' competition to control Min, and it widened even further when Wu Yüeh later joined in the Chou invasion of Southern T'ang.

Despite Wu Yüeh's difficulties with some Northern as well as Southern states, it conducted trade and offered tribute throughout the early tenth century. We have already seen that Wu Yüeh started to trade with Min and Nan Han after the creation of diplomatic ties. Merchants also crossed the border between Wu/Southern T'ang and Wu Yüeh. The three coastal states of Min, Nan Han, and Wu Yüeh undoubtedly enjoyed a thriving trade over both land and sea routes. Some of Wu Yüeh's tribute items to the North, such as spices, ivory, and other exotica, originated from the South.

Wu Yüeh trade followed its tribute to the five Northern states. It was probably the North's largest trading partner and vice versa. Wu Yüeh was renowned for its lavish tribute offerings. In 937, for example, some of the major items in Wu Yüeh's tribute included the following: 4,000 bolts (*p'i*) of pongee (*chüan*) or 10.5 percent of the total amount of pongee presented to the Chin court from both domestic and foreign subordinates; 5,000 taels of silver, or 47.5 percent of the total of all tribute silver; and 1,000 bolts of patterned damask (*wen-ling*) for which Wu Yüeh was famous. In 938 Wu Yüeh presented 20,000 bolts of pongee, or 30 percent of the total; 10,000 taels of silver, or 8.5 percent of the total; 90,000 taels of floss silk (*mien*), or 76 percent of the total; and 8,000 bolts of patterned damask.[77] From these few figures we can easily imagine the extent of trade.

The extensive trade and tribute between Wu Yüeh and the other domestic states strongly suggest a growing degree of economic interdependence. Nothing better demonstrates this than the mosaic of currency systems in operation across China at that time.[78] Changes in one state's currency, a shift for example to a different specie, had repercussions in neighboring states. In 948 a proposal to introduce iron currency came up for debate at the Wu Yüeh court. The plan was vigorously opposed by the ruler's younger brother, who marshalled an eight-point argument.[79] His first major point, a formulation of what came to be known six centuries later in the West as Gresham's Law, was that the less intrinsically valuable iron coins would drive out the more valuable copper cash, which would be hoarded by other states. The second argument was that the new coins would not be negotiable in other states, thereby impeding commerce or even bringing it to a halt.

Domestic Multi-State Relations, 956–978

The second phase of domestic multi-state relations differed significantly from the first in one crucial respect: the growing power of the two Northern states, the Chou and the Sung, and their encroachment upon the Southern kingdoms. Wu Yüeh was increasingly forced into real, not just nominal, alignment with the North. Otherwise it would have become an adversary of the Chou and Sung.

In 955 the Chou began its invasion of the Southern T'ang. This was the first major effort in half a century by a Northern state to extend its border below the Huai River. At the same time Ch'ien Shu sent a tribute mission to the Chou. The Wu Yüeh envoy, who perhaps not by coincidence was a member of Ch'ien's military staff, returned to his homeland with a Chou plan to attack the Southern T'ang.[80] The strategy was for Wu Yüeh to put pressure on the rear flank of Southern T'ang while the Chou attacked in force from the north.

The Chou order for Wu Yüeh to join the attack precipitated an intense policy debate in Hang-chou. No matter what the decision, the implications for Wu Yüeh's future diplomatic relations, and even its continued existence, were momentous. This was to be a true test of the degree of its

professed subservience to the Northern states. One Wu Yüeh prime minister favored taking up arms immediately, arguing that the invasion was an
unparalleled opportunity, presumably to cripple its old rival. The other
prime minister feared Southern T'ang reprisals if the Chou attack failed;
there was, after all, little evidence at that time of the effectiveness of Chou
military capabilities.[81]

Ch'ien Shu opted to join with Chou against the Southern T'ang, but
judging by Wu Yüeh's ineffectiveness, its commitment seemed to be less
than wholehearted. In 956 he dispatched expeditions against two prefectures across the border, Ch'ang-chou and Hsüan-chou (modern Hsüan-
ch'eng in the province of Anhui). The failure of the attack against Ch'ang-
chou persuaded the commander of the force marching to Hsüan-chou to
withdraw before he engaged the enemy.[82] This effort was the extent of Wu
Yüeh's participation in the invasion until two years later when the victory
of the Chou was assured.[83] In 958 a Wu Yüeh marine force of 20,000 linked
up with the Chou for the final push of the war.[84]

The Chou victory had far-reaching economic, military, and diplomatic
consequences. Chou acquired all Southern T'ang territory between the
Yangtze and Huai rivers. This area produced large quantities of salt, the
revenue from which was invaluable to the Southern T'ang economy.
Southern T'ang's fiscal loss was Chou's gain. For the first time in half a
century, a Northern power had sufficient revenue to fuel a large military
machine that could be used to reintegrate the empire. Another economic
advantage for the Chou was the ability to reopen the Grand Canal, which
facilitated the transport of trade and tribute from the South to the North.

The diplomatic effects of the war were dramatic. First, the Southern
T'ang formally declared itself subordinate to the Chou and abandoned the
title of emperor in favor of the term "ruler of a kingdom" (*kuo-chu*), whose
connotation was less prestigious than Wu Yüeh's *kuo-wang*, "king of a
state." Second, diplomatic relations between Wu Yüeh and Southern T'ang
dwindled. The Chinese records do not reveal any contact between the two
states until 975 when the Southern T'ang was on the verge of collapse
before the Sung invaders. Despite its antagonism, Southern T'ang no
longer posed a military threat to Wu Yüeh, because it was weakened and,
more important, because any retaliatory attacks would probably have
provoked a strong response from the Chou or the Sung.

Finally, the Chou victory altered Wu Yüeh's relationship with the
Northern states. The territory north of the Yangtze, though controlled by
the rival Southern T'ang, had served Wu Yüeh as a buffer against the
North. Now geographic proximity forced Wu Yüeh to develop a more
extensive tributary relationship with the Chou and later the Sung. The
tribute Wu Yüeh sent to the Chou in 958, the year that the Chou emperor
reached the banks of the Yangtze, testifies to the changed relationship

between Wu Yüeh and the Northern states. Ch'ien Shu sent six tribute missions to the Chou that year, offering the following: 150,000 taels of floss silk, at least 28,000 taels of silver and silver objects, 200,000 *tan* (each *tan* amounted to 120 catties) of rice, 81,000 bolts of pongee, 20,000 bolts of damask, 34,000 *chin* or catties of tea, 2,000 pieces of fine cloth for clothing, 1,000 strings of cash, and countless other items whose quantities are not recorded.[85] The amounts in this offering exceed by far that given in any single previous year, and not until the Sung threatened to dissolve Wu Yüeh twenty years later were such large quantities bestowed.

After Sung T'ai-tsu's accession to the throne in 960, Wu Yüeh increased the number of tribute missions to the North.[86] Many of the tribute missions were headed by one of Ch'ien Shu's sons or other family members. In return, the Sung often sent gifts of sheep, horses, and camels, which it probably obtained from the Khitans, and honored Ch'ien Shu on the anniversaries of his birth. Envoys from Wu Yüeh often received special favors and treatment at the Sung court.[87] Other honors, gifts, and titles were regularly bestowed on members of the royal household and on officials.

Mutual dependence was the basis of the harmonious relations between Wu Yüeh and Sung. While Sung T'ai-tsu's attention was focused on the subjugation of other states (Ching-nan and Ch'u in 963, Shu in 965, and Nan Han in 971), he needed the loyalty of Wu Yüeh on his southern flank to blunt any aggressive impulses the Southern T'ang may have had. But he was not fully confident of Wu Yüeh's intentions. For its part, Wu Yüeh wanted to curry favor with the Sung to protect its own existence. As a token gesture of support for Sung reunification campaigns, Ch'ien Shu sent some troops from his personal guards to join in the Sung invasion of Shu.[88] In 971 Wu Yüeh sent lavish gifts to the influential Sung prime minister, Chao P'u, presumably to win his sympathies.[89]

After the defeat of Nan Han in 971, Sung T'ai-tsu turned his attention to conquest of the Southern T'ang. The Sung emperor ordered Ch'ien Shu to join the attack.[90] Historical accounts do not record any debate about the advisability of invading the Southern T'ang. There was little to debate, for the consequences of ignoring the order were plain.

Wu Yüeh did not launch its attack until 976, with Ch'ang-chou again the target. This expedition differed from that during the Chou in one telling respect. The Sung appointed one of its officers, with a force of several thousand troops, to serve as Inspector General of the Infantry and Cavalry on Expedition (*hsing-ying ping-ma tu-chien*).[91] Sung T'ai-tsu never trusted the loyalty of any military force beyond his direct control in the capital and had less reason to trust an expedition to a foreign state. Ch'ien Shu personally led the attack against Ch'ang-chou and after two attempts emerged victorious.[92]

Meanwhile, the ruler of Southern T'ang appealed to Wu Yüeh for assistance. Desperation evidently impelled him to seek some accommodation and alliance with his rival of many decades. He wrote Ch'ien Shu: "Today without me, how will there be you tomorrow? As soon as you exchange [my] territory for reward as a meritorious king, you too will be just an ordinary citizen of K'ai-feng." Ch'ien dared not respond, but forwarded the letter directly to Sung T'ai-tsu.[93] The Southern T'ang ruler's prediction eventually proved accurate.

Even before his victory over Southern T'ang, Sung T'ai-tsu began to urge Ch'ien Shu, the last remaining major Southern ruler, to travel to K'ai-feng for an audience. The Sung emperor wrote Ch'ien that he was eager to see him and promised to let him return freely to Hang-chou.[94] Ch'ien, his wife, and the crown prince left for K'ai-feng in 976 and were showered with gifts from T'ai-tsu all along the route. When Ch'ien reached the Sung capital, the emperor personally accompanied him to a specially constructed mansion, entertained him publicly and privately, and granted him exceptional privileges. He was allowed to wear his shoes and a sword at court and permitted to sign his personal name to official documents.[95] The emperor also gave Ch'ien's wife the title of imperial consort (*fei*), over the objections of his prime minister.[96]

The consequences of not abdicating and not dissolving his state were subtly but pointedly made clear to Ch'ien. He prepared to return to Hang-chou, leaving his son behind in K'ai-feng. Before he set out for Wu Yüeh, the emperor secretly gave him a yellow bag and told him to examine the contents privately on the return journey. Inside the bag he found all the memorials officials had sent to Sung T'ai-tsu urging him to detain Ch'ien in K'ai-feng.[97]

Ch'ien's days as an independent ruler were obviously numbered, but Sung T'ai-tsu's death in 976 postponed the inevitable for another year and a half. During 977 Ch'ien pursued a policy of buying his independence through presentation of lavish tribute and offers to relinquish some of the special privileges given him by the Sung. When he sent his son with tribute in the same year, he requested permission to increase the amount of regular tribute.[98] A month later he requested that he be referred to by his personal name in imperial edicts.[99] Sung T'ai-tsung, who succeeded T'ai-tsu, refused both petitions. To have consented would have reduced Ch'ien's obligation to the Sung court and weakened the pressure on him to relinquish his kingdom.

Ch'ien traveled to K'ai-feng for a second and final time in 978. He was accorded the same profuse hospitality as during his first visit. Soon after Ch'ien's arrival, Ch'en Hung-chin, the ruler of two prefectures in what was formerly the state of Min, surrendered to the Sung. This made Ch'ien the last Southern holdout and intensified the pressure on him to follow suit. He offered to disband his army and to renounce his titles and privileges if he could be allowed to return to Wu Yüeh.[100] T'ai-tsung refused, whereupon it became obvious that Ch'ien no longer could bargain for Wu Yüeh's survival.

Capitulation came later in 978. Ch'ien was given the honorary title of King of Huai-hai (*Huai-hai kuo-wang*), and his sons and officials all received titles and ranks of one sort or another.[101] So ended Wu Yüeh, the longest-lived of the Five Dynasties/Ten Kingdoms states and the only one to capitulate without military intervention.[102] Diplomatic strategy was its primary means of survival, and when there was no longer room to man-euver, Wu Yüeh simply surrendered.

The importance of Wu Yüeh to the Sung, and by implication to the previous five Northern states, can be measured by the amount of its tribute offerings. The Sung maintained a careful record of the tribute received from Wu Yüeh during the reigns of T'ai-tsu and T'ai-tsung. The following are among the major items: over 95,000 taels of yellow gold; over 1,012,000 taels of silver; over 280,000 bolts of various types of silk; more than 797,000 bolts of colored pongee; more than 140,000 gold-and-silver decorated utensils for wine; 70,000 silver-decorated weapons; 1,500 gold-adorned tortoise shell implements; 200 gold and silver dragon and phoenix ships; and other rare and exotic items too numerous to mention.[103] This stagger-ing sum of tribute over the years unquestionably contributed to the Sung war chest and to its fiscal stability.

International Multi-State Relations

Functioning like any Chinese regime ruling a unified empire, Wu Yüeh conducted relations with states beyond Chinese territory. It was in touch with Japan, the Khitan state north of the Great Wall, and all three Korean states of the time, Silla, Koryŏ, and Later Paekche. These ties between Wu Yüeh and overseas states were the natural outgrowth of its geographic location and of its well-developed maritime commerce.

Wu Yüeh initiated a tributary relationship with Kyŏn Hwon, the mili-tarist who ruled the state of Later Paekche in the southwestern tip of the Korean peninsula. Even before the fall of the T'ang dynasty, Wu Yüeh had bestowed several titles on him. As early as 900 Kyŏn sent an envoy to Wu Yüeh, and Ch'ien Liu responded by promoting him to the titular rank of Honorary Grand Protector (*chien-chiao ta-pao*).[104] In 918 Kyŏn presented horses to Wu Yüeh, and Ch'ien conferred another promotion.[105]

This relationship between Wu Yüeh and Later Paekche offered mutual benefits to both states in their quest for domestic legitimacy. Later Paekche needed to bolster its position vis-à-vis rivals seeking to unify Korea, and Chinese recognition and titles served its purpose. In 925 Kyŏn also declared himself a subordinate of the Later T'ang for the same reason.[106] By the same token, if Wu Yüeh was to be perceived as a state with imperial or quasi-imperial status, it needed to fulfill the traditional role of the "central kingdom" to which all foreign states theoretically looked for the source of authority and legitimation.

Relations were also maintained with Later Paekche's enemies, Koryŏ and Silla. At least one envoy from Koryŏ traveled to Wu Yüeh in 937.[107] In 925 Ch'ien Liu granted a Chinese title to the ruler of Silla.[108] Commerce between Wu Yüeh and the Korean states no doubt developed, but we know little about it. The Chinese sources yield few details about this trade. One incident pertaining to trade is, however, recorded. In 961 a ship from Koryŏ landed in Wu Yüeh. One rare object on board particularly appealed to Ch'ien Shu, who offered to buy it, but for some unexplained reason the ship's captain refused to sell it.[109]

No other state during the T'ang–Sung transition period developed such extensive relations with Japan. Unlike Wu Yüeh's relations with Korea, Wu Yüeh seems, on the surface, to have gained little from its exchanges with Japan. From the middle of the ninth century, Japan did not send official missions to China and never sent any to Wu Yüeh. But Wu Yüeh sent several embassies to Japan. Although the texts of Wu Yüeh's notes to Japan are not preserved, it appears that Wu Yüeh did not attempt to establish a tributary or other formal relationship with Japan. The political benefit to Wu Yüeh of its missions to Japan was enhancement of its status as an imperial state.

Chinese merchants were the principal quasi-official intermediaries between the two states, indicating that commerce was essential to their relationship. Wu Yüeh would either deputize a ship's captain as an envoy or else use one simply as a bearer of messages and presents. The Japanese court, which was happy to receive Chinese goods, used the same merchants to reciprocate Wu Yüeh's diplomatic dispatches and gifts. Because of their frequent trips, Chinese merchants knew the most about both states and could interpret the events and messages of one to the other.[110]

In 935 Ch'ien Yüan-kuan sent the first recorded mission to Japan. His envoy, who was also a merchant, presented some sheep to the Japanese court.[111] In the following year the same envoy and two others from Wu Yüeh arrived in Japan with a communiqué. The powerful Minister of the Left (*sadaijin*), Fujiwara Tadahira, sent a reply to Ch'ien Yüan-kuan.[112] In 940 Japan sent another diplomatic note to Wu Yüeh.[113] Five years later, three ships from Wu Yüeh with a hundred men aboard landed in Hizen prefecture (modern Nagasaki), but they apparently had no explicit diplomatic mission.[114]

In 953 the same merchant who had first traveled to Japan in 935 returned with gifts of silk and other goods together with a missive for

Fujiwara Morosuke from Ch'ien Shu. The Fujiwara leader responded in deferential terms to Wu Yüeh and Ch'ien.[115] Curiously, this diplomatic note as well as others to Wu Yüeh's rulers were signed by a member of the Fujiwara clan, not the emperor. Perhaps the Japanese emperors could not or would not respond because of the breach in Sino-Japanese relations. Or the Fujiwaras may have understood that the Wu Yüeh rulers controlled only a region and thus were not equal in rank to the Japanese emperor. Relations between Ch'ien Shu and the Fujiwaras continued, nonetheless. Missions from Wu Yüeh are recorded in 957 and 959.[116]

Buddhism fostered diplomatic relations between Wu Yüeh and both Japan and Korea. The rulers of Wu Yüeh, particularly the first and the last, were devout believers.[117] The T'ien-t'ai sect of Buddhism had originated several centuries before in the territory later controlled by Wu Yüeh, and attracted many foreign monks on study missions. Japanese and Korean monks were known to have passed through or sojourned for long periods in Wu Yüeh.[118] And monks from Wu Yüeh went to Japan and Korea to spread the word.[119]

During the turmoil of the Huang Ch'ao rebellion and its aftermath, many Buddhist texts were evidently destroyed or lost in Wu Yüeh. Devotees that they were, the Wu Yüeh rulers sought to obtain the missing sutras. Consequently, they dispatched official delegations and letters to Korea and Japan for this purpose. In 947 Ch'ien Tso learned from merchants that the T'ien-t'ai sect flourished in Japan. He immediately sent a message to the Japanese court, presenting some books and offering to buy any available sutras. Fujiwara Saneyori replied and enclosed 200 taels of gold but did not mention the sutras.[120] In 961 Ch'ien Shu sent fifty kinds of precious objects and a letter to Koryŏ seeking the missing sutras. The Koryŏ ruler commissioned the monk Chegwan to take many texts to Wu Yüeh, where he remained until his death.[121] In the mid-950s, Ch'ien Shu manufactured 84,000 miniature pagodas which contained a seal with his name and title. A Japanese monk happened to be passing through Wu Yüeh at the time and took 500 of the pagodas back to Japan with him.[122] The propaganda effect in Japan was dramatic. Although we do not know how Ch'ien disposed of the remaining pagodas, it is not hard to imagine that he sent many of them far and wide in China and overseas. Intentional or not, the subtle result was to demonstrate not only Ch'ien's piety but also Wu Yüeh's prosperity, political power, and cultural achievements.

Wu Yüeh's dealings with the Khitans were the most significant aspect of all its foreign relations. Wu Yüeh was the first of the Chinese states to establish relations with the Khitans. In 915 Ch'ien Liu dispatched an envoy, who probably was a merchant, to present "tribute."[123] Whether or not Wu Yüeh actually presented tribute (*kung*), as the dynastic history of the

Liao dynasty indicates, is a matter of political perception; it is highly unlikely, though, that Ch'ien thought he was, as the term "tribute" implies, subservient to the Khitans.

From 915 to 943, Wu Yüeh and the Khitans exchanged seventeen missions, thirteen from Wu Yüeh to the north and four from the Khitans to the south.[124] All but one of these appear to have been routine. In 941, however, Wu Yüeh sent a letter in a wax ball, the usual way for transmitting secret messages.[125] At this time Hang-chou had suffered a devastating fire and Ch'ien Yüan-kuan had suffered a mental breakdown, prompting some advisers at the Southern T'ang court to advocate an invasion. It is reasonable to speculate that Wu Yüeh hoped to persuade the Khitans to intercede with the Southern T'ang.

This incident suggests the role that the Khitans could play in Chinese domestic politics. The Southern T'ang developed its alliance with the Khitans to counter the strong links between Wu Yüeh and the Northern states.[126] In its own relations with the Khitans, Wu Yüeh may have wanted to neutralize the Khitans' ties with the Southern T'ang. More likely, though, it may have intended to use the Khitans to offset the power of the Northern states. Wu Yüeh's relationship with the Khitans was recognized in the North. In 918 the envoys from Liang and Wu Yüeh appeared together at the Khitans' court.[127] Information about Wu Yüeh's contacts with the Khitans could easily have reached the Liang court.

When the Chin dynasty, under Shih Ching-t'ang, gained control of North China with the support of the Khitans, Wu Yüeh would presumably seek to strengthen its relationship with the Khitans. The Chin, after all, officially admitted its subservience to the Khitans, and Wu Yüeh nominally recognized the sovereignty of the Chin and by extension should so recognize the Khitans. During this period, Wu Yüeh increased the number of its missions to the Khitans. It sent seven embassies between 939 and 943. The Khitans stood to gain from diplomatic and commercial relations with the wealthy state of Wu Yüeh. Thus they encouraged merchants and officials from Wu Yüeh to exchange goods with them. Trade did, for some time, flourish between the two states.[128]

Conclusion

This essay has portrayed a segment of the Byzantine pattern of tenth-century Chinese history. The reader might well perceive of this period as an era of chaos, characterized by usurpations, wars, and unstable coalitions. Yet if the events of the time are interpreted in light of a balance of power, they can fit into a comprehensible pattern.

The protagonists in this system were Wu Yüeh, Wu/Southern T'ang, the succession of five Northern states (which are collectively considered one actor), the Khitans, Ching-nan, Ch'u, Min, and Nan Han.[129] The first five were the primary actors while the other three played subsidiary roles. Before 956 a fairly stable balance of power system operated. Each state was eager to expand its power at the expense of the others but was also willing to negotiate rather than fight. Some even chose non-belligerent tactics to strengthen themselves. Wu Yüeh's entire diplomacy rested on this premise. By carefully attempting to remain in the good graces of the Northern states, Wu Yüeh capitalized politically on the privileges it received and used the fiction of its loyalty to the North as protection against attacks from Wu/Southern T'ang. Yet the states showed no hesitation to fight, because their existence ultimately depended upon military power.

The basic rule in a balance of power system is: cease aggression before annihilating an actor. This requires a conscious commitment on the part of the states to maintain the system. It also means that the actors realize that their self-defense is best served by preserving the system. Wu/Southern T'ang's hesitancy to bring Wu Yüeh to its knees in 919 and 941 is an example of the operation of this rule. Even when Southern T'ang and Wu Yüeh were competing for territory in the state of Min, they did not seek its total destruction; the remnants of the Min state were allowed to regroup in two prefectures. The Southern T'ang and Wu Yüeh rulers clearly appreciated the necessity for maintaining the balance of power system. The collapse of one state would have meant the same fate for the other, as the last Southern T'ang ruler pointed out to Ch'ien Shu. Similarly, rulers in the North understood, for example, that Wu Yüeh was the key to stability in the South and to their own security.

National reunification and political legitimacy, which are closely intertwined, were the primary supranational organizing principles in premodern Chinese political thought. All the states expected eventual reintegration of the empire, but none of the Southern kingdoms maintained any serious pretense that they would or could achieve this objective. The Northern states, on the other hand, were the ones to make the most forceful but not always accepted claims to legitimacy. Because of this, as well as their military strength, they were the actors whom, in one way or another, all other states tried to constrain militarily and diplomatically.[130]

As soon as the Chou met success across the Huai River, the fragile balance-of-power system that existed until then was destabilized. The Chou gained new resources and control of the major north–south transportation artery. These two factors, together with the growing Chou and Sung drive for national hegemony, spelled the eventual collapse of the system. In the face of these pressures, Wu Yüeh's exquisitely equivocating diplomacy could no longer assure its survival.

NOTES

1. For a recent description of early Koryŏ history, see H. W. Kang, "The First Succession Struggle of Koryŏ, in 945: A Reinterpretation," *Journal of Asian Studies* 36, 3 (1977): 411–428.

2. George Sansom describes this period's changing diplomatic and internal political scene in *A History of Japan to 1334* (Stanford, 1974), pp. 136–150.

3. The interactions among states of the Spring and Autumn period have often been examined as a system of international relations. Richard L. Walker has written the most authoritative account in English: *The Multi-State System of Ancient China* (Westport, Conn., 1971; reprint of 1953 ed.)

4. Ch'ien Yen, *Wu Yüeh pei shih* (hereafter *WYPS*), 4.30b, describes the size of Wu Yüeh's population and territory.

5. Opinions vary about the date when Wu Yüeh, as well as some of the other ten kingdoms, was "founded" and thus how many years it existed. Ou-yang Hsiu et al., *Hsin Wu-tai shih* (hereafter *HWTS*), 67, 844, says it lasted 84 years, fixing the beginning in 895. Lu Chen, *Chiu-kuo chih*, 5, 1a (*Pi-chi hsiao-shuo ta-kuan* edition), says Wu Yüeh existed 98 years. Clearly, no single specific event indisputably can be designated as marking the beginning of the state. Many scholars accept the year 907 when Ch'ien was named *Wu Yüeh wang* and when the T'ang fell.

6. For an account of Ch'ien's rise to power, see Watanabe Michio, "Goetsu koku no kenkoku katei," *Shikan* 56 (September 1959): 93–104. Also see Ch'ien's biography in Hsüeh Chü-cheng et al., *Chiu Wu-tai shih* (hereafter *CWTS*), 133, 1766–1768, and Wu Jen-ch'en, *Shih-kuo ch'un-ch'iu* (hereafter *SKCC*), 77, 1a–30b. The only study in a Western language of Wu Yüeh is by Édouard Chavannes, "Le royaume de Wou et de Yue," *T'oung Pao* 17, 2 (May 1916): 129–264. He translates the biographical materials from T'o T'o et al., *Sung shih* (hereafter *SS*), CWTS, HWTS, and other sources.

7. Two articles survey the general and political history of Wu Yüeh. Sakurai Haruko, "Godai jūkoku no Goetsu ni tsuite," *Nara shien* (February 1967), pp. 11–24. Watanabe Michio, "Goetsu koku no shihai kōzō," *Shikan* 76 (October 1967): 33–51.

8. For the standard account of political developments in North China during the late T'ang and the first four of the five northern "dynasties," see Wang Gungwu, *The Structure of Power in North China during the Five Dynasties* (Kuala Lumpur, 1963).

9. Ssu-ma Kuang, *Tzu-chih t'ung-chien* (hereafter *TCTC*), 266, 8675–8676, reveals the courses of action some military governors or princes considered against Chu Wen.

10. *TCTC*, 266, 8676; *WYPS*, 1, 40b–41a; *HWTS*, 67, 839.

11. *TCTC*, 264, 8632; 266, 8680; *WYPS*, 1, 41a; *SKCC*, 77, 31a.

12. *SKCC*, 78, 1b.

13. *SKCC*, 77, 32ab; 78, 1ab; *WYPS*, 1, 41a–42b.

14. *TCTC*, 266, 8684; *WYPS*, 1, 41a; *SKCC*, 77, 31b.

15. *TCTC*, 267, 8703; *WYPS*, 1, 41b; *SKCC*, 78, 1b.

16. In the late T'ang, Ch'ien had to seek aid from Chu Wen in order to fend off Yang Hsing-mi; *CWTS*, 133, 1768.

17. Robert J. Krompart has studied the Wu and early Southern T'ang in his Ph.D. dissertation, entitled *The Southern Restoration of T'ang: Counsel, Policy, and Parahistory in the Stabilization of the Chiang-Huai Region* (University of California, Berkeley, 1973), pp. 887–943.

18. For accounts of some of the major campaigns, see *WYPS*, 1, 42a, 50a, 54b–55a; *SKCC*, 78, 1b, 8b, 12a–12b; Wang Ch'in-jo, *Ts'e-fu yüan-kuei* (hereafter *TFYK*), 217, 28a, p. 2607.

19. Hino Kaisaburō has imaginatively analyzed the overland communication networks in the Five Dynasties. See his "Godai no namboku Shina rikujō kōtsurō ni tsuite," *Rekishigaku kenkyū* 11, 6 (June 1941): 372–402.

20. *TCTC*, 269, 8802 lists the main points in the route.

21. The perils of the sea voyage are described in *TCTC*, 278, 9089; *CWTS*, 134, 1792; and *TFYK*, 168, 17a, p. 2031.

22. The campaign is described in *SKCC*, 78, 12b; *WYPS*, 1, 54b; *TCTC*, 270, 8824, 8833, 8835.

23. *TCTC*, 270, 8836–8837.

24. *TFYK*, 197, 23a, p. 2381.

25. *WYPS*, 1, 52b; *TCTC*, 270, 8803; *SKCC*, 78, 9b–10a.

26. *WYPS*, 1, 49b; *TCTC*, 268, 8760; *SKCC*, 78, 8a.

27. *SKCC*, 78, 11b; *WYPS*, 1, 54a; *TCTC*, 270, 8819, 8824; *CWTS*, 9.131. *TCTC* and *CWTS* list this post as *yüan-shuai*, while *SKCC* and *WYPS* give the title of *tu yüan-shuai*. I follow the latter pair of sources. In a recently discovered document dated 922, Ch'ien indicates his title as *tu yüan-shuai*. See Wang Shih-lun, "Wu-tai Wu Yüeh te liang-chien wen-shu," *Wen wu* (January 1960), pp. 65–66.

28. *TCTC*, 269, 8799. Liang T'ing-nan, *Nan Han shu* (Hong Kong, 1967 reprint of 1830 woodblock ed.), 2, 4a, p. 12. Liang T'ing-nan, *Nan Han shu k'ao-i* (same edition) 2, 6b–7c, pp. 106–107.

29. *TCTC*, 274, 8954; *SKCC*, 78, 17b.

30. *TFYK*, 219, 30a, p. 2635; *TCTC*, 277, 9073; *CWTS*, 134, 1792. In the only work in a Western language on Min, Edward H. Schafer describes this incident; see his *The Empire of Min* (Rutland and Tokyo, 1954), p. 39.

31. *WYPS*, 1, 52a; *SKCC*, 78, 9a; *Nan Han shu*, 2, 3b, p. 12; *Nan Han shu k'ao-i*, 215–6a, p. 106. Edward H. Schafer has the only account in a Western language of Nan Han; see his translation of *HWTS*, ch. 65, "The History of the Empire of Southern Han," *Silver Jubilee Volume of the Zinbun-Kagaku-Kenkyusyo* (Kyoto, 1954), pp. 339–369.

32. *WYPS*, 1, 55a–56b; *SKCC*, 78, 13a; *CWTS*, 9, 139.

33. *WYPS*, 1, 52b; *SKCC*, 78, 10a; *TCTC*, 269, 8808; Schafer, *The Empire of Min*, p. 34. Tanaka Seiji has described the relations between Wu Yüeh and Min; see his "Goetsu to Bin to no kankei, Binkoku no nairan o chūsin toshite," *Tōyōshi kenkyū* 28, 1 (June 1969): 28–51.

34. *WYPS*, 1, 57a; *TCTC*, 271, 8865; *SKCC*, 78, 13ab.

35. *WYPS*, 1, 55a; *SKCC*, 78, 13a; *TCTC*, 290, 8846–8847, 8849.

36. *WYPS*, 1, 57a; *SKCC* 78, 13b; *HWTS*, 67, 840.

37. Chavannes, op. cit. (n. 6 above), pp. 164–66, describes the evolution of this privilege and some incidents when it was conferred. See also Wang P'u, *Wu-tai hui-yao* (hereafter *WTHY*), 11, 143.

38. *TCTC*, 272, 8880; *SKCC*, 78, 14ab; *WYPS*, 1, 58ab. Chavannes, op. cit., p. 167, quotes an inscription from the *Liang-che chin-shih chih* which dates the use of the title *Wu Yüeh kuo-wang* as early as 921. However, in one of the recently discovered Wu Yüeh documents dating from 922 (cf. Wang Shih-lun, op. cit., n. 27 above), Ch'ien Liu designates his title simply as *Wu Yüeh wang*. I follow this latter document.

39. *CWTS*, 133, 1768 dates the granting of this title a year or two later, but *TCTC*, 272, 8880 more appropriately gives a date of 923. Surely Ch'ien Liu would not have wanted to retain the title of regional military governor after he was made a *kuo-wang*.

40. The *TCTC* commentator Hu San-hsing notes, though, that even in his day (the thirteenth century) the people residing in what was Wu Yüeh's territory still referred to Ch'ien Liu as Ch'ien T'ai-tsu. *TCTC*, 275, 8879—8898. This same source, as well as *SKCC*, 80, 14a, quoting *Chien-yen i-lai ch'ao-yeh tsa-chi*, gives examples of the first two rulers having posthumous titles.

41. Ssu-ma Kuang must receive some credit for pointing out that Ch'ien did change reign titles (*TCTC*, 275, 8997), but he grasped only part of the picture. The great Southern Sung scholar Hung Mai was the first to examine the issue thoroughly; see his *Jung-chai sui-pi* (Peking, 1959), part 4, *chüan* (hereafter ch.) 5, pp. 47—48. In the Ch'ing period Wang Ming-sheng amplified on Hung; *Shih-ch'i-shih shang-ch'üeh* (Ts'ung-shu chi-ch'eng ed.), 97, pp. 1121—23. Ch'ien Ta-hsin also studied the matter; *Shih-chia-chai yang-hsin lu* (Peking, 1957), ch. 15, pp. 264—265.

42. This supposition by Hung Mai and Wang Ming-sheng can be corroborated by the recently discovered Wu Yüeh document of 922 (cf. Wang Shih-lun, op, cit.) which uses a Liang reign title.

43. Chung Yüan-ying cites *Yü hai* for this reign title. *Li-tai chien-yüan k'ao* [*Shou-shan-ko ts'ung-shu* (Shanghai, 1889)], 2, 19b—21a.

44. *WYPS*, 1, 55a, 65b—66a; *SKCC*, 78, 13a.

45. *TCTC*, 273, 8926; *CWTS*, 32, 449; 133, 1768; *WYPS*, 1, 61a; *SKCC*, 78, 15a; *WTHY*, 4, 49; 11, 143. The exact chronology of this event is somewhat confused in the sources, some indicating that it occurred in 924 and others in 925. I rather think that Ch'ien's request was made in 924 but that no action was taken on it until 925. The documents in *WTHY* tend to confirm this.

46. *CWTS*, 133, 1768; *SKCC*, 78, 17a.

47. *TFYK*, 664, 7a, 7645; *WYPS*, 1, 63a; *SKCC*, 78, 20ab; *TCTC*, 276, 9032—9033; *CWTS*, 40, 554; *HWTS*, 24, 253.

48. *CWTS*, 133, 1768.

49. *WYPS*, 1, 63a; *TCTC*, 276, 9032—9033; *SKCC*, 78, 20ab; *CWTS*, 133, 1768.

50. *CWTS*, 40, 554.

51. *SKCC*, 78, 20b; *CWTS*, 40, 554.

52. *WYPS*, 1, 63a; *SKCC*, 78, 20b.

53. *CWTS*, 133, 1768.

54. *CWTS*, 133, 1786—1770; *TCTC*, 277, 9048; *SKCC*, 78, 20b. The text of Ch'ien Yüan-kuan's memorial to the T'ang is preserved in *CWTS*.

55. *WYPS*, 1, 63b; *SKCC*, 78, 21a. *CWTS*, 42, 577, and *TCTC*, 277, 9058 date this in the third month.

56. *TCTC*, 277, 9066; *SKCC*, 78, 23a.

57. *WTHY*, 11, 144; *CWTS*, 44, 606.

58. *CWTS*, 45, 616; *TCTC*, 278, 9100.

59. *TCTC*, 281, 9172.

60. Sources disagree on whether Ch'ien received the title King of Wu Yüeh before establishing state, as opposed to provincial, institutions. *WYPS*, 2, 8b, and *SKCC*, 79, 7ab claim that the title came first, but *WTHY*, 11, 145, *CWTS*, 76, 1009, and especially *TCTC*, 281, 9184, more convincingly suggest the chronology I follow.

61. *CWTS*, 134, 1783 gives a brief summary of Wu and Later T'ang relations.

62. *TFYK*, 232, 17a–19a, pp. 2763–2764, offers details on the gift-bearing missions from Wu to T'ang.

63. *WYPS*, 1, 57a; *SKCC*, 78, 13a.

64. *WYPS*, 2, 6b; *SKCC*, 79, 5a.

65. *SKCC*, 79, 7b.

66. Lu Yu, *Nan T'ang shu* (*Ssu-pu pei-yao* ed.), 1, 3b.

67. *Nan T'ang shu*, 1, 5a; *SKCC*, 79, 9b.

68. *Nan T'ang shu*, 1, 6a, 7a.

69. *WYPS*, 3, 1b; *SKCC*, 80, 2a.

70. *TCTC*, 282, 9226; *SKCC*, 15, 15ab; 79, 11b. For a discussion of this incident and Wu Yüeh–Southern T'ang relations, see Tanaka Seiji, "Nantō to Goetsu to no kankei," *Shiryū* 16 (March 1975): 1–18.

71. *Nan T'ang shu*, 1, 6b; *SKCC*, 15, 15b.

72. *TCTC*, 274, 8954.

73. *TCTC*, 274, 8971; *SKCC*, 78, 17b.

74. *TCTC*, 278, 9096. Schafer, *The Empire of Min*, pp. 40–65 passim, discusses this and other conflicts between Wu/Southern T'ang and Wu Yüeh over the Min.

75. *TCTC*, 285, 9312–9314, 9349; *WYPS*, 3, 9a, 11a; *SKCC*, 80, 6a, 7ab.

76. *TCTC*, 289, 9425; *SKCC*, 81, 5a.

77. Hino Kaisaburō has conveniently compiled tables comparing the quantities of major tribute items submitted to the northern court during certain periods of the Five Dynasties era. "Godai hanchin no kyoshiken to Hokosōchō no yobaiken" (part 1), *Shien* 15 (March 1937): 114–124. For the full list of Wu Yüeh tribute presented in 933 and 938, see *TFYK*, 169, 13a, p. 2038; 169, 15b–16a, p. 2039; *SKCC*, 79, 7b–8a. There are a few minor differences between the two sources.

78. For a discussion of the currency systems, see Miyazaki Ichisada, *Godai Sōshō no tsūka mondai* (Tokyo, 1943), pp. 13–82.

79. *TCTC*, 285, 9313; *WYPS*, 3, 10a.

80. *WYPS*, 4, 11b; *TCTC*, 292, 9543; *SKCC*, 81, 7ab.

81. *WYPS*, 4, 12ab; *TCTC*, 292, 9540–9541; *SKCC*, 87, 3ab.

82. *WYPS*, 4, 12a; *TCTC*, 293, 9549–9550; *SKCC*, 81, 7b–8a.

83. *SS*, 480, 2a, notes that before 958 Wu Yüeh was told to withdraw its troops because the Southern T'ang had already begun to sue for peace. I can find no references in other sources to such an order from the Chou and must question the accuracy of the *SS* on this point.

84. *WYPS*, 4, 13b; *SKCC*, 81, 9a. For a full account of the war, see Chung-kuo li-tai chan-cheng-shih pien-tsuan wei-yüan-hui, *Chung-kuo li-tai chan-cheng-shih* (Taipei, rev. ed., 1976), vol. 10, pp. 314–326.

85. *TFYK*, 169, 26b—27a, pp. 2044—2045.

86. *WYPS*, 4, 16a; *SKCC*, 81, 11a.

87. Li T'ao, *Hsü Tzu-chih t'ung-chien ch'ang-pien* (hereafter *HCP*), 10, 1b.

88. *WYPS*, 4, 17b; *SKCC*, 81, 13a.

89. *HCP*, Yung-lo ta-tien, 12360, 7a. *SKCC*, 82, 3b dates this incident as 973, but *HCP* seems more reliable. Chao P'u was dismissed from office in 8th month of 973.

90. *WYPS*, 4, 20b; *SKCC*, 82, 3a.

91. *WYPS*, 4, 22a; *SKCC*, 82, 4a.

92. *WYPS*, 4, 22b, 27b; *SKCC*, 82, 4b—5a.

93. *HCP*, Yung-lo ta-tien, 12307, 4b; *SS*, 480, 3ab; *Nan T'ang shu*, 3, 4b. *SKCC*, 82, 5a, incorrectly gives 975 as the date for this event.

94. *HCP*, Yung-lo ta-tien, 12308, 2a; *SS*, 480, 3b.

95. *WYPS*, 4, 25ab—26a; *SKCC*, 82, 5b—7a.

96. Wang Ch'eng, *Tung-tu shih-lüeh* (Taipei, 1967 reprint), 24, 1b.

97. *WYPS*, 4, 26ab; *SKCC*, 82, 7ab.

98. *WYPS*, 4, 27b; *SKCC*, 82, 9b.

99. *SS*, 480, 5b; Sung Shou (attributed compiler), *Sung ta chao-ling chi* (Peking, 1962), 277, 878.

100. *HCP*, 19, 7a.

101. *WYPS*, 4, 28a—30a; *SKCC*, 82, 9b—11a.

102. Although Ch'en Hung-chin surrendered without a struggle, he had a small satrapy that is not considered a state.

103. *WYPS*, 4, 41a.

104. *Samguk sagi* (Seoul, 1972), ch. 50, p. 785.

105. *Samguk sagi*, 50, 785; *SKCC*, 78, 12ab.

106. *Samguk sagi*, 50, 785.

107. *SKCC*, 79.7b. Korean souces do not mention this mission.

108. *SKCC*, 78, 17a; *CWTS*, 133, 1768.

109. *SKCC*, 81, 11b.

110. In a rather extended study, Hino Kaisaburō masterfully discusses, among other points, the connections between merchants and envoys in the Five Dynasties. See his "Godai jidai ni okeru Kittan to Shina to no kaijō bōeki," *Shigaku zasshi* 52, 7 (July 1941): 1—47; 52, 8 (August 1941): 60—85; 52, 9 (September 1941): 55—82.

111. *Nihon kiryaku*, in vol. 8, *Kokushi taikei kōhen* (Tokyo, 1895), ch. 2, p. 820. Nishioka Toranosuke has written a helpful article about Wu Yüeh-Japanese relations. "Nihon to Goetsu to no kōtsū," *Rekishi chiri* 42, 1 (July 1923): 32—62.

112. *Nihon kiryaku, kōhen*, ch. 2, p. 821.

113. Ibid., p. 827.

114. *Honchō seki*, vol. 5, *Kokushi taikei* (Tokyo, 1896), pp. 124—125.

115. *Honchō bunsui* (Tokyo, 1648 woodblock ed.), 7, 26a—27a.

116. *Nihon kiryaku, kōhen*, ch. 4, pp. 869, 875.

117. For a study of Ch'ien Liu and Buddhism, see Andō Tomonobu, "Goetsu Bushuku-ō Sen Ryu to Bukkyō—shimpi-e no heikōshō to ōkō-e no yabō," *Ōtani gakuhō* 50, 4 (March 1971): 28—46.

118. *SKCC*, 89, 4a, 7a.

119. *Fo-tsu t'ung-chi* (*Taishō Daizōkyō* 2035, vol. 49), ch. 42, p. 391c.

120. *Honchō bunsui*, 7, 25a—26a. *Dai Nihon shi* (1851 woodblock ed.), 232,

24b–25b, mentions this episode but mistakenly confuses Ch'ien Shu for Ch'ien Tso.

121. *Fo-tsu t'ung-chi*, ch. 10, p. 206ab; ch. 43, pp. 294c–295a; *SKCC*, 89, 5b–6a.

122. Ono Gemmyō explains this story in some detail. *Bukkyō no bijutsu oyobi rekishi* (Tokyo, 1916), pp. 614–640.

123. T'o T'o et al., *Liao shih* (hereafter *LS*), 1, 10. For a simple summary of Wu Yüeh–Khitan intercourse, see Lu Tai-tseng, "Wu-tai shih-kuo tui Liao te wai-chiao," *Hsüeh-shu chi-k'an* 3, 1 (August 1954): 25–51, esp. pp. 36–37. Hino Kaisaburō, op. cit. (n. 110 above) also provides much helpful information and inter-pretation.

124. Both Lu and Hino overlook the fact that a Wu Yüeh envoy accompanied his Khitan colleague to the north in 933; *SKCC*, 79, 5a. I do not know the source of *SKCC*'s entry.

125. *LS*, 4, 50.

126. In addition to Lu and Hino on this subject, see Wang Chi-lin, "Ch'i-tan yü Nan T'ang wai-chiao kuan-hsi chih t'an-t'ao," *Yu-shih hsüeh-chih*, 5, 2 (December 1966): 1–15.

127. *LS*, 1, 11.

128. *LS*, 37, 437. See also a brief discussion in Hino, op. cit. n. 110 above.

129. Although certainly a national actor, Shu, because of its geographic location, interacted primarily with the northern dynasties and infrequently with the southern or lower Yangtze states. Thus it is not included in this particular model of the balance of power system.

130. My analysis of the balance of power system is based on the work of Morton A. Kaplan, *System and Process in International Relations* (New York, 1957), pp. 22–36.

PART II

The Sung Dynasty in a Multi-State System

The Rhetoric of a Lesser Empire: Early Sung Relations with Its Neighbors

WANG GUNGWU

The tenth century in China was one of many kingdoms, empires, and dynasties, and each one of them sought to inherit what was perceived as the grand imperial heritage of the T'ang dynasty. This was true up to the first two decades of the Sung dynasty. Until the end of Sung T'ai-tsu's reign (960–976), every claim to that heritage, if not obviously hollow, was greeted with suspicion and was challenged by some other, rival claim. This was particularly true of the claim to T'ang greatness in the known world around China, even thought that claim by the T'ang itself had become more rhetorical than real by the end of the eighth century. The point is that, for some one hundred and fifty years after the An Lu-shan rebellion, while the T'ang was struggling to survive as a military empire, the imperial style in the dynasty's relations with foreign kingdoms and tribes seems to have been sustained.[1] It would not have occurred to T'ang officials that there should be any need to reconsider this style in the face of threat and danger. On the contrary, it was probably unthinkable that the T'ang court should have considered any dilution of its claims to superiority just because the imperial writ did not cover as large an area as it did at the height of the empire's power. This reduction in size and the concomitant reduction in power and wealth to the court could, after all, be looked upon as temporary, with the full recovery of past glory still a possibility. In short, the loss of physical means to dominate its neighbors should not be the grounds for reviewing the philosophical and political basis for T'ang's "foreign" relations.

All the same, after the fall of T'ang, it is difficult to see how the "empires" and kingdoms of the Five Dynasties period could have been credible users of the T'ang rhetoric and methods. Did the rulers and officials of lesser empires acknowledge that there might be a gap between the rhetoric and reality and that this gap would be apparent to their neighbors? Even for the Sung dynasty, which brought the period of confusion to an end, despite its success in unifying most of China, there were times during its three hundred years of existence when reality so departed from rhetoric and was so different from the T'ang imperial image for so long that it is a wonder how the rhetoric was preserved and justified as worth preserving. This essay attempts to explain this by looking at some of the rhetoric during the early years of the Northern Sung (960–1125) when one state, that of the Khitans, at least could claim equal status with it.

Let me begin with the main characteristics of the T'ang imperial rhetoric, which are enshrined in early T'ang edicts and memorials.[2] I ignore the obvious literary flourishes and consider only words which seem to have had meaning and purpose down to the end of the dynasty. They appear to divide into five broad groups:

- language that was largely moral and cosmological and expressed inclusiveness;
- the rhetoric dealing specifically with tribute;
- derogatory language justifying the use of force;
- routine communications stressing realism and flexibility;
- the rhetoric of contractual relations.

They may be briefly illustrated with a few examples.

The first stressed the all-embracing and superior responsibilities of the Son of Heaven in the following terms: "Heaven covers all and Earth supports all. We will nurture all those who seek us." This was fairly representative of the inclusive approach. It was fundamental because it affirmed that the emperor had to adopt this approach if he did not want to oppose the Way of Heaven. An extension of this would be to say that everyone far and near was equidistant before the Son of Heaven and that no one would be left out, no one was beyond the pale where the imperial virtue (te) was concerned.[3]

The rhetoric of tribute seemed to follow from the first, but it really included quite distinct ideas with different implications. It used terms denoting the levels of hierarchy in tributary relations and would appear to contradict the inclusive rhetoric. It discriminated between states that were near from those far away, those that were more sinicized from those that were less so or not so at all, and those that were vital to the empire from those that were irrelevant. The rhetoric was more subtle than the first group, but having evolved over the centuries, it can be said to have reached its highest development during the T'ang.[4]

The third group derived from increasingly hostile Chinese attitudes toward non-Chinese cultures and the "inferior" people such cultures produced. In its extreme form, the language that was used asserted the exclusiveness of what was Chinese and led to declarations such as this: "The Hsiung-nu with their human faces and animal hearts are not of our kind. When strong, they are certain to rob and pillage; when weak, they come to submit. But their nature is such that they have no sense of gratitude or righteousness."[5] These formulations led to the view that China could not depend on virtue and moral superiority, but needed to use force against recalcitrance and barbarism.

The language of realism and flexibility was based on calculations of relative strength and weakness. This might be described at one level as the strategic approach, which accepted that times changed and that China might have to use one kind of rhetoric when strong and another kind when weak. It would use a wide range of techniques to "hold a loose rein" (*chi-mi*) over all peoples.[6] Depending on circumstances, it employed the rhetoric both of inclusiveness and of exclusiveness as well as the language of the tributary system in order to keep the initiative at all times. This was routine language needed between China and its neighbors, neither aggressive nor submissive but flexible and neutral enough for practical purposes.

As for the rhetoric of contractual relations, there had always been ambiguity as to whether this was really meant to be binding or whether it was merely a variation of the strategic approach, that is, merely a temporary device to gain time, regain initiative, and help outmaneuver the enemy. If the treaties and various kinds of alliances were binding, it would be assumed that some rulers were willing and able to arrive at negotiated agreements and that equality was possible between such rulers. As T'ang T'ai-tsung put it, "Once the treaty was made, it would not only be beneficial to you but would bring long-term prosperity to your descendants." The rhetoric certainly demanded that the Chinese emperor always keep his word and might also insist that the non-Chinese ruler should do the same.[7] This contractual approach differed from the strategic one in that it did not depend on hardheaded calculations of strength and weakness alone, but also involved ideas about friendship, about legitimate interests, about agreed frontiers, about the behavior and duties of envoys, and even about long-term peace and prosperity and what might be described as the rudiments of modern diplomacy.

One final word about rhetoric. There was obviously a difference between the rhetoric of "inter-state relations" (or the language used between rulers) and that within the Chinese court among officials discussing what was to be done in "foreign" relations. For each of the five sets of rhetoric summed up above, we may further distinguish between internal and external communications. Where the data is available and significant, I shall note this distinction wherever it occurs.

The Sung dynasty began as just another one of the short-lived dynasties (it could well have been the Sixth after the Five Dynasties) of North China. Until the beginning of the second emperor T'ai-tsung's reign (976–997), no one could have been confident that it would be much different from its unstable predecessors. Thus, for the first twenty years or so, the dynasty's use of the T'ang imperial rhetoric toward its neighbors could be, and often was, challenged. The rhetoric was, at this time, mainly a way of expressing the aspirations of yet another hopeful unifier of the Chinese empire, the seeking of the norm and the ideal that had been lost for a hundred years. Sung T'ai-tsu, the founder, was more fortunate than most of his pre-decessors in that he inherited the momentum of unification started by Chou Shih-tsung (954–959). Shih-tsung had conquered the northern prefectures of his most powerful southern neighbors, the "empire" of Nan T'ang, and had begun to recover territories that had been lost to the Liao dynasty of the Khitans in 936.[8] But Nan T'ang and Liao were still T'ai-tsu's strongest enemies. Both of them also claimed the right to use the imperial rhetoric of the T'ang. Liao was the more dangerous in that one of its subordinate states, the Northern Han, as well as sixteen of its southern prefectures, were well within Chinese traditional borders. No less dangerous was the fact that Liao had successfully used the T'ang imperial rhetoric to apply to the "Chinese" court between 936 and 947 after the T'ang Restoration of 923–936 had finally collapsed. This was when Shih Ching-t'ang (who reigned as Chin Kao-tsu 936–942) had memorialized as a minister of the Liao, paid respect to the Liao emperor as his "father," and paid a tribute of 300,000 rolls of silk.[9]

Fortunately for Sung T'ai-tsu, the Liao empire was ruled by the incom-petent Mu-tsung (951–969) during the first decade of the Sung when T'ai-tsu concentrated on conquering south and west China. His military suc-cesses there confirmed for his court that he had finally inherited the mandate of T'ang. Thus when indirect contacts were made in 974 to establish peaceful relations between the two empires, T'ai-tsu had already been using the whole range of the imperial rhetoric for his relations with neighbors to the south and west, including those he had not conquered and those controlled by non-Chinese tribal leaders.[10] It is interesting to see how careful both the Sung and the Liao courts were about making official contact. Relations were initiated by prefects along the border in the Ho-pei region. The Khitan prefect Yeh-lü Ts'ung had written, "Why not gener-ations of friendly alliance and regular gifts?" He explained that the second ruler of Later Chin (942–946, Shih Ching-t'ang's successor) had been badly advised and that this was what had led to war between the two courts. That tragedy had been due to the Chin emperor's ingratitude, but where Sung was concerned, "There has never been the slightest fissure between our two courts; if envoys were exchanged and the intentions of our rulers were bared, this would rest our weary people and restore our good relations."[11] To this conciliatory note, his Sung counterpart, Sun Ch'üan-hsing, was authorized to write a favorable reply.

This turned out to have been a good start. The next year, the Liao sent envoys, and the Sung ministers congratulated Sung T'ai-tsu on having the Khitans coming to seek good relations. But T'ai-tsu was modest about the old rhetoric, speaking of *mu-hua er-lai* ("coming because they admire us") but immediately adding that this was not so much because of the "little virtue" (*liang te*) that he had but really because of good fortune (*shih-yün*).[12] For the next four years, Sung-Liao relations could not have been better. In 975 alone, the Liao dispatched several missions. When T'ai-tsu forced the Nan T'ang ruler to surrender, the Khitan envoy was present to congratulate him. The next year, when T'ai-tsu died, a special Liao envoy brought condolences, and then Liao sent another mission on the occasion of T'ai-tsung's accession. Envoys from Liao arrived again in 977 and in 978, and they were all feted and presented with rich gifts. Only the mission at the end of 978 and early 979 was described as *lai-kung* ("come [to offer] tribute"). But the context of each mission shows that the Liao envoys did not admit that their state was inferior; the use of the terms *hsien* ("to offer up"), for presenting gifts to the Sung, and *tz'u* ("to confer upon an inferior"), for returning gifts to the Liao, was for the Sung record, and this was true of *kung*, which certainly could not have been accepted by the Liao.[13] What emerges clearly is that the relationship was based principally on the exchange of gifts between equals.

Liao Ching-tsung (969–982) was probably aware that the Sung was planning to attack Liao's subordinate state of Northern Han, and sought friendly relations in order to restrain the Sung. If so, his policy did not succeed for long. Early in 979, Sung T'ai-tsung personally launched an attack on the Northern Han. The Liao envoy who had recently arrived in Sung territory was entertained at the expeditionary headquarters.[14] Soon after, despite an attempt by Liao to save the Northern Han, the Sung was victorious, and T'ai-tsung was encouraged by this to embark on his first campaign against Liao. He marched his troops to the siege of Yu-chou (modern Peking), but when the Khitan main force arrived, he was soon badly defeated. According to Khitan sources, T'ai-tsung barely escaped with his life.[15]

The 979 campaign meant that T'ai-tsung claimed the right to start a war to regain lost territories, even though good formal relations existed between Liao and Sung. Using a similar rhetoric, Liao claimed the right to defend a subordinate state against attack. The Liao also asserted that it had the right to defend its territory in Ho-pei (part of the sixteen prefectures) which had been presented to Liao more than forty years earlier. Indeed, Liao could contend that the Sung, by exchanging embassies and gifts from 974 on, had accepted the status quo in Ho-pei. Thus it was Sung that betrayed that understanding.

T'ai-tsung's confidence in declaring war on the Khitans was not unjustified. The year 979 represented the climax of Sung power. Non-Chinese states and administrations had been arriving with tribute (*lai-kung*), most notably Korea since 962 and 963, Champa since 961 and 962, the Tanguts since 960; and not least, after a period of some confusion, the new Vietnamese leader could be recorded in 973 as having submitted to Sung authority. Some of these early examples, especially in the edict of 963 to the King (*kuo-wang*) of Korea and in that of 972 to the Prince of Chiao-chih (Vietnam), had given the Sung the chance to use the traditional inclusive rhetoric in external communications.[16] Also, at least in the case of Korea, the Tanguts, and Chiao-chih, the Sung was able to formalize a close tributary relationship based on the conferring of Sung titles and the appointment to Sung regular and honorary offices. Although the Liao emperors had been doing the same with Liao titles and offices for the tribal groups that they had subdued to their east, north, and west, the Sung emperors could well believe that such peripheral areas of the Liao could not be compared with some of the well-organized states that acknowledged the superior position of the Sung.

Thus the first and second types of rhetoric, that of inclusiveness and that of the hierarchy of tributary states, were those applied in times of growing strength. The relationship based on equality and the exchange of gifts which the Sung had established with the Liao between 975 and 979 was exceptional and was obviously meant to be temporary. The language used in external communication with the Liao was that of realism and flexibility. It certainly served the function of gaining time and deceiving the opposition while relative strength and weakness were being calculated.

After the defeat by the Liao in 979, however, Sung T'ai-tsung and his ministers appear less restrained in both external and internal communications. Let me take the examples of the views of Sung ministers in 980, the edict to a Po-hai tribal leader in 981, an edict to the King of Korea before T'ai-tsung ordered the disastrous campaign of early 986, and the memorials of Sung Ch'i (917–995) and Chang Chi (933–996) of 989.

In 980, Li Fang (925–996) and Hu Meng (915–986) advised T'ai-tsung not to renew the war against the Liao but to concentrate on training and armaments and on the accumulation of financial resources.[17] In short, they did not think that the Sung had the capacity to fight again at that time. But they described the Khitans as recalcitrant "barbarians" who dragged their "smell of sheep and goats" with them in attacking China, as rascals who would run away when faced with authority, and as "minor evil spirits" whom the emperor could easily frighten away. This is an internal discussion when the need to flatter the emperor probably overrode that of analyzing the enemy's real threat, hence the use of violent words to denigrate the Khitans. Of a different nature was the edict to a Po-hai chieftain the following year.[18] This was for external consumption, and it begins, "We grandly possess all the ten thousand states; our light covers all four directions. However far it reaches no limit; there is no one who does not submit. Only the rascal Khitans bordering on the Northern Wastes have gathered together the crafty and the cruel to attack our borders." It then goes on to invite the Po-hai tribes to join in a campaign to destroy the Khitans and promises to reward them with the Khitan lands north of the Great Wall after the inevitable victory.

My third example comes from an edict a few years later, just before the campaign of 986.[19] This is an edict calling upon the King of Korea to support the effort to destroy the Khitans, appealing to the defense of their common culture so that they might together save the Chinese people from "falling into barbarous customs" and "eradicate the evil exhalations." Korea, of course, could not save T'ai-tsung from a disastrous defeat. After the defeat, an edict of regret was promulgated which spoke of inhuman "barbarians" behaving like "dogs and goats" when violating the imperial borders.[20] Although this edict was for internal purposes only, it echoes what had already crept into external use.

Finally, the memorials of Sung Ch'i and Chang Chi of 988: Sung Ch'i's long memorial was thorough but somewhat ambiguous.[21] He advocated the need for better intelligence and logistics, but he also considered the alternatives of either seeking peace or launching a full-scale war. Since he did not expect T'ai-tsung to sue for peace at this point, he concentrated on the tactical problems of taking the former Chinese territories of the Liao empire and on how to divide the "barbarians" and use the many subject tribes of the Liao empire to destroy Khitan power once and for all. His colleague Chang Chi was more honest about what the Sung could and should do.[22] He weighed the pros and cons of various methods of dealing with strong enemies. The best policy was that of active forward defense, which was based on this sage advice: "If they [the enemies] come, be fully prepared to resist them; if they depart, resist the temptation to pursue them." But he thought that Sung was not strong enough to adopt this policy. Also, he clearly showed why he opposed an aggressive, or what he called the "worst," policy, that is, the policy of war that had failed twice in a decade. He concluded that, given Sung's present condition, the only practical policy was to sue for peace, not as an act of submission but as a necessary step toward the eventual ideal policy of forward defense.

In presenting his arguments, Chang Chi was arguing in terms of a diplomacy that was indeed "war by other means." Where forward defense was not possible, and where war would have courted disaster, the only course open was diplomacy. But the only diplomacy he knew was "to put away one's armor and bows and use humble words and send generous gifts, to send a princess to obtain friendship, to transport goods in order to establish firm bonds; although this would diminish the emperor's dignity, it could *for a while* end fighting along the three borders." He argued that this was a good time to pursue such diplomacy. He cited the successful examples of Han Kao-tsu and T'ang T'ai-tsung and appealed for flexibility in order "to turn danger to safety." But the rhetoric still demanded that he say that this was *not*, as it was with the early Han emperors, a question of lacking strength and of being unable to project virtue, but one of viewing the "barbarians" like animals. He then continues:

> Who would wish to exhaust China's resources to serve the worthless barbarian and harm our *jen* and *i* to quarrel with serpents and swine? Barbarian attacks in earlier times were merely compared with the sting of gadflies and mosquitoes. What achievements can one find amongst them? Examining the official documents and studying the great plans concerning danger and security, only the sages have understood this. Now is the moment for binding friendship and resting the people. If indeed Heaven above regrets calamity and [causes] the rogues to appreciate our humaneness [*jen*] and they thus accept our wish for friendly alliance and extinguish the beacons on the frontiers, that would indeed be a great fortune to our ancestral altars.[23]

But there was, of course, no way that Chang Chi could have recommended this course of diplomacy except as a temporary expedient. He used thus the example of T'ang T'ai-tsung to emphasize this point, illustrating how T'ai-tsung indulged the greed of the T'u-chüeh (Turkic) ruler for several years and enfeebled the tribesmen until he was ready to send forces to destroy them. This was proof of how effective was the policy of enduring disgrace and biding time until victory was certain. Chang Chi believed that the Khitans were of the same ilk and therefore recommended that the empire temporarily bow low in order to save itself from danger.

The two memorials did not lead to any firm decisions, but they prepared Sung T'ai-tsung and his successor, Chen-tsung, for what was yet to happen. Hostilities along the northern border continued, but T'ai-tsung was ready to talk peace if the occasion arose. However, it had to be "peace with honor," and the Khitans did not oblige. On the contrary, they disdained the limited trading facilities offered by the Sung and stepped up their attacks. In 1004 they launched a full-scale war on the Sung.[24] The war ended predictably with a series of Sung defeats, and a humiliating "treaty of alliance" was signed. The Sung did not have to send a princess to the Liao, but everything else was based on the diplomacy that Chang Chi had recommended.

Sung sources assert that it was the Khitans who wanted to end the war. But it was the Sung who bought off the Khitans with an annual subsidy of silks and silver. What was important were the diplomatic steps that led to agreement, and the rhetoric Chen-tsung and his ministers used to justify submission.

The roles of the two Chinese negotiators, Wang Chi-tsung on behalf of the Khitans and Ts'ao Li-yung (d. 1029) on behalf of the Sung, are well known.[25] The two "diplomats" performed well, the former Sung official understanding the rhetoric of the strong and knowing how far he could advise the Khitans to go, and the Sung diplomat minimizing the rhetoric on behalf of the weaker side and doing well enough to please Emperor Chen-tsung. What remains interesting is the language recorded for the Sung court itself. When Wang Chi-tsung's secret message seeking peace was brought to Emperor Chen-tsung, the emperor mentioned that the periods of great prosperity in the past had been those when the rulers saw profit in making peace with the "barbarian" enemy. But he reaffirmed conventional rhetoric that unless the "barbarians" were embraced with great virtue and overawed with strong troops, they could not be made to submit. Since he thought that his virtue was not great enough to influence the Khitans nor his majesty strong enough to recover lost territories, he doubted if the message was sincere. All the same, he responded positively to Wang Chi-tsung's message, and the negotiations began, but not without several references to his duty to bring peace and security to his people (*an-min*). The rhetoric of *an-min* was a useful antidote to that of "controlling animals," which he continued to use in internal debate. Thus alternating between defiance and "yielding to circumstances," he sent his envoy back and forth to deal with the Khitans. But by this time he was careful to confine his more threatening words to oral communications and put as little down on paper as possible.[26]

The treaty was signed in 1005, and there followed years of peace with the Liao. Although uneasy at times, especially when the Sung tried to assert itself against the Tangut Hsi Hsia in 1042, it was a peace that lasted almost one hundred and twenty years. Liao's relations with the Sung were the nearest thing to equality in Chinese history until modern times. This exceptional equality was based on the claims of both states to use T'ang rhetoric, and some of the new procedures, therefore, had to be clothed in a neutral language. But by adopting kinship terms like "elder" and "younger brother," "uncle" and "nephew," "grand-uncle" and "grand-nephew," some of the old rhetoric could still be preserved.[27] In particular, the equality was carefully treated by the Sung rulers as unique to their relations with the Liao, and this enabled them to maintain some of the majesty expected of them in their dealings with other states.

There is no space here to consider how the Sung dealt with other states. What I will show is how Sung officials reviewed the history of Chinese "foreign relations" in the immediate wake of the treaty of 1005 with the Khitans. This emerges most clearly in the work *Ts'e-fu yüan-kuei*, compiled by officials like Wang Ch'in-jo (960–1025) and others, who had been personally involved with Chen-tsung's decision to seek peace. The work was begun in 1005, within months of the signing of the treaty of Shan-yüan

(1005), and completed eight years later. It was one of the most thorough surveys of the many facets of Chinese relations with foreign states and peoples.[28] The last forty-five *chüan* of this large compilation are important not only for their neat arrangement of well-known verifiable data but also for their inclusion of new data on the decades before the foundation of the Sung. But what is of special interest here are the thirty-five prefaces that the editors themselves wrote, for they reveal as systematically as one could expect what the state of mind was of some of the highest Sung officials.

The first is the longest, the General Preface to the Section on Subordinates or "Outer Ministers" (*wai-ch'en*), the title of which is itself revealing.[29] Despite the recent conclusion of a treaty that made quite clear that the Khitan ruler was in no sense a "minister" of the Sung, this was the title given to the section on relations with non-Chinese states and peoples. This can be compared with the earlier Section on "Being Commissioned" (*feng-shih*), which included all envoys to the non-Chinese together with all types of imperial commissioners to various regions, provinces, and prefectures within the Chinese empire itself.[30] Both titles seem to reaffirm the claims of the orthodox imperial rhetoric and reject the possibility of equality between the Son of Heaven and other rulers. But could the editors sustain this view throughout?

Given the context of the Shan-yüan treaty of 1005, the General Preface on Subordinates is an extraordinary historical document. It begins with the classic description of the four types of "barbarians" to the east, south, west, and north, how they were regulated and deemed to have been "subordinates" in ancient times. The sage Emperor Shun laid the foundation for their control by sending officials in the four directions to transform the "barbarians." During the Hsia dynasty, one of the rulers lacked virtue (*shih-te*), and the "barbarians" began to revolt. They had to be pacified before they would submit, but soon after, they came to admire superior values and offered tribute. When the last Hsia ruler did not follow the Way, the Shang successors had to reestablish control. When the Shang ruler was decadent and corrupt, various "barbarians" again invaded "China," and it was left to Chou to reassert control and to induce the frontier peoples to become tributaries again. Thus long before the empire was united, all the main ingredients of the inclusive and universalistic rhetoric of the future empires are noted as having existed. Although some of the language used was anachronistic, the attitudes represented were probably genuine.

The next stage witnessed the consolidation of China's northern boundaries as the states of Ch'in, Chin, and Yeh drove out the "barbarians" and built walls. Simultaneously, its southern boundaries were extended as the state of Ch'u seized the lands of the southern Man and Yüeh. By the time the Ch'in and Han empires reached their fullest extent, the pattern was set: the north and west had to be defended by strong armies; the south and east could ultimately be conquered and populated by Chinese. The idea of subordinate states, however, was revived, and the kingdom of Chao-hsien (mainly northern Korea and southeastern Manchuria) was made the "outer minister" defending the passes.[31] China's vision, up to this point, was one of inexorable advance, of "manifest destiny." But, ironically, it was also at this point, when the empire had virtually reached its peak, that the limitations of the classical rhetoric became apparent.

Han Kao-tsu was not strong enough to defeat the Hsiung-nu. A peace treaty based on a marriage alliance (*ho-ch'in*) was therefore devised. Suitable "princesses" were married to the Hsiung-nu ruler, rich gifts of fine silks and provisions were sent annually, and kinship ties between elder and younger brothers became part of the new rhetoric.[32] For some sixty years, an uneasy peace was maintained. But new problems had clearly emerged: treaties could be broken and needed renewals and renegotiation; frontier markets had to be established to cope with increased trade; large expeditionary armies could be sent far outside the passes; and, not least, treaties of alliances could be made with one's enemy's enemies. Thus the whole spectrum of trade, diplomacy, and war opened up choices in policy, and new kinds of decisions had to be made to cope with different situations.[33] For a while, with the opening up of the Western Region under Han Wu-ti, it appeared that the old rhetoric of submissions and tribute could be extended indefinitely, but this proved to be illusory, and by the second century A.D. it had become obvious that the rhetoric was based on strength and was meaningless during periods of weakness and disorder. The authors of the General Preface clearly admitted this by dismissing the period of nearly three hundred years between the fall of Western Chin and the rise of Sui in five lines (out of 190 lines). As they put it, "The names of tribes and kingdoms increased daily, and matters concerning submissions, rebellions, and tributary relations cannot all be recorded."[34]

The last part of the Preface deals with the period most vital to the Sung, the period of T'ang glory, which the successor empires claimed to inherit. Obviously, the rhetoric describing subordinate states submitting to majesty and virtue and paying tribute was appropriate for some of the relations with non-Chinese. But it was clear that the centuries of rule by various tribal leaders between the fourth and sixth centuries had modified some of the rhetoric of the Han empire. For example, where marriage alliances in the Han had been agonizing, those of the T'ang had continued the tribal traditions of the Northern dynasties and appear to have been made painlessly with the T'u-yü-hun, the T'u-chüeh, and the Uighurs, and with Tibet (T'u-fan), simply and even cynically according to relative strength and to need.[35] When such alliances had become the norm, it is not surprising that they came to be treated as an integral part of the rhetoric. Thus, the Preface could say that T'ang T'ai-tsung (626–649) "agreed to the marriage alliance, and from then on, Tibet was in a state of submission." It did not comment on the inherent contradiction here, because the "alliance" was not seen as one between equals. Indeed, in 625, one official had advised T'ang Kao-tsu (618–626) to agree to a marriage alliance with the western T'u-chüeh as a matter of expediency.[36] T'ai-tsung himself, when he was advised not to break his promise in dealing with the Hsüeh-yen-t'o in 642, drew a sharp distinction between the Han and the T'ang: "Formerly during the Han, the Hsiung-nu were strong and China was weak; therefore the daughters were richly adorned and married to the *Shan-yü*. Now China is strong and the Northern Ti are weak and a thousand Chinese soldiers can defeat their several tens of thousands."[37] Thus the "alliance" was regarded as merely another device to enable China to execute the long-term policy of "controlling the barbarians with loose reins" (*chi-mi*).

But the contradiction was there, not perhaps in T'ai-tsung's tough speech, but certainly in the words of the Preface. For there was no doubt that T'ai-tsung agreed to the marriage alliance with Tibet in 641 because that state posed a serious threat. There was no question of Tibet's submitting to T'ang authority in any sense.[38] And the the contradiction is even more evident in another statement in the Preface about the decision of T'ang Su-tsung (r. 756–762) to initiate a marriage alliance with the Uighurs in 758. Su-tsung was in great danger and sought Uighur help. Yet the Preface says that after the marriage alliance was contracted, "the Uighurs sent troops to help the empire against the rebels and, from then on, paid tribute without cease"; again, no sign of recognizing the contradiction in terms.[39] Here contemporary documents like the edict promulgated by Su-tsung for the occasion contributed to the blurring of the words by treating the Uighurs as subordinates who came to help out of loyalty and allegiance. The Uighurs did not, in truth, "pay tribute without cease."

The Preface also records other important changes in institutions and historical circumstances. The most significant for the Sung in the context of the Treaty of Shan-yüan was the sworn oath (*meng-shih*). Here, too, the meaning is blurred, when Tibet is described as seeking a sworn treaty and then is said to have "continuously sent tribute from then on."[40] The record is clear here. T'ang rulers rarely agreed to sworn treaties, especially when these treaties suggested equality. As far as Tibet was concerned, however, the T'ang had acquiesced, and it protested when the T'ang resorted to emperor-vassal rituals. Tibet insisted that "the rites were originally between equals." T'ang Te-tsung (r. 779–804) was forced to treat Tibet as an equal in the terms he used in addressing its envoys.[41] T'ang rulers only agreed to the sworn treaty when in great danger and under duress. Indeed, the oath-taking by smearing the mouth with animal blood in order to seal the "alliance" with Tibet in 783 merely served to reveal both T'ang reluctance and weakness.[42] Neither side was satisfied, and the treaty was easily broken, but Tibet did not perceive of itself as a tributary. The authors of the Preface knew that the Sung-Khitan treaty in 1005 was sworn between equals, all letters of greeting were written between equals, Khitan envoys were treated with considerable respect, and, if anything, the annual "gifts" of silks and silver had been negotiated, or rather bargained for, with such great difficulty that they could easily be described as Sung tribute to the Liao.[43] Yet the Preface could portray the sworn oath as something connected with other states paying tribute to China.

Enough said about the distortions of the imperial rhetoric in the years after 1005. The Preface also records other points of interest which are worth noting here. The T'ang had established several protectorates (*tu-hu-fu*) to control the "barbarians," first in the north and west; but eventually, after the disastrous An Lu-shan rebellion, in the south in An-nan (northern Vietnam), it recognized that its control over An-nan was tenuous and that a new arrangement was necessary.[44] Another point was the belated acknowledgment that other empires controlled their subordinate states in ways similar to those of China. The Preface mentions the T'u-chüeh and Tibet as having their own subordinates. It also cites the Khitans, who had caused the submission of the Tatars, the Hsi, and the Shih-wei after 885.[45] These two points can be related to a third, which referred to the fall of the Sui after 617: "China was in great disorder. Many Chinese escaped to join the T'u-chüeh, and these tribes thus began to prosper."[46] All three points hint at the most important development during the T'ang: that the "barbarians" had become more sophisticated in political, administrative, and technical skills mainly through closer association with China, learning to employ the Chinese, participating in protectorate government, and using the rhetoric and the methods of "tributary" control. All these changes were relevant to the way the Khitans built their empire, as the Sung learned to its cost. This development must have impinged firmly on the minds of the authors of the Preface. Perhaps not unrelated is their comment on how Shih Ching-t'ang, later Chin Kao-tsu, bribed the Khitans with the sixteen prefectures, "and there was no reason for trouble for the whole of Kao-tsu's reign."[47] Were they vaguely conscious that Sung Chen-tsung had just done something similar and felt that there was now no reason for trouble for the Sung as well?

The General Preface to the section on subordinates is an overview of relations between Chinese and non-Chinese which reflects the preoccupations of Sung officials after the Treaty of Shan-yüan. It tries hard to show the continuity from the ancient sage-kings to the Sung, but it also records new developments; it reaffirms the imperial rhetoric, but is also honest with data that does not fit that rhetoric and even contradicts it. In presenting the data, the editors divided the material into thirty-four topics in forty-five *chüan* (see the Appendix to this chapter). These topics may be divided into nineteen that largely describe the chief characteristics of the non-Chinese (13 *chüan*) and fifteen that stress China's attitudes and policies toward them (32 *chüan*). The first nineteen include rhetoric that ranges from the sympathetic and tolerant to the hostile and suspicious. But much more relevant here are the other fifteen topics. These in turn may be divided into the nine that record the inferior position of the non-Chinese who paid tribute, sought audiences, and could easily be rewarded and rebuked, and the six that were more ambiguous, some admitting China's relative weakness and others implying at least equality between China and other states.

The longest of these fifteen topics are "Preparing Defenses" (7 *chüan*), "Quelling Rebellion" (6 *chüan*), and "Tributary Relations" (5 *chüan*), and the length of these sections reflects the quantity of data in the official record for each topic. Of the 32 *chüan*, less than half (15 *chüan*) assume Chinese superiority, while the others accept that a more ambiguous position existed from time to time. Again, in the context of Sung military weakness, these 17 *chüan* are of special interest, since they include the 7 *chüan* of "Preparing Defenses" and the 6 *chüan* of "Quelling Rebellion."[48] The latter, of course, recorded periods of decisive strength as well as of relative equality, but these were periods when non-Chinese empires did not acknowledge Chinese superiority. The remaining four topics consisted of slightly more than 4 *chüan*, and these were "Marriage Alliances," "Seeking Good Relations," "Oath-taking," and "Trade" (significantly, the shortest).[49]

The fifteen Prefaces, which were actually written in the decade after the Treaty of 1005, are of special interest. The classical rhetoric was fully represented, and many of the ideas of the General Preface are repeated. What is important, however, is the emergence of one clear thread running through all fifteen of the Prefaces as the ideal policy toward non-Chinese; this was expressed in two ways: as "control by loose reining" (*chi-mi*) and as "winning their confidence through kindness" (*huai-jou*).[50] Neither phrase was new, and the Sung editors were merely reaffirming what they thought the historical record had shown to have been the most successful policy. But they went further by showing, on the one hand, the many facets of such a policy and, on the other, the relationship it had with alternative policies, such as bribing the insatiable "barbarians," seeking to assimilate them, pacifying and trying to annihilate them, and devising reliable defenses against them. In Preface after Preface, the subtleties are woven together into a sophisticated amalgam of the rhetoric of inclusiveness, of tribute, of retaliation and punishment, which was, at the same time, combined with a sharp awareness of relative strength and weakness and a readiness, whenever really necessary, to negotiate treaties and alliances with equals. Despite some apparent contradictions, the authors of the Preface reveal how astutely they had studied the official histories, how well they understood that there was no single way of dealing with China's neighbors, how important it was to cultivate a rich and flexible vocabulary to cover dfferent types of relationships, and not least, how desirable was the traditional rhetoric which expressed China's ideals and the ultimate goal of securing and enhancing the standards of civilization in an uncertain world of "inferior" cultures.

After 1005, the Sung was relatively weak compared with one empire, the Liao, and relatively strong compared with its other neighbors. The Prefaces emphasize that war is the least desirable policy, to be resorted to only for the defense of one's frontiers. At the same time, a defensive policy must be an active and a forward one, to be conducted with close attention to good intelligence, to facts, to reality. Such a policy could ensure peace only if accompanied with strategic thinking and diplomatic flexibility. China could, in this way, gain its neighbors' respect and admiration, and when it had that, the neighboring states and tribes would voluntarily come to submit to its authority and pay tribute. China's authority needed to be supported by trust, by virtue, and by the proper rites, all adding responsibility and predictability to China's moral position. Thus the policy of *chi-mi* was not, as it might appear, merely one of keeping a distance, being generous with gifts and official titles, and having "spheres of influence" and strong defenses. It was also, as several of the Prefaces emphasize, one of not becoming isolated and of maintaining unceasing relations with neighbors. There is a perception of the need to conduct active diplomacy.[51]

Finally, some comments on the limitations of this rhetoric of active diplomacy. Relations with the Liao had been reestablished as an "alliance" on the basis of an expensively bought equality. Indeed, the years between T'ai-tsung's first campaign in 979 and the Treaty of Shan-yüan in 1005 were years of adjustment, of scaling down Sung ambitions to attain the full glory of T'ang. All the peoples of the north and northeast were cut off from the Sung; even Korea had to send its tribute to Liao instead of to Sung.[52] And almost immediately after the 979 defeat, T'ai-tsung was to discover that already his was a lesser authority among the Tanguts and the Vietnamese. The Tanguts saw the light and began to play the Liao against the Sung, which eventually led to the rise of an independent empire.[53] The Vietnamese were less fortunate in not having another "big brother" to manipulate, but they soon discovered how weak Sung really was when T'ai-tsung's armies failed again in 980–981. There was also the model of independent Ta-li, and there were the various tribes who could be made to pay their tribute to the Vietnamese rather than to the Sung. Vietnam's southern neighbor Champa, for all its close relations with China, found that the Sung could not really help it in a crisis, and the Vietnamese realized that they were free to manage their western and southern neighbors as they pleased.[54] The consequences of all this were clear. Although Tanguts and Vietnamese both continued to accept the Chinese rhetoric of tribute for some decades afterwards, the foundations had been laid for their own independent empires of Hsi Hsia and Ta Yüeh. Thus the de facto situation around Sung China soon after 1005 was one of several states that did not "submit" to Sung authority but allowed the rhetoric of tribute to be used until they were ready to reject it.[55] What had become clear was that the Sung demanded that the rhetoric be used because, as the editors of *Ts'e-fu yüan-kuei* have shown, this was the key to the policy of *chi-mi*, the safest and most successful of the approaches inherited from the T'ang.

Until 979 the Sung emperors were out to equate rhetoric and reality. Hence, when faced with a border or territorial dispute, they were ready, if necessary, to threaten or start a war. Afterwards, slowly and with reluctance, there was an admission that rhetoric could not always reflect reality, and by 1005 there was a readiness to modify some of the more grandiose claims in the rhetoric. After 1005, as they contemplated the continuities of Chinese history, Sung officials began to see that there had been a respectable tradition of dealing with reality separately so that there was no need to change the rhetoric. When all you could do was to try to hold the line, there was obviously no Chinese world order. But even for a lesser empire, perhaps especially for one so perceived, the rhetoric of tribute was immensely comforting and reassuring.

APPENDIX
The Thirty-four Topics in the Wai-ch'en Section of Ts'e-fu yüan-kuei

Nineteen on the non-Chinese states and peoples (number of *chüan*)

Native Customs (3)
States and Peoples (2)
Hereditary Ranks (2)
Tribes (1)
Mutual Attacks (1)
Treachery (1)
Official Titles; Talent; Virtuous Acts (1)
Strength and Prosperity; Grievances; Destruction (1)
Appearance; Skills; Bravery; Rebelliousness; Resentment; Cruelty (1)
Translation (part of 1 *chüan*)

Fifteen on Chinese attitudes and policies (number of *chüan*)

Chinese superiority asserted

Tribute (5)
Appointing to Fiefs (3)

Rewarding the Unusual (3)
Assistance in War (1)
Returning to the Fold (1)
Hostages; Rebukes (part of 1 *chüan*)
Seeking Audience; Making requests (part of 1 *chüan*)

Chinese position ambiguous

Preparing Defenses (7)
Quelling Rebellion (6)
Marriage Alliances (2)
Seeking Good Relations (1)
Oath-taking (1)
Trade (part of 1 *chüan*)

NOTES

1. The evidence that this was so is slender for the years after 860, but the fragments that have survived suggest that the style did not change; see Sung Min-ch'iu, *T'ang ta chao-ling chi* (Taipei reprint), ch. 1, 30, 72, 107, 110. Similarly with the documents for the successor dynasties in North China: Liang, 907–923, and Later T'ang, 923–936; see Ssu-ma Kuang, *Tzu-chih t'ung-chien* (Peking, 1956), ch. 250–278, and *Chiu T'ang shu* (Peking, 1975), ch. 194A–199B.

2. The most obvious sources are the sections on foreign peoples and states of *Chiu T'ang shu* and *T'ung-tien* (Taipei, 1959), ch. 185–200; also *T'ang ta chao-ling chi*, ch. 128–130.

3. *Chiu T'ang shu*, 194A, 5162. The idea of equidistance and imperial virtue is discussed in the background section of my "Early Ming Relations with Southeast Asia: A Background Essay," in John K. Fairbank (ed.), *The Chinese World Order* (Cambridge: Harvard University Press, 1968), pp. 34–62.

4. Although there were refinements during the Ming dynasty, the basic tribute system departed little from the rhetoric of the early T'ang; see the discussions during T'ang T'ai-tsung's reign, the results of which were summarized by T'ang historians commenting in the foreign states' sections of *Chin shu* (Peking, 1974), ch. 97; *Liang shu* (Peking, 1973), ch. 54; *Chou shu* (Peking, 1971), ch. 49–50; and *Sui shu* (Peking, 1973), ch. 81–84.

5. *Chiu T'ang shu* 194A, 5162. These are the words of Wei Cheng (580–643), one of T'ang T'ai-tsung's closest advisers.

6. For a full discussion, see Yang Lien-sheng, "Historical notes on the Chinese World Order," in Fairbank (ed.), *The Chinese World Order*, pp. 20–33.

7. *Chiu T'ang shu*, 194A, 5158; 196B, 5263–5265.

8. *Tzu-chih t'ung-chien*, ch. 292–293.

9. The literature on this topic is large. The basic documents may be found in *Tzu-chih t'ung-chien*.

10. For example, *Sung ta chao-ling chi* (Taipei reprint, 1972), ch. 225 and 227; T'o T'o et al., *Sung shih* (Peking, 1977), 487, 14036; 492, 14152–14153.

11. *Sung Hui-yao chi-kao* (Peking, 1957), vol. 8, 7673. The Sung records suggest that it was the Liao that sought relations; the Liao records say that it was the Sung that sent an envoy to seek peace—a clear example of how the use of T'ang imperial rhetoric on both sides affected the writing of history. I have not been able to ascertain from the surviving fragmentary records which side really took the initiative.

12. *Sung Hui-yao chi-kao*, 7673.

13. *Sung shih*, 3, 43–46; 4, 54–55; T'o T'o et al., *Liao shih* (Peking 1974), 9, 94–101.

14. *Sung Hui-yao chi-kao*, 7674–7675. This is not mentioned in *Sung shih*, but *Liao shih* records that the Liao envoy was told, "If the northern court does not aid [Northern Han], the peace treaty remains. Otherwise there will be war"; 9, 101.

15. *Liao shih*, 9, 102.

16. *Sung shih*, 487, 14036; 489, 14079–14080; 485, 13982–13983; 488, 14058.

17. Li T'ao, *Hsü Tzu-chih t'ung-chien ch'ang-pien* (Taipei, 1964), 21, 11a–12a; *Sung Hui-yao chi-kao*, 7676.

18. *Sung Hui-yao chi-kao*, 7765.

19. *Sung ta chao-ling chi*, 237, 924; *Sung shih*, 487, 14038. A similar version is recorded in *Koryŏ-sa* (Yonhui University, 1955), 3, 68, for the end of 985.

20. *Sung Hui-yao chi-kao*, 7678.

21. *Sung Hiu-yao chi-kao*, 7679–7682; *Sung shih*, 264, 9125–9128.

22. *Sung Hui-yao chi-kao*, 7682–7683. For another version of this memorial, see *Hsü Tzu-chih t'ung-chien ch'ang-pien*, 30, la–5b.

23. *Sung Hui-yao chi-kao*, 7682.

24. *Liao shih*, 14, 160; *Sung shih*, 7, 125–127; *Hsü Tzu-chih t'ung-chien ch'ang-pien*, ch. 57–58.

25. The Liao accounts differ from the Sung accounts; see n. 24 above. For the documents concerning the negotiations, *Sung ta chao-ling chi*, 232, 903–904, and 228, 882. There are further details in *Sung Hui-yao chi-kao*, 7686–7689. See also the study by C. Schwarz-Schilling, *Der Friede von Shan-yüan (1005 n. Chr.)* (Wiesbaden, 1959), pp. 40–54, 108–137.

26. *Sung Hui-yao chi-kao*, 7688. The wording of the treaty is recorded in *Hsü Tzu-chih t'ung-chien*, 58, 22b–23a.

27. See *Sung ta chao-ling chi*, chüan 228–232, for a variety of examples.

28. The edition used here is the Taiwan reprint, Taipei, 1967.

29. *Ts'e-fu yüan-kuei* (hereafter *TFYK*), 956, 11237–11241.

30. *TFYK*, ch. 652–664.

31. *TFYK*, 956, 11238.

32. *TFYK*, 978, 11486–11488.

33. See Yü Ying-shih, *Trade and Expansion in Han China* (Berkeley, 1967), especially chapters 5 and 6.

34. *TFYK*, 956, 11239–11240.

35. *TFYK*, 956, 11240; also *Chiu T'ang shu*, ch. 194A–196B.

36. *TFYK*, 978, 11495; *Hsin T'ang shu* (Peking, 1975) 100, 3933–3934.

37. *TFYK*, 978, 11496–11497.

38. *Chiu T'ang shu*, 196A, 5221–5222.

39. *TFYK*, 956, 11240, and 979, 11504–11505; see also *Hsin T'ang shu*, 217A, 6115–6116.

40. *TFYK*, 956, 11241.

41. *Chiu T'ang shu*, 196B, 5246, and *TFYK*, 981, 11528.

42. One Chinese envoy was ashamed of having to conduct the oath-swearing ceremony and sabotaged the proper rituals by persuading the Tibetan ruler not to use the necessary sacrifices of cattle and horses but to use dogs and goats instead; *TFYK*, 981, 11529, and *Chiu T'ang shu*, 196B, 5247–5248. For a more satisfactory *equal* treaty with Tibet in 821, see also 196B, 5264–5265.

43. The chief negotiator of the treaty was warned not to exceed 300,000 units of silk and silver annually. Emperor Chen-tsung was delighted when the negotiator succeeded in keeping to that figure; *Hsü Tzu-chih t'ung-chien* 58, 176.

44. *TFYK*, 956, 11240–11241. On An-nan, see *Sung shih*, 488, 14057, and *Wen-hsien t'ung-k'ao* (Taipei, 1959), 330, 2591.

45. *TFYK*, 956, 11241.

46. *TFYK*, 956, 11240.

47. *TFYK*, 956, 11241.

48. *TFYK*, ch. 988–994 and 982–987 respectively.

49. *TFYK*, ch. 978–979, 980, 981, and 999 respectively.

50. *Chi-mi* appears in thirteen of the fifteen Prefaces; *TFYK* 963, 11326; 968, 11376; 973, 11427; 974, 11437; 977, 11472; 978, 11486; 981, 11524; 982, 11534; 988, 11597; 996, 11694–11695; 999, 11719 and 11725. *Huai-jou* or some idea of gentle protective concern appears in nine of them, all the above except 968, 978, 982, 996; and in addition, in 980, 11508.

51. *TFYK*, 968, 973, 974, 977, 978, 981, 982.

52. The Korean king used the Sung reign title from the end of 963 and the Liao reign title from the middle of 994; *Koryŏ-sa*, 2, 62, and 3, 79.

53. *Sung shih*, 485, 13986–14000.

54. *Sung shih*, 488, 14058–14067; 489, 14079–14083.

55. The Tanguts did this in 1034. The Vietnamese were not so open, but in effect rejected Sung supremacy in the 1060s before adopting its own reign-titles; Kawahara Masahiro, "Ri-chō to Sō to Kankei (1009–1225)," in *Betonam Chūgoku Kankei shi*, ed. Yamamoto Tatsurō (Tokyo, 1975), pp. 41–42, 70. See also *Sung shih*, 488, 14069.

THREE

Barbarians or Northerners:
Northern Sung Images of the Khitans

TAO JING-SHEN

This essay will survey the views of Northern Sung rulers, scholar-officials, Neo-Confucian thinkers, and private writers on the Khitans, with emphasis on their images of their northern neighbors within the framework of equal diplomatic relations between the two states.

The traditional attitude toward the alien peoples was based largely on the *Ch'un-ch'iu* (or *Spring and Autumn Annals*). China and her neighbors were divided into two worlds: the internal or the "civilized" center was surrounded by the uncivilized world of the "barbarians."[1] The "barbarians" who admired Chinese civilization and wished to reside in the Chinese world and to adopt Chinese customs were permitted to do so. They would eventually be transformed into Chinese.[2] Those who refused absorption into the Chinese world were expelled from China.

Judging from the persistence of this basic attitude, historians have asserted that in premodern times the Chinese always believed themselves to be the only civilized people in the world and regarded the peoples outside of China's borders as inferior. Scornful of these non-Chinese, the Chinese developed a strong sense of ethnocentrism, which eventually resulted in an antagonistic response to the West in modern times. This thesis, however, should be tested by case studies of China's foreign relations. In recent years excellent studies of China's traditional world order have appeared, but most of them deal with the Middle Kingdom in the Ch'ing period.[3] The traditional theory that China was the center of the universe and that the neighboring "barbarian" states were tributaries developed early in the Han dynasty. During the long history of Chinese foreign relations, there have been different patterns and changes.[4] The tribute system does not adequately describe these fluctuations in China's relations with foreigners.

My thanks to my colleague Professor William R. Schultz, who carefully read the original version of the paper and made valuable suggestions.

Map 2. East Asia, 1141 A.D.
Based on Albert Herrmann, *An Historical Atlas of China*, pp. 38–39.

And even the tribute system masked what were really relations between equal and independent states. The relationship between the Han and the Hsiung-nu, for example, was at first conducted on the basis of equality. During the period of disunity which followed the fall of the Han, diplomatic parity characterized the relations of the Northern Wei (386–532) and the Southern dynasties.[5] Many diplomatic practices in the Sung, in fact, were patterned after those of the Northern Wei period, which in turn had their origins in ancient times. Even in the T'ang, Sino-Turkish and Sino-Tibetan relations were often marked by a sense of equality between the parties. In 821–822, the T'ang and the Tibetan rulers negotiated a treaty based on diplomatic parity. The treaty was ratified in court ceremonies held in both Ch'ang-an and Lhasa. According to the treaty, kinship relations were to be established, and both rulers were to have the title of "Great Emperor."[6]

Before the establishment of the Sung, the Five Dynasties had formed an international order which differed considerably from the tribute system. First of all, four of the five states maintained relations with the Khitans, the dominant foreigners of that time, on a basis of full equality; only the fifth was subordinate to the Khitans. Yeh-lü A-pao-chi, the founder of the Khitans' Liao dynasty, had initially requested investiture from the emperor of the Later Liang. He later demanded treatment as a fellow sovereign. Second, when A-pao-chi allied himself with Li K'o-yung of Shansi against the Liang in 905, the two agreed that they would become sworn brothers. Third, the Later Chin paid annual indemnities to the Khitans.[7]

China has had a long tradition of upholding a world order with herself at its center. But she has had an equally long tradition of conducting relations with neighboring countries on a basis of equality whenever circumstances made that necessary. China often adopted pragmatic and flexible policies. The views of the T'ang statesman Lu Chih reflect the realistic bent of some officials. Lu's appraisal of traditional Chinese foreign policy led him to conclude that success or failure depended on the strength of the "barbarian" tribes. When China was strong and the "barbarians" were weak, it was possible to promote "virtue" or to attack the foreigners. When China was weak and the "barbarians" were strong, the court ought to be conciliatory or even ought to appease the "barbarians" to prevent incursions. If the "barbarians" were as powerful as the Chinese, China's frontier defenses should be strengthened and limited military operations employed to ward off foreign raids.

Proper timing and a balanced policy (*ch'eng*) were, according to Lu, essential for success. There were no fixed rules, and no set policies would ensure success. The government should always analyze the general conditions realistically. Rulers should seek the assistance of competent officials and not act on whim. Those who employed competent officials and adopted the policies recommended by their advisers would be successful.[8] Some, if not all, of Lu's views influenced the officials and scholars of the Northern Sung.

The Official Attitude: Diplomatic Parity

Diplomatic relations between the Sung and the Liao were based on two treaties concluded in 1005 and 1042 respectively. The first treaty consisted of the following:

- the establishment of a friendly relationship between the two states;
- annual payments of 100,000 taels of silver and 200,000 bolts of silk to the Khitans by the Sung as "military compensation";
- the demarcation of borders between the two states;
- an agreement that neither side should detain robbers and fugitives;
- an agreement that neither side should disturb the farmlands of the other;
- an agreement that neither side should construct new fortifications and canals along the border;
- a pledge of a solemn oath with a religious sanction in case of contravention.[9]

The treaty of 1042 confirmed the brotherly relationship sworn to by the emperors of the two states. It also increased the annual payments to a total of 500,000 units of silver and silk.[10]

Diplomatic parity is revealed in practices not stipulated in these treaties. A fictitious kinship relationship, which extended to members of the imperial households, was established between the emperors of the two states. The diplomats and writers of the time often referred to them as "brotherly states." Official ceremonies were, on occasion, performed by both imperial families as if they were actually related. On receiving the news of the death of an emperor of the neighboring state, the other emperor would immediately send envoys to offer his official condolences. Meanwhile, funeral ceremonies were held at both courts, and for seven days officials would be denied audiences with the emperor, who was mourning the death of his "brother." The emperor, Chinese or Khitan as the case may be, would forbid the playing of music for seven days. The name of the deceased emperor became taboo not only in his own state but also in the neighboring state.[11]

Moreover, after the treaty of 1005 had been concluded, a new diplomatic language of equality came into general use. The two states often addressed each other as "the northern dynasty" (*pei-ch'ao*) and "the southern dynasty" (*nan-ch'ao*). The Liao, on occasion, referred to the Chinese dynasty as "the Southern Sung."[12] The rules of etiquette which applied to visits of Khitan envoys differed from those which were applied to other "barbarians."[13] Diplomatic missions were exchanged regularly to celebrate the New Year's Day and the birthdays of the emperors, to mourn the death of an emperor, and to celebrate the enthronement of a new emperor. Every meal, every prostration, and all seating arrangements were carefully managed, and diplomatic protocol was maintained.[14] In 1007 the Sung established a State Letters Bureau (*Kuo-hsin ssu*), under the Internal Service Department (*Ju-nei nei-shih sheng*), to handle the exchange of state letters with the Khitans and to provide its ambassadors with knowledge of diplomatic precedents and practices.[15] The Bureau of Military Affairs (*Shu-mi yüan*) handled foreign affairs, but the Secretariat-Chancellery (*Chung-shu men-hsia*) and the Bureau of Military Affairs always worked together on major issues.[16] Although neither treaty mentioned trade between the Sung and the Liao, commerce was regulated after 1005 and was conducted only at specific trading posts. Since neither the Sung nor the Liao offered tribute to the other, trade between the two states was based on equality.[17]

Diplomatic equality characterized official communications between the Sung and the Liao. Terms such as "the Great Sung" and "the Great Liao" or "the Great Khitans" appear throughout Northern Sung official writings, and range from state letters,[18] various imperial edicts promulgated to be read to foreign envoys,[19] local governmental correspondence with visiting foreign envoys,[20] brief letters from Sung envoys acknowledging the receipt of gifts from the Liao government and expressing appreciation for banquets,[21] to announcements declaimed by actors in court performances attended by foreign embassies.[22] Immediately after the conclusion of the treaty of 1005, Emperor Chen-tsung abolished all the place names with characters such as "caitiffs" (lu) and "barbarians" (jung). Thus, the military prefecture of Wei-lu (literally: "Showing military power to the caitiffs") was changed into Kuang-hsin ("Extending faith"), and Ching-jung ("Pacifying the barbarians") into An-su ("Peaceful and silent").[23] Other taboos concerning the Liao imperial family were also observed.

Li T'ao's Hsü Tzu-chih t'ung-chien ch'ang-pien, the monumental compilation of Northern Sung chronicles, is a good example of the official rendering of terms concerning the Khitans. This work, which faithfully preserves terminological usage in official documents and the veritable records, among other sources, reveals a remarkable change from the use of terms of disparagement to the use of neutral ones with regard to the Khitans after 1005. The most commonly used term is "Khitans." Another is "the Northerners" or "the Northern dynasty." This usage is important insofar as it implies a change of official attitude toward the Khitans, although the change in attitude, if in fact it represented that at all, was by no means general.[24]

Another official work illustrates the same trend. In 1081 Su Sung was commissioned to compile the state letters and documents concerning the "Northern dynasty." The work was completed in two years and submitted to the throne in the sixth month of 1083. This compilation of all the statutes and accounts on the Liao included descriptions of its government and customs, illustrations of the routes through which Sung envoys reached the Liao court, and maps. Unfortunately, the work was lost. According to the preface written by Su Sung, which is extant, the chapters on the Liao envoys, state letters, and documents were compiled under the headings of "northern envoys," "northern state letters" (pei-hsin), and "northern correspondence" (pei-shu). In the chapters on Liao imperial genealogy and customs, there were sections on "Khitan genealogy" (shih-hsi) and "Khitan national customs" (kuo-su). Occasionally, the terms "barbarian troops and horses" (fan-chün ma) and "barbarian country" (fan-chieh) were also employed, but the most commonly used terms throughout the work seem to have been "northerners" (pei-jen), "Northern envoys," and so forth.[25]

In the first exchange of missives between two local officials of the Liao and Sung border areas in 974, the Sung letter proposes that the two states should become "eternal allies" (yü-kuo).[26] During the negotiations of the treaty of 1005, a Sung letter indicates the hope of the court that the two states (erh-kuo) would be friendly neighbors.[27] Subsequently, the goal of friendship between the neighbors was reiterated in an exchange of state letters, and the term "two states" was occasionally used.[28] These letters often refer to "brotherly states" (*hsiung-ti chih kuo*).[29] In Li T'ao's work the terms "China" (*Chung-kuo*) and "Liao" or "the Northern dynasty" frequently appeared in pairs.[30] The Liao is referred to as a "foreign state" (*wai-kuo*) by the renowned Sung official Fan Chung-yen.[31]

In addition to its recognition of Liao as an independent state, the Sung was concerned about its boundaries. The Treaty of Shan-yüan stipulated that both states should not violate each other's borders. Sung scholars and officials were proud that their court neither sent princesses to marry foreign chieftains nor ceded land to them.[32] From 1074 to 1076, the Sung and the Liao had disputes over certain border areas, and prolonged negotiations followed. Shen Kua, a famous scholar and scientist, was appointed as a special ambassador to negotiate with the Khitans. Shen did thorough research in the State Letters Bureau and gathered the relevant documents and maps in favor of the Sung claim. In a series of six meetings with Liao representatives, Shen insisted that the Sung maps on the areas in dispute were correct, and he was able to keep Liao demands to a minimum.[33] In the final settlement, however, the Sung lost large parcels of land, and Han Chen, the official responsible for the final negotiations, was condemned by his colleagues. Even the renowned Wang An-shih was held responsible for this loss because he had insisted that the Sung should not provoke war with the Liao over minor matters.[34]

Many Sung rulers and officials were determined to reconquer the Yen-Yün region. Emperor Hui-tsung adopted a policy of seeking aid from another "barbarian" group, the Jurchens, in order to regain this region. The policy failed, and the Jurchens invaded North China in 1126, but the Sung court refused to relinquish this territory. Even after three garrisons in Ho-pei and Ho-tung had been ceded by treaty to the Jurchens, the Sung court still attempted to attain them. The issue of territory was so important that it was a factor in the final collapse of the Northern Sung. The Sung's tenacious hold on the three garrisons was used by the Jurchens as an excuse to launch another expedition, which destroyed the Northern Sung.

The Myth of Sung Superiority over the "Barbarians"

In contrast to the polite state letters sent to the Liao court or presented orally to Liao diplomats, official records not intended to be read or heard by the Khitans were not respectful. In these documents, officials asserted that the Sung attained legitimacy by reunifying all of China. A memorial submitted by high-ranking officials in 978 noted that the Sung had extended its power to a thousand *li* beyond its borders and was in control of ten thousand countries. Remote "barbarian" kingdoms and peoples beyond the northern desert had come to pay tribute.[35] The edict that changed the reign title of Emperor Chen-tsung in 1004 stated that the dynasty had received the Mandate of Heaven and that the four seas had submitted to its benevolence.[36] The obituary of Emperor T'ai-tsung praised him for his military exploits, which had extended Sung civilization to the rest of the world and led to his unification of all its peoples.[37] In the obituary of Emperor Jen-tsung, the first ruler Emperor T'ai-tsu was lauded for using military power to unite the lands in all four directions (*ssu-fang*). The same document condemned the northern enemy and western "barbarians." Emperor Jen-tsung was credited with suppressing and pacifying them by employing the snare (*chi-erh*).[38]

The Sung government repeatedly attempted to legitimize itself. By 984 the imperial court had recognized the historical existence of the Five Dynasties and had adopted the element of fire to replace the element of wood, which symbolized the Later Chou.[39] Emperor Chen-tsung asserted the Sung's political and cultural superiority over the Liao. A general amnesty, which implied that the war had ended and that peace had been attained within the four seas, was announced. This announcement also stated that all peoples would now appreciate the customs of China and would enjoy bountiful harvests.[40] Ou-yang Hsiu, in his famous essay on legitimacy, pointed out that by rectifying wrongdoing with virtue and by reunifying the whole of China the Sung had attained legitimacy.[41]

In Sung documents issued exclusively to its own officials, more often than not the Khitans were termed "barbarians." In 1037, for example, Emperor Jen-tsung required the candidates who were taking a special examination to discuss this problem: Why did the "barbarians," having been sinicized, still violate the frontiers?[42] In imperial edicts concerning official appointments, and especially in cases of local officials whose posts were close to the border, the terms "barbarians" and "caitiffs" are often found.

Foreigners are referred to as inferior peoples in many official and private writings. In the *History of the Five Dynasties* (*Chiu Wu-tai shih*), the emperor of the Khitans is called "chief of the caitiffs" (*lu-chu*), and the people are called either "Khitans" or "caitiffs." The authors of the *Ts'e-fu yüan-kuei*, compiled during the reign of Emperor Chen-tsung, used terms such as "Khitans," "caitiffs," "barbarian caitiffs" (*jung-lu*), and "northern caitiffs" (*pei-lu*). In private works, the terms range from such neutral expressions as "Khitans," which is used most commonly in Northern Sung collected works, "the Liao," "the northerners," "the northern dynasty," "the northern country" (*pei-kuo*), "the northern enemy," "the northern neighbors," to insulting terms, such as "ugly caitiffs" (*ch'ou-lu*), "violent caitiffs" (*k'ung-lu*), "wolves," "owls" (*hsiao-ch'ih*), and simply "animals." Ancient terms used to designate "barbarian" people, such as *Hsün-yün* and *Hsiung-nu*, were also employed in referring to the Khitans. A passage in Yeh Meng-te's *Shih-lin yen-yü* reads: "Since the Khitans [and we] established familial relations . . . when Empress Dowager Ming-su reigned, the caitiffs sent embassies with letters to congratulate her on New Year's Day and her birthday." The author apparently did not feel that he would offend the imperial family by describing its Khitan "relatives" as "caitiffs."[43]

The *sung*, or hymn, a special genre of literature that was dedicated to praising the deeds of emperors and the achievements of a dynasty, deserves attention in this connection. One early Sung dynasty hymn dedicated to the imperial court and lauding accomplishments in causing the "barbarians" to submit is the "Hymn on the Northern Barbarian Submission" (*Pei-ti lai-ch'ao sung*), written by Wang Yü-ch'eng (954–1001). In the preface, Wang describes the savage customs of the "barbarians" and traditional Chinese policies toward them. He asserts that the Sung dynasty employed the best policy in its relations with them, superseding that of the ancient Chou dynasty. It relied on benevolence in dealing with the states lacking an advanced culture. Not only did this policy rally the people of China to support Sung rule, but it also attracted "barbarian" envy of Chinese culture. The emperor, intending to gain the allegiance of peoples of remote places and to pacify other states, treated foreigners with propriety (*li*) and taught them the virtues (*te*). In this hymn, the Khitans are referred to as "Hsiung-nu," and they are to submit to the Sung in the fashion of the "barbarian" submissions to the ancient sage kings. Such military men as Wei Ch'ing and Ho Ch'ü-ping (famous generals of the Han) were needed to suppress them. Although it was not dated, the hymn was clearly written to praise Emperor T'ai-tsu's efforts to normalize diplomatic relations with the Khitans in and after 974.[44] The conclusion of the treaty of 1005 was also applauded by scholar-officials. Chang Fang-p'ing (1007–1091), in his "Hymn to the Sung" (*Sung sung*), describes the so-called "submission of the barbarians" in 1004–1005 as nothing but a glorious victory for the Sung.[45]

Somewhat different from the hymns is the prose essay "Admonitions for the Throne" (*Fu-i chen*), submitted to Emperor Jen-tsung by Ts'ai Hsiang (1012–1067).[46] In the opening sentences, Ts'ai points out that the rulers should change their policies in response to climatic changes and natural calamities, which are caused by the *yin* and *yang* forces. Specifically, *yang* is represented by the ruler, and *yin* by his subjects, "barbarians," and women. The ruler must revise his policies so as to curb the excessive growth of the forces of *yin*. The "barbarians" were thus identified with the dark forces in the universe. Han Yü, the pioneer of Neo-Confucianism, attacked Buddhism as a foreign, "barbarian," and hence inferior religion. He distinguishes between the teachings of the ancient sages and the institutions of the "barbarians."[47] In his essay "What Is the True Human Being?" he concludes that "human beings [i.e., the Chinese] are the masters of the 'barbarians' and animals."[48]

Sung thinkers continued to make this distinction between the civilized

Chinese and the savage "barbarians." Since the Khitans posed a serious menace to the existence of the Sung, attacks on "barbarians" naturally included the Khitans. "The institutions [*fa* or *dharma*] of foreign countries have caused turmoil in China, and "barbarian" rulers have resisted the Son of Heaven."[49] The former refers to Buddhism whereas the latter alludes to the Khitans. There was an unmistakable trend in the Northern Sung to assign an inferior position to all "barbarians." The Neo-Confucian Shao Yung wrote two poems about the "barbarians":

> *Thinking about Calamities*
> Servants and slaves insult their masters,
> "Barbarians" invade China.
> This injustice has been so since ancient age,
> To resolve the problem there is no way.[50]

> *On the Central Plain*
> On the Central Plain, the armies
> Base themselves on benevolence and righteousness.
> When these virtues are lost,
> "Barbarians" come with their insults.[51]

The Ch'eng brothers, who were renowned Neo-Confucian thinkers, also wrote about foreign affairs. They agreed with Han Yü's view of the three levels of beings: the civilized Chinese practice the *li*. If it is partially lost, the Chinese will be degraded into "barbarians." If the *li* is completely lost, they will sink to the level of animals.[52] The Ch'eng brothers were critical of the Han and T'ang governments. The dynasties since the Han, they contended, only "seized" power.[53] In the period of disunity from 220 to 589 the *li* and the way of government (*fa*) were both lost, so that only the way of the "barbarians" prevailed. Though the Sui and the T'ang reunified China, numerous "barbarian" customs survived.[54] The Han and T'ang rulers ruled by force, not by benevolence.[55]

The Ch'eng brothers believed in the forces of *yin* and *yang*, which, when not in harmony, resulted in natural calamities. The lack of harmony of *yin-yang* was in turn caused by misgovernment.[56] Ch'en Shun-yü (d. 1074), a pupil of Ou-yang Hsiu, established a connection between *yin-yang* and the "barbarian" menace. In a memorial submitted to Emperor Shen-tsung on portents in the heavens, Ch'en theorized that supreme *yin* leads to changes in the heavens, and that *yin* symbolizes war, conspiracy, recalcitrant officials, "barbarians," eunuchs, and women in the imperial palaces. Celestial changes, therefore, are an indication that one or more of the above will adversely affect state affairs.[57]

As early as 1002 another Neo-Confucian thinker had already discussed the relationship of the *yin-yang* system to the "barbarians." He contended that China is *yang* and the "barbarians" are creatures of *yin*. There is nothing surprising about "barbarian" invasions of China, because *yin* inevitably clashes with *yang*. The rulers should cultivate happiness (*yang*) among the Chinese people and achieve harmony in the state, and then they will be able to control the "barbarians."[58]

By the end of the Northern Sung, the *yin-yang* concept as it related to the rise of the "barbarians" had become a popular belief. The introduction to the *Ta-Sung Hsüan-ho i-shih*, or *Stories of the Hsüan-ho reign* (1119–1125), which formed the basis for the Ming novel *Shui-hu chuan*, tells us that in the 3,000 years of China's history peaceful years were by no means as many as troublesome ones. The principle behind history is *yin-yang*. *Yang* is represented by China, gentlemen, and the way of Heaven, whereas *yin* symbolizes "barbarians," inferior people, and human desires. When the latter dominates, however, "barbarians" encroach upon China, inferior people become powerful, and natural calamities occur. Changes in *yin-yang* are closely related to the character of the emperor.[59]

Finally, the myth of Sung superiority loomed large in foreign policy considerations. Most officials favored the use of peaceful tactics in dealing with "barbarians." The traditional concept of cultivating virtue as an effective means to bring about "barbarian" submission was central to this line of thinking.[60] Chao P'u, who served at the court of both Emperor T'ai-tsu and Emperor T'ai-tsung as prime minister, opposed the use of military power to conquer the "barbarians." He pointed out in his memorials submitted during and after T'ai-tsung's military campaigns against the Khitans that since ancient times wise rulers had adopted a policy of pacification and had not interfered in "barbarian" affairs. Their policy consisted of a defensive use of military power and the cultivation of virtue.[61] T'ien Hsi, another ranking official at the court of T'ai-tsung, also recommended a policy that combined military power (*wei*) with virtue (*te*).[62]

A corollary of these views is the belief that the "barbarian" menace was not as serious as internal problems. Since the "barbarians" could be transformed by Chinese virtues, the primary concern of Chinese rulers should be the cultivation of virtue and the pacification of the Chinese people. The sage kings of ancient times had successfully cultivated the virtues, and the "barbarians" were so tenderly cherished that they no longer desired to invade China.[63] Even Emperor T'ai-tsung, the most militant emperor of the Northern Sung, emphasized internal Chinese problems in 991 in these words: "External threats are only frontier matters which can be prevented from occurring beforehand. But wickedness is without observable form, and when villains make internal trouble it is very frightful. Rulers should pay attention to this."[64] T'ai-tsung's views were probably influenced by such ministers as Chao P'u and Chang Ch'i-hsien.

Both argued that the ancient sage kings did not compete with the "barbarians" in military prowess but were preoccupied with fundamental policies (*pen*). Ancient rulers considered the maintenance of peace and order in China to be the first priority of the state, and foreign affairs to be unimportant (*mo*). Only when the Chinese enjoyed peace would the remote peoples voluntarily submit.[65]

Such statesmen as Han Ch'i, Fan Chung-yen, Wang An-shih, and Ssu-ma Kuang also shared this view. Han Ch'i held that all external threats originated in internal problems, for the "barbarians" were always alert to China's inner problems and waited for a proper time to launch invasions.[66] Fan Chung-yen argued that vicious elements in the government were more detrimental to the state than "barbarian" encroachment. Wang An-shih, whose reforms aimed to enrich the state and to strengthen its military power, advocated that internal reforms be implemented before external expansion was attempted.[67] During the Sung-Liao negotiations of their border disputes in 1074–1076, Wang allegedly said, "If we want to acquire the land in dispute, we could give it away first," because the Sung was not ready to take a strong stand against the Liao.[68] Ssu-ma Kuang pointed out that the sage kings always emphasized internal affairs. He contended that when nearby places were stabilized remote places would then be pacified.[69] The treaty of Shan-yüan was perceived as an ideal example of a successful policy that combined power and virtue. Emperor Chen-tsung had marched his armies to the frontiers and showed the Khitans the Chinese determination to fight. Meanwhile, he was sincere in negotiating with them to promote the well-being of both peoples.[70]

Even in times of crisis, some officials continued to stress the cultivation of virtue by the Chinese emperor and the insignificance of "barbarian" disturbances. On the eve of the Jurchens' conquest of the Northern Sung, Ch'en Kung-fu, a censor, memorialized the throne that the most pressing priorities were the cultivation of virtue and some necessary political reforms. If the government implemented internal reforms, the "barbarians" would cherish Chinese virtue and fear Chinese military power.[71]

Realistic Appraisals of the Northerners

Sung officials were realistic enough to assess accurately the power of the Khitans and flexible enough to change their policies toward the enemy. Circumstances forced them to concede that there was little hope of conquering the Khitans. The best policy would be to accept the provisions of the treaty of Shan-yüan.

Emperor T'ai-tsung apparently knew that he had not achieved a true reunification of China. In his refusal to accept an honorary title from his officials, he indicated that since the Northern Han had not yet been annexed and the prefectures of Yen and Chi had not yet been recovered, it would be an exaggeration to talk about unification.[72] When Ssu-ma Kuang discussed the presentation of an honorary title to Emperor Shen-tsung in 1086, he reviewed the precedents and concluded that the practice was not found in ancient times but had been introduced by the T'ang emperors. He praised Emperors T'ai-tsu and T'ai-tsung for their refusal to accept honorary titles (T'ai-tsung accepted only a modest one) and lamented the fact that Emperor Chen-tsung had accepted such titles.[73]

Sung official documents that circulated internally are not entirely hostile to the Khitans. In an edict of 1074, the emperor asked a few ranking officials for their opinions about the Khitan demand for some border territories. The first sentence reads: "Our court has made peace with the *northerners* for about eighty years."[74] Numerous edicts and reports from local governments on the border refer to the Khitans as "northerners," rather than as "barbarians," "caitiffs," or other pejoratives, and their land as the "northern side" (*pei-chieh*).[75] Even in the comments made by Emperor Shen-tsung at the end of reports and memorials submitted by his officials, there are few hostile terms, and the Khitans are simply designated as "enemies" and "northerners."[76]

The *Tzu-chih t'ung-chien*, one of the most important contemporary histories, often describes the Khitans but never depicts them as inferior "barbarians." Its author, Ssu-ma Kuang, writes of them simply as "Khitans." He knew that the emperors and officials at the Sung court, as well as foreigners, would read his work. With this in mind, he naturally would not want to provoke protests from readers living in the Khitan state, who at that time were buying and smuggling into their kingdom books published in Sung territory. It is also possible that Ssu-ma Kuang, being a conservative statesman, wanted to maintain peaceful relations with the Khitans and the Hsi Hsia.[77] Scholars and officials in the eleventh century accurately assessed Khitan affairs based on careful study and examination of the enemy. A number of officials made direct, firsthand observations of the Khitans after 1005, when the Sung and the Liao began to exchange ambassadors. Sung envoys were required to write reports on their missions to the Liao, and these reports were invaluable to the court.

The Sung concluded that the Khitans differed from the ancient "barbarians." Emperor T'ai-tsung once noted that "the Hsün-yün today are different from ancient barbarians in their numerical strength, their constant changes in policy, and their deceitful tricks."[78] By the eleventh century, the court recognized that the Khitans were the most advanced of any of China's neighbors throughout history. Many officials spoke of the "Great Liao," "the powerful neighbors," "the powerful enemy," and "the enemies of the north and the west."[79] Han Ch'i pointed out that the Khitans had adopted Chinese culture and considered themselves superior to all foreign states of the past. The Khitans had subdued Koryŏ and had competed with Chinese dynasties for hegemony for more than a hundred years. Therefore, they had even come to believe that they were superior to the Sung.[80]

Sung officials often distinguished between the northern enemy and the western "barbarians." Fan Chung-yen insisted that equal status in international relations should not be granted to the Hsi Hsia, but the Khitans had been treated as equals since the Five Dynasties.[81] One official differentiated between the "powerful neighbors in the north" and the "recalcitrant caitiffs in the west."[82] Another official states that the northern enemy was China's cancer whereas the western bandits were only scabies.[83] The Khitans were frequently referred to as the "northern enemy" or the "Khitans," but the Hsi Hsia of the west were called the "western bandits" or the "rebellious *Ch'iang*" (the character *Ch'iang* was written with a sheep radical).[84]

A memorial by an official named Fu Pi was one of the more well-reasoned presentations of the Chinese view. He pointed out that the Khitans possessed unprecedented military power, which the Chinese could not match. They had learned much from the Chinese, from government organization to architecture, from language and literature to the employment of Chinese officials. In short, the Khitans had not only adopted Chinese institutions but also had a formidable military machine, which the Chinese did not have. Fu Pi thus maintained that the Khitans should not be considered in the same way as the "barbarians" of ancient times.[85] He implied that the Liao dynasty ought to be regarded as another state. China was one state among several in its area, though it was, of course, the most civilized one.

Sung policy toward the Liao tended to be realistic. Ou-yang Hsiu, for example, asserted that no dynasty in the long history of Sino-foreign relations had been completely successful in dealing with the "barbarians." Whether the "barbarians" would invade China was an issue over which the Chinese did not exercise full control. Ou-yang Hsiu pointed out that when China had the *tao*, the barbarians would not necessarily submit; when China lost the *tao*, the barbarians would not necessarily invade. The management of foreign affairs should be extremely cautious, concluded Ou-yang, for the best management would not benefit China, but mishandling of the "barbarians" would mean disaster.[86] A policy of nonintervention and pacification, based on practical considerations, developed. While Emperor T'ai-tsung was preparing for his second expedition against the Khitans in 986, many officials opposed an aggressive policy. One expert on Khitan affairs maintained that peaceful relations with the Khitans were preferable to war.[87] Following T'ai-tsung's defeat in a battle in the same year, Chao P'u several times remonstrated with the emperor that no further military action be taken against the Khitans. Chao argued that the ancient sage kings had not interfered with "barbarian" affairs and that military adventures were detrimental to the people and the state.[88] The prime minister and other officials offered similar advice to the emperor.[89] In 989 Emperor T'ai-tsung issued an edict asking his officials to present their views on national defense and foreign policy. Most officials still favored peaceful tactics. They pointed out that attacks against the "barbarians" were not always successful and that war was actually the worst policy.[90]

Sung rulers and officials realized that it was more economical to make annual payments to the Liao than to wage war. Their payments constituted less than one or two percent of military expenditures in wartime.[91] The advantages of peace far outweighed those of war. These officials did not ignore the disadvantages of a policy of peace. They lamented the annual payments, which enriched the Khitans but drained the resources of the Chinese people. Fan Chung-yen wrote in 1044, "Yen and Yün are lost. This is the greatest insult inflicted on China by the barbarians in a thousand years, but it has not been avenged."[92] Wang An-shih deplored the fact that Emperor Shen-tsung addressed the Liao emperor as "uncle" and sent annual gifts to him, considering such actions humiliating to China.[93]

Many officials worried that the enemy's greed would lead to a resumption of hostilities at any time, especially in the mid-eleventh century after the Khitans allied themselves with the Hsi Hsia. In 999 a certain Ho Liang first expressed the fear of a union between the Khitans and the Hsi Hsia.[94] Ou-yang Hsiu warned the throne in 1035 that the nature of the enemy was so unpredictable that peaceful relations could never be considered permanent.[95] The Sung was also concerned about national defense because the Sung-Liao border did not follow natural geographical lines that were easily defensible. The construction of waterways, strategic posts, and even willow trees was essential to block Khitan cavalry in case of war.[96]

A few officials argued that, since the Sung-Liao treaties were unreliable, the Sung should strengthen national defenses in preparation for the stoppage of annual payments and a final solution of the problem by military means.[97] Not all officials held pacificist attitudes toward the Khitans. Sung Ch'i contended that the only effective way to deal with the "barbarians" was to use military force.[98] Ou-yang Hsiu was hostile to the northern and western enemies in the 1040s. Wang An-shih's reforms of military institutions and implementation of policies to strengthen the national defense are well known and need not be discussed here.

It should be noted that many of the views expressed at that time on Sino-foreign problems are combinations of traditional clichés and new insights. Fan Tsu-yü's comments on T'ang foreign policy illustrate this point nicely. Fan, a renowned historian who cooperated with Ssu-ma Kuang in the latter's historical projects, presents his own views on foreign affairs in his

Mirror of the T'ang (*T'ang chien*).[99] Fan is critical of the T'ang emperor T'ai-tsung's policy of expansionism. He notes that whenever there is mis-government in China, the four "barbarians" encroach upon her territories. The ancient sage-kings developed a strategy to deal with the "barbarians." They attracted foreigners by appointing competent officials and by con-stantly paying close attention to the proper governing of the people. When China herself enjoyed good government, and when proper foreign policies were implemented, the "barbarians" admired Chinese customs and righteousness and submitted to Chinese leadership, without being enticed by the lure of profit or without being forced to do so by military power. Those who wanted to submit were indulgently cherished; those who did not want to do so were not forced to submit. The people of China were not exploited, and their resources were not exhausted to suppress the "barbarians."

Fan criticizes the rulers of later ages who desired to destroy the "barbarians" in order to avenge their wrongdoings, or to entice them to submit because the rulers liked them. Both policies were inadequate, Fan points out, because the "barbarians" were similar to the Chinese people. They also loved profit, avoided losses, and cherished life. "Are they different from human beings?" Fan asks. The sage-kings would not kill them, because these ancient rulers loved birds, animals, grass, and trees, not to mention other human beings. How could the sage-kings ever cause the deaths of their own subjects in order to suppress the "barbarians"? The "barbarians" differed from the Chinese in environment, customs, languages, and desires. Even if China acquired their lands she could not make use of them. In order to maintain control over "barbarian" lands, Emperor Yang of the Sui exhausted his manpower and resources and eventually brought about the fall of his dynasty. Emperor T'ai-tsung of the T'ang, concludes Fan, attempted to unify China and the "barbarian" states. This was not an adequate policy to bequeath to posterity, because it would never bring peace to China.

In sum, Fan portrays and treats the "barbarians" as human beings. And he objects to the unification of the world at the expense of human lives and resources.

Conclusion

During the Northern Sung there were two opposing views of the Khitans, which probably derived from the two major traditions in China's foreign relations. The belief in Chinese superiority, not only in cultural but also in political and military terms, corresponded with and largely derived from the long tradition of Sinocentrism. The formal writings of many scholars and officials often upheld the myth of Chinese superiority. The interpretation of the peace with the Liao as the successful application of the elements of power and virtue by the Chinese reflects this myth. Theories of legitimacy and *yin-yang* cosmology also supported this view.

The other interpretation was based on realistic observation and careful assessment of Liao power. Men such as Fu Pi made accurate evaluations of the Khitans and recommended a rational course of action toward them. The rational approach to foreign policy decision-making is best exemplified in the diplomacy of the Ch'ing-li period (1041–1048), when open discussions of foreign affairs and collective decision-making contributed to successful solutions to foreign policy problems.[100]

These views, however, do not represent a clear-cut dichotomy. It was possible for scholars and officials to hold both views simultaneously. On the one hand, they might believe in China's cultural and even military superiority; on the other hand, they could make fairly reasonable appraisals of foreign affairs. A good example is Su Ch'e, who was a fine observer of events at the Liao court and of the personality of the emperor, but who also described the nature of the "northern barbarians" as that of animals.[101]

Such conservative scholar-officials as Ssu-ma Kuang and Ch'en Kung-fu often clung tenaciously to the concepts of power and virtue and favored appeasement. The more progressive elements, represented by Fan Chung-yen and Wang An-shih, were more hostile to the Khitans. Even so, the policies of the latter were rational and cautious, emphasizing internal reforms which would eventually help to eliminate the foreign menace.

The image of the Khitans as a powerful enemy, capable of building a huge empire, forced the Sung Chinese to reevaluate the international situation. They understood the difficulties entailed in changing the status quo and turned their attention to internal affairs. Under these circumstances, the more practical officials constantly warned against the dangers of an eventual "barbarian" invasion and urged the strengthening of national defense, whereas those of a more idealistic turn of mind urged the cultivation of virtue in order to gain the submission of the "barbarians."

NOTES

1. *Ch'un-ch'iu Kung-yang Ch'uan Chu-su* (Taipei: I-wen ed.), p. 231, 15th year of Ch'eng-kung.

2. Mencius says, "I have heard of men using the doctrines of our great land to change barbarians. But I have never yet heard of any being changed by barbarians." See James Legge (tr.), *The Chinese Classics Vol. Two: The Works of Mencius* (Oxford, 1895), pp. 253–254.

3. John K. Fairbank (ed.), *The Chinese World Order: Traditional China's Foreign*

Relations (Cambridge, Mass., 1968).

4. For the Han tribute system, see Yü Ying-shih, *Trade and Expansion in Han China: A Study in the Structure of Sino-Barbarian Economic Relations* (Berkeley and Los Angeles, 1967); for a statement about the Sung period, see Yang Lien-sheng's article, "Historical Notes on the Chinese World Order," in Fairbank (ed.), *The Chinese World Order*, pp. 20–21.

5. Cf. Lu Yao-tung, "Pei-Wei yü Nan-ch'ao tui-chih ch'i-chien te wai-chiao kuan-hsi," *Hsin-ya shu-yüan hsüeh-shu nien-k'an*, no. 8 (1966), pp. 31–61.

6. Li Fang-kuei, "The Inscription of the Sino-Tibetan Treaty of 821–822," *T'oung Pao* 44 (1956): 1–99.

7. T'ao Chin-sheng, "Sung-Liao chien te p'ing-teng wai-chiao kuan-hsi," *Shen Kang-po hsien-sheng pa-shih jung-ch'ing lun-wen chi* (hereafter *SLPT*) (Taipei, 1975), pp. 225–227.

8. Lu Chih, *Lu Hsüan-kung tsou-i ch'üan-chi* (Shanghai, n.d.), ch. 3, pp. 61–68. The general observation cited here is translated from pp. 61–62.

9. The text of the treaty is in Li T'ao, *Hsü Tzu-chih t'ung-chien ch'ang-pien* (hereafter *CP*) (Taipei, 1964), ch. 58, pp. 22b–23a; also see T'ao Chin-sheng and Wang Min-hsin (eds.), *Li T'ao Hsü Tzu-chih t'ung-chien ch'ang-pien Sung-Liao kuan-hsi shih-liao chi-lu* (hereafter *CPSL*) (Taipei, 1974), p. 253.

10. Cf. *SLPT*, p. 232.

11. Ibid., pp. 239–241.

12. In the report made by a special ambassador to the Sung court in 1099, the term "Southern Sung" (Nan Sung) was used. When the Sung government protested the usage, the Liao ambassador replied that it was an official usage in Hsi Hsia state letters to the Liao. See *CP*, ch. 507, pp. 9a–11a; ch. 509, p. 7a; also *CPSL*, pp. 847–849, 854.

13. Such an edict was issued in 1082; see *CP*, ch. 326, p. 3b; *CPSL*, p. 762.

14. Cf. *SLPT*, pp. 239–241; also the statement made in 1090, in *CP*, ch. 496, p. 17a; *CPSL*, p. 835.

15. The earliest appearance of the *Kuo-hsin ssu* is reported in *CP*, ch. 64, p. 12b; also *CPSL*, p. 277. In 1054, its name was changed to *Kuo-hsin so*; see *CP*, ch. 256, p. 6b; also *CPSL*, p. 671. The escorting officials also submitted reports on the activities of foreign envoys; see *CP*, ch. 509, p. 6b; *CPSL*, p. 854, for the records of conversations with foreign envoys.

16. T'ao Chin-sheng, "Pei-Sung Ch'ing-li shih-ch'i te wai-chiao cheng-ts'e", *Bulletin of the Institute of History and Philology, Academia Sinica*, (hereafter *PSCL*), vol. 47, no. 1 (1975), pp. 54–56.

17. *SLPT*, pp. 233–241.

18. Examples of state letters are found in *Sung ta chao-ling chi* (Peking, 1962).

19. There are numerous such documents in the collected works of the Northern Sung period. Examples are: Wang Kuei, *Hua-yang chi* (*Ssu-k'u ch'üan-shu chen-pen* ed., hereafter *SKCS*), 4th ser., chs. 18, 21, 23–25, 30–32; Sung Ch'i, *Ching-wen chi* (*SKCS*, *pieh-chi*), ch. 33; Hu Su, *Wen-kung chi* (*SKCS*, *pieh-chi*), ch. 27; Su Sung, *Su Wei-kung wen-chi* (*SKCS*, 4th ser.), chs. 25, 26; Fan Tsu-yü, *Fan T'ai-shih chi* (*SKCS*, 1st ser.), chs. 28–32; Han Wei, *Nan-yang chi* (*SKCS*, 2nd ser.), ch. 15; Sung Hsiang, *Yüan-hsien chi* (*SKCS*, *pieh-chi*), ch. 30; Ch'iang Chih, *Tz'u-pu chi* (*SKCS*, *pieh-chi*), ch. 33.

20. The first correspondence occurred in 974, and served as a diplomatic overture to normalize relations between the two states. Cf. *SLPT*, p. 228. Another example is found in Liu Chih, *Chung-su chi* (*SKCS, pieh-chi*), ch. 9, p. 9a: a letter from the city of K'ai-feng to Liao envoys.

21. Examples are found in Yang Chieh, *Wu-wei chi* (*SKCS*, 5th ser.), ch. 11; Wei Hsiang, *Ch'ien-t'ang chi* (*SKCS*, 5th ser.), ch. 10; and Han Ch'i, *An-yang chi* (*SKCS*, 4th ser.), ch. 39.

22. Fan Tsu-yü, *Fan T'ai-shih chi*, ch. 33, p. 15a.

23. *CP*, ch. 58, p. 24a; *CPSL*, p. 253. Cf. *SLPT*, p. 239.

24. *SLPT*, pp. 235–236; see also the index in *CPSL* under the entries of "Ch'i-tan," "pei-jen," "pei-chieh," "jung-jen," "i-ti," etc.

25. Su Sung, *Su Wei-kung wen-chi* (*SKCS*, 4th ser.), ch. 66, pp. 1a–5a. For the compilation of the work and its continuation, see *CP*, ch. 315, pp. 1b–2a; ch. 339, pp. 10b–11a; ch. 509, p. 15a; also *CPSL*, pp. 755, 772, and 856.

26. See *Sung Hui-yao chi-kao*, vol. 8, p. 7673. In *CP*, the term "neighboring state" (*lin-kuo*) is used. See *CP*, citing *Yung-lo ta-tien*, ch. 12307, p. 5a; also *CPSL*, p. 56.

27. *Sung ta chao-ling chi* (Peking, hereafter *STCL*) ch. 228, p. 882.

28. Ibid., chs. 228–232, pp. 882–903.

29. For such usage, see *CP: Yung-lo ta-tien*, ch. 12400, p. 5b (*CPSL*, p. 419); *CP*, ch. 151, p. 14a (*CPSL*, p. 477).

30. One official told Khitan officials that "China has made peace with the northern dynasty" (*CP*, ch. 105, p. 20a; *CPSL*, p. 354). Another official reported to the court that "the enemy . . . was afraid of China's attack" (*CP*, ch. 115, p. 17b; *CPSL*, p. 380). Ou-yang Hsiu mentioned the "northern caitiffs" four times, the "two caitiffs" (Liao and Hsia) twice, the "two states" (*erh-kuo*: Liao and Hsia) three times, and China once, in a memorial submitted in 1042 (*CP: Yung-lo ta-tien*, ch. 12399, pp. 17a–21b; *CPSL*, pp. 408–409).

31. In 1021 an edict states that "the Khitans, Po-hai, and Jurchens [in China] were originally foreigners (*wai-kuo jen*)" (*CP*, ch. 77, p. 10a; *CPSL*, p. 306). In 1044 Fan Chung-yen discussed government policy toward the Hsia, saying that "once China lost her superior position [as overlord] over the Hsia, the foreign state [Liao] would look down upon China" (*CP*, ch. 151, p. 4a; *CPSL*, p. 473).

32. Cf. *PSCL*, 62–64. According to Henry Serruys, the Ming never sent princesses to marry Mongol rulers either. See his *Sino-Mongol Relations during the Ming, II: The Tribute System and Diplomatic Missions (1400–1600)* (Brussels, 1967), p. 18.

33. Cf. Chang Chia-chü, *Shen Kua* (Shanghai, 1962), pp. 82–101; Chang Ya-ch'in, "Shen Kua yü Sung Liao hua-chieh chiao-she," *Shih-i*, no. 12 (1975), pp. 10–25.

34. Cf. my paper presented to the American Oriental Society meeting held in Tucson in 1977, entitled "Peace with the Barbarians: Wang An-shih's Policy towards the Khitan."

35. *STCL*, ch. 2, p. 6.

36. Loc. cit.

37. *STCL*, ch. 10, p. 45.

38. *STCL*, ch. 10, pp. 46–47.

39. Li Jo-shui et al., *T'ai-tsung huang-ti shih-lu* (*Ssu-pu ts'ung-k'an* ed., hereafter *SPTK*), 3rd ser., ch. 29, pp. 14a–15b.

40. *STCL*, ch. 117, p. 397.

41. Cf. James T. C. Liu, *Ou-yang Hsiu: An Eleventh-Century Neo-Confucianist* (Stanford, 1967), p. 111; also Ch'en Fang-ming, "Sung-tai cheng-t'ung-lun te hsing-ch'eng chi-ch'i nei-jung," *Shih-huo yüeh-k'an*, vol. 1, no. 8 (1971), p. 425.

42. Chang Fang-p'ing, *Lo-ch'üan chi* (*SKCS*, 1st ser.), ch. 18, p. 31a. The entry is dated the fifth year of *ching-yu*; however, there was only a fourth year of *ching-yu*, or 1037. See also Lu Tien, *T'ao-shan chi* (*SKCS*, *pieh-chi*), ch. 9, p. 13a, for an essay written for the state examination, which in part states: "Now that the 'barbarians' have submitted to us and there are no troubles internally and externally." Another example can be found in Hu Su, *Wen-kung chi*, ch. 29, p. 4b.

43. Cf. *SLPT*, p. 234, n. 3. My impression that the most commonly used term to designate the Khitans is "caitiffs" is based on the reading of more than sixty collected works of the Northern Sung period.

44. Wang Yü-ch'eng, *Hsiao-hsü wai-chi* (Shanghai, n.d.), ch. 10, p. 475.

45. *Lo-ch'üan chi*, ch. 5, pp. 4b–5a.

46. Ts'ai Hsiang, *Tuan-ming chi* (*SKCS*, 4th ser.), ch. 9, pp. 3ab.

47. *Chu Wen-kung chiao Ch'ang-li wen-chi* (*SPTK*, 1st ser.), ch. 11, pp. 95–96.

48. Ibid., p. 98.

49. Li Kou, *Chih-chiang Li-hsien-sheng wen-chi* (*SPTK*, 1st ser.), ch. 27, pp. 196–198, letter to Fan Chung-yen.

50. Shao Yung, *I-ch'uan chi-jang chi* (*SPTK*, 1st ser.), ch. 16, p. 117.

51. Ibid., ch. 18, p. 137.

52. *Erh-Ch'eng i-shu*, in *Ssu-pu pei-yao* ed. (hereafter *SPPY*), ch. 2a, p. 226.

53. Ibid., ch. 11, p. 8a.

54. Ibid., ch. 18, p. 39b.

55. Ch'eng Hao, *Ming-tao hsien-sheng wen-chi*, ch. 2.

56. *I-ch'uan hsien-sheng wen-chi*, ch. 1, p. 2b. This is a memorial written by Ch'eng I on behalf of his father.

57. Ch'en Shun-yü, *Tu-kuan chi* (*SKCS*, 3rd ser.), ch. 4, pp. 19b–20a.

58. Chao Ju-yü, *Sung ming-ch'en tsou-i* (*SKCS*, 2nd ser.), ch. 4, pp. 1a–7a.

59. Anon., *Hsin-pien Hsüan-ho i-shih* (*SPPY*), p. 1a.

60. Cf. Wang Gungwu, "Early Ming Relations with Southeast Asia: A Background Essay," in Fairbank (ed.), *The Chinese World Order*, p. 43.

61. Chao Ju-yü, *Sung ming-ch'en tsou-i*, ch. 129, pp. 8a–15b, a memorial submitted to Emperor T'ai-tsung appealing for the withdrawal of the armies.

62. T'ien Hsi, *Hsien-p'ing chi* (*SKCS*, 4th ser.), ch. 1, pp. 15b–16a; ch. 22, p. 9b. Cf. also Ch'en Hsiang, *Ku-ling chi* (*SKCS*, 3rd ser.), ch. 21, p. 14a.

63. James Legge's translation of *Tso chuan*, Book X, Duke Chao, Year XXIII, is "Anciently, the defences of the sons of Heaven were the rude tribes on every side of the kingdom" (p. 700). The famous Sung prime minister Wang Tan's reference to it is found in Lo Ts'ung-yen, *Lo Yü-chang chi* (Shanghai, n.d.), ch. 5, p. 59; Su Shun-ch'in, *Su Shun-ch'in chi* (Shanghai, 1961 ed.), ch. 11, p. 156.

64. *CP*, ch. 32, p. 9a; *CPSL*, p. 149.

65. T'o T'o et al., *Sung shih* (Po-na ed.), ch. 265–266. Cf. also Yen Shu, *Yüan-hsien i-wen* (*SKCS*, 7th ser.), pp. 1ab.

66. *SLPT*, p. 248; for other views, see p. 246.

67. I have discussed Wang's scheme of reforms in my unpublished paper,

"Peace with the Barbarians: Wang An-shih's Policy towards the Khitan." The Chinese version is entitled "Wang An-shih te tui Liao wai-chiao cheng-ts'e," *Bulletin of the Institute of History and Philology, Academia Sinica*, vol. 50, pt. 4 (1979), pp. 657–677.

68. Ibid.

69. *Wen-kuo wen-cheng Ssu-Ma-kung chi*, ch. 57, p. 431; also ch. 45, p. 351. For a general assessment of Neo-Confucianists' views, see Ch'en Ch'ing-hsin, "Sung-ju ch'un-ch'iu tsun-wang yao-i te fa-wei yü ch'i cheng-chih ssu-hsiang," *New Asia Journal*, vol. 10, no. 1, part 1 (1971), pp. 269–368. For Southern Sung concentration on internal issues, see Charles A. Peterson, "First Sung Reactions to the Mongol Invasion of the North," in John W. Haeger (ed.), *Crisis and Prosperity in Sung China* (Tucson, 1974), pp. 249–251.

70. Cf. *CP*, ch. 67, pp. 9b–10a, for the opinion of Ma Chih-chieh; *CPSL*, p. 282.

71. Chao Ju-yü, *Sung ming-ch'en tsou-i*, ch. 150, pp. 36b–37a.

72. *STCL*, ch. 3, p. 11.

73. *CP*: *Ch'ang-pien Shih-pu*, ch. 3A, pp. 21a–21b; *CPSL*, pp. 606–607.

74. *STCL*, ch. 213, p. 810.

75. See *CPSL*, pp. 723–640, for examples for 1072 (*CP*, chs. 232–237).

76. Cf. ibid., pp. 668–724, for Shen-tsung's comments in 1074–1076 (*CP*, chs. 253–276). In nineteen endorsements in which the emperor made reference to the Khitans, "caitiffs" and "bandits" are found in three of them (two on p. 706 and one on p. 723; *CP*: *Yung-lo ta-tien*, ch. 12507, pp. 4a, 5a; ch. 274, p. 16a).

77. In a memorial submitted in 1067, Ssu-ma Kuang favored maintaining peace with the Khitans. He talked about the "Khitans" or the "caitiffs." See *CP*: *Yung-lo ta-tien*, ch. 12429, pp. 12ab (*CPSL*, pp. 587–588). However, in other memorials submitted in 1065 (*CP*, ch. 205, pp. 7a–8b; *CPSL*, pp. 600–601), 1085 (*CP*, ch. 363, pp. 13b–14b; *CPSL*, pp. 782–783), and 1086 (*CP*, ch. 364, pp. 33b–34a; *CPSL*, p. 784), he used only the names "Khitans" and "enemy."

78. The comment was made in 991; see *CP*, ch. 32, pp. 4b–5a; *CPSL*, p. 148.

79. Cf. Ch'in Kuan, *Huai-hai chi* (Commercial Press, n.d.), ch. 18, p. 117, for the term "the Great Liao" (Ta-Liao); P'eng Ju-li, *Po-yang chi* (*SKCS*, 2nd ser.), ch. 4, p. 18b, for "powerful enemy" in a poem; Chang Lei, *K'o-shan chi* (*SKCS*, 4th ser.), p. 8a, for "powerful neighbors," also in a poem.

80. *CP*, ch. 142, pp. 16b–17a; *CPSL*, pp. 438–439. Cf. also *SLPT*, p. 244.

81. *Sung ming-ch'en tsou-i*, ch. 133, pp. 28ab.

82. *CP*: *Yung-lo ta-tien*, ch. 12400, pp. 10b–11a; *CPSL*, p. 424.

83. *K'o-shan chi*, ch. 40, p. 4a.

84. See *CP*, ch. 141, p. 9b (*CPSL*, p. 433), for Ou-yang Hsiu's memorial submitted in 1043, in which Ou-yang talked about "northern enemies" and "western bandits"; *CP*, ch. 142, pp. 13ab (*CPSL*, p. 437), for Han Ch'i's renditions of "northern dynasty" and "bandits"; *CP*, ch. 151, p. 15b (*CPSL*, p. 478), for Yü Ching's usages of "northern enemy" and "western barbarians"; *CP*, ch. 151, pp. 25ab (*CPSL*, p. 482), for Fan Chung-yen's uses of the same terms as those employed by Yü Ching.

85. *CP*, ch. 150, pp. 16a–17a; *CPSL*, pp. 459–460.

86. Ou-yang Hsiu et al., *Hsin Wu-tai shih*, ch. 72, "Preface." Su Sung also made a similar observation; see *CP*, ch. 284, p. 7b; *CPSL*, p. 732.

87. *CP*, ch. 27, pp. 1b–6a; *CPSL*, pp. 102–106.

88. *CP*, ch. 27, pp. 11b–14b; *CPSL*, pp. 111–113.

89. *CP*, ch. 27, pp. 15ab; *CPSL*, p. 114.

90. *CP*, ch. 30, pp. 1a–13b; *CPSL*, pp. 129–137.

91. *CP*, ch. 150, p. 16a; *CPSL*, p. 459.

92. Chao Ju-yü, *Sung ming-ch'en tsou-i*, ch. 134, p. 26a.

93. *CP*, ch. 237, p. 6a; *CPSL*, p. 637.

94. *CP*, ch. 44, pp. 16a–20a; *CPSL*, pp. 172–176.

95. *CP*, ch. 119, p. 6b (*CPSL*, p. 383); *CP*, ch. 141, pp. 9a–11a (*CPSL*, pp. 433–435). For similar views, see Hsia Shu, *Wen-chuang chi*, ch. 13, pp. 18a–19b; Chang Fang-p'ing, *Lo-ch'üan chi*, ch. 18, p. 31b; Liu Ch'ang, *Kung-shih chi* (*SKCS, pieh-chi*), ch. 40, pp. 15b–18a; Lü T'ao, *Ching-te chi*, ch. 19, pp. 1a–7b; Liu Chih, *Chung-su chi*, ch. 6, p. 21a: Hua Chen, *Yün-ch'i-chü-shih chi* (SKCS, 1st ser.), ch. 18, pp. 12a–14a.

96. Sung Ch'i wrote a detailed analysis of the problem of peace and national defense in his "Ho-jung lun" and "Yü-jung lun," in *Ching-wen chi*, ch. 44. Similar discussions are found in Hu Su, *Wen-kung chi*, ch. 8, pp. 6b–7a; also pp. 9b–12a. Hu was in charge of national defense as Deputy Commissioner of the Bureau of Military Affairs in 1061–1066. See also Lü T'ao, *Ching-te chi*, ch. 5, pp. 15b–16a. An earlier view is *CP*, ch. 30, pp. 1a–2b (*CPSL*, pp. 129–130).

97. For examples, see Ch'en Shun-yü, *Tu-kuan chi*, ch. 1, pp. 10a–11b, and Lü T'ao, *Ching-te chi*, ch. 19, pp. 6a–7a.

98. Sung Ch'i, *Ching-wen chi*, ch. 44, p. 13b.

99. *T'ang chien* (Shanghai, n.d.), ch. 6, pp. 49–51. Concerning the first view, Wang An-shih also regarded the "barbarians" as equals, and he believed they were treated by the ancient kings equally. See *Chou-kuan hsin-i* (*Yüeh-ya-t'ang ts'ung-shu*), ch. 13, p. 10a. In a debate at the imperial court in 1072 on whether the Liao emperor was sincere in keeping the peace, Wang insisted that judging from the records of twenty years the Liao emperor was clearly not a stubborn character who would disregard reason. See *CP*, ch. 236, p. 9b (*CPSL*, p. 631). Wang's attitude was markedly rational.

100. *PSCL*.

101. *Luan-ch'eng hou-chi* (*SPTK*, 1st ser.), ch. 11, p. 583; *Luan-ch'eng ying-chao chi* (*SPTK*, 1st ser.); also ch. 11.

PART III

Institutions for Foreign Relations in the Multi-State System

FOUR

Sung Foreign Trade: Its Scope and Organization

SHIBA YOSHINOBU

Medieval Commercial Revolution: 8th–13th Centuries

Before going into a detailed description of the scope and nature of Sung foreign trade, it is necessary to look briefly at the major features of "the medieval Chinese commercial revolution" which underlie the advent of the mercantile era in East Asia.[1] After a period of stagnation in the Six Dynasties, which was marked by the decline of both interregional and international trade, China was reunified by the Sui and the T'ang, and the subsequent period, extending roughly from the eighth to the thirteenth century, was, by contrast, a time of economic growth.

Improvements in the offical transportation system, which facilitated the movement of taxes, officials, troops, and documents, contributed greatly to the integration and maintenance of unity.[2] The most significant effect of this consolidation of the official system was the concomitant improvement and extension of the unofficial transportation network, that it brought about, particularly within the areas served by the official system. Contemporaneously with these changes, marked advances were made in the technology of navigation and in the publication of handbooks on tides and currents, as well as in the sphere of land and naval warfare. The quality of maps of foreign countries also improved.[3] Indeed, the Sung and Yüan dynasties were the golden age of Chinese geography and cartography.

A regular and extensive maritime trade between China and the Indian Ocean littorals had begun in T'ang times. Initially, the Arabs took the leadership in this trade, but within a few centuries they were overtaken by rivals.[4] Chinese people thus entered an era of colonial ventures and voyages of discovery. Driven partly by population pressure and its attendant economic, social, and political stresses, and partly by the spirit of adventure and the desire for wealth, the Chinese embarked upon their first large-scale maritime emigration. The first permanent Chinese settlements in Southeast Asia were established at this time.[5]

These developments were the first indication of the breakdown of China's time-honored theory of foreign relations. China had been accustomed to foreign relations across a land frontier. While Chinese expansion to the north was limited by geographic factors, there were no such limits toward the south. With the onset of a new epoch in which Chinese vigorously began to move southward by sea, their concept of a self-sufficient Middle Kingdom and the diplomacy linked to it gradually came into conflict with the new reality. This is the phase described by J. K. Fairbank as "the eclipse of the tribute system by trade." [6]

The colonization of the plains and hills of the Yangtze valley and the southeast littoral considerably enlarged the geographic scope of economic exchange, which was also stimulated by an increase in population and in rural productivity. There was an abundance of untapped but accessible natural resources in the south, and exploitation of this new frontier gave a dynamic impulse to the medieval Chinese economy. From the fourth century, when the Northwest was beginning to be replaced as the economic center of the nation, there was a steady migration of the population toward the south. From the tenth to the thirteenth century, this population shift increased in tempo. [7] This migration helped to diffuse new technology and contributed to urban growth. Thus higher productivity in the new region created a larger marketable surplus, stimulated internal trade by causing a greater demand, and augmented the rate of saving and the formation of capital. The way was paved for the burgeoning commercialization of China's most advanced regional economies.

There were also revolutionary developments in market structure and urbanization. The components of this revolution, as recently summarized by G. W. Skinner, [8] were (1) a relaxation of the restriction that each county could maintain only one market, which had to be located in the capital city; (2) the breakdown and eventual collapse of the official marketing organization; (3) the disappearance of the enclosed marketplace, along with the walled-ward system, and their replacement by a "much freer street plan in which trade and commerce could be conducted anywhere within the city or its suburbs"; (4) the rapid expansion of particular walled cities and the growth of commercial suburbs outside their gates; and (5) the emergence of a "great number of small and intermediate-sized towns" with important economic functions.

Coupled with these developments were important shifts in governmental policy, which resulted in the increased monetization of taxation and trade, and a general decline in official regulation of commercial affairs. Faced with the rising secular trend that characterized this transitional age, the government changed its policy to exploit commerce as a source of revenue. [9] This particularly became evident from the first inauguration of the "two tax" system in 780. The four principles adopted by this new financial system show how vital was the change in financial policy. That is, (1) all taxes should be collected, in principle at least, in cash; (2) assessment of tax-farming should be made according to the amount of property held by each household; (3) the total amount of tax collected in a particular year should be calculated beforehand, based on the rough estimate of government expenditures for that year; and (4) no taxes other than the single farming of the "two taxes" should be permitted.[10]

As a result, the proportion of surplus agricultural production which passed directly into government hands as tax was reduced. Also, the government's direct involvement in local affairs was reduced.[11] On the whole, a qualitative change in the nature of internal trade thus took place during the T'ang–Sung transition. The essential elements of this change were these: (1) commodities collected and distributed by itinerant merchants were, from Sung times on, no longer limited to luxury goods for the rich, but grew to include daily necessities for a broader base of the population, including petty rural landowners and the poor; (2) farmers in various regions of China were no longer economically self-sufficient, but were involved in a network of internal trade; and (3) internal trade was no longer confined to urban and quasi-urban areas, but was extended to include border villages located far from major cities.[12]

Since the regional economies still exhibited significant diversity in their evolution and structure, however, the degree of commercialization was different from place to place and was not as high as in late imperial times. Government trade through the exchange of goods with neighboring people at the trading posts on the border, and through the provisioning of a large amount of its standing army, played a far from negligible role in the rise of long-distance trade. In short, at this stage of the commercialization of Chinese society, both technological advance and foreign, or long-distance, trade were the main stimuli for the growth of cities and trade. When foreign trade was conducted, it was in response mainly to the demands of the upper classes and the population of the most urbanized areas.

Throughout this period, intercourse between the regions became increasingly regular, and the circle of exchange continuously widened. An interregional and international trade of a regular character emerged, and China's economic relations with other East Asian countries were intensified.[13]

In this period, which saw the rebirth of trade, a large part of the non-agrarian wealth consisted of circulating capital; the need for ready cash was great. Both private traders and the government sought to accumulate money. The chief medium of exchange in the international trade of the day was bullion, especially silver, whereas in China's internal trade copper money was widely used, along with, to a lesser extent, silk, silver, and other monies of inferior quality. With the monetization of the economy, a threefold division of money into silver, copper money, and other inferior quality money also developed in domestic trade.[14] In the Five Dynasties period, the use of silver as the medium of exchange in the sale of precious goods became an established practice in the regional economies of the south and hence made its way into the north.[15]

By the end of the Northern Sung, the government's total silver holdings in the capital reached the sum of approximately forty million taels.[16] Meanwhile, the circulation of inferior quality money, which also began in the Five Dynasties period, resulted from two related factors: the general deficiency in ready cash (i.e., copper money) relative to the growth in demand for it, and the government's unwillingness to permit the flow of its holdings of copper cash beyond its borders. As a result of this deficiency the state of Min (in Fukien) adopted a lead currency, which undermined the monetary systems of other states that exchanged their copper cash and silver for inferior Min coins. The dynasties of the North China plain and the Wu Yüeh kingdom (in Chekiang and southern Kiangsu) attempted, by contrast, to hoard large reserves of copper for strategic reasons. In this context, the question of how to acquire the largest share of "international" trade, and how then to manage the share so acquired in order to produce more wealth, were the main tasks to which most of the governments of the day addressed themselves. And the Sung, in the process of reunifying the empire, learned about monetary and commercial policies from the experiences of the Five Dynasties period.[17]

When China was reunified, the Sung established control over commodities in high demand in both internal and external markets. The production of tea, salt, and a few mineral resources and the import of precious spices and incenses were placed under government supervision, and merchants served as intermediaries in the circulation of these goods.[18] The government also tried to further economic integration by the circulation of large amounts of copper money to be used as legal tender. Annual output of copper cash rose to 1.83 million strings early in the eleventh century, reaching a maximum of 5.06 million strings in 1080.[19] Bills, promissory notes, and paper money were also more frequently used.[20] Partly because of the availability of large copper deposits within its borders, and partly because of the convenience of paying its standing army with copper cash, the Sung consistently (and successfully) employed copper money as legal tender. The Sung accumulated copper money, bullion, and other kinds of currencies in sufficient quantities to maintain its economic integrity. This economic unity, which was strengthened by the interregional and international commerce enabled the Sung to survive for about three centuries, despite the military pressure from its bellicose neighbors.

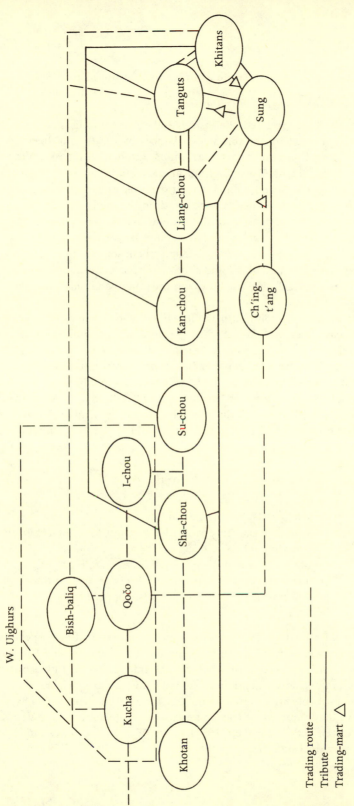

Figure 1

Trading route ----
Tribute ———
Trading-mart △

Areas, Trade Routes, and Commodities

Trade across the Northern Border

As the T'ang declined, the eastern end of the transeurasian trade routes was fragmented by the repeated advances of various northern peoples. There were, from east to west, the Khitans, Jurchens, Tanguts, Ch'ing-t'ang or Western Ch'iang, Kansu Uighurs, and Khotan Uighurs. In rough outline, their geographical and economic relationships are depicted in Figure 1.

The semi-nomadic people who lived on the fringes of China were not uncivilized "barbarians," nor did they derive from a single ethnic stock. They had already developed states composed of various ethnic groups, including Han colonists who had taught them something of Chinese technology as well as of military and administrative techniques. Chinese philosophical and ideological teachings, on the other hand, made little headway among these peoples.

Because of the political instability noted above, the main artery of the west–east trade was forced to divide into several branch routes in the Kansu Corridor before finally reaching the terminus towns on China's northern frontier. Though this instability interrupted China's political relations with the states of East Turkestan, exemplified by the sudden decline of the oasis town of Tun-huang, trade between China and the west continued to thrive, with the northern peoples serving as intermediaries. The following commodities were exchanged through this transcontinental route.[21]

Goods from the West

- horses, camels, sheep, asses
- jade, pearls, amber, emerald, coral
- frankincense,[22] myrrh, ambergris, musk, sodium chloride (i.e., borax),[23] yellow alum
- yak's tail, antelope's horn, white marten, ivory
- fine white carpets, Persian silk brocade, fine cotton cloth
- iron suits of armor, steel swords, copper utensils
- bullion

Such products as frankincense, myrrh, ambergris, fine carpets, ivory, coral, and Persian silk came from the far west (i.e., the Red Sea, eastern Africa, and the Persian Gulf), and were transported to China by Arabs, Turks, or Persians. Other items, like jade, borax, yak's tail, and fine cotton cloth, probably arrived from Central Asia and Tibet. The list below, which shows the frequency of tribute missions dispatched by the states of East Turkestan to the Sung (960–1063), is arranged by type of commodity and by individual state.[24]

	Liang-chou	Kan-chou	Tun-huang	Turfan	Kucha	Khotan
horses	9	17	14	3	18	5
jewels	0	26	23	3	11	10
incense	0	6	10	1	10	2
others	0	6	2	0	2	4

Goods from China

- raw silk, silk, silk brocade
- incense, spices, tortoise shell, ivory, pearls, rhinoceros horn, cassia (mainly products from Southeast Asia and South China)
- bullion, gold or silver or copper ornaments, lacquerware, porcelain
- tea, ginger, orange peel
- paper, stationery, printed items[25]

Together with the exchange of commodities with the Liao, Hsi Hsia, and Ch'ing-t'ang, which will be examined below, China's trade with the states of East Turkestan during the Northern Sung, which was in the form of tributary trade, persisted. Once a year, envoys from at least one of these states arrived in China.[26] Tribute envoys from East Turkestan were accompanied by Uighur merchants, who in most cases remained for long periods in one of the cities of North China and sold their valuable goods in exchange for bullion.[27] At the height of the Northern Sung, the parity of gold and silver in China fluctuated between 6 : 1 and 10 : 1, while the parity in the eastern Muslim states was around 9.6 : 1. Sung gold was cheaper than that of the Islamic world. Hence merchants from East Turkestan traded for Chinese bullion.[28] The Uighur merchants also profited through their money-lending activities in K'ai-feng.[29]

International trade, conditioned by fluctations in supply and demand and by fluctuations in price of bullion, developed, but this is only a part of the picture. It is necessary to explain why China, with such an abundance of resources and with its technological achievements, continued to show interest in foreign trade with unfriendly states in the north and did not attempt to seal off its northern border.

First, China had a continuing need for cavalry horses, which were obtained in the north. The Middle Kingdom never had sufficient horses.[30] Second, both the Sung and the Northern dynasties needed additional wealth to finance military expenditures. The Northerners benefited greatly from their role as "middlemen" in the transeurasian trade; the Sung received a handsome profit as well as provisions for its army.[31] Third, the merchants and the upper classes of both sides benefited from international trade. The demand for luxury goods on the part of the upper classes and the most urbanized segments of the population rapidly increased.[32]

Sung officials, whose wealth was based on the intensive and highly productive agriculture of their tenants, and who could gain access to government positions principally through the imperial examinations, differed from the aristocrats of the preceding dynasties. As officials, they had to make their own way, and most of the privileges of status which they enjoyed could not be bequeathed to their children. It cannot have been easy for them to maintain their families at a high standard of living in the urbanized and commercialized society of the times. Their official prerogatives, however, and laws that tolerated official investment in commerce, particularly in the covert form of investment of funds with others, meant that they had opportunities to make money. As their rank and wealth increased, they tended to move into the cities, where their extravagant expenditures provided the basis for the flowering of a distinctive official-gentry culture.[33]

Extravagance spread downward from officialdom into the lower classes and outward from the capital to the provinces. This may be inferred from the sumptuary legislation repeatedly issued by the Sung government, especially that relating to dress, furniture, and housing. These laws were widely disobeyed, as may be seen from the observations of one contemporary: "These days the families of artisans and merchants trail white silks and brocades, and adorn themselves with jades and pearls. In nine cases out of ten, if one looks a person over from head to foot, one will find that he is breaking the law." Wang Mai, a thirteenth-century official, wrote:

> The customs of the empire have now become extravagant. Limitless sums are squandered on the construction of lofty and elegant mansions, something which used to be forbidden. These days such is the practice of spendthrift emulation that roof beams confront each other in unbroken succession. There is no end to the waste of money on gilding and kingfisher feathers, something on which restrictions used to be imposed. There are at present rows of shops which do gold-plating, competing with each other for profit. One drinking-bout among the gentry may squander property worth ten pieces of gold. It is not only officials of long standing who do this; the pernicious practice is imitated by those who have just entered the government service. Trifles like women's ornaments and clasps may cost up to a hundred thousand cash. Nor does this happen only in the great households; those of moderate means also strive to do the same. Adornments which make their appearance in the Rear Palace in the morning will have become the fashion among the commoners by evening. What is manufactured yesterday for those in high places will be spread throughout the capital tomorrow.

Gold-foil costume jewelry, although it was illegal, was worn not only by powerful and titled individuals but also by commoners who had little money. Gold and silver vessels were much used, being found even in the wine-shops, tea-houses, and restaurants of larger cities. Silversmiths and shops that dealt in gold and silver were found in many prefectural and county capitals and even in some market towns. In some areas, ordinary townsfolk and villagers wore gold and silver ornaments.[34]

Both Buddhist and Taoist festivals, as well as the theatrical performances closely connected with them, often held at market towns, afforded opportunities for the purchase of such foreign goods as drugs, perfumes, incense, and spices.[35] The drugs acquired by the government through international trade were also sold at official medical treatment bureaus established in major cities.[36]

Luxurious tastes were also prevalent among the upper classes of the various peoples who constituted China's neighbors.[37] They obtained Chinese goods they needed either through trade or in the form of gifts made by the Sung in return for tributary offerings.

Trade with the Liao

The Liao, which ruled eastern Inner Mongolia and part of northern China, was divided into five provinces, each having its own capital. It was not as integrated as the Sung. The Liao exhibited a great deal of diversity from province to province. Most of its territory, however, was linked by an effective network of overland routes, which connected the main roads of neighboring provinces.[38] The main Liao port at the mouth of the Liao River was linked with the ports of China along the coast of the Shantung Peninsula and at the mouth of the Yangtze River.[39] This sea route was particularly useful when military disturbances or political unrest impeded overland trade missions between the Sung and the Liao.

The commodities exchanged included, from the Liao, horses, sheep, white marten fur, white fox fur, woolen cloth, carpets, brocade, silver and golden ornaments, iron suits of armor, slaves, and lumber; and from China, silk, silk brocade, tea, military weapons, marine products, ginger, orange peel, *caesalipinia sappan* (dye), medicines, and silver and golden ornaments. The Chinese also shipped goods from Southeast Asia to the Liao.[40] Above all, the Chinese desired horses from the Liao and the Jurchens, who were their principal suppliers of studs.[41]

The Liao, from its inception, depended on trade. As early as 909, Yeh-lü A-pao-chi, its founder, established a trading post that set a precedent for the later development of commerce throughout his domain.[42] Shortly thereafter, during the reign of T'ai-tsung, thriving markets in each of its four state capitals developed.[43] Later, the Liao dispatched military expeditions against the Koreans, the Jurchens, the Tanguts, the Uighur states in Kansu, and China. As a result of the expeditions against the Jurchens and the Koreans, the Liao succeeded in controlling the lines of communication between the Jurchens, Korea, and China, and thus in monopolizing the trade in furs, horses, pearls, and ginseng. At the same time, the Liao received regular tribute missions from the Jurchens, Korea, the Uighurs, Khotan, and Kucha, which offered jade, amber, agate, frankincense, fine carpets, cotton cloth, and bullion.[44]

After these successes in acquiring new territory and in expanding commerce, the Liao sought to improve its trade relations with China, which had been carried on amicably, but on a limited scale. The Liao was induced to do so because the presence of Chinese specialists and craftsmen in its domain had stimulated an increased demand for luxury goods from China.[45]

By the treaty of Shan-yüan in 1005, the Sung agreed to open five permanent trading posts located close to the border.[46] The Liao reciprocated by opening three of its own markets.[47] Officially sanctioned trade between the two states could be conducted at these posts. Lack of sources thwarts any effort to describe this system of frontier markets. But a few Sung records enable us to see at least part of the picture.[48] The distinction between official transactions and private trade was rigidly maintained. Official trade dealt with commodities subject to governmental monopoly, which were sent from K'ai-feng. Government officials supervised the trade. Sung merchants offered tea, silk, lacquerware, porcelain, and grains. Officials stationed at these markets watched for espionage activities and settled disputes over prices which arose as a result of improper trade practices.

Certain goods were not traded. The Sung prohibited the export of salt, books, maps, and weapons, whereas the Liao forbad the sale of horses. Needless to say, notwithstanding attempts at enforcement, it was impossible for either country to prohibit the contraband trade that was carried on actively along the entire frontier.[49]

The exchange of goods at these official frontier markets was only a part of the total flow of goods between the two countries. The Sung had agreed to send 100,000 taels of silver along with 200,000 bolts of silk to the Liao as annual tribute. The amounts were later raised to 200,000 and 300,000, respectively.[50] But this did not result in an increase in Liao's bullion holdings.[51] Sung exports normally exceeded imports by a great margin. On the average, Sung's foreign trade with the Liao showed an annual favorable trade balance of 800,000 strings of cash, of which the government's share through official trade accounted for about 400,000 to 500,000 strings.[52] This excess of exports over imports enabled the Sung to regain all of the silver sent to the Liao as tribute.

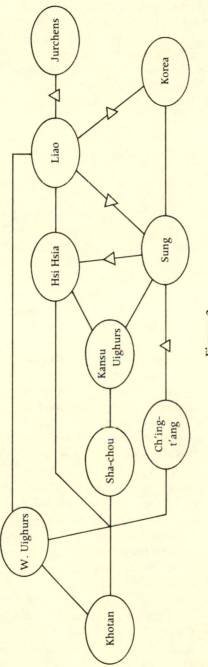

Figure 2

Some of the silk cloth and silver obtained from the Sung was exported by the Liao to its neighbors. For example, when the Tanguts were at war with the Sung the price of silk in the Hsi Hsia state was forty times higher than that of the Sung.[53] Even in peaceful times it was three or four times higher than that of the Sung.[54] The Liao exploited this situation by exporting its silk to the Hsi Hsia at a price merely twice as high as that of the Sung. The trade relations centering around the Liao can be shown schematically in Figure 2.

Trade with the Hsi Hsia

Like other of China's northern and western neighbors, the Hsi Hsia was economically dependent on the transeurasian trade. The Hsi Hsia domains stretched south of the great bend of the Yellow River, but it also controlled important sections of caravan routes that ran from East Turkestan to the frontier towns of China.[55] Despite its strategic location, the Hsi Hsia had less trade with the Chinese dynasty than that which the Sung conducted with the Liao. The Hsi Hsia had few resources, including camels, sheep, cattle, horses, licorice, yellow wax, musk, fine salt, and medicines.[56] Although the Tanguts produced fine salt, which they could sell to people in Shensi and Kansu, Sung China's rigid enforcement of its salt monopoly system in these areas effectively excluded Hsi Hsia salt.[57] The Tanguts could, of course, have exported horses and such western commodities as jade, borax, fine carpets, amber, coral, and incense, which they obtained from neighboring tribes in the north and the Kansu Uighurs to the west. But they were on bad terms with the latter for a long while. As a result, trade did not expand.

The Sung then made a conciliatory gesture. In return for sending horses and sheep to China, Hsi Hsia envoys were granted the right of free trade while they were in the Middle Kingdom.[58] With the consolidation of the Hsi Hsia kingdom, however, warfare broke out between the two. The Sung, eager for peace, was forced to change its policy, and by the treaty of 1007, it established trading markets.[59] In 1026 it opened two additional markets.[60] Meanwhile, the Hsi Hsia expanded into the Kansu Corridor to strengthen its control of trade with the west. Before long, the Uighur states at Kan-chou and Liang-chou succumbed to the Hsi Hsia pressure (in 1028 and 1031, respectively), and thereafter Tun-huang, Kua-chou, and Su-chou submitted to the Tanguts.[61] In 1035 the Hsi Hsia dispatched a military expedition against the Ch'ing-t'ang tribesmen who lived in the upper reaches of the Yellow River.[62] These people garnered enormous profits from the trade in horses and western commodities which flowed along southern caravan routes through East Turkestan, bypassing the Kansu Corridor.[63]

The Tanguts' aggression led to hostilities between them and the Sung. A treaty in 1044 ended the fighting. Under this agreement, the Sung was forced to send the Hsi Hsia 50,000 taels of silver, 130,000 bolts of silk, and 30,000 catties of tea as an annual gift, along with 22,000 taels of silver, 23,000 bolts of silk, and 10,000 catties of tea under the guise of annual presents in return for gifts from the Hsi Hsia.[64] The Sung also agreed to establish two new trading markets and to reopen eight horse-purchasing marts that had already been set up at the border.[65] Hsi Hsia merchants traded horses (about 20,000 annually), sheep (several tens of thousands), cattle, camels, dyes, licorice, yellow wax, musk, medicines, and such other western goods as borax, jade, fine carpets, amber, coral, and frankincense, while Sung merchants and officials offered tea, silk, silver, exotic items from Southeast Asia, porcelain, lacquerware, and silver and gold ornaments.[66]

The exchange of illicit goods was also carried on at the border. Printed texts, weapons, tea, and copper and iron money were smuggled out from the Sung, and fine salt from the Hsi Hsia. Some of the copper and iron money entered the Hsi Hsia domains as a result of exchanges designed to level out the balance of payment. This influx provided a stimulus for the gradual monetization of the Tangut economy. Since iron and copper in its territory were scarce, the import of iron and copper money provided the state with an indispensable means of minting its own currency.[67]

The balance of payment between the two countries resembled that between the Sung and the Liao. One sheep, for example, was valued at several catties of tea, and the total amount of tea imported by the Hsi Hsia through trading marts in 1044 was estimated at a little more than 200,000 catties, 10 percent of which it obtained as gifts from the Sung.[68] Hsi Hsia's export of several tens of thousands of sheep was nearly sufficient to cover the cost of importing the tea. The Tanguts' demand for silk was great, because the Sung was almost the sole supplier. Since a horse was valued at 20 bolts of silk at the horse-purchasing marts, the Hsi Hsia could obtain about 400,000 bolts of silk for the 20,000 horses it sold annually.[69] But the Tanguts' export of horses decreased year after year because of the advent of a new source of supply, the Ch'ing-t'ang. To obtain the Chinese products they craved, they were compelled to buy them with the silver that the Sung offered them as tribute. The silver that the Sung had relinquished to both the Khitans and the Tanguts simply flowed back into China as a result of trade.

Trade with the Ch'ing-t'ang

During the last half of the Northern Sung, the government annually purchased from 15,000 to 20,000 horses for military use from the Ch'ing-t'ang.[70] The Sung was forced to do so because the other sources of supply, the Liao and Hsi Hsia, had placed an embargo on the export of their own horses. In order to finance the purchase of such a huge number of cavalry mounts, the Sung government initiated a system of exchanging Ch'ing-t'ang horses for Chinese tea, produced in the area of present-day Szechwan and Shensi.[71] As a result, both the production and the circulation of the Szechwanese tea, which hitherto had been free of government restriction, was placed under much tighter official control. The export of tea from southern China into these areas was also prohibited. The government purchased the tea directly from the estates and sent it to the border markets by merchants or officials. At these markets, some of the tea was sold by officials to the Chinese and the other inhabitants of the area. Of the 30 million catties produced in Szechwan, about 25 million were sold for local consumption, while 5 million catties were bartered for the horses of the Ch'ing-t'ang people. The average price of one Ch'ing-t'ang horse was 100 catties of Szechwanese tea.[72]

The Ch'ing-t'ang also supplied mercury, musk, and fur. They served, in addition, as "middlemen" for the trade in western goods that came through East Turkestan by way of the southern caravan routes.[73]

Trade with the Chin

After the Jurchens' destruction of the Northern Sung in the 1120s, international trade went through a period of change. The trade routes from the west were now largely dominated by the Mongols and the Hsi Hsia. The Sung, however, was compensated for the loss of this trade by the growing seaborne trade with Southeast Asia and the Arabs in the Indian Ocean littorals. The drying up of the Sung's main source of military horses was not so easily remedied, though the tribal peoples of Yunnan and Kwangsi supplied the Middle Kingdom with some.[74] The Sung also made greater use of its navy for defense.

The Jurchens, who founded the Chin dynasty, were enriched after the surrender of the Northern Sung capital. They acquired an enormous amount of the Sung silver reserve, valued at 40 million taels, along with 3 million *ting* of gold, 8 million *ting* of silver, 54 million bolts of silk, and 15 million bolts of silk brocade.[75] They also inherited the latter's advanced and diversified industries and developed monetary system, as well as a commercial economy.[76] The diffusion of silver through commercial transactions and the spread of paper money into parts of North China enabled the Chin to establish a monetary system based on paper currency, which almost entirely ended the use of iron and copper cash.[77] All of these advantages permitted the Chin to sustain itself economically for about a hundred years.

The Sung traded regularly with the Chin,[78] even when they were at war.[79] In a peace treaty signed in 1141, both parties agreed to maintain commercial relations by the reestablishment of trading markets. Although these markets resembled those of Northern Sung times, they were more extensive and more highly organized. They functioned rather well until they were disbanded in 1206, with only minimal disturbances during the years of war, 1159–1165.[80]

The two states opened about twenty markets for trade. Trade was carried on through both official and private channels. Official trade entailed the exchange of commodities under government control, such as silk produced by official industries, spices, and incense. Officials in charge of this trade were provided with capital or goods for the exchanges. Private trade was conducted by merchants who were required to pay the government a fixed commercial tax and a brokerage fee. The Sung prohibited trade in copper cash, salt, weapons, books, silver, rice, or provisions for the army, while the Chin forbade the exchange of horses, salt, and copper cash. But neither side was able to eliminate the contraband trade. The Sung exported tea, silk, valuables from Southeast Asia, ginger, orange peel, cotton cloth, rice and other grains, lacquerware, porcelain, wooden furniture, gold and silver ornaments, writing brushes, ink, copper money, silver, books, and weapons. The Chin reciprocated with horses, copper money, silver, silk, pearls, drugs, marten fur, dyes, and salt.

The Southern Sung annually offered the Chin silver and silk as a subsidy or gift, just as the Northern Sung had sent "gifts" to the Liao and the Hsi Hsia. By the treaty of 1141, the Sung agreed to send the Chin 250,000 taels of silver and 250,000 bolts of silk as annual tribute.[81] In 1165 the amount was decreased to 200,000 taels and 200,000 bolts respectively.[82] In 1208 the amount of silk was once again increased to 300,000 bolts.

The Chin consistently imported more than it exported during this whole period. The Sung's import of large amounts of silk was balanced out by its extensive export of tea and other goods from the south.[83] It appears that the silver which entered the Chin as tribute or through smuggling soon flowed back to the Sung, either as a result of Chin purchases at the trading markets or through the contraband trade.[84] The direction of the flow of copper cash is still controversial. Katō Shigeshi insists that copper money must have flowed into the Chin, while Sogabe Shizuo postulates that the flow was in the other direction.[85] Both states, however, experienced a serious drain of copper. Although the Chin acquired enormous quantities of copper money from the Northern Sung, it lacked sufficient copper deposits to mint additional coins. The Southern Sung's exploitable copper deposits decreased.

Trade across the Sea

For a long time the Chinese had lagged behind in the development of the maritime technology needed for transoceanic trade. During the T'ang regular coastal trade had developed among the many seaports of the China coast, Po-hai Bay, the Korean Peninsula, and the Japanese islands. But the Chinese ships used in this trade were small and vulnerable to the hazards of the sea. They were only suited for the navigation of shallow coastal water, being essentially nothing more than slightly modified versions of the ships originally used in the inland waterways. Thus the T'ang was content to rely on Southeast Asian, Persian, and Arabian ships for trade with Vietnam, Cambodia, Malaya, Java, and India. The Arabs were the most important of the intermediaries in the transoceanic trade. They plied the Indian Ocean in large ships, trading at the major ports of India, Ceylon, Java, and China, where the port of Canton was the distribution center for spices, incense, silk, pearls, jasper, gold, silver, lacquerware, and porcelain. Goods from the east were brought back by these same vessels to the Persian Gulf or the Red Sea by means of the monsoon winds. This precious freight was then sent to inland countries by the transcontinental caravan routes or unloaded at the port of Alexandria.

By Sung times, the Chinese had made great advances in the construction of seagoing junks.[86] The ships were built with iron nails and waterproofed with a special oil. Their equipment included watertight bulkheads, buoyancy chambers, floating anchors, axial rudders in place of steering oars, scoops for taking samples off the sea floor, and small rockets propelled by gunpowder. The Chinese learned many of their techniques of navigation and shipbuilding from Arabs, and in their use of iron nails, watertight bulkheads, pinewood planks, and floating anchors surpassed their teachers. Their ships were, in fact, more seaworthy than those of the Arabs.[87] It is not surprising, therefore, that from the tenth century on, foreign merchants chose, when possible, to travel on Chinese ships. The recent excavation of a sunken Southern Sung junk, off the shore of Ch'üan-chou Bay, Fukien, has revealed the general features of a large-sized seagoing vessel of the era.[88]

> total length, 39.55 meters   maximum width, 9.9 meters
> height at bow, 7.98 meters   height at stern, 10.5 meters
> displacement tonnage,   (actual weight, ca. 250 tons)[89]
>   ca. 154.40 tons

The outstanding characteristics of these oceangoing vessels were their large capacity and speed. Such bulky goods as rice, porcelain, pepper, lumber, and minerals, which were always difficult to handle, could now be transported by Chinese seafarers. For instance, large quantities of rice from the Yangtze River ports could regularly be supplied to Chekiang, Fukien, and Shantung.[90] As an example of the huge carrying capacity, more than 10,000 pieces of ceramic ware have been recovered so far from a fourteenth-century Chinese junk excavated off the shore of Sinan, Korea.[91] The average capacity of such seagoing junks is estimated to have been between 200 and 600 tons. As for speed, from Fukien to Korea took five to twenty days,[92] and from Canton to Champa eight days,[93] and the journey from Ningpo to Mi-chou in southern Shantung could take as little as three.[94]

The large-scale colonization of the Southeast Asian coast and South China and the resultant movement of the Chinese into the tropics provided a further stimulus to the growth of seaborne trade.[95] Chinese attracted by the profits to be made began to participate in this commerce. The Chinese merchants who reached the trading ports of Southeast Asia had to remain there for some time, waiting for the next monsoon for the trip home. Owing partly to this enforced stay and partly to the lure of profits, many Chinese became permanent residents in various areas of East Asia, Champa, Srivijaya, Tonking, Cambodia, and Korea.[96]

The T'ang initiated a shift in government policy toward seaborne trade. It abandoned strict control over commerce and began to exploit it as a source of revenue.[97] The subsequent increase in the volume and tempo of maritime trade encouraged the Sung to reestablish the same system. As early as 977, a few years after the Southern Han kingdom's submission to the Sung (971), an Office of the Monopoly of Trade (*Ch'üeh-i chü*) was established in K'ai-feng,[98] and in the same year an Office of Overseas Trade was created at Canton. This was followed by the inauguration of similar offices at other ports, including Hang-chou (989), Ningpo (992), Shanghai (1074), Ch'üan-chou (1087), Mi-chou (1088), and Wen-chou (before 1132).[99] Of these, Hang-chou and Ningpo were mainly for trade with Korea and Japan, whereas the trade with Southeast Asia was funneled through Canton and Ch'üan-chou.

The regulations for the Office of Overseas Trade resembled those of the frontier trading market system. The officials were expected to do the following: (1) Inspect incoming vessels and collect maritime customs in kind. The officials deducted, in advance, a portion of the goods in kind, and then farmed out customs duties proper and monopoly taxes. The tariff rate fluctuated from time to time, but in general it was fixed at one-tenth of the cargo. In late Sung, higher rates were applied to precious goods. (2) Use public funds to purchase foreign goods. They bought such special commodities as pearls, tortoise shells, rhinoceros horns, steel, brass, coral, agate, frankincense, and large pieces of ivory. As for the rest of the cargo, the officials could purchase it at their own discretion; the remainder could be freely sold to private merchants. (3) Issue certificates that allowed traders who had already paid custom duties to sell their cargos at markets within China. (4) Issue certificates to foreign ships, allowing them to depart from China. Officials were to make sure that Chinese vessels returned to the same port from which they departed. (5) Increase the volume of seaborne trade by encouraging foreign merchants to come to China. (6) Enforce the

embargo placed on the export of copper cash and other illicit items.
(7) Supervise the rescue of wrecked ships and dispose of the property left
by foreign merchants.[100]

The profits the government derived from this trade were far from
negligible. In the early Northern Sung, government revenue from the
maritime trade amounted to 300,000 to 500,000 strings of cash, accounting
for 2 or 3 percent of the total revenue.[101] It was very difficult to prevent illegal trade in the ports where the Offices of Overseas Trade were
established, particularly in the Southern Sung. The government was eager
to attract as many foreign vessels as possible, and it needed private ships as
naval auxiliaries in times of war. The scope of this trade is reflected in travel
accounts of contemporary writers,[102] and in the archaeological discoveries
of such Chinese products as porcelains and copper money. Ordinarily, the
western limit of the Chinese junks was the Malabar Coast of India, but
sometimes they reached the Persian Gulf and the Red Sea.[103] A total of
1,364 Sung copper coins were discovered in northern Ceylon, along with
many Sung porcelains, as a result of archaeological expeditions in 1911 and
1949.[104] Similarly, many Sung porcelains have been discovered in East
Africa,[105] Egypt,[106] the Persian Gulf,[107] Istanbul,[108] Mesopotamia,[109]
the eastern coast of the Mediterranean, and India. Sung ceramics are also
widely distributed throughout East Asia, particularly in Japan. Kamakura
Japan was probably the largest importer of Chinese porcelains and copper
money.[110] Some scholars argue that the cargo of more than 10,000 pieces of
porcelain found in the remains of the Chinese junk sunk off the southwest
coast of Korea must have been on its way to Japan and the Philippine
Islands. Korea at that time did not need these Chinese porcelains, because
its own ceramic industry could meet most of the domestic as well as the
foreign demand. Large numbers of Sung porcelains have also been discovered in the Philippine Islands,[111] Sarawak in North Borneo,[112] Singa-
pore, and Malaya.[113]

Sung copper cash has been found in Ceylon, East Africa, the rim of the
Persian Gulf, and the Malabar Coast.[114] Since the main international
currency for the settlement of trade accounts was bullion, the circulation of
copper money was quite limited. Cambodia imported Sung copper cash,
according to the Chinese sources, as a luxury item for the use of the upper
classes.[115] In Java, Sung copper cash was used to some degree as a medium
of exchange.[116] In Japan, too, it was widely used as legal tender. In the
early eleventh century, when Japanese government control over maritime
trade with China was relaxed, there was an increased demand for the
import of Chinese coins. This demand was further stimulated by the rapid
growth of domestic industries in central Japan and by the increased
monetization of Japanese society.[117] Regular trade between the two countries thus developed.

In sum, there was a steady increase in regular seaborne trade between China and the surrounding countries. Japan, for example, provided gold, silver, copper, sulfur, mercury, drugs, lumber, pearls, steel swords, and fine furniture, while China reciprocated with silk, silk brocade, cotton cloth, aloe wood, sandalwood, ambergris, materials for fine furniture, books, dyes, porcelains, and copper cash.[118] China's official maritime trade with Korea was frequently interrupted by political tensions between the two. The private seaborne trade, mainly served by Chinese vessels, thrived, however, after the early eleventh century. The main items exported by Korea were silver, lacquerware, matting, copper ware, celadons, pongee, linen, fur, musk, dyes, ginseng, and medicines, while China exported myrrh, incense, spices, rhinoceros horn, ivory, rare birds and flowers (all from Africa and Southeast Asia), silk, mercury, and books.[119]

China's export of goods to Southeast Asian countries, as recorded by Chao Ju-kua, may be summarized as follows:[120]

silver and gold	Cambodia, Srivijaya, modern Malaysia, Sumatra
silk, silk brocade	Srivijaya, modern Malaysia, Java, Malabar, Brunei, Philippines
porcelains	Champa, Cambodia, Srivijaya, modern Malaysia, Java, Malabar, Brunei, Philippines, Zanzibar
lacquerware	Champa, Java, Brunei
parasols	Champa, Cambodia, Brunei
ironware	Srivijaya, modern Malaysia
matting	Champa, Brunei
silk fans	Champa
leather drums	Cambodia
glass and pearl ware	Brunei
cochineal	Brunei
wine	Champa, Cambodia, Srivijaya, modern Malaysia, Philippines, Brunei
rice	Srivijaya, modern Malaysia, Philippines
sugar	Champa, Cambodia, Srivijaya, modern Malaysia
salt	Brunei
Indian red	Java

The Sung was eager to obtain spices and incense.[121] Frankincense from East Africa and western Asia was most in demand, followed by aloe wood, sandalwood, cloves, and pepper. The Chinese definitely preferred aloe wood of the different types of incense.[122] It was much more suited to their taste and was more accessible. South China, Hainan, North Vietnam, Malaya, and Sumatra all supplied it to the Sung. Frankincense and other perfumes or incense reaching Chinese ports by sea were often transshipped to neighboring countries. There was a steady demand for pepper among the general populace and the upper classes,[123] but China consumed less of that spice than the West.

A wide variety of commodities flowed into China via the seaborne trade: incense (including amber, myrrh, and musk in addition to those mentioned above), spices (including nutmeg and cassia), cotton, yellow wax, rhinoceros horn, ivory, pearls, silver, gold, tortoise shells, and sulfur. The Sung exported silver, gold, silver and gold ornaments, copper money, copperware, tinware, lacquerware, ironware, mercury, pottery, porcelain, silk, silk cloth, linen, matting, books, and stationery.

The question of the balance of trade in the seaborne trade is difficult to answer. Since few official records of trade have survived, there is no way to answer the question with confidence. The Sung must have profited from the tremendous number of porcelains and copper coins sent abroad. On the other hand, there was a continuous flow of Chinese silver and gold into the tropics, resulting from the excessive import of luxury items such as incense and spices.[124]

The Organization of Sung Foreign Trade: A Conclusion

Large-scale trade was often initially unorganized, hazardous, and seasonal, and the merchants were for the most part itinerants. These traders needed to pool their resources to raise the capital to carry on trade by sea or by land.

Temporary partnerships were formed by merchants and sailors for trading ventures in Korea, Japan, the East Indies, and Southeast Asia. Wealthy merchants often hired an agent to manage these ventures for them.[125] Such merchants as a Muslim from Southeast Asia, who owned eighty seagoing vessels, clearly had either to employ agents or to hire out ships.[126] In at least one instance, a Yüan dynasty law code distinguished between the financial backer, the owner of the ship, and the person immediately in charge of an overseas trading venture when considering the punishment for misconduct.[127] Under the Southern Sung a kind of collective ownership was formed among the shipowners in Ming-chou, Wen-chou, and T'ai-chou.[128] Crude forms of *commenda* and *societas maris* were also found.[129] In a *commenda*, a wealthy person or a merchant entrusted money or goods to another merchant who then used it for commercial purposes.[130] The *societas maris* differed from the *commenda* in that the capital employed was at least partially supplied by merchants who participated directly in the management of the venture. The profits in this temporary arrangement were shared in proportion to the sum invested by each partner.

Trade, however hazardous and mobile, obviously could not be conducted without fixed markets. With the growth in size and scope of foreign trade, many fairs, which combined international wholesale and retail trade, emerged.[131] The great fair of Shao-hsing provided a place for the exchange of such luxuries as jades, white silks, pearls, rhinoceros horns, perfumes, precious medicines, silk damasks, lacquerware, Buddhist books, paintings, bells, tripods, ritual vessels, and amusing rarities.[132] Fairs specializing in incense and medicine were found in Hang-chou, K'ai-feng, and Ch'eng-tu (Szechwan).[133] For example, Tu Cheng, who lived in about the beginning of the thirteenth century, has left these verses on the autumn medicine fair in Ch'eng-tu:

> Coming in a palanquin to visit the Medicine Fair, our bearers' knees are caught in the press of the crowd. Little by little we inch our way up to the gate, already surrounded by a diversity of goods. Passing the arcades under a careful scrutiny, there is such a profusion it cannot all be detailed: Orpiment, seeds of aconite piled on mats on the ground, ginseng and glutinous millet waiting on tray after tray. Mica and frankincense the color of sparkling crystal, aloe and sandalwood wafting their fragrant scents. The river herbs are thick and dense. From the aquatic genera come leeches. Some things are costly, such as cinnabar . . . others yet are bitter, like sulphate of copper . . . some are stale like pemmican and mince-meat pickled in brine. Some fresh, like dates and chestnuts. Many are products of barbarian tribes, yet all have come to answer China's needs. Merchants have buffeted the sea-winds and the waves, and foreign merchants crossed over towering crags drawn onwards by the profits to be made. . . . Six thousand ounces of silver is the least they carry, and sometimes as much as two thousand ounces of gold. The fair begins in the earliest hours of morning, and closes in the last hours of dusk. Here are the rich and powerful with numerous bond-servants . . . carriages and horses in grand array, scattering in clouds of dust. When evening comes they get completely drunk, and then go home, their bags and boxes bulging.[134]

The commodities of long-distance trade were sold at huge fairs. Then the drugs and incense were distributed in local markets by petty itinerant dealers, in many cases Taoist priests who made their living by trading in drugs, incense, and stationery.

The booming international trade under the Sung was by no means isolated or exceptional in China's economy. It was, in fact, accompanied by a substantial development in overall commercial organization.

The main mechanisms for China's official trade with the rest of the world were the tributary system and border markets (including the Office of Overseas Trade). On the whole, both of these mechanisms worked rather well. In this period when China was weak, the tribute system's ritual or cultural value was generally less appreciated by her neighbors than in T'ang times. Still, China's rich resources and cultural achievements attracted neighboring peoples, who continued to send envoys to the Middle Kingdom. China's neighbors were interested not only in pecuniary gain but also in maintaining cultural contacts with the Middle Kingdom. They were eager to learn about China's refined life-style, organizational skills, metal technology, navigational techniques, methods of warfare, textile manufacturing, earthenware industry, astronomy, medical science, philosophy, and, to a lesser extent, religion. At the same time, once the scope of trade relations was enlarged by improvements in transportation, the economic value of the system was bound to increase. Developments in transportation enabled seafarers from Arabia, India, and Southeast Asia, who lived at the remote periphery of the Chinese world, to arrive in China for trade.

China's trade with the Liao, the Hsi Hsia, and the Chin was accompanied by political and diplomatic relations which the Chinese found humiliating. But China's balance of trade with its northern neighbors was favorable to the Sung. Despite its military weakness, the Sung benefited from its commercial relations with the northerners. To improve its economic position, it began to use copper currency, mint coins on a vast scale, issue paper money, increase its bullion reserves, monopolize highly marketable commodities, relax its strict control over merchants, and promote foreign trade. Sung mercantile policy sought by all means to increase the national wealth through expansion of trade. This resulted in the rapid economic development of China and a booming trade with its neighbors, and hence in the gradual "eclipse of the tribute system by trade."

NOTES

1. Katō Shigeshi, *Shina Keizai-shi gaisetsu* (Tokyo, 1944), pp. 89–156; Denis Twitchett, "Merchant, Trade, and Government in Late T'ang," *Asia Major*, n.s. 14,

part 1 (1968), pp. 63–95; Mark Elvin, *The Pattern of the Chinese Past* (Stanford, 1973), pp. 131–178.

2. Aoyama Sadao, *Tō-Sō jidai no kōtsū to chishi chizu no kenkyū* (Tokyo, 1963); Elvin, op. cit., pp. 131–145.

3. Joseph Needham, *Science and Civilisation in China* (Cambridge, 1971), vol. IV: 3; Shiba Yoshinobu, *Sōdai shōgyō-shi kenkyū* (Tokyo, 1968), translated by Mark Elvin as *Commerce and Society in Sung China* (Ann Arbor, 1970) (hereafter Shiba/Elvin), pp. 4–14; Elvin, op. cit., pp. 131–145.

4. Ibn Battūta, *Voyages d'Ibn Batoutah*, ed. C. Defremery, vol. 4 (Paris, 1927), pp. 86, 88; Kuwabara Jitsuzō, *Hojukō no Jiseki* (Tokyo, 1935), pp. 84–97.

5. Lo Jung-pang, "The Emergence of Chinese Sea Power during the Late Sung and Early Yüan Periods," *Far Eastern Quarterly* 14 (1954–55): 489–503; see Wada Hisanori, "Tōnan Ajia ni okeru Shoki Kakyō shakai (960–1279)," *Tōyō gakuhō* 42, 1 (1959): 76–106, and his "Tōnan Ajia ni okeru Kakyō shakai no seiritsu," in *Sekai no Rekishi* (Tokyo, 1961), pp. 111–148; Herold Wiens, *China's March Toward the Tropics* (Hamden, Conn., 1954).

6. John K. Fairbank, *Trade and Diplomacy on the China Coast* (Cambridge, Mass., 1954), pp. 23–38. J. K. Fairbank (ed.), *The Chinese World Order* (Cambridge, Mass., 1968), pp. 3–4.

7. Aoyama Sadao, "Zui, Tō, Sō sandai ni okeru kōsu no chiiki teki kōsatsu," *Rekishigaku kenkyū* 6, 4 (1936): 441–446; 6, 5 (1936): 529–554; Elvin, *Pattern*, pp. 204–210; Chi Ch'ao-ting, *Key Economic Areas in Chinese History* (London, 1936); Sudō Yoshiyuki, "Nansō tōsaku no chiikisei," *Sōdai keizaishi kenkyū* (Tokyo, 1962), pp. 74–138.

8. G. William Skinner, "Urban Development in Imperial China," in G. W. Skinner (ed.), *The City in Late Imperial China* (Stanford, 1977), pp. 23–25.

9. Twitchett, "Merchant, Trade," pp. 80–81.

10. Denis Twitchett, *Financial Administration Under the T'ang Dynasty* (Cambridge, 1963), pp. 111–123. Hino Kaisaburō, "Ryōzei-hō no kihonteki yongen-soku," *Hōsei-shi kenkyū*, no. 11 (1960), pp. 40–77.

11. Denis Twitchett, "The T'ang Market System," *Asia Major*, n.s. 12, 2 (1966): 207.

12. Fujii Hiroshi, "Shin-an shōnin no kenkyū," *Tōyō gakuhō* 36, 1 (1957): 2–7; Nishijima Sadao, *Chūgoku keizai-shi kenkyū* (Tokyo, 1966), pp. 732–736.

13. Miyazaki Ichisada, *Godai Sōsho no tsūka mondai* (Tokyo, 1943), pp. 3–4.

14. Katō Shigeshi, *Tō-Sō jidai ni okeru kin, Gin no kenkyū*, vol. 1 (Tokyo, 1925), pp. 1–283; P'eng Hsin-wei, *Chung-kuo huo-pi shih* (Shanghai, 1965), pp. 323, 417–428; Yang Lien-sheng, *Money and Credit in China: A Short History* (Cambridge, Mass., 1962), pp. 40–50.

15. Miyazaki, op. cit., pp. 169–240.

16. *Ta-Chin Kuo-chih*, ch. 32.

17. Miyazaki, op. cit., pp. 118–121.

18. Ch'üan Han-sheng, "T'ang-Sung cheng-fu sui-ju yü huo-pi ching-chi te kuan-hsi," in his *Chung-kuo ching-chi-shih yen-chiu* (Hong Kong, 1976), vol. 1, pp. 203–263..

19. P'eng, p. 451; Hino Kaisaburō, "Hoku-Sō jidai ni okeru dō, tetsu-sen no chūzō-gaku ni tsuite," *Shigaku zasshi* 46, 1 (1935).

20. P'eng, op. cit., pp. 428–440; Katō Shigeshi, "Kōshi no kigen ni tsuite," in his *Shina keizaishi kōshō* (Tokyo, 1953), vol. 2, pp. 1–13.

21. The data are derived from *Sung Hui-yao: "Tan-i, Li-tai Ch'ao-kung."* See also Maeda Masana, *Kasei no rekishi-chirigaku teki kenkyū* (Tokyo, 1969), pp. 522–524; Nagasawa Kazutoshi, "Godai Sō-sho ni okeru Kasei chihō no chukei-kōeki ni tsuite," *Tōzai bunka kōryū-shi* (Tokyo, 1975), pp. 109–119.

22. As to frankincense, see Theophrastus, *Enquiry into Plants*, IX, IV. 4–6, trans. A. Hort (London, 1916), II, pp. 237–238; also see Yamada Kentarō, *Tō-zai kōyaku-shi* (Tokyo, 1956); Lin T'ien-wei, *Sung-tai hsiang-yao mao-i shih-kao* (Hong Kong, 1960).

23. See Ibn Hauqal, *Kitab surat al-ard*, ed. T. H. Kramers (Leiden, 1938), II, 2, pp. 505–506; Matsuda Hisao, *Kodai Tenzan no rekishi chirigakuteki kenkyū* (Tokyo, 1956), pp. 400–403.

24. Maeda, op. cit., p. 524.

25. The data are obtained from various authors' works on the Sung overland trade with northerners. These sources will be cited below.

26. Maeda, op. cit., pp. 493–499.

27. Li T'ao, *Hsü Tzu-chih t'ung-chien ch'ang-pien* (hereafter *HCP*) (Taipei, 1964), ch. 75, p. 11b; ch. 111, p. 8b. *Sung Hui-yao chi-kao* (Peking, 1957), "Fan-i," 4, pp. 8b, 9a; and 4, pp. 9b, 10ab, 11a. Also see Miyazaki, op. cit., pp. 235–240; Satō Keishirō, "Hokusō jidai ni okeru Kaikitsu shōnin no tōzen," in *Chūgoku-shi Ronsō* (Yamagata, 1978), pp. 89–106.

28. Satō, ibid., pp. 332–334.

29. Satō, ibid., pp. 336–338

30. Umehara Kaoru, "Seitō no uma to Shisen no cha," *Tōhō gakuhō* (Kyoto) 45 (1973): 202–205. For a later period, see Morris Rossabi, "The Tea and Horse Trade with Inner Asia during the Ming," *Journal of Asian History* 4, 2 (1970): 136–168.

31. Shiba Yoshinobu, "Sō-dai shiteki seido no enkaku," in *Sōdai-shōgyō-shi ronsō* (Tokyo, 1974), pp. 123–159.

32. Karl A. Wittfogel and Feng Chia-sheng, *History of Chinese Society, Liao (907–1125)* (Philadelphia, 1949), pp. 219–225. Tamura Jitsuzō, "Ryō-Sō no kōtsū to Ryō kokunai ni okeru keizai teki hattatsu," *Seifuku-ōchō no kenkyū* I (Kyoto, 1964); Shimada Masao, *Ryō-dai shakai-shi kenkyū* (Kyoto, 1952), pp. 209–343; for the Hsi Hsia, see Okazaki Seirō, *Tangūto Kodai-shi kenkyū* (Kyoto, 1972), pp. 239–252. For the Chin, see Mikami Tsugio, *Kin-shi kenkyū* III: *Kin-dai Joshin shakai no kenkyū* (Tokyo, 1973), pp. 208–211; and Toyama Gunji, *Kinchō-shi kenkyū* (Kyoto, 1970), pp. 37–39.

33. Shiba/Elvin, pp. 202–203.

34. Ibid., pp. 203–205.

35. Ibid., pp. 156–164.

36. Elvin, op. cit., pp. 184–192. Miyashita Saburō, "Sō-Gen no iryō," in Yabuuchi Kiyoshi (ed.), *Sō-Gen jidai no kagaku-gijutsu-shi* (Kyoto, 1967), pp. 141–142.

37. See note 32 above.

38. Tamura, op. cit. pp. 171, 228–236, 249–256.

39. Hino Kaisaburō, "Godai jidai ni okeru Kittan to Shina to no kaijō-bōeki," *Shigaku zasshi* 52, 7 (July 1941): 1–47; 52, 9 (September 1941): 55–82.

40. Loc. cit.

41. Hino Kaisaburō, "Godai no ba-sei to tōji no uma-bōeki," *Tōyō gakuhō* 29, 1 (1942): 372–375; Hino Kaisaburō, "Sō-sho Joshin no santō raikō to bōeki," *Chōsen gakuhō* 37 and 38 (1966): 372–375; 371–404; and his "Sō-sho Joshin no santo raikō no taise to sono yurai," *Chōsen gakuhō* 33 (1964): 45–46.

42. Hirashima Kiyoshi, "Kittan no bokkō-ki ni okeru Chūgoku to no kankei," *Shien* 53 (1952): 88–89.

43. T'o T'o et al., *Liao shih* (Po-na ed.), 60, 1a–1b.

44. Wittfogel and Feng, op. cit. (n. 32 above), pp. 219–225.

45. Shimada, op. cit., pp. 253–267.

46. *HCP*, 59, 6a–7b. T'o T'o et al., *Sung shih* (*SS*), 38, 26b–27a; 186, 23a–23b; Tamura, op. cit., p. 239.

47. Tamura, op. cit., p. 240.

48. *Sung Hui-yao chi kao* 38, pp. 5480–5482.

49. Tamura, op. cit., pp. 242–245.

50. Hino Kaisaburō, "Gin ken no jukyū jō yori mita Godai Hokusō no Sai-hei Sai-shi," *Tōyō gakuhō* 35, 1 (1952): 15–21; 35, 2 (1952): 154–166.

51. The Sung presents to the Northerners were well balanced by the vast amounts of profits gained at trading posts on the border. See, for example, Hsü Meng-hsin, *San-ch'ao pei-meng hui pien*, ch. 8, the sixth month of the fourth year of the Hsüan-ho era.

52. *SS* 186, 23a–23b. See also Hino Kaisaburō, *op. cit* (n. 50 above), 1–21. Hatachi Masanori, "Hokusō Ryō kan no bōeki to saizō to ni tsuite," *Shien* 111 (1974): 127–133.

53. *HCP*, 404, 23b. Hino, *Tōyō gakuhō* 35, 2. (1952): 75.

54. Hatachi, op. cit., p. 122.

55. Maeda, op. cit., pp. 584–614.

56. Okazaki, op. cit., (n. 32 above), pp. 240–244.

57. Miyazaki Ichisada, "Seika no Kōki to Seihaku-en mondai," in his *Ajia-shi no kenkyū* I (Kyoto, 1959), pp. 293–310.

58. Okazaki, op. cit., pp. 240–242.

59. *SS* 186, 24a, b; 66, 2b.

60. *HCP*, 104, 3b.

61. *SS*, 485, 12b; *HCP*, 111, 16b.

62. *HCP*, 117, 17b, 18a; 119, 16b, 17a.

63. Maeda, op. cit., pp. 558–570; Okazaki, op. cit., pp. 299–305.

64. *HCP*, 152, 9b, 10a.

65. *HCP*, 153, 12a. Hino, *Tōyō-gakuhō* 35, 2 (1952): 173–174

66. Okazaki, op. cit., pp. 240–242.

67. Nakajima Satoshi, "Seika ni okeru dō Tetsu-sen no chūzō ni tsuite," *Tōhō gakuhō* (Tokyo) 7 (1936): 187–208.

68. *HCP*, 149, 15a–15b, 16a–16b, 17a. Hino, *Tōyō gakuhō* (1952): 173.

69. *HCP*, 339, 2b. Hino, ibid., pp. 173–175.

70. Umehara, op. cit. (n. 30 above), p. 205; Lin Shui-han, "Sung-tai pien-chün chih ma-shih ma chih kang-yün," *Ta-lu tsa-chih* 31, 9 (1965): 258–265.

71. Umehara, op. cit., pp. 198–202.

72. Ibid., pp. 210–212.

73. Maeda, op. cit. (n. 21 above), pp. 626–678.

74. Fujimoto Hikaru, "Nansō Kōba kō," *Tōyōshigaku rōnshū* 1 (1953): 205–215

and his "Zoku Nansō Kōba kō," *Shichō* 57 (1955): 1–13.

75. *Ta Chin kuo-chih*, ch. 32.

76. Mikami, op. cit. (n. 32 above), pp. 208–211.

77. T'o T'o et al., *Chin shih* (Po-na ed.), 48, 15a.

78. Katō Shigeshi, "Sō to Kin-koku to no bōeki ni tsuite," in *Shina Keizaishi Kōshō* II (Tokyo, 1953), pp. 253–262. Ōsaki Fujio, "Sō-Kin bōeki no keitai," *Hiroshima Daigaku Bungakubu Kiyō* 5 (1954): 159–182.

79. Li Hsin-ch'üan, *Chien-yen i-lai ch'ao-yeh tsa-chi chia-chi*, ch. 20, 186. See also Ōsaki, op. cit., pp. 162–163.

80. Also see Katō Shigeshi, "Sō-Kin bōeki ni okeru cha sen oyobi kinu ni tsuite," in *Shina Keizaishi Kōshō* II, pp. 284–316.

81. *SS*, 29, 18b.

82. *SS*, 33, 16a–16b.

83. See note 80.

84. Katō Shigeshi, *Tō-Sō jidai ni okeru kin gin no kenkyū*, II, ch. 10, and his *Kin-koku ni okeru gin* (Tokyo, 1926), pp. 614–626. Ch'üan Han-sheng, "Sung Chin chien te ssu-tsou mao-i," *Bulletin of the Institute of History and Philology, Academia Sinica* 11 (1947), pp. 425–447.

85. Sogabe Shizuo, *Nichi Sō Kin Kahei Koryū-shi* (Tokyo, 1949), pp. 109–126; 195–206.

86. Shiba/Elvin, pp. 4–40.

87. Kuwabara, *Hojukō no Jiseki*, pp. 88–92. Needham, op. cit. (n. 3 above), pp. 412, 450, 459.

88. "Ch'üan-chou Wan Sung-tai Hai-ch'uan Fa-chüeh chien-pao," *Wen-wu* 10 (1975): 28–35.

89. Thomas H. C. Lee, "A Report on the Recently Excavated Song Ship at Quanzhou and a Consideration of Its True Capacity," *Sung Studies Newsletter* 11–12 (1976): 4–9.

90. Shiba/Elvin, pp. 58–63.

91. Kungnip chungang pangmulgwan, *Sinan haejō munmul* (Seoul, 1975).

92. Shiba/Elvin, p. 9.

93. Wada Hisanori, op. cit. (n. 5 above), p. 87.

94. Shiba/Elvin, p. 9.

95. Wada, op. cit., p. 87.

96. Wada, op. cit., p. 87, and Mori Katsumi, *Nissō Bōeki no Kenkyū* (Tokyo, 1958), pp. 284–285. *SS*, 187, 17b; 19b, 20a. Shiba/Elvin, pp. 187–188.

97. Fujita Toyohachi, "Sō-dai no Shihaku-shi oyobi Shihaku jōrei," in *Tō-zai kōshō-shi no kenkyū, Nankai-hen* (Tokyo, 1943), pp. 288–289.

98. *HCP*, 18, 9a.

99. Shih Wen-chi, "Sung-tai Shih-po-ssu te she-chih," in *Sung shih yen-chiu chi* (Taipei, 1970), pp. 341–402.

100. Satō Keishirō, "Nan-Sō jidai ni okeru Nankai bōeki ni tsuite," in *Isurāmu shōgyō-shi no kenkyū* (Kyoto, 1981), pp. 344–366.

101. Li Hsin-ch'üan, op. cit. (n. 79 above), ch. 15.

102. For example, Chou Ch'ü-fei's *Ling-wai tai-ta* and Chao Ju-kua's *Chu-fan chih* (F. Hirth and W. W. Rockhill, *Chau Ju-kua*, St. Petersburg, 1911).

103. Chou Ch'ü-fei, *Ling-wai tai-ta*, ch. 3.

104. D. H. Devandra, *Guide to Yapahuva* (Colombo, 1951).

105. G. Mathew, "Chinese Porcelain in East Africa on the Coast of South Arabia," *Oriental Art* new series 2, 2 (1956).

106. Loc. cit.

107. Sakurai Kiyohiko, "Perusha Wan Minabu fukin no Chūgoku tōji," in *Matsuda-hakushi Koki-kinen Tōzai Bunka Koryū-shi* (Tokyo, 1975), pp. 276–298; R. L. Hobson, "Pottery Fragments From Southern Persia and Northern Punjab," in A. Stein, *Archaeological Reconnaissances in North-Western India and South-Eastern Iran* (London, 1937), Appendix A.

108. J. A. Pope, *Fourteenth-Century Blue and White: A Group of Chinese Porcelains in the Topkapu Sarayi Müzesi, Istanbul* (Washington, 1952).

109. Friedrich Sarre, *Die Keramik von Samarra* (Berlin, 1925); Mikami Tsugio, "Chūgoku tōji to Isuramu tōji no kankei ni kansuru nisan no mondai," *Seinan Ajia Kenkyū* 14 (1965): 6–7.

110. Kamei Akinori, "Sō-dai no yushutsu tōji—Nippon," in *Sekai Tōji Zenshū* (Tokyo, 1978), vol. 12. Mori Katsumi, op. cit. (n. 96 above), pp. 474–489.

111. Cheng Te-k'un, "The Study of Ceramic Wares in Southeast Asia," *Chung-wen Ta-hsüeh Chung-kuo wen-hua yen-chiu-so hsüeh-pao* (Hong Kong, 1972), vol. 5, no. 2, pp. 302–205. L. Locsin and C. Locsin, *Oriental Ceramics Discovered in the Philippines* (Tokyo, 1967).

112. Cheng, op. cit, pp. 305, 306. T. Harrison, "Trade Porcelain and Stoneware in South-East Asia," *Sarawak Museum Journal* 10 (1961).

113. Cheng, op. cit., pp. 297–299.

114. Henry Yule, *The Book of Ser Marco Polo*, 3rd ed. rev. By Henri Cordier; vol. 2, p. 337.

115. Ch'en Cheng-hsiang, *Chen-la Feng-t'i-chi Yen-chiu* (Hong Kong, 1975), p. 58.

116. See J. V. G. Mills (trans.), *Ma Huan: Ying-yai Sheng-lan, The Overall Survey of the Ocean's Shores* (Cambridge, 1970), pp. 86–97.

117. Mori, op. cit. (n. 96 above), pp. 474–489. Akiyama Kenzō, "Sō-dai no Nankai bōeki to Nissō bōeki to no renkei," *Shigaku zasshi* 44, 12 (1933): 1487–1528.

118. Mori, op. cit., pp. 263–279.

119. Mori, op. cit., pp. 280–292.

120. See Hirth and Rockhill, op. cit. (n. 102 above)

121. Lin T'ien-wei, op. cit. (n. 22 above), pp. 166–215.

122. Yamada Kentarō, *Kōryō no Michi* (Tokyo, 1977), pp. 157–205.

123. Shiba/Elvin, p. 206. Yamada Kentarō, *Tō-zai kōyaku-shi* (Tokyo, 1956), pp. 319–333.

124. *HCP*, 85, 19b.

125. Shiba/Elvin, pp. 189–201.

126. Ibid., p. 28.

127. Ibid.

128. Ibid.

129. Shiba/Elvin, pp. 191–200, 31–34.

130. Ibid., p. 191.

131. Ibid., pp. 156–164.

132. Ibid., pp. 159–160.

133. Ibid., pp. 161–163.

134. Ibid., pp. 162–163.

FIVE

Sung Embassies:
Some General Observations

HERBERT FRANKE

<table>
<tr><td>

When I was at home I was
in a better place: but
travellers must be content.

As You Like It, IV, 16
</td><td>

An ambassador is an honest
man sent to lie abroad for
the good of his country.

Sir Henry Wotton
(1568–1639)
</td></tr>
</table>

This essay proposes to study Sung embassies to other states. It does not deal with the multiple problems of foreign politics encountered by Sung ambassadors. Instead, a survey of the institutional side of Sung diplomacy, as opposed to political content and motivation, will be attempted.

Sources on Sung embassies are overabundant. We have, in the first place, the voluminous corpus of documents preserved in the *Sung Hui-yao,* along with the corresponding brief outlines in the relevant chapters of the *Sung shih.* For the states of Liao, Koryŏ, and Chin the institutions in charge of welcoming the foreign embassies are described in the chapters on officialdom of the respective national histories. An extremely useful and easy-to-handle survey of Sung-Chin relations is in chapters 60 and 61 of the *Chin shih* where a chronological list of missions in both directions from 1116 to 1233 is given. This list is paralleled by a similar chronology of Chin intercourse with Koryŏ and Hsi Hsia. No such handy chronology exists for the relations between Liao and Sung in any of the extant historical works; it had to be supplied by modern scholarship.[1]

Another important category of sources are the reports of Sung envoys, their diaries and travelogues.[2] These texts provide a lively picture of the actual problems encountered by the envoys who set out on their sometimes hazardous journeys. Related sources are works of a more systematic and even encyclopedic character describing a foreign country and its institutions, which were written after the successful completion of a diplomatic mission. To this category belongs, for example, the *Kao-li t'u-ching* by Hsü Ching (1093–1155), which gives a comprehensive account of Korea based on an embassy in the year 1124.[3] Another firsthand account of a similar nature is the *Meng-ta pei-lu,* a text written perhaps by a certain Chao Kung after a mission in 1221 when a Sung embassy visited the court of the Mongol general Mukhali.[4] Such texts contain information on the treatment of Sung envoys by foreigners. Finally, an enormous amount of information can be gathered from the collected works of Sung authors. Many famous Sung literati-officials had, at some time or other in their careers, taken part in an embassy, either as an accredited envoy or as a supernumerary family member accompanying a relative on a diplomatic mission. For this reason the reader will find much interesting information even when casually glancing through the pages of works of Sung authors, including, of course, works recording miscellanea (*pi-chi*). Poetry, too, sometimes contains relevant information on embassies, particularly if the poems are dated and describe a certain event or outlandish customs. Countless poems of this nature can be found in Sung works, sometimes grouped together in the poetry sections of collected works. Examples of poetry written during an embassy to Liao are the series of twenty-eight poems written by Su Ch'e (1039–1112),[5] and the many poems composed by Fan Ch'eng-ta (1126–1193) when he served as envoy to the Chin in 1170.[6]

This sketchy survey of sources will have shown that an exhaustive study is nearly impossible in view of the wealth of materials that could be consulted. But we must not forget that there are many recurrent and repetitive features reported in these sources and that certain patterns become apparent.

A word or two should be said about the problem of statehood, which plays such an important role in Sung foreign relations. In selecting Liao, Koryŏ, and Chin as main topics, we are concerned with foreign nations or multi-ethnic states which were set apart from the minor "barbarians" in the Sung political system. These states, and also to some extent Hsi Hsia, form a special category of Sung partners in foreign relations, with formalized diplomatic channels and regular embassies dispatched at certain specific occasions, in accordance with pseudo-familial relationships. All other foreign nations, tribes, or states had to be content with treatment as mere tribute-bearers to the Sung court.[7] It is not quite clear to what extent the status of a state (*kuo*) was reflected in the Sung ambassadorial system. There does not seem to exist a definition of which states were accorded formalized treatment, like Liao, Koryŏ, Hsi Hsia, and Chin, and which states were only admitted to the Sung court as bearers of tribute.

A recurrent problem for Sung was the correct address of state letters. Should, for example, the Chin court be addressed as "Great Chin" or just "Chin"? This question turned up in 1177.[8] The insistence on the correct name of a foreign state is reflected in those passages of descriptions of foreign states where the problem of "state name" (*kuo-hao*) is dealt with.[9] For the rulers of Annam the status of *kuo* was something desirable in the twelfth century: an Annamite envoy wrote—in Chinese—this verse on the walls of a hostel: "Our journey would be a full success if we were honored with the name 'state.'" And indeed the expectations of the Annamite envoys were fulfilled.[10] Annam was, however, a state that belonged to Sinitic civilization, and one where the ruling elite, including the king himself, knew about the importance of ritually correct titles and the rectification of names, which played such a great role in East Asian politics—as it does in modern diplomatic relations too.

But other less sinicized political entities in Sung times experienced difficulties in their correspondence with the Sung court. Sung writers who were deeply imbued with traditional Chinese notions of propriety some-times report condescendingly the ignorance of foreigners when addressing the Sung court and its envoys. Some examples are given by Chou Hui, who had himself served as an envoy to the Chin in 1177 and thus knew about the rules of the game.[11] He tells us that when a Sung envoy was sent to the Tibetans the foreigners were ignorant of the proper title of the Sung emperor. They referred to him as the "Son of Heaven of the Chao Family" (*Chao-chia T'ien-tzu*) and to the Sung crown prince as "[Our] Maternal Uncle of the Chao Family" (*Chao-chia A-chiu*). This name for the Sung emperor goes back to the T'ang dynasty when the royal Tibetan family had married Chinese princesses.[12] Also, the kings of Khotan are referred to as examples of "barbarian" ignorance of diplomatic etiquette. A letter from Khotan to the Sung emperor in 1081 addressed him as "Great Official and Maternal Uncle of the Han Family (*Han-chia a-chiu ta-kuan-chia*) Who Reigns over the Lands in the Great World in the East Where the Sun Rises"[13]—certainly a colorful name for the Sung ruler but not suited for addressing a Chinese emperor. One can easily imagine the disgust of Chinese officials who had to handle a document where an emperor was addressed in such a disrespectful and intimate way. The same problem was encountered by the Sung when they first encountered the Mongols. This was at a time when the Mongols had not yet developed a formal ceremonial in their communications with other powers. The Sung envoy sent to the Mongols in 1221 reported that their words were very simple and straight-forward. Mukhali, or rather, his interpreters, addressed the Sung envoy thus: "You dear (*hao*) chancellor of the dear emperor of the Great Sung." In the same passage of the text the Sung emissary deplored the future Mongol loss of simplicity and honesty because of the influence of former Chin officials in their service.[14] All this is in sharp contrast to the highly formal ceremonial that had been developed between the Sung and their northern neighbors, Liao and Chin, and also for the relations between the Sung on the one hand and Koryŏ or Hsi Hsia on the other.

Types of Embassies

The types of embassies exchanged between Liao and Sung have been studied in great detail,[15] so that it may suffice here to give a short summary. There were twelve different types of Sung embassies. After the ratification of the Shan-yüan treaty (1005), ambassadorial relations between the two states had become regularized, and either at fixed dates or in the case of specific events the Sung court dispatched embassies. The embassies sent out at fixed dates were those for the New Year festival and the birthday of the northern ruler or reigning empress. Special embassies announced the accession of a new Sung ruler, and others congratulated the Liao for the enthronement of a new ruler. A special type of embassy was dispatched when a Liao empress took up the regency for a juvenile crown prince.

The death of a ruler, too, was formally announced through a special embassy, which was followed by another embassy offering presents to the northern court. If a Liao ruler died, a mission of condolence was obligatory, and another type of embassy was entrusted with offering sacrificial gifts for the deceased. The receipt of congratulations or condolences was acknowledged by a special embassy. These ten types of embassies were all concerned with ritual matters and left no room for political negotiations on a governmental level. This was reserved for Emissaries for State Letters (*Kuo-hsin shih*), who presented written statements containing inquiries or requests. The general term for political ad hoc embassies was "floating embassies" (*fan-shih*). It should be noted that political as well as ritual embassies consisted, on both sides, of traveling emissaries. The modern Western notion of permanent representation abroad by resident diplomats was unknown in the Far East. Only as late as the sixteenth century did the system of permanent diplomatic representation evolve in Europe, first in the Italian states of the Renaissance period.[16]

Diplomatic relations through traveling envoys, as sanctioned by the Shan-yüan treaty of 1005, also characterized contacts between the Sung and the Chin.[17] Sung sources repeatedly stress the importance of following Liao precedents with the Chin, which regarded itself as the legitimate successor of the Liao. Some of the designations of embassies changed, however, after the emergence of the Chin as an independent power. Thus we find the term "Envoy for General Inquiry" (*t'ung-wen shih*), which was changed in 1127 to "Supplication Envoy" (*ch'i-ch'ing shih*).[18] This points to the political nature of the embassy; the change of designation indicated the nearly hopeless military situation of the Sung after the fall of K'ai-feng and the desire of the Sung to appear humble vis-à-vis the victorious Chin. But this remained an exception. After the resumption of peaceful relations with the Chin in 1141, relations between the two states followed—with occasional interruptions—the pattern established by the treaty of Shan-yüan, which must therefore be regarded as crucial in the history of Sung foreign relations.

Sung Agencies for Diplomatic Intercourse

Another characteristic of Chinese foreign policy is that no equivalent of a Foreign Office existed in medieval China. Foreign relations were treated as a part of politics in general with no special agencies for handling interstate problems. The decision-making process at court was the same for domestic and for foreign politics. A specialized government agency, which handled the formal side of intercourse with foreigners and their states, did exist. This was the Court of Diplomatic Reception (*hung-lu ssu*), the functions of which corresponded roughly to what would be termed in modern times a department of protocol.[19] Under the *hung-lu ssu*, which was in turn subordinate to the Ministry of Rites, was the Department for Ingoing and Outgoing State Credentials (*wang-lai kuo-hsin so*). This agency was, however, not in charge of diplomatic correspondence in general, but was only concerned with the Liao, including the reception of Liao envoys and with their audiences at the Sung court. The State Letters Bureau therefore served not only as the office from which orders and regulations concerning Sung embassies emanated but also as a visitors' department or travel agency, which cared for the Liao envoys as long as they were on Sung territory. This office dealt exclusively with the Liao and, after 1122, the Chin. A special place was thus accorded to relations with Liao.[20]

Different agencies were responsible for other states. Relations with the "barbarian tribes west of the River" (*Ho-hsi fan-pu*), principally the Hsi Hsia, were managed by the *kuan-kan so* and the Directorate of the Western Postal Stations (*tu-t'ing hsi-i*).[21] Matters concerning audiences, tributes, hostels, and mutual trade with the Uighurs, Tibetans, Tang-hsiang, Jurchens (before 1122 and the founding of the Chin), and other peoples were administered by the Hall of Welcoming Guests (*li-pin yüan*),[22] which also provided interpreters for the respective languages. The Postal Stations Cherishing the Distant Ones (*huai-yüan i*)[23] managed visits from the "Southern Barbarians," Annam, "Western Barbarians" (*Hsi-fan*), Kucha, Ta-shih (Arabs or Persians), Khotan, the Kan-chou and Sha-chou Uighurs, and the Tsung-ko,[24] a Tibetan tribe living in the region of Lake Kuku Nor. Finally, the *t'ung-wen kuan* and the *kuan-kan so* handled relations with Korea (Koryŏ). The *hung-lu ssu* also had jurisdiction over such agencies as the supervisory offices for Buddhist temples and the Buddhist clergy, including a translation office for Buddhist sutras. The Buddhist religion was somehow regarded as bound up with foreign relations. After 1127 the *hung-lu ssu* was abolished, and all the agencies formerly under its jurisdiction were directly administered by the Ministry of Rites.

In the Sung bureaucracy, foreign relations, in particular the handling of foreign envoys, were strongly differentiated according to status. Liao, and later Chin, relations came under the *kuo-hsin so*. Hsi Hsia fell into a special category, and so did Koryŏ. Their diplomatic status was certainly lower than that of the Liao or Chin. The *li-pin yüan* and *huai-yüan i* were concerned with minor foreign states to the south, west, and north of the Sung. Chinese officials clearly devised a hierarchy of foreign states based upon power and wealth.

Diplomatic Correspondence

For each of the solemn occasions when courtesy embassies were exchanged, a text was composed and presented to the other court. The purpose of these documents was purely ceremonial, and no political content appears. For those who had to draft such documents, it must have been difficult to say nothing in wellphrased and polite words without becoming repetitive. But we should nevertheless not scorn these works of the Sung literati and their Liao or Chin counterparts. Even today in Western societies one might find it difficult to write a letter of congratulation or condolence, and invariably the same phrases and words will crop up. It is not easy to give individual expression to formal occasions, and perhaps not even expected. Moreover, modern diplomatic correspondence is full of conventional phraseology, and it may even amount to a breach of etiquette if the appropriate phraseology is not used.

A good survey of the diplomatic letters sent from the Sung court to the Liao may be obtained from the collection of Northern Sung documents, *Sung ta chao-ling chi*, where the texts of 113 letters to the Liao are given.[25] Subsequent sections of this work are devoted to correspondence addressed to Hsi Hsia (ch. 233–236). Documents issued to Koryŏ are found in chapter 237, while letters to all other nations and tribes are collected in chapters 238–240. Here we find documents issued to Annam, the Ta-li kingdom in Yunnan, and the Tibetans in the Kuku Nor region (*Hsi-fan*). The section on miscellaneous barbarians (*chu-fan*) includes documents written to various aboriginal tribes in the southwest, to Khotan, and to several minor chieftains in the northwestern border regions. The special role of Liao in Northern Sung times is evident from the category of letters sent to them. State letters (*kuo-shu*) were reserved for the Liao, whereas the letters sent to Koryŏ and Hsi Hsia—both were nominally under Chinese suzerainty— were edicts (*chao*), decrees (*ch'ih-shu*), or documents of investiture (*chih*).[26]

The political state letters entrusted to "floating embassies" were not empty stylistic exercises. Here the formalism is limited to the initial and closing phrases and to some formulas normally used in official correspondence.[27] In Sung diplomatic correspondence, the proprieties of dealing with a foreign court were observed, particularly the correct titles of the foreign ruler, but this did not prevent Sung officials and statesmen from referring to the Liao and Chin as "slaves" or "caitiffs" (*lu*) for domestic consumption. Many if not most Sung politicians continued to look down upon the powerful Liao and Chin states as "barbarians." The principle of reciprocity in diplomatic relations with these states was nothing more than an enforced concession, which was but grudgingly granted because of the Sung's military weakness. On the other hand, this reciprocity proved to be a stable element in Sung politics, which lasted for well over two hundred years and could, if the situation demanded it, easily have been extended to other parties as well. The system was flexible and allowed a considerable adaptation to changing circumstances. Differences in political power could be expressed by a corresponding difference in pseudo-familial status. The lower the power and prestige of Sung, the lower its adopted family status in relation to the foreign ruling family and vice versa. Diplomatic relations were expressed, both by correspondence and by embassy ceremonials, within a hierarchical but adaptable system. The Sung collected the existing rituals into a sort of diplomatic handbook. In 1081 Su Sung (1020–1101), who had been an envoy to the Liao in 1077, was ordered to gather all the written materials about state letters after the establishment of peaceful diplomatic relations with the Liao.[28] In 1195 the Sung minister Chao Ju-yü proposed that the precedents from the Lung-hsing reign (1163–1165) on be compiled into a companion volume. Each Sung envoy and each official escorting the Chin envoys would be given a copy. An edict sanctioned Chao Ju-yü's request, and the compilation was sent to the Bureau of Military Affairs (Shu-mi yüan).[29]

Unfortunately, both Su Sung's work and the later compilation seem to be lost. The table of contents of Su Sung's compilation is preserved in his collected works.[30] The book was voluminous, consisting of 200 chüan, some of which had to be divided into sub-chapters. The emperor received the work on June 22, 1083. It was an encyclopedia on Sung relations with Liao after 1005, with a rich collection of documents arranged according to topics. Every aspect of diplomatic intercourse was illustrated by the relevant official documents, including such practical matters as a list of hostels and postal stations and a description of the Liao state and its customs. Su Sung's political philosophy, which coincided with that of the Sung court, consisted of an apology for the appeasement policy followed by the Sung in relaions with the Khitans. With some pride, Su Sung pointed out that the establishment of peaceful relations with Liao permitted the people in the border regions to live a normal life and reach old age without ever having been troubled by military actions.[31]

Diplomatic Personnel and Its Recruitment

Each embassy from the Sung court could be assigned to one specific category. Its duties were in each case narrowly circumscribed, and there was no room for political conversations. Political envoys had to follow strictly the instructions for negotiations, as laid down by the court in the state letters.[32] But it would be wrong to conceive of the Sung envoys as mere letter-carriers. The envoys invariably had some room for negotiations within the limits set by the court. They were representatives of the Sung emperor and had to enhance the prestige of their state in a foreign and sometimes hostile environment. This duty required men who were able to maintain their dignity in adverse circumstances, who had mastered the rules of etiquette, who had a classical education and skill in debates, and who were physically healthy. Great attention was therefore paid to the proper selection of embassy personnel, not only as far as the envoys (*shih*) and their deputies (*fu-shih*) were concerned, but also to that of the military escort attached to each embassy, the "three ranks" (*san-chieh*). Normally, the envoy was a civilian official and his deputy a military official. The Bureau of Military Affairs chose the envoys.[33] Again and again, edicts urged officials to select only talented and able persons. But there was no professional diplomatic corps and no career personnel employed exclusively for embassies, so that the problem of recruitment was a recurrent one. The Sung was apparently successful in appointing capable envoys. A surprisingly large number of prominent Sung military and civilian officials served as envoys, among them not a few future prime ministers. Successful envoys were occasionally reappointed in subsequent years. Yü Ching (1000–1064), for example, served three times as envoy to the Liao.

The selection of clerical and military personnel was, to a large extent, left to the envoys themselves. But there were problems. In 1148 the *san-chieh* escort soldiers were accused of improper behavior leading to unpleasant incidents.[34] In 1156 the court ruled that the selection of *san-chieh* should not be made on the spur of the moment, and that the names of candidates should be submitted in advance to the Bureau of Military Affairs through the State Letters Bureau.[35] These soldiers should not be former convicts, and they ought to be good-looking, able-bodied, and well-trained men.[36] Nor should the officers be too old or. too young; only officers between the ages of thirty and fifty years ought to be considered as candidates.[37]

The escort personnel attached to the embassy varied greatly. The embassy of 1133, which negotiated with the Chin, had fourteen men in the *shang-chieh* ("upper ranks") category (including one physician), fifteen men in the *chung-chieh* ("middle ranks") category (including, among others, men to carry the flags and letters), and seventy soldiers in the *hsia-chieh* ("lower ranks") category, which included two riding teachers, one head-cook, one carpenter, and one embroiderer.[38] The escort consisted of one hundred men, to which we must add the conscripted local labor serving as carrier coolies, grooms, cart-drivers, and so on. In 1189 the escort was even more numerous: two hundred infantry men, one hundred cavalry men, and ninety-five grooms for the horses, or a total of almost four hundred men.[39]

Officials at the court repeatedly complained that the embassies were too large.[40] People frequently wished to be included among the embassy personnel. To take part in an embassy brought prestige and sometimes promotion to a higher rank. Travel in the retinue of an envoy or as an envoy could be profitable, not only because of the customary presents received in the host country, but also because of the chance to conduct private trade with foreigners. Escorts were, on occasion, approached by outsiders who bribed them and traveled in their place. In 1162 the censorate was permitted to impeach the envoys if unauthorized military escorts traveled to foreign lands.[41] Su Ch'e (1039–1112), on returning from his embassy to the Liao, complained that there were too many personal retainers (whom he denounced as persons of no merit, hsiao-jen) attached to the embassy. He urged the court to reduce the number of such retainers.[42] An envoy or his deputy could appoint family members as supernumerary embassy personnel—a good chance for adventurous young relatives to see the world. An edict of 1097 permitted the envoy and his deputy to appoint one family member each as a servant to his staff.[43] Under the Southern Sung, the number of accompanying family members was limited to two.[44] The tendency to fill up the embassy with family members seems to have been widespread. An edict of 1195 states that in the past too many county magistrates had applied for their sons to be attached to embassies.[45] The number of clerks and other secretarial personnel was limited by statutes (e.g., for a first-class embassy, five clerks (li), one scribe, and one secretary), though more were allotted if they were needed.[46]

All these regulations were more or less observed in practice. An embassy to the Chin in 1125, for example, had eighty people, among them one physician, two interpreters, and three riding-teachers. About half of the eighty men were soldiers. For the transport of their baggage they had three carts, ten camels, and twelve horses.

Travel Money and Other Allowances

We have many detailed figures for the money and commodites paid to the embassy personnel, apart from their normal salary to which they were entitled. Only a few examples will be given here. For the 1133 embassy to the Chin, the envoys each received 60 bolts of silk, 100 strings of cash, and 50 ounces of silver. For a military escort of the upper rank (shang-chieh), the sums paid were lower: 40 bolts of silk, 10 strings of cash, and 20 ounces of silver. The lower officers of this group and the embassy physician each received 30 bolts of silk, 40 strings of cash, and 10 ounces of silver, the middle and lower ranks (chung-chieh, hsia-chieh) correspondingly less. The physician received an extra allowance of 100 strings of cash for emergencies. The expenditures for travel expenses (money for accommodations, shan-chia ch'ien, and money for meals, shih-ch'ien) were also prescribed. Regular officials could spend 30 strings of cash a month for accommodations and 500 cash daily for food. For the soldiers, money for accommodations amounted to 8 strings of cash a month, and the daily food allowance was 500 cash.[47] After the resumption of regular relations with the Chin, new regulations were issued. Each envoy now received 200 bolts of silk, 200 ounces of silver, and 1,000 strings of cash. His deputy received the same amounts of silk and silver but only 800 strings of cash. The military escorts or the upper ranks (*shang-chieh*) were each entitled to 15 bolts of silk and 15 ounces of silver, the middle ranks to 15 bolts and 10 ounces, and the lower ranks to 10 bolts of silk and 5 ounces of silver.[48] These payments were, however, regarded as excessive, and in 1148 a 50 percent cut was ordered for the silk and silver payments to the envoys.[49] After the completion of their mission, the envoys had to present, within ten days after their return, an account showing their expenditures.[50]

The court enacted detailed provisions for the daily allowances for food, cooking supplies, and other utensils. Regular officials were entitled to four ounces of oil and five catties of charcoal daily for cooking, with an additional load of coal in winter. The daily food allowance for clerks was 200 cash, for junior secretaries, 150 cash, and for kitchen boys and rank-and-file soldiers, 30 cash. The payments clearly differed according to rank and status. A simple clerk received almost seven times as much as an ordinary soldier. These payments must, nonetheless, have been attractive or at least sufficient, for there were always volunteers for the embassies. The court even regulated the amount of office equipment and stationery. Envoys had at their disposal 200 envelopes, 300 sheets of double paper, 300 cards, and 30 sheets of yellow paper from Hsüan (in Anhui province). Even the stamp color was not forgotten: envoys received 5 ounces of red color. Thirty letter boxes, or rather, letter tubes for the transport of documents, were also provided.[51] An embassy therefore was almost an office on wheels, with all the paraphernalia required for conducting business by correspondence.

Agencies for Reception in the Host Countries

The Liao diplomatic agencies responsible for the reception of Chinese envoys resembled the Sung institutions, but the formal bureaucracy of the Liao was much less developed. The titles of officials and the names of offices, as given in the sources, were perhaps only a Chinese tag attached to rather simple and rustic institutions without the high specialization of functions found in the Sung.[52] Even late in the eleventh century, a Sung envoy noted the minimal ceremonies at official audiences.[53] The Liao had a Court of Diplomatic Reception (*hung-lu ssu*) modeled on that of the Chinese, but our sources do not tell us much about its special activities and functions.[54] Care for foreign emissaries was entrusted to the Bureau for Visiting Guests (*k'o-sheng chü*), which was established in 938.[55] The reception of Sung envoys at the border and their journey to the residence of the Liao ruler followed the Sung system. The Liao capitals had hostels for the foreign envoys, and the Chinese sources referred to these attendants with the same official title as that of the Sung, namely, Hostel Escort Commissioner (*kuan-pan shih*). Attendants cared for the Sung envoys and accompanied them to the audience hall.[56] The Liao provided an official escort, who also had a counterpart on the Chinese side, the Parting Escort Commissioner (*sung-pan shih*).

The relative paucity of material for the Liao contrasts with the abundance of details in the sources for the Chin bureaucracy. The Chin followed the Sung system throughout. We know that it too had a *hung-lu ssu*, though the chapters on officials in the *Chin-shih* do not mention that agency. The Ministry of Rites took charge of the reception of envoys. The Bureau for Visiting Guests, under the aegis of the Department of Court Etiquette (*hsüan-hui yuan*), welcomed and escorted foreign envoys.[57] Ushers (*yin-chin*) handled tributes and presents from foreign countries.[58] The Chin followed Sung precedents in the escort of foreign envoys. Welcoming Escort Commissioners (*chieh-pan shih*) met the foreigners at the border and led them to the ruler's residence. There the Hostel Escort Commissioners (*kuan-pan shih*) received them and acted as their hosts during their stay in the capital, and on their way back they were in the care (and, we might add, under the supervision) of the Parting Escort Commissioners (*sung-pan shih*).[59] The hostel for the Sung envoys in the capital of the Chin (modern Peking) was called *Hui-t'ung kuan*, and the envoys from Hsi Hsia and Koryŏ had separate hostels opposite the *Hui-t'ung kuan*.[60] The Chin generally appointed a Chinese and a Jurchen or native as hostel commissioners. The Chin government selected persons who knew Chinese and who could be regarded as educated by a Chinese envoy. Not infrequently, the government appointed officials who had already served as ambassadors to the Sung and were therefore familiar with Chinese etiquette. Indeed, some Sung envoys report that they were impressed by their hosts, though they occasionally came across an inadequate hostel commissioner. In 1170–1171 the envoy Fan Ch'eng-ta was displeased with an illiterate commissioner. He wrote a poem satirizing the poor Khitan hostel attendant.[61]

The commissioners and their deputies who acted as hosts to the Sung envoys were assisted by auxiliary personnel. No less than seventy persons constituted the normal retinue when the Chin officials set out to receive the Sung envoys at the border. This number included not only officials with specialized functions but also such service personnel as stewards, kitchen boys, cooks, runners, and insignia bearers. A special official was assigned to explain court rituals to the Sung envoys. The hostel in the capital where embassies stayed was guarded by thirty soldiers. The kitchen personnel in the hostel numbered forty. Three physicians looked after the health of the guests, one specializing in pharmacology, another in pulse diagnosis, and still another in general ailments (*fang, mo, tsa*). The horses of the guests could, if necessary, be treated by a veterinarian, who also belonged to the standard personnel attached to the hostel.[62]

The Koreans followed the Chinese models, perhaps not so much those of the Sung as those of the T'ang. The Ministry of Rites handled the diplomatic relations of Koryŏ.[63] An agency known as the *T'ongye mun* handled the ceremonials for foreign ambassadors, and the *Yepin sa* arranged banquets for foreign guests.[64] The Koreans also had a translators' office, named *T'ongmun kwan*, to train scholars under the age of forty in Chinese.[65]

The travel account of the Sung envoy Hsü Ching offers a vivid portrayal of the Koreans' reception of foreign emissaries. The Sung envoy describes first the hostel where he was lodged, the *Sunch'ŏn kwan*, a sumptuous building, which was better built than the royal palace itself. It contained outer galleries where the less prestigious embassy personnel were entertained; it had a pavilion for a band in the courtyard, and many sidewings and galleries. In the late eleventh century, the Korean king converted the hostel into a separate palace. Hsü Ching, together with the Sung embassy, was lodged in a guesthouse behind the *Sunch'ŏn kwan*, which was a slightly smaller building. The Khitan envoys were lodged in the *Inŭn kwan*, a building opposite the Sung hostel. The Jurchens were lodged somewhere else, in the *Yŏngsŏn kwan*, and Chinese merchants were lodged in the *Hŭngwi kwan*.[66] But Hsü notes with a touch of complacency that all the other hostels were rather primitive and not at all as comfortable as the building where his own embassy resided.

The *Koryŏ-sa* yields few specific details on Sung embassies. Sung-Koryŏ relations were, for most of the time, a halfhearted affair because of Koryŏ's fear of Liao and of Chin. The great expense and trouble involved also prevented the Sung government from imposing itself and its own views on the Koreans.[67]

During the early years of their state the Mongols had no special officials to deal with foreign envoys. Even after the accession of Khubilai, they did not have an office comparable to the State Letters Bureau of the Sung, though the term *Kuo-hsin shih* (Emissary for State Letters) is used once in connection with a mission to Annam.[68] The obvious reason that no State Letters Bureau existed under the Yüan is that an institution like the Sung *Kuo-hsin so* was based on mutual and somewhat equitable relations. For the Mongols no such relations were conceivable. There was no need to establish such an agency. The Yüan government did, however, have special institutions for receiving foreign envoys. It created a *Hui-t'ung kuan*, under the Ministry of Rites, which escorted foreigners to court and handled tribute missions and their audiences. The office was established in 1276, abolished in 1288, and reestablished in 1292.[69] The Yüan text, which describes the functions of the *Hui-t'ung kuan*, is clearly scornful of the foreign envoys. Guest bureaus (*k'o-sheng*) developed, similar to those of the Liao and Chin, but under the Mongols they had a different function. They were attached to the Central Chancery, to the Military Bureau, and to the Department of Buddhist and Tibetan Affairs.[70] Each of these highest central offices had its own guest department but without specific diplomatic functions. The Mongol government in China certainly practiced hospitality, but it did not develop a special machinery for dealing formally with foreign states and did not grant a special status to other states as the Sung had done with the Liao and Chin.

Journeys of Sung Embassies

The Sung government was responsible for foreign envoys as long as they were on Sung territory. It devised numerous regulations for these embassies. Envoys could not travel a distance of more than two postal stations a day. They were not allowed to stay more than three days in any station, though envoys traveling in the provinces of Szechwan and Kuang-tung could stay up to five days.[71] Travel was slow, even if the envoys proceeded along well-established roads. Hsü K'ang-tsung needed over half a year for his trip to the Supreme Capital of Chin in Manchuria. Within China he traveled 1,150 *li* in twenty-two stages from K'ai-feng to the Chin border. From the border to the Supreme Capital took another thirty-nine stages, covering 3,120 *li*.[72] Travel from Hang-chou to Peking was very much shorter. Several months absence was normal. The Sung embassy of 1169–1170 departed on the eighteenth day of the tenth month in 1169, crossed the Huai River border on the twenty-eighth day of the eleventh month, and arrived in Peking on the twenty-seventh day of the twelfth month, just in time for the New Year festivities. The envoys left Peking on the sixth day of the first month and were back in Hang-chou in the fourth month after an absence of almost half a year.[73] The extant diaries all show that the embassies' residences in the Liao or Chin capitals were relatively short, normally about one week or ten days. Most of the time was spent on the road.

After a Sung embassy had crossed the border its transport, including provision of food, lodging, and animals for the carts and carriages became the responsibility of the host country. As early as the eleventh century, the Liao had provided rest houses and restaurants for travelers. These were sometimes cared for by soldiers from a local tribe who had been given fields in the vicinity in which they lived. The Khitan officials provided not only meals for the embassy personnel and fodder and hay for their horses, but also the vessels, cups, and plates for their meals.[74] We do not know what provisions the Khitans gave to Sung envoys, but we have a detailed account of the Chin's daily food rations to Sung envoys. The rations were plentiful and could easily feed a whole family, not to mention servants. The envoy and his deputy were entitled daily to twenty bottles of fine wine, eight pounds of mutton, five hundred coins in lieu of fresh fruit, five hundred coins for incidental expenses, three pounds of white noodles, one-half pound of oil, two pounds of vinegar, one-half pound of salt, three pints of fine white rice, one-half pound of meal-sauce, and three bundles of fire-wood. The military escort personnel received much less, but even a member of the lowest ranks (*hsia-chieh*) received three bottles of wine, two pounds of mutton, one pound of noodles, one and a half pounds of white rice, and one hundred coins for incidental expenses. The Chin certainly did not skimp in providing for Sung envoys.[75]

Diplomatic Ceremonial for Sung Embassies

As soon as the Sung envoys entered foreign territory, they were feted with countless official banquets, culminating in the banquets at the Liao and the Chin courts. The ceremonies at these occasions followed Chinese customs, but the food was of Khitan or Jurchen origin and therefore foreign to the Chinese.[76] One difference between northern and Chinese culinary customs was that the northerners always served hot soup first and tea later, a fact noted by several Sung envoys.[77] Under the Chin there were minor or "country" banquets (*ch'ü-yen*) and "flowery" or "ornate" banquets (*hua-yen*).[78] Sung travelers offer first-rate accounts of these banquets. The term "flowery" has to be taken literally. After the wine was served, the guests were given flowers made of colored silk, which they placed on their heads.[79] The guests were entertained with music, dances, and theatrical performances. The music performed at the northern courts seemed strange to the Chinese guests; the melodies sounded to them melancholy and almost like a funeral dirge.[80] It is not clear whether the music played at the Chin court was native Jurchen music or just Northern Chinese music with which the Southern Chinese were unfamiliar. As was noted above, the Liao court ceremonies were relatively primitive. The Chin, however, tried hard to imitate the Chinese, and as early as 1125 Hsü K'ang-tsung reported that the Chin ceremonies resembled those of the Chinese. The ceremonies for audiences and for the reception of foreign envoys were elaborate under the later Chin and followed the pattern set by the Sung. The audiences with the emperor were the most well regulated. The bowing, advancing, retreating, and greeting were prescribed to the most minute detail.[81] The regulations for the audiences and receptions read like the script for a ballet. They are extremely detailed and reveal the formalities to which foreign envoys had to conform.[82] The evidence suggests that the Sung envoys enjoyed a higher status at the Chin court than those from Hsi Hsia and Koryŏ. During the reign of Hsi-tsung (1135–1149), the Sung envoys were seated in the row reserved for third-rank officials while the Hsi Hsia and Koryŏ emissaries sat behind them in the rows reserved for officials of the fifth rank.[83]

A traditional part of the court rituals were the shooting contests, a friendly and sportive occasion where wine was served as a matter of course. After the contests, the envoys were given embroidered garments and saddled horses as presents. The whole ceremony was more or less public; princes of the imperial clan and high officials mingled with the crowd and watched the shooting.[84] In 1221 the Mongols invited the Sung envoys to take part in their native sports of hunting and polo. When the envoys politely declined, they were fined six cups of wine.[85]

An anonymous painting in the Palace Museum shows the reception of Khitan envoys at the Sung court.[86] The formal reception of foreign ambassadors was an impressive and colorful ceremony with large crowds taking part or observing the scene. Some of the envoys did not make a good impression on the Sung. One Chinese author notes, with considerable condescension, that the Po-hai emissaries, who reached China in 1177, looked strange, behaved without discipline, were noisy, and laughed loudly in the presence of Chin officials.[87] Another Chinese writer described what he perceived to be the boorishness of a Hsi Hsia embassy to the Chin court. He noted that the Hsi Hsia envoys all came from the princely family and that they were correctly attired with golden caps and red robes, but their retinue was, in contrast, clad in the "barbarian" way, with the hair tied up in a knot, a small kerchief, and a pointed cap. The Hsi Hsia presented twelve loads of presents, twenty-four horses, seven hunting falcons, and five small dogs to the Chin emperor. When these gifts were lined up in the courtyard, the horses neighed, the dogs barked, and the whole ceremony was disrupted.[88]

Exchange of Presents

The great number of banquets which the Sung envoys attended was matched by the number of occasions when presents were exchanged. The basic presents were those which the Sung court gave to the foreign court and which the foreign court offered the Sung. The number of presents was considerable even for routine embassies, and it was staggering in cases when the embassy congratulated a new ruler or mourned a deceased ruler. A few examples will suffice to prove the point. Hsü K'ang-tsung's embassy of 1125 transported the following goods to the Chin emperor: three horses with bridles adorned with gold and silver, and for each horse a whip made of ivory and tortoise shell, eight gilt cups and silver vessels of varying shape and size, three incense-burners shaped like a lion, three throne garments, ten baskets of fruit, ten jugs of honey, and three pounds of young tea-leaves.[89] A detailed list of presents to the North is given on the occasion of Sung Jen-tsung's death (1063): gold vessels totaling 2,000 ounces in weight, silver vessels 20,000 ounces in weight, and objects made of jade, ivory, and other precious materials.[90] In 1187 after the death of Sung Kao-tsung, the presents sent to the Chin totaled gold vessels weighing 2,000 ounces, silver vessels weighing 20,000 ounces, and 2,000 bolts of silk. The transport of these commodities could be a problem; therefore in 1187 additional boats had to be requisitioned in Huai-nan and Liang-Che.[91]

The Sung almost always sent tea to the Northern courts. When Su Sung was an envoy in 1077–1078, his deputy objected to giving the Khitans the best tea, called *hsiao-t'uan ch'a* (tea pellets), a brand that was normally reserved for the Sung imperial table. But other members of the embassy said that the Khitans would only accept *t'uan-ch'a*.[92] Some of the Khitans had apparently become connoisseurs in tea, and they were no longer content with cheaper brands. In the twelfth century, the Sung escorts used to take tea presumably for trade during their journey in Chin territory. The Northerners, however, demanded tea of the highest quality.[93]

The official gifts from court to court must be differentiated from the presents to which the envoys and their retinue were customarily entitled. No one came home from an embassy without having received presents according to his rank. These presents consisted of silver, textiles, garments, belts and sundry articles, and occasionally horses with bridles and saddles. The Chin History enumerates the standard presents for the Hsi Hsia envoys. The envoy and his deputy each received 3 garments and 140 bolts of textiles. In the early years of the dynasty, they were given 2 sable furs; if sable was not available, the envoy received 150 ounces of silver and his deputy 60 rolls of textiles. These generous gifts were later eliminated. Instead of "live animals for sacrifice" (*sheng-hsi*) (that is, as provisions), the envoys received 39 rolls of thin silk, 62 rolls of textiles, 4 rolls of linen, 3 golden belts, 3 gilt silver belts, and 3 saddles and bridles inlaid with gold and silver, among other gifts.[94] The presents for the Sung envoys and their retinue were probably more numerous and valuable than those for the representatives of the Hsi Hsia. On special occasions, the gifts accorded by the Chin were greater than normal, which prompted the Sung to increase the gifts for the Jurchen envoys who came to Hang-chou. Reciprocity was traditional, if only as a matter of prestige.[95] In the late twelfth century, a Sung envoy and his deputy expected a minimum of 7 garments and 7 belts as a farewell present, and the escort personnel 5 each.[96] But this was a bare minimum; the existing embassy diaries, for obvious reasons, are silent on the individual gifts received from the Northern court.

The Sung envoys and their personnel were, according to the letter of the law, forbidden to engage in private trade during their mission. The punishment for such illegal trade was two years of hard labor (*t'u*).[97] Even if subordinates were the culprits, envoys and their deputies who did not investigate received the same punishment.[98] The temptation to trade Southern goods was great, because they could fetch a high price on Northern markets, twice as much as their original price in Sung territory. The escorts provided by the Chin sold presents which they had received from the Sung embassy. No wonder that the local usher attached to the Sung embassy could be happy with an orange left over from the meal in the hostel.[99] The export of copper coins to the North was strictly forbidden. An edict was issued in 1195 against this widespread practice, which was one of the great problems of the Sung economy.[100] One provision required a search of the baggage and clothing of the embassy personnel in order to prevent the illicit export of coins.[101] Another provision forbade envoys and their personnel from accepting farewell presents in the Sung towns while en route to the North.

Problems of Propriety

Innumerable Sung regulations dealt with propriety and etiquette for embassies to foreign lands. Several of these concerned the appropriate dress for the emissaries, particularly if they were sent to offer condolences for a ruler's death.[102] In 1197 a discussion about the proper attire for envoys was initiated. The prefect of Hang-chou wrote that his office was responsible for the official uniforms worn by embassy personnel. The cloth for these garments was dyed in the color red (*fei*) known as "barbarian red." The prefect pointed out that the Chin envoys now wore garments in red imitating the Chinese fashion and that Sung envoys to the Jurchens reported that the higher Chin officials wore uniforms of a deep purple color as in China. It was intolerable that the Sung envoys wore "barbarian red." He sought permission, therefore, to instruct the dyeing manufacturers of Hang-chou to produce a Chinese type of red to distinguish the Sung from the Chin. His request was granted.[103] This is not much different from modern times, where dress regulations for diplomats are taken seriously.

Another problem which, like dress regulations, was crucial at that time concerned seating arrangements. In 1076 the Sung envoy Ch'eng Shih-meng arrived at the Liao border. The Khitan official had arranged the seats for the welcoming banquet so that he faced south, the prefect of the town west, and the Sung embassy east. Ch'eng protested and refused to take his seat. After a long quarrel lasting into the evening Ch'eng succeeded in being seated opposite his host, both facing east and west respectively. Ch'eng's protest was motivated by the traditional Chinese notion that "facing south" was the prerogative of the ruler and therefore implied superiority.[104]

Part of the diplomatic routine between the Southern and Northern courts was the exchange of imperial portraits. Even this could cause squabbles between protocol experts on both sides. The emperor Hsing-tsung of Liao (r. 1031–1055) had sent a portrait of himself to the Sung and requested a portrait of the Sung emperor in return. He died, however, before the Sung had sent their portrait, and his son who succeeded him renewed the request. The Sung, on their part, asked for a portrait of the new ruler, but the Khitans insisted on receiving the Sung portrait first. The Sung envoy protested and pointed out that the relations between the Sung and the Liao were like those between uncle and nephew. This argument, together with a reference to classical precedents, impressed the Liao court so that its officials sent the portrait of their new ruler before they received the one of the reigning Sung emperor.[105]

The taboo on the use of imperial names was another concern. In 1094 a Sung envoy to the Khitans was dismissed because he quarreled with his personnel over the taboo name P'u-wang, the name of a nephew of the Sung emperor Jen-tsung.[106] In the twelfth century the Sung government insisted that a Chin envoy whose name contained the character *yüan* should change it to *shang*. The character *yüan* was part of the name of Emperor Ying-tsung's grandfather.[107] On the other hand, the Sung government also tried to observe the taboos of the Chin imperial family. A Sung hostel attendant in 1188 had to change his name Cheng Ssu-tsung into Cheng Ssu-ch'ang because the character *tsung* was part of the name of the Chin emperor Shih-tsung's father, Wan-yen Tsung-yao.[108] For the same reason, the Sung envoy Chang Tsung-i was told in 1191 to change his name temporarily by dropping the character *tsung*.[109] Even place names were temporarily changed in order to respect a taboo. When the Hai-ling emperor of Chin appointed Wan-yen Kuang-ying crown prince, the Sung changed the name of the prefecture Kuang-hua into T'ung-hua and that of Kuang-chou into Chiang-chou.[110] (Refer to the Glossary for the Chinese characters.) Such cases show how strongly the Sung and their counterparts insisted on mutual respect for their rulers' name taboos. The adoption of these traditional Chinese customs by the Liao and Chin courts also points to a full-scale absorption of the northerners into the Sinitic ritual orbit.

Risks and Hardships for Envoys

An appointment as ambassador could bring prestige, promotion, and to some extent, material rewards through the numerous presents received from foreign governments. But there were also potential risks and hardships. One risk was the possibility of detainment by the other state if the embassy was dispatched at a time when no treaty guaranteeing normal diplomatic intercourse was in effect. From 1127 to 1141, when the Sung and the Chin were in conflict, several Sung envoys were kept in a state of semi-captivity. The Chin authorities were probably practicing a form of political blackmail, but it may also be that they were sometimes impressed by the Sung envoys and tried to secure their services. Indeed, the promise of employment and promotion tempted some of the Sung emissaries. Yü-wen Hsü-chung (1079–1146), a Sung envoy, preferred to remain with the Chin and later played some role in spreading Chinese literary influence under the Chin. Other Sung emissaries, however, remained adamant in the face of Chin promises and pressure. T'eng Mao-shih, for example, sought to accompany the Sung emperor Ch'in-tsung on his voyage to the North, but the Chin refused to let him proceed with his deposed emperor. T'eng is said to have died in 1128 as a result of his grief. In 1132 the Sung government rewarded him posthumously by promotion to a higher rank.[111]

Other Sung envoys were detained for many years by the Chin. Wang Lun was sent to the Chin in 1139 in order to negotiate the return of the coffin of the emperor Hui-tsung who had died in captivity in 1135. He steadfastly refused all of the Chin's offers of a government post and was either killed or forced to commit suicide in 1144.[112] Hung Hao, who had been sent to the Chin in 1129, was only released by an edict of the Chin emperor in 1142 after a new treaty with Sung had been signed.[113] The prolonged involuntary sojourn of Hung Hao (1088–1155) in the North resulted in several monographs on the Chin which contain much valuable information, above all his *Sung-mo chi-wen*.[114] It must have been a very slight consolation for the unfortunate captives to learn that the Sung government had in 1132 sanctioned the continued payment of their salaries to their families.[115] The issue was still alive in 1159 when someone complained that sons or grandsons of envoys who had not returned did not receive their compensation. A benevolent decision on such cases was urged, and in 1161 another edict to the same effect was issued.[116]

Another more natural risk was death or illness during a mission. The government in whose territory the death had occurred contributed to the funeral expenses. In 1092 the Liao government, for example, gave 300 ounces of silver for coffins and funeral garments when the deputy of a Sung envoy died in the North.[117] In the same year, by sheer coincidence, a Liao envoy died in Sung territory, and the Sung government followed the example of the Liao by providing financial assistance for the funeral.[118]

Under the Southern Sung, a deputy envoy died during his mission in 1167 on his way home. He was promoted posthumously, and his only son was promoted to a higher rank in recognition of his father's merits.[119] Cases of illness are repeatedly reported in the sources. In 1200 the deputy envoy announcing the death of the Sung emperor Kuang-tsung to the Chin fell ill on his way to the border. The prefect of a Sung border town was instructed to send a government physician to care for the envoy before he crossed the border into Chin territory. At the same time an official was appointed who would take the envoy's place if his health did not improve.[120] But he recovered in time, for the Chin History mentions him as a member of the embassy.[121]

Another risk was the ever-present possibility of disciplinary action if an envoy did not abide by one of the numerous Sung regulations. In 1097, for example, a military escort of the lower rank misbehaved in K'ai-feng by starting a fight and was severely punished.[122] Three years later, a fine was imposed on envoys who had not duly taken notice of the death of Emperor Che-tsung when they returned to the border.[123] In the following year, several Sung envoys were demoted by two ranks because they had not ensured that their underlings were properly dressed.[124] In other cases, accusations against embassy personnel were less specific. Degradation was decreed for "disgracing the mandate" (1106) or for "not observing the statutes" (1117) or for arrogant and negligent behavior during the mission (1122).[125] Such disciplinary actions against Sung envoys were paralleled by cases where foreign envoys misbehaved in Sung territory and thus caused trouble.

The journeys which the Sung envoys made were not pleasure trips. Their diaries occasionally contain graphic descriptions of the hardships of traveling by carriage and boat. When Chou Hui went to Peking in 1176, the Chin authorities provided four luxury carriages for the envoys and their escorts. They were beautiful to look at and adorned with two lanterns made of gauze. Each was drawn by fifteen donkeys and accompanied by five or six grooms. Yet these carriages were not comfortable; Chou tells us that the travelers were constantly tossed about and that it was like riding in a boat on high waves. An additional hardship on his journey resulted from the Chin's thoughtfulness. The Chin had commissioned a band of Tibetan flute-players whose melancholy and dreary music wafted over the embassy day and night.[126] A particular problem for a Chinese who, like Chou Hui, came from a milder climate was the biting cold in the North. The embassies presenting New Year congratulations to the Liao and Chin courts traveled during the coldest months. Chou Hui later complained that his ears froze and almost fell off. He tried to protect his ears as much as possible and even tells us what to do if an ear really freezes. He warns against exposing it to warmth too quickly and says it should be warmed only gradually. He consoles himself with the thought that north of Peking the winter cold is even worse than the plains of northern China which he had to cross.[127] Other envoys furnished themselves with such warm clothing as felt caps and wadded robes.[128]

Unfamiliar food, together with the endless rounds of wine, contributed to the discomfort of the Sung travelers. The northern "barbarian" food is frequently described as ranging from mediocre to bad. Hsü K'ang-tsung found the food served to him by his Jurchen hosts disgusting and inedible.

He particularly disliked hearts, intestines, and leek boiled in a sort of soup, which was eaten out of wooden bowls.[129] Hsü found the food a little better when his host was a Grand Preceptor of the Chin and a very cultured man of Po-hai ancestry who had visited Sung China as an envoy in 1123.[130] Chou Hui complained that the wine served by his Chin hosts was dreadful. He also tells us that a favorite dish of the "barbarians" was cakes made of flour and honey and fried in oil. The meat served was formed into various shapes, such as rolls, rings, balls, and dumplings. Other dishes which Chou endured were breads, a blood soup, boiled mutton, a rice broth, and a soup with shredded meat and noodles. His breakfast consisted of little cakes swimming in lung fat, jujube pastry, and a gruel made of flour.[131] A detailed description of the meals served at the imperial banquets in Peking may be found in Lou Yüeh's diary.[132] Lou was happy, however, when he could buy fresh perch from the Yellow River on his way to Peking. He notes that this was the first time on his travels that he had had good food.[133] Hsü Ching found Korean tea almost unpalatable because it was so bitter. The food provided for his embassy by the local Korean authorities consisted mostly of noodle dishes.[134] A humorous incident concerning Khitan food customs is reported by Chang Shun-min. He reports, with some displeasure, that the Liao envoys who came to the New Year and imperial birthday audiences were given 1,500 ounces of silver, but that the Sung envoys to the Liao were presented with a gift of ten sheep and ten steppe-marmots. He did not know what to do with them and set them free. The Khitan hostel attendant was dismayed and told Chang that the marmots were valuable presents. The attendant feared a reprimand if the court learned that the Sung envoy had not received his present.[135]

The Sung travelers always had to drink with their hosts.[136] The hardest drinkers seem to have been the Mongols. They were pleased when their guests got drunk, clamored loudly, vomited, and finally fell to the floor in a stupor. "If our guests get drunk, they are of one heart with us and no longer different." When the Sung envoys took leave, Mukhali instructed their escorts: "In all good towns you should stay several days. If there is good wine, give it them to drink, and if there is good food, give it them to eat. Good flutes and good drums should be played and beaten."[137] This kind of good-natured but coarse hospitality might not have been popular among highly refined Sung officials.

Did the hospitality provided for Sung envoys include the services of young women? The Jurchens practiced the custom of guest prostitution vis-à-vis the Liao envoys traveling in their country. They lodged the envoys with families with unmarried girls who waited on them.[138] Some Sung envoys found in their hostels, in addition to food and drink, female companionship. The Sung diaries are silent on this particular point. But when Chou Hui's embassy entered the prefectural town of Kuei-te in

Honan province, they were met not only by the local dignitaries but also by courtesans (*chi*, sing-song girls).[139] We can only speculate whether these girls amused the Sung guests just with music or with other skills as well.

Among the few amenities of traveling, extensive sightseeing should be mentioned, both in Sung territory and beyond. The diaries reveal that the authors visited places of historical or antiquarian interest, particularly in northern China. But the local population through whose districts the huge caravans passed—those both of the Sung and of foreign states—was always faced with extravagant demands by the government authorities. In 1145 the court acted to prevent such abuses. It issued regulations to the local governments meant to curb demands on the people in the prefectures between the capital and the border.[140] The embassy personnel sometimes behaved arrogantly and were censured.[141] The hardships for the local people consisted chiefly in the conscription of local labor for transport and other services. When an embassy in 1191 crossed the Yangtze River, an auxiliary corvée force of 2,000 men was mobilized. The court, believing such recruitment to be excessive, decreed that in the future only 1,000 men should be conscripted, 800 for the escort personnel and their needs, and 200 to provide for the official banquets.[142] No more than the statutory number of carts and horses should be requisitioned.[143] Similar services were exacted from the population in the northern states as well, and we would certainly find many complaints on the hardships endured by the people if we had a source like the *Sung Hui-yao* for the Liao or the Chin.

Envoys as Spies

As a rule, embassies, after their return, offered reports on what they had heard and seen, on the customs of foreign lands and their resources, and on foreign rituals. It seems likely that they were also to offer intelligence information. This included personality profiles of the foreign dignitaries with whom they dealt. Thus Hsü Ching records not only the names and titles of the Korean officials whom he met but also their backgrounds and personalities.[144] He seems to have been favorably impressed by the education of his hosts.

Military information was essential for the Sung in case peaceful relations were replaced by political and military disturbances. Indeed, much of the data in the existing diaries were intended to provide information useful for the military. To this category belong above all the detailed itineraries with exact distances between the major places and the geographical descriptions of the countries themselves. Knowledge of the road system was necessary if a Sung army should ever try to advance into foreign territory. The state of repair of fortifications and the defense facilities of the towns were of interest for the Sung military. The importance of information on the land north of the border was enhanced by the hardly concealed hope that one day the lost territories might be regained by the Sung. We find this expressed in the postscript to Lu Chen's report. He asserted that the lands south of the passes were all former Chinese (Han and T'ang) territory which might in the future be returned by the Liao to the Sung.[145] In 1125 Hsü K'ang-tsung carefully noted the fortifications of the towns which he had passed on his way, the locations of watchtowers, the height of the walls, and the position of gates.[146] Another author reported, for example, that the garrison of the Eastern capital of Chin consisted of 21 ch'ien-hu (chiliarchs), each with 300 to 400 men, totaling 8,000 soldiers. The garrison of Kung prefecture consisted of only 3 chiliarchs, with 1,200 soldiers.[147] Also, Chou Hui's diary yielded items of military importance. He crossed the Yellow River on a floating bridge which consisted of eighty-five boats, each of which was 17 feet long and about 10 feet distant from the next boat. He described the technical details of the construction and added that the bridge would be extremely useful should the Sung ever reconquer the North.[148] Such remarks show that despite the peaceful relations sanctioned by treaty there existed much latent revanchism among Sung officials.

Such reports as the Kao-li t'u-ching and the Meng-ta pei-lu devoted special chapters to the foreign armies, their equipment, and their training. It is not surprising, then, that foreign states became conscious of their security. The Chin, for example, for a time prohibited its Chinese subjects from talking to Sung envoys. This regulation was abolished before 1170, perhaps because it could not be adequately enforced.[149] Sung envoys, nevertheless, had numerous opportunities to talk to the native Chinese population in the towns through which they passed, and conversations with local people are repeatedly recorded in their diaries. Such contacts enabled the envoys to gather information on the domestic situation in the Northern states. Even political gossip was sometimes recorded if it was thought to be useful. Lou Yüeh reports that the Prince of Yüeh, the eldest son of Chin Shih-tsung, was enraged that his younger brother, not he, had been appointed as heir apparent. He was given ten servant-girls (concubines), but he refused to accept them and said that even if a child would be born to him one day it would be of no use. When the Mongols invaded the border regions, the prince was entrusted with the defense, but he was unable to restore peace and had to withdraw.[150] The eldest son of Shih-tsung thus is represented as deeply disillusioned, and indeed he was later killed because of an alleged plot against his nephew, the emperor Chang-tsung.[151]

Observations on the internal stability of the Northern states are also found in these diaries. Fan Ch'eng-ta wrote about the Chin construction projects in Peking.[152] Eight hundred thousand civilians and 400,000 soldiers were mobilized, and Fan learned that many had died in the course of their labor service.[153] Chou Hui also cited the figure of 1,200,000 workers, and he too mentioned the large number of casualties during the construction work. He added that the "blood and sweat" of the people were misused for the reconstruction of the capital, though he conceded that the palace buildings were imposing.[154] Dissatisfaction with the Chin regime is thus indirectly reported. Travel through K'ai-feng, the former Sung capital, saddened the Sung envoys. They repeatedly deplored the decay of the former Sung palaces. Chou Hui, after his visit to K'ai-feng, expressed his hope that the Sung would one day reconquer the lost Central Plains and regretted that he was too old to see the day of liberation.[155] Here again is an example of the revanchist attitude of many Sung literati and officials.

The role of embassies in collecting information was also reflected in the security measures which the Sung adopted for foreign embassies. The Liao and Chin envoys naturally tried to obtain military and political information while traveling in Sung territory. In 1015 a Sung edict prohibited unauthorized talk with Liao envoys and their personnel and forbade drinking and joking with the foreigners, even when Sung officials were seeking information about the Liao state.[156] If Sung interpreters or other personnel traded privately with Liao embassy people and inadvertently divulged state secrets, they were to be punished according to martial law.[157] When the Sung fought a war against the Hsi Hsia in 1081–1082, spies informed the Chinese dynasty that a Khitan official, as deputy envoy, would try to elicit information about the situation at the northwestern border. To prevent such leaks, the Military Bureau, as the highest agency for national security, determined which Chinese officials would come into contact with the Khitan envoy and that written guidelines would be handed to the Chinese hostel attendants.[158] The concern about possible leaks in the security system and the role of foreign envoys as potential spies appears also in a memorial written by Su Shih in 1089. He feared that Korean envoys might "chart and sketch our mountains and rivers and buy books" and then pass this information to their Khitan overlords.[159] The role of books to which Su Shih alludes was interesting. He was concerned lest the "barbarians" should learn too much about Chinese statecraft. Thus the Koreans were prevented until 1101 from buying the *T'ai-p'ing yü-lan*, an encyclopedia, which certainly cannot be regarded as a military work, but which offered some insight into Chinese political history.[160] In sum, it is clear that espionage and intelligence work were, for both sides, an integral part of the diplomatic game.

Some General Conclusions

The general characteristics of Sung diplomacy, in particular the ritual and ceremonial aspects, derive from a much earlier period in Chinese history. The formative period was that of the Spring and Autumn and Warring States (ca. 800–200 B.C.), which saw "the emergence of many of the concomitants of a multistate system, including a rudimentary science of international politics."[161] The various contending states of that era had already exchanged embassies and had devised elaborate ceremonies. One whole sub-chapter entitled "Audiences" (ch'ao-shih) in the ritual compilation *Tai-Tai li-chi* is devoted to the ceremonies at court receptions for the king and the nobility.[162] This sub-chapter describes many practices which are later also found in the Sung. Each year the states sent envoys to inquire about neighboring lands. Embassies were dispatched to elicit intelligence, to announce auspicious events, and to offer congratulations. As in Sung times, the host country was responsible for lodging and feeding the envoys. When the envoys arrived in the outskirts of a town, they were met by commissioners with refreshments. The guests were entitled to at least one festive banquet and two normal banquets, in addition to a multitude of minor celebrations. In the hostels, the foreign envoys received food, meat, grain, hay, and wood for fuel. The archery contests, which were a standard feature of diplomatic receptions under the Sung, derive from this time.

The *I-li* offers more details about the ceremonies regulating the missions of the lords, starting with the appointment of envoys and the preparation of presents.[163] Numerous specific instructions are given for the proper gifts and presents, those for the host state and its dignitaries and those for the envoys to compensate them for their efforts. Silk was a standard gift. Guests received both slaughtered and live animals (sheep, in particular), which is reminiscent of the Khitan presents of sheep and marmots to Sung envoys.[164] The rules of mourning were similar to those of the Sung. If an envoy died, the host state provided the coffin and shroud for the corpse. As in the Sung, envoys rehearsed the proper ceremonies before they entered another state.[165] In 1169 a Sung embassy to the Chin specifically arranged a dress rehearsal of their ceremonies in a border town before it crossed the Huai River into the Chin state.[166]

Gifts were always an integral and important part of diplomacy. The lavishness of the presents depended upon the relative status of the diplomatic partners. Equal status demanded equal gifts. States of relatively equal status vied with each other in the extravagance of the presents they gave to foreign envoys. Lavish presents were a way of enhancing national prestige. In archaic times and in so-called primitive societies, the exchange of gifts sometimes assumed the form of a contest where the partners tried to surpass each other.[167] The detailed regulations of the Chinese Warring States period may be seen as a more advanced stage of development. Boundless exchange had been replaced by ritually determined differentiation. The notion of exchanging presents is interrelated with the idea of hospitality.

No visit without an exchange of presents: this has been traditional in the Far East until modern times, and it was certainly true when envoys paid formal visits in a foreign state or when they were visited by officials in their hostel. The presents given to the envoys were not meant for trade. It is not easy to imagine a Sung envoy selling the garments and belts which he had been given in the North in China.[168]

From earliest times in Chinese history, therefore, we notice the all-pervading importance of rituals. Propriety (*li*) governed the exchange of embassies. But the rules of propriety could only be effective if both sides "knew the rites." Common recognition of the rules and equality of status was required. The partner had to be a state (*kuo*) with institutions that paralleled those of the Sung. It made no difference if the other state had a tributary status under a more or less hypothetical Sung suzerainty (e.g., Annam, Hsi Hsia, or Koryŏ) or if it was a fully independent imperial state recognized as such by the Sung (e.g., Liao and Chin). With the latter, the relative status of the partners was expressed in pseudo-familial relationships sanctioned by treaties. The Sung, the Liao, and the Chin were partners in a bilateral, balanced power system, although the Sung may have perceived this as a temporary and politically expedient arrangement. Direct control of the other states was out of the question.[169] Thus the bilateral relations with Liao and Chin, and the multilateral relations with Annam, Hsi Hsia, and Koryŏ provided for a diplomacy that was modeled on patterns inherited from antiquity, and which created a carefully if precariously balanced Chinese world order.

NOTES

1. Nieh Ch'ung-ch'i, "Sung-Liao chiao-p'ing k'ao," *Yen-ching hsüeh-pao* 27 (1940): 1–51; Fu Lo-huan, "Sung-jen shih-Liao yü-lu hsing-ch'eng k'ao," *Kuo-hsüeh chi-k'an* 5, 4 (1935): 165–194, and "Sung-Liao p'ing-shih piao-kao," *Bulletin of the Institute of History and Philology, Academia Sinica* 14 (1949): 57–136; Chang Liang-ts'ai, *Pu Liao-shih chiao-p'ing piao* (Peking, 1958). The data on Sung-Liao relations contained in the *Hsü Tzu-chih t'ung-chien ch'ang-pien* of Li T'ao have been conveniently assembled by T'ao Chin-sheng and Wang Min-hsin in *Li T'ao Hsü Tzu-chih t'ung-chien ch'ang-pien Sung-Liao kuan-hsi shih-liao chi-lu*, 3 vols. (Taipei, 1974). For more relevant literature, see chapter 3 in this volume.

2. Édouard Chavannes has translated into French the following itineraries and diaries of Sung envoys: Hu Ch'iao, *Hsien-lu chi*, "Voyageurs chinois chez les Khitan et les Joutchen," *Journal Asiatique* (hereafter *JA*) (1897), pp. 390–411; Wang Ts'eng, *Wang I-kung hsing-ch'eng lu*, *JA* (1897), pp. 412–419; Fu Pi, *Fu Cheng-kung hsing-ch'eng lu*, *JA* (1897), pp. 430–436; Sung Shou's relation, *JA* (1897), pp. 437–442; Hsü K'ang-tsung's itinerary, *JA* (1898), pp. 361–439; Chou Hui, "Pei Yüan

Lou. Récit d'un voyage dans le Nord. Écrit sous les Song par Tcheou Chan," *T'oung Pao* (hereafter *TP*) 5 (1904): 163–192. Lu Chen's *Ch'eng-yao lu* has been translated by Joseph Mullie, "Tch'eng Yao lou. Relation de Voyage de Lou Tchen," *Geografiska Annaler* 17 (Stockholm, 1935): 413–433. The itinerary of Ch'en Hsiang has been the subject of study by Barry Till, "A Sung Embassy to the Liao Nation (1067)," *Canada-Mongolia Review* 1, 1 (1975): 57–66.

3. On this work, see also Inaba Iwakichi, "Kōri zukei wo yomishite," *Ichimura Hakase kohi kinen tōyōshi ronsō* (Tokyo, 1933), pp. 149–168. The book was originally illustrated, but by the twelfth century the pictures were lost.

4. The book has been attributed to Meng Kung (1195–1246), a famous Sung general, but it has been shown that he was not the author (see Charles A. Peterson in Herbert Franke, ed., *Sung Biographies* [hereafter *SB*], Wiesbaden, 1976, p. 786). It was probably written by Chao Kung, who is otherwise unknown. It has been translated into Russian and annotated by N. Ts. Munkuev, *Men-da bei-lu "Polnoe Opisanie Mongolo-Tatar"* (Moscow, 1975). This work contains also a facsimile of the original Chinese text with Wang Kuo-wei's annotations.

5. Su Ch'e, *Luan-ch'eng chi* (Ssu-pu ts'ung-k'an ed.), ch. 16, 11b–16b. The poem which Su composed on a chieftain of the Hsi tribe has been translated in Karl Wittfogel and Feng Chia-sheng, *History of Chinese Society—Liao, 907–1125* (Philadelphia, 1949), p. 220. Interesting political reports and memoranda on the Liao by Su Ch'e are in *Luan-ch'eng chi*, ch. 41, 10b–16a. On Su Ch'e, see also Yoshinobu Shiba in *SB*, pp. 882–885.

6. Fan Ch'eng-ta, *Shih-hu chü-shih shih-chi* (Ssu-pu ts'ung-kan ed.), ch. 12. On Fan Ch'eng-ta, see Sadao Aoyama in *SB*, pp. 308–309.

7. On tribute missions to the Sung court and the regulations for their reception and traveling, see Werner Eichhorn, "Bestimmungen für Tributgesandtschaften zur Sung-Zeit," *Zeitschrift der Deutschen Morgenländischen Gesellschaft* 114 (1964): 382–390. The same author has also given an account of audiences at the Sung court, "Notiz betreffend Audienzen am Sung-Hofe," ibid. 108 (1958): 164–169. On risks and hardships suffered by Sung envoys, see Herbert Franke, "Einige Bemerkungen zu Gesandschaftsreisen in der Sung-Zeit," *Nachrichten der Gesellschaft für Natur- und Völkerkunde Ostasiens* 125 (1979): 20–26.

8. *Sung Hui-yao chi-kao* (hereafter *SHY*), Peking, 1957, ed., 3561/I. On titles of Liao rulers, see also Wittfogel and Feng, op. cit., p. 354, n. 44.

9. *Meng-ta pei-lu* (hereafter *MTPL*), in Wang Kuo-wei (ed.), *Wang Kuan-t'ang ch'üan-chi* (Taipei, 1968), 4a, trans. Munkuev, op. cit., pp. 50–52, notes pp. 121–125.

10. Almut Netolitzky, *Das Ling-wai tai-ta von Chou Ch'ü fei. Eine Landeskunde Südchinas aus dem 12. Jahrhundert* (Wiesbaden, 1977), p. 30.

11. Chou Hui, *Ch'ing-po tsa-chih* (hereafter *CPTC*), Shanghai, n.d., ch. 6, 3a–3b.

12. The embassy referred to by Chou Hui was that of Liu Huan (1000–1080) in 1038 (T'o T'o et al., *Sung shih*, Po-na ed. (hereafter *SS*), ch. 492, 13b. A list of embassies exchanged between Sung and the Tibetan states is included in Liao Lung-sheng, "Pei Sung tui T'u-fan te cheng-ts'e," *Sung-shih yen-chiu*, vol. 10 (Taipei, 1978), pp. 119–123.

13. This address is also recorded in *SS*, ch. 490, 7b. In the *SHY* we do not find a Khotanese embassy for the year 1081, only one for 1080 (*SHY*, 7721/II).

14. *MTPL*, 13b. Munkuev op. cit., pp. 78–79, with notes pp. 189–190.

15. See the literature quoted in n. 1 above. A good survey is given by Christian Schwarz-Schilling, *Der Friede von Shan-yüan (1005 n. Chr.). Ein Beitrag zur Geschichte der chinesischen Diplomatie* (Wiesbaden, 1959), pp. 78–94. On types of embassies, see pp. 79–80.

16. For references, see Schwarz-Schilling, op. cit., pp. 88, n. 51.

17. On pre-Chin relations between the Jurchen and the Sung, see Herbert Franke, "Chinese Texts on the Jurchen," *Zentralasiatische Studien* 9 (1975), Appendix I, "Early Sung-Jurchen Relations," pp. 167–171.

18. This was on the ninth day of the fifth month in 1127; see *SHY*, 3540/II–3541/I, and also 3560/II.

19. *SS*, ch. 165, 5b–6a. The *SHY* does not have a special chapter on the *hung-lu ssu*.

20. On the *Kuo-hsin so*, see also the entries in *SHY*, 3087/I–3107/I.

21. See also the brief entries in *SHY*, 7479/I.

22. There are a few entries on the *li-pin yüan* in *SHY*, 2917/I–II.

23. *SHY*, 7479/II has two brief entries dated 1006 and 1075 on the *Hui-yüan i.*

24. Tsung-ko is a Chinese rendering of the Tibetan name Cong-kha or Cong-ka, the region east of the Kuku Nor. See Rolf Stein, *Recherches sur l'épopée et le barde au Tibet* (Paris, 1959), pp. 230–231 and passim.

25. Sung Shou, *Sung ta chao-ling chi* (Peking, 1962), chapters 228–232. These chapters are also reprinted in facsimile in the *Liao-shih hui-pien*, vol. 6 (Taipei, 1973), sec. 58, pp. 1–28.

26. The diplomatic handbook by Su Sung discussed below (see notes 28–35) distinguishes for Sung-Liao relations oath-letters (*shih-shu*) state-letters (*Kuo-shu*) and state-credentials (*Kuo-hsin*). The latter accompanied gifts to the Liao, which served to improve relations, such as the annual payments, whereas the term *Kuo-shu* seems to apply to matters entrusted to routine embassies.

27. For a discussion of epistolary formulae in Sung diplomacy, see Dagmar Thiele, *Der Abschluss eines Vertrages: Diplomatie zwischen Sung-und-Chin Dynastie 1117–1123* (Wiesbaden, 1971), pp. 146–152. An analysis of state-letters exchanged between Sung and Chin is also given in Herbert Franke, "Treaties between Sung and Chin," *Études Song in Memoriam Étienne Balázs*, edited by Françoise Aubin, Sér. I, 1, *Histoire et Institutions* (Paris: La Haye, 1970), pp. 55–84.

28. *SHY*, 3537/I, where, however, the title is given as *Hua-i Lu-Wei lu* instead of *Hua-jung Lu-Wei lu*. The expression Lu-Wei goes back to *Lun-yü* XIII, 7, "The governments of Lu and Wei are brothers." On Su Sung, see also S. Miyashita in *SB*, pp. 969–970.

29. *SHY*, 3556/I.

30. *Su Wei-kung wen-chi* in *Ssu-k'u ch'üan-shu chen-pen IV chi* (Taipei, n.d.), ch. 66, 1a–5a. The compilation of this work is also mentioned in Su's biography. See *SS*, ch. 340, 28b–29a.

31. *Su Wei-kung wen-chi*, ch. 66, 4b.

32. D. Thiele, *Der Abschluss eines Vertrages*, p. 145.

33. *SHY*, 3536/II (edict of 1039). See also, on the recruitment of envoys, Christian Schwarz-Schilling, *Der Friede von Shan-yüan*, p. 82 and n. 53.

34. *SHY*, 3444/II.

35. *SHY*, 3545/II.

36. *SHY*, 3554/I (1189). This edict was repeated in 1198. *SHY*, 3556/II–3557/I.

37. *SHY*, 3557/I/I (1199).

38. *SHY*, 3541/II.

39. *SHY*, 3553/II.

40. See, for example, *SHY*, 3544/I–II (1146).

41. *SHY*, 3545/II–3546/I.

42. *Luan-ch'eng chi*, ch. 41, 15b.

43. *SHY*, 3539/I.

44. *SHY*, 3542/II.

45. *Ch'ing-yüan t'iao-fa shih-lei* (hereafter *CYTFSL*) (Tokyo, 1968), ch. 5, 38/I.

46. Loc. cit.

47. *SHY*, 3541/II–3542/I.

48. *SHY*, 3542/I–II.

49. *SHY*, 3544/II.

50. *CYTFSL*, ch. 5, 35/I.

51. Ibid., 26/II–38/II.

52. Wittfogel and Feng, op. cit., p. 358, n. 60. For a detailed study of government agencies concerned with foreigners, see Paul Pelliot, "Le Hōja et le Sayyid Ḥusain de l'Histoire des Ming," *TP* 38 (1947): 207–224.

53. Chang Shun-min, *Hua-man lu* (hereafter *HML*) (Taipei, n.d.), 4b.

54. T'o T'o et al., *Liao shih (hereafter LS*), Po-na ed., 47, 13a. Wittfogel and Feng, op. cit., p. 487, translates the name of the office as "Hall of State Ceremonial."

55. *LS*, ch. 47, 11a; Wittfogel and Feng, pp. 445 and 486.

56. *LS*, ch. 50, 5b.

57. T'o T'o et al., *Chih shih* (hereafter *CS*), Po-na ed., 56, 3b.

58. Loc. cit.

59. *CS*, 38, 13b–14b.

60. Lou Yüeh, *Pei-hsing jih-lu* (hereafter *PHJL*), in *Pai-pu ts'ung -shu chi-ch'eng* (Taipei, n.d.), 33a. For a graphic description of the envoys' hostel in the Chin Supreme Capital in Manchuria, see Hsü K'ang-tsung, *Hsüan-ho i-ssu feng-shih hsing-ch'eng lu* (hereafter *HKT*), in *San-chao pei-meng hui-pien* (Taipei, 1962), translated in *JA* (1898), pp. 427–428. The hostel had 300 rooms, built like tents—that is, the walls were hung with draperies. The Sung envoys slept on *k'ang* brick-beds, covered with a thick carpet, some silk, furs, and huge pillows. The hostel was over twelve *li* from the imperial palaces.

61. *Shih-hu chü-shih shih-chi*, 12, 10b.

62. *CS*, ch. 38, 14a-b. This passage comes from a chapter dealing with the reception of envoys from Hsi Hsia, but we may safely assume that the same regulations also applied to the Sung envoys.

63. *Koryŏ-sa* (hereafter *KRS*) (Seoul, 1972 ed.), 76, 19a.

64. *KRS*, 65, 1a ff.

65. *KRS*, 76, 46b–47a. The translator's office was later renamed *sayŏk wŏn*.

66. Hsü Ching, *Hsüan-ho feng-shih Kao-li t'u-ching* (hereafter *KLTC*), in *Pai-pu ts'ung-shu chi-ch'eng* (Taipei, n.d.), 27, 1a–6a.

67. For a fundamental discussion of relations between Sung and Koryŏ, see Michael C. Rogers, "Sung-Koryŏ Relations: Some Inhibiting Factors," *Oriens* 11 (1958): 194–202.

68. Sung Lien et al., *Yüan shih* (hereafter *YS*), Po-na ed., 15, 12b.

69. *YS*, 85, 25b.

70. *YS*, 85, 7a.

71. *CYTFSL*, ch. 5, 35/II. This statute applied also to messengers traveling within Sung territory, not only to diplomatic envoys. For a study of the Sung postal system, see Peter H. Golas, "The Courier-Transport System of the Northern Sung," *Harvard University Papers on China* 20 (1966): 1–22.

72. *HKT*, trans. E. Chavannes, *JA* (1898), p. 376.

73. *PHJL*, passim. The day of departure for the envoys who traveled to the New Year audience in Peking was fixed for the ninth day of the eleventh month of each year in 1179 (*SHY*, 3561/II).

74. Lu Chen, *Ch'eng-yao lu* (hereafter *CYL*), in *Pai-pu ts'ung-shu chi-ch'eng* (Taipei, 1965).

75. Hung Hao, *Sung-mo chi-wen, hsü* (Yü-chang ts'ung-shu ed.), 7b.

76. On Liao food, see also Wittfogel and Feng, op. cit., p. 255, n. 40. Food served to Sung envoys by the Chin is described in *PHJL, shang* 18a-b, and in Chou Hui, *Pei-yüan lu* (hereafter *PYL*), in *Shuo-fu* (Taipei, 1963), trans. E. Chavannes in *TP* 5 (1904): 167–168.

77. For the Liao, see *HML*, 4b; for the Chin, *PYL*, trans. E. Chavannes in *TP* 5 (1904): 167.

78. *CS*, 38, 2a–3a. The Chin history describes the "minor" banquets but not the "flowery" banquets.

79. *HKT*, trans. E. Chavannes, *JA* (1898), p. 435.

80. *PHJL, hsia* 3b.

81. According to *PHJL, shang* 35b, the ceremonials at the Chin court had been introduced chiefly by Ching Ssu-hui, who had himself been an envoy to Sung (in 1156, *CS*, 60, 27b) and who imitated the Sung regulations. Ching, who died in 1170, has a biography in *CS*, 91, 16b–17b.

82. *CS*, 38, 5b–14b describes the treatment of envoys from Hsi Hsia at the Chin court.

83. *CS*, 38, 3a.

84. *HKT*, trans. E. Chavannes, *JA* (1898), pp. 435–436. The archery contest is also mentioned in *PHJL, hsia* 4b.

85. *MTPL*, 15a-b; Munkuev, op. cit., p. 82.

86. The title of the painting is *Ch'i-tan-shih ch'ao-p'ing* and depicts an audience held in 1005. It is reproduced in *Arts of China. Painting 1* (Taipei, 1955).

87. *CPTC*, 12, 3a.

88. *PHJL, shang* 35a.

89. *HKT*, trans. E. Chavannes, *JA* (1898), p. 375.

90. *CPTC*, 6, 5b.

91. *SHY*, 3563/I–II.

92. *HML*, 20a-b.

93. *CPTC*, 4, 3a.

94. *CS*, 38, 14b.

95. The presents in kind were converted into gifts of silver, totaling 5,390 ounces; *SHY*, 3553/II–3554/I (1189).

96. *PYL*, trans. E. Chavannes, *TP* 5 (1904): 191.

97. *CYTFSL*, 5, 34/I.

98. Edict of 1148; *SHY*, 3544/II.

99. *PYL*, trans. E. Chavannes, *TP* 5 (1904): 177.

100. On the prohibitions against export of coins, see Yang Lien-sheng, *Money and Credit in China: A Short History* (Cambridge, Mass., 1971 ed.), p. 38.

101. *SHY*, 3556/I–II.

102. *SHY*, 3552/II–3553/I.

103. *SHY*, 3556/II. For other incidents concerning proper dress, see *SS*, 316, 6a; 318, 17b–18a; 333, 4a.

104. *SS*, 331, 20b. For another case in 1027 when the Sung insisted successfully on proper seating arrangements for the Liao envoys at their own court, see *SS*, 288, 5b.

105. *SS*, 318, 11b.

106. P'u-wang (995–1059) was the father of emperor Ying-tsung. On his biography, see M. Chikusa in *SB*, pp. 843–845.

107. The Jurchen envoy's name was Wan-yen Yüan-i. He had been an envoy to the Sung in 1150 (*CS*, 60, 22b). The document referring to this case in *SHY*, 3561/I is dated 1174.

108. *SHY*, 3564/I.

109. *SHY*, 3555/I.

110. *CS*, 82, 18a.

111. T'eng Mao-shih and his fate are the subject of a monograph by Sung Lien (1310–1381); see F. W. Mote in L. C. Goodrich and Fang Chaoying (eds.), *Dictionary of Ming Biography* (New York, 1976) p. 1230. T'eng is not mentioned in the *CS*. His posthumous promotion is recorded in *SS*, 27, 2a.

112. On Wang Lun, see Herbert Franke in *SB*, pp. 1124–1128.

113. *CS*, 4, 9a.

114. On Hung Hao's biography, see Chang Fu-jui in *SB*, pp. 464–465.

115. *SHY*, 3541/I–II.

116. *SHY*, 3546/I and 3546/II.

117. Wittfogel and Feng, op. cit., p. 303, n. 26.

118. *SHY*, 3538/II.

119. *SHY*, 3548/I. The envoy mentioned in *SHY* is also listed in the chronology of embassies in the Chin History, *CS*, 61, 8b.

120. *SHY*, 3557/II.

121. *CS*, 62, 13a.

122. *SHY*, 3539/I.

123. *SHY*, 3540/I.

124. Loc. cit.

125. For all three cases, see *SHY*, 3540/II.

126. *PYL*, trans. E. Chavannes, *TP* 5 (1904): 169.

127. *CPTC*, 5, 2b. Chou Hui also reports that the weather in the middle and last decades of the third month in North China had been unbearably hot and dusty (*CPTC*, 3, 2a).

128. Fan Ch'eng-ta, *Ts'an-luan lu* in *Shou-fu* (Taipei, 1963), 41, 4b.

129. *HKT*, trans. E. Chavannes, *JA* (1898), pp. 295–396. On Jurchen food, see also Herbert Franke, "Chinese Texts on the Jurchen," p. 132, and Appendix II, "Jurchen Food Recipes," pp. 172–177.

130. *HKT*, trans. E. Chavannes, *JA* (1898), p. 423. On Li Ching, see *CS*, 60, 6b, and also Hung Hao, *Sung-mo chi-wen*, Yü-chang ts'ung-shu ed., 6a–6b.

131. *PYL*, trans. E. Chavannes, *TP* 5 (1904): 167–168, 177. Honey-cakes fried in oil are repeatedly mentioned as a favorite Northern dish; see e.g., *Sung-mo chi-wen*, 12b.

132. *PHJL*, *shang* 18b–19a.

133. *PHJL*, *shang* 22a.

134. *KLTC*, ch 33, 2b.

135. *HML*, 24a–24b. The steppe people used to catch the "yellow rats" (*huang-shu*) for food and sell them at meat markets.

136. On wine-drinking among the Jurchens and in the Chin state, see Herbert Franke, "A Note on Wine," *Zentralasiatische Studien* 8 (1974): 241–246; also 9 (1975): 129.

137. *MTPL*, 15a-b; Munkuev, op. cit., pp. 82–83.

138. *Sung-mo chi-wen*, 8b–9a; Wittfogel and Feng, op. cit., p. 370, n. 18.

139. *PYL*, trans. E. Chavannes, *TP* 5 (1904): 174.

140. *SHY*, 3544/I.

141. This happened in 1155; *SHY*, 3545/I.

142. *SHY*, 3555/I.

143. *SHY*, 3560/I (1160). For a complaint made in 1199, see also *SHY*, 3557/II.

144. *KLTC*, 8, 3b–5a.

145. *CYL*, 4b–5a, trans. J. Mullie, *Geografiska Annaler* 17 (1935).

146. *HKT*, passim, esp. p. 392. On the fortifications of K'ai-feng, see *PHJL*, *shang* 17b.

147. *PHJL*, *hsia* 8b.

148. *PHJL*, trans. E. Chavannes, *TP* 5 (1904): 177.

149. *PYL*, *shang* 15a.

150. *PHJL*, *hsia* 8b.

151. On Shih-tsung's eldest son, Wan-yen Yün-chung, see, *CS*, 85, 1b–4b. On Wan-yen Yün-kung (1146–1185), who had been appointed as heir apparent but who died before his father, see *CS*, 19, 3b–10b. He was the father of the emperors Chang-tsung and Hsüan-tsung.

152. K'ung Yen-chou (1107–1161) was a former Sung soldier who reached high offices under the Chin; see *CS*, 79, 3b–4b. His biography does not mention, however, that he devised the construction of the imperial palaces in Peking under Hai-ling.

153. Fan Ch'eng-ta, *Lan-p'ei lu*, in *Ts'ung-shu chi-ch'eng* (Shanghai, 1936).

154. *PYL*, trans. E. Chavannes, *TP* 5 (1904): 189–190.

155. *CPTC*, 3, 2a.

156. *SHY*, 3088/II.

157. *SHY*, 3090/II.

158. *SHY*, 3537/II.

159. Michael C. Rogers, "Sung-Koryŏ Relations," *Oriens* 11 (1958): 198.

160. Ibid., p. 201.

161. Benjamin I. Schwartz, "The Chinese Perception of World Order, Past and Present," in John K. Fairbank (ed.), *The Chinese World Order. Traditional China's Foreign Relations* (Cambridge, Mass., 1968), pp. 278–279. For a general discussion of

diplomacy in early China, see also Richard Louis Walker, *The Multi-State System of Ancient China* (Westport, Conn., 1971 reprint).

162. *Ta-Tai li-chi pu-chu*. Basic Sinological Series (n.p., 1941), ch. 12, Section 77, pp. 139–146. For a German translation, see Richard Wilhelm, *Li Gi. Das Buch der Sitte* (Jena, 1930), pp. 327–332. Subchapter 7 of Section 7 in the *Ta-Tai li-chi* is identical with *Li-chi*, Section *p'ing-i*, 48, 1–10, which deals with the intercourse between princes. Additional material can also be found in the *Chou-li*.

163. *I-li*, in *Shih-san ching chu-shu* ed. (Shanghai, 1935), ch. 8 of the text, ch. 19–24 of the *chu-shu* commentary. For an English translation, see John Steele, *The I-li or Book of Etiquette and Ceremonial* (London, 1917), vol. 1, pp. 189–242.

164. See above, n. 134. The old custom of presenting envoys with living animals is obliquely alluded to in the Chin regulation for presents to Hsi Hsia envoys. It is said there that in lieu of living provisions (*sheng-hsi*, i.e., cattle and fowl) textiles were given (*CS*, 38, 14b).

165. *I-li*, translated by J. Steele, vol. 1, p. 193.

166. *PHJL*, *shang* 10b.

167. The classical study on the exchange of gifts in early and primitive societies and its sociological meaning is Marcel Mauss, *Essai sur le don* (Paris, 1925). An English translation is *The Gift: Forms and Functions of Exchange in Archaic Societies* (Glencoe, 1954). Marcel Granet has dedicated his *Danses et Légendes de la Chine Ancienne* (Paris, 1926) to Marcel Mauss. His book contains many perspicacious insights into the social functions of ritual spending and conspicuous consumption in ancient China, in particular in his chapter "Le Prestige au temps des Hégémons," pp. 79–104.

168. For a discussion of this problem, see Mark Mancall, "The Ch'ing Tributary System: An Interpretive Essay," in John K. Fairbank (ed.), *The Chinese World Order*, p. 76.

169. John K. Fairbank, *The Chinese World Order*, p. 13, distinguishes Control, Attraction, and Manipulation as three distinctive features in traditional Chinese foreign relations.

PART IV

Foreign Lands and the Sung

SIX

National Consciousness in Medieval Korea: The Impact of Liao and Chin on Koryŏ

MICHAEL C. ROGERS

It's a truism that a state's foreign policy owes its shape and dynamism to the ideological premises of the ruling elite, or the dominant faction, at any given time. In the case of Koryŏ (918–1392), decisions concerning the official stance to be adopted vis-à-vis the continental powers were matters of no small moment. Such decisions were sometimes distilled with considerable struggle and anguish and tell us much about the development of national and cultural consciousness in medieval Korea. The fact that such decisions were made in the context of rapid and far-reaching change in the interstate relations in East Asia is another reason why they repay careful scrutiny—as careful, that is, as the often frustratingly meager documentation will permit. Especially for the tenth and early eleventh centuries, the *Koryŏ-sa* (virtually our only Korean source) is thin in its coverage, owing to the destruction of the dynastic archives in Kaesŏng in 1011 by Khitan invaders.

In general treatments of Korean history the Liao and Chin are usually mentioned in the same breath, both described as powerful non-Chinese states in Manchuria which exacted a reluctant tributary allegiance from the kings of Koryŏ.[1] On a superficial level these two more or less sinified powers had much in common, the more so since the Jurchen regime, in its concern for the legitimization of its rule, was keenly aware of Liao precedents and demanded for itself all the prerogatives that Liao had enjoyed on the international scene. Not least of the latter was the status of suzerain over both Koryŏ and the formidable Tangut principality of Hsi Hsia, the perennial scourge of Sung's northwestern frontier. Though Koryŏ and Hsi Hsia were poles apart in their political and cultural orientations, they were often paired in the official histories, probably owing to the tributary status that linked them in the mind of the historian.[2] Similarly, the differences between Liao and Chin were obscured by the application of another political stereotype—that of "rival state" (*ti-kuo*, i.e., vis-à-vis China).

Its integrity and irredentist aspiration were inherent in the very name Koryŏ (Ch. Kao-li), which, being a shortened form of Koguryŏ (Ch. Kao-chü-li), summed up the state-founding ideology: Koryŏ, as descendant of the powerful Manchurian kingdom that had extended its rule deep into the Korean peninsula only to succumb, eventually (668), to Silla and its imperial allies from T'ang.[3] The spiritual heirs of Koguryŏ could never forget the ancestral lands in Liaotung and beyond; chafing at peninsular constriction, they regarded Koryŏ's phase of state-founding and consolidation as but a period of preparation for recovery of those vast domains. From the peninsular standpoint, however, Koryŏ was clearly the successor of Silla, the peninsula's first unifier. Throughout the eighth and ninth centuries, Silla's kings had fulfilled in exemplary fashion their tributary obligations to the T'ang emperor and had reaped enormous benefits by participating in the Chinese world order. The attitudes and ideals symbolized by Silla were antithetical to those conjured up by Koguryŏ. Silla's effective rule had never extended beyond the thirty-ninth parallel—to the Taedong River, on the shore of which Koguryŏ's last capital, Sŏgyŏng (mod. Pyongyang),[4] was located. Hence Sillan tradition could provide no motivation for expansion even as far as the Yalu, much less beyond it; on the contrary, such expansionism was perceived as fraught with danger to the aristocratic rule that had evolved during the two and one-half centuries of Unified Silla. The military leaders of the new state of Koryŏ badly needed the learning and expertise in administrative affairs which the aristocracy of the defunct Silla state could offer.[5] The Silla ethos quickly gained the ascendancy in Kaesŏng after the unification of the peninsula in 936 and retained that position until 1170. For purposes of foreign relations, on the other hand, the Koryŏ court presented itself as heir of Koguryŏ.[6] This dualism profoundly conditioned the history of Koryŏ down to the Mongol conquest.

The above sketch is of course simplistic. Polarization, with Koryŏ's "true" identity as the burning issue, occurred only in times of national crisis (usually precipitated by pressures from the continent). The most notable such crisis resulted from the rise of Chin and the fall of the Northern Sung. It was then that the rivalry between Silla-successionism and Koguryŏ-successionism flared up and elicited the classic historiographical and literary responses. Since the twelfth century is more fully documented, it would perhaps be well to cast a forward glance at those materials before proceeding to comment on Koryŏ's relations with Liao.

In 1145, a decade and a half after Koryŏ's relations with Chin had been regularized, the sinified scholar Kim Pusik (1075–1151) produced his synthesis of pre-Koryŏ history, Historical Records of the Three Kingdoms (Samguk Sagi).[7] He found the basic structure of official Chinese historiography adequate to his purposes, which clearly included the presentation of Silla as Koryŏ's dynastic predecessor, in both spirit and fact. With Chin as suzerain-state, Koryŏ was relatively insulated from the pull of the Chinese world order, and this relief from pressures exerted from abroad afforded Koreans both stimulus and opportunity for continuing reassessment of Koryŏ's place in the world. The "Annalist Records" (*P'yŏnnyŏn T'ongnok*) is a product of this period. Composed by Kim Kwan'ŭi, this fanciful reconstruction, which is preserved in a prefatory chapter of the *Koryŏ-sa*, represents a concerted effort to assert Koryŏ's autonomous legitimacy on the basis of popular cult and lore (notably shamanism and geomancy, i.e., *p'ungsu*) and to reconcile its dual heritage stemming from Silla and Koguryŏ.[8] In 1193 the poet-statesman Yi Kyubo (1168–1241) celebrated a national ethos rooted in the heritage of Koguryŏ with his "Ode to King Tongmyŏng" (*Tongmyŏng Wang P'yŏn*), based on an "Old Three Kingdoms History."[9] That work—designated "old" because it antedated Kim Pusik's work—has not survived save for that portion, pertaining to Koguryŏ's legendary founder King Tongmyŏng, in which Yi Kyubo found inspiration. Even with regard to the "Historical Records," an extant work, there is scholarly debate as to the degree to which the two opposing outlooks (Silla vs. Koguryŏ) conditioned the presentation and interpretation of events.[10] The rise of Chin produced a shock-wave in which the pragmatism and entrenched privilege of the Silla-Confucianistic orientation clashed with the visionary and adventuresome inclinations of the Koguryŏ-oriented nativists. The rationale of the former was a China-centered universalism, and the latter's outlook was particularistic (state/*kuo* or Korean oriented), and drew heavily upon geomancy and other folkloristic elements for legitimacy.[11]

The development of Koryŏ's self-image in the face of the Liao and Chin challenge is an intriguing, if somewhat nebulous, subject. Chinese influences, notably the then rapidly developing "science" of dynastic legitimacy, ought not to be ignored.[12] Under the Northern Sung the subject of "Orthodox Hegemony" (*cheng-t'ung*) provoked lively discussion, characterized by a great deal of tortuous reasoning; this continued under the Southern Sung with a considerable—and understandable—increment of anguish and outrage. There can be little doubt that Korean statesmen were well aware of this issue together with its ideological and historiographical dimensions; they undoubtedly saw the question of Koryŏ's identity as one in which the Koguryŏ option was suffused with nativist (non-Chinese) myth and symbol, while the Silla protagonists were intent upon shoring up the crumbling foundations of Chinese universalism. The controversy was a political struggle rather than a learned polemic. There was no Korean counterpart to the urbane rationalism of an Ou-yang Hsiu,[13] or to the xenophobic fulminations of a Fang Hsiao-ju.[14] The disintegration of the Chinese world order, however, was not without specific repercussions northeast of China.[15] Since dynastic legitimacy was part of the "higher culture" for which the Koreans looked to the Middle Kingdom, we are not surprised to find scholars and statesmen of Koryŏ adapting it to their own purposes.

In Koryŏ's pre-Sung existence of forty-two years, the Korean kings affiliated themselves successively with most of the "Five Dynasties," while resolutely rebuffing overtures made by the Khitans, whose conquest of Po-hai in 926 had touched a sensitive nerve in Koryŏ.[16] The people of Po-hai, being "remnant people" of Koguryŏ, were related to the Koryŏ dynasts, and in the latter's aspiration to recover the old Koguryŏ territory they were potential allies. As one after another of the Five Dynasties fell, the Koryŏ court responded pragmatically, assuming an independent stance by promulgating a year-title of its own.[17] In short, by the time Koryŏ entered upon relations with Sung, three foreign policies were well established: an affinity with China, alternating with independence as the situation warranted, and an attitude of hostility toward the Khitans.

The period from 962 to 1020 was inaugurated by Koryŏ's first mission to Sung,[18] and terminated by the Korean king's declaration of vassalage to the Khitan emperor.[19] Throughout this period, the Khitans loom threateningly in the background, providing Sung with its only practical motivation for maintaining relations with Korea. The Koreans never actually fielded an army to act in concert with the Sung against the Khitans, nor did the Chinese respond in Koryŏ's hour of need. Joint Sino-Korean action always seemed possible, but was thwarted by the Khitan strategists' refusal to be drawn into engagements on Chinese and Korean fronts at the same time; indeed, hostilities against the one always seemed to coincide with an olive branch extended toward the other.

In 993, after Sung and Koryŏ had on at least two occasions failed to enlist the other's aid against the Khitans, the court of Koryŏ shifted its tributary allegiance to the Khitan emperor. This realignment reflected Sung's inability to control Liaotung in the face of the eastward expansion of Liao power. The official Korean account of this realignment reveals the ideological tensions in the Koryŏ court and illustrates how Koryŏ's relations with Liao were inextricably intertwined with the relations that both states had with Sung.[20] The confrontation which Sŏ Hŭi, representing the court of Sŏngjong (r. 982–997), had with the commander of a powerful Khitan invading force is generally considered to represent a turning point in Koryŏ's history. The account may be summarized as follows.

In response to an invasion launched by the Khitans, Sŏ Hŭi was given command of the Central Army, with the mission of defending the northern frontier. To direct the defense, the king proceeded north to P'yŏngyang, and as far as Anbuk-pu, but fell back (presumably to P'yŏng-yang) upon hearing that the Khitan general Hsiao Sung-ning had conquered Pongsangun. As Sŏ Hŭi was en route to rescue that city, Hsiao Sun-ning proclaimed that his state was annexing the territory that had been ruled by ancient Koguryŏ. He added that his invasion had been precipitated by the Korean incursions on that territory. He demanded that they surrender. Sŏ Hŭi, however, discerned evidence in this missive that the invaders would be amenable to a peaceful settlement. Another letter from Hsiao Sun-ning announced that he had an army of 800,000 and that the king and court of Koryŏ faced the alternatives of immediate surrender or annihilation. A Korean envoy was unable to modify this ultimatum. At this point, the king of Koryŏ opted for pacifism and would have ceded the disputed territory to Liao had it not been for the advice of Sŏ Hŭi. The latter argued that the real expectations of the Khitans were much more modest. Moreover, the proposed cession of territory would only lead to further demands in the name of ancient Koguryŏ. He favored making a fight of it. Of like mind was Yi Chibaek, who argued passionately for an unyielding stance, describing the territorial integrity of the realm as a sacred ancestral trust. The only valid basis for Koryŏ's response was nativistic. Koryŏ should turn to the national spirits, such as those associated with Silla's *hwarang* cult, rather than to the "strange usages of an alien region." (The historian comments that Yi Chibaek's use of such extreme terms reflected the dissatisfaction of the Koryŏ court with King Sŏngjong's Chinese ways.) Meanwhile, Hsiao Sun-ning, despite a military setback at Anyung-jin, renewed his demand for surrender. Koryŏ dispatched a peace emissary (*hwat'ongsa*), but Hsiao rejected him, apparently because he wanted a plenipotentiary spokesman.

Sŏ Hŭi rose to the occasion. He alone responded to the king's call for a man who might "establish millennial merit by driving back troops with mouth and tongue." Upon Sŏ Hŭi's arrival at the enemy camp, the formal negotiations were delayed by a lengthy dispute about the protocol appropriate for their meeting. At issue was the dignity of Koryŏ, and Sŏ Hŭi successfully upheld it. By staging a sit-in his quarters he forced Hsiao Sun-ning to acquiesce in his demand for equal status. The proceedings opened with the two men "sitting face-to-face on east and west." Hsiao began by enunciating the premise underlying his earlier charge of Koryŏ encroachment: that is, he identified Koryŏ with Silla and Liao with Koguryŏ. He complained that Koryŏ, despite its proximity to Liao, "crossed the sea to serve Sung." These two issues had prompted Liao's invasion. The price of peace would be Koryŏ's cession of territory to Liao and Koryŏ's cultivation of diplomatic relations with Liao (rather than with Sung). Sŏ Hŭi, in a classic statement of Koryŏ's irredentist ideology, vehemently asserted Koryŏ's claim to Koguryŏ territory on both sides of the Yalu. He justified Koryŏ's relations with Sung and noted that hostile Jurchen tribes in the Yalu region prevented similar relations with the Liao. If Koryŏ were permitted to establish forts in strategic locations to control the Jurchens it would seek to cultivate relations with Liao. Sŏ Hŭi's response, reported in full to the Khitan emperor, elicited the latter's acquiescence, at least to the extent that he ordered his troops withdrawn because Koryŏ had "asked for peace." During the next two years, Sŏ Hŭi led several expeditions into territory east of the Yalu to build forts to regulate the Jurchens. Such an expansion fit in with the agreement that had been reached with the Khitans.

The agreement has ever since been hailed as a diplomatic triumph. The Koreans exacted a heavy price for their shift of tributary affiliation. They halted a massive Khitan invasion already launched against them, and justified their claim to Koguryŏ's cis-Yalu territorial legacy. This account, however, makes rather heavy demands on the reader's credulity. Theatrical trimmings aside, the story would seem to consist of three "acts": (1) the Khitan invasion and demands, (2) the panic-stricken reaction of the Korean king and some of his advisers, and (3) Sŏ Hŭi's exploit. The Liao history, the *Liao-shih*, confirms acts one and three. Unfortunately, it cannot be relied upon in this matter. The *Liao-shih* reveals that its source for Liao's relations with Koryŏ and the Jurchens was the *Ta-Liao chih-chi*, a work that had been presented to the Yüan court by Koryŏ.[21] Another work, the *Ch'i-tan kuo-chih*, antedates the *Liao-shih* by about a century and is, in fact, the only one extant of the three major sources used in the compilation of the *Liao-shih*. The *Ch'i-tan kuo-chih* plainly refers to Koryŏ, and even its brief section devoted to that state is entitled "Silla."[22] This is an implicit negation of Koryŏ's claim to the legacy of Koguryŏ, and it no doubt reflects the contemporary attitude of the Khitans toward Koryŏ. It tells us nothing about 993 specifically. The *Ch'i-tan kuo-chih*, in fact, does not mention any dealings, whether hostile or friendly, between Liao and Koryŏ in or about 993. There appears to be no corroboration for the agreement secured by Sŏ Hŭi. Liao's expansion into the Yalu region in the 980s and 990s is well documented, however, and there is nothing inherently implausible in an agreement being reached in 993 between Liao and Koryŏ concerning boundary and tributary arrangements. Nor is it unlikely that the Khitan emperor decreed a show of force in order to expedite such an agreement.

This account may mirror the Sung's relations with the Liao.[23] In 993 Liao's energies were directed primarily against Sung, and continued so until 1005. In that year Sung representatives negotiated the famous treaty of Shan-yüan with the Khitans.[24] Though this pact formally placed a foreign ruler on a footing equal to that of the Chinese emperor, it laid the foundations for the peace that prevailed between Sung and Liao until both were overwhelmed by the Jurchen founders of the Chin dynasty. The treaty numbed Sung's interest in its northeastern tributary, an interest that had always been primarily strategic in character. It also enabled the Khitans to concentrate on their eastern frontier with a minimum of concern about their southern border. Within a few years, the Liao, capitalizing on the peace treaty, launched a series of highly destructive invasions of the peninsula. During this time of troubles, Koryŏ repeatedly but in vain appealed to Sung for help against the aggressors.[25] This indifference to the fate of its tributary in the peninsula was, from Sung's standpoint, a side effect of the Shan-yüan treaty, deplorable no doubt, but inevitable. The resulting bitterness and disillusionment of the Koreans found allegorical expression in the story of Sŏ Hŭi's exploit.

The Sung-Liao agreement, apart from the equality of status that constituted its formal framework, had two essential terms: (1) an annual payment by Sung to the Khitans and (2) evacuation by the Khitans of the North China area known as Kuan-nan ("South of the Passes"). The parallel with the two terms of the Koryŏ-Liao transaction is obvious. Koryŏ's acceptance of a tributary relationship with Liao corresponds with Sung's annual payments. For King Sŏngjong's inclination to cede the northern part of his realm to the Khitans, there is the parallel of the Sung emperor Chen-tsung's desire to move his capital to the south or west to escape the Khitan menace; for the iron-willed and histrionically talented Sŏ Hŭi, there is Sung's negotiator, the similarly endowed Ts'ao Li-yung; the concept of territorial integrity as a matter of national honor and loyalty to ancestors, invoked by Sŏ Hŭi and Yi Chibaek, finds vigorous expression also in the councils of Sung when negotiations with Liao were discussed; and prominent in both cases (i.e., 1005 and 993) are conflicts of historically grounded territorial claims. Less substantive but no less revealing are certain parallels in rhetorical flourishes and flamboyant gestures. The dispute about the protocol appropriate to the meeting of Sŏ Hŭi and Hsiao Sun-ning has its Shan-yüan precedent. The description of the Korean diplomat and the Khitan general "sitting face-to-face, one on the east and one on the west," comes into focus when it is seen as lampooning the official designations of Liao and Sung as "Northern Court" and "Southern Court" respectively.

The Sŏ Hŭi story is not only a biting satire on Sung's relatively weak capability on its northern frontier; it points the finger of scorn at the whole idea of Chinese universalism. The *real* Khitan invasions—those of the eleventh century—cut the Sino-Korean umbilical cord with fire and sword. The legend of Sŏ Hŭi, whose real prototype may well have been a tenth-century military figure active on Koryŏ's northern frontier, was probably evolved during the period of reconstruction in the 1020s following the invasions. The account is an interesting illustration of the extent to which, particularly for the poorly documented tenth century, history could be fashioned from legend and the resulting need for justification and reassurance. The Treaty of Shan-yüan and its aftermath (i.e., the Khitan invasions of Korea) made it obvious to both Sung and Koryŏ that for the time being at least, little was to be gained, and much might be lost, from maintaining a relationship. The request which Hyŏnjong's envoy Han Cho made of Sung in 1022 for "books on *yin-yang*, geomancy (*ti-li*) and medical prescriptions"[26] is noteworthy, contrasting with the classical titles that the Korean court was eager to acquire in happier times. The occult works were probably sought as aids for mobilizing the spiritual resources of Korea, now that it was clear that the small state could no longer look to Sung for even moral support, much less material.[27] The poem with which Hyŏnjong is said to have honored Kang Kamch'an (b. 968), hero of the triumphant Korean defense against the invading Khitans, evokes the mood of the 1020s:

> In the year *kyŏng-sul* (1010) the dusty horde did roar
> As their arms swept even to the Han River shore.
> Had we not then in Duke Kang our savior found,
> Evermore would our coats on the left be bound.[28]

With his classic reference to barbarism ("left lapel"), the king likens himself and Kang Kamch'an to Duke Huan and Kuan Chung of old, celebrating their success in manning the ramparts of (Chinese) civilization. The implication is clear that the issue had, thanks to Kang Kamch'an and others, been decided in favor of civilization, uncompromised by the Korean king's enforced vassalage to the Khitan emperor. A renewal of the Sung connection was, after all, not inconceivable; hence there continued to be a tension between ideal and reality. This is one respect in which the Liao-Sung Gestalt differs fundamentally from the Chin–Southern Sung period that followed. That is to say, Liao coexisted with a well-established Chinese government which, being based in the Central Plain of North China, asserted a convincing claim to possession of the Mandate of Heaven. The Koreans perceived the Khitan state as an eruption of barbarism that would eventually be contained. Embattled though it might be, Chinese universalism was still seen as viable. The Koreans helped to make it so, by demonstrating their ability to repel, unaided, full-scale Khitan invasion, and by their patent unreliability as allies of the Khitans. Thus one may say that Koryŏ during Liao played an essential role in the maintenance of the balance of power on the continent.

In Koryŏ, during the four-decade period of severance of relations with Sung (c. 1030 to c. 1070), the idea that the peninsular kingdom was no longer a satellite but had developed an independent orbit and was a planet (a "Little China") in its own right seems to have emerged. When the question of reopening relations with Sung was raised in 1058, it was decided negatively, on the grounds that Koryŏ had nothing to gain.[29] Such relations were in fact resumed a decade later on Sung initiative as part of the reform program instituted by the reformer Wang An-shih.[30] This Sung impulse, which capitalized on Liao decline,[31] represents an effort to recapture the spirit of universal sway through virtue. It indeed brought about a resurgence of the old Sung-Koryŏ relationship. The resurgence was short-lived, however, coming to an inglorious end with the fall of the Northern Sung and the rise of the Jurchen Chin dynasty. It was replaced by a mutual disillusionment more pervasive than that of the post–Shan-yüan years.

In the northeast Asian world ushered in by the Jurchens we no longer see the stark contrast between civilization and barbarism that had characterized the tenth and eleventh centuries. The relative absence of tension in Koryŏ's relations with the Jurchens[32] reflects the Chin's qualifications, as perceived by the Korean court, for possession of the Mandate of Heaven. The Jurchen emperor's superiority to his Khitan predecessor can be attributed to both cultural and geographical factors. The Jurchens were indeed less "barbaric," by traditional Chinese norms, than the Khitans had been. Still more far-reaching in its practical and psychological effects was Chin's conquest of North China: by shifting the zone of sino-"barbarian" confrontation from Hopei southward to the Huai, that triumph of Jurchen arms moved Koryŏ much further out on the periphery of events, making the Koreans essentially spectators in a two-way balance, where previously they had consituted a third party. Thus for all the stress and trauma of their inception, Koryŏ's relations with Chin produced a stable détente that left the Koreans free to concentrate on internal development and cultural pursuits with little fear of interference or harassment from abroad.[33]

The disintegration of Chinese universalism set in motion a quest for origins among the peoples on the periphery. Chin and Koryŏ had one important thing in common: the founders of both states claimed for their efforts the auspices of ancient Koguryŏ. That was still a name to be conjured with in twelfth-century northeastern Asia, retaining ideological potency centuries after the state itself had been wiped out by the T'ang-Silla axis (668). In fact it had never been permitted to lapse into oblivion. In the eighth century it had been kept alive by Po-hai (Kor. Parhae), whose court referred to itself as "Kao-li" in official communications with Japan.[34] Shortly before the fall of Po-hai to the Khitans in 926, the hallowed name got a new lease on life as Wang Kŏn staked his claim to Koguryŏ's legacy by naming his new state Koryŏ. With its rule barely extending as far as the Yalu, however, Koryŏ did not truly resemble Koguryŏ, since the latter, despite its push into the peninsula early in the fourth century, had until its fall retained vast continental domains. A claim to Koguryŏ ancestry also fortified the state-founding ideology of the Jurchens in eastern Manchuria two centuries after the founding of Koryŏ; apparently the apologists of the ruling Wan-yen clan perceived that the "raw" (*sheng*) or less civilized Jurchens, themselves the "remnant people" of Po-hai, would rally more readily to a cause that could invoke the name of Koguryŏ.[35] The prior claim of Wang Kŏn's Koryŏ in this matter seems to have glamorized the peninsular kingdom in the eyes of the Chin and enhanced the value of a Korean declaration of tributary allegiance. Conciliation, rather than overt threat, was the keynote of Chin's Koryŏ policy in its initial phase.

More than a century had elapsed since the "Northern" and "Southern" courts (Liao and Sung, respectively) had exchanged "sworn letters" (*shih-shu*) solemnly swearing to abide by the terms of the Treaty of Shan-yüan. Both parties had recognized the prevailing realities by resorting to the egalitarian tradition of the "Covenant" (*meng*), relinquishing that of the hierarchical "Mandate" (*ming*).[36] The latter tradition was still less applicable to the relations between Sung and Chin after the empire had been divided into a "barbarian" north and a Chinese south, with the latter being forced to acknowledge an inferior status.[37] The dominant faction in the Koryŏ court had no choice but to recognize that the sun of Sung, having been definitively eclipsed in the Central Plain, could no longer command their allegiance. But the Koreans would be disoriented and demoralized until a replacement luminary, invested with the authority of a Son of Heaven, had been installed.

The transactions between the Sung and the Liao were equitable. They differed from the course of Sung's relations with Hsi Hsia. In corresponding with the Tanguts, the Sung employed a "sworn vassal-letter" (*shih-piao*) and a "sworn decree" (*shih-chao*). The Sung court attempted in this way to preserve the Mandate of Heaven framework, while injecting a note of realism in the form of an imprecation. Statesmen and scholars of Sung seem to have regarded such a hybrid instrument with some distaste. This is not surprising, since the juxtaposition of the Mandate and the Covenant made a mockery of the spirit of the Mandate of Heaven. For the aggressive Tangut leader Li Yüan-hao (r. 1032–1048), who had a cynical view of Chinese paternalism, such an instrument must have carried more weight than any amount of high-flown universalistic rhetoric would have done.[38] Needless to say, the chancellery of Sung in its diplomatic practice had never confused the truculent chieftains of the Tanguts with the elite of the Korean peninsula's "Little China." A Jurchen chancellery, however, was another matter. Being themselves "barbarian" and still at an immature stage of state consolidation, the Jurchens could hardly be expected to make sophisticated distinctions in their dealings with neighboring states. The need they felt most keenly in conducting their foreign affairs was precedent; and that need was amply satisfied by the usages that had developed in the course of Sung's interaction with Hsi Hsia and Liao during the previous century and a half.[39] Since those usages sanctioned a documentary hybrid of hierarchy and parity, they saw no need to question it. They had never been immersed in the Mandate of Heaven tradition. For them, the oath-formula was simply an affirmation of good faith that was appropriate, even indispensable when two states were laying the foundations for a long-term relationship.

The perceptions of Koryŏ's aristocracy, conditioned by a century and a half of ceremonious relations with continental powers, were very different from those of the still rather "raw" or uncivilized Jurchens. In their foreign relations, the Koreans had been able to preserve, outwardly at least, a naive idealism in their dedication to Chinese universalism; Koryŏ's policy of non-involvement in continental power politics was well served by such a posture. The elite owed its privileged status to an acknowledged role as custodians of Confucian virtue and wisdom within the framework of the Chinese world order. That order was called into question when the Chin envoy Ssu Ku-te in 1129 demanded an imprecation by which the Korean king would make himself and his house liable to the wrath of spiritual powers should they not fulfill their tributary obligations.[40] The Koreans insisted that they had already pledged their loyalty to their new suzerain. There was no need for a formula they regarded as impious, even blasphemous. A "covenant-oath" (*meng-shih*) was, for them, a device resorted to by "rival states" (*ti-kuo*) who couldn't trust each other. Now, however, "a Sage (i.e., the Chin emperor), having received the Mandate, has wrought a vast unification, in light of which this lowly buffer-state had joyfully submitted from its heart's core and was respectfully fulfilling its tributary obligations."[41]

Nearly a year elapsed—a period of intense ideological ferment within Koryŏ—before envoys were commissioned to bear King Injong's oath of allegiance to the Chin emperor (December 24, 1130).[42] The Koreans undertook to educate the Jurchen ruler concerning the crucial difference between Covenant and Mandate, identifying him with the latter because of his position as the Son of Heaven. The concluding formula ("If anyone violate this covenant, may the spirits strike him dead!") represents minimal compliance with the demand for an oath. The "barbaric" Liao, by securing at sword's point Koryŏ's compliance with universalistic norms, had shielded the Koreans from a multistate reality; it was left to the Chin, whose emperors were both more sinified and better qualified for the Mandate of Heaven, to introduce them to the new international order. The Chin History's brief coverage of the oath controversy depicts, with what seems to be a tinge of sarcasm, the Koreans being dragged, kicking and screaming, into the bleak and forbidding political landscape of the twelfth century. The task of managing that transition was assigned to a Chinese literatus named Han Fang (*chin-shih* of 1112), who had held office under the Liao and was well qualified to serve as a cultural intermediary. He debated the oath issue with Korean erudites and, by means of threats veiled in classical allusions, persuaded them that they would be wise to comply with the demand.[43]

Chin's conquest of North China and abduction of Sung's imperial family dealt the universalistic mystique a blow from which it could never fully recover. "Barbarians" had appropriated the Mandate of Heaven. This was obviously a setback for the sinified Korean elite, who probably felt themselves tarred with a "barbarian" brush, for all their acquired dexterity with a Chinese one. But this development was not without its compensation. It stimulated the Korean quest for an autonomous national legitimacy, one that would be unbeholden to traditional sanction, hence unshaken by whatever upheavals might take place on the continent. Needless to say, such a stimulus was lost upon the dominant faction, which was Silla-successionist; the reaction of its members was, as we have seen, to do their utmost to shore up the old order, even with a non-Chinese Son of Heaven presiding. It was the political "outs" in Koryŏ who refused to make that adjustment; on the contrary, they saw in the breakup of the old order an opportunity to assert their country's claim to its "birthright" in Manchuria, the legacy of Koguryŏ. To that end, an improvement of their position within the state was an essential first step.

The nativist-irredentist movement that acquired momentum in the late 1120s was led by the monk Myoch'ŏng, who was able to gain influence over the young king Injong by virtue of his thaumaturgic reputation.[44] The objectives of this movement, whose ideological overtones continued to reverberate long after its suppression, included removal of the capital from Kaesŏng to Sŏgyŏng and a declaration of Koryŏ's sovereign status. The fielding of a military expedition against Chin was a part of the program, at least as envisaged by some participants. The struggle also had a regional dimension: the very name "Western Capital," where open rebellion flared in 1135, proclaimed the irredentist aspiration of the city.[45] The commander-in-chief of the government forces which eventually put down the rebels was the then dominant figure in Kaesŏng, Kim Pusik. His triumph and that of his Confucianist faction in this struggle inaugurated three and a half decades of dominance by the civil officialdom, the prestige of the military officials being at a low ebb. This rebellion did not disrupt the comfortable Koryŏ-Chin relationship.[46] The northern frontier was stabilized on a basis more favorable to Koryŏ than had been the case during Liao (when the frontier had been a perennial source of friction); this must have facilitated the downgrading of Koryŏ's military establishment to the advantage of the civil officialdom. Civilian control lasted until the military coup of 1170.

This milieu of civil dominance is strikingly reminiscent of the situation in the Southern Sung at about the same time. By 1141, Sung scholar-officials had gained unquestioned ascendancy, especially in the formulation of policy toward the Jurchens.[47] Six years later Kim Pusik was entrusted with the compilation of the "Veritable Records" (sillok) of King Injong's reign.[48] Not surprisingly, the scholar ideal is prominent in the relevant portion of the Koryŏ-sa, the sources for which Kim Pusik controlled by virtue of his sillok commission. Similar problems faced the governments of Sung and Koryŏ in their confrontation with Chin. They both chose civilian control as the solution. For Koryŏ, it seemed to work. Kim Pusik lived to see Korea accept a status as subordinate to the Jurchens. He also witnessed the acquiescence of the Southern Sung to the Chin hegemony.

Was Kim Pusik's *Historical Records*, completed in 1145, affected by these events? Considerable scholarly controversy rages over this question.[49] I believe that Kim Pusik the historian is inseparable from Kim Pusik the ideologue. He was intent upon buttressing the "serve-the-greater" ideology, undeterred by the fact that the "greater" state in question was of non-Chinese origin. He did this by emphasizing the dedication of Silla's rulers to the Chinese world order and to their own status as subordinates of the T'ang Son of Heaven, and by documenting Koryŏ's identity as culturally and genealogically anointed heir of Silla. Kim Pusik, who was himself of royal Silla descent, sought to minimize the rupture between Silla and Koryŏ, constructing a bridge between them by asserting certain questionable genealogical and cultural linkages.[50] He presented the Silla–Koryŏ transition as a type of conquest-by-culture pattern commonly associated with dynasties of conquest in Chinese history. Though abandoned by Heaven, the last Silla king had still responded to Wang Kŏn's charismatic virtue; and for his part the Koryŏ ruler, acknowledging the cultural values that Silla had exemplified, had accepted many of these values in the organization of his state.[51] As far as possible, Kim Pusik wanted to see the change of dynasty as essentially a change of name.

Kim Pusik was entirely satisfied with Koryŏ's peninsular setting. He was well aware that Koguryŏ's vast continental domains and population had formed the basis for the state of Po-hai, Silla's contemporary.[52] He, nonetheless, ignored the history of Po-hai and included the two and one-half centuries of Unified Silla history in his "Historical Records of the Three Kingdoms." It can be argued that, from an "objective" standpoint, the historical realities of northeast Asia in the eighth and ninth centuries would have been better served by the compilation of two distinct historical works: a "Northern History" and a "Southern History," dealing, respectively, with Po-hai and Silla. Kim Pusik was taken to task by scholars of the late Yi period for his failure to give Po-hai its due, since an officially compiled history of that state would have laid a historiographical foundation for a de jure claim on the part of Korea to the old continental territories of Koguryŏ.[53]

Such complaints are of course otiose. These critiques fail to heed his concept of historical legitimacy. It was a concept that placed no special value on territory as such; there can be little doubt that he viewed the portion of Koguryŏ which was not influenced by Silla as having relapsed into barbarism, hence beyond the reach or concern of a self-respecting historian. To him, the Koryŏ unification meant a northward expansion of the values of civilization (that of T'ang-Silla) from the Taedong River (the approximate northern boundary of Silla) to the Yalu; those values assert a higher claim upon him than anything the "barbaric" Manchurian waste-lands offered. This orientation accorded well with a reluctance, widespread among men of Sung, Liao, and Chin, to acknowledge that Silla had really been replaced, especially by a state whose name invoked the auspices of Koguryŏ.[54] Koryŏ's own elite, by their stress on an ongoing Silla tradition when dealing with representatives of continental powers, fostered the myth of a Silla still alive and well in the peninsula. Po-hai was the obvious link between Koguryŏ and Koryŏ, and by ignoring Po-hai Kim eliminated any duality or ambiguity regarding Koryŏ's spiritual origins and the source of its legitimacy. Silla was, in his view, the sole fountainhead.

This attitude is surely reflected in Kim's choice of documents for inclu-sion in his "Historical Records." In his biography of Ch'oe Ch'iwŏn (857–?), a paragon among sinified Silla scholars, he reproduced only one writing from Ch'oe's voluminous literary collection, one in which Ch'oe describes Po-hai as "a gang of bastards left over from Koguryŏ."[55] In Kim's consigning of Manchuria to oblivion one can also see a gesture of contempt for the Jurchens and the rude empire they had put together on foundations laid by the hated Khitans. Given his background, Kim's attitudes are understandable enough; one can, however, sympathize with later gener-ations of Koreans as they seethe with frustration at the spectacle of Injong's court, by its sponsorship of Kim's work, divesting Koryŏ of even a theoret-ical claim to Koguryŏ's continental domains. Korea was thus relegated to peninsular status. On the other hand, the verdict of posterity tends to ignore the fact that Kim's ideological sword was double-edged: if Silla was a mirror for Koryŏ, then T'ang served that function for Sung and Chin. The lesson that emerged from Kim's history was that the glory of T'ang was a thing of the past. It behooved Koryŏ to look to its survival in a post-universalistic world by using its considerable diplomatic skills, with a keen awareness of the distinction between rhetoric and reality.

Chong Chungbu's coup of 1170, which inaugurated the military dic-tatorship, may perhaps be viewed as a delayed reaction to the fall of the Northern Sung. As a role-model for Koryŏ, Silla had never been very convincing; indeed, as we have seen, it had always given place to the Koguryŏ persona when important issues were at stake in foreign affairs. The dramatic collapse of the old order in 1126 made it plain to all but the die-hard Silla-ists that the T'ang-Silla Gestalt, however idealized in concep-tion (as by Kim Pusik), was simply irrelevant to the twelfth century. In the ideological dialectic of that century one might regard the nativist move-ment associated with Myoch'ŏng (itself a reaction to the "Catastrophe of Ching-k'ang") as a thesis which elicited a two-pronged anti-thesis: the

Samguk Sagi with its sinified (*sadae*-ist) orientation designed for elite consumption, and the *P'yŏnnyŏn T'ongnok*, which exploited for the benefit of a de-sinified Silla-successionism the same sort of popular cult and lore that had served Myoch'ŏng so well. Both works can be seen as Silla-successionist counterattacks launched by royal order against the still seething Western Capital ideology; they represent efforts to prevent chronic ideological conflict from erupting into violence such as that which had already shaken the dynasty in the 1130s. These efforts were unsuccessful, thanks to the coup d'etat of 1170, which initiated a military dictatorship. It was under the aegis of this regime that Yi Kyubo wrote his "Ode to King Tongmyong" (*Tongmyŏng-Wang P'yŏn*) in 1193.

Yi Kyubo was one of the "newly advanced literati" who came to maturity under the dictatorship. Unlike the court-dependent aristocracy of early Koryŏ, whom they replaced as a rèsult of the coup, these were self-reliant and "progressive" men whose literary skills made them useful to the military regime. Yi's "Ode to King Tongmyŏng" narrated the heroic and marvelous exploits of the mythical founder of Koguryŏ; it represented the last stratum of the ancient legend of the King. By his own account, Yi composed the poem in 1193, after reading the Annals of Tongmyŏng as given in the "Old Three Kingdoms History." The thirty-odd quotations from this work which he used as commentaries to his poem are all that remains of it. In his preface, Yi deplored the shortened version of Tongmyŏng's Annals which Kim Pusik had incorporated in his "Historical Records of the Three Kingdoms," surmising that Kim pruned it of what he regarded as popular tales of the marvelous—elements unsuited, by Chinese norms, for inclusion in a standard history. Yi Kyubo admits that such was initially his own reaction to the Annals, alleging that it was only after profound reflection that he recognized in the story the divinely inspired foundation of the Korean state. "It was for this reason that I have recorded it in the form of a poem, desiring that all under heaven should know that our country is from the very beginning the city of a sage." This observation reflects the new consciousness of the dictatorship period, which recognized only Koguryŏ-successionism, and moreover, rejected the validity of Chinese norms for the expression of Korean historical truth.

But a preoccupation with the cultural traditions of one or another of the Three Kingdoms was inherently divisive, inasmuch as it fostered regional "iconographies" within the peninsula. With the Tangun story of the following century (*Samguk Yusa* and *Chewang Ungi*), the Three Kingdoms were transcended and attention was focused on the pre–Three Kingdoms heritage of all Koreans. Koryŏ's relations with Liao and Chin undoubtedly helped to set the stage for this development, but the major "credit" must go to the Mongols. For it was only after the long drawn-out and unprecedentedly devastating invasions of the Mongol cavalry in the thirteenth century that Korean national consciousness was raised to the point where a mythic basis for national unity could be forged.

NOTES

1. Koryŏ's manner of "serving" Liao in formal relations was expressly invoked by Chin as the precedent to be followed (e.g., communication presented by Chin envoy to Koryŏ court in 1126: *Koryŏ-sa* (hereafter *KRS*) (Yonhui University edition, 1955), 15, 19a-b; cf. *Chin shih*, Wan-chien ed. of 1529, 135, 5a–5b. Nevertheless, it is misleading to say, as does Chŏn Haejong in his *Han-Chung Kwankye-sa Yŏngu* (Seoul, 1970), p. 47, that Chin was no less coercive in its attitude toward Koryŏ than Liao had been. In the two sets of relations, the underlying spirit was significantly different.

2. See E. I. Kychanov, *Ocherk Istorii Tangutskogo Gosudarstva* (Moscow, 1968), and his article, "Les guerres entre les Sung du Nord et le Hsi Hsia," *Études Song*, ser. I, no. 2 (1971), pp. 102–118.

3. The historians of the *Sung shih*, *the Liao shih*, and the *Chin shih* were not expansive in their historical comment on foreign relations; concerning the dearth of such comment, see Wang Gungwu, "Early Ming Relations with Southeast Asia: A Background Essay," in J. K. Fairbank (ed.), *The Chinese World Order* (Cambridge, Mass., 1968), pp. 44 ff. In the relevant monograph-titles of those histories, the objective term "outside" (*wai*) is used, replacing the several terms for "barbaric" used in the earlier histories; this of course indicates a new, more realistic world-outlook; for discussion, see Koh Pyŏng'ik, "Chungguk Chŏngsa-ŭi Woeguk Yŏlt-chŏn," in his collection *Tong' a Kyosŏ-sa-ŭi Yŏn'gu* (Seoul, 1970), pp. 36 ff. In *Liao shih* and *Chin shih*, separate "foreign nations" coverage is given only to Koryŏ and Hsi Hsia. Hsi Hsia is treated in greater detail than is Koryŏ. The critique (*tsan*) appended to *Chin shih* 135 (Kao-li) is very brief and perfunctory, with nothing to say about Koryŏ-Chin relations as such; this contrasts with the comment appended to *Chin shih* 134 (Hsi Hsia), where the historian disscuses in substantive terms the history of the Tangut state and its people, particularly as these affected relations with Chin. The *Sung shih* devotes only one chapter (487) to Koryŏ, with no appended comment; on the other hand, its two chapters on Hsi Hsia (485–486) are provided with a lengthy comment. Despite such relative stress on Hsi Hsia, the *Sung shih* compilers, as Kychanov notes (*Ocherk*, p. 5), ignored important and still extant Chinese sources, to say nothing of Tangut sources that were at their disposal. *Sung shih* 487 (on Koryŏ) is probably based on a *Sung Hui-yao* chapter devoted to Koryŏ, though that chapter has unfortunately been lost. For Koryŏ, one can only rejoice in the existence of the *Koryŏ-sa* and regret the lack of a Hsi Hsia counterpart to it.

4. Wang Kŏn restored the name Koryŏ, which had been temporarily adopted by Kong Ye, the rebel leader whom he overthrew (see Kim Sanggi, *Koryŏ Sidae-sa*, p. 2). Pak Hansŏl has made an interesting case for the name Kong Ye as signifying "Descendant of Chu Mong" (Chu Mong = "archer"), in line with Kong Ye's claim to represent a resurgence of Koguryŏ ("Kong Ye sŏngmyŏnko—Koguryŏ kyesŭng

p'yobanggwa kwallyŏn hayŏ"), *Hanguk Hangnon-ch'ong* (Seoul, 1974, pp. 75–87). In any case, the "iconography" represented by Koguryŏ had been exploited for ideological purposes well before Wang Kŏn's ascendancy.

5. We leave aside the question of the degree and quality of the political and cultural unification actually achieved under Silla. A negative indication in this regard is the pattern of insurrection preceding the fall of Silla: this shows a notable absence of rebel bases located in the territory of pre-unification Silla. For discussion of this and related matters, see Ellen S. Unruh, "Reflections on the Fall of Silla," *Korea Journal* 15, 5 (May 1975): 54–62.

6. That Wang Kŏn designated P'yŏngyang as "Western Capital" between 919 and 921 can be inferred from notices in his annals in *Koryŏ-sa* (see Yi Pyŏngdo, *Hanguk-sa, Chungse-p'yŏn*, p. 38). The epithet "Western," which has scant geographical warrant, evokes the memory of (Former) Han's "Western Capital," Ch'ang-an, contrasted with (Later) Han's "Eastern Capital" of Lo-yang; and behind this is the model of Chou, whose history is similarly bisected by removal of the capital, in 700 B.C., from Hao-ching, in the Wei Valley, which had been overrun by the Jung barbarians, to Lo-yang. The relevance of this Chinese analogy, which has gone unnoticed by Korean scholars (too obvious?), is certified by the fact that P'yŏngyang was temporarily named Hogyŏng. *KRS* 58, 30a; cf. *Hsü Tzu-chih t'ung-chien ch'ang-pien* (Taipei, 1961), 36, 4b, *sub* A.D. 1083, summary of Koryŏ's political geography, stating that P'yŏngyang is called Hoju and is considered to be the Western Capital. In the context of tenth-century Korea, "Western Capital" is an ideologically loaded name: asserting Koryŏ's Koguyrŏ heritage, it summarizes the geopolitical difference between Koryŏ and Silla. Therefore the degree to which Wang Kŏn and his successors accorded special status to Sŏgyŏng is considered to be one important indication of the intensity of their commitment to a policy of northward expansion.

7. Concerning the *Samguk Sagi*, see Kim Tai-jin (ed. and tr.), *A Bibliographical Guide to Traditional Korean Sources* (Seoul, 1976), pp. 11–17.

8. Not extant as an independent work, the *P'yŏnnyŏn T'ongnok* makes up the bulk of the "Koryŏ Segye," a prefatory chapter of the *Koryŏ-sa*. For discussion, with references to recent scholarship, see Ha Hyŏn'gang, "Kŏn'guk-chŏn Wangssi Seryok-ŭi Silt'ae," in the National History Compilation Committee's *Han'guk-sa*, vol. IV (Seoul, 1964), pp. 17 ff. Several scholars have treated the historicity (or lack of it) and symbolism of this work, but the significance of the timing of its appearance (i.e., the special circumstances of Ŭijong's reign as conducive to the production of such a work) has not, so far as I know, been pointed out.

9. Yi Kyubo's poem is contained in ch. 3 of his literary collection, *Tong-guk Yi Sangguk Chip* (for which see Kim Tae-jin, op. cit., pp. 26–30). A woodblock ed. is reproduced in *Koryŏ Myŏnghyŏn Chip*, vol. I (Seoul, 1973; the poem on pp. 33–37); introducing this edition is an informative essay by Prof. Yi Usŏng on Yi Kyubo and his work. For a translation of the "Ode" into Korean, see Hwang Sun'gu, *Tongguk Un'gi* (Seoul, 1967), pp. 141–184. For a free translation of the "Ode" into English, see R.Rutt, "A Lay of King Tongmyŏng, "*Korea Journal* 13, 7 (July 1973): 48–54.

10. For the hypothesis of *Samguk Sagi's* "Silla-ism" replacing a putative "Koguryŏ-istic" orientation of the "Old Three Kingdoms History," and the related claim made by Kim Pusik of royal Silla blood in the line of Koryŏ's kings, see

Suematsu Yasukazu, *"Kyu-Sangoku-shi* to *Sangoku-Shiki," Seikyū Shisō* (Tokyo, 1966), pp. 1–27. To the plausibility of the earlier work's being Koguryŏ oriented (since that was, after all, in accordance with Koryŏ's state-founding ideology), Suematsu adds his conclusion about the founding dates of Koguryŏ and Silla as given in the *Samguk Sagi:* Kim Pusik, lacking any documentation for his unrealistic Silla chronology, simply derived it by predating from the Koguryŏ founding date, which *is* realistic, and was probably documented in the "Old History." Appended to Suematsu's article are the relevant texts—the "Ode," the "Old History's" Annals of King Tongmyŏng, and the corresponding annals in the *Samguk Sagi*— tabularly organized to facilitate comparison. A cursory comparison of the versions of the two histories reveals that from the standpoint of *cheng-t'ung* Kim Pusik emasculated the earlier one, toning down its mandate claims by presenting them in a hearsay fashion or omitting them altogether. I believe that Yi Kyubo's "Ode" rests upon a well-developed mythic tradition wherein Koguryŏ was paramount among the three kingdoms, and, as a corollary, the Koryŏ unification was seen as representing, not a northward expansion of civilization (as the Silla-successionists would have it), but a southward expansion of the political power and cultural spirit of a resurgent Koguryŏ. Prof. Yi Pyŏngdo, in the "Explication" (*Haesŏl*) introducing his translation of the *Samguk Sagi* (vol. I, Seoul, 1956, pp. 7 ff.) refrains from speculating about the issue of Silla-ism vs. Koguryŏ-ism, contenting himself with remarking that the "Old History" was probably not much different from Kim Pusik's work, for which, indeed, it served as the basic framework. Folkloristic analyses have been made by M. I. Nikitina, in his *Ocherki Istorii Koreiskoi Literaturyi do XIV v.* (Moscow, 1969), pp. 46–53; Russian translations appended, pp. 226–232; and by Kim Ch'ŏltchun in his article "Koryŏ Chunggi-ŭi Munhwa Ŭisikgwa Sahak-ŭi Sŏnggyŏk," in Yi Usŏng and Kang Man'gil (eds.), *Han'guk-ŭi Yŏksa Insik*, vol. I (Seoul, 1976), pp. 96 ff.

11. See Yi Pyŏngdo, *Koryŏ Sidae-ŭi Yŏngu* (Seoul, 1958), pp. 3 ff. A particularly interesting recent addition to the Korean scholarship on the "consciousness" prevalent in the late Silla–early Koryŏ period is an article by Ch'oe Pyŏnghŏn in *Han'guk-sa Yŏngu* 11 (1975): 101–146. Focusing on the late Silla monk Tosŏn, Ch'oe describes the role of Sŏn Buddhism, allied with geomantic (*p'ungsu*) theories, in the sociopolitical transition from Silla to Koryŏ. An important source for these matters is the *P'yŏnnyŏn T'ongnok* (n. 8 above), which, in responding to the ideological needs of the reign of Ŭijong, collected legendary material that had been current at the time of the dynasty's founding.

12. For a good selection of references concerning the concept of dynastic legitimacy, see Hok-lam Chan, *The Historiography of the Chin Dynasty: Three Studies* (Wiesbaden, 1970), pp. 54 ff.

13. See R. Trauzettel, "Ou-yang Hsius Essays über die legitime Thronnachfolge," *Sinologica* 9 (1967): 226–249.

14. See John Fincher, "China as Race, Culture, and Nation: Notes on Fang Hsiao-ju's Discussion of Dynastic Legitimacy," in D. Buxbaum and F. Mote (eds.), *Transition and Permanence: Chinese History and Culture. A Festschrift in Honor of Dr. Hsiao Kung-ch'uan* (Hong Kong, 1972), pp. 59–69.

15. For some general observations on the Chinese perception of world order, with reference to its effects on the self-perceptions of the non-Chinese people on the

periphery of the empire, see B. I. Schwartz, "The Chinese Perception of World Order," in J. K. Fairbank (ed.), *The Chinese World Order* (Cambridge, Mass., 1968), pp. 280 ff.

16. For Liao's conquest of Po-hai, see K. Wittfogel and C. S. Feng, *History of Chinese Society: Liao (907–1125)* (Philadelphia, 1949), pp. 576 ff. The chronicler of Taejo's reign notes the conquest, *sub* 925, in terms sympathetic to Po-hai, which "was neighbor to us and generation after generation was hostile to the Khitan" (*KRS*, 1, 18a-b). There was a considerable influx of Po-hai refugees into Koryŏ.

17. In fact, it would appear that Koryŏ was inaugurated with an independent reign-title, "Heaven-bestowed" (*Ch'ŏn-su*), which Wang Kŏn adopted upon his assumption of power in 918 (*KRS*, 1, 8b, 1a) and retained until he accepted investiture from the Later T'ang in 933 (*KRS*, 2, 3b–6a; 86, 3a). Kwangjong (r. 950–975), who is credited with placing the dynasty on a firm foundation, adopted the reign-title "Radiant Virtue" (Kwangdŏk) in 950 (*KRS*, 2, 26b) and retained it until 952 (investiture from Later Chou: *KRS*, 2, 27a); regarding chronological discrepancies between *KRS* and a contemporary inscription, see Imanishi Ryū, *Kōrai-shi Kenkyū* (Keijō, 1944), pp. 187–200, and Akiura Hideo in *Seikyū Gakusō* 12 (1933): 108–147. Responding to the extinction of the Later Chou in 960, Kwangjong adopted the reign-title *Ch'unp'ung* ("Lofty Abundance"; Imanishi's surmise, op. cit., pp. 180 ff., that *Ch'unp'ung* was merely a taboo variant of the first Sung reign-title, *Chien-lung*, is unconvincing). It is noteworthy that *Ch'unp'ung*, unlike the earlier cases, is attested only in inscriptions (not in *KRS*). This absence of literary evidence undoubtedly reflects the official historians' effort to shield their state from the opprobrium of rebellion against the Sung; in the case of the Five Dynasties, whose charisma was so much less, such suppression wasn't felt to be necessary.

18. Koryŏ's first envoy to Sung, Yi Hŭng'u, was sent in 962 (for references, see Marugame Kinsaku, "Korai to So to no Tsuko Mondai," *Chōsen Gakuhō* 17 [Oct. 1960]: 2 and 6). In the following year Kwangjong received a patent of investiture recognizing him as "King of the State of Kao-li."

19. In the Koryŏ-Liao peace settlement, which was formalized in 1022, the Korean King's acknowledgment of his subordination to the Khitan emperor was basic. Regarding this, and the subterfuge (replacing Hyonjong with a fictitious king) to which the Koryŏ court shortly afterwards resorted in its relations with Liao, see M. Rogers, "Some Kings of Koryŏ as Registered in Chinese Works," *Journal of the American Oriental Society* 81, 4 (1961): 419 ff.

20. *KRS*, 94, 1b–5b.

21. Cf. Feng Chia-sheng, *The Sources of Liao Dynasty History* (in Chinese), *Yenching Journal of Chinese Studies*, Mon. Ser. No. 5 (1933), pp. 32 ff.

22. See note 54.

23. Yi Chehyŏn (1287–1367) in his critique of Sŏngjong (appended to the latter's annals, *KRS*, 3, 3b, f.) pointedly alludes to the threats to which the Sung court was subjected prior to the Shan-yüan treaty as paralleling the experiences of the Koryŏ court before Sŏ Hui undertook his heroic diplomacy. The territory which the Later Chin had ceded to the Khitans (936) was apt to be referred to when Sung or Koryŏ requested aid of the other (*KRS*, 3, 8a; T'o T'o et al., *Sung shih* [hereafter *SS*], Po-na edition, 487, 3a–3b), and in 1003 by the Koryŏ envoy Yi Song'gu, who alleges

that the Yen-Chi territorial cession was a factor in facilitating the Khitans' approach to Koryŏ (*SS*, 487, 8a).

24. See Christian Schwartz-Schilling, *Der Friede von Shan-yüan* (1005 n. Chr.) (Wiesbaden, 1959).

25. On this point Sung's policy was predetermined. The intention of the Khitans to invade Koryŏ was made to the Sung court by a Liao envoy who was received on Nov. 14, 1010. Chen-tsung, having conferred with his chancellor, Wang Tan (957–1017), ordered the magistrate of Teng-chou (Shantung) to inform any Korean envoys who might ask for military aid that he dare not forward the request to the court.

26. *KRS*, 4, 38a.

27. An impulse toward self-sufficiency was evident a few years earlier (1017), when Hyŏnjong decreed that special honor be done to the tombs of the kings of Koguryŏ, Silla, and Paekche (*KRS*, 4, 24b). This was clearly an appeal to the several peninsular loyalties to join in resisting the common Khitan foe.

28. Kyŏngsul yŏnjung yu nojin
   Kan'gwa sim'ip Han'gang pin
   Tangsi pul'yong Kanggong ch'aek,
   Kŏguk kae wi chwaim-in. (*KRS*, 94, 9b).

29. *KRS*, 8, 11a-b; cf. Kim Sanggi, *Koryŏ Sidae-sa*, p. 163.

30. M. Rogers, "Factionalism and Koryŏ Policy under the Northern Sung," *Journal of the American Oriental Society* 79, 1 (1959): 16–25.

31. In the case of Liao's peninsular tributary, for example, no remissions of tribute are recorded for the period 1054–1071 (see Wittfogel and Feng, op. cit., pp. 320–324).

32. M. Rogers, "The Regularization of Koryŏ-Chin Relations (1116–1131)," *Central Asiatic Journal* 6, 1 (1961): 52–84. In general works coverage has been limited to this initial phase of the relations between the two states: e.g., Yi Pyŏng-do, *Han'guk-sa, Chungse-p'yŏn* (Seoul, 1961), pp. 404–418; Mikami Tsugio *Kinshi Kenkyū, San: Kindai Joshin Shakai no Kenkyū* (Tokyo, 1973), pp. 438–486. I. V. Vanin ignores Chin almost entirely in his *Feodal'naia Koreia v XIII–XIV Vekakh* (Moscow, 1962), mentioning the Jurchen state only in connection with the Mongol invasions. Granted that Koryŏ does not loom nearly so large on Chin's horizon as the latter does on Koryŏ's, the Koreanist cannot but feel some disappointment on noting that Koryŏ does not even appear in the index of Toyama Gunji's large volume on Chin history, *Kinchō-shi Kenkyū* (Kyoto, 1970).

33. The period encompassed by the reigns of Injong (1123–1146) and Ŭijong (1147–1170) has been described as one of remarkable cultural achievement in Koryŏ (Inaba Iwakichi, "Sangoku Shiki no Hihan," *Chōsen* 192 (1931): 135–150; Kim Sanggi, *Koryŏ Sidae-sa*, pp. 400–413).

34. Po-hai's identification of itself with Koguryŏ in diplomacy with Japan in the eighth century is well attested in the *Shoku Nihongi* (see Mikami *Kindai-shi*, p. 40, nn. 20–23, for references pertaining to the years 727, 759, and 761). Apart from the matter of Po-hai's state-founding ideology being Koguryŏ oriented, it is likely that Po-hai's seventh-century overtures to Japan, stressing affiliation with Koguryŏ so as to utilize that state's former good relations with Japan, was Po-hai's response to pressures exerted at that time by T'ang and the latter's peninsular vassal-state of Silla (for this observation I am indebted to my colleague John C. Jamieson and

his unpublished paper, "The Manchurian Kingdom of Pohai," presented at the Regional Conference on Korean Studies, University of British Columbia, Feb. 17−19, 1978). Texts of the official communications between Po-hai and Japan have been brought together by Chin Yü-fu in his *Po-hai kuo-chih ch'ang-pien*, Ch'ien-hua shan-kuan, ed., ch. 18, 5b−24a (reprinted as no. 55 of Hua-wen shu-chü's *Chung-hua Wen-shih ts'ung-shu*).

35. For the above interpretation of "Kao-li" in the context of the rise of Chin, I am indebted to Mikami (op. cit., pp. 22−26), though I would agree with Prof. Yi Pyŏngdo (*Hanguk-sa, Chungse-p'yon*, p. 376) that the matter merits further investigation. See also the discussion of Pak Hyŏnso in the National History Compilation Committee's *Hanguk-sa*, IV, pp. 324 ff.

36. Regarding the distinction between *ming* and *meng*, see W. A. C. H. Dobson, "Some Legal Instruments of Ancient China: The Ming and the Meng," **Wen-lin**, *Studies in the Chinese Humanities*, edited by Chow Tse-tung (Madison, 1968), pp. 269−282. It was a distinction of which the Koreans were all aware, as is clear from their stated grounds for dissociating themselves from the *meng*.

37. The oath-letters that were exchanged between Chin and Sung in 1142 leave no doubt about the latter's subordinate status. (See H. Franke, "Treaties between Sung and Chin," *Études Song in Memoriam Étienne Balázs*, Ser. I, 1 [1970], pp. 77 ff.)

38. I refer to the Sung−Hsi Hsia transaction of 1044. Li Yüan-hao felt compelled to seek peace with Sung because he was faced with a hostile Liao (see Kychanov, *Ocherk*, pp. 153 ff., and "Les Guerres . . . ," pp. 109−111; Tao Jing-shen, "Yü Ching and Sung Policies toward Liao and Hsia, 1042−1044," *Journal of Asian History* 6, 2 (1972): 114−122).

39. In 1118 Aguda presented Liao with a series of demands, including the remission of documents pertaining to Liao's relations with Sung, Hsia, and Korea. The Liao government complied with this in 1118; see Wittfogel and Feng, op. cit., p. 596.

40. Rogers, "Regularization," pp. 72 ff.

41. *KRS*, 15, 41b.

42. *KRS*, 16, 4b: Injong 7th year, 11th month, *ping-ch'en* day.

43. Rogers, "Regularization," pp. 75−77. Han Fang's biography, which is the first one given in *Chin-shih*, 125, stresses this episode, which is conspicuously absent in the other relevant sections of *Chin-shih*—the Annals (ch. 3), the Diplomatic Tables (ch. 60), and the Monograph on Koryŏ (ch. 135). Evidently, the compilers of the official history found the episode admissible as a personal exploit (indeed, it seems to be Han Fang's chief claim to fame) but not as a diplomatic issue. The Manchu court took a very different attitude in the 17th century: in the officially commissioned précis of the *Chin-shih*, done in the 1640s, Han Fang's exploit is all that is given concerning Chin's relations with Koryŏ (C. de Harlez, *Histoire de l'Empire de Kin: Aisin gurun-i-suduri bithe* [Louvain, 1887] pp. 57 ff.).

44. For bibliography concerning this movement, see Yi Kibaek, *Han'guk-sa Sillon* (Seoul, 1976, rev. ed), p. 168.

45. See note 5.

46. There was concern in the Koryŏ court lest Kim Pusik's protracted siege of the Western Capital provoke armed intervention from Chin (see Rogers, "Regularization," p. 81, n. 141). Nothing of the sort happened, and as it turned out, the

annual embassies exchanged by Chin and Koryŏ (as tabulated in *Chin-shih*, ch. 60–62, and noted in the annals of the *Koryŏ-sa*), were uninterrupted from 1127 to 1212.

47. See James T. C. Liu, "Yüeh Fei (1107–1141) and China's Image of Loyalty," *Journal of Asian Studies* 30, 2 (1972): 197.

48. *KRS*, 98, 19a.

49. See *Chindan Hakpo* 38 (Oct. 1974): 203–227.

50. The linkages in question (for the most part supplied by Kim Pusik in his commentaries) were analyzed in 1920 by Ogiyama Hideo in *Tōyō Gakuhō* 20, 3. For more recent observations, see Koh Byŏng'ik, "Samguk Sagi-e issŏsŏ-ŭi Yŏksa Sŏsul," in his *Tong'a Kyosŏpsa-ŭi Yŏngu*, pp. 69–101, esp. pp. 93 ff. (the article is reprinted in *Hanguk-ŭi Yŏksa Insik*, vol. I, no. 8, pp. 31–63); see also Yi Usŏng's contribution to the "*Samguk Sagi* Symposium," pp. 2–6.

51. There was of course a basis of fact here: Wang Kŏn did adopt Silla practices in the organization of his state. See Ha Hyŏn'gang, "Koryŏ-sisae-ŭi Yŏksa Ŭisik," *Yihwa Sahak Yŏngu* 8 (1975): 12, n. 2 (references to *Samguk Sagi* 33, *Koryŏ-sa Chŏl'yo* 1, and *Koryŏ-sa* 76).

52. *Samguk Sagi* contains seven references to Po-hai, all in contexts apparently derived from Chinese sources. In his Monograph on Geography, Kim Pusik twice notes that Po-hai fell heir to Koguryŏ territory (ch. 37, pp. 2 and 11 of 1928 Chōsenshi Gakkai ed.).

53. An early exponent of the view that the history of Korea should include that of Po-hai was Yi Sŭnghiu (1224–1300), who represents it as a bridge linking Koguryŏ with Koryŏ, in his *Chewang Un'gi* ("Rhymed Record of Theocrats and Kings"), the standard edition of which is included in *Koryŏ Myŏnghyŏn chip*, vol. I, pp. 627–644; cf. Yi Usŏng, "Koryŏ Chunggi-ŭi Minjok Sŏsasi," *Sŏnggyun-gwan Taehakkyo Nonmum chip* 7 (1962): 94 ff. Yu Tukkong (1748–?) in his *P'arhae-ko* (quoted in Yi Usŏng, op. cit., p. 108) deplored Koryŏ's failure to compile "Northern" and "Southern" Histories so as to claim Po-hai; cf. Yi Usŏng, "A Study of the Period of the Northern and Southern States," *Korea Journal* 17, 1 (Jan. 1977): 28–33. The nationalist historian Sin Ch'aeho (1888–1936) endorsed this, claiming Po-hai as an integral part of the history of the Korean people (*Collected Works of Sin Ch'aeho*, vol. I [Seoul, 1972], p. 502; cf. Cha Kipyok, "Political Thought behind Korean Nationalism," *Korea Journal* 16, 4 [April 1976]: 13.)

54. Koryŏ was often referred to as "Silla" by men of Sung, Liao, and Chin (see Yi Pyŏngdo, *Koryŏ Sidae-ŭi Yŏngu* [Seoul, 1954], p. 180, and Wittfogel and Feng, op. cit., pp. 261–318). In the case of the Manchurian kingdoms one can readily see self-serving reasons (i.e., territorial implications) for denial of the name Koryŏ to the peninsular state. Thus, in the *Ch'i-tan kuo-chih*, ch. 26, Koryŏ is named "Silla" and is described as being to the east of Kao-li, occupying the territory of Han's Lo-lang. On the other hand, Hsü Ching's *Kao-li t'u-ching* (A.D. 1123) clearly traces Koryŏ's descent from Koguryŏ, through Po-hai (ch. 1, p. 12, of the *Han-p'an Yi Sangok* Festschrift ed. [Seoul, 1970]). Since Hsü Ching's testimony undoubtedly reflects what he was told at the Koryŏ court, one may conclude that the latter, however Silla oriented in domestic ideology, regarded their state's Koguryŏ persona as more effective when confronting an international crisis.

55. "Koguryŏ chan'ol yuch'wi" (*Samguk Sagi*, 46; p. 3; cf. *Koun Sŏnsaeng Munjip* in *Ch'oe Munch'ang-hu Chŏnjip* [Sŏnggyn'gwan Univ. ed., Seoul, 1972], p. 70).

SEVEN

Tibetan Relations with Sung China and with the Mongols

LUCIANO PETECH

With the murder of the anti-Buddhist king Glang-dar-ma in 842, the Tibetan monarchy collapsed. The outer dominions in western and northwestern China and in Central Asia were lost. Tibet itself disintegrated into a number of principalities ruled by families descended from the two sons of Glang-dar-ma. By the beginning of the tenth century, the process of fragmentation was complete. Already in that century, but mainly in the next one, the Buddhist monasteries, which were scattered all over the country, entered the political arena. Some of them became wealthy, thanks to pious foundations and donations, and tried to play a role in the contest for power. At first they sought the support of some noble family; later they used their own economic power for political action. It was then the turn of the neighboring princes to look to the monasteries for protection. Several monasteries came to form centers of ecclesiastical principalities ruled by abbots who were originally chosen by the monks themselves. Later the succession was often based on heredity. One brother usually became the spiritual leader, while another married in order to produce children. The succession went normally from uncle to nephew (e.g., abbots of Sa-skya who were from the 'Khon family). This could even lead to the establishment of two separate branches, one restricted to spiritual leadership and the other wielding administrative powers (e.g., the P'ag-mo-gru-pa). Another possibility was for the abbot to marry and to bequeath his position to his son, though such cases of succession were infrequent. The rNying-ma-pa and other Red Sects permitted a transfer of power from father to son.

From the ninth to the thirteenth century there was no Tibetan state. No single government ruled all of Tibet. A study of international relations between Tibet and neighboring countries is thus difficult. No one Tibetan kingdom maintained relations with China, Central Asia, and the northern Indian states; a number of local principalities among the various frontiers dealt with neighboring countries. Only with Mongol control of Tibet did one single state emerge.

A particular difficulty is caused by the nature of our sources. Any historian dealing with Tibetan events from the ninth to the thirteenth century is bound to draw an unbalanced picture. The tiny scraps of information relating to the years from about 900 to about 1230 are in sharp contrast with the relatively plentiful evidence available for the rest of the thirteenth century. There is little hope that fresh material on the political history of those "black centuries" will be made available.

Another obstacle is that the texts dealing with this period are exclusively religious, being written by monks for monks. They concentrate on the religious aspects of foreign relations. They refer primarily to Indian scholars who came to Tibet to revive and reform Buddhism, local kings who patronized Tibetan scholars and sent them to study in the Indian universities, and the comings and goings of Tibetan monks to and from Mongolia and China on the invitation of the Mongol rulers.

Similarly, the Chinese sources for the Five Dynasties and Sung periods practically ignore Tibet, with the exception of the small principalities in Amdo, which had little influence except in a restricted local area. On the other hand, both Chinese and Tibetan texts covering the Yüan period are copious and complementary. Under these circumstances, selection among the Tibetan texts is essential; in principle, I have utilized the earlier texts only, those nearer to the events. Accordingly, such well-known works as the *dPag-bsam-ljon-bzang* of Sum-pa mKhan-po and the *Hor Chos-'byung* of 'Jigs-med-rig-pa'i-rdo-rje are quoted only in those rare instances where they do not wholly depend on their predecessors.

The essay ends with the last decades of the thirteenth century because by that time there are no international relations. Tibet had become a dependency of Mongol China and lacked the independent status required to develop its own foreign policy.

The Tsong-kha Kingdom and the Sung

After the end of both the T'ang dynasty and the Tibetan monarchy, the Chinese continued to refer to their western neighbors as the T'u-fan but now in a restricted sense. Whereas in the T'ang period T'u-fan indicated the huge Tibetan kingdom, under the Five Dynasties and the Sung it was applied to a small territory in Amdo, on the Kansu border, occupied by some splinter principalities. Some of them were inhabited by Tibetans, while others were formed by fragments of various populations formerly subject to Tibet but set free by the collapse of the monarchy. The Tibetans called these groups 'od-'bar, transcribed in Chinese as Wu-mo or Hun-mo.[1]

In 906 the Tibetans attacked the Wu-mo, who were in partial control of Hsi-liang-fu (Liang-chou). They apparently met with success, and in 908 and 911 the Wu-mo envoys who presented themselves at the Chinese court did so on behalf of their Tibetan masters. The second embassy, coupled with one from the Kan-chou Uighurs, was received with particular honors. After an interval, other embassies from T'u-fan came to court between 927 and 933. By then, these so-called embassies were simply messengers sent by the local Tibetan gentry seeking appointments in the provincial official-dom of Liang-chou. After 933 the Chinese texts register them as missions from Hsi-liang-fu, dropping the mention of T'u-fan; Liang-chou was con-sidered an imperial town, governed by Tibetan officials who bore the local title *che-pu* (Tib. *c'ed-po?*). After 950 the raids and invasions of the Tanguts and the Uighurs temporarily severed this area's relations with China.[2]

When the Sung gained the throne, communications with Liang-chou were reopened. The main importance of the so-called T'u-fan tribes for China consisted in the thriving horse trade, which was particularly lively in the years between 990 and 995, under the Liang-chou chiefs *che-pu* A-yü-tan (d. 993) and his brother and successor *che-pu* Yü-lung-po.[3] At the end of the tenth century, some changes took place. Sung China was the paramount power, and the Uighur khanate of Kan-chou continued to be its good neighbor; the Tibetan clans usually maintained friendly relations with both because of trade. But farther east the Tangut state was in the process of formation, which eventually led to friction and open warfare.

The main center of Tibetan population in the Liang-chou district was the Liu-ku (Six Valleys) region, to the west of the town.[4] At the dawn of the eleventh century, the eastern section of the region was ruled by the *che-pu* Yü-lung-po. In about 1001, in the western section, a new leader named P'an-lo-chih appeared; this name is possibly a transcription of *'Phan bla-rje*, and he may have been a member of the famous Rlangs family. He very quickly became the foremost figure in the politics of that outer fringe of the Chinese empire. The extent of his wealth is revealed by the tribute of five thousand horses he sent to K'ai-feng in 1002. In the following year his power reached its zenith when the thirty-two clans of the upper Wei rallied to him, and the Sung government awarded him the title of Shuo-fang *chieh-tu-shih*.[5]

The Sung sought to gain the support of P'an-lo-chih against Li Chi-ch'ien, the founder of the Tangut state, who was threatening China's northwestern borderlands. In 1003 Li marched his troops into Liang-chou. P'an-lo-chih tendered his submission, and Li Chi-ch'ien, not suspecting treachery, accepted it. Almost at once, the Tibetan chieftain gathered the Liu-ku clans, attacked his new overlord by surprise, and utterly defeated him. Li Chi-ch'ien was hit by an arrow during his flight and died of his wound (February 1004). This success was of little use to P'an-lo-chih, who was murdered some months later.[6]

At the end of 1004, the Liu-ku tribes elected P'an-lo-chih's younger brother Ssu-to-tu as their leader. He was immediately appointed Shuo-fang *chieh-tu-shih* by the Chinese government, and continued to be loyal to the Sung, sending tribute at frequent intervals. His people were weakened by a serious outbreak of plague which in 1006 decimated his clans. He sent tribute for the last time in 1015, and late in the same year the Uighurs attacked and occupied Liang-chou, killing Ssu-to-tu in the process.

In the meantime a new center of power was building up outside the ill-defined border, in the purely Tibetan district of Tsong-kha (i.e., the region around Hsi-ning). A prince from Western Tibet, named Chüeh-ssu-lo (997–1065), was elected ruler at the age of twelve (i.e., in 1008). After some dispute about the seat of government, a Lama called Li Li-tsun or Li Tsun kidnapped Chüeh-ssu-lo and brought him to the town of Tsong-kha, east of Hsi-ning, where he installed him as king and became his minister (*lun-po*, Tibetan *blon-po*).[8]

Chüeh-ssu-lo's real name was Ch'i Nan-lu Wen Ch'ien-pu, and we are expressly told that the last two syllables were a local pronunciation of *btsan-po*, the royal title of the old Tibetan monarchy. *Wen* seems to correspond to Tibetan *dbon*, "nephew," and occurs in several other names in that area. The first three syllables may transcribe Khri gNam-lde, a name which agrees with the pattern prevailing in the lineage of Khri bKra-shis-rtsegs-pa. His country of origin, called Wu-san-mi or Kao-ch'ang Mo-yü, was situated far to the west of the Kuku Nor. Professor Stein goes so far as to suggest that Mo-yü = Mar-yul (i.e., Ladakh); but this would encounter a series of historical and geographical difficulties.[9]

Chüeh-ssu-lo entered the political arena in 1014, when he and Li Li-tsun were strong enough to collect an army of about 60,000 to 70,000 men against the advance of the Tanguts. In the following year they for the first time sent tribute to the Chinese court, including high-bred horses and 7,000 ounces of gold. As a rule, the new kingdom followed a policy of friendship with the Chinese emperor as well as with the Uighur ruler of Kan-chou. This policy was briefly interrupted in 1015, when Chüeh-ssu-lo, having assisted the Uighur ruler against the Tanguts, asked for a daughter of his in marriage. When he was rebuffed, he retaliated by preventing commerce and diplomatic relations between Kan-chou and Chinese territory. In the following year, the Uighur ruler died, and his successor gave way, leading to the restoration of relations.[10]

In the same year Li Li-tsun renounced his religious vows and returned to a lay state, marrying eighteen women. At the beginning of 1017 he petitioned the Sung court to be granted the title *btsan-po*. But the K'ai-feng government—noting that Chüeh-ssu-lo, although higher in status and birth than Li Li-tsun, had made no such request—rejected his request. This may have led to a cooling of relations beeween the ruler and his ambitious minister. After 1019 we hear nothing about Li Li-tsun, who disappeared from the scene. Then Chüeh-ssu-lo retired to Miao-ch'uan (now Lo-tu hsien), where he appointed the local chief Wen-pu-ch'i as his new minister.[11]

Meanwhile, the menace of the new Tangut chief Li Yüan-hao had increased rapidly. Chüeh-ssu-lo himself led 45,000 men against the Tanguts. But it was all to no avail. In 1028 the Tanguts took the Uighur capital Kan-chou and soon completed the conquest of the whole Uighur Khanate. Liang-chou too, which had been seized by the Uighurs in 1016, fell into the hands of the Tanguts (1031), whereupon the Tibetan clans who formerly obeyed P'an-lo-chih migrated southward and joined Chüeh-ssu-lo. Li Yüan-hao then turned against the Sung and succeeded in cutting direct communications between Tsong-kha and China by his occupation of Lan-chou and other towns in eastern Kansu. Shortly after, Wen-pu-ch'i rebelled against his master, but was overpowered and killed; on this occasion (1032) Chüeh-ssu-lo shifted his residence to Ch'ing-t'ang (modern Hsi-ning). The most critical moment came in 1035, when Li Yüan-hao launched a direct attack against Chüeh-ssu-lo's new capital, but was stopped and compelled to retreat. Chüeh-ssu-lo's active help was fully recognized by the Sung emperor, who in 1041 granted him the title of Ho-hsi *chieh-tu shih*.[12]

The rise of the Hsi Hsia empire of the Tanguts, officially proclaimed in 1038, turned out to be a blessing in disguise for Tsong-kha. It diverted the Central Asian trade to the Hsi-ning region, since the normal route to China via Liang-chou or the Ordos was barred by the Tanguts. The Central Asian traders now had their terminus at Hsi-ning. About the same time there was a brisk trade of horses from Ch'ing-t'ang in exchange for tea from Szechwan.[13] Amdo was presumably one of the main tea suppliers to Central Tibet, where that beverage was beginning to be appreciated.

The last years of Chüeh-ssu-lo witnessed a serious crisis. The son of the murdered minister Wen-pu-ch'i had become a center of disaffection. He found allies in two of Chüeh-ssu-lo's sons, who were asserting their authority and who had since 1046 sent tribute to the Sung independently from their father. In 1058 the two princes rebelled, but were defeated and killed, and in the following year the same fate befell Wen-pu-ch'i's son. The disaffected tribes returned to the fold. In 1058 Chüeh-ssu-lo fought with success against the Tanguts.[14] He also received a Khitan princess as wife for his third son, Tung-chan. The old Tibetan ruler died on November 3, 1065. The greatest figure in the medieval history of Amdo had passed from the scene.[15]

Chüeh-ssu-lo was the only Tibetan leader able to organize a semblance of a state and to play a role in the long struggle between Uighurs, Tanguts, and Sung. His kingdom supported Buddhism and often employed Tibetan monks in their relations with the Chinese empire.[16]

Chüeh-ssu-lo was succeeded by Tung-chan, who is probably the Tsong-kha *btsad-po* sPyan-snga Don-chen of the *Red Annals*. Like his father, he was known to the Chinese as the Miao-ch'uan chief, although his residence had been moved to Ch'ing-t'ang. Tung-chan, until his death in 1086, entertained good relations with the Sung, and in 1081, upon the request of the emperor, he mobilized his warriors to repel an attack by Hsi Hsia.[17]

His successors as Miao-ch'uan chief and Ho-hsi *chieh-tu shih* were his adopted son A-li-ku (1040–1096) and the latter's son-in-law Hsia-cheng. With Hsia-cheng, a cruel and incapable man, the kingdom plunged into turmoil. His uncle was accused of plotting against him; Hsia-cheng dared not put him to death, but sternly punished his followers. All the tribes south of the Yellow River broke away from Tsong-kha. One Ch'i-pa-wen, being exiled by Hsia-cheng to the Lung-pu (Rong-po) tribes, rebelled, occupied Ch'i-ko (Tib. Khri-kha), and proclaimed himself king there. In 1099 the Sung capitalized on this civil war and occupied Miao-ch'uan. Hsia-cheng fled from Ch'ing-t'ang and submitted to the Sung; he died in China in 1102. His rival Ch'i-pa-wen occupied Ch'ing-t'ang, but the town was retaken by the Sung forces in the following month. Most of the kingdom fell into Chinese hands and was organized into regular districts with new names: Miao-ch'uan became Huang-chou, Ch'ing-t'ang was given the name Chan-chou, and the town of Tsong-kha became Lung-chih ch'eng.[18]

This first Chinese occupation was merely a phase. A general revolt broke out at once and after one month the garrison of Tsong-kha was cut to pieces and the town fell into the hands of Ch'i-pa-wen; Miao-ch'uan too was evacuated. Some years later the Sung mounted an offensive, and in 1104 the Chinese recovered Ch'ing-t'ang; the town was given the name Hsi-ning by which it is still known. Ch'i-ko was fortified by the Sung in 1105. The rest of Ch'i-pa-wen's short-lived kingdom was organized in 1009 as the Chi-shih *chün*. This unexpected revival of Sung authority in Amdo was a result of the aggressive policy carried out by the K'ai-feng government between 1102 and 1105 on the initiative of the eunuch T'ung Kuan. Sung paramountcy in Amdo, however, came to an end after their ill-advised attack upon the Hsi Hsia (once more upon the advice of T'ung Kuan), which ended with disastrous defeats southeast of Hsi-ning (1115) and south of Lan-chou.[19] Shortly thereafter, the advance of the Jurchens culminating in the conquest of K'ai-feng (1126) eliminated Sung influence from Amdo. The last tribute mission from T'u-fan to the Sung was received in 1136.

Amdo seems to have remained for a long time a no-man's-land between Hsi Hsia and Chin. In 1182 the Chin finally incorporated Tsong-kha into its empire.[20] By that time the region had lost much of its significance in Tibetan-Chinese relations, and very little is known of its history in the twelfth and thirteenth centuries.

The Tibetans also maintained relations with the Khitans during this same time. According to the Liao annals, the Tibetan tribes were divided into four groups: Hsi-fan, Ta-fan, Hsiao-fan, and T'u-fan.[21] The Liao History lists tribute missions from T'u-fan in 953, 989, 1051, 1054, 1069, 1071, 1075, 1103, and 1104.[22] No details beyond the bare fact of their arrival are available, and we do not know which Tibetan tribes were responsible for these missions. No part of Tibet bordered on the Liao empire. Liang-chou first and Tsong-kha afterwards presumably tried to foster trade relations by sending envoys with presents.

The Sa-skya-pa and the Mongols

According to Mongol accounts, the Mongols and Tibet were in touch as early as Chinggis Khan's proclamation as Supreme Khan in 1026. No trace of this is found in the early historical works written by Tibetans.

An earlier version, contained in the *Shira Tuji* (written ca. 1655–1660) and Saghang Sechen's *Erdeni-yin tobci* (written in 1662), reports that in 1206 Chinggis Khan marched against the king of Tibet Külüge Dorji Khaghan.[23] The latter sent Ilughu Noyan as envoy with three hundred men, presenting tribute of countless camels and offering to submit. Chinggis accepted the tribute and sent Ilughu Noyan back to Tibet bearing a letter for Sa-skya Chag Lotsawa Ānandagarbha (= Tib. Kun-dga'-snying-po). In this way he became master of the whole of Tibet.

Külüge Dorji seems to refer to rDo-rje-dpal or Tho-ci, the Tibetan name of the ninth Tangut ruler, killed in 1227.[24] Ilughu Noyan is actually Ilughu Burkhan, which appears to have been a general title of all the Tangut rulers until Chinggis Khan changed the name of the last one to Shidurghu before ordering his execution.[25] A tribute of camels points unmistakably to the Hsi Hsia. Accordingly, the main portion of this account was recognized long ago as a mistaken reference to Chinggis Khan's second campaign against the Tangut kingdom, which took place in 1207.[26] In 1206 or 1207 Chinggis Khan's dominions did not border with Tibet at all, as the Tangut kingdom lay between the two.[27] As to the Chag Lo-tsawa, this is either dGra-bcom (1153–1216) or his nephew C'os-rje-dpal (1197–1264),[28] while Kun-dga'-snying-po is the name of the Sa-skya abbot who lived from 1092 to 1158 and who is said to have prophesied the birth of Chinggis Khan.[29] A good deal of confusion has clearly crept in here.[30]

A later version appears first in Sum-pa mKhan-po's *dPag-bsam-ljon-bzang* (1748), followed by 'Jigs-med-rig-pa'i-rdo-rje's *Hor Chos-'byung* (1819), the first perhaps and the second certainly being a Mongol writing in Tibetan. They assert that in 1206 or 1207 Chinggis Khan marched to dBus (Central Tibet). The *sde-srid* Jo-da' and Tshal-pa Kun-dga'-rdo-rje with a following of three hundred men held a great feast (*dga'-ston*) and sent a messenger to the conqueror to submit, to present their homage, and to recognize him as sovereign of Western, Central, and Eastern Tibet. Thus Chinggis Khan became lord of all of Tibet. He sent a letter to the Sa-skya Lama Kun-dga'-snying-po, expressing his intention to invite him soon to Mongolia.[31]

sDe-srid Jo-dga' is listed among the princes of Yar-klungs, but no date is given. Kun-dga'-snying-po, as was mentioned above, lived from 1092 to 1158. Tshal-pa Kun-dga'-rdo-rje was the author of the *Deb-ther dmar-po*, compiled in 1346. Thus the whole account is a tissue of chronological and historical absurdities.

As far as the Tshal-pa are concerned, this may be a later development of an earlier tradition according to which the first Tibetan monks to penetrate Mongolia were gTsang-pa Dung-khur-ba and six pupils of his. They led an ascetic life and worked miracles among the herdsmen, but as they did not know the language they could express themselves only by signs. They reached Mongolia three or four years after the proclamation of Chinggis Khan as ruler of the Mongols (i.e., 1209–1210). The hostility of the Taoists (their presence in Mongolia is surprising) and of the Nestorian Christians compelled gTsang-pa and his followers to move to the Tangut kingdom. Chinggis Khan found them there when he invaded that country in 1215. gTsang-pa talked with the conqueror through an interpreter and explained to him the main tenets of Buddhism, obtaining eventually a document (*'ja'-sa*) granting protection to the Buddhist monks.[32] This tradition may have some historical foundation only so far as the Tshal-pa activities in the Tangut kingdom are concerned.

In sum, the theory that a parliament of the Tibetan lay and ecclesiastical princes assembled in 1206 to tender voluntary submission to Chinggis Khan is invalid.[33]

Chinggis's son and successor, Ögödei (1229–1241), sought relations with Tibet. Tibetan sources note that after ascending the throne Ögödei advised his family to invite the Lama (Tshal) Gung-thang-pa. His sister-in-law, the "Holy Mother" (Sayin eke) Sorghakhtani and her sons (Möngke, Khubilai, etc.), who had already patronized gTsang-pa in 1215, received Gung-thang-pa and acted as his benefactors. He granted them spiritual powers, "and this was the beginning of the quest of religion by the Mongols." The Lama also prophesied the future greatness of Khubilai, and the Tshal-pa monks continued in favor for some time.[34] Whether this account is legendary or contains some factual elements is more than we can tell.

Muslim sources assert that immediately after his election Ögödei dispatched expeditions against Tibet and Korea. After the conquest of the Chin empire in 1234 he again sent an army toward Tibet.[35] Neither Chinese nor Tibetans confirm these alleged expeditions.[36]

A few years later we reach solid ground. In 1236 Köden, Ögödei's second son, had led an unsuccessful campaign in Szechwan, which caused fear of an impending Mongol invasion in Tibet.[37] Köden returned north, and in 1239 settled in Byang-ngos (i.e., the Liang-chou region).[38] Whether on his own initiative or acting on orders from his father, he turned his attention toward Tibet. The country was then in great turmoil, with feuds raging everywhere between princes and monasteries.[39] In 1240 Köden sent a small army under the command of Dor-ta (Dor-tog, Dorda Darkhan), who penetrated as far south as the 'Phan yul valley. This first Mongol inroad caused great damage to the bKa'-gdams-pa convents of rGyal Lha-khang, where five hundred men were butchered, and of Rva-sgreng. Two bKa'-brgyud-pa monasteries were spared. One was sTag-lung, which was covered by such a heavy fog that the Mongols could not see it; the other was 'Bri-gung, which the abbot Grags-pa-'byung-gnas (on the see 1234–1255) is said to have defended by causing a miraculous shower of stones. Dor-ta wished to carry the abbot away with him, hoping that the latter would instruct the Mongols in the Buddhist religion. The abbot refused and instead suggested the name of Sa-skya Paṇḍita Kun-dga'-rgyal-mtshan (1182–1251). As the terrible fame of the Mongols had preceded them, the 'Bri-gung abbot was probably trying to save his life or his freedom. He did not suspect that his refusal would be extremely significant for the future of Tibet.[40]

Köden waited until 1244 to send envoys, probably with an escort but without an army, to summon the Sa-skya Paṇḍita to his camp. His letter was dated on the full moon of the eighth month and was accompanied by presents. It was courteous in tone but also contained a clear threat of invasion in case of noncompliance.[41] A refusal was out of the question, and the 'Bri-gung abbot himself urged the Sa-skya Paṇḍita to accept the invitation. The elderly Sa-skya abbot (he was sixty-two at the time), accompanied by his nephews 'Phags-pa and Phyag-na-rdo-rje, respectively nine and seven years old, set out on his journey.[42] The Tibetans had not elected him or conferred a mandate on him. The Mongols simply wanted an influential monk to employ for their own purposes in Tibet. The 'Bri-gung-pa was their first choice, but he succeeded in deflecting this unsought-for honor to the Sa-skya-pa; and the latter, perhaps more clear-sighted than his colleague about the ultimate effects, accepted the invitation, or rather the summons.[43]

Sa-skya Paṇḍita started in a leisurely manner on his voyage; he went to dBus and stayed there during the whole of 1245. The objections and fears prevailing in some circles were voiced by the bKa'-gdams-pa monk Nam-mkha'-'bum, whose sect had suffered most from Dor-ta's raid in 1240. Sa-skya Paṇḍita had to explain and justify his undertaking.[44] In the following year Sa-skya Paṇḍita reached Byang-ngos (Liang-chou). Köden was absent, having gone to attend the great *khuriltai* (assembly of Mongol nobles), which in that year elected Güyüg as the successor to Ögödei. He returned to Liang-chou in 1247 and met the abbot there. They agreed without difficulty on the main points of their future relations. The Sa-skya Paṇḍita entered into a new role as an agent of Mongol policy in his home country. He sent a circular letter to the ecclesiastical and lay notables of Tibet, advising them to submit and to allow the Mongols to exact taxes and to levy troops.[45] To cement the agreement, the boy Phyag-na-rdo-rje was promised in marriage a daughter of Köden's. Moreover, Güyüg sent substantial presents to the Tibetan monasteries: 4 bre-chen of gold (1 bre-chen = 20 bre; 1 bre = ca. 2 pints), 20 bre-chen of silver, and 200 precious robes.[46]

By his agreement with the Sa-skya abbot, Köden laid the foundations of Mongol influence in Tibet. Before the two partners could embark upon any serious activity, three events changed the political situation. Güyüg died in 1248, Tolui's son Möngke was elected as his successor on July 1, 1251, and Sa-skya Paṇḍita died at Byang-ngos at the end of 1251.[47] The Mongol throne passed to another branch of the family of Chinggis Khan, and this fact, coupled with the death of the Sa-skya abbot, deprived Köden of any possibility of playing an independent role in Tibetan politics. His arrangements having gone askew, Mongol policy in that region had to be redefined.

Möngke immediately intervened in Tibet. On the one hand, he perhaps intended to secure for himself a zone of influence hitherto reserved to the Ögödei branch of the family; and on the other hand, Tibetan opposition may have increased during the Mongol interregnum and the illness of the Sa-skya Paṇḍita. Whatever the motive, soon after his election, Möngke appointed one Khoridai to command the Mongol and Chinese troops in the T'u-fan region (northeastern Tibet).[48] In the same year or in 1252, Köden sent another army from Liang-chou led by Du-pe-ta or Do-be-ta (Dörbetei?).[49] This two-pronged invasion wrought havoc in Tibet. In 1253, the Mongols under Hur-ta killed an otherwise unknown teacher named rGyal-tsha Jo-'ber and the Mongol advance prevented rGyal-ba Yang-dgon-pa (1213–1258) from meeting the master Khro-phu Lotsawa. The invaders penetrated as far as 'Dam, "killing, looting, burning houses, destroying temples and injuring monks." Because of the invasion of Hur-tang, rGyal-ba Yang-dgon-pa had to advise the prince of La-stod to agree to the Mongol demands.[50] Hur-ta and Hur-tang are evidently Tibetan transcriptions of Khoridai. His campaign lasted about two years and had serious consequences.

Simultaneously, several members of Möngke's family took over the patronage of Tibetan sects. The Khaghan himself protected the 'Bri-gung-pa and the gTsang mGur-mo-ba; the Sa-skya-pa were left to the care of Köden; the Tshal-pa were entrusted to Möngke's younger brother Khubilai; the g. Ya'-bzang-pa, Phag-mo-gru-pa, and Nyamg-pa were to be under the jurisdiction of his brother Hülegü; the sTag-lung-thang-pa were protected by the youngest brother, Arigh Böke.[51] One possible interpretation of this apportionment is that Möngke tried to introduce in Tibet the appanage system that was found in the Mongol-occupied regions of China. At the same time he attempted to exert his influence upon the largest possible number of great monasteries and sects.

This distribution was reshuffled almost at once. The 'Bri-gung abbot sPyan-snga Grags-pa-'byung-gnas "in the second half of his life accepted many presents from king Hu-la-hu [Hülegü]."[52] In 1253 Khubilai asked Köden to hand over 'Phags-pa and his brother.[53] They went to Khubilai's camp accompanied by Köden's second son, Mönggedü, who probably served as a hostage for his father.[54] Nothing further is heard of Köden; he died at some time between 1253 and 1260; his descendants kept their rank in the peerage and their appanage of Liang-chou.[55]

In addition to these changes, one of the "protectors" soon left Central Asia for good. In the *khuriltai* of 1253, Hülegü was entrusted with the command of the Mongol army in Iran. He delayed his departure for some time and traveled slowly, crossing the Amu-Darya as late as January 2, 1256. Meanwhile, he continued to maintain his Tibetan connections and repeatedly sent presents to the Phag-mo-gru-pa abbot rGyal-ba Rin-po-che (on the see 1235–1267).[56] His successors, the Il-Khans of Iran, kept up these contacts. They patronized Buddhist monks and built and endowed temples in their territories. Khan Arghun (1284–1291) was surrounded by Buddhist (probably Tibetan) monks. After his death, however, the dynasty accepted Islam, and in 1295–1296 Buddhism was suppressed and its temples and monasteries were destroyed.[57]

'Phags-pa was well received at Khubilai's court.[58] But the Mongol prince left at once for his successful campaign in Szechwan and Yunnan (1253–1254). Even after his return to his fief, he does not appear to have paid much attention to the young Sa-skya-pa scholar.[59] Shortly thereafter, Khubilai became interested in a quite different sort of holy man, Karma Pakshi (1206–1283), the second incarnation of the Black Hat (Zhvanag) section of the Karma-pa sect, one of the most famous miracle-workers in the history of Tibetan Buddhism. In 1255 Karma Pakshi received an invitation from Khubilai; he started at once and met the prince in Amdo,[60] not far from Khubilai's residence. He stayed with Khubilai for a short time, performing several miracles. Then he departed, much to Khubilai's displeasure, and traveled to Liang-chou and Kan-chou. In 1256 he was received by Möngke in the Shira Ordo palace not far from Karakorum. He gained the favor of the Khaghan and probably participated in a disputation between Buddhists and Taoists held in that year. Possibly in connection with that meeting, the Mongols contacted other religious leaders, such as rGod-Tshang-pa (1189–1258) and Chag Lotsawa Chos-rje-dpal

(1197–1264). The latter was invited to Mongolia, but declined because of poor health. The death of Möngke in 1259 put an end to these approaches to other Tibetan schools. His death also led to a brief period of chaos.

A struggle for the succession erupted between Khubilai and his younger brother Arigh Böke. Most of the Tibetan monasteries sided with Khubilai, as did their administrators, such as the Sa-skya *dpon-chen* Shākya-bzang-po. The 'Bri-gung *khri-dpon* rDo-rje-dpal, however, had become a partisan of Arigh Böke when he visited Möngke's court. He had a face-to-face dispute (*gdong-bsheg*) with Khubilai and treated him with utter contempt.[61] This confrontation marked the beginning of the opposition of the 'Bri-gung-pa against Khubilai and the Sa-skya-pa which persisted, secretly or in the open, for thirty years.

As for Karma Pakshi, he returned to China during Khubilai's war with Arigh Böke. But Khubilai had not forgotten his abrupt departure from his camp and lent a ready ear to rumors which accused the master of hoping for the victory of Arigh Böke. Karma Pakshi was arrested and, according to legend, was kept for three and a half days on a burning pyre, remaining, however, unscathed. He was then banished "to the shores of the Ocean," and two of his pupils were sentenced to death. After two years and eight months he was brought back to court, and in 1263 he was exonerated. He obtained leave to return to Tibet and remained there the last years of his life.[62]

Karma Pakshi's departure from Khubilai in 1256 had left the path free for 'Phags-pa, who in the meantime had concluded his studies and was ordained as a full monk in that year.[63] He was at once admitted to Khubilai's inner circle and in 1258 began to initiate the Mongol prince in the Buddhist religion. The Sa-skya-pa considered this event to be the real beginning of the Lamaist mission in the Mongol world.[64] In the same year, 'Phags-pa participated in the Buddhist-Taoist disputation held in the presence of the prince.[65] From this moment on, his rise was spectacular; apparently Khubilai had found in him the tool he needed for his designs on Tibet. After his own proclamation as khaghan and Chinese emperor, Khubilai granted to 'Phags-pa the title of "National Preceptor" (*kuo-shih*) and appointed him the supreme chief of the Buddhist clergy (January 9, 1261).[66] With the end of his war with his younger brother in 1264, the emperor granted to 'Phags-pa the famous "pearl document" (*'ja'-sa mu-tig-ma*), which confirmed the exemptions and privileges conferred on Buddhist monks.[67]

Why did Khubilai select the young Sa-skya hierarch? The choice was due, in part, to his blood relation to Sa-skya Paṇḍita. Yet the latter had died long before. Moreover, the house of Ögödei and Köden, in particular, had initiated relations with the Sa-skya-pa. When Möngke ascended the throne, he had no special obligations to the Sa-skya-pa; he had, in fact, distributed all the Tibetan sects among the members of his own family.

Khubilai had a completely free hand. His selection of 'Phags-pa can be better understood if we remember that the Tibetan Budddhist had arrived in the Mongol camp, practically as a hostage, at the age of nine. Although he received a careful Tibetan education and went through extensive religious and philosophical studies, he must have been greatly influenced by Mongol views. He must also have recognized the overwhelming force of their still-expanding empire. He was less hesitant to cooperate than other Lamas, such as Karma Pakshi, who came to Mongolia as adults. This may have been the main reason for Khubilai's choice. It could not have been dictated by any Sa-skya-pa preeminent position or influence in Tibetan society before the rise of the Mongols. 'Phags-pa as the political leader of Tibet was simply "invented" by Khubilai because he was the religious chief who offered the best guarantees of intelligent subservience to the aims of the new ruler of China.[68]

At about that time Khubilai started to pay closer attention to the Tibetan-speaking regions. The geographical terms employed in the Chinese texts for these regions are three: T'u-fan, Hsi-fan, and Wu-ssu-tsang, which were not synonymous. Mongol administration followed Sung precedent in designating T'u-fan as the extreme northeast of Tibet, reaching to the old Tsong-kha kingdom and neighboring zones. Hsi-fan was a general name for the Tibetan border tribes in western Szechwan and southern Kansu. The new, purely Tibetan term Wu-ssu-tsang (dBus-gTsang) was adopted for Central Tibet.

In 1264 Khubilai started to pacify the Hsi-fan. In that year, the eighteen Hsi-fan clans were organized as the An-hsi *chou*. In 1265 prince Yesü-bulcha, a grandson of Köden, fought the Hsi-fan, and the troops under his command received a reward of 300 *liang*. But the campaign was concluded only in 1268 when Khubilai ordered the general Mangghudai to lead six thousand men into the Hsi-fan country, to pacify it, and to establish an administrative center there (*chien-tu*).[69] The result of those campaigns was the creation of a civilian and military command (*yüan-shuai fu*) for the Mongol-Chinese and Hsi-fan troops at Wen-chou in southernmost Kansu.[70]

Meanwhile, in 1264, 'Phags-pa had left for Tibet, apparently charged with the task of establishing Mongol sovereignty on lines acceptable to the Tibetans, with due regard to their national peculiarities and traditions. He may have encountered some opposition at the frontier on his return, because in that year the troops, who under the command of the myriarch (*wan-hu*) Khongridar had conquered T'u-fan (i.e., Amdo), received a reward of 450 *liang* for their meritorious service.[71]

Little is known of 'Phags-pa's activities after his arrival at Sa-skya. His younger brother Phyag-na-rdo-rje was appointed "head of all Tibet" (*Bod-spyi'i steng-du bkos*) probably in 1265. The emperor also granted him the title of Prince of Pai-lan, a golden seal, and the rank of *t'ung-chih* of the right and left. The texts emphasize that this was the first time the emperor had offered an official seal (*tham-ga*) to Tibet in general and to Sa-skya in particular.[72] Khubilai may have intended to establish a lay principality in central Tibet, under Mongol suzerainty, and propped up by the spiritual authority of the Sa-skya abbot. This project was cut short by the untimely death of Phyag-na-rdo-rje in 1267 at the age of twenty-nine.

His death dealt a heavy blow to the whole unfinished and untried structure, and 'Phags-pa was unable to prevent its collapse and had to retire to 'Dam. The 'Bri-gung-pa order led the resistance against both the Sa-skya-pa and their imperial protector. Khubilai acted expeditiously to destroy this opposition. In the same year, 1267, Mongol troops under Kher-khe-ta (or prince Kher-tha), possibly advancing from Amdo, entered Tibet and crushed all resistance, paving the way for the establishment of an administrative structure which ruled the country for the next eighty years.[73] The year 1268 may be accepted as the date of the establishment of Mongol domination in Tibet. Characteristically, 'Phags-pa was not permitted to stay in Sa-skya while the imperial officers carried out their task. During 1268 he was kept in western China.

The work of organization followed a pattern well known in the history of Mongol empire-building. The office of *dpon-chen* was probably created at this time, as the actual head of the Sa-skya government, under the direction of the *kuo-shih* (later known as *ti-shih* or Imperial Preceptor) and within the frame of imperial bureaucracy.[74] The first holder of the office was Grum-pa Shākya-bzang-po, who had managed the temporal affairs of the monastery after the departure of the Sa-skya Paṇḍita in 1244, and had given ample proof of his administrative capacities. The Mongols gave him the title and seal of *zam-klu gun-min dben-hu* (i.e., *san-lu chün-min wan-hu*), civil and military myriarch for the three circuits of Tibet. As such, he not only headed the administration, but also commanded the militia of Central Tibet. He started the construction of the Lha-khang chen-mo at Sa-skya. This building, a huge fortress-like palace, was apparently intended as the seat of the government.[75]

A preliminary measure, in keeping with the normal procedures of the Mongols in newly acquired territories, was the taking of a census (*dud-grangs rtsis-pa*). In 1268 the census was entrusted to two teams of Tibetan officials, one headed by the imperial envoys (*gser-yig-pa*) A-kon and Mi-gling for the districts from mNga'-ris to Zha-lu (i.e., gTsang), and the other by Su-thu A-skyid for the districts from Zha-lu to 'Bri-gung (i.e., dBus); they worked closely with the *dpon-chen* Shākya-bzang-po. The territory included in the census was Central Tibet; Eastern Tibet and practically all of Western Tibet were excluded.[76]

Another measure that followed Mongol practice was the establishment of a regular postal service (Mong. *jam*)[77] as a necessary means for enabling the faraway imperial government to receive timely information and to forward prompt and adequate orders. The organization of the service was entrusted to the official Das-sman (Mong. Dashman), who was expressly charged by Khubilai with the task of creating the postal network and of proclaiming the sovereignty of the emperor over Tibet. He was granted ample resources from the imperial treasury for this purpose. He was also appointed *rtsa-ba'i dpon-chen* (president; Chinese *yüan-shih*) of the *son-bying dben* (*hsüan-cheng yüan*, Court for the Administration of Buddhist Affairs; but this name was not given until 1288). This was the first instance of the permanent stationing of an imperial official in Tibet. After him, the official I-ji-lag (Turk. Ejilik?) was sent to Tibet as postmaster-general with the title of *thong-ji* (Chinese *t'ung-chih*). The service was based on a chain of twenty-seven postal stations, classified as major (*'jam-chen*) and minor (*'jam-chung*), running from the Chinese border to Sa-skya. A number of families who were obliged to perform compulsory service (*'u-lag*) were apportioned to each *'jam*. In practice the countryside along the mail route was divided into a number of territorial units or postal districts, which were part of the thirteen myriarchies (*khri-skor*) of the civil adminis-tration.[78] The service was headed by one or more officials called *'ja-mo-che* (Mong. *jamchin* or *jamuchin*).[79]

Militia, census, and mail service, along with taxation, were the main-stays of Mongol rule in subordinate states. Most of these administrative measures were introduced in Tibet in 1268–1269, although no direct information on the militia and taxes is available in extant sources.

In 1269 'Phags-pa returned to China, entrusting Tibet to the experi-enced hands of Shākya-bzang-po. Khubilai had requested that the abbot devise a new script to be used both for Mongolian and for Chinese. 'Phags-pa based his script on the Tibetan alphabet. In the second month of 1269 it was declared to be the national script, and its use was made compulsory in official documents. 'Phags-pa was now in even higher favor with Khubilai. At the end of that year, or early in 1270, the emperor granted him the title of Imperial Preceptor (*ti-shih*).[80] But soon after, he left the court again; during the following years (1271–1273), his normal residence was at Shing-kun (Lin-t'ao). His personal contacts with the emperor were limited, and we are entitled to entertain some doubts about the extent of his political influence with Khubilai.[81]

In 1274 'Phags-pa obtained leave to return to Tibet, and his nephew Rin-chen-rgyal-mtshan succeeded him as *ti-shih*. Once more the return of the Sa-skya abbot was accompanied by the advance of a Mongol army. In the third month of 1275, the emperor ordered three princes to send their Mongol contingents to reinforce A'urughchi, prince of Hsi-p'ing, who was fighting against the T'u-fan. A'urughchi was apparently escorting 'Phags-pa, whose return to Tibet was meeting with some opposition. The Prince and the Lama finally reached Tibet in 1276.[82]

Before their arrival, the Sa-skya temporal administration had changed hands. The *dpon-chen* Shākya-bzang-po had died in 1275 and was succeeded (perhaps in 1276) by Kun-dga'-bzang-po.[83] Our sources do not allow us to decide whether the change at Sa-skya was connected with the resistance met by Prince A'urughchi at the frontier. In 1277 Prince A'urughchi killed one Zangs-che-pa, perhaps reflecting some turbulence in the country.[84] In the same year 'Phags-pa summoned at Chu-mig a general conference of the ecclesiastical leaders of the country.[85] Although the sources describe it as a purely spiritual affair, it may have had some political implications, such as the final recognition of Mongol sovereignty in Tibet.

Meanwhile, a new official had come to the fore at the Yüan court. The Chinese sources call him Sang-ko and the Tibetan ones Sam-gha, Zam-gha, or Zam-kha. He was not an Uighur, as is usually believed, but a Szechwan Tibetan of the bKa'-ma-log clans descended from garrisons stationed on the border by the ancient kings of Tibet. He was first noticed and employed by 'Phags-pa as interpreter. Then he entered the imperial service and was employed in the financial department; his later career as favorite of the emperor and unscrupulous financier and statesman, as well as his downfall and execution in 1291, is an important episode in the history of the Yüan dynasty.[86]

In 1280 'Phags-pa died at Sa-skya at the age of forty-five.[87] His death gave rise to suspicions of foul play, the more so as it was common knowledge that there was no love lost between the abbot and the *dpon-chen* Kun-dga'-bzang-po. A Sa-skya official accused the latter of having poisoned 'Phags-pa.[88] The emperor sent Sam-gha (Sang-ko), at the head of a force of 7,000 Mongols and numerous militia from Amdo, to Tibet. Sam-gha imprisoned Kun-dga'-bzang-po and put him to death in 1281. Then Sam-gha went to Sa-skya, where he undertook a partial reorganization of the Mongol structures in Tibet, concentrating on the posting of Mongol garrisons in several strategic locations throughout the country. He also turned his attention to the postal service, which was regarded as such a burden by the local Tibetans that many of them had fled. The garrisons he had posted in the north were also charged with the supervision of the six major postal stations (*'jam-chen*) of the region. He enjoined the dBus district headmen to supply them with fodder, food, furniture, and medicine.[89]

'Phags-pa was succeeded on the Sa-skya see (*gdan-sa*) by Phyag-na-rdo-rje's son Dharmapālarakṣita, born in 1268, who had been brought up as a Mongol and came to Tibet for the first time in 1281. His stay there was short, however, because in 1283 he was appointed *ti-shih* and went back to China. He resigned as Imperial Preceptor in 1286 and started for Sa-skya, only to die en route in 1287.[90]

During those years three *dpon-chen* followed the unfortunate Kun-dga'-bzang-po, each holding office for a short time: Zhang-btsan, Phyag-po-sgang-dkar-ba, and Byang-chub-rin-chen. The latter won the special appreciation of the emperor, who granted him a crystal seal and the title of *hsüan-wei shih*. He was followed by Kun-dga'-gzhon-nu, and by gZhon-nu-dbang-phyug.[91]

In 1287, during the tenure of gZhon-nu-dbang-phyug, two imperial commissioners came to Tibet to carry out a revision (*che-gsal*) of the basic census of 1268. This mission did not conduct a fresh census but simply examined the functioning of the Tibetan financial administration.[92]

Perhaps as a result of the 1287 mission, the *hsüan-wei shih* gZhon-nu-dbang-phyug was charged with providing for the needs of the poor families inscribed in the registers of the postal and military services in the territory under his jurisdiction. Sang-ko sent 2,500 *liang* of silver for this purpose.

The Yüan policy in Tibet continued to be directed by Sang-ko, until his intolerable pride, coupled with widespread corruption, led to his downfall and execution in 1291.[93] After the death of Dharmapālarakṣita the emperor appointed 'Jam-dbyangs Rin-chen-rgyal-mtshan of Shar-pa as regent (*bla-ch'os*) of Sa-skya, but not as titular abbot; he held this post until 1303 when he was appointed *ti-shih* and left for the Chinese capital, where he died in 1305.[94]

In the 1280s a new outbreak against Mongol domination took place. Its center was, as usual, 'Bri-gung. In 1285 the 'Bri-gung forces attacked and destroyed a rival monastery. In succeeding years they became bolder because they obtained the support of a certain sTod Hor king Hu-la.[95] It seems likely that the intervention of the sTod Hor troops was connected with the long-lasting feud between Khubilai and Khaidu, the head of the house of Ögödei. The war between the two rulers reached its climax precisely in those years, with Khaidu's advance toward Karakorum and the revolt of Chinggiskhanid princes in Manchuria and Eastern Mongolia. Khubilai himself had to take to the field in 1288 to crush the rebels. In the fourteenth century sTod Hor in the Tibetan texts designates East Turkestan,[96] and King "Hu-la" can only be Du'a (1274–1306), the staunch ally of Khaidu and head of the house of Chaghadai. "Hu-la" cannot be Khaidu himself, because his territory was too distant from Tibet and had no direct contact with it.

The 'Bri-gung–sTod Hor coalition represented a serious threat and necessitated a full-scale intervention of Mongol forces. According to the Tibetan sources, the Mongol expeditionary corps was led by Prince Temür Bukha. In 1290 his army, combined with the militia of Central Tibet under the *dpon-chen* Ag-len (or Ang-len) rDo-rje-dpal, defeated the 'Bri-gung-pa and sTod Hor troops led by the sTod Hor prince Rin-chen. The monastery of 'Bri-gung was stormed and put to the torch with the loss of about ten thousand lives. After the victory, the imperial army sent detachments to pacify several districts of Southern Tibet, and all members of the opposition were stamped out.[97]

As usual, the mail routes were affected by the war. On November 6, 1292, the dBus gTsang *hsüan-wei ssu* reported that after the 'Bri-gung revolt the mail service had been interrupted, as its personnel was utterly impoverished and desperate. The imperial government ordered officials to provide the five mail stations of dBus gTsang with 100 horses and 200 yaks, and their 736 serving families with 150 *liang* of silver each. Early in 1293 the court sent on an additional sum of 9,500 *liang* for the relief of the families at the postal stations.[98]

Tibet subsequently remained more or less calm under Mongol and Sa-skya domination. The imperial authorities gradually lost interest in the country, so that few entries concerning Tibet are found in the basic annals of the *Yüan-shih*.

Relations between the Yüan emperors and Tibet were complicated. From the Tibetan point of view it was a relationship between teacher and pupil, protégé and protector, recipient and donor, expressed in the short term *yon-mchod*. Khubilai had "donated" to 'Phags-pa, first, the thirteen *khri-skor* (myriarchies of Central Tibet), and on a second occasion, the three *chol-kha* (Mong. *chölge*) of dBus, gTsang, and mNga'-ris. The traditional dates for these events vary and are much too early; the most commonly accepted are 1254 and 1260. The first date must be ruled out, as Khubilai in 1254 was simply a prince and had no authority to make such a gift. If any "donation" was actually made, I suggest that the first one preceded 'Phags-pa's first return trip to Tibet in 1265, and the second before his final return in 1276.

The Chinese texts do not offer any additional details. Even if we understand these "donations" as delegation of local power, it is clear that only Central Tibet was really affected;[99] Sa-skya-pa authority in Western Tibet was largely theoretical, while Amdo and Khams were directly controlled by the imperial authorities.

From the Mongol point of view, Tibet was an autonomous province of the empire with special institutions. The country was under the rule of the emperor, who exercised his authority through the Court of General Administration of Buddhism (*hsüan-cheng yüan*). The orders of the emperor and of the Imperial Preceptor had the same force in Tibet.

The history of the Court of General Administration of Buddhism is complex. It is described in a section of the monograph on bureaucracy (*po-kuan chih*) of the *Yüan-shih*.[100] It was established at the beginning of the Chih-yüan period (i.e., in 1264) as the *tsung-chih yüan*, under the overall authority of 'Phags-pa. Its task was to exercise control over the Buddhist cult, monasteries, and monks in China, and over the administration of

Tibet. As often in the monographs of the *Yüan-shih*, however, this account is compressed and not wholly correct; several scattered pieces of information in the *pen-chi* and other texts point to a different history for the *hsüan-cheng yüan*. Although there is no mention in the *pen-chi* of the creation of the *tsung-chih yüan* in 1264, we may accept this date. There was, however, another agency, the *tsung-t'ung so*, which appeared for the first time in 1265 and was not abolished until 1311. It superintended the affairs of the Buddhist clergy in the provinces.

An agency charged with Tibetan affairs was not formed until February 14, 1280. On that date the emperor created an office called *tu kung-te-shih ssu*, with a rank of 3b, "to deal with all the monks subject to the *ti-shih* as well as with the civil and military affairs of Tibet."[101] By 1281 it served as the normal official channel between the Buddhist clergy and the government.[102] The rise of Sang-ko brought the *tsung-chih yüan* again to the fore. In a document dated March 21, 1284, a monk called *toyin* Hsiao-yeh-ch'ih appears as the head of the *tu kung-te-shih ssu*, while Sang-ko is mentioned in the same document as head of the *tsung-chih yüan*, charged also with the supreme direction of the affairs of the other office (*ling kung-te-shih ssu shih*).[103] When at the end of 1287 Sang-ko was appointed to a rank equivalent to prime minister, *ch'eng-hsiang* of the right, he continued to concern himself with Buddhist affairs and with Tibet.[104]

In 1288, at Sang-ko's suggestion, the *shih-chiao tsung-chih yüan* was given the new name *hsüan-cheng yüan*, with the enhanced rank 1b. Sang-ko continued as its head.[105]. This is the first time we find the new form *shih-chiao tsung-chih yüan*. We cannot avoid the suspicion that this is a case of loose employ of official terms, and that really the *shih-chiao tsung-t'ung so* is intended, and that the *tsung-chih yüan* lingered on as a shadow office without functions. This supposition is turned into a near certainty by the following piece of information: "On May 22nd, 1291, the *tsung-chih yüan* was merged into the *hsüan-cheng yüan*."[106] This means that it had survived after 1288. After 1295 there were frequent changes in the personnel of the *hsüan-cheng yüan*. By 1330 there were ten heads (*yüan-shih*) in the agency. It is not clear how the influence of the Imperial Preceptor could be preserved under this structure.[107] After 1291 the *kung-te-shih ssu* was practically merged with the *hsüan-cheng yüan*. It was resurrected in 1303,[108] but was apparently no longer concerned with Tibet. It dealt mainly with Buddhist rites and ceremonies at the court. It was exempted from the wholesale abolition of the religious agencies decreed in 1311.[109] But in 1326 it was abolished, and its duties were handed over to the *hsüan-cheng yüan* in 1329; in 1332 it was reestablished once more.[110]

In sum, a special agency for Tibetan affairs at the Chinese capital was organized in 1280 and took its final shape in 1288. The partnership of the Sa-skya sect and the court found its practical expression, at least until the end of the thirteenth century, in that one of the heads of the *hsüan-cheng yüan* was for all intents and purposes a nominee of the Imperial Preceptor.

Contrary to the usual scholarly view, it was not the Sa-skya abbots, as such who ruled Tibet in the period from 1275 to 1350. The spiritual succession following 'Phags-pa was complicated. After the death of Dharmapālarakṣita in 1287, the legitimate successor was his cousin bDag-nyid-chen-po bZang-po-dpal (1262–1322). Since the latter was suspected of having poisoned Dharmapālarakṣita, he was exiled for sixteen years. On his return to Sa-skya in 1305, he was restricted to spiritual activity. He had several wives, and his numerous sons founded four different branches of the 'Khon family, each with its own palace in Sa-skya and with landed property in its district. They did not administer Tibet, except when one of the members of the family was appointed *ti-shih* and as such had to reside at the Yüan capital in Peking. Of the nine *ti-shih* who held office after the retirement and death of Dharmapālarakṣita, only five were members of the 'Khon family. The rest belonged to the Shar-pa and Khang-gsar-pa families, who had been pupils of Sa-skya Paṇḍita and of 'Phags-pa.[111] The lack of a proper law of succession played a role in preventing the Sa-skya hierarchs from becoming the real rulers of a united Tibet. The titular head of the Tibetan government was the *ti-shih* and not the abbot, a fact clearly shown by the extant contemporary documents preserved in the Zha-lu monastery. They bear the imprint of the official jade seal of the *ti-shih*, and they always begin with the words "by the order (*lung*; Mong. *jarligh*) of the King, [this is] the word (*gtam*; Mong. *üge*) of the *ti-shih*."[112]

The head of the Tibetan administration was, at least in the eyes of the Tibetans, the *dpon-chen*, nominated by the *ti-shih* and appointed by the emperor. He governed in his own right within the domains of the Sa-skya monastery; outside them, he acted in his capacity as imperial official within the administration created in Tibet by the Mongols.[113]

The administration consisted basically of one of the Offices for Pacification (*hsüan-wei ssu*; Tib. *swon-we-se* or similar transcriptions), created by Khubilai as an intermediary between the province and the districts. In the frontier regions the officers also held military powers, including the office of regional commander (*tu yüan-shuai*).[114] Northeastern Tibet had a separate administration under the *hsüan-wei ssu* of the T'u-fan zone. This zone included the district of Ho-chou, starting point of the important route for mDo-khams and dBus gTsang. The T'u-fan *hsüan-wei ssu* had jurisdiction over the T'u-fan and T'o-ssu-ma (mDo-smad, Amdo) circuits (*lu*), receiving its authority from the *hsüan-cheng yüan*.[115]

We do not know when the Central Tibetan *hsüan-wei ssu* was established. The most probable date is about 1268, (i.e., at the same time when the census was taken and the mail service was introduced), but neither the monograph on bureaucracy nor the *pen-chi* of the *Yüan-shih* give a date. We know only that it was in existence during the 1270s, when its members met Karma Pakshi.[116] Its authority extended over the three circuits (*lu*) of dBus, gTsang, and mNga'-ris sKor-gsum. After the 'Bri-gung revolt and the reconstruction of the mail service by the *dpon-chen* gZhon-nu-dbang-phyug, the imperial government thought it advisable to give Tibet a permanent military organization in order to avoid the repeated expensive military expeditions. Accordingly, on November 9, 1292, following a proposal of the *hsüan-cheng yüan*, the administration of dBus, gTsang, and mNga'-ris sKor-gsum was converted into a combined *hsüan-wei-shih ssu tu yüan-shuai fu*.[117] As described in the monograph on bureaucracy, it was staffed by five *hsüan-wei shih*, two *t'ung-chih*, one *fu-shih*, and some lesser officials. The civil personnel included also a land transport officer of the dBus-gTsang zone.[118] The purely military personnel included two generals (*tu yüan-shuai*), who commanded the Mongol units in dBus and gTsang, and two commanders (*yüan-shuai*) who were posted in mNga'-ris sKor-gsum (Western Tibet), presumably to guard the frontier toward sTod Hor (Turkestan). One commissioner for the "punishment of the rebels" (*chao-t'ao shih*), who acted as head of a military police in unruly or newly pacified tracts, headed the military agency (*kuan-chün*) in Tan ('Dam).[119] On the district level, Central Tibet was divided into thirteen myriarchies (*khri-skor*), each under a hereditary myriarch (*khri-dpom*, Chin. *wan-hu*). With the decay of Mongol administration, they came to form the core of a new Tibetan aristocracy.[120]

This sketch represents merely the final shape taken by the *hsüan-wei ssu* of Central Tibet at the end of Khubilai's reign, but we know next to nothing of its operation. The documents seem to show that a good deal of it did, in fact, exist and function.[121] Two doubtful matters are the number of Mongol officials who actually resided in Tibet, and the site of the headquarters of the *hsüan-wei ssu*. It appears that the *hsüan-wei ssu* was located in Sa-skya itself because it was the terminus of the mail route in the fourteenth century and served as residence for exiled Korean princes.[122]

The relation of the Sa-skya *dpon-chen* with the Tibet *hsüan-wei ssu* is not clear, the first *dpon-chen* Shākya-bzang-po was merely allowed the title of *san-lu chün-min wan-hu*, "civil and military myriarch of the three circuits." The first *dpon-chen* to appear in the Chinese texts with the title *hsüan-wei shih* is gZhon-nu dbang-phyug in 1288.[122] The Tibetan sources note that the first was Byang-chub-rin-chen (about 1285). After that time, each *dpon-chen* probably received this appointment as a matter of routine. But he would have been only one of the five in the *hsüan-wei ssu*. The Zha-lu documents never even mention the *dpon-chen*. The highest ranking officials to whom they are addressed are the *mi-dpon*(= *shih*) of the dBus-gTsang *swon-we-se* (*hsüan-wei ssu*).[123]

Another doubtful point is the tenure of office of the *dpon-chen*. There were twenty-seven *dpon-chen* between 1268 and ca. 1350. Some of them twice occupied the office, which amounts to an average of about three years. This time tallies with the regular triennial tenure of office of the high provincial officials under the Yüan dynasty. The *dpon-chen* may have been subject to the same official regulations as any other member of the Yüan bureaucracy. However, this is merely a working hypothesis. Finally, in the fourteenth century, the rank of general (*tu yüan-shuai*; Tib. *du-dben-sha*) was frequently granted to Tibetans.[124]

The results of this study may be summarized as follows. There was no contact between Central Tibet and the Mongols before 1240. The Mongol rulers tried to obtain political influence in Tibet through the Lamaist clergy, eventually, probably around 1260, giving preference to the Sa-skya-pa sect. In the years 1268–1270, Tibet was organized as a special region of the Yüan empire, ruled jointly by the emperor and the Sa-skya-pa sect, which was represented by the Imperial Preceptor residing in Peking. This partnership functioned both at court and on the local level. The abbot of Sa-skya, when he was not identical with the *ti-shih*, was apparently restricted to a spiritual role. The status of Tibet was thus different from that of such subordinate states as Korea or the Uighur *iduq qut* in Central Asia because it had no local ruler residing in the country itself. An underground opposition headed by the 'Bri-gung abbots flared up on occasion. They were finally crushed in 1290. After that date, the country was virtually integrated into the Yüan empire until the middle of the fourteenth century. The revolt of the Phag-mo-gru-pa, who were the heirs to the 'Bri-gung-pa, practically severed the links of Tibet with China, except for ceremonial missions, and restored the independence of Tibet for almost four centuries.

NOTES

1. *T'ang shu* (Po-na-pen edition), 216B, 9b. After the Tibetan occupation of the Kansu cities, most of the population of Liang-chou was composed of Tibetans, or Tibetanized Chinese; Paul Demiéville, *Le concile de Lhasa* (Paris, 1952), p. 185.

2. See the materials collected by James Hamilton, *Les Ouighours à l'époque des Cinq Dynasties d'après les documents chinois* (Paris, 1955), pp. 20–60.

3. *Sung Hui-yao chi-kao* (hereafter *SHY*) (Peking, 1957), Fang-yü 21, 15b–16a; *Sung shih* (hereafter *SS*) (Po-na edition), 492, 4a–5a; *Wen-hsien t'ung-kao* (hereafter WHTK) (Shanghai, 1936), 335, 2629b-c.

4. See M. Maeda, "Godai oyobi Sō-sho ni okeru Rokkoku no chiiki kōzō kansuru ronkō," *Tōyō gakuhō* 41 (1958–1959): 439–472.

5. *SHY*, Fang-yü 21, 16a–17b; *SS*, 7, 1a; 492, 5b–7a. On the origins of P'an-lo-chih, see T. Iwasaki, "Seiryōfu Hanrashi seiken shimatsu kō," *Tōhōgaku* 47 (1974),

chiefly pp. 29–32, based on Z. Yamaguchi, "Hakuran to Sumpa no Rlangs shi," *Tōyō gakuhō* 52 (1969–1970): 31–34.

6. *SHY*, Fang-yü 21, 17b–20a; *SS*, 7, 3a; 485, 9a; 492, 7a-b; *WHTK*, 335, 2629b-c.

7. *SHY*, Fang-yü 21, 20b–23b, and Fan-pu 6, 2a; *SS*, 7, 5b; 7, 11a; 8, 9a; 492, 8a–10a; *WHTK*, 335, 2629c. For the events of those years, see also S. Okazaki, "Kasai Uiguri shi nikansuru kenkyū," *Oriental Studies in Honour of Juntarō Ishihama* (Osaka, 1958), pp. 73–74.

8. *Deb-ther dmar-po* (hereafter *DTMP*) (Gangtok, 1961), 20b; *SS*, 492, 11b; Chang Fang-p'ing, *Lo-ch'üan chi* (Peking National Library ms.), 22, 17a-b; *WHTK*, 335, 2630A. See R. A. Stein, *Recherches sur l'épopée et le barde au Tibet* (Paris, 1959), p. 145, who showed that Chüeh-ssu-lo was a transcription of the Tibetan title *rgyal-sras*, meaning "prince." The private name of Li Li-tsun was Ying-ch'eng Lin-pu-ch'ih. Its first part occurs also elsewhere and seems to be either a title or a clan name; the second part transcribes Tibetan *rin-po-che*. Chüeh-ssu-lo's origin is explained in the *Red Annals* (compiled 1346). Khri bKra-shis-rtsegs-pa, a descendant of the last Tibetan king Glang-dan-ma, had three sons, of whom 'Od-lde was the second. 'Od-lde, in turn, had four sons, the second being Khai-lde, whose descendants were the dynasty of nDo-smad (Ando). The chiefs of Ando searched for a scion of the old Tibetan dynasty and elected him their ruler. This was Chüeh-ssu-lo.

9. Stein, op. cit., pp. 230–231.

10. *SHY*, Fan-pu 6, 1b–2a; *SS*, 8, 11s; 8, 12a–12b; 492, 12a; *WHTK*, 335, 2630a. See Elisabeth Pinks, *Die Uiguren von Kan-chou in der frühen Sung-Zeit (960–1028)* (Wiesbaden, 1968), pp. 42–44, 46.

11. *SHY*, Fan-pu, 6, 2b; *Lo-ch'üan-chi*, 22, 18a; *SS*, 258, 9b–10b; 492, 12a-b; *WHTK*, 2630a.

12. *SHY*, Fan-pu, 6, 2b; *Lo-ch'üan chi*, 22, 18a–b; *SS*, 11, 1a; 485, 14b; 492, 13a-b; Pinks, op. cit., p. 88. On the progress of the Tangut conquest of the Uighur Khanate of Kan-chou and of the semi-Tibetan principality of Liang-chou, see K. Nagasawa, "Saika no Kasai shinshutsu to Tō-sai kōtsū," *Tōhōgaku* 26 (1963), chiefly pp. 56–63.

13. See K. Umehara, "Seitō no uma to Shisen no cha," *Tōhō gakuhō* 45 (1973): 195–244, especially 202–209.

14. *SHY*, Fan-pu, 6, 3b–4a; *Lo-ch'üan chi*, 22, 19b–20a; *SS*, 10, 11a; 11, 6b; 11, 13b; 12, 2a; 12, 11b; 492, 13b. The Khitan marriage, for which *SS*, 492, 14a, is our sole source, was apparently no state affair. The *Liao shih* ignores it, and *Lo-ch'üan chi*, 22, 21a, merely states that Tung-chan "took as concubine a Khitan woman."

15. *SHY*, Fan-pu 6, 4a–5b; *SS*, 492, 13a–15a; *WHTK*, 335, 2630a-c. See also S. Okazaki, "Kasai Uiguri shi," p. 77. For short sketches of Chüeh-ssu-lo, see Stein, op. cit., pp. 231–233, and H. Wakamatsu, in H. Franke (ed.), *Sung Biographies* (Wiesbaden, 1976), pp. 255–257, and Luc Kwanten, "Chio-ssu-lo (997–1068). A Tibetan Ally of the Northern Sung," *Rocznik Orientalistyczny* 39 (1977): 92–106. A good deal of material is gathered in K. Nagasawa, "Saika no Kasai shinshutsu," pp. 63–65.

16. *Fan-sêng* Ching-tsun was sent to K'ai-feng in 1019; *fan-sêng* Ma-ch'u-po-ssu-chi died in 1063, and his heir was his nephew *fan-sêng* Seng-chieh-pa; *fan-sêng* Li-pa-shan-po is mentioned in 1075. *SHY*, Fan-pu 6, 2b; 6, 4b; 6, 11b. See R. A. Stein, *Les tribus anciennes des marches sino-tibétaines* (Paris, 1959), pp. 73–77.

17. *SHY*, Fan-pu 6, 6a–29b; *SS*, 16, 4b; 18, 7b; 18, 12b; 328, 19b–20a 492, 15b–18a; *WHTK*, 335, 2630c, 2631a.

18. *SS*, 18, 15a 19, 12b; 87, 25a-b 87, 26a; 492, 18b, 21a. These operations were a marginal episode of the war of 1096–1099 against Hsi Hsia; see E. I. Kychanov, "Les guerres entre les Sung du Nord et le Hsi Hsia," *Études Song in Memoriam Étienne Balázs* (The Hague, 1971), p. 112.

19. Otto Franke, *Geschichte des chinesischen Reiches*, IV (Berlin, 1948), pp. 182–183, 196–198.

20. T'o T'o et al., *Chin shih* (Po-na ed.), 26, 16a.

21. T'o T'o et al., *Liao shih* (Po-na ed.), 46, 27b; K. Wittfogel and Feng Chia-sheng, *History of Chinese Society: Liao (907–1125)* (Philadelphia, 1949), pp. 108–109.

22. See the table in Wittfogel and Feng, op. cit., pp. 321–325.

23. N. P. Shastina (trans.), *Shara Tudzhi, mongol'skaja letopish' XVII veka* (Moscow-Leningrad, 1957), pp. 128–129; I. J. Schmidt, *Geschichte der Ost-Mongolen und ihres Fürstenhauses* (St. Petersburg, 1829), p. 89.

24. dPa'-bo gTsug-lag, *mKhas-pa'i-dga'-ston* (hereafter *KPGT*), ed. Lokesh Chandra (Delhi, 1959–1961), p. 789.

25. Luc Kwanten, "Chingis Khan's Conquest of Tibet: Myth or Reality?" *Journal of Asian History* 8 (1974): 15–17. H. Okada, "Mōko shiryō ni mieru shoki Mō-Zō kankei," in *Tōhōgaku* 23 (1962): 99, identifies Ilughu with Nilkha Senggüm, the son and heir of the Ong Khan of the Kereyid, whom the *Sheng-wu Ch'in-cheng-lu* says escaped to Hsi Hsia, then wandered in Po-li T'u-fan (Döri Tibet), and eventually fled to Kucha, where he was killed (translated by P. Pelliot, "À propos des Comans," *Journal Asiatique* 15 [1920]: 181–182). Sung Lien et al., *Yüan shih* (hereafter *YS*) (Po-na edition), 1, 13a, tells almost the same story. The identification of Ilughu Noyan with Nilkha Senggüm can hardly be accepted.

26. See Okada and Kwanten, as cited in n. 25 above. This mistake may be due to a confusion between Tibet and Böri-Tibet, a name which seems to have designated the Tsaidam region or portions of the Tsong-kha kingdom of the eleventh century. See P. Pelliot, "À propos des Comans," pp. 182–193. "Buri Thabet" was known also to the Papal envoys of 1246. See John of Pian del Carpine, in A. van den Wyngaert (ed.), *Sinica Franciscana*, I (Quaracchi, 1929), pp. 60–61, and C. de Bridia, in A. Önnerfors (ed.), *Historia Tartarorum C. de Bridia monachi* (Berlin, 1967), p. 14.

27. This has been justly pointed out by T. V. Wylie, "The First Mongol Conquest of Tibet Reinterpreted," *Harvard Journal of Asiatic Studies* 37 (1977): 105.

28. G. N. Roerich (trans.), *The Blue Annals* (hereafter *BA*) (Calcutta, 1949–1953), pp. 1054–1055.

29. Blo-bzang-bstan-'dzin's *Altan Tobci*, quoted by W. Heissig, *Die Familien-und Geschichtsschreibung der Mongolen*, I (Wiesbaden, 1959), p. 63.

30. There is an item of information that seems to connect Chinggis Khan with Tibet. The Russian translation of Rashīd Al-dīn, *Sbornik letopisei* (Moscow-Leningrad 1952), I, 2, p. 273, contains a list of the ninety-five Mongol commanders appointed by Chinggis Khan in 1262 (parallel to the *Secret History of the Mongols*, p. 202). We are told that the conqueror sent Shiku-Güregen to Tibet with 4,000 men of the Khongirat. But actually the *Tubat* of the text followed by the Russian translator is a mistake for Tumat (i.e., the Tümed tribe), then dwelling to the west of Lake Baikal. Not only had this been recognized by the nineteenth-century trans-

lator Berezin, but the same mistake is duly avoided in a parallel text in *Sbornik letopisei*, I, 1, p. 162. Tibet is not concerned here.

31. Sum-pa mKhan-po, *dPag-bsam-ljon-bzang*, III (ed. Lokesh Chandra) (New Delhi, 1959), 139. The *Re'u-mig* (21) says that in 1206 Chinggis Khan became master of the whole of dBus in Tibet, with the exception of Mi-nyag (i.e., Hsi Hsia). *Hor Chos-'byung*, Tibetan text (*Mōko ramakyō-shi*, Tokyo, 1940), pp. 23–24; translation (G. Huth, *Geschichte des Buddhismus in der Mongolei*, Strassburg, 1896), p. 24.

32. *KPGT*, pp. 792–793.

33. See G. Tucci, *Tibetan Painted Scrolls* (hereafter *TPS*) (Rome, 1949), pp. 8–9; J. Bacot, *Introduction à l'histoire du Tibet* (Paris, 1962), p. 46; W. D. Shakabpa, *Tibet: A Political History* (New Haven and London, 1967), p. 61; D. Schuh, *Erlasse und Sendschreiben mongolischer Herrscher für Tibetische Geistliche* (St. Augustin, 1977), p. xvi.

34. *KPGT*, pp. 394, 793–794. Sorghakhtani-beki (d. 1252) is known to have been a Christian. Incidentally, the list of the sons of Tolui in *KPGT*, p. 792, is corrupt.

35. Juvaini, as translated by J. A. Boyle, *The History of the World Conqueror* (Manchester, 1958), pp. 190, 196.

36. The campaign of 1235 is described in the Chinese texts (*YS*, 2, 5a; *Hsü Tzu-chih t'ung-chien* [Peking, 1958], 168, 4580); but it did not touch Tibet, nor even approach its border. See the discussion by S. Kuchera, ''Mongoly i Tibet pri Chingiskhane i ego preemnikakh,'' in S. L. Tikhvinskii (ed.), *Tataro-Mongoly v Azii i Evrope: Sbornik statei* (Moscow, 1970), p. 259.

37. Life of sTag-lung-pa (1190–1236) in sTag-lung Ngag-dbang-rnam-rgyal's *Chos-'byungngo-mtshar rgya-mtsho* (Tashijong, 1972 reprint), 54bis a-b (I, pp. 371–372); Life of Chos-lding-pa (1180–1240) by U-rgyan-pa, in *BKa'-brgyud yid-bzhin nor-bu-yi 'phreng-ba* (Leh, 1972 reprint), 277b (553).

38. The identity of Byang-ngos with Liang-chou is now well established.

39. See the interesting passage in the Life of Lha-gdong-pa (1213–1258), in *bKa'-brgyud gser-phreng chen-mo* (Dehra Dun, 1970 reprint), 37a-b (I, pp. 616–617).

40. *BA*, pp. 91, 517–518, 629; *KPGT*, pp. 449, 794; Life of sTag-lung-pa in *Chos-'byung ngo-mtshar rgya-mtsho*, NYA, 73b (510). According to G. Tucci, *Deb-ther dmar-po gsar-ma* (hereafter *DMSM*) (Rome, 1971), pp. 181, the sgom-pa (adminis-trator) of 'Bri-gung, Shākya-rin-chen, was made prisoner by the Mongols. T. V. Wylie, ''The First Mongol Conquest of Tibet Reinterpreted,'' pp. 107–108, suggests that the different affiliations of the damaged and of the spared monasteries are of historical significance, but the evidence on this point seems insufficient.

41. For Köden's letter, see now the critical study by D. Schuh, op. cit., pp. 31–41, who concludes that the extant version is a forgery.

42. *KPGT*, p. 449. The departing abbot left at Sa-skya as his spiritual vicars (*chos-dpon*) 'O-yug-pa bSod-nams-seng-ge and Shar-pa Shes-rab-' byung-gnas, and as temporal administrator the nang-gnyer-ba Grom-pa Shākya-bzang-po; see *rGya Bod yig-tshang* (hereafter *GBYT*) (University of Washington ms.), p. 195a.

43. See also the discussion by D. Schuh, ''Wie ist die Einladung des fünften Karma-pa an den chinesischen Kaiserhof als Fortführung der Tibet-Politik der Mongolen-Khane zu verstehen?'' in *Altaica Collecta* (Wiesbaden, 1976), pp. 227–229, n. 17.

44. *De-bzhin-gshegs-pa thams-cad kyi bgrod-pa gcig-pa'i lam-chen gsung-ngag rin-po che'i bla-ma brgyud-pa rnam-thar*, 62b; Ngor Kun-dga'-bzang-po's Biography of Sa-skya Paṇḍita, 67a-b. Nam-mkha'-'bum was the author of a life of 'Phags-pa written in 1267 and extensively quoted in *'Dzam-gling byang-phyogs kyi thub-pa'i rgyal-tshab chen-po dpal-ldan Sa-skya-pa'i gdung-rabs rin-po-che ji-ltar byon-pa'i tshul gyi rnam-par thar-pa ngo-mtshar rin-po-che'i bang-mdzod kun-'byung*, 75a–93a.

45. The letter, dated 1249 according to the *Re'u-mig*, 26, is found in the *'Dzam-gling . . . Sa-skya-pa'i-gdung-rabs*, 57b, and in the collected works (*gsung-'bum*) of the Sa-skya Paṇḍita, NGA, 214a. A first translation is in *TPS*, pp. 10–12. New detailed summary in D. Schuh, "Wie ist die Einladung des fünften Karma-pa . . . ," pp. 230–233, n. 20.

46. Life of Zur thams-cad-mkhyen-pa (by the Fifth Dalai-Lama), 20b.

47. On the 'Phrul-pa'i-sde monastery where Sa-skya Paṇḍita died, see G. N. Roerich, "Mun-mkhyen Chos-kyi-'od-zer and the Origin of the Mongol Alphabet," in *Journal of the Asiatic Society of Bengal*, Letters, 11 (1945), pp. 53–54.

48. *YC*, 3, 3a. Khoridai is a fairly common name among the Mongols; see P. Pelliot and L. Hambis (trans.), *Histoire des campagnes de Gengis Khan*, I (Leiden, 1951), pp. 62–64. It was also the name of the fifth son of Khubilai, not found in the genealogies of the *Yüan-shih*, but given by Rashīd al-Dīn; L. Hambis, *Le Chapitre CVII du Yuan-che* (Leiden, 1945), p. 116, and P. Pelliot, *Notes on Marco Polo* (Paris, 1959), p. 568. This identification presents some difficulties, as the fifth son of Khubilai may have been rather young in 1251 to lead an army.

49. *KPGT*, 449, 796; *Kha-rag gNyos kyi rgyud-pa byon-tshul mdor-bsdus* (Toyo Bunko manuscript), 16b.

50. *KPGT*, p. 796; Life of Lha-gdong-pa in *bKa'-brgyud gser-phreng chen-mo*, DA, 18a, 33a, 37a (I, 578, 608, 616).

51. *KPGT*, pp. 449, 794, where the date is wrongly given as 1239. Rectification in D. Schuh, *Erlasse und Sendschreiben*, pp. xxi–xxii.

52. *DTMP*, 37a.

53. *Fo-tsu li-tai t'ung-tsai* (Taishō 2036), IL, 725-C; *YSS*, 202, 1b.

54. *DTMP*, 21a, has Mong-gor. But the original manuscript has Mo-go-du or Mo-ge-du; S. Inaba, "The Lineage of the Sa-skya-pa: A Chapter of the Red Annals," *Memoirs of the Research Department of the Toyo Bunko* 22 (1963): 116, n. 44. *KPGT*, p. 795, has Mu-gu-du.

55. H. Okada, op. cit., pp. 101–102.

56. *BA*, p. 580; *KPGT*, p. 409.

57. B. Spuler, *Die Mongolen in Iran* (Berlin, 1955 ed.), pp. 180–187. In 1289 the Dominican friar Ricoldo da Montecroce found Buddhist monks (*baxites*) in Asia Minor; U. Monneret de Villard, *Il Libro della Peregrinazione nelle Parti d'Oriente di Ricoldo da Montecroce* (Rome, 1948), pp. 47–54.

58. An attempt by 'Phags-pa to go back to Tibet in the same year was abandoned mainly on the intervention of Khubilai's wife Chabui; *'Dzam-gling . . . Sa-skya-pa'i gdung-rabs*, 67b (translation in D. Schuh, *Erlasse und Sendschreiben*, p. 89).

59. The famous privilege purported to be granted by Khubilai in 1254 has been shown to be largely a later fabrication, at least as far as its date and present form are concerned; D. Schuh, *Erlasse und Sendschreiben*, pp. 103–118.

60. On Rong-yul or Rong-po, see T. V. Wylie, *The Geography of Tibet according to the 'Dzam-gling rgyas-bshad* (Rome, 1962), p. 106 and nn. 720 and 721. Biography of rGod-tshang-pa (ISHED Manuscript), K138b. G. Roerich, *Biography of Dharmas-vamin* (Patha, 1959): 39–40. Roerich's translation is partly wrong and has been corrected by J. DeJong in his review in *Indo-Iranian Journal* 6 (1972), p. 173.

61. *Ngo-mchil btab*, lit. "spat in his face." Lokesh Chandra's edition has *ro-mchil*, which yields no meaning. I owe thanks to *dge-bshes* 'Jam-dpal-seng-ge Ati for his kind help with this difficult passage.

62. *BA*, pp. 485–487; *KPGT*, pp. 432–433, 446–447, 450, 797; H. Richardson, "The Karma-pa Sect: A Historical Note," *Journal of the Royal Asiatic Society*, (1958), pp. 143–145.

63. *BA*, p. 214; *DMSM*, p. 184; *KPGT*, pp. 410, 446–453.

64. *KPGT*, pp. 792, 796.

65. J. Thiel, "Der Streit der Buddhisten und Taoisten zur Mongolenzeit," *Monumenta Serica* 20 (1961): 37–46. On the participation of 'Phags-pa in the third conference, see Y. Imaeda, "Pa-ku-pa 'Phags-pa zō *Dōshi chō-fukuketsu* ni tsuite," *Tōyō gakuhō* 56 (1974): 41–48.

66. *YS*, 4, 12, where *ti-shih* is a palpable mistake for *kuo-shih*.

67. Edited and translated by D. Schuh, *Erlasse und Sendschreiben*, pp. 118–124. About the same time Khubilai granted to the rNying-ma-pa *gter-ston* Zur Shākya-'od (1205–1268) a privilege exempting the Tantrics of dBus and gTsang from taxation and military service. See Pema Tsering, "rNying-ma-pa Lamas am Yüan Kaiserhof," In L. Ligeti (ed.), *Proceedings of the Csoma de Körös Memorial Symposium* (Budapest, 1978), p. 516.

68. According to T. V. Wylie, "The First Mongol Conquest of Tibet Reinter-preted," p. 113, the main reason for the Mongol choice of the Sa-skya-pa was the need for a guarantee of continuity of control, and in this respect the Sa-skya-pa were uniquely qualified because religious and economic power was a prerogative of the 'Khon family. But the same conditions prevailed with the Phag-mo-gru-pa, the 'Bri-gung-pa, the Lha-pa (Kha-rag), and probably other sects. In addition, succes-sion to the Sa-skya see was not regulated by any strict law, as the history of that sect amply shows.

69. *YS*, 5, 20a 6, 16a, 5a. Of course, Hsi-fan has nothing to do with Tibet proper, as was believed by T. V. Wylie, "The First Mongol Conquest of Tibet Reinter-preted," p. 125.

70. *YS*, 87, 10b-11a. Later the Hsi-fan country came under the jurisdiction of the *hsüan-cheng yüan*; T. Fujishima, "Genchō senseiin kō, sono nimenteki seikaku o chūshin to shite," in *Ōtani gakuhō* 46, 4 (1967): 66–67.

71. *YS*, 6, 2b.

72. *DTMP*, p. 22a; *GBYT*, 199a. According to the latter text, the title of prince of Pai-lan was repeatedly granted to lay members of the 'Khon family. However, only one instance of such an appointment is recorded in the *Yüan-shih*, under the date of 1321; L. Hambis, *Le chapitre CVIII du Yuan-che*, p. 137.

73. *KPGT*, pp. 410, 747, 796. A 'Dam-pa-ri-pa appears in the *Kha-rag gNyos kyi rgyud-pa byon-tshul mdor-bsdus*, 16b–17a. He lived from 1200 to 1263 and was a disciple or attendant (*nye-gnas*) of the head of the Lha-pa sect (Kha-rag gNyos family). In 1234 and the following years he collaborated in the building and

completion of some monasteries, chiefly of Gye-re, which became the headquarters of the sect and was inaugurated in 1246. 'Dam-pa-ri-pa acted as *spyi-dpon* (chief administrator, apparently of the monastery and of the sect) from 1245 to his death. An interlineary note adds to *spyi-dpon* the words *dBus-gTsang gi*, i.e., of Central Tibet. But this interpolation is without authority; a 'Dam-pa-ri-pa as administrator of central Tibet is unknown to all sources. In any case, the date of his death precludes an identification with the 'Dam-pa-ri-pa killed by the Mongols in 1267.

74. *DTMP*, 24b; *GBYT*, 197a; *DMSM*, 185–186. The sequence of events was correctly recognized by T. V. Wylie, "The First Mongol Conquest of Tibet Reinterpreted," pp. 124–125, and before him by the Tibetan scholar Sherab Gyaltsen Amipa, *Historical Facts on the Religion of the Sa-skya-pa Sect* (Rikon, 1970), p. 44.

75. *DTMP*, 24b; *BA*, p. 216. For the title *chün-min wan-hu*, see P. Ratchnevsky, *Un code des Yüan*, I (Paris, 1937), p. 14 on. Chinese *lu* corresponds to Mongol *kölge* (Tib. *chol-kha*).

76. *GBYT*, 181a–183a; Autobiography of the Fifth Dalai-Lama, 20b–21a (translated in *TPS*, pp. 251–252); Klong-rdol Bla-ma, *gsung-'bum*, 'A, 5a. Western scholars usually speak of two censuses. But I believe that there was only one census in 1268, followed in 1287 by a financial inspection or revision of the administrative practice based on it. See L. Petech, "The Mongol Census in Tibet," in M. Aris (ed.), *Tibetan Studies in Honour of Hugh Richardson* (Warminster, 1980), pp. 233–238.

77. On the Mongol word *jam*, see W. Kotwicz, "Les termes concernant le service des relais postaux," *Rocznik Orientalistyczny* 16 (1950): 329–336. On the institution in general, see P. Olbricht, *Das Postwesen in China unter der Mongolenherrschaft* (Wiesbaden, 1954).

78. Practically our sole source is *GBYT*, 166a–168a and 197a, on which the above sketch is based; it is usually known through the rather muddled translation by S. Ch. Das, "Tibet under the Tartar Emperor of China," in *Journal of Asiatic Society of Bengal*, Extra Number (1905), pp. 95–98, who translates *jam* as "district," thus confusing the whole issue. The bare fact and date are recorded also in *KPGT*, p. 796: "In the Earth-Snake year [1269] the postal route was established" ('*jam lam gtsugs*). The *hsüan-cheng shih* Dashman was the father of Büretü who married a daughter of Üsh-Temür (d. 1295), prince of Kuang-p'ing (L. Hambis, *Le chapitre CVIII du Yuan-che*, p. 148). I-ji-lag may be the same as the *mi-chen* E-ji-lag sent by the emperor at some date between 1282 and 1292 to invite to China the famous scholar and traveler O-rgyan-pa (1230–1309); *bsGrub-brgyud Karma Kam-tshang brgyud-pa rin-po-che'i rnam-par thar-pa rab-'byams nor-bu zla-ba chu-shel gyi phreng-ba* (New Delhi, 1972) 85b (I, 176). For the insertion of the *jam* in the frame of the administrative districts (*khri-skor*), which was carried out concurrently, see *GBYT*, 183a–184a, where the operations are described according to the ledgers (*deb-ther*) compiled by the *nang-chen-pa* of Sa-skya and the *du-dben-sha* (Chin. *tu yüan-shuai*) gZhon-nu-mgon.

79. Zha-lu documents in *TPS*, pp. 747–754. On the *jam* in Tibet, see also G. N. Roerich, "Mongol Tibetan Relations," p. 48.

80. The date 1270 is given in *Fo-tsu li-tai t'ung-tsai*, XLIX, 705B–C, but it was probably in 1269. The title *ti-shih* was reserved for the heads of the Sa-skya-pa sect. It alternated between the members of the 'Khon family and the Shar-pa and Khang-gsar-pa lineages descended from disciples of 'Phags-pa. On the *ti-shih* of the Yüan

dynasty, see *TPS*, p. 15; S. Nogami and S. Inaba, "Gen no teishi ni tsuite," in *Oriental Studies in Honor of Juntarō Ishihama* (Osaka, 1958), pp. 430–448; and S. Inaba, "Gen no teishi ni tsuite, Oran-shi wo shiryō toshite," in *Indogaku Bukkyōgaku kenkyū* 8 (1960): 26–32; S. Inaba, "Gen no teishi ni kansuru kenkyū," in *Ōtani daigaku kenkyū nenpō* 17 (1964): 79–156; S. Inaba, "An Introductory Study on the Degeneration of Lamas: A Genealogical and Chronological Note on the Imperial Preceptors in the Yüan Dynasty," in G. H. Sasaki (ed.), *A Study of Klésa: A Study of Impurity and its Purification in the Oriental Religions* (Tokyo, 1975), pp. 526–553 (20–47).

81. Information on 'Phags-pa's movements is available in his complete works (*Sa-skya bka'-'bum*, Tokyo edition, vols. 6 and 7), which almost always give date and place of composition.

82. *YS*, 8, 20b; *BA*, pp. 212, 973; *De-bshin-gshegs-pa*, ect., 164b–165a; *'Dzam-gling* . . . *Sa-skya-pa'i gdung-rabs*, 75a. On this prince, see L. Hambis, *Le chapitre CVII du Yuan-che*, p. 114, and *Le chapitre CVIII du Yuan-che*, p. 141. Hambis spells the name Oghruqci; but considering the Tibetan transcription A-rog-che, I prefer to follow on this point L. Ligeti, review of Hambis's book in *Acta Orientalia* 5 (1955): 319. A'urughci's biography in *YS*, 131, 11a–13a, makes no mention of his activity in Tibet; but we know that later he gave to O-rgyan-pa the means for the restoration of the sPud-tra monastery in La-stod, which had been well-nigh destroyed by the *dpon-chen* Kun-dga'-bzang-po; *bsGrub-brgyud Karma* . . . *brgyud-pa*, 87a (I, 173).

83. See the discussion by T. V. Wylie, "The First Mongol Conquest of Tibet Reinterpreted," p. 128n.

84. *KPGT*, p. 796.

85. *BA*, p. 212; *DMSM*, p. 186. It was presided over by the Karma-pa master mChims Nam-mkha'-grags, and the expenses were borne by the Mongol heir apparent, Chen-chin; *DTMP*, p. 26b.

86. For the Chinese sources on Sang-ko, see H. Franke, "Seng-ge, das Leben eines uigurischen Staatsbeamten zur Zeit Qubilais, dargestellt nach Kap. 205 der Yüan Annalen," *Sinica* 17 (1942): 90–113 (but Sang-ko does not transcribe Seng-ge). See also L. Petech, "Sang-ko: A Tibetan Statesman in Yüan China, "*Acta Orientalia* 34 (1980): 193–208.

87. A scholarly study of the life of 'Phags-pa is still a desideratum. M. Nakano, "An annotation on the *Ti-shih Pa-pa hsing-chuang*" (in Chinese), in *Hsin-A hsüeh-pao* 9, 1 (1969): 93–119, hardly satisfies this need.

88. *DTMP*, 24b; *BA*, pp. 216, 582; *DMSM*, p. 186; *KPGT*, p. 796; Life of 'Ba'-ra-pa (1310–1391) in *bKa'-brgyud gser-phreng chen-mo*, PHA, 6a–b (II, 31–32). The connection between Kun-dga'-bzang-po and the death of 'Phags-pa is obscure and the sources contradict themselves. See the long discussion by W. D. Shakabpa, *Bod kyi srid-don rgyal-rabs* (Kalimpong 1967), pp. 295–299, omitted in the English version of the same work: *Tibet: A Political History* (New Haven and London, 1967).

89. *GBYT*, 176a–178a. As in the case of prince A'urughci, Sang-ko's biography in the *Yüan shih* does not mention his Tibetan campaign, which of course is no proof that he did not undertake it. His expedition was accompanied by some amount of looting and hardship for the Tibetan peasantry; see *Chos-'byung ngo-mtshar rgya-mtsho*, 83b (430). According to rNying-ma-pa tradition, the intervention of Zur Shākya-'od's son Shākya seng-ge avoided wholesale bloodshed after the execution

of Kun-dga'-bzang-po; Biography of Zur Thams-cad-mkhyen-pa by the Fifth Dalai-Lama, 19a.

90. S. Inaba, "An Introductory Study, p. 536.

91. *DTMP*, 24b; *BA*, 216.

92. The so-called census of 1287 is mentioned in *GBYT*, 181a, on which is based the confused account of S. Ch. Das, "Tibet under the Tartar Emperors of China," pp. 101–102. See note 76.

93. S. Nogami, "Gen no senseiin ni tsuite," pp. 785–788.

94. Inaba, op. cit., p. 536.

95. *DMSM*, p. 187.

96. To give an example: "sTod Hor king Thu-mug Themur" is the Chaghataid Khan of Turkestan Tughlugh Temür (1347–1363); see D. Schuh, *Erlasse und Send-schreiben*, p. 144 and n. 114. The name Hu-la is a shortened form of Hülegü, but this identification is impossible. Hülegü had died in 1265.

97. *BA*, p. 217; *KPGT*, p. 750; *DMSM*, pp. 187 and 205. According to the Biography of Zur Thams-cad-mkhyen-pa by the Fifth Dalai-Lama, 19b, and to the Autobiography of the Fifth Dalai-Lama, 21b, both the *sgom-pa* and the sTod Hor prince Rin-chen were taken prisoners. As to the names and titles quoted here: Temür Bukha was almost certainly the son of A'urughci of that name, who in 1291 was given the title of prince Su-yüan; *YS*, 16, 15b; L. Hambis, *Le chapitre CVII du Yuan-che*, pp. 120–121, and *Le chapitre CVIII du Yuan-che*, pp. 142, 154. *Zhal-ngo*, usually a monk-official, designates here the religious head of the sect; at that time this was Chos-sgo-ba rDo-rje-ye-shes (1225–1293; on the see since 1288). The *sgom-pa* was the civil and military administrator, a charge similar to the *dpon-chen* of Sa-skya.

98. *YS*, 17, 15a-b.

99. See, e.g., G. Tucci, *Indo-Tibetica* IV, 1 (Rome, 1941)̄, p. 91.

100. *YS*, 87, 8b–9a. Translated by P. Ratchnevsky, *Un code des Yüan*, I, p. 151, and by F. W. Cleaves, "The Sino-Mongolian Inscription of 1346," *Harvard Journal of Asiatic Studies* 15 (1953): 41–42. The standard studies on this office are: S. Nogami, "Gen no senseiin ni tsuite" in *Asiatic Studies in Honour of Tōru Haneda* (Kyoto, 1950), pp. 779–795; T. Fujishima, "Genchō," in *Ōtani gakuhō* 46, 4 (1967): 60–72, and "Genchō ni okeru kenshin to senseiin," in *Ōtani gakuhō* 52, 4 (1973): 17–31; the last mentioned article concerns only the post-Khubilai period and does not deal with Tibetan matters. See also *YS* 6, 2a; 130, 15b; *Yüan Tien-chang* 33, 1a–1b.

101. *YS*, 11, 3a. The *kung-te-shih ssu* went back to the times of the T'ang dynasty, when it was in charge of Buddhist temples and monks; R. Des Rotours, *Traité des fonctionnaires et Traité de l'armée* (Leiden, 1947), pp. 389–309.

102. *Fo-tsu li-tai t'ung-tsai*, XLIX, 707c.

103. *Pien-wei-lu* (T. 2116), LII, 776A; *Fo-tsu li-tai t'ung-tsai*, XLIX, 708B, 709A. More or less the same position is shown in *YS*, 205, 20b, and 205, 5b.

104. *YS*, 14, 20b.

105. *YS*, 15, 13a.

106. *YS*, 16, 17a.

107. *YS*, 87, 8b–9a; P. Ratchnevsky, *Un code des Yüan*, I, pp. 151–152. Cf. *TPS*, pp. 32–33; S. Nogami, "Gen no senseiin ni tsuite," pp. 785–788.

108. *YS*, 202, 8b.

109. P. Ratchnevsky, *Un code des Yüan*, I, pp. lxxx–lxxxi; cf. *YS*, 24, 4b; *Yüan Tien-chang* 33, 1a–1b.

110. *YS*, 30, 7a; 33, 22b; and 36, 4b. I could not consult S. Nogami, "Gen no kudokushishi ni tsuite," in *Shina-Bukkyō shigaku*, VI, 4.

111. S. Inaba, "An introductory study," passim.

112. *TPS*, pp. 747–764.

113. The Zhalu decress issued by the *ti-shih* from Peking or Shang-tu are always addressed to the commissioners (*mi-dpon*) of the *hsüan-wei ssu*, and never to the *dpon-chen* as such. Typical on this point is Doc. V (*TPS*, p. 750), giving instructions to "the officials of the *hsüan-wei ssu* beginning with 'Od-zer-seng-ge'"; the latter was the twelfth *dpon-chen*, but this title does not appear in the document.

114. For the *hsüan-wei ssu* in Yüan China, see *YS*, 91, 4b, translated in P. Ratchnevsky, *Un code des Yüan*, I, p. 93. For the *hsüan-wei ssu tu yüan-shuai fu* in the frontier regions, see *YS*, 91, 5a–b, translated in P. Ratchnevsky, op. cit., p. 235.

115. *YS*, 60, 10a; 60, 11a; 87, 9b; 87, 10a; 87, 11a; 87, 12b; 87, 14a. Cf. *GBYT*, 168a. In 1283 the emperor ordered the *an-ch'a ssu* to inspect the papers of the T'u-fan *hsüan-cheng yüan*; *YS*, 12, 21b.

116. *KPGT*, p. 454.

117. *YS*, 17, 12b.

118. According to P. Ratchnevsky, *Un code des Yüan*, I, pp. and 170, *chuan-yün* is merely an abbreviation of *chuan-yün yen-shih ssu*, "direction of the salt ponds and of the salt monopoly," but this would be rather unexpected in Tibet. It has been remarked that in several instances names "such as *chuan-yün ssu* seem to designate transportation rather than salt administration functions"; see H. F. Schurmann, *Economic Structure of the Yüan Dynasty*, (Cambridge, Mass, 1956), p. 188, n. 10.

119. On the *chao-t'ao shih*, see O. Franke, *Geschichte des chinesischen Reiches*, IV, pp. 460, 561, and V, p. 229; also the meagre notice in *YS*, 91, 7a–b.

120. The Mongol organization of Tibet is tabulated in *YS*, 87, 14a-b, translated in *TPS*, p. 681.

121. L. Hambis, "Notes sur l'historie de Corée à l'époque mongole," *T'oung Pao* 45 (1957): 194.

122. *YS*, 15, 11a.

123. Same formula in *KPGT*, p. 454.

124. *TPS*, p. 687, n. 106.

EIGHT

Old Illusions and New Realities: Sung Foreign Policy, 1217–1234

CHARLES A. PETERSON

The Mongol invasions of Hsi Hsia in 1209 and Chin in 1211 opened a new era in East Asian history. They also ushered in a new phase in the foreign relations of the Sung state to the south, the surviving Chinese dynasty. As the fine balance among these reigning powers was upset, Sung found itself drawn increasingly into the struggle for North China until in 1234 the entire north passed into the lands of the Mongols. This set the stage for the long Sung-Mongol duel for rule over all of China which terminated only with the final Mongol victory in 1279. The premise underlying the present study is that the initial phase of the Mongol conquest in China, from 1209 to 1234, was the last to hold out genuine foreign policy options for the Sung government. Decisions made by Sung during this period, that is, in the course of the Mongol-Chin conflict, not only helped shape contemporary developments but also drastically reduced the options open to Sung thereafter. From 1234, with no other powers present to influence events and with the Mongols bent on total conquest, the decisions facing Sung were in the sphere of defense rather than foreign policy. Sung could only defend itself; it could not negotiate its survival.

Our focus here, then, will be Sung foreign policy in this critical period, more specifically from 1217 to 1234. We shall begin with a summary of the earliest Sung responses, already treated in detail elsewhere,[1] and then trace the complex, turbulent course of developments surrounding the principal objects of Sung policy: Chin, the northern rebels, and the Mongols.[2] Hsi Hsia, save for a couple of flirtations over a possible military alliance, remained on the periphery of Sung concerns until its fall to the Mongols in 1227. Consequently, it will not come in for discussion.[3]

The First Years of the Crisis

News of the Mongol attacks on Chin was met with a mixture of caution and *Schadenfreude* by Sung to the south. There was little sense of new opportunities opening up, of a new promise for recovery of the north. In view of the strength of irredentism in twelfth-century Sung China, how can we account for this mild and negative response? The answer lies in the searing memory of the 1206–1208 war with Chin, that great irredentist crusade which ended so disastrously.[4] Having been lulled by reports of Chin's internal and border problems into believing that its armies were no longer to be feared, Sung planners led by Chief Councillor Han T'o-chou mounted an invasion of North China, which soon resulted in Sung armies heading rapidly back home. The greatest cost of this failure, greater than the huge reparations or the execution of Han himself as demanded by the peace agreement, was to Sung self-confidence and its self-image as the legitimate government for *all* Chinese. For not only were Sung armies decisively beaten, but the Chinese population in the North signally failed to rise in support of the native dynasty. The North was subsequently not formally written off, and no one dared *say* that recovery was out of the question. Yet, destabilizing new developments there were not likely to be greeted with enthusiasm and hope.

By early 1214, however, it was clear that significant changes were under way. Mongol armies had overrun Hopei and placed the Chin capital of Yen-ching (Peking) under siege. In Manchuria the Khitans were in open revolt, and in Shantung large bands of Chinese rebels challenged Chin authority. With Chin control apparently disintegrating everywhere, the regular exchange of diplomatic missions between Sung and Chin courts, as stipulated by treaty, could hardly be maintained. This continued to be the case even after the removal of the Chin court to the greater security of its southern capital at Pien-ching (K'ai-feng). The parallel with events of just a century earlier, when the Jurchens rose and, with Sung cooperation, overturned the Khitan Liao dynasty, was too obvious for Southern Sung analysts to miss. But what did it mean? What lessons did it teach? Above all, it was taken to mean and to teach that any form of cooperation with a "barbarian" power, at least on or near Chinese soil, was dangerous and absolutely to be avoided. Yet, as the Jurchens were the perpetrators of the treachery that cost the Sung dynasty possession of the traditional Chinese heartland, they were Sung's inveterate enemy, which in turn ruled out any form of cooperation with the "old" barbarian in order to control the "new" one. Only a tiny minority of officials at Hang-chou, therefore, argued for bolstering Chin as a buffer state against the newly risen power to the north. But, as for taking strong measures against the old enemy, the memory of the fiasco of 1206–1208, as was suggested above, was still too fresh to permit any sanguine expectations.

An additional feature of Southern Sung psychology stands out. For many of the decision-makers, and evidently for a large part of the populace as well, Sung had become an essentially southeastern (or south-central) state. It lay securely nestled behind the Yangtze, extending only a neglected frontier zone northward to the Huai River, the formal boundary with Chin. One major group of officials in particular stressed the advantages of Sung's southern position, espousing a "fortress Yangtze" strategy. For them, recovery of the North had become a matter of rhetoric, not a serious policy objective. This group seems to have been most influential at court, and usually, though not always could count on having the dominant minister Shih Mi-yüan (d. 1233) in its camp. The other major group, uncompromising and passionately irredentist in spirit was distinguished by its call for a hard line in foreign affairs, by its insistence on military reform, and not least, by its intense interest in the Huai region. This area, which had been allowed to go to seed over the course of previous decades, was esteemed for its capacity, real or presumed to serve both as the main line of defense and a springboard for recovery of the North. The arguments of this group—which included some of the most prominent intellectual luminaries of the whole period—strike us today as highly persuasive. Well they should, since the arguments of their opponents have been so poorly preserved.

The first visible step taken by the Sung government to adapt its policy to the new realities in the North came in 1214 when it suspended payment to Chin of the annual subsidy stipulated under the terms of the existing treaty. In principle this abrogated the treaty, though no such assertion was made. The motivation for this step was threefold. Primarily, the Sung court took the opportunity of its neighbor's difficulties to withdraw from an agreement it had always considered humiliating. Second, denying its erstwhile enemy funds that it so badly needed was no doubt intended to weaken it. Finally, this was probably an attempt on Sung's part to disengage itself altogether from existing arrangements in the North so as to leave its hands unfettered for future contingencies. That suspension of payments might well lead to war was not overlooked.

A second step or series of steps, initially covert, was taken along the border and resulted in Sung logistic support for rebel armies operating in Shantung and Honan. These measures probably date from 1215 or 1216, by which time some of these armies had attained considerable size. Their formation and operations, in fact, caused deep apprehension among Sung observers, who regarded them as potential invaders, as a general source of chaos, and, should any of them become truly powerful, as possible rivals to Sung for the allegiance of the Chinese population in the North. The persistent skepticism which characterized attitudes toward them—Sung loyalists by another definition—reveals, incidentally, how shallow ethnic identification was in the China of that day. The provision of funds and rations to these groups was probably first undertaken as a limited tactical move—that is, as a way of controlling a potential danger along the border and of sustaining them for use against the "barbarian" power(s) to the north. Only in the next phase of Sung-Chin relations did they achieve a new and stronger focus in Sung strategic thinking.

The War with Chin, 1212–1224

The year 1217 marked a new phase in the struggle for the North. Though in the south Sung held to its passive course, to the north Mongol operations were drastically affected by the departure of Chinggis and his preparations for the Khwārazmian campaign. Taking the flower of the Mongol army with him, Chinggis left Mukhali to pursue the war against Chin. Whatever the change in quality of leadership, Mukhali was left with only a limited number of Mongols and otherwise a mixed force of defectors and surrendered troops.[5] Mongol military pressure was drastically reduced as a result. In 1216 Chin had already begun to recover some of the locations previously lost and now was consolidating its position as a Honan-based state. But its condition was far from enviable. Having endured six years of invasion and disorder, lost most of its northern territories, and relocated the seat of government, it had few resources on which it could call. Moreover, in regions such as Shantung and eastern Honan where economic recovery was expected, rebel armies remained out of control. Nor could the degree to which these forces were sustained by the foreign power to the south long remain a secret.

Despite this provocation and Sung's suspension of subsidy payments in 1214, diplomatic relations had been maintained between the two courts.[6] After all, it cost each side little to dispatch the usual three or four ceremonial embassies per year, and they served a useful function in intelligence. But by 1217 physical need was pushing Chin toward an aggressive position, one now in fact permitted by the breather enjoyed in the war with the Mongols. It is almost certain that the Chin missions to Hang-chou of late 1216 and early 1217 applied pressure on the Sung court to resume subsidy payments, agreement on which would surely have avoided new hostilities. In any event, the Chin emperor Hsüan-tsung's complaint to the Sung envoy Ch'en Po-chen in early 1217 about Sung provocations along the border was surely intended both as an ultimatum and as a justification for commencing hostilities.[7] In the fourth (lunar) month, following some debate at court, Chin launched attacks along the Sung frontier, thereby involving itself in a second war and opening a second front. This was a calculated risk and, in view of the tremendous losses of men and material which Chin had suffered against the Mongols, perhaps a surprising one. Certainly, it reveals in what low esteem Chin leaders held Sung arms. Yet, if the objectives are assumed to have been goods and a favorable settlement rather than significant territorial expansion, they were by no means un-realistic.[8] Although Sung armies performed better in the event than was expected, they showed little inclination toward such offensive action as might have threatened the heart of Chin itself. And throughout the next decade and more, the Mongols could not give the beleaguered state their undivided attention.

Sung's response to the growing tensions with Chin is characterized by the lack of any serious last-ditch efforts to avoid the rupture and war. The routine embassy to present birthday greetings to the Chin monarch Hsüan-tsung was dutifully dispatched, and received in Pien-ching in the third month. It might have pursued negotiations toward the maintenance of peace.[9] But the overwhelming impression conveyed by the sources is that the Sung government left the initiative to Chin and consciously accepted the drift into war. The reason for this was of course its conviction that Chin was a doomed state, further accommodation with which would be more costly than a war. Though an ideal spokesman for this position is difficult to find,[10] the memorials for this period of the scholar and court official Yüan Hsieh reveal some of the considerations underlying it.[11] In its present reduced circumstances, Chin is seen as a dangerous distraction and a source of instability. Occupying an untenable and indefensible location in Honan, it is bound to seek expansion at Sung's expense. It was not in fact universally accepted that Chin was bent on conquest; some found the need to secure the adherence of Honan's population as the principal reason for its fighting.[12] But Yüan's view that the maintenance of formal relations, acceptable to Chin, would only prolong an intolerable condition does seem to have been widely shared. Moreover, Sung's attention should be focused on the rising power in the North, the Mongols, who must not be misled by any Sung pussyfooting with the common Jurchen enemy. In addition, accommodation with the latter threatened to alienate the Chinese "loyal-ists" in the North, who could neither forgive nor trust a government which again came to terms with their "barbarian" overlords.

Yet, opinion at the Sung court was by no means undivided, and Yüan Hsieh makes explicit reference to advocates of peace. Though none of their arguments have survived, they must have supported the alternative of resuming subsidy payments to Chin in order to avert war. Whatever the strength of the arguments, they did not capture the ears of Shih Mi-yüan and Emperor Ning-tsung (r. 1195–1224).[13] But did the leadership under-estimate Jurchen capabilities at this stage? Possibly, since only the com-mand of Chao Fang is said to have been well prepared upon the opening attacks, and this was as a result of his own initiative.[14] The government pinned some of its hopes on draining popular support away from Chin, for one of its earliest wartime acts was to issue a proclamation to personnel and subjects living under the Northern regime to abandon it and come over to the Sung.[15] The first of a series of such proclamations, this was clearly an attempt to rally Northerners on the basis of a proto-nationalistic appeal.

We shall not attempt to pursue here the course of the war, which, though not a success for Chin, showed this truncated state in possession of astonishing resilience and determination.[16] Every spring from 1217 to 1222, with the apparent exception of 1220, it launched major offensives against Sung positions. The attacks in the Huai region to the east were moderately successful, but, as that region was relatively unproductive at this point, and in its northern reaches subject to the instability of Shantung, net gains were few. Attacks to the west also met with some success and resulted in the acquisition of large stocks of needed provisions; however, they never quite penetrated the Szechwan basin. The strategic key to victory for Chin, even a conditional one, lay in the destruction of the backbone of the Sung defense system in the Han valley, and this proved beyond its powers to achieve. This was the one sector in which Sung armies were properly organized, supplied, and led. After serious fighting in 1217 and 1218, the decisive engagement there took place in late summer of 1219 when a major Jurchen army was destroyed following a long, unsuccessful siege of Tsao-yang. Chin's most dramatic success came in the spring of 1221 with penetration of Huai-nan west all the way to the Yangtze and capture of the prefectural capitals of Huang and Ch'i. But there was no possibility of maintaining such an advanced position.

Chin was of course able to spare only one part of its army for the southern front, since it was at the same time engaging Mongol forces in Shantung, Hopei, Shansi, and Shensi. Chin strategy called for a holding action in the north while pursuing, as was already observed, the offensive in the south. The former objective seems to have been achieved. Though the precise course of the campaign waged by Mukhali from 1217 to his death in 1223 is not clear, it appears that early success, especially in Shansi, gave way to a stalemate by late 1221. Then, probably impelled by successful Jurchen resistance, he revised his strategy and moved with his main army to the west, principally Shensi. This left, as we shall see, an odd assemblage of forces battling it out in the east, which now became a secondary theatre for the Mongol China campaign, itself secondary to Chinggis's operations in Central Asia. While Mukhali made steady progress in the west, his death in the spring of 1223 was another setback for the Mongols. Thus, Chin hopes of holding off its northern enemy while pursuing attacks against Sung to the south were effectively realized.[17]

Throughout the period of hostilities, the Sung government remained opposed to a negotiated settlement and committed to a defensive struggle. At the end of 1218 the Chin court, seeking to exploit its early victories, had sent envoys to discuss the possibilities for a new peace accord; at that time they were not even permitted to proceed beyond the frontier region.[18] Yet, within six months fears at Hang-chou over the influence of peace proponents were sufficiently strong to spark a student protest against one high official.[19] Time was of course on the side of Sung, with its territory largely intact, its ample population, and its productive economy. But its conservative and reactive policy entailed a ruthless neglect of the population living north of the Yangtze, subjecting it year after year to the cruelties of war.[20]

The war must have become a losing proposition for Chin after 1222, if indeed it had not already been so. In the spring of 1224 the Chin court attempted to open peace talks with Sung, but was rebuffed. Sung leaders clearly had no intention of entering into any further agreements with the old enemy. But Chin, seeking peace unconditionally, dispatched emissaries in the middle of that year to advise Sung frontier commanders that it was ceasing hostilities. The Sung court agreed to do likewise, and a truce was realized.[21] At the same time the Mongols found it necessary to regroup following Mukhali's death and the disaffection of the Tanguts. Thus, by late 1224 hostilities among the three main powers in China had declined to the lowest level in many years. But, if Sung's unwanted war with Chin was over, it had other commitments in the North, which were expanding rapidly, surely more rapidly than its abilities to deal with them.

The Dilemma of the Northern Loyalists, 1217–1231

Of almost equal concern to Sung policy-makers at this time as defense against the Chin was proper management of the rebels—"loyalists"—in Shantung and areas adjoining the border.[22] Indeed, many Sung officials had been insisting for some time that the future of the North would be determined between the "new barbarians" and these rebel bands. We have observed that the court adopted a policy of cautious support for at least some of these bands. Once hostilities with Chin broke out, there was excellent reason for expanding it. But as the promise for successful use of these troops grew, by no means excluding the tantalizing dream of their spearheading a Sung recovery of the North, so too did the problems surrounding them. The principal ones were how much support to provide, to whom to provide it, and what kinds of political and administrative ties to create. The latter problem was particularly difficult and reveals the deep divisions that rent the Chinese world at this time.

Vis-à-vis these rebels, the Sung court desired the best of both worlds, maximum control and minimum responsibility. To this end it was prepared to give them official titles and provide logistic support. But it was quite unprepared to absorb them into its own military establishment or even let them cross the border to the South. Part of the reason for this attitude was financial, with the military budget already felt to be staggering, but the more fundamental reason was a deep distrust of them as political aliens. It was probably not only that the rebels had never lived as Sung subjects but also that they had rebelled against established authority, even though a "barbarian" one. Incidentally, the same writers who view the rebels with distrust exhibit great sympathy toward *refugees*, whose lack of organization evidently qualified them as less dangerous and more loyalist. But a more critical point is that the rebels were not wholly Sung's to control, regardless of the titles and rations with which it provided them. They were a marginal group who, whatever the hardships they might suffer, did enjoy other options than serving Sung. The Chin and the Mongols appeared at one time or another as equally good or even better masters, and some figures successively served all three. The rebels can hardly, therefore, be considered an internal problem. On the contrary, they formed a marginal element functionally comparable to the sinified tribes living on the frontiers of China, who sometimes were and other times were not amenable to control by the dynasty in power.

The headquarters for liaison and supply with the rebels was Ch'u-chou (Huai-an), the most easterly settlement of any size on the Huai River frontier. The first commander at Ch'u to open up relations with the rebels was Ying Ch'un-chih, an otherwise obscure figure, who then handled affairs there through 1218.[23] On the authorization of Chief Councillor Shih Mi-yüan, he channeled supplies to several rebel groups, nicely designated the Loyalist Army (Chung-i chün). To judge by later criticisms, this must have been a time of rather generous support, especially once the war began. Moreover, Ying's role as a broker for the loot carried south by the rebels made Ch'u-chou a popular location.[24] As a result, large numbers of them flocked there for trade and employment, creating a situation which shortly began to trouble observers to the south. At this point there were many distinct groups, each with its own leader and none yet truly dominant. Conflict between them was not infrequent, a feature which would eventually prove the bane of Sung policy.

A second phase in Sung policy toward these rebels began in 1219. Relative lack of results and mounting costs led to the installation of a new commander, one Liang Ping, apparently with instructions to put a rein on the rebel leaders and to reduce expenditures. A memorial from this year by Liang's successor Chia She pinpoints the problem: the rebels must be formed into a single army, confined to the area north of the river, and reduced in number to the point where they were not a wasteful drain on Sung finances.[25] Liang's administration proved less than satisfactory, and he was soon replaced. It is during his period, nevertheless, that several major loyalist successes are recorded. In the spring of the same year, the army of the increasingly important leader Li Ch'üan scored two successive victories over an invading Chin column, forestalling the success of this eastern offensive.[26] Then in the summer Li's gains in Shantung were such as to induce the pivotal Chin commander at Ch'ing-chou, Chang Lin, to surrender with a reported twelve prefectures.[27] Chang was then given formal Sung appointment confirming his authority over the territory under his control. It is critical to note that this, in the same manner as all areas north of the Huai which were "surrendered" to the Sung by rebels and defectors, represented only a potential gain. Tactically and to a considerable degree logistically, the armies on the spot continued to operate independently. This was also true of defectors to the Mongols. By the end of the year, the Sung court was sufficiently encouraged by these developments to summon its top-ranking commanders for a formal deliberation on the feasibility of lauching a northern expedition which would seek support from rebels in the North.[28] It is not clear what came of the deliberation, but there was no slackening of interest in using the rebels.

Chia She was appointed to the command at Ch'u late in 1219 and, as a measure of the expanded responsibilities of this post, given the additional title of Commander of Troops and Horses in Ching-tung and Ho-pei (i.e., all of northeast China). Already known as a critic of operations here, Chia must have been expected to apply a firm hand to them. But evidently he was also expected to promote the Sung cause among potential friends to the north. In the spring of 1220, for example, he issued an appeal to the "braves" of the northeast to switch their allegiance to Sung.[29] However, among the groups around Ch'u, frictions and rivalries came to a head for the first time in 1220. In one instance Li Ch'üan instigated the murder of the leader of another group, favored by the court as a possible overall commander. In another, and more damaging instance, Shih Kuei, a particularly rambunctious figure, mutinied, seized control of the troops at one key location, and finally fled to the Mongols. Most of his men fell eventually into the hands of Li Ch'üan, who by the end of 1220 had clearly become the dominant rebel leader.[30]

Some of these problems were attributable to Chia She and his policies. Preoccupied with the issues of cost and control, he eliminated support for some 30,000 men, presumably saving the government 30 to 40 percent in costs. The remaining force of approximately 60,000 was thus brought safely below the number of regular troops in this sector (ca. 70,000). Moreover, Chia enforced a divide-and-rule policy, dividing the irregular forces into several separate contingents.[31] It is impossible to know how much of this was done on Chia's own initiative, but given the centralized character of Sung government, it is difficult to believe that the court had not provided at least a general policy directive. Numbers, organization, supply, and direction were all pertinent to the effective use of the loyalists. But these hinged in turn on which of two strategic alternatives the court adopted. It could build up their strength, establish greater cohesion, and employ them offensively to acquire territory for permanent occupation. Or it could maintain them in a reduced, divided condition to act essentially as a defensive screen before the main Sung lines. The latter clearly was the course chosen and one which did in fact bear some fruit. In the strong Chin attack of spring 1221, which penetrated the western Huai section, Li Ch'üan and the "Loyalist Army" helped provide relief for defense forces under attack; then they inflicted a sharp defeat on the invaders as they attempted to recross the Huai.[32] But it had severe limitations too. When the important Chin general Yeh Shih came over to the Sung in the summer of 1220 with considerable territory in western Shantung, largely as a result of Li Ch'üan's pressure, there were no means available to consolidate this gain. Consequently, upon the appearance of the Mongols in force late in the year, Yeh understandably rallied to them rather than attempt an isolated defense for a shadowy master to the south.[33]

Moreover, it was impossible for Sung authorities to maintain close control over rebel leaders whom they wished at the same time to operate effectively across the border. Naturally, when these leaders began to enjoy success, they developed bases and interests of their own. Li Ch'üan is the best example here. Coming to control much of eastern Shantung, he made Ch'ing-chou (I-tu) his Northern headquarters, corresponding to Lien-shui (northeast of Ch'u), his Sung-affiliated, southern headquarters. The acquisition of this Northern base occurred after his split with Chang Lin, which drove the latter into the arms of the Mongols late in 1221 and which came about for explicitly financial reasons. Together with Chang and with his own brother Li Fu, Li had been pursuing a highly lucrative trade in goods from the South, imported by sea into Chiao-hsi (approximately at modern Chiao county, across the bay from Ch'ing-tao). Caught in a profit squeeze because of the high cost of land transport for which he was responsible, Chang drew most of his profits from local salt production— until Li Fu muscled into that too and provoked the rupture.[34] To the extent that the Sung court refused to accept responsibility for these marginal areas, it had to accept such freewheeling and self-seeking conduct.

Chia She seems to have become increasingly ineffective in the latter part of his service at Ch'u-chou and, to judge by the surviving fragments of his memorials, increasingly disillusioned as well.[35] He may well have influenced the selection in 1223 of his successor, Hsü Kuo, a hard-line military man known for his contempt of the rebels and his distrust of Li Ch'üan in particular. It is notable that his very competence for the job was questioned by one high official.[36] Hsü represents the culmination of the court's effort to keep a short rein on the rebels and also the final failure of that policy. Perhaps the court felt that the time was especially propitious for stiff measures in view of the gradual winding-down of the war with Chin. Moreover, it had been under heavy internal pressure to find an effective formula for achieving stability on the frontier and, beyond that, for preparing to reassert Sung's rightful claim to the North. Since the Northern loyalists remained an issue in Sung politics for nearly two decades, it is not surprising to find attitudes in the early stage differing sharply from those in the later. Up to 1225, there was some optimism over the possibility of successful employment of the Northerners; after the events of that year, and especially after 1227, there could be none at all.

Sung officials distinguished, as we implied above, between the population of North China as a whole and those segments in active and organized opposition to the Chin regime. The Northern Chinese were assumed to be fundamentally Sung in sentiment; but by now, in contrast to the hopes of such early enthusiasts as Liu Yüeh,[37] there was no expectation that they could be drawn into an active role in determining the fate of the North. For some critics, the government had missed its chance to mobilize such latent support. Yüan Hsieh, always among the most sympathetic observers of refugees and defectors, contrasted Sung practice with that of Chin. He found the latter, on what empirical grounds we do not know, far more successful than Sung's policy of keeping them at arm's length.[38] Ts'ao Yen-yüeh, a provincial official throughout these years, was also deeply troubled by the government's handling of the refugee problem. A rigid policy up to 1217 of not granting admittance or succor gave way to profligate and wasteful recruiting by border commanders once the war began. But, even more important in Ts'ao's eyes, the ruthless indifference of the court and the armies toward the people of Honan had thoroughly alienated them. In their penetrations to the North, Sung armies behaved as though they were operating among an enemy population, with the result that this population looked upon the imperial forces as mere bandits. Caught in the middle, the Honanese drew back from the governments of both North and South.[39]

The Northern rebel armies fell into a different category altogether.[40] Far from sanguine at the outset, attitudes here only became more critical as problems of cost and control grew. Shortly before his death in 1223 and still in professional exile, Yeh Shih bitterly took the government to task for its support of these forces. Initial skepticism toward them, it is claimed, gave way to complacent acceptance of their utility in protecting Sung's borders. In view of Shih Kuei's mutiny and Li Ch'üan's growing power, it was folly to sponsor these large, well-organized armies, shower them with titles and offices, and let them operate with a free hand. This was not only a shortsighted, costly solution, but it posed, Yeh warned, direct dangers to Sung itself. Moreover, Sung's deep involvement gave these forces significant influence on Sung policy, a point also made by Wei Liao-weng.[41] But if distrust of the rebels ran deep among civil officials, it was far more pronounced among military men. Chao Fang's sons, K'uei and Fan, both of whom served in the Huai sector, typified this view, holding that Li Ch'üan and the others were genuine rebels in sheep's clothing who would un-questionably not remain loyal to Sung.[42] How self-serving such a view might have been is difficult to say; it must have rankled that Li and his officers received high appointments, diverted funds from the regular army, and yet operated with such freedom. The events of 1225 seemed destined to confirm such doubts. However, the reports submitted by the frontier officials themselves had decidedly influenced opinion and policy-formation at court in the interval.

The information available permits a relatively clear reconstruction of the situation at Ch'u-chou at the outset of 1224, when Hsü Kuo assumed command. It was a situation which, unbeknown to most contemporary observers, was steadily moving out of control. Hsü, as we have already suggested, entered the scene with the intention of bringing these irregulars into line and showing them who was boss. His failure was so complete that we can only conclude he was ill-suited for the job. But the events of the next few years reveal Ch'u-chou as a frontier town on the order of those of the American Old West, one which simply could not be administered in the same manner as the average, even frontier, Sung prefecture. As a military post, it was dominated by troops, which were of two kinds. The term "Northern army" designated the irregulars enrolled in the various "loyal-ist" contingents, who were all no doubt Northern Chinese, primarily Shantungese. By and large, they were kept in camps outside the town and north of the river, but there were clearly many inside as well. Moreover, the rebel leaders and their families had domiciles in town and probably entrepôts for themselves and their armies too. "The Southern army" designated the Sung regular units, probably composed of men both from the Huai-Yangtze region and from the south. These troops were intended mainly to form a defense line against the Chin, but they were also there to act as a check on the "Northern army." There was, in fact, considerable attention paid to the relative strengths of these forces. We noted above how Chia She brought the number of irregulars down below that of the regulars. Ts'ao Yen-yüeh, no opponent to the use of the former, even asserted that they should constitute no more than one-third the number of regulars.[43] Cost was naturally a factor, as well as security. The operation of loyalist contingents beyond the border to the north further complicated matters, and commanders out in the field unquestionably recruited as they wished and as their means permitted.

We shall pass over the details of the series of steps taken by Hsü Kuo to assert his and the court's dominance.[44] These included public humiliation of Li Ch'üan, confiscation of some of the loyalist bonus funds, and an attempt at intimidation by a grand assembly of all the troops under his command. There are indications that Hsü was going farther in this direction than the court wished, for Li continued to receive new honors and in the spring of 1224, together with former protégé P'eng I-pin, was given a bonus of 300,000 strings of cash.[45] Moreover, this was a period when loyalist arms carried farther to the north than ever. While Li remained dominant in eastern Shantung, P'eng steadily expanded his territory in western Shantung. His position here dated from 1222, probably when he first began operating independently of Li Ch'üan. By 1224, holding several important locations, his army had become one of the two major mercenary forces employed by the court to stake out a military claim to the North. Early in 1225, however, the situation at headquarters in Ch'u-chou collapsed. A year and more of friction between Hsü Kuo and the unruly elements from the North came to a head in a mutiny, which left Hsü dead and the town in disorder. Observers were quick to blame agents of Li Ch'üan, who in any event attempted to exploit the occasion by asserting his authority over P'eng I-pin. P'eng not only rejected this claim but, in a message to the court, accused Li of treason. This led in turn to clashes between the armies of the two, which, though indecisive, were somewhat to P'eng's advantage. The possibility of any joint action by these advance armies was, to say the least, shattered. Yet in mid-1225 P'eng's army moved northward, whether on his own initiative or not is not clear. After advancing as far as Chen-ting, which he took, he suffered a major defeat against a Mongol army and was killed in the pursuit. This was a significant loss to the Sung, but it was a loss of potential rather than of real power. Whether P'eng was a committed Sung loyalist or a warlord carving out a domain of his own simply cannot be determined.[46]

At Ch'u-chou, Hsü Kuo was replaced by Hsü Hsi-chi, known as a sympathizer of Li Ch'üan's, as the court now sought merely to restore some semblance of order. If Shih Mi-yüan and his colleagues suspected Li's involvement in the mutiny, they betrayed no sign of it. Not only was there no open inquiry, but according to one source, Li was given the honorary designation of "Lesser Protector" (shao-pao) in this same year.[47] Clearly unprepared to risk an open break, the leadership sought to retain his adherence with blandishments. With other possible masters waiting in the wings, compromise with this marginal element was the only alternative to a dangerous confrontation. The possibility of interference by Li in internal matters was even foreseen by one official. Writing with reference to Shih Mi-yüan's manipulation of the imperial succession in 1224, resulting in Li-tsung's accession, he had the temerity to suggest that Li Ch'üan might well use his army to challenge the legitimacy of the emperor.[48] Indeed, Li had been approached in early 1225 by a group from Hu-chou (Wu-hsing), subsequently executed, with the proposal to supply the force to enthrone the rightful heir; but he made no move.[49] In the inner councils of the court, talk evidently revolved around the possibility of setting up another high loyalist officer, Shih Ch'ing, as a counterpoise to Li. However, in a statement that reveals the relative helplessness of the court, the high official Ch'iao Hsing-chien argued that Shih could not possibly survive long against Li and that reliance on any of these self-made strong men was a self-defeating policy. The best course was clandestinely to recruit a few reliable old hands in Shih's army to take charge upon his assassination—which was apparently not to be discouraged—and build upon them to insinuate court control.[50] Whether there was indeed anybody willing to play this dangerous game and whether the court made any efforts in this direction is quite uncertain. On the surface, at least, the court did nothing until given an opportunity by the Mongols.

In the spring of 1226, Mongol forces besieged Li at Ch'ing-chou, and reports soon began circulating of his difficult straits and even of his death. Significantly, there was not even the breath of a suggestion to send a relief force to assist him. On the contrary, the court appointed a new commander, Liu Cho, at Ch'u-chou in the fall of 1226 with the aim of finally eliminating the troublesome loyalist presence. Once again an involved struggle ensued as Liu cut off supplies and attempted to expel loyalist leaders and troops. These measures failed when, in the second month of 1227, a revolt flared up which expelled the court's representative instead. And again a tough administrator was replaced by an easygoing one. But it no longer mattered. Having been under siege for more than a year, Li Ch'üan surrendered and took office under the Mongols. The final chapter in the story of Sung's ambivalent relationship with the Shantung rebels had begun. At Ch'u-chou a final struggle of nerves ensued, the court suspending supplies in order to bring the loyalist cliques to heel, the loyalists fencing with Sung officials and with each other for personal advantage. At last, in mid-1227, the court abandoned Ch'u as a command headquarters, and thus as a center of supply and coordination for loyalist forces. Headquarters was withdrawn to Yang-chou, with corresponding military adjustments, and Ch'u, reduced in status to an "army" seat (*chün*), was treated, in the words of one historian, like a location on the most distant frontiers of China.[51]

In a sense, the worst had come to pass. The main loyalist commander and army had gone over to the Mongols. Many of the remaining loyalists were scattered and in the service of various masters, including the Chin. Most had surely become wholly cynical about any connection with the Chinese regime at Hang-chou. With respect to territory not only were no positions north of the Huai retained, but the outer perimeter fixed on Ch'u was severely weakened. There was, it is true, no immediate danger threatening the eastern frontier as a result of this failure of policy. The Mongols were busy elsewhere, and the truce was holding with Chin. Li Ch'üan posed something of a threat, but Sung garrisons were adequate to check his army, and it soon emerged that Li wanted to "fence-sit" for a while anyhow. In the fall of 1227 he actually returned to Ch'u-chou as Mongol regional commander for Shantung and Huai-nan with Mongol advisers in tow. Though we cannot pursue here this involved epilogue in the saga of Li's relations with the Sung court, we should note that he remained there, essentially as an independent warlord, from this time down to the end of 1230. Eventually, he reopened relations with the court, asked for and received provisions, and was even offered high rank again. But from the court's point of view these were all mere gestures, tactical devices which it employed to keep him quiet. It did not seriously consider entrusting him with any responsibilities that were at its disposal to confer. Yet, a case can be made for Li Ch'üan, who appears as something more than a mere renegade, and on occasion even as a genuinely tragic figure. The book closes on him at the outset of 1231. Relations with the court having soured, he was provoked into fighting his own little war and moved southward to launch an attack on Yang-chou. The attack failing, he was killed and his army dispersed. Sung then seized the opportunity afforded by his demise to reoccupy its old lines.[52] Thus it was back to square one for Sung. Or not even that, for a decade and a half of effort and untold sums had been lost, and very likely an opportunity for significant gains in the northeast as well.

The Mongols: Allies and Foes, 1221–1234

To say that early Sung-Mongol relations are shrouded in mystery is no overstatement. A number of signposts are evident, marking the uneven course of these relations, and one event, the campaign to destroy the last vestige of the Chin state, is even well documented. But otherwise we must speculate and infer as to the content of communications and particularly the nature of any agreements reached. Apparently, many materials did not survive the historiographic filter applied under the Mongol regime, and no doubt the withdrawal of other materials feared as compromising from the Chinese point of view reduced still further the pool of relevant sources.

There are no attested direct contacts between Mongol leaders and the Sung state before 1221. On at least two occasions in the initial period of their conquest of Chin, probably in 1213 and then again in 1214, the Mongols attempted unsuccessfully to reach the Sung court with their envoys. For their part the Sung in these early years showed little interest in establishing contact and, as I have argued previously, reveal a laggardly growth of knowledge per se about the Mongols. Though it would be hazardous to assume that whatever was known was written down, the fact is that no Chinese text containing substantial information on this northern people dates from before 1221 (or at least one claiming an anterior date which is above suspicion).[53] In terms of normal kinds of military and political intelligence, Chin refugees, defectors, and prisoners would of course have provided useful information, but it could have been only fragmentary.

It was probably owing to Mongol initiative that the first Sung embassy was sent to a Mongol khan, as well as the first embassy to the khan's viceroy in China, resulting in the earliest extant work on the Mongols in any language. Chinggis's dispatch of one Su (or Chu)-pu-han to the Sung court, as Wang Kuo-wei has suggested, apparently prompted this court's dispatch of a return mission under Kou Meng-yü to the khan's court, then in Central Asia, in 1221. Kou's account of this embassy, the *Shih-pei-lu*, unfortunately has been lost. But an apparently related mission to Mukhali at Yen-ching that same year resulted in the well-known *Meng-ta pei-lu* by a member of the mission, Chao Kung.[54] Like Kou, Chao was an official active in military administration along the border throughout these years rather than a court official. While invaluable as a source of information on the Mongols, his work has relatively little value for the nature of diplomatic exchanges at this time. Though the *Yüan shih* records that Kou came "to request a peace agreement [or treaty]," it is unlikely, given prevailing attitudes at Hang-chou, that Kou and Chao conducted any more than exploratory talks. But these stimulated enough interest in the South to send Kou forth on a second mission two years later.[55] The common interest was, of course, the elimination of Chin. By no means averse to the use of diplomacy, and having made repeated efforts to contact the Sung court, the Mongols were surely more open than Sung to the idea of an alliance. Another possible area of discussion was the fate of specific regions which were falling out of Chin control. Shansi and northern Shensi posed no problem, but Shantung and southern Shensi were potentially or actually contested areas. Was there an attempt at a gentleman's agreement not to engage, in view of the desirability of destroying the common enemy? We do not know. What we can safely assert is that the Sung court had by the early 1220s gained firsthand, though still limited, knowledge of the Mongols as a political and military force. It is true that no Sung Chinese had as yet gone to Mongolia itself, or had gone and recorded any impressions that survive.

Opinion among the Sung intelligentsia, as we have seen, continued to focus on immediate issues and dangers despite the menacing specter of the Mongols. Chin and its prospects persisted as the main object of concern, even though predictions of its imminent demise had gone on for years now. Second only to Chin was concern over the Northern rebels, such as we have examined at some length. Obviously, these were related problems, for, as long as Chin survived as a state with vastly reduced power and control, such marginal groups outside the law were bound to persist. Faced with this conditon of instability in the North, most observers found that the only sure answer was to strengthen the defense of the country. There was tremendous interest in analyzing the country's military situation and proposing solutions for its various problems.[56] How well informed many of these analysts were and how well their proposals would have worked is difficult for the modern observer to assess. But they all shared a common assumption: Sung could do little to determine the fate of the North, but with the right men, measures, and plans it could defend itself against come what might. With regard to the Mongols, all writers remained vague and reserved. There were some calls to be wary of this rising power and avoid provoking it. But the key ingredient in their attitude was the conviction that the Mongols were simply another brand of "barbarian." They were bound to act in their characteristically aggressive and ravenous way, amenable if at all only to material inducements. The true potential of the Mongols was by no means clear at the time, as their effort to conquer China was retarded by a number of serious interruptions: by Chinggis's departure westward, by Jurchen resurgence, by Mukhali's death in 1223, by Chinggis's death in 1227, and then by the interregnum preceding Ögödei's election in 1229. Without understanding the causes behind the reduced pace of conquest, Sung observers could reasonably have questioned either Mongol will or Mongol power.

As was suggested above, there were possible areas of contention between Sung and the Mongols both in the east and in the west. Shantung was obviously one of them. We have seen a kind of war by proxy in the early 1220s as Chin (and eventually Sung) defectors struggled under Mongol banners with loyalist-mercenary armies in Sung pay. Defections from the Sung side to the Mongol, such as that of Yeh Shih and Chang Lin, seem to have occurred through the presence or pressure of the Mongol army rather than as a result of combat. Nor do any of the quasi-Sung armies ever appear to have fought an army under the immediate command of Mukhali or his successors. The two powers had, in effect, a direct confrontation upon P'eng I-pin's advance into Hopei in 1224–1225, resulting, as we have seen, in the destruction of P'eng's army. Were there any diplomatic repercussions of these events? We know of none; but Sung could easily have disowned P'eng altogether or explained away his indiscreet advance as a matter of exceeding orders. Subsequently, Sung remained clear of Li Ch'üan and his predicament, and once he went over to the Mongols, there was no longer even a quasi-Sung presence north of the Huai.

The picture in the west was quite different. The Mongol interest in southern Shensi and the Han River valley was in the strict sense strategic. We should recall here Chinggis's deathbed counsel to his sons in the summer of 1227: since Chin has the western approach to K'ai-feng so well fortified at T'ung-kuan and adjoining key points, the Mongols should seek rights of passage from the Sung and, outflanking the T'ung-kuan fortress, attack K'ai-feng from the south.[57] It is doubtful that the Mongol attacks on Sung positions in southern Shensi and northern Szechwan in the opening weeks of 1228 were an attempt to realize this plan.[58] More likely, they were raids carried out by local commanders; but they do represent the first Sung-Mongol armed conflict in the west.

The death of Chinggis brought Mongol military operations to a virtual halt. Ögödei was elected Grand Khan first in the fall of 1229, and only after this did the campaign against Chin again get under way. Still Chin refused to play the corpse, and two more years of mixed success on the battlefield persuaded the Mongol leaders indeed to adopt the strategy of Chinggis. In a well-known episode of mid-1231 they dispatched envoys to the Sung court to request free passage for the army, but the envoys were killed by the local Sung commander. This seemingly foolhardy act has been plausibly explained by one modern commentator as an endeavor to prevent the Mongol envoys from sowing the seeds of dissension and treachery for which they were well known. Another envoy was dispatched, this one to Szechwan, but with results that are unknown.[59] In any case, the Mongols retaliated for the murder with widespread attacks on Sung positions, seized the passes, and proceeded eastward according to plan without Sung approval or, apparently, resistance. There must have been considerable alarm at court and among the frontier commanders, but our sources are reticent about this. The event called forth another in a series of memorials on the inadequate defense of Szechwan but little discussion of the political aspects.[60] The Mongols evidently meant what they said on the matter of passage; no Sung positions are recorded as having been permanently lost to them at this time.

It is surprising that the chronicles ignore diplomatic contacts for the interval 1223–1231; yet, it is probable that some occurred. Even had the talks of 1221 and 1223 been unproductive, matters of common interest were likely to stimulate other exchanges within a few years. Chinggis is said by one source to have sent one of his officials, Hao-ho-shang pa-tu, four times on missions to the Sung, and yet no Sung source preserves any record of them. It would not be surprising if Sung had sent an envoy with condolences upon Chinggis's death, even in the absence of treaty relations between the two courts. In 1230 a Mongol mission was dispatched to Sung to propose a treaty, but it was turned back with no result.[61] In any event, the next significant diplomatic exchange occurred at the outset of 1233, initiated again by the Mongols in their frustration over the endless struggle against Chin.

The major development in this war had been the success of the Mongols' eastern campaign of 1231–1232, which left the Chin capital at K'ai-feng exposed to a Mongol army. Though the latter was unable to maintain an airtight siege, by the end of 1232 the city was nevertheless reduced to dire straits.[62] At this point Chin control scarcely exceeded the area of eastern Honan and perhaps failed to extend that far. Yet, Ögödei and his advisers were sufficiently wary of Chin's resilience to turn to Sung for aid. Early in 1233 they dispatched Wang Chi, who was to become the principal envoy to Sung for the next several years, to open discussions for a joint attack on their common enemy. Wang was received by the frontier commander at Hsiang-yang, Shih Sung-chih, who communicated the offer to the throne.[63] The first crucial point of decision for Sung in its relations with the Mongols had been reached.

The Mongol offer reached Hang-chou at a time when a gradual but significant change of leadership was under way. After nearly a quarter of a century, Shih Mi-yüan's period of dominance was drawing to a close. In external relations at least, Shih's byword had been caution, and whether consciously or not, he was true heir to Ch'in K'uei's policy of peace abroad and prosperity at home (the latter conceived, incidentally, as China below the Yangtze).[64] Shih died late in 1233, well after the issue of collaboration with the Mongols had been decided. But there are clear signs of his political and probably approaching physical demise prior to this, of which Sung's positive response to the Mongols can itself be read as an additional sign.[65] Perhaps a cause and most certainly a result of Shih's weakening hold was the increasingly active role played by Li-tsung, who now found it time to assert his independence from his political mentor. Contemporary records abound with references to his assuming "personal control of government" (ch'in-cheng). Another result was the first, tentative reshuffling of alliances at court, leading to the subsequent minor purge of Shih's Ming-chou clique at the beginning of 1234.[66] Still, considerable continuity was maintained by Cheng Ch'ing-chih, a useful ally of Shih's in his deposition of the heir apparent in 1224, a former tutor of Li-tsung's, and an occupant of high central positions since 1228, who became Shih's successor as Chief Councillor in late 1233.[67]

Unfortunately, nothing survives of the actual court deliberations over the joint attack on Chin which would acquaint us with the positions adopted and the reasons for them. We are told only of broad agreement to undertake this action, with opposition being limited to the rising military commander Chao Fan, perhaps supported by his brother K'uei, on the grounds of Sung's catastrophic experience a century earlier with a "barbarian" alliance.[68] On the one hand, of course, the decision was wholly consistent with Sung policy of uncompromising hostility to the Chin regime. On the other, it represented a critical change, primarily in that it called for active cooperation with a foreign power, but also in that it featured, for the first time since the debacle of 1206, a major military initiative across the border by imperial forces. Sung moves in the recent war with Chin, even when tactically offensive, had been essentially defensive in aim.

What lay behind this departure by the emerging new leadership from the former distinctly conservative political and military policy? First, the Sung court and military seem to have felt a new confidence following the defeat in 1231 of Li Ch'üan, the result of a new, get-tough line forced upon Shih Mi-yüan by Cheng Ch'ing-chih and the shadowy Yüan Shao with the emperor's backing.[69] A good deal of self-congratulation accompanied this elimination of "the Northern army," which, from the Sung perspective, greatly stabilized the eastern Huai region. Then too, the painful prolongation of the Mongols' effort to destroy Chin, which had lasted now for over twenty years, surely made it easier for Sung leaders to underestimate the Mongols and the problems which future dealing with them would pose. Indeed, the Mongols' request for an alliance could hardly have been read as other than a sign of their limitations. Finally, the role of the Sung policy of revanche must not be neglected, either as an emotional force or as a mainspring of strategic planning. The Sung desire for revenge against the nation that had stolen its homeland, still felt hotly in some quarters, stood closer to realization than at any time in the last century. But calculation as well as passion entered into the decision, for the campaign to destroy Chin must have been recognized as Sung's best available opportunity to stake a claim to any part of the North. This was all the more true since the failure of its policy of using rebel mercenary armies to establish this claim. Emotional commitment and pragmatic considerations must, therefore, have reinforced each other once the alternative was faced and the question posed: how can we *not* take this opportunity? The reported unanimity at court is, in this light, not difficult to understand.[70]

Was there not a more tangible inducement to Sung to join the campaign, namely, the promise of the return of specific territory? One of the lesser chronicles of the period indeed makes such an assertion, stating that the Mongols agreed to the return of Honan to Sung. This was then picked up and reported by later compilers, no doubt in an effort to justify Sung's subsequent course of conduct.[71] While we shall return to this issue in the light of the postwar settlement (so far as it can be discerned), we can safely assert that nothing in the surviving contemporary literature suggests the existence of such a "deal"—or, at the very least, any awareness of it among contemporary writers and officials.[72] But is it reasonable to assume that the Sung representatives bargained for nothing at all? Perhaps not, but they might have been led by their eagerness to finish Chin off to accept only a vague commitment.

If we lack precise information about the content of Sung-Mongol negotiations, we are also unsure about their mechanics. The Mongol emissary

bearing the offer of an alliance reached the Hsiang-yang frontier headquarters at the outset of 1233, and it was long assumed that the responding
Sung embassy under Tsou Shen-chih set off shortly afterwards. A recent
study suggests, however, that Tsou's embassy left Hsiang-yang only in the
sixth month of that year, not reaching Ögödei's court until late winter in
1234.[73] Negotiation of the most critical issues could hardly have waited
until then, for the campaign was not only already scheduled to begin but
had by that point indeed been completed. Clearly, then, a basic understanding between the two parties had been reached at Hsiang-yang, with
close reference no doubt to Hang-chou. Tsou's mission was, as a result,
dispatched to seal this agreement and to fulfill the demands of protocol. It
was, incidentally, from this embassy that the second early Chinese work on
the Mongols issued, the Hei-ta shih-lüeh by one of Tsou's aides, P'eng Ta-
ya. Considerably better informed than Chao Kung's pioneering account of
1221, this work was subsequently provided with a rich commentary by a
member of Tsou's second, or 1235, embassy, Hsü T'ing.[74]

Meanwhile, Chin fortunes continued to decline. In the spring of 1233,
the emperor Ai-tsung forsook his starving, beleaguered capital and fled
with part of his court to Kuei-te. Remaining there until approximately mid-
year, he moved again, this time to Ts'ai-chou, where the final act in the
drama was to be enacted. The lone hope of this remnant of the once mighty
Chin empire was to gain time for rallying the loyalty and support still
believed to exist among the chiefly Chinese population. To do this, the
assistance of Sung was indispensable. The truce between the two states had
remained intact after 1224; but sporadic engagements now broke out as
Sung armies moved into more advantageous positions. Still, grasping at a
last straw, Ai-tsung in the ninth month sent emissaries to Sung to plead for
provisions in order to sustain his efforts. The appeal was made partly on
moral grounds and partly on grounds of self-interest. The Chin emperor
emphasized how well he had kept the truce since ascending the throne (in
1223) and how humane his conduct had been toward Sung subjects, drawing a contrast with Sung's current opportunism. He observed too that,
having extinguished some forty countries already, including most recently
Hsi Hsia, the Mongols would inexorably move on from Chin to Sung.[75] But
the appeal was ignored, and late in autumn the joint Mongol-Sung attack
on Ts'ai-chou began.[76] It is noteworthy that, in addition to sending an
army of 20,000, Sung made some 300,000 shih of grain available to the
Mongol forces, revealing the latter's major weakness in the last phase of the
war and probably the principal reason for its alliance with Sung. Again, the
Chin resisted stoutly, but they were overcome after the first of the year
(1234), and the Jurchen dynasty reached its appointed hour.

If there were any conflict or bitterness between the victorious parties
over the territorial division of spoils, none is recorded. Shih Sung-chih's

victory announcement, in addition to reporting the circumstances attend-
ing the triumph, described a division of territory along a line drawn
through Ts'ai and Ch'en prefectures, the Mongols gaining possession of
lands lying to the west, effectively northwest, of it.[77] The clear implication
is that Sung received the lands to the east, or southeast. The fate of Ts'ai and
Ch'en is not spelled out, though the former, its walls systematically destroyed after its fall, must have been in ruins. Actually, some of the
locations in eastern Honan never came into Sung hands, and there are no
indications that the territory of the Mongols' satrap in Shantung, Yeh Shih,
was affected. The disposition of the forces of the Hsiang-yang command
following the battle suggests too that Sung gains were made only in the area
of the former Chin prefectures of T'ang and Teng.[78] In effect, neither Sung
nor the Mongols acted *as if* there had been an understanding on the return
of Honan to the Chinese dynasty or, for that matter, even a division along
the lines suggested in Shih Sung-chih's report.[79] But this by no means
precludes the presence of a strong sentiment in some Sung circles that
Sung's share was wholly inadequate and that the hallowed ground of "the
three capitals" must inevitably return to Sung possession.[80] In fact, one of
the few early instances of friction reported between the two new neighbors
occurred when Sung sent an official north to K'ai-feng to sacrifice at the
imperial graves. Initially blocked by Mongol authorities, this official was
able to accomplish his mission only by leaving his retinue and proceeding
by stealth.[81]

A period of some uncertainty ensued in those freshly conquered areas of
the former Chin domain, for which there were several reasons. In part it
was because of the time required for the completion of Mongol mopping-up
operations.[82] In part it was because of the widespread devastation and
depopulation that had resulted from the war. But mostly it was because of
the dilatory fashion with which the Mongols established their machinery of
rule. It was of course only now that ideas of the means of rule proper to a
sedentary population such as the Chinese were beginning to make headway
among Mongol leaders. So basic a measure as registration of the population
for taxation only came up for consideration in the autumn of 1234, though
the Mongols had controlled many parts of North China for twenty years or
so.[83] Meanwhile, the main Mongol armies withdrew to the North, their
leaders summoned to a *khuriltai* in the summer of that year, where cele-
bration of the great victory would take place and stock would be taken of
conditions facing the now vastly extended empire.[84] Honan was left under
military rule, though of a quite anemic kind. The Mongols, evidently
convinced that the fighting was over, left behind altogether negligible
garrisons.[85] In all probability, they assigned rather low priority to this area
because of the slim pickings it offered for the moment. But they unquestionably considered it wholly and truly theirs by right of conquest.

Unfortunately, the signs were read differently in some quarters south of the border where the minimal Mongol presence was perceived as evidence of indifference, ultimately a misapprehension of enormous consequences.

Sung jubilation over the destruction of the Jurchen regime was initially tempered by uneasiness over the real strength and intentions of the new "barbarian" neighbor. But the news grew encouraging as refugees from Honan reported that the Mongols were seemingly abandoning the province. Many of these reports were transmitted (and perhaps embellished) by the Chao brothers, commanding the Huai sector, to an emperor who was becoming increasingly sanguine about Sung's prospects to recover part of the North and who was no longer saddled with a nay-saying chief councillor. Cheng Ch'ing-chih was indeed equally sanguine. By the middle of the fourth month, 1234, prospects seemed to justify the calling of a great debate at court on whether to adopt a new aggressive foreign policy or to maintain an essentially defensive one, with provincial officials invited to memorialize their views.[86] Characteristically, we are well informed on the views of the "right" side in the debate, the side proven right by subsequent events and according to the canons of Confucian historiography—that is, those who opposed any move northward; and we are largely ignorant of the views of those officials who favored it—the "wrong" side. As a result, it is simply not possible to do justice to the latter.

Led on by reports of the Mongols' withdrawal, the revanchist camp put forth a proposal which outlined the feasibility, first, of seizing Honan and, then, of successfully defending it.[87] It argued that Sung armies advancing through Honan up to "the three capitals" would encounter no resistance, which in the event proved correct. It also argued that this region could be adequately defended by establishing a defense line along the Yellow River from T'ung-kuan in the west to Ch'ing-ho (Ch'ing-ho *hsien*) in the east. Sung forces would be significantly expanded by the recruitment of able-bodied Northerners, whose willingness to support this endeavor was apparently not questioned. What was foreseen for the Chinese warlords in Mongol service in Shantung is not clear; but presumably Sung success would have induced them to change sides.

In terms of purely Chinese precedent, it is difficult to find support for the defensive strategy proposed. However, its proponents may have had in mind the recent performance of Chin after the removal of its court from Yen-ching to K'ai-feng.[88] While the Jurchens watched Hopei, Shansi, and Shensi gradually go under, they maintained themselves in this secondary position for over a decade and a half—and with nothing like the kind of support the whole of the Sung realm could provide. Yet, in the context of Chinese history as a whole one finds little to commend a defensive strategy centered on the Yellow River. By implication the Mongols were far from being perceived as an irresistible force. Was this not perhaps because of the difficulties of mastering siege warfare which they encountered in China? The sheer length of the Mongols' campaign against Chin plus the need eventually to call upon Sung for aid, as was observed above, may also have tempered Sung's estimate of their military prowess. But it was also genuinely hoped that the Mongols would give up Honan without a fight, as unrealistic as that might now seem.

Having by contrast survived largely intact, the contra arguments strike the modern reader as informed, thorough, and incisive. Indeed, they provide a useful corrective—though many other Sung examples can be found—to the notion that Chinese statesmen dealt merely in moral homilies rather than in practical realities. Several themes are common to the statements of officials such as Chen Te-hsiu, Ch'iao Hsing-chien, Wu Ch'ien, and others, which may be summarized as follows.[89]

A first objection is to the miscalculation being made of the Mongols' current posture and of their likely reaction to any such unilateral action by Sung. Most certainly they will react instantly and harshly to the seizure of their newly won territory and with who knows what consequences for the Southern regime. Wu Ch'ien warns the advocates of action that, once provoked and with their might-is-right credo, the Mongols will not be easily put off from further conquest. He also takes issue with the claim that they had abandoned the area, observing that they had only dispersed to small, separate garrisons. As Wu was serving at the time in the western Huai region, this raises pointed questions about the quality of intelligence on which the pro group was relying.

Virtually all writers stress the inadequate state of Sung military preparedness for the proposed operation. In all respects, from leadership and training to weapons and supplies, the Sung army is simply not in the condition required. It is hardly able to defend us, Li Tsung-mien observes; how can it possibly take the offensive? The vast new manpower demands of the proposed strategy of garrisoning the length of the Yellow River are also pointed out by Wu Ch'ien, requiring no fewer than 150,000 first-line troops. Where can they be obtained? Quality is equally important; far tougher than Sung soldiers, the Jurchens were not able to resist the Mongols.

Again, the devastated condition of Honan comes in for attention from virtually all memorialists. Existing stores have been exhausted, and the region, suffering major depopulation and a total collapse of production, cannot offer any logistical support in the immediate future. In the words of Chen Te-hsiu, Sung armies will have performed the pointless exercise of moving north to seize and protect a wasteland. Obviously, they would have to carry needed supplies with them and thereafter be continually supplied from the south. Wu Ch'ien goes into great detail on this question, estimating that a million *shih* of grain a year would have to be moved north to support the armies installed there, and in view of the completely useless condition of the Grand Canal, transport would have to be by land. This situation would also have important bearing on the response of the towns to the north, which would adhere to Sung only as long as the supply link to the south held. Once cut off by the Mongols, they would quickly switch sides again.

Not only Honan beyond but some areas within the border are regarded as in no condition to support a major military initiative. All writers stress the unsettled, depressed state of the Huai region, long subject to conflicts along the border, to the movement of troops and refugees, and to requisitions, while Shih Sung-chih points out the incidence of famine in the Han valley prefectures. Most significantly, these writers, especially Ch'iao Hsing-chien and Wu Ch'ien, emphasize that the necessary means and manpower can be obtained from an already hard-pressed populace only at the risk of inciting active resistance. Few words are minced in informing the emperor about the state of the country under his rule, as revolt and disorder are held out as serious possibilities.[90]

Finally, opponents believe that historical and ethical considerations do not justify an aggressive Sung move against the Mongols. Present circumstances are in contrast to those surrounding Sung's relationship to the Jurchens, who had betrayed Sung and taken possession of the Central Plain. Revenge, now realized, had been incumbent on Sung in that connection. However, the Mongols seized North China not from Sung but from the Jurchens. And, as thus far Sung and its new neighbor have been allies and friendly neighbors, Sung should not violate this relationship and the existing state of peace. This argument was advanced to counter the very core of the revanchist rationale for the expedition, and while those who made it fully subscribed to Sung's moral and legal claim to rule all of China, their position came down to tacit acceptance of Mongol rule over the North.

These were persuasive arguments,[91] which were in Wu's case buttressed by a concrete, explicit analysis of conditions and contingencies, and in Chen's by a broad historical perspective. Chen's comparison of the current situation with that at the end of the Northern Sung may not appear highly original, but, by drawing analogies between the corrupt leadership and unstable conditions of the country then and now, he was leveling powerful criticisms at his superiors. Even more penetrating in its criticism is the memorial of Ch'iao Hsing-chien, which is nothing less than an indictment of the Sung regime—for its inability to eliminate social inequities and obtain the firm adherence of the entire populace, for its unreliable and unresponsive bureaucracy, and for its incompetent military establishment. Virtually all of these critics called for basic reforms, which alone could produce a healthy army, state, and society. On this score a fundamental difference, surely in part ideological, separated the two sides, for the pro-recovery group clearly felt it possible to achieve its goal by military and political means without the delay of thorough internal reforms. Opinion differed even more dramatically over the quality of the army. The pro-recovery group could hardly have promoted its policy without a fair degree of confidence in Sung arms. It is true that Sung forces had secured the eastern frontier through their defeat of Li Ch'üan and had contributed significantly to the final destruction of Chin. Yet, even if the bad press of the Sung army is somewhat discounted, it is difficult to conceive how imperial planners expected to supply the troops sent north. There was simply no solution short of massive support from the Yangtze valley. In this respect, it is ironic to contemplate the prospect of Southern Sung's encountering the same logistic problems in conducting a campaign into North China that Chinese governments always had encountered in sending armies out into the steppe. Events suggest that some of the skills needed to meet them had, indeed, been lost.

This opposition proved, of course, unavailing, but perhaps what we see of it is misleading. Perhaps the northern expedition had broad support, signs of which vanished as some officials later successfully covered their tracks and others were saved embarrassment by friendly editors and compilers.[92] But one ingredient was essential to the enterprise, the support if not the actual initiative of the emperor. No doubt nurtured on the same revanchist ideology as his predecessors,[93] Li-tsung emerges from about 1230 as an increasingly activist monarch. Before the final campaign against Chin had been completed, he had begun consultations on the possibility of recovering part of the North.[94] From 1233 he had in Cheng Ch'ing-chih a Chief Councillor whom he perhaps knew best of all the regular officials and who was clearly prepared to support his aims.[95] Li-tsung is also known to history as a sponsor of Neo-Confucianism, having begun a recall to court of such idealistic critics as Chen Te-hsiu, Wei Liao-weng, Ts'ui Yü-chih, and others whom Shih Mi-yüan had consigned to long periods of exile in the provinces. The new phase in his reign introduced by this recall earned from Confucian historians the designation "little Yüan-yu," evoking the period 1086–1093 when the conservatives led by Ssu-ma Kuang succeeded Wang An-shih's reformers in power. Is not the pattern that emerges one of, in Franke's phrase, a "völlig weltfremder Literat" who, disregarding the pragmatic considerations laid before him, pursued policies which were more feasible on paper than they ever could be in practice?[96] To be sure, this is only one-half of the equation explaining the decision to move north. The other half is the ambition and unwarranted confidence in their forces of the Chao brothers and their Huai-tung group. They supplied, if this thesis is correct, the practical "expertise" on which the emperor and his closest advisers at court felt they could rely.[97]

The dénouement came quickly, putting an abrupt end to over a century of Sung dreams of recovery and provoking the hostilities that would eventually destroy the dynasty. Within eight weeks the armies that had been sent forth to seize the region of "the three capitals" met defeat and were forced to return in ignominious flight.[98] They had, as critics predicted, found a wasteland where their rations were rapidly exhausted and no more were forthcoming. The major battlefield defeat, at Lo-yang, is said in fact to have occurred because Sung troops were weak with hunger. The failure of the expedition did not mean that an immediate crisis faced the country; as in their war against Chin, the Mongols' effort to conquer Sung proved highly sporadic. But there is no doubt that in Sung politics and foreign relations, and probably in the national psyche as well, a new page had been turned.

Conclusion

Sung provocation of the long and deadly war with the Mongols should not obscure the achievement of one of its foreign policy goals, destruction of the Jurchen state of Chin. This objective was never modified, though Sung did not actively pursue it at all times. It is noteworthy that active measures followed closely upon the first perception of serious problems in Chin around the turn of the century, namely, Sung's attack of 1206. It has in hindsight struck observers since the thirteenth century that, with the Mongols rising in the rear of Chin, it was not a good idea to assist in the destruction of that regime. But was there ever a genuine choice? The Sung were prisoners of a powerful revanchist heritage which in turn rested on fundamental conceptions of their place in the world and in the cosmos. The former demanded unremitting efforts to recover the ancient Chinese heartland, the latter, uncontested Chinese supremacy over the nations of the world, morally and politically.

Policy toward the new power to the north showed less consistency. Despite their common interest in eliminating Chin, Sung long kept clear of any closer, potentially troublesome relationship with the Mongols, haunted by the disastrous results of collaboration with the Jurchens a century earlier. Only in 1233 was this posture changed, permitting short-term cooperation for the purpose of eliminating Chin; but the reversal of 1234 followed immediately with Sung's attempted occupation of Honan. Faulty intelligence, overconfidence in current military capabilities, and wishful thinking combined to produce this rash step, which Sung leaders were soon to rue. It is curious that both attempts, in 1206 and in 1234, to throw off the defensiveness of mind and strategy which characterized Southern Sung and to take military initiatives against the North proved total failures. One suspects historiographic bias in the treatment of the plans and preparations for these operations, but this suspicion admits of no easy confirmation in face of the evidence that has survived.

The third important targets of Sung policy in this period were the would-be Shantung loyalists, whom it held at arm's length and yet attempted to exploit. These irregular forces operated freely in the Huai region, a critical one both for Sung security and for Sung hopes to recover the North. Sung policy sought, negatively, to neutralize any threats posed by these groups and, positively, to use them as an outer defensive shield against turbulence or attacks from the north. Their ethnic Han identity seems to have made only a minor difference to Sung planners, who were at no time prepared to welcome them with open arms. Still, it is far from certain that the loyalist leaders truly desired full incorporation into the Sung political order, and many seemed only too well prepared to exploit Sung support to strengthen their own hands as independent warlords. Sung policy here succeeded in pushing some of the most powerful ones into the arms of the Mongols. It is difficult today to avoid the impression that Sung missed a golden opportunity to strengthen its position in the northeast and even to lay the basis for the occupation of parts of Honan, Kiangsu, and Shantung. Nevertheless, contemporary writings, on the whole, reveal little enthusiasm among Sung officials toward taking strong initiatives designed to shape the future of the North, and correspondingly, a tacit acceptance of the division of the Chinese world.

This examination of foreign policy has been inhibited by our inadequate knowledge of two important areas. First, finances and economic conditions, aspects of which surface among several of our writers, have still been so little studied that we simply cannot gauge the extent to which they influenced policy. But it must not have been negligible. Second, the structure of politics at the Sung court in the thirteenth century, indeed during the whole of Southern Sung, has never been analyzed in sufficient depth and detail. The differences in position discerned here in foreign policy should most certainly be considered in light of those which separated officials on domestic issues. Similarly, the nature of political relationships claims high priority as a subject for extended research. Given the preoccupation of most officialdom with internal affairs, the results promise to be rewarding.

NOTES

1. See Charles Peterson, "First Sung Reactions to the Mongol Invasion of the North, 1211–1217," in J. W. Haeger (ed)., *Crisis and Prosperity in Sung China* (Tucson, 1975), pp. 215–252, which forms the basis for the paragraphs that follow.

2. It is not possible here to treat these developments from the perspectives of these other powers or groups. Source material of an "internal" character is scarce for the rebels and the Mongols. For Chin, it is ample, yet no thorough study of this

final phase of Chin history has been done. Valuable discussions and translations into Western languages of some late sources can be found in the following: Hok-lam Chan's study of Liu Ch'i's *Kuei-ch'ien-chih* in *The Historiography of the Chin Dynasty: Three Studies* (Wiesbaden, 1970), pp. 121–188; the same author's "Prolegomena to the *Ju-nan i-shih*: A Memoir on the Last Chin Court under the Mongol Siege of 1234," *Sung Studies Newsletter* 10 (Dec. 1974): 2–19; Erich Haenisch, "Die Ehreninschrift für den Rebellengeneral Ts'ui Lih, "*Abhandlungen der Deutschen Akademie der Wissenschaften: Philosophischhistorische Klasse*, no. 4 (1944); and the same author's "Zum Untergang zweier Reiche: Berichte von Augenzeugen aus den Jahren 1232–33 und 1368–70," P. Olbricht (ed.), *Abhandlungen für die Kunde des Morgenlandes* 38, 4 (1969).

3. Hsi Hsia's fortunes in this period are treated in H. Desmond Martin, *The Rise of Chingis Khan and His Conquest of North China* (Baltimore, 1950), chaps. 5, 9, and 10, and in Luc Kwanten, *Imperial Nomads: A History of Central Asia, 500–1500* (Philadelphia, 1979), pp. 113–124.

4. See Corina Hana, *Bericht über die Verteidigung der Stadt Te-an* (Wiesbaden, 1970), especially pp. 21–65.

5. Igor de Rachewiltz, "Muqali, Bōl, Tas and An-t'ung," *Papers on Far Eastern History* 15 (March 1977): 50, gives a figure of 23,000 for the number of Mongol troops left to Mukhali, with indications that this was well under half his total force. For a good general account of the Mongol-Chin war, see Yao Ts'ung-wu, "Meng-ku mieh-Chin chan-cheng-te fen-hsi," in Chang Ch'i-yün (ed), *Chung-kuo chan-shih lun-chi* (Taipei, 1954).

6. See *Chin shih* (hereafter *CS*), 62, 28a, and *Sung shih* (hereafter *SS*), 41, 11b. All dynastic histories are cited from the Po-na ed.

7. See *CS*, 15, 1a.

8. There is wide agreement among modern scholars on material need as the real reason for Chin's attack. See I. Miyazaki, *Ajiashi no kenkyu*, vol. 2 (Kyoto, 1959), p. 187; Chin Yü-fu, *Sung-Liao-Chin shih* (Shanghai, 1946), p. 109; and Tōyama Gunji, *Kinchō-shi Kenkyū* (Kyoto, 1964), p. 54.

9. *CS*, 62, 30b–31a, and *SS*, 40, 1a, record this mission but reveal nothing beyond the names of its two principal officials.

10. In the first installment of this study, I considered the methodological problems of determining the context for and process of foreign policy formation in late Southern Sung (see the reference in n. 1, pp. 216–218). The central problem is simply a result of the lack of adequate material. State papers fall far short of what is available for other periods in Sung, and the private papers of the most important decision-makers have not on the whole survived, a condition which I believe applies to all the significant chief councillors of Southern Sung. In addition, however, to the standard sources, in chronicle and biographical forms, we do possess the papers of several middle- and high-ranking officials who were both representative and in a general way influential. I have drawn here as much as possible on such papers in order to determine, on the one hand, the context of opinion and, on the other, the options seen available to the Sung government. In the process of identifying items of possible use in this body of material, I enjoyed the valuable assistance of Mr. Kam Tak-him, a recent Cornell University Ph.D.

11. The memorials in question can be found in Yüan's works *Chieh-chai chi* (Ssu-

k'u ch'üan-shu chen-pen ed., *pieh-chi*, no. 341), 2 (10a–11b), 3 (4a–12a, and 14b–17a), 4 (passim), and 7 (13b ff.), and are datable to 1217–1219 by reference to Chen Te-hsiu's obituary of Yüan in *Hsi-shan hsien-sheng Chen Wen-chung kung wen-chi* (*SPTK* ed.), 47, 12b–19b. Yüan, who was at this time (Provisional) Executive in the Ministry of Rites and a Han-lin academician, enjoyed some familiarity with the emperor at this time, as can be seen in the discussions reported not only in Chen's obituary but also in *Sung Hui-yao chi-kao* (hereafter *SHY*), 186:29, 50a-b. His *SS* biography, ch. 400, is almost worthless.

12. See, for example, Ts'ao Yen-yüeh's memorial in his *Ch'ang-ku chi* (Ssu-k'u ch'üan-shu chen-pen ed.), 6, 1a, datable to ca. 1218–1219.

13. Biographical sketches of Shih and Ning-tsung by Herbert Franke and Miyazaki Ichisada, respectively, may be found in *Sung Biographies*, ed. Herbert Franke (Wiesbaden, 1976), vol. II, pp. 872–873 and 802–804.

14. See my biographical sketch of Chao Fang in *Sung Biographies*, I, pp. 54–56, with references. Also see Otto Franke, *Geschichte des chinesischen Reiches*, IV (Berlin, 1948), p. 273.

15. *SS*, 40, 1b. An example of such a proclamation can be found in *SHY*, 186:29, 50b–51a.

16. The most convenient collection of source material on the war is in *Sung-shih chi-shih pen-mo* (hereafter *SSCSPM*), 86. Also see Liu Po-chi, *Sung-tai cheng-chiao shih* (Taipei, 1971), vol. 1, pp. 433–437, and Shen Ch'i-wei, *Sung-Chin chan-cheng shih-lüeh* (Wuhan, 1958), pp. 172–178.

17. For readers accustomed to relying on Martin's admiring account of Mongol progress in these years (*The Rise of Chingis Khan*, Chap. 8), this sketch may be surprising. However, Mukhali's western movement is inexplicable if one accepts a record of uniform success in the east. In all probability, he lacked the manpower to overcome the main Chin positions. For more up-to-date, though still positive, assessments of his campaigning, see de Rachewiltz's article cited in n. 5 above, and Sun K'o-k'uan, *Yüan-tai Han wen-hua chih huo-tung* (Taipei, 1968), pp. 51–54. Luc Kwanten presents a revisionistic account in "The Career of Muqali: a Reassessment," *Bulletin of Sung and Yüan Studies* 14 (1978): 31–38, which falls short, however, of an exhaustive treatment of the evidence.

18. *CS*, 62, 31a-b; *SSCSPM*, 86, 754.

19. *Hsi-shan wen-chi*, 47, 20a.

20. On the disastrous effects of the war, see Yeh Shih's remarks in his *Yeh Shih chi* (*Shui-hsin pieh-chi*), "Hou-tsung" (Peking, 1961 ed.), p. 846.

21. On these developments, see *CS*, 62, 32b–33a.

22. In developing the following discussion, particularly regarding the career of Li Ch'üan, I have benefited greatly from seminar work submitted by Dr. Richard W. Bodman of St. Olaf's College. An excellent treatment of the loyalists, and one suitably critical of the sources, can be found in Sun K'o-k'uan, *Meng-ku Han-chün yü Han wen-hua yen-chiu* (Taipei, 1958), pp. 11–43. Martin's incidental treatment of them in *The Rise of Chingis Khan*, chap. 8, seriously misrepresents the situation as it evolved in this area.

23. See Peterson, "First Sung Reactions to the Mongol Invasion," p. 245.

24. *SS*, 476, 2a.

25. For the administration of the little-known Liang Ping and Chia She's

memorial, see the latter's biography, *SS*, 403, 5a-b. Chia, who is treated by A. Levy in *Sung Biographies*, I, pp. 201–203, was himself serving on the frontier at the time.

26. *SS*, 40, 5b–6a, and 476, 3b–4a. The surviving material on Li Ch'üan is very rich, principally a remarkably long, two-*chüan* biography in *SS*, 476–477. Dr. Bodman has called my attention to the valuable account of him and the events at Ch'u-chou by Chou Mi in his *Ch'i-tung yeh-yü*, ch. 9 (the Ts'ung-shu chi-ch'eng edition of which will be used). Much useful material is collected in *SSCSPM*, 87. For a reliable brief treatment, see F. Aubin's notice in *Sung Biographies* II, pp. 542–546.

27. *SS*, 476, 4a: *Ch'i-tung yeh-yü*, 9, 108.

28. *SS*, 40, 7a.

29. *SS*, 40, 7b, and 403, 6b.

30. On these events, see *Ch'i-tung yeh-yü*, 9, 108; *SS*, 476, 6a; *Sung-shih ch'üan-wen hsü Tzu-chih t'ung-chien* (hereafter *HTCTC*), 30 (1969, Wen-hai reprint), p. 2414. Sun, *Meng-ku Han-chün chi Han wen-hua yen-chiu*, pp. 26–27, regards Shih Kuei's mutiny and defection, coming at the time it did, as a catastrophic blow to the loyalist-Sung cause.

31. *SS*, 403, 6a.

32. *SS*, 40, 9b, and 476, 7b.

33. Sun, *Meng-ku Han-chün yü Han wen-hua yen-chiu*, pp. 34–35, providing further detail, agrees in holding Sung policy responsible for such losses. A great patron of Chinese literati under the Mongols, Yeh Shih has a biography in *Yüan-shih*, 148. For the view from the other side and a demonstration of the critical role in ultimate Mongol success of such defectors, see Igor de Rachewiltz, "Personnel and Personalities in North China in the Early Mongol Period," *Journal of Economic and Social History of the Orient* 9 (1966): 88–144.

34. *SS*, 476, 8a-b.

35. *SS*, 403, 7a-b.

36. A little background on the attitudes of Hsü Kuo, a veteran of service on the Huai frontier, is provided by *SSCSPM*, 87, 764. The dissenting official was Ch'iao Hsing-chien; see *SS*, 417, 3b.

37. See Peterson, "First Sung Reactions to the Mongol Invasion," pp. 232–233.

38. See *Chieh-ch'ai chi*, 3, 8b and 15b.

39. See *Ch'ang-ku chi*, 6, 5b–9a, and 10, 9b–10b. Also, cf. Peterson, "First Sung Reactions to the Mongol Invasion," pp. 221–222. Ts'ao, who has a biography in *SS*, 410, took up important positions at court only a year or two before his death in 1228.

40. The concern here and throughout this paper is with the *eastern* rebels, by far the most numerous and important. Limitations of space and time preclude my dealing with the rebel groups active in Shensi, eastern Kansu, and northern Szechwan.

41. *Yeh Shih chi*, 845–850. Yeh's own proposal for positive action, namely a series of self-sustaining colonies in the Huai region, is discussed by Winston W. Lo, *The Life and Thought of Yeh Shih* (Hong Kong, 1974), pp. 105–107. Though this is a useful discussion, the charge of "racism" leveled by the author against Yeh is unacceptable. The grounds for it, that Yeh urged payment of bounties to the northern Chinese for each Jurchen they killed, falls far short of sustaining any such

label. Suggested by a remark by Sung T'ai-tsu, the idea was by no means rare. See *Chieh-chai chi*, 2, 5a-b. For Wei's point here, see *Ao-shan ta-ch'üan wen-chi* (Ssu-pu ts'ung-kan edition), 16, 11b.

42. *SS*, 417, 12a and 20a–21a.

43. *Ch'ang-ku chi*, 6, 7b.

44. On conditions at Ch'u-chou and this sequence of events, see *Ch'i-tung yeh-yü*, 9, 109–110; *SS*, 476, 10b–12b; and *SS*, 417, 12a-b.

45. *SS*, 40, 12b.

46. Sun, *Meng-ku Han-chün yü Han wen-hua yen-chiu*, pp. 25–26, does not appear to share these doubts.

47. *Ch'i-tung yeh-yü*, 9, 110.

48. *SSCSPM*, 88, 779–780. The thrust of this memorial was, in fact, to deliver a sharp attack on Shih Mi-yüan.

49. *SSCSPM*, 88, 778.

50. *SS*, 417, 3b–4a. Li Ch'üan did eventually kill Shih Ch'ing (late in 1227), but under significantly altered circumstances.

51. *HTCTC*, 164, 4462.

52. The main sources for the remaining phase of events at Ch'u and of Li Ch'üan's career are again the latter's biography, *SS*, 476–477, and *Ch'i-tung yeh-yü*, 9, whose account is particularly graphic. Considerable information also survives in other biographies and in contemporary memorials.

53. On early contacts and knowledge, see Peterson, "First Sung Reactions to the Mongol Invasions," pp. 247–248, including notes.

54. On these missions and the authorship of the surviving work, see Wang Kuo-wei's colophons (dated 1925–1926) to his annotated edition of the *Meng-ta pei-lu* (Meng-ku shih-liao ssu-chung ed.), also summarized by P. Pelliot in *T'oung Pao* 26 (1929): 165–167. A Russian translation of the *Meng-ta pei-lu* has been done by N. T. Munkuev (Moscow, 1975), and one into German by Peter Olbricht and Elisabeth Pinks has appeared—*Meng-Ta Pei-lu und Hei-Ta shih-lüeh* (Wiesbaden, 1980). Martin evidently misread Pelliot's note, asserting that Kou Meng-yü also went only to Mukhali's headquarters in Hopei (*The Rise of Chingis Khan*, p. 261, n. 50). As the *Yüan shih* (hereafter *YS*) Annals record this mission, surely it was realized at the Mongol court.

55. *YS*, 1, 20b–21a; 22a.

56. Military analyses can be found in the works of virtually every official discussed in this paper and in many others besides. Particular ones need hardly be cited for present purposes.

57. *YS*, 1, 23a-b. I acknowledge the possibly apocryphal origins of this anecdote, especially as *SSCSPM*, 90, 790, attributes this strategy to the Chin defector in Mongol service, Li Ch'ang-kuo, also known as Li Pang-jui (also see below, n. 61).

58. *HTCTC*, 164, 4468.

59. On these events see *YS*, 1, 2b–3a; *SSCSPM*, 90, 790; and Franke, *Geschichte* IV, p. 286. In a section on the Mongols' successful use of a fifth column, Sun K'o-k'uan speculates that the murder of the envoys was done in calculated fashion; see *Yüan-tai Han-wen-hua chih huo-tung*, pp. 22–23.

60. *HTCTC*, 165, 4507.

61. Hao-ho-shang's missions are reported in his *Hsin Yüan-shih* biography, 148,

1a (1922 ed.). The 1230 mission was headed by Li Ch'ang-kuo; see *YS*, 153, 12a. Franke, *Geschichte*, V, pp. 154–155, treats the latter as the follow-up to the one aborted by the murder of the envoys, explaining away the date given of 1230 as the time when Li was commissioned. However, Li's biography makes it clear that he was received in Huai-tung by Li Ch'üan who, we have seen, was killed at the outset of 1231. If Li Ch'ang-kuo is correctly reported to have been sent to Szechwan in 1231 (see above, n. 59), then certainly two different missions are involved.

62. See the contributions of Chan and Haenisch cited in n. 2 above.

63. Wang's biography in *YS*, 153, 5a, and also *SS*, 41, 14a-b, record this embassy, the latter implying that this was not the first such Mongol bid. Further on Wang, see de Rachewiltz, "Personnel and Personalities in North China," n. 90. On Shih Sung-chih, a nephew of Shih Mi-yüan's, see E. V. Mende's sketch in *Sung Biographies*, II, pp. 876–879.

64. Ch'in K'uei (1090–1155) is only now undergoing a more objective reassessment. See M. Yamauchi's account in *Sung Biographies*, I, pp. 241–247.

65. Shih hardly appears, for example, in the chronicles for 1232, and in the fall of that year he vainly sought permission to retire from court (*HTCTC*, 166, 4525). Note the point made below on policy toward Li Ch'üan.

66. On the purge of Shih's cronies, see *HTCTC*, 167, 4554. M. Yamauchi has pointed out the regional basis of this power bloc in "Nan-Sō seiken no sui-i," *Sekai rekishi* (Tokyo, 1970), 9, pp. 250 ff.

67. See the biographical essay on Cheng by R. Bodman and C. A. Peterson in *Sung Biographies*, I, pp. 156–163.

68. *SSCSPM*, 91, 803. But *HTCTC*, 167, 4551, places Chao Fan's objection a whole year later. He has a brief notice by K. Umehara in *Sung Biographies*, I, pp. 52–53, while Chao K'uei is treated by E. V. Mende on pp. 64–69.

69. See Liu K'o-chuang's epitaph in *Hou-ts'un hsien-sheng ta-ch'üan-chi*, 170, 3b–4a (Ssu-pu ts'ung kan edition). Despite the availability of scattered information (see sources given in Ch'ang Pi-te et al., *Sung-jen chuan-chi tzu-liao so-yin*, 3 [Taipei, 1975], p. 1858), little that is substantial can be said about Yüan Shao, though he occupied high offices at court and served as principal administrator of the metropolitan district and circuit for at least a decade prior to this time. His disgrace in 1234 on the grounds of corruption was surely politically inspired, even if some evidence supporting the charge was turned up.

70. The contemporary and near contemporary historiography of Sung court politics at this time reveals some intriguing disagreements over who was responsible for the decision. Wang Mai, for example, in a piece written in 1235 (see his works, *Ch'ü-hsüan chi*, 2, 1a–7a [Ssu-k'u ch'üan-shu chen-pen ed., 1st ser.], claims that Yüan Shao was the one who really persuaded the emperor to join the attack and that Cheng Ch'ing-chih could not counter his influence. However, this piece is really an apologia for Cheng, who was still in power and who was something of a sponsor of Wang's . A more balanced view is presented by Chao Ju-t'eng who, writing in 1252, gives Cheng responsibility both for keeping in office unsavory cronies like Yüan and for encouraging the emperor to take this action against Chin. See his works, *Yung-ch'i chi*, 4, 2b–5a (Ssu-k'u ch'üan-shu chen-pen ed., 1st ser.).

71. The *Sung-chi san-ch'ao cheng-yao*, 1, 8 (TSCC ed.), reports this agreement as the result of Tsou Shen-chih's mission. It is also related in the Ming compilation,

SSCSPM, 91, 803, and the Ch'ing work, *HTCTC*, 166, 4528.

72. Huang K'uan-ch'ung in his article "Pien 'Tuan-p'ing ju-lo pai-meng,'" *Shih-i* (Sept. 1973), pp. 54–65, confirms and indeed has gone beyond my own research here. See pp. 54–55 for a brief review of the views of previous writers on the subject. There is, of course, the distant possibility that historiographers working under the Mongol regime scrubbed clean all references to such a deal, as suggested by Chang Yin-ling (see the "Shih-ti chou-k'an" of the *Ta-kung pao* for Nov. 20, 1936, or Huang's article) and Franke (*Geschichte*, IV, p. 288, and V, p. 156). But it is doubtful that Mongol "censorship" could have been so thorough and complete (cf. below n. 79). Not surprisingly, Mongol sources contain no mention of an agreement along these lines.

73. See Chang Huan-feng, "Sung ku Ssu-ch'uan ... P'eng Chung-lieh kung shih chi," *Sung-shih yen-chiu chi*, 5 (Taipei: Chung-hua Ts'ung-shu Pien-shen Wei-yüan hui, 1970), pp. 73–78. In this careful examination Chang takes issue with Wang Kuo-wei, who had accepted the timing suggested by the *Sung shih* Annals (see n. 63). While there is not space here to review his evidence, attention may be drawn to the *Ssu-k'u ch'üan-shu tsung-mu t'i-yao* notice on Tsou's own account of the embassy, since disappeared, the *Shih-pei* (or, *Yen*) *jih-lu*, where quite explicit information on dates is provided.

74. The best edition of this work is Wang Kuo-wei's (see n. 54 above), whose view that Hsü went on the second embassy is generally accepted. Professor Olbricht has translated the *Hei-Ta shih-lüeh* as well as the earlier account (see N. 54). The valuable use to which the work can be put is shown in Yao Ts'ung-wu's article, "*Hei-Ta shih-lüeh*-chung so-shuo Wo-k'uo-t'ai han shih-tai Hu ch'eng-hsiang shih-chi k'ao," *Sung-shih yen-chiu chi*, 5, pp. 95–118.

75. *CS*, 18, 9a.

76. Ample material on this campaign is collected in *SSCSPM*, 91.

77. Shih's *lu-pu* is an elusive document not quoted in substance in his biography or any other expected source. In fact, it turns up, to my knowledge, only in the biography of the late Southern Sung figure Chia Ssu-tao, where it is cited to give the background of the Sung-Mongol conflict. See *SS*, 474, 13b (and, as subsequently transmitted, *SSCSPM*, 91, 810). We can only speculate why not only this but the whole body of Shih's papers have been lost. Was it essentially the result of Confucian political opposition or Mongol suppression (despite n. 72) or both?

78. Li Tsung-mien makes reference to Sung's "obtaining" Ts'ai-chou in a memorial submitted probably in the spring of 1234, but whether this is suppositional or fact is not clear. See *SS*, 405, 2a. As for the former Chin locations in the east, the progress of the Sung army northward later in 1234 (see below) as described in *Ch'i-tung yeh-yü*, 5, pp. 52–53, reveals that none had come under Sung control. *SS*, 41, 17b, gives a brief but explicit indication of the disposition of forces following the campaign. Sung's acquisition of the "empty towns" of T'ang and Teng is confirmed by Wu Ch'ien in *Lü-chai i-chi*, 4, 14a (Ssu-k'u ch'üan-shu chen-pen ed., 2nd ser.).

79. I find it difficult to dispute Chin Yü-fu's contention that evidence, even if only indirect, revealing a Sung-Mongol agreement on the return of Honan would have turned up somewhere else (besides the *Sung-chi san-ch'ao cheng-yao*) if there had ever been one. Cf. *Sung-Liao-Chin shih*, pp. 109–110.

80. Besides Pien-ching (K'ai-feng, the Eastern Capital), the designation "three capitals" included Lo-yang (the Western Capital) and Sung-chou (the Southern Capital). The strength of the charisma of the Central Plain as the true locus of the Heavenly Mandate is nicely exposed in Hoyt C. Tillman's "Values in History and Ethics in Politics: Issues Debated between Chu Hsi and Ch'en Liang," chap. 7, Ph.D. dissertation, Harvard University.

81. *SSCSPM*, 91, 810.

82. For example, the Mongol capture of Hsü-chou followed by a month or more the fall of Ts'ai, and the loyalist Chin general Wu Hsien was killed only in the fifth month. See *HTCTC*, 167, 4557 and 4561.

83. See Yao, "*Hei-ta shih-lüeh*-chung . . . shih-chi k'ao," pp. 102–104, and for a more general sketch, I. de Rachewiltz, "Yeh-lü Ch'u-ts'ai (1189–1243): Buddhist Idealist and Confucian Statesman," in A. F. Wright and D. C. Twitchett (eds.), *Confucian Personalities* (Stanford, 1962), pp. 201–207. Although some information is available on developments at the Mongol court, very little is known about conditions in the various parts of North China, including Honan, in the early Mongol period.

84. *YS*, 4, 4a-b, and Rashīd al-Dīn's account in *The Successors of Genghis Khan*, trans. by John Boyle (New York, 1971), pp. 54–55. Kwanten (in *Imperial Nomads*, p. 133) places at this meeting the Mongol decision and plans to attack Southern Sung as well as other countries. However, both of the above sources make it clear that this program of conquest was determined only at a second grand assembly the following year, 1235. The site of the 1234 meeting, Dalan-Daba, is located by Kwanten on the Orkhon River.

85. All Sung sources, but especially *Ch'i-tung yeh-yü*, 5, make this clear.

86. Only *Sung-shih ch'üan-wen*, 32, 2499 (Wen-hai reprint), records this event, which in view of the absence of external tensions, must have been inspired by the prospects for positive action. Actually, the issue of an initiative into the north had been smoldering at least since the first of the year, since it is mentioned by Chen Te-hsiu in his memorial of the second month (see below, n. 89). The entire reconstruction presented here is based on fragmentary information contained in *Ch'i-tung yeh-yü*, 5, biographies, and various memorials submitted at the time. There is widespread attribution in these materials of responsibility for the ensuing campaign to Cheng and the Chao brothers.

87. This proposal is cited in very abbreviated fashion by Wu Ch'ien in *Lü-chai i-chi*, 4, 15a, and in *Hsü-kuo kung tsou-i*, 1, 7a (TSCC ed.).

88. Indeed, Wu Ch'ien, *Lü-chai i-chi*, 4, 17a, takes up this very point.

89. The principal document from Chen's hand dates from the second month of 1234, still prior to his recall from his service as Prefect of Fu-chou. It is found in *Hsi-shan wen-chi*, 13, 1a–9a, followed by a lengthy memorial of the ninth month also containing much relevant material. Ch'iao Hsing-chien's memorial is preserved in *SS*, 417, 4b–7a. In view of his high office, occupying the posts of Assistant Executive of the Secretariat-Chancellery and of Administrator of the Bureau of Military Affairs, he may have submitted his highly critical statement for the emperor's eyes only. Two of Wu Ch'ien's memorials (already cited above) are relevant. The one in *Hsü-kuo kung tsou-i*, 1, 7a-b, must be posterior to the fourth month, since it refers to another memorial of that time. The beginning of the other,

in *Lü-chai i-chi*, 4, 14a–18a, has evidently been excised, making the dating problematic. Wu came under accusation in the fifth month, along with his brother, for financial irregularities, and as a result lost his post. One would not have expected him to express himself with such freedom and bluntness under such circumstances; but it is not out of the question. He had had responsibilities in military administration in Huai-hsi. Other relevant views are preserved in abbreviated form: of Li Tsung-mien, at this time a censor, in *SS*, 405, 2a; of Shih Sung-chih from Hsiang-yang, in *SS*, 414, 9b; of an obscure provincial official, Tu Kao, in *HTCTC*, 167, 4560; and of a member of Chao Fan's own staff, in ibid., 4563.

90. Fear of popular reaction to the harsh financial measures which an ambitious and aggressive foreign policy would require has not received adequate attention as a constraint on Sung military performance on the whole.

91. My discussion does not, of course, exhaust them—e.g., the expected charge that military leaders were promoting the expedition for the sake of fame and advancement.

92. The biographies in the *Sung-shih* are notorious for excluding negative material on their subjects—e.g., Chao Fan's in *SS*, 417, ignores his responsibility for the decision to make the northern expedition, and Wu Ch'ien's in *SS*, 418, omits mention of his cashiering in 1234.

93. Cf. Édouard Chavannes, "L'Instruction d'un futur empereur de Chine en l'an 1193," *Mémoires concernant L'Asie Orientale* 1 (1913): 19–64.

94. *HTCTC*, 167, 4551.

95. See *Sung Biographies*, I, pp. 157–158.

96. Franke, *Geschichte*, IV, p. 301.

97. Is there any possibility that the decision was taken in the light of new intelligence on the Mongol position and intentions provided by Tsou Shen-chih's embassy? If so, it could not have been by Tsou himself, since he only reached Hsiang-yang in return in the seventh month (see Chang article, cited in n. 73). But he could conceivably have sent a messenger with up-to-date information. A complication here is that Tsou was a subordinate of Shih Sung-chih's, who himself strongly opposed the expedition.

98. On the northern expedition no secondary work conveys the tragicomic quality of the event so well as Chou Mi's account in *Ch'i-tung yeh-yü*, 5, a precise and vivid relation. Again, *SSCSPM* in ch. 92 has brought together much useful material.

PART V

The Mongol Hegemony

NINE

The Yüan Dynasty and the Uighurs of Turfan in the 13th Century

THOMAS T. ALLSEN

Subordinate States in the Mongol Empire

At its apogee in the mid-thirteenth century, the "Great Mongol State" (*yeke mongghol ulus*) was the largest contiguous land empire in the history of mankind. It controlled an expanse of territory stretching from the Pacific Ocean to the eastern shores of the Mediterranean and ruled over a multitude of peoples and states differing widely in language, cultural traditions, and forms of social and economic organization.

At the center of the empire sat the person of the Grand Khan or Khaghan, surrounded by his closest kinsmen, the "golden lineage" (*altan urugh*), and the imperial clan (*obogh*). This clan, the Borjigins, dominated a tribe (*irgen*), the Mongol, composed of related clans. Other tribes were federated with and subordinate to the Mongols. Those who joined the confederation voluntarily (called *khari* or *il irgen* by the Mongols) enjoyed greater privileges than did "rebellious tribes" (*bulgha irgen*) who resisted incorporation.[1] Outside these "inner" and "outer" tribes were various dependent social groups: slaves, craftsmen, and most important, the sedentary populations of the cities and villages subject to Mongol authority.[2]

The sedentary sector, which contained a substantial majority of the total population of the empire, was in some cases ruled directly by the khaghan and his agents, and in others indirectly through local ruling houses whose right to existence was recognized by patents of investiture issued by Mongols. By the end of the thirteenth century a large number of sedentary states had become subordinates.[3] These were generally, but not exclusively, located on the frontiers of the empire and ranged in size and population from the Koryŏ kingdom of Korea[4] to the tiny Sultanate of Mārdīn, a town in Mesopotamia. The sedentary subordinate states were also ranked, like the inner and outer tribes, according to the sequence and condition of their entry into the empire. The Mongols treated nomadic subordinates somewhat differently than sedentary ones. Only the latter will be considered here.

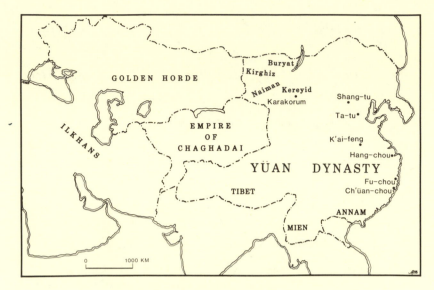

Map 3. The Mongol Domains, 1290 A.D.
Based on Albert Herrmann, *An Historical Atlas of China*, p. 43.

Native dynasts were allowed to retain their thrones and territories as subjects of the khaghan for a variety of reasons. In some instances, distance (e.g., Bulgaria), inaccessibility (e.g., Kashmir), or climatic conditions (e.g., Burma) made the military effort necessary to force capitulation very costly. In order to avoid such campaigns, the Mongols, prior to the commencement of hostilities, customarily issued orders of submission that in essence offered local rulers physical and institutional survival in return for submission to the khaghan. The choice given potential vassals is graphically expressed in a *jarligh* issued in the name of the Grand Khan Möngke (r. 1251– 1259) that his brother Hülegü caused to be sent to the ruling houses of the Middle East on the eve of the Mongol campaign against the Assassins:

> If you come of your own accord and support our army with men and supplies, your countries, armies and households will remain with you and your efforts on our [behalf] will be looked upon with favor. But, if you are negligent and cultivate remissness in carrying out the order, then as soon as we, with God's power, finish with them [the Assassins], we, without fail, will head in your direction and deal with your households and countries in the same manner we dealt with them.[5]

Obviously, such offers were also a valuable diplomatic tool for weakening the resolve of an enemy and a means of detaching his subordinates and allies. Despite Chinggis Khan's injunction, reported in the *Tartar Relation*, that the Mongols should "make peace with none unless they surrendered unconditionally and without treaty,"[6] his successors retained a degree of flexibility in dealing with foreign states that proved useful for diplomatic purposes. For example, Möngke granted Hetum, the king of Lesser Armenia, certain concessions which were formalized by treaty, in order to gain the latter's support for the attack on Baghdad.[7]

Another and perhaps more compelling reason for the toleration of dependent states was the Mongols' lack of experienced administrative manpower. Since very few of the Mongols' estimated population of 700,000[8] were literate, and still fewer were familiar with the "customs and laws of cities," the retention of a local dynasty and its attendant administrative apparatus was often the most practical method of controlling and exploiting the population and resources of a newly surrendered territory. In several instances, the Mongols even created new dynasties—for example, the Kart of Harāt, headed by a family familiar with local languages, conditions, and administrative practices.[9] Similarly, the Sa-skya, the Lamaist sect that ruled Tibet in the thirteenth and fourteenth centuries, was also a creation of the Mongols.[10]

Among the vassals of the Mongols, the Uighurs, as Rubruck correctly notes, "were the first dwellers in towns to be subject to Chingis Chan [*sic*]."[11] Because of their early adherence to the empire, as well as their proximity to the Mongol homeland and their administrative and clerical skills, the Uighurs had a close and continuous relationship with the Mongol Grand Khans for nearly a hundred years. It is the purpose of this essay to examine the evolution of this relationship, with particular reference to the kinds of demands placed upon the Uighurs for goods and services, as a means of elucidating the role of subordinate states in the rise of the Mongol Empire. In the conclusion, I will make some comparisons between Chinese and Mongol systems of tributary relations.

Historical Background

In 840 the Kirghiz destroyed the Uighur state that had dominated Mongolia for nearly a century. Most of the Uighur tribes declined to serve the conquerors and abandoned their native land, seeking refuge in China, Kansu, and East Turkestan. The tribes who reached Turkestan soon established a new state that embraced the eastern half of the T'ien Shan range and the northern fringes of the Tarim Basin. In this new homeland, the Uighurs gradually gave up the nomadic way of life and merged with the indigenous Indo-Iranian-speaking populace. Major urban centers developed, principally Khara Khocho in the Turfan Depression and Besh Balikh on the northern slopes of the T'ien Shan, which were witness to one of the most impressive cultural achievements in the medieval history of Eurasia.[12]

With the exception of their frequent conflicts with the Tanguts, the Uighurs maintained amicable relations with their neighbors and enjoyed an independent existence until the rise of the Karakhitay, or Western Liao, in the early twelfth century. Sometime around 1130, the Uighur ruler acknowledged his subordination to the *gurkhan*, Yeh-lü Ta-shih, the founder of the Karakhitay state, by handing over to the latter several relatives as hostages.[13] The Karakhitay do not seem to have exercised very stringent control over their new subordinates, at least not initially, since the Uighurs continued to maintain tributary relations with the Chin dynasty for another forty years.[14] This loose form of control came to an end in the first decade of the thirteenth century, when the *gurkhan* dispatched a new representative to the court of the *iduq qut* (*i-tu-hu*), the Uighur ruler.[15]

Chinggis Khan and Barchukh Art Tegin[16]

The new Karakhitay resident among the Uighurs was a Buddhist monk bearing the title Junior Supervisor (*shao-chien*).[17] According to Rashīd al-Dīn, "when he took power, he extended the hand of tyranny over the *Iduq qut*, the amirs and the Uighur tribes. He demanded unreasonable taxes and they [the Uighurs] came to loathe him."[18] His greed and arrogance so alienated the Uighurs that the *iduq qut*, Barchukh Art Tegin, after consultation with his chief minister (*kuo-hsiang*), Bilge Bukha, and other civil and military officials, resolved to have him murdered.[19] From the accounts of their deliberations, it is clear that the decision to do away with the Karakhitay representative was predicated on gaining the protection of Chinggis Khan, that is becoming a subordinate of the Mongols.

The murder of the *shao-chien* took place in 1209 in Khara Khocho. Pursued by Uighur officials and the populace, the hated monk was forced to take refuge in a large building or tower, where he was subsequently killed.[20] Shortly afterwards, just as the *iduq qut* was preparing to send an embassy to Chinggis Khan, the latter's representatives unexpectedly arrived at his court. The Mongols were warmly received, and a return embassy was dispatched,[21] conveying the *iduq qut's* pledge that he wished to become Chinggis Khan's "servant and son."[22]

Barchukh was soon offered an opportunity to demonstrate his fidelity to the Mongols. Sometime in 1209, along the Irtysh River, Chinggis Khan defeated a contingent of Merkid, who then fled toward the Uighur country in the hope of finding sanctuary. The *iduq qut* rebuffed their entreaties and, following a fierce engagement, succeeded in driving them off. The incident was duly reported to Chinggis Khan, who approved of the Uighurs' action, but demanded that the *iduq qut* personally deliver tribute to the Mongol court as a sign of his sincerity. In compliance with this order, Barchukh immediately sent various valuable items to the Mongols. His personal audience with Chinggis Khan, however, was delayed until 1211, when the latter returned from a campaign against the Tanguts. In the meantime, a Mongol garrison was established in the *iduq qut's* domain to ensure continued loyalty.[23]

When he finally had his audience, held somewhere on the Kerülen River, the *iduq qut's* profession of loyalty so pleased the Mongol ruler that he ordered Barchukh "to be [his] fifth son, to be bound as a brother with the emperor's sons."[24] Chinggis Khan also bestowed upon him one of his daughters in marriage.[25]

Once his status as a subordinate was formalized, Barchukh was required to participate in the Mongol campaigns of conquest. He was first called upon in 1216 to accompany Jebe on an expedition against Küchlüg, Chinggis Khan's Naiman rival, who had made himself master of the Karakhitay state. Thereafter, the *iduq qut* paticipated in the attack on the Khwārazm Shāh, fighting at Utrār and distinguishing himself at Nīshāpūr.[26]

In 1225, following his return from Central Asia, Chinggis Khan mounted a punitive expedition against the Tanguts for refusing to send contingents in support of the Mongol armies in the west. Barchukh once again accompanied his sovereign, and the experience of witnessing the destruction of the Tangut nation must have served as a forceful reminder, if any were necessary, of the dire consequences of refusing to comply with Mongol demands.[27]

The Uighurs' Status in the Early Mongol Empire

There are a number of indications that the Uighurs and their ruler enjoyed a special status during the reign of Chinggis Khan. Certainly, Barchukh (as well as his successors) held an honored place among the subordinates of the Mongols. The reason for this precedence is clearly revealed in a statement that Khubilai made to the Koryŏ ruler and his son in 1270:

> You [the Korean monarch] submitted later, therefore [you] are ranked low among the princes (*wang*). During the reign of our T'ai-tsu [Chinggis Khan], the *Iduq qut* was the first to submit, accordingly it was ordered that [he] be ranked first among the princes. Arslan [A-ssu-lan][28] next submitted, therefore [he] was ranked below him [the *Iduq qut*]. You ought to know this.[29]

Moreover, because the *iduq qut* yielded "gracefully, without causing the men of . . . Cinggis Qaghan [*sic*] to suffer and without causing his geldings to sweat,"[30] he further improved his credit with the Mongols.

The most visible sign of the Mongols' esteem for Barchukh was the distinction of being designated as Chinggis Khan's fifth son; he was the only subject ruler honored in this manner.[31] In a society in which kinship was an essential structural element, such a designation served to underscore the closeness and, at the same time, the subservience of the *iduq qut* to the Mongol emperor. That this distinction was honorary in nature and did not signify that Barchukh was in actuality treated as a natural son is demonstrated by the fact of his betrothal to one of Chinggis Khan's daughters, that is, to one who was nominally his "sister."[32] Although the Persian sources state that the marriage between the Uighur chief and his intended spouse, variously called Al Altun or Altan Beki, never occurred, owing to the demise of the principals, the essential point is that she was deemed a suitable mate for Chinggis Khan's "fifth son."[33] If Barchukh was really thought of as "one of the family," such a union would hardly have been contemplated. Regardless of the outcome in this instance, the offer was still a great honor and one later bestowed upon many of Barchukh's successors. In the latter cases there is no doubt that the marriages were actually carried out.[34]

In addition to these honors, which were mainly symbolic in nature, a more concrete manifestation of Mongol favor can be cited. Because they were employed extensively in the Mongol army and administrative apparatus, the *iduq qut's* subjects had become widely scattered throughout Central and East Asia. Consequently, when Chinggis Khan returned from Transoxania in 1224 or 1225, he was approached by Barchukh with the request that "all his people be returned home." This request was granted,[35] and individuals stationed as far away as Peking were allowed to go back to Uighuristan.[36] Even though it is quite unlikely that *all* the Uighurs, as is implied in the request, were actually reunited in their homeland, especially in the face of increasing demands for manpower to garrison and administer newly acquired territories—nonetheless, this was a concession that the Mongols seldom, if ever, made to their subject states.

The Division of the Empire

With the death of Chinggis Khan in 1227 and the resulting lull in Mongol expansion, the *iduq qut* and his people were furnished a respite after a decade of incessant campaigning. The demise of the Mongol emperor also brought about a division of the empire among his four eldest sons, which led ultimately to the establishment of regional khanates. While the basic outlines of the division are disclosed in the sources, it is not at all clear to which appanage, if any, the Uighur land was assigned.

Vaṣṣāf and Mustawfī list Besh Balikh (i.e., Uighuristan) as one of the territories included in Chaghadai's domain, but this is flatly contradicted by Juvainī.[37] This author manifestly excludes Uighuristan from the possessions of Chaghadai. He states that the latter received the territory extending "from the frontiers (*hudūd*) of the Uighur country to Samarkand and Bukhara,"[38] and in another place describes Chaghadai's holdings as stretching "from Samarqand to the boundary (*kanār*) of Besh Baliq."[39]

It also has been suggested that Uighuristan formed a part of Ögödei's appanage, but this assertion is not supported by any of the sources known to me.[40] Juvainī states that Ögödei received the region of the Khobakh and Emil rivers, an area in Zungharia to the northwest of the Uighur country.[41] The only indication we have that connects the Uighurs with Ögödei's appanage is that portions of their country were granted to two of his offspring: his sixth son, Khadan, received the area of Besh Balikh during the reign of Möngke,[42] and several Uighur towns were temporarily subordinated to his second son, Köden, whose main appanage, however, was in the Tanguts' land.[43]

Which of these conflicting assertions is to be preferred? In my view, Juvainī, who has left the most complete account of the division and who traveled through the territories in question, has the greater claim on our confidence. His work was written only thirty years after the division of the empire took place, while those of Vaṣṣāf and Mustawfī were not completed until the fourteenth century. By this time the Uighur kingdom had, in fact, become part of the Chaghadai khanate, and these two historians' understanding of Chinggis Khan's territorial assignments may have been influenced by this development.

If this surmise is correct, and Uighuristan, as Juvainī clearly implies, was not among the territories bestowed upon any of Chinggis Khan's sons, what then was the political status of the *iduq qut's* domain in the thirteenth century? One possible solution to this problem has been advanced by Abe Takeo. He argues that the kingdom of the *iduq qut*, Chinggis Khan's "fifth son" by adoption, constituted a "fifth khanate, occupying a position next to the fiefs of [the Mongol emperor's] four sons."[44]

As evidence for his claim, Abe refers the reader to Chinggis Khan's remarks to the Tangut and Khwārazmian rulers,[45] remarks which he feels illustrate the important political implications of this adoption. In his statement to the Tangut ruler, which goes back to Rashīd al-Dīn,[46] Chinggis Khan agrees to "treat him as a son" and to allow him an opportunity to bring supplies into the beseiged Tangut capital in return for formal submission. Chinggis Khan's comments to the Khwārazmian ruler, Muḥammad, which go back to the Arabic historian Nasawī,[47] deal with the Mongol leader's proposal to divide the known world between himself and the Khwārazm Shah, whom he calls his most favored son, and to encourage trade between their respective spheres of influence.[48]

These remarks, Abe claims, demonstrate that the act of adopting (i.e., treating him as a son) "signified more than anything else the securing of the territory ruled over by the adopted person."[49] But allowing a ruler to remain in his lands in return for submission, a diplomatic technique frequently employed by the Mongols, is in no way equivalent to placing that ruler, even one enjoying the honorific title "son," on an equal footing with the emperor's own sons. Thus, while it is true that Chinggis Khan "showed [the Uighurs] greater favor than any other state,"[50] none of the sources, including those invoked by Abe, provide any support for the view that the *iduq qut* was formally invested as the head of a "fifth khanate."

Since Uighuristan was not established as a separate khanate nor, apparently, bequeathed to any of the emperor's sons, how is the question of its political status to be resolved? In my opinion, the most plausible explanation is that the Uighur kingdom had its continuity guaranteed as a state directly subordinate to the Grand Khan.[51]

Whatever the formal disposition of Uighuristan, all the available evidence strongly suggests that during the thirteenth century the Uighur kingdom was under the effective control of the Grand Khan. He selected and confirmed all its rulers in office, and its populace was subject to the administrative jurisdiction of officials appointed by him. There is nothing to indicate that any regional khan or appanage prince exercised appreciable influence in these matters. So long as the empire was unified (i.e., to 1259), this generally held true for other subordinate states as well, even those located within the boundaries of regional khanates. In other words, down to Khubilai's reign, it really made little difference in practice whether the Uighurs or any other peoples were nominally subordinated to a regional khan, since the right of investiture and selection of Mongol residents (*darughas*) was in the hands of the Grand Khan.

Barchukh's Successors

When Barchukh died, apparently late in the reign of Ögödei (r. 1229–1241), a son, *Kesmes (K. shmash),[52] came to the Mongol court and was appointed as his father's successor. Shortly thereafter, *Kesmes also expired and by order of the regent, Töregene, the widow of Ögödei, another of Barchukh's sons, Salindi, replaced him. According to the Persian sources, the new Uighur ruler became a powerful and much honored figure at the Mongol court.[53] But in consequence of his involvement in the intrigues that surrounded the enthronement of Möngke as Grand Khan, Salindi did not enjoy this status for long.

The growing tension among Chinggis Khan's descendants following Ögödei's death finally resulted in an open rupture over the issue of selecting a successor to the Grand Khan, Güyüg (r. 1246–1248). In this contest for control of the imperial throne two candidates were put forward. Shiremün, a grandson of Ögödei, was backed by his own kinsmen and those of

Chaghadai, while his rival, Möngke, the eldest son of Tolui, relied on the support of his own relatives and those of Batu, the khan of the Golden Horde. In the ensuing struggle Möngke and his allies emerged victorious.

Once in power, the new emperor initiated a massive purge directed against all who had opposed his enthronement. The series of trials and executions that followed resulted in the near destruction of the lines of Ögödei and Chaghadai. When it became known through an informer that Oghul Khaimish, Güyüg's widow and the regent in the period 1249–1251, had secured Salindi's agreement to support the candidacy of Shiremün with 50,000 troops, he too was brought to trial at the emperor's camp.[54]

At the judicial unquiry (*jarghu*) presided over by Mengeser, Möngke's chief judge (*yeke jarghuchi*), Salindi admitted his complicity when confronted with the confessions of his co-conspirators. The *iduq qut*, together with several other Uighur noblemen who had been party to his understanding with Oghul Khaimish, was then returned to Besh Balikh, where he was beheaded before the entire population. Salindi's brother and successor, Ögrünch, served as his executioner.[55] Although in this instance only a few members of the Uighur ruling elite were affected, future entanglements in the internal disputes of the Mongols were to prove extremely costly to the Uighur nation as a whole.

Not much is known about Salindi's replacement, Ögrünch.[56] He died sometime during Möngke's reign, and his son, *Mamula, *Mamulagh, or *Mamura, was named as his successor, probably in 1257.[57] The latter accompanied Möngke on his campaign against the Sung and later returned to Khara Khocho at an undisclosed date after the death of the emperor in southwest China in 1259.[58]

Administrative Arrangements

Although Chinggis Khan appointed two Uighurs as *darughachi* of two small villages in their homeland, there is no evidence that the Mongol ruler placed such residents in the larger Uighur towns during his lifetime.[59] For example, in the enumeration of the towns of Central Asia to which *darughachi* had been assigned by Chinggis Khan, which is found in paragraph 263 of the *Secret History*, the major Uighur cities of Besh Balikh and Khara Khocho are conspicuous by their absence.[60] Similarly, the various other accounts of the Uighurs' submission to the Mongols are also silent on this point.

Apparently, the governance of the country was left in the hands of the *iduq qut's* retinue (*mulāzim*), a body composed of "his tribe, family and servants," which he had been allowed to establish by imperial order following his return (ca. 1218) from the expedition against Küchlüg.[61] It was members of this body, the officers and family of the absent "Uighur

King" (Hui-ho *wang*), who met and entertained the Taoist monk Ch'ang-ch'un when he passed through Besh Balikh in 1221 on his way to see Chinggis Khan.[62] At his next stop, Jan Balikh, a town farther to the west, Ch'ang-ch'un was again received by the local Uighur ruler and his family.[63] In contrast to the portrayal of his reception in Uighuristan, the account of his travels, the *Hsi-yu chi*, reports that Ch'ang-ch'un was welcomed to Almalikh, one of the principal cities of the Kharlukhs, by a Mongol *darughachi* in the company of the local ruler.[64] Thus, while the sources indicate that *darughas* were stationed in the major population centers of Central Asia (and North China)[65] during Chinggis Khan's lifetime, so far as can be judged from the *Hsi-yu chi*, Mongol residents had not yet been assigned to Uighuristan, or at least played no visible role there.

From the information contained in the Uighur civil documents, it appears that Mongol residents began to take an active part in the administration of the *iduq qut's* lands during the reign of Ögödei.[66] One of these documents refers to a *darugha* of this period, a certain Tughlugh, who was engaged in the collection of agricultural taxes.[67] Another makes mention of a proposed presentation of "camels to the army of Ögödei [and] horses suitable for saddling to the *darughas* of [Yangi?] Baliq,"[68] a city on the northwestern frontier of Uighuristan.

These *darughas*, who were concerned primarily with the control and exploitation of the local populations to which they were assigned, were not in a position to deal with problems that affected the administration of the Uighur realm as a whole. This was the responsibility of one of the three large regional administrations that Ögödei had created to exercise authority over the sedentary population of the empire in 1229. The Uighur kingdom was under the jurisdiction of Maḥmūd Yalavach, a Khwārazmian Turk, whose administrative authority extended over most of East and West Turkestan. In 1241 Maḥmūd was put in charge of North China, and his son, Mas'ūd Beg, replaced him as the Mongol's chief administrative officer in Central Asia. The dividing line between their respective jurisdictions ran along the Uighur-Tangut frontier.[69] Mas'ūd Beg was forced to abandon his office during Töregene's regency, but subsequently was reinstated by Güyüg. Because of his experience and his early support for Möngke, Mas'ūd Beg was retained in office when the new emperor came to power.[70]

In the *Yüan shih's* account of his reappointment, it is stated that Möngke "selected Nokhai, Tarakhai, Mas'ūd and others to be the governors (*hsing-shang-shu sheng-shih*) of Besh Balikh and other places [and] *Amdulla Usun, Aḥmad, and Yeh-te-sha to assist them."[71] Although he was mentioned third in the list of officials, the Persian sources, which give a much fuller account, leave no doubt that Mas'ūd Beg was the head of the Mongol administration in Central Asia. The Chinese account also implies that Mas'ūd Beg's administration was headquartered in Besh Balikh. Several

Middle Eastern sources mention his presence in the Uighur capital follow-ing his confirmation in office, but do not explicitly state that his head-quarters was there.[72] On the contrary, they leave the impression that Mas'ūd Beg spent most of his time in Samarkand and Bukhara. Since the chief characteristic of these regional administrations, however, was their mobility, as is implied by their Chinese name, such impressions can be very misleading. Nothing is known about the other officials mentioned in the *Yüan shih* passage, but it is possible that some were directly concerned with the administration of Uighuristan.

At the same time that these officials were appointed, a Mongol army under the command of *Bürilgitei was dispatched toward Besh Balikh. As Barthold has suggested, the purpose of this move was to link up the forces of Möngke with those of Batu, in order to complete the destruction of the rival Ögödeid and Chaghadaid lines.[73]

Arigh Böke, Khaidu, and Uighuristan

When the khaghan died in 1259, the Mongol princes for the second time in a decade failed to find a successor acceptable to all factions. Their inability to act in concert on this occasion further sharpened the divisions and rivalries that had plagued the Mongols since the death of Ögödei. In fact, the Mongols never fully recovered from the clash of arms that broke out between the two rival claimants for the throne, Arigh Böke and Khubilai, both younger brothers of the deceased khaghan, Möngke.

Unfortunately, the Uighurs' part in this latest outbreak of hostilities within the Mongol imperial family is not well known. At the outset, the forces of Arigh Böke, who controlled Mongolia, occupied the Kansu Corridor, thereby preventing direct communication between the Uighur kingdom and China proper. Within Uighuristan itself, there was scattered fighting between the supporters of the two claimants. Neither side was able to gain the upper hand, but from the biography of Yeh-lü Hsi-liang in the *Yüan shih*,[74] it appears that Khubilai's backers were generally on the defensive. Cut off from China, they were initially forced to retire westward and only reached Khubilai's court, via Kashgar and Khara Khocho, in 1263. By this time, Arigh Böke's hold on Kansu was broken, thanks mainly to the efforts of Khadan.[75] Meanwhile, Arigh Böke's cause had suffered other setbacks, and in 1264, defeated in the field and abandoned by his principal ally, the Chaghadai khan, Alghu, he surrendered to Khubilai, recognizing his brother as the rightful heir to the throne.

The attitude of the Uighur ruling family toward this struggle is nowhere recorded. Even the whereabouts of the reigning *iduq qut*, *Mamula, during this period is unknown. Though he died in Khara Khocho, there is no information to indicate when he returned to his homeland from southwest

China, where he had been campaigning with Möngke, and what role, if any, he played in the contest between Arigh Böke and Khubilai.

In any event, *Mamula's son and successor, Khochkhar Tegin,[76] who was installed as the *iduq qut* in 1266, was not in office long before the Uighur land again became a battleground as a result of yet another breach among the Mongol princes. The semblance of unity that Khubilai had managed to restore to the empire following the surrender of Arigh Böke was soon shattered by Khaidu, a descendant of the deposed line of Ögödei.[77] Khaidu, who was proclaimed khaghan around 1269 by a coalition of Mongol princes in Central Asia, proved to be a much more formidable opponent for Khubilai than Arigh Böke had been. After this enthronement, which took place beside the Talas River, Khaidu set about reorganizing his own realm (in western Zungharia) and that of the Chaghadai khans, who became his subordinates. He successfully reintroduced discipline into his armies and brought about a revival of urban life in Central Asia, which greatly benefited the imperial coffers.[78]

The exact sequence of events that led to an open break between Khaidu and Khubilai is obscure, but it appears that the first step was taken by Khaidu, who attacked toward Pei-t'ing in 1268. In the Chinese sources this name is usually applied to Besh Balikh, but on occasion it also refers to Karakorum. In this instance it most likely refers to the Mongol rather than the Uighur capital.[79] Whatever the actual direction of Khaidu's thrust, the Uighur ruling house was sufficiently concerned for its security to abandon Besh Balikh, on the exposed northern slopes of the T'ien Shan, for the more defensible Khara Khocho in the Turfan Depression.[80] Besh Balikh was not, however, occupied by the enemy and continued to be used as a major Yüan outpost for some time.[81] The precise date of the *iduq qut*'s departure is not known, but it must have occurred about 1270 and certainly before 1275.

In the latter year, two Chaghadaid princes, Du'a and Busma, presumably acting in concert with Khaidu, besieged the *iduq qut*, Khochkhar, in Khara Khocho for six months. Du'a finally withdrew after receiving a daughter of the *iduq qut* in marriage. Khubilai, who was still occupied with the final conquest of the Sung, was pleased with Khochkhar's successful resistance. He gave the *iduq qut* a Mongol princess in marriage and 100,000 *ting* of paper money for the relief of his subjects. Several years later Khochkhar was killed in another clash with the Central Asian Mongols in the vicinity of Khamil, where he had again moved his court to be closer to Chinese territory.[82]

When Khochkhar met his death, a son, Ne'üril Tegin, petitioned Khubilai for troops to strike back at his father's enemies. Because of his youth and inexperience, the Yüan authorities refused the request, and around 1283 established him and his court in Yung-ch'ang, a walled city in Kansu.[83] From this point on, the Uighur ruling family, now essentially a government in exile existing solely at the sufferance of the Yüan court, exerted little influence on events in their homeland.

Khaidu continued to put pressure on Uighuristan after the *iduq qut*'s court had taken up residence in Kansu. In 1286 he launched a large-scale attack on Besh Balikh, which overwhelmed the Yüan defenders, and in February of 1290 Jangkhi, a Jalayir commander in the service of Khaidu, penetrated farther to the east, plundering Khamil.[84] Despite the military successes, Khaidu seemed unable, or more likely uninterested, in permanently occupying Uighuristan at this time.

In order to deal with the threat posed by Khaidu, Khubilai mounted a counterattack along two lines of advance. In the north, starting from Karakorum, the emperor's fourth son, Nomukhan, in command of an army of Mongol cavalry, led a drive toward the Chaghadai capital, Almalikh. This force, though initially successful, soon was seriously weakened by dissension, and by the late 1270s finally disintegrated completely, owing to numerous defections. The other line of advance led through the oases of Central Asia. This thrust, which relied on the extensive deployment of garrison troops and the development of the economic resources of the Kansu Corridor for logistical support, proved to be the stronger of the two.[85]

The military defense of the Uighur kingdom, which was closely supervised from Peking, was entrusted to the Chinese general Ch'i Kung-chih in 1280. By the following year he had established his command, composed largely of Chinese military colonists from Kansu, in Besh Balikh. In 1282 additional military supplies were dispatched to Ch'i Kung-chih, and he was granted special permission to inflict severe punishment on all deserters (i.e., branding on the face). By 1283 the Besh Balikh garrison apparently was constituted as a military colony.[86]

In the period 1285–1287 the garrisons in Besh Balikh and in other cities in Uighuristan were heavily reinforced with Chinese, Mongol, and "recently surrendered" troops. Elite units such as the Right Alan Guard were also posted to the area. In the spring of 1289, military colonies in the region of East Turkestan were reorganized and consolidated, following the setback suffered by the Yüan forces near Besh Balikh in 1286, in which the commander, Ch'i Kung-chih, was captured. New garrisons in Besh Balikh and in the Tarim Basin are also reported for the year 1295.[87] This seems to have ended Yüan efforts to defend the Uighur land.

Growing Uighur Dependence on the Yüan

The complete Yüan takeover of the defense of Uighuristan[88] had been accompanied by a series of administrative changes that gradually excluded the Uighur ruling family from active participation in the affairs of their homeland. In fact, once the move to Yung-ch'ang had been completed, the Uighur people can be described accurately as wards of the Yüan dynasty.[89]

Nothing is known of the administrative arrangements in Uighuristan in the decade after the surrender of Arigh Böke. Mas'ūd Beg, who governed East Turkestan on behalf of Ögödei and Möngke, does not appear to have played any further role in the area once Khubilai was firmly in power.[90] So far as I am aware, the earliest references to matters relating to the governance of the Uighur kingdom in Khubilai's reign are from 1274, when the office of Uighur Judge (*Wei-wu-erh tuan-shih-kuan*) was established, and from 1278, when a Surveillance Office (*an-ch'a-ssu*) was set up.[91]

In early 1281 the office of Uighur Judge was transformed into the Protectorate (*tu-hu-fu*) of Pei-t'ing, that is, Besh Balikh. A certain Tokh Temür and other unnamed individuals were charged with the conduct of its affairs. Finally, in 1283, at about the time the Uighur court left for Kansu, a Pacification Office (*hsüan-wei-ssu*) for Besh Balikh, Khara Khocho, and "other places" was formed to provide unified direction to the Yüan military, political, and economic efforts in Uighuristan.[92] Whether this latter body superseded or complemented the Surveillance Office and Pei-t'ing Protectorate is not made clear in the sources.[93]

As the new bureaucratic machinery was put in place, the Yüan state steadily brought the social and economic life of the Uighur kingdom under its direct control. For example, laws were promulgated in 1275 and 1287 that minutely regulated hunting within the Uighur lands.[94] Also, in 1276 an imperial edict was sent to the *iduq qut* and his officials in Khara Khocho, to the *darughas* (*kuan-jen*) "of the twenty-four cities" (i.e., Uighuristan), and to the Buddhist and Christian communities, ordering them to suppress the practice of drowning unwanted female infants. Those caught committing such acts in the future would have one-half of their property confiscated. If a slave (*nu*) exposed the guilty party, he acquired "hundred families" (*pai-hsing*) status, that is, became a freeman.[95]

More important, the monetary system was integrated with that of the Yüan. In the early 1280s a central bureau (*chiao-ch'ao t'i-chü-ssu*) and a treasury (*chiao-ch'ao-k'u*) were established to oversee the administration and exchange of paper money in Uighuristan.[96] This does not, however, mark the first appearance of this type of currency in Uighuristan, since sizable sums were granted the *iduq qut* and his subjects during the 1270s. It is even possible that paper notes may have circulated in this region as early as the reign of Möngke.[97]

In Uighur civil documents, paper money is called *chao*, a transcription of its Chinese name, *ch'ao*, and the amount calculated in terms of *yastukh* (lit. "pillow"), the equivalent of the Chinese *ting* ("ingot"). For lesser sums, the enumerators were *bakhir* and *satir*, which correspond, respectively, to the Chinese *liang* ("ounce") and *ch'ien* (one-tenth of an ounce).[98] Even particular issues of notes are mentioned: In a land sale deed the famous "precious note of the Chung-t'ung era" (in Chinese, *Chung-t'ung pao-ch'ao*; in Uighur, *Chung tung bao chao*), first issued in 1260, is used for payment.[99] From the frequent references in these documents it is apparent that Yüan paper money was in common use in Uighuristan for all kinds of personal and business transactions in the last half of the thirteenth century.[100]

The social and economic dislocation occasioned by Khaidu's invasions of Uighuristan was considerable. An agricultural economy based on the extensive use of irrigation is extremely sensitive to the disturbances of war. Vital facilities such as canals and dams are destroyed not only directly by military action, but indirectly by the dispersal of the agricultural population, which results in the disruption of the regular service and repair work necessary to prevent silting. The sources leave little doubt that this is exactly what happened in Uighuristan in the last three decades of the thirteenth century.

Many Uighur families fled their homes, especially those living on the northern slopes of the T'ien Shan, and settled in China.[101] The precise number is not known, but references in the *Yüan shih* to recurrent attempts to reassemble the Uighurs leave the impression that the migration was quite extensive. For example, in the biography of Khochkhar it is stated that in consequence of the rebellion of Khaidu:

> the Uighur people had met with disorder and were dispersed; consequently there was an order given to the *Iduqqut* to collect and succor them [i.e., his subjects]. These of his people who are in establishments of the Imperial Princes and [Imperial] In-laws are all to be returned to their homeland [lit., to their tribe]: All of the Uighurs are again to be united![102]

This attempt, which was initiated in the late 1260s, was still continuing in 1291 when Khubilai ordered a halt to further efforts in this direction. In 1296 the new emperor, Temür, ordered Ne'üril, who succeeded Khochkhar, to try again.[103] The problem had become so severe as to defy solution.

The decline in agricultural productivity which accompanied the dispersal of the Uighur people led to repeated famines and to outbreaks of banditry.[104] According to Rashīd al-Dīn, the situation in Uighuristan was comparable to that which prevailed in the most devasted regions of the Il-khan realm on the eve of the reforms of Ghāzān (r. 1295–1304):

> Because some provinces were on the frontier and armies frequently passed through, their inhabitants were totally destroyed or had fled and [the land] remained uncultivated as in Uighuristan and other provinces which are on the frontier between the Grand Khan and Khaidu.[105]

As conditions deteriorated the Uighur people became increasingly dependent on Yüan assistance and support.

Attempts were made to strengthen and restore the local economy. In 1282 Ch'i Kung-chih established a foundry to manufacture agricultural implements in Besh Balikh, and two years later a new market was built in the same city with government funds. The Yüan authorities also granted a large amount of relief in the hope of stabilizing the situation. Aid was first dispensed to the people of Besh Balikh in 1278 and thereafter became a regular practice. In 1285 and 1286, Khara Khocho and Khamil received famine relief. Besh Balikh and Khamil received aid in 1289, and Khamil again in 1303. The stricken areas received cattle, grain, paper money, and silk, most of which came from the province of Kansu.[106]

Chaghadai Occupation of East Turkestan

The Yüan make no further mention of relief and defense measures in Khara Khocho and Besh Balikh after 1295. This also seems to be the date of the last Yüan administrative orders concerning Uighuristan.[107] Because of the virtual silence of the Chinese sources on the Uighur kingdom in the first decades of the fourteenth century, little is known of its incorporation into the Chaghadai Khanate. Sinologists have usually taken 1329–1332 as the *terminus post quem* for this event because in that period the Yüan government issued a map of Central and West Asia depicting all of Uighuristan up to Khamil as part of the Chaghadai domains.[108] Fortunately, a more detailed account of the political status of the Uighur kingdom, at least up to 1316, can be pieced together from the Persian sources.

Rashīd al-Dīn, speaking of the end of Khubilai's reign, remarks that Khara Khocho "is between the frontiers of the Qa'an (i.e., Qubilai) and Qaidu and the people are on good terms with them both and render service to both sides."[109] He goes on to report that the Central Asian princes continuously raided the frontiers, but always withdrew, avoiding a major confrontation—a tactic Khubilai and his commanders found most vexing. This situation persisted into the early years of Temür Khaghan's reign, for the same source relates that the Yüan still maintained a large military force along the frontier at Khara Khocho to ward off these raids.[110]

Between 1298 and 1301, Temür fought a series of battles with the Chaghadaid and Ögödeid armies, in which Khaidu was killed and Du'a seriously wounded.[111] Despite their victory in the field, the Yüan forces withdrew from Uighuristan, allowing their antagonists to occupy the area (the reasons for this will be discussed below).

The Chaghadai occupation must have occurred shortly after these battles, since Du'a, whom the Persian historian Naṭanzī credits with seizing "many of the dependencies [muzāfāt] of the kingdom of China,[112] already counted Khara Khocho among his possessions by A.H. 704/1304–1305. In a message to Chabar, Khaidu's successor, Du'a speaks of a *khuriltai* to be held "between Qara Qocho, which is the frontier of Besh Baliq [i.e., Uighuristan] and the pride [*khāsah*] of our state [*mulk*] and *ulus* and the country of Qara Qorum, which is the center of the empire and the fount of good fortune."[113] Thus, Khara Khocho, after a period of neutrality in the 1290s, finally gravitated into the orbit of the Chaghadai khans in the first years of the fourteenth century. Besh Balikh, because of its exposed geographical position, probably fell into their hands somewhat earlier.

As a result of the above mentioned *khuriltai* and subsequent meetings between the representatives of Temür Khaghan and the regional khans, a temporary halt was called to the chronic warfare among the Mongol princes. Though fighting soon broke out between the lines of Ögödei and Chaghadai, allies of thirty-five years in the struggle against Khubilai, this does not seem to have involved the Yüan directly, nor resulted in any change in the frontier between the Chaghadai khanate and China.[114]

This relatively peaceful interlude ended in 1316, as a result of disagreements over grazing and camping rights between the Yüan and Chaghadai frontier garrisons in Zungharia and Uighuristan. In his account of this dispute, the historian Qashani, who served at the court of the Il-khan Öljeitü (r. 1304–1318), and who was very knowledgeable about Chinese and Central Asian affairs, provides a detailed description of the dispositions along this frontier as of A.H. 716/1316–1317.[115] The Yüan had large garrisons stationed along the Khobakh River[116] and the Esen Muren (a tributary of the Irtysh) in Zungharia and similar detachments in Bars-kul (the Barkol of modern maps), Khamil, and along the Tibetan frontier. According to Qashani, directly opposite each of these garrisons, Esen Bukha, the Chaghadai khan (r. ca. 1310–1318), had posted his own contingents of roughly similar strength. From this description it is clear that the Chaghadai troops were still in control of the major Uighur population centers and that the Yüan forces were to the north and east of them.

Fighting first erupted in the Zungharian sector, where Esen Bukha had his camp. A Yüan force of five *tümen* pushed him back up the Irtysh the distance of a three-month journey. In the area of Khamil, the Yüan armies drove their opponents back the distance of a forty-day journey, where they established a roadblock to prevent the return of the Chaghadai troops.[117] Since Khara Khocho is only fifteen or sixteen stages to the west of Khamil,[118] the Yüan forces must have reoccupied this city, as well as the entire Turfan Depression. That the Yüan armies actually took possession of Khara Khocho is confirmed by one of the few references to this episode in the Chinese sources. In the biography of the *iduq qut*, Ne'üril, it is stated that he "led an army to Huo-chou [Khara Khocho] and again established [it as] an Uighur city."[119] No date is given, but as this is his last reported act prior to his death in 1318, the chronology seems right.

Following his defeat, due largely to faulty logistic measures,[120] Esen Bukha undertook a campaign in Khurāsān in order to compensate himself for his losses in the east. However, the Yüan forces increased their pressure in Zungharia and reached the Talas River in 1317, forcing Esen Bukha to withdraw his forces from northern Iran to defend his eastern frontiers.[121] These spectacular Yüan advances do not appear to have been the result of a planned attempt to regain control of east Turkestan, but rather a matter of Yüan local commanders exploiting an advantageous situation in order to chastise the Chaghadai armies and to seize territory that added depth to their defensive position.

It is difficult to determine precisely when the Chaghadai khanate finally regained full control of the Uighur lands. On the one hand, the fact that Ne'üril died in Yung-ch'ang in 1318 and his son and successor, Temür Bukha, so far as we know, never set foot in the Uighur kingdom, suggests that the Yüan hold on the area was not long-lasting. On the other hand, since Khara Khocho sent tribute to the Yüan court in 1330,[122] it would appear that the Uighur capital still enjoyed some independence of action, even after the Yüan had recognized it as a Chaghadai possession. Perhaps Khara Khocho went through another period of neutrality.[123]

The first clear evidence that Chaghadai rule was firmly reestablished in Khara Khocho comes from the Mongol documents recovered in Turfan,[124] two of which, issued in the name of the Chaghadai khan Yisun Temür, in 1338 and 1339, are addressed to Mongol officials stationed in Khara Khocho.[125] The document of 1339 also mentions a [Khara] Khocho *iduq qut* whom the Chaghadai khans installed in place of the departed Yüan line. While this new line ruled in Uighuristan, the "Yüan" *iduq qut*s remained in Kansu, supported by and serving the Yüan dynasty.

Ne'üril, who was formally invested as *iduq qut* in the reign of Wu-tsung (r. 1308–1312), concurrently held the post of *p'ing-chang cheng-shih*, an important position within the Yüan government. His dual status was officially recognized by the emperor, Jen-tsung (r. 1312–1321), who gave him two seals, one which authorized him to function as a Yüan official within China proper and one which authorized him to act as the *iduq qut* within the confines of his homeland. In 1316, obviously in conjunction with his triumphant return to Khara Khocho, the emperor made him Prince of Kao-ch'ang. All his successors, who also served the Yüan court in important administrative capacities, bore this title.[126]

The Yüan government continued to support the many Uighur refugees in China. In 1311 some recently registered Uighur families were given three months' provisions and an amount of land in the province of Honan, on which they were to sustain themselves.[127] That the number of immigrants was substantial is indicated by the fact that special courts were set up to deal with litigation involving Uighurs in China.

Causes of the Yüan Withdrawal

There are various reasons why the Yüan dynasty, despite the defeat of Khaidu and Du'a, failed to hold Uighuristan and Central Asia. Dardess isolates several important factors. First, the Mongols decided to concentrate their efforts on defending Mongolia, for both psychological and strategic reasons. Whereas control of Mongolia was essential for the security of the new capital, Peking, Besh Balikh, which was 1,400 miles distant, was not. Second, Uighuristan became an economic liability to the Yüan dynasty. While the military efforts of Khaidu and his associates in Uighuristan brought economic gains in the form of plunder and tribute, those of Khubilai and Temür were a financial drain. The economic base established in Kansu to support the Yüan presence in East Turkestan proved to be inadequate for the task.[128]

The Yüan dynasty experienced the same problems other Chinese dynasties faced in defending Turkestan from the inroads of steppe peoples; in the long run, the Central Asian Mongols were able to make the defense of the area too costly for the Yüan dynasty to bear, since there was no effective means of permanently forcing Khaidu, Du'a, and their followers to discontinue their hit-and-run raids.

Uighur Obligations to the Mongols

The basic set of demands that the Mongols imposed on all their subordinate states is succinctly stipulated in Khubilai's order of 1267 to the Annam ruler: (1) the ruler must come personally to court, (2) sons and younger brothers are to be offered as hostages, (3) the population must be registered, (4) militia units will be raised, (5) taxes are to be sent, and (6) a *darugha* is to take charge of all affairs.[129] Another set of instructions for surrendering states, directed to the Korean monarch in 1262, contains the same demands, but requires additionally the establishment of postal relay stations, *jams*.[130]

Taken together, these two decrees provide a basic blueprint of the Mongol method of controlling and exploiting the human and natural resources of surrendered states. As Henthorn indicates,[131] such decrees consistently attribute these "instructions" to Chinggis Khan. While it is undoubtedly true that he is responsible for the basic elements, there are good reasons to suppose that two of the requirements—the submission of population registers and the establishment of postal relay stations—ought to be credited to his successor, Ögödei.

Although there are no records indicating that such instructions were ever presented to their rulers, there is no doubt that the Uighurs were subject to the same set of demands as were the people of Annam and Korea.

Since Barchukh's journey to the court of Chinggis Khan and the posting of *darughas* and other officials in Uighuristan have already been discussed, I will concentrate my attention here on population registration, the imposition of taxes, the establishment of the postal relay stations, and military recruitment.[132]

Population Registration

Census taking was the key to Mongol efforts to mobilize the human and financial resources of the sedentary regions of the empire. The object of the registration was to facilitate the assessment of taxes, to identify skilled craftsmen and technicians, and to recruit military personnel.

In Chinggis Khan's time, the Mongols maintained a register of the lands and peoples assigned to various princes and military leaders,[133] but it was not until Ögödei's reign that systematic registration of the non-nomadic population took place. The first census was carried out in North China in 1234–1236 and the next in 1252–1259. The latter census, initiated by Möngke, was on a vast scale covering the whole of the empire. Because of deficiencies in the first two registrations, Khubilai ordered another to be conducted in 1271.

There is no evidence that the Uighur population was counted in the first of these registrations, but it is fairly certain that they were included in the second. Juvainī reports that in 1252 Möngke directed Mas'ūd Beg to survey the population of the territories under his jurisdiction and then to return "in haste to court."[134] While there is no way to verify that a census of the Uighurs was actually carried out, it seems highly unlikely that they would have been excluded from Möngke's tally, since the inhabitants of North China, Iran, Afghanistan, Armenia, Georgia, and the Russian principalities were counted at this time. As for the census of 1271, it must certainly be connected with Khubilai's order to the *iduq qut*, Khochkhar, issued sometime before 1275, to reassemble his scattered subjects. Finally, further registrations in Uighuristan are mentioned in 1284 (limited to Besh Balikh) and in 1296.[135]

Following the completion of the census, the Mongols organized the population into administrative/military units based on the decimal system. The references to leaders of ten, *onlugh*, leaders of a hundred, *yüzlügh*, *yüz-begi*, leaders of a thousand, *ming-begi*, and leaders of ten thousand, *ülchi tümen*, in the Uighur civil documents indicate the presence of such a system in the Uighur kingdom, but the problems encountered in dating many of those documents make it difficult to determine if these offices reflect Mongol or pre-Mongol practice.[136]

Taxation and Tribute

Upon surrending, local dynasts were required to present themselves at the Mongol court with appropriate tribute. The intrinsic worth of the tribute initially offered was of less importance to the Mongols than the symbolic value of its presentation as an act of submission. Thus, when Barchukh submitted, Chinggis Khan made it clear that the *iduq qut's* willingness to send tribute in coin and in kind was to be the test of the sincerity of his professed desire to serve the Mongols.[137]

Until the reigns of Ögödei and Möngke, when efforts were made to regularize the collection of taxes, the Mongol practice was to demand a "tenth of everything" from their subjects, or to exact supplemental or extraordinary levies to meet specific needs. Even after the institution of a regular program of taxation, extraordinary exactions continued. An excellent illustration of the latter is related by Sayf ibn Muhammad in his history of Harāt.[138] He records that when Tolui returned from his campaign in Khurāsān, he distributed many prisoners among the members of the imperial family. A number of these prisoners, robe-makers by profession, came into the possession of Ögödei. They were well treated and handsomely rewarded; by imperial order, they were given annually a substantial sum (*mablaghi*) from the revenues (*mahsul*) of Besh Balikh. Irregular levies of this sort are still mentioned in the reign of Möngke. In 1257 the Uighurs presented the Mongol ruler with a number of gifts. The Grand Khan refused them and issued an order that they were no longer to send irregular tribute to the court.[139]

Ögödei first attempted a systematization of tax collecting in North China, but his efforts were not totally successful. In Möngke's reign, another attempt was made, and a fairly unified system was introduced throughout the empire. While the same set of taxes was collected in the three major administrative regions of the empire—Turkestan, North China, and Iran—the rates varied slightly, presumably to take into account differing economic conditions.[140] The three basic taxes adopted at this time were retained by Khubilai and became the basis of the Yüan revenue system. These included the *khubchiri*, a tax collected in cash from each sedentary household (among the nomads it was collected in cattle); the *khalan*, an agricultural tax from which the nomads were exempt, and the *tamgh*, a duty on trade and comerce, which fell mainly on the urban population. *Tamgha*, as a tax term, is not mentioned in Uighur civil documents of the Mongol era, but there are references to *khubchiri* and *khalan*, several of which evidently predate the Mongol era.[141]

Although the *khubchiri* levied on the sedentary population was ostensibly collected in cash, Uighur documents show that goods were often accepted in lieu of currency. In one case; millet was substituted, and in another, horses. The agricultural tax, *khalan*, which was assessed in kind, was collected in the Uighur kingdom from Ögödei's time on.[142] According to a document published by S. E. Malov, peasant households, formed into groups of ten, were held collectively responsible for the payment of this tax, and perhaps of others as well.[143]

Before Khubilai's reign, *darughas* collected the Uighurs' taxes under the general direction of the governor of Turkestan, Mas'ūd Beg, who then delivered them directly to the Grand Khan's treasury.[144] Subsequently, this responsibility was assumed by the new administrative machinery installed in the Uighur kingdom in the 1270s and 1280s.

Postal Relay Stations

Because of the vastness of the empire, the Mongols found it necessary to develop an elaborate network of postal relay stations (*jam*) in order to ensure rapid communication between the rulers and their subordinates. Because of its importance in disseminating orders, reports, and intelligence in time of war, the *jam* was closely tied to the Mongol military establishment. This famous institution, described by many European travelers, was officially founded early in the reign of Ögödei.[145]

Maintenance of the stations was a heavy burden on the sedentary populace. Households assigned to a *jam* were responsible for the upkeep of the physical facilities, and for the needs of the relay horses, permanent staff, and official travelers. They were burdened as well by numerous unauthorized travelers (e.g., merchants and religious officials). Repeated orders banning unauthorized travel testify to its frequency.

Although they were not mentioned before the 1270s, relay stations were certainly established in Uighuristan before then, since Besh Balikh was on one of the main east-west communication routes. Arghun Akha, the Mongol governor of Iran, his assistant, the historian Juvainī, and King Hetum of Armenia, all of whom passed through Besh Balikh in the early 1250s on their way to Karakorum to conduct official business, must have traveled by official post.

As the conflict between Khaidu and the Yüan dynasty intensified, the postal relay network was extended and reorganized. In 1278 a certain Basa Chaghri was placed in charge of postal affairs in Uighuristan. In this same year, a new head was appointed to the station at Jan Balikh, the westernmost outpost of the Yüan forces.[146] Three years later, on the recommendation of Prince Ajikhi, a descendant of Chaghadai in the service of the Yüan, a new network of thirty relay stations, running from Besh Balikh to T'ai-ho ling in northern Shansi, was established in order to improve communication between the metropolitan area and this sensitive frontier.

Subsequently, in 1283 and 1285, additional stations were established in East Turkestan.[147]

This new network of stations in the Uighur kingdom was essentially an early warning system designed to keep the local commanders, as well as officials in Peking, well informed on the movements of Khaidu and Du'a. Its primary purpose is plainly brought out in Rashīd al-Dīn's description of the system. He states that *jams* and military patrols were stationed at every *sübe* (Mongol for a strategic point) to give warning of the approach of hostile troops. He also mentions a string of relays running between the *sübe* of Ajikhi in the extreme west and the *sübe* of Mukhali in the east, a clear reference to the network of 30 *jams* connecting Uighuristan with China proper.[148]

The inhabitants of Uighuristan made one other contribution to the communications system of the empire: a branch of the Bekrin, a tribe of mountaineers living in the Uighur kingdom, whom Rashīd al-Dīn describes as neither Mongols nor Uighurs, were sent to Iran during Hülegü's time to serve as messengers in the mountainous regions of the Il-khan realm.[149]

Military Recruitment

The astounding series of military victories that the Mongols achieved in such rapid succession in the thirteenth century was not due solely to the fighting qualities of the Mongol soldiers and the tactical, logistical, and organizational abilities of their leaders; of equal importance was their success in mobilizing and organizing the subject populace, both sedentary and nomadic, to meet the continuous demand for additional military manpower, a demand that Mongol society could not by itself satisfy.[150]

The Mongols obtained this additional manpower because Chinggis Khan, as the author of the *Tartar Relation* expresses it, adopted the policy "of conscripting the soldiers of a conquered army into his own, with the object of subduing other countries by virtue of his increased strength, as is clearly evident in his successors, who imitate his wicked cunning."[151] Soldiers conscripted in this manner either continued to fight under the command of their own leaders or were formed into new, often ethnically mixed, units under the control of Mongol-appointed officers. In one form or another, all surrendered states were required to support the Mongol's military ventures. Failure to fulfill this obligation, as the Tanguts discovered, brought terrible retribution.

The Uighurs, despite the fact that they were reputed to be poor fighters,[152] served in large numbers in the Mongol armies. When Chinggis Khan attacked Khwārazm, Barchukh accompanied him with 10,000 Uighur troops. Apparently, these were for the most part infantrymen, since Bar Hebraeus contrasts the *iduq qut*'s "army of peasants" with the "horsemen" of Sughnakh Tegin, the Kharlukh leader.[153] This Uighur unit fought at Utrār and in Khurāsān, and was later involved in supply operations.[154] Other Uighur contingents, whose leaders had submitted to Chinggis Khan independently of the *iduq qut*, also participated in the campaigns in the west.[155]

In Möngke's reign, the *iduq qut*, *Mamula, led a force of 10,000 against the Sung. The ethnic composition of the unit is not stated, but presumably many Uighurs were included.[156] Other members of the Uighur ruling house also commanded units of their countrymen on behalf of the Mongols. Ne'üril's brother, *Sösö[k] Tegin, led a contingent of 1,000 Uighurs who were posted to Yunnan in 1285 as frontier guards. Another Uighur garrison of the same size (or perhaps the same one) is mentioned in Yunnan in the early years of the fourteenth century.[157]

Uighur troops not only fought as a group with their own leaders, but were drafted into composite units as well. Rashīd al-Dīn relates the history of one such unit, a *tümen* composed of Uighurs, Kharlukhs, Turkmen, and inhabitants of Kashgar and Kucha. Formed, apparently, shortly after Chinggis Khan's conquest of East Turkestan, this unit was commanded by a series of Sönid Mongol officers from the same family. This *tümen* was attached ultimately to Hülegü and fought, without distinction, in Ked Bukha's Egyptian campaign. As a result of their poor performances, the *tümen* commander was dismissed and executed, but the unit itself was kept intact. Together with the 1,000 Uighurs of another unit posted to Iran, these troops very probably formed the nucleus of the sizable Uighur community which flourished in Khurāsān down to the sixteenth century.[158]

Lastly, the aforementioned tribe of mountaineers, the Bekrin, provided the Mongols with 1,000 men.[159]

Cultural Resources

In addition to military recruits and tribute, the Mongols made heavy demands on the special skills—administrative, technological, and artistic—of their subjects. Although this demand for specialists of all kinds is not mentioned in any of the extant orders of submission, nonetheless, the Mongols made a systematic effort to identify and use the particular talents of all who fell under their power. Their use of the Bekrin as messengers in mountainous areas is a case in point.

Because the Uighurs were the first of the advanced sedentary societies to come under Mongol control, they exercised a profound influence on the institutional and cultural life of the empire in its formative stages. Uighur cultural influences, however, began penetrating Mongolia even before the submission of Barchukh. When the Naimans were defeated in 1204, Uighur scribes who had been serving at their court fell into Mongol hands. One of them, T'a-t'a T'ung-a, who was the head of the Naiman chancellery, first introduced the Mongols to the use of the seal in the conduct of government affairs.[160]

The Uighur alphabet, which was one of their more significant contributions to the Mongols, was also transmitted prior to the *iduq qut's* surrender.[161] The exact circumstances under which it was borrowed are not known, but once adopted, the new script became an important instrument of Mongol statecraft. Knowledge of this script was a valuable asset for anyone seeking a position in the Mongol administrative system. Juvainī notes with derision that many equated mastery of this alphabet with great knowledge and learning, and that it was the means by which numerous individuals gained access to high office.[162]

Because of the importance of their script, the Uighurs played an important role in the education of the Mongol ruling class. T'a-t'a T'ung-a was given the task of teaching Chinggis Khan's sons the Uighur alphabet, so that they might "write the national language."[163] In an edict issued in 1271, Khubilai ordered that the education of imperial princes and important military commanders adhere to the program of training followed by Uighur learned men (*bakhshi*).[164]

The Uighurs were also active in the administration of the empire. For example, of the 277 *darughas* mentioned in the *Yüan shih* whose ethnic background can be established, 34 are Uighurs. Only the Mongols themselves, with 104, and the North Chinese (*Han-jen*), with 46, can claim more. In other parts of the Mongol domains, the situation was the same, especially in the Chaghadai khanate, where Uighur *bakhshis* wielded great influence at the court in the fourteenth century.[165]

While the Uighur kingdom, like all other dependent states, provided the Mongols with troops and taxes, it was Uighur administrative and cultural skills that the Mongols prized most highly. Uighuristan functioned as a reservoir of trained administrative personnel, which the Mongol khans drew upon extensively. As one Chinese writer put it, after Barchukh placed himself under Mongol authority, "all [Uighurs] with talent or skill served the court."[166]

Conclusion

Although it is admittedly dangerous to generalize on the basis of a single example, I should like to offer some tentative conclusions about the role of dependent states in the Mongol empire. Perhaps the best way to proceed is to compare Mongol and Chinese methods of dealing with dependent states.

On the ideological level, the Mongols and the Chinese shared common ground. From Chinggis Khan on, the Mongols consistently advanced a claim to universal dominion. In their view, all peoples and nations were potential members of the Mongol empire-in-the-making, and everyone, after being duly informed of the requirement, was obliged to submit to the Mongol khaghan. Those who failed to do so were considered rebels and treated accordingly. In Mongol terms this usually meant the destruction of the offending state and the partial annihilation and enslavement of its subjects.[167] In such a political system, there was no place for relations between equal, sovereign states, such as developed between the Sung and its northern neighbors, the Liao and the Chin.

As justification for their claims, the Mongols invoked a heavenly mandate, which they alleged gave them the right, and indeed the duty, to bring the entire world under their sway. Evidence for this claim they found in the good fortune that accompanied Chinggis Khan through many perilous times. Their idea of a divinely anointed, universal sovereign was quite likely derived from the well-known Chinese concepts of the Mandate of Heaven (*t'ien ming*) and the Son of Heaven (*t'ien-tzu*). Whether the Mongols borrowed these ideas directly from the Chinese or indirectly through the Turks has not been established.[168]

While the Chinese and the Mongols held common assumptions concerning the origin, character, and extent of their right to rule, in actual practice their relationships with subject states differed markedly.[169] In contrast to the Mongols, who relied almost exclusively on military force in their dealing with foreign states, the Chinese usually preferred to bring foreign rulers into their orbit by more peaceful means—gifts, grants of titles, and favorable trade relations. Beyond acknowledging Chinese suzerainty through various symbolic acts (e.g., adopting the Chinese calendar and sending in local products), the subordinate ruler was subject to few additional demands and retained a large measure of autonomy within his own territory. As long as the surrendered state refrained from hostile acts, the Chinese were content with employing this "loose rein" (*chi-mi*) policy, one which the subordinate party often found economically advantageous.

The Mongols, on the other hand, required much more from their dependent states. Service to the Mongol khaghan was expressed mainly not in terms of symbolic acts of submissiveness, but in providing, punctually, the numerous goods and services stipulated in the instructions to surrendered states. To ensure that their demands were met, the Mongols stationed officials, backed up by military garrisons, in their dependent states. In fact, there was very little difference between the obligations of the subject populace directly subordinated to Mongol rule and those living in subordinate states. A Uighur farmer in Turfan bore the same burdens as the Chinese peasant in Honan or his Persian counterpart in Khurāsān. Even the administrative setup was basically the same. In both cases, native officials, who knew the local languages and customs, worked alongside

Mongol-appointed residents, usually foreigners, who looked after the interests of the khaghan. The Mongols, unlike the Chinese, granted little administrative autonomy to their subordinate states.

To make their claim of universal dominion a reality required a continuous and intensive effort, one akin to the modern concept of total war. Chinggis Khan's levée en masse of the "peoples who live in felt tents" established the pattern. His immediate successors undertook a similar mobilization of the human, natural, and financial resources of the sedentary societies under their control. All their subjects—nomadic tribesmen, agriculturalists, and urban dwellers—were expected to contribute fully toward the realization of their great enterprise. Therefore, the Mongols were not satisfied with passive or symbolic acquiescence to their rule; they demanded the active participation of dependent states in the effort to carry out their mandate.

NOTES

1. For examples of the term *khari* used in the sense of "subordinates," see Klaus Sagaster, "Herrschafstideologie und Friedensgedanke bei den Mongolen," *Central Asiatic Journal* 17 (1973): 231–232; and F. W. Cleaves, "The Sino-Mongolian Inscription of 1338," *Harvard Journal of Asiatic Studies* (hereafter *HJAS*) 14 (1951): 53–54 (where the term is translated as "principality"). For the terms *il* and *bulgha irgen*, see A. Mostaert and F. W. Cleaves, "Trois documents mongols des archives secrètes vaticanes," *HJAS* 15 (1952): 485–495. In the Chinese sources of the period, subordinates are usually called "dependent states" (*hsia-kuo*) or "newly surrendered states" (*hsin-fu kuo*).

2. See Paul Buell, "Mongolian Social and Political Organization and the Mongolian State in China," unpublished paper presented to the Yüan Workshop, Princeton, June 1975; and Wolfram Eberhard, *Conquerors and Rulers*, 2nd ed. (Leiden, 1970), pp. 116–118.

3. In addition to the examples cited in the body of the paper, the following countries, cities, peoples, and dynasties were subordinates: Russian principalities, Mosul (city in Syria), Seljuks of Rum, Greater Armenia, Georgia, the Shirvan Shāhs (Azerbaijan), Atabegs of Fārs, Qūtlūgh Shahs of Kirmān, Trebizond, Māzandarān, Volga Bulgars, Kashmir, Ta-li, Annam, Burma, and Java.

4. For a useful study of Mongol rule in Korea, see W. E. Henthorn, *Korea: The Mongol Invasions* (Leiden, 1963).

5. Rashīd al-Dīn, *Jāmi' al-tavārīkh* (ed. B. Karīmī) (hereafter Rashīd/Karīmī) (Tehran, 1959), vol. II, p. 688; see also E. Voegelin, "The Mongol Orders of Submission to the European Powers," *Byzantion* 15 (1941): 406.

6. R. A. Skelton et al., *The Vinland Map and the Tartar Relation* (New Haven, 1965), p. 90. See also the parallel passage in Carpini, Christopher Dawson (ed.), *The Mongol Mission* (New York, 1955), p. 38.

7. See A. G. Galstian (trans. and ed.), *Armianskie istochniki o Mongolakh* (Moscow, 1962), pp. 67–70, for a Russian translation of the agreement.

8. N. Ts. Munkuev, "Zametki o drevnikh mongolakh," in S. L. Tikhvinskii (ed.), *Tataro-Mongoly v Azii i Evrope* (hereafter *TMAE*) (Moscow, 1970), p. 367. This estimate is for Chinggis's time.

9. See V. M. Masson and V. A. Romodin, *Istoriia Afganistana*, vol. I (Moscow, 1964), pp. 291–302.

10. See Turrell Wylie, "The First Mongol Conquest of Tibet Reinterpreted," *HJAS* 37 (1977): 103–133. See also chapter 7 in this volume.

11. Dawson, op. cit., p. 141.

12. On the historical geography of Uighur territory, see Akira Shimazaki, "On Pei-t'ing (Bišbaliq) and K'o-han Fu-t'u-ch'eng," *Memoirs of the Research Department of the Toyo Bunko* 32 (1974): 99–114; and James Hamilton, "Autour du manuscript Stael-Holstein," *T'oung Pao* (*TP*) 46 (1958): 142–150. On Uighur cultural history, see the works of A. von Gabain, *Das Leben im uigurischen Königreich von Qočo, 850–1250* (Wiesbaden, 1973); and Monique Maillard, "Essai sur la vie matérielle dans l'oasis de Tourfan pendant le haut moyen âge," *Arts Asiatique* 29 (1973): 3–185.

13. See Karl A. Wittfogel and Feng Chia-sheng, *History of Chinese Society: The Liao* (Philadelphia, 1949), pp. 621–622 and 635–637 for details.

14. A. G. Maliavkin, *Materialy po istorii Uigurov v ix–xii vv* (Novosibirsk, 1974), p. 76. See also Wittfogel and Feng, op. cit., pp. 665–668, for a discussion of the Karakhitay system of subordinate states.

15. The Uighurs borrowed the title *iduq qut* or *iduqut*, which means "holy fortune" or "luck," from the Basmil, another Turkish-speaking people. See R. Rahmet, "Der Herrschentitel Iduq-qut," *Ural-Altaische Jahrbucher* 35 (1964): 150–157.

16. There are several studies of Mongol-Uighur relations available: See M. Kutlukov's article in *TMAE*, pp. 85–99; and Cha-ch'i Ssu-ch'in, "Yüan-tai te hsi-yü," in *Hsin-ch'iang yen-chiu* (Taipei, 1965), pp. 39–68. As for Japanese works, which I am unable to read in the original, I have consulted Liu Mau-tsai's review of Takeo Abe, *Nishi-Uiguru kokushi no kenkyū*, *Central Asiatic Journal* 4 (1958), pp. 73–81; and Joachim Glaubitz, "Japanische Arbeiten über Zentralasien," *Der Islam* 35 (1960): 129–139, which summarizes the works of Abe and Saguchi.

17. Sung Lien et al., *Yüan shih* (hereafter *YS*) (Peking, 1976 ed.), 124, p. 3044. In the Persian sources, Rashīd/Karīmī, p. 309, he is called a *shahnah*, which is the Arabo-Persian equivalent to the Mongol *darugha* and the Turkish *basqaq*. His Chinese title, in the form of *Shawkam*, is understood as a personal name.

18. A, A. Ali-zade, A. S. Romaskevich, and A. A. Khetagurov (eds.), Rashīd al-Dīn, *Jāmi' al-tavārīkh* (vol. I, pt. 1, hereafter Rashīd/Ali-zade) (Moscow, 1968), pp. 338–339.

19. *YS*, 124, pp. 3049–3050; 135, p. 3271; 137, p. 3319; and F. W. Cleaves, "The Sino-Mongolian Inscription of 1326 in Memory of Prince Hindu," *HJAS* 12 (1949): 31, 85.

20. The Chinese sources, "Kao-ch'ang Hsieh shih-chia chuan," in *Yüan wen-lei*, ed. Su T'ien-chüeh (Shanghai, 1958), ch. 70, p. 1016, state that he was killed by the chief minister, Bilge; and the Persian sources, John A. Boyle (trans.), *The History of*

the World Conqueror (hereafter, Juvainī/Boyle) (Manchester, 1958), vol. I, pp. 42–43, indicate that the building was pulled down around him.

21. *YS*, 124, p. 3064. Barchukh also sent an ambassador to the *gurkhan*, apparently to inform him of his change of allegiance.

22. Rashīd/Karīmī, vol. I, pp. 309–310, and *Sheng-wu ch'in-cheng lu*, ed. Wang Kuo-wei (hereafter *SWCCL*) (Taipei, 1975), pp. 151–152, both state that Chinggis initiated the first contact. In fact, the accounts of the submission of the Uighurs offered by these two sources are in complete accord. It is clear that they were translated from a common Mongol source. The biography of the *iduq qut* in the *YS*, 122, p. 3,000, also agrees with them. Juvainī/Boyle, vol. I, pp. 44, and the *Secret History* (hereafter *SH*), para. 238, mention only the *iduq qut's* return embassy. (My understanding of the *SH* text is based on the translations of Haenisch, de Rachewiltz, and Pelliot.) See also *YS*, 1, p. 14.

23. The establishment of the Mongol garrison is related in the biography of A-t'a Hai-ya, which is found in *Chung chou ming hsien wen-piao*, quoted from Feng Chia-sheng et al., *Wei-wu-erh tsu shih-liao chien-pien*, vol. I (Peking, 1958), p. 102.

24. Chao Meng-fu, *Sung-hsüeh chai-wen chi*, 7, 12a. Unless otherwise noted, all literary collections are cited according to *Ssu-pu ts'ung-k'an* ed.

25. Rashīd/Karīmī, vol. 1, pp. 310–311, 320; *SWCCL*, pp. 152–157; and *YS*, 1, p. 15, and 122, p. 3,000, provide a full and consistent account of Uighur-Mongol contacts in the period 1209–1211.

26. Rashīd/Ali-zade, pp. 340–341; Rashīd/Karīmī, vol. I, p. 454; Juvainī/Boyle, vol. I, pp. 46–47; and *YS*, 122, p. 3,000.

27. For a concise account of the fate of the Tanguts, see E. I. Kychanov, "Nekotorye suzhdeniia ob istoricheskikh sud'bakh tangutov posle nashestviia Chingiskhana," *Kratkie soobshcheniia Instituta narodov Azii* 76 (1965): 154–165.

28. Arslan Khan, the ruler of the Kharlukh Turks, also traveled to the Kerülen River in 1211 to submit to Chinggis Khan. See Rashīd/Karīmī, vol. I, p. 320.

29. *YS*, 7, p. 128.

30. See Cleaves's translation of "The Sino Mongolian Inscription of 1362," p. 85, the Mongol text.

31. This fact is mentioned in Islamic, Mongol, and Chinese sources. See, for example, Yü Chi, *Tao-yüan hsüeh-ku lu*, 24, 7b. This is the source of the biographies of *iduq quts* found in *YS*, 122. Chinggis Khan offered to treat the Khwārazm Shah and the ruler of the Tanguts as sons. But in both cases the Mongols found it necessary to destroy these ruling houses (see below). There were, however, at least two other individuals, neither rulers of foreign states, who bore the title "fifth son": the Tatar foundling Shigi Khutukhu (see Rashīd/Karīmī, vol. I, p. 414) and the Tangut official, Uchaghān Nūyān (see Rashīd/Ali-zade, p. 326). It should also be kept in mind that Chinggis Khan did have a fifth (and a sixth) son, but only the four offspring of his senior wife, Börte (Jochi, Chaghadai, Ögödei, and Tolui), were given major political or military responsibilities and received large appanages (*ulus*) from their father. Not much is known of Chinggis's other two sons, *Urukhuchi and Kölgen.

32. The offer is mentioned in all the sources, including para. 238 of the *SH*.

33. See Rashīd/Ali-zade, p. 341; Juvainī/Boyle, vol. I, p. 47, n. 17; *YS*, 109, p. 2760; and Dawson, op. cit., p. 141, where it is stated that Chinggis Khan "gave his

daughter in marriage to their (the Uighurs') king."

34. See Louis Hambis, *Le Chapitre CVIII du Yuan-che* (Leiden, 1954), tableau 11, facing p. 130. For marriages between the Mongol and Korean ruling houses, see Louis Hambis, "Notes sur l'histoire de Corée a l'époque mongole," *TP* 45 (1957), tableau I, facing p. 212.

35. Chinggis Khan responded favorably to this petition despite the fact that he recently had found it necessary to execute a number of Uighur nobles for unspecified crimes. See Juvainī/Boyle, vol. I, p. 140.

36. See *YS*, 130, p. 3174, the biography of A-lu-hun Sa-li (Arghun Sali). His grandfather, A-t'ai Sa-li (Atai Sali), was one of those allowed to return home. On the form of these names, see the discussion of Louis Ligeti, "Sur quelques transcriptions sino-ouigoures des Yüan," *Ural-Altaische Jahrbucher* 33 (1961): 235–238.

37. Vaṣṣāf, *Kitāb-i mustatāb-i Vassaf al-hazrat* (Bombay, 1852–1853), p. 580, and Ḥamd Allāh Mustawfī Qazvīnī, *Tarikh-i guzīdah* (Tehran, 1960), p. 586.

38. 'Ata-Malik-i-Juwaynī, *Ta'rīkh-i-Jahān-gushā* (3 vols.), ed. Muḥammad Qazvīnī (hereafter Juvainī/Qazvīnī) (London, 1913–1937), vol. I, p. 31. Cf. Juvainī/Boyle, vol. I, pp. 42–43, where the word "frontiers" (*hudud*) is not translated. See also V. V. Barthold, *Dvenadtsat leksii po istorii tureskikh narodov Srednei Azii*, in his *Sochineniia*, vol. V (Moscow, 1968), p. 146.

39. Juvainī/Qazvīnī, vol. I, p. 226. Cf. Juvainī/Boyle, vol. I, p. 271, where again the word for boundary (*kanār*) is not reflected in the translation.

40. Barthold, in his *Turkestan down to the Mongol Invasion*, 3rd ed. (London, 1968), p. 393, n. 4, refers to, but does not embrace, the suggestion of Veselovsky (whose work is not available to me) that Ögödei was given Uighuristan.

41. Juvainī/Boyle, vol. I, p. 43. When Ögödei became khaghan, he moved to Karakorum and transferred his appanages in Zungharia to his son Güyüg.

42. *YS*, 3, p. 45. Cf. Juvainī/Boyle, vol. II, p. 595; and Rashīd al-Dīn, *The Successors of Genghis Khan*, trans. J. Boyle (hereafter, Rashīd/Boyle) (New York, 1971), p. 217, where it is implied that the territories assigned to his descendants, including Khadan, were originally part of Ögödei's appanage. Khadan, Khadaghan, and Khada'an are variants of this name (which means "nail" in Mongolian).

43. *YS*, 63, p. 1569. The towns in question were detached from Besh Balikh sometime before Köden's death (during the reign of Güyüg, 1247–1249) and later restored in 1284. In his translation of this passage, E. Bretschneider, *Mediaeval Researches from East Asiatic Sources* (hereafter Bretschneider) (London, 1967 reprint), vol. II, pp. 27, 28, mistakenly identifies K'uo-tuan with the city of Khotan, not with Köden, Ögödei's second son. See also Rashīd/Boyle, pp. 20, 21.

44. Abe Takeo, "Where Was the Capital of the West Uigurs?" in *Silver Jubilee Volume of the Zinbun Kagaku Kenkyusyo, Kyoto University* (Kyoto, 1954), p. 435.

45. Abe quotes these remarks through the translation of C. D'Ohsson, *Histoire des Mongols*, vol. I (La Haye et Amsterdam, 1834), pp. 202–203 and 378.

46. Rashīd/Ali-zade, p. 325.

47. Muḥammad al-Nasawī, *Sirah Jalāl al-Dīn Mankabirtī*, ed. Ḥafiz Ḥamdī (Cairo, 1953), p. 83.

48. For further information on these negotiations, see V. V. Barthold, *Turkestan v epokhu mongol'skogo nashestviia chast pervaia Teksty* (hereafter *Turkestan*) (St. Petersburg, 1898), pp. 397–444; and Jūzjānī, *Tabakat-i Nāsārī*, vol. II, trans. H. G.

Raverty (New Delhi, reprint ed., 1970), pp. 965–967.

49. Abe, op. cit., p. 435.

50. Chao Meng-fu, op cit., 7, 12a.

51. This is the position of the Soviet scholars Kutlukov in *TMAE*, p. 90, and D. I. Tikhonov, *Khoziaistvo i obshchestvennyi stroi Uigurskogo gosudarstva* (hereafter *Khoziaistvo*) (Moscow and Leningrad, 1966), p. 59.

52. Also read K.smayn, Juvainī/Qazvīnī, vol. I, p. 34; and Rashīd/Ali-zade, p. 342. I have adopted the reconstruction suggested by Boyle, Juvainī/Boyle, vol. I, p. 47, n. 19. *Kesmes means "he who does not cut."

53. Juvainī/Boyle, vol. I, pp. 47–48; and Rashīd/Ali-zade, p. 342. His name appears to mean "the discarded," *Drevnetiurkskii slovar* (hereafter *DTS*) (Leningrad, 1969), p. 482.

54. Juvainī/Boyle, vol. I, pp. 585–590. Juvainī emphasizes the anti-Muslim aspects of the agreement in order to picture Möngke as a defender of the faith, but it is clear that the main purpose was political, i.e., to oppose the enthronement of Möngke.

55. Juvainī/Boyle, vol, I, pp. 48–53; and Rashīd/Boyle, p. 215. His name means "joy" or "gladness," *DTS*, pp. 380–381.

56. *YS*, 122, pp. 3000–1. In the Chinese sources Ögrünch is depicted as the direct successor to Barchukh; neither *Kesmes nor Salindi is mentioned. I have preferred the Persian accounts of the succession to the Chinese for several reasons. Juvainī, our main source, was a contemporary of the events. He was in Besh Balikh in 1253–1254, only a year after the execution of Salindi. While it is hard to conceive of a reason for Juvainī to fabricate such a story if it were not true, there are obvious reasons why the Chinese accounts, which go back to an inscription prepared in honor of the Uighur ruling house, might prefer to pass over in silence the events leading to the execution of Salindi. The event is in no way unique; the head of at least one other subordinate state, i.e., the Khūtlūgh Sultans of Kirmān, suspected of sympathizing with the Ögödeids, was replaced by a relative who also served as the deposed ruler's executioner.

57. *Mamula is mentioned as *iduq qut* for the first time in this year. Also, in the fall of this same year, the Uighurs sent Möngke various expensive presents, including a pearl-encrusted parasol (see *YS*, 3, p. 50). Since the umbrella is a well-known Buddhist symbol of kingship, it may be that this gift was connected with *Mamula's investiture.

58. *YS*, 122, p. 3000.

59. On these two *darughachi* (*ta-lu-hua-ch'ih*), see *YS*, 124, p. 3047, and 134, p. 3246.

60. This passage has been translated by Francis W. Cleaves, "*Daruya* and Gerege," *HJAS* 16 (1953): 241–244. The towns mentioned are Bukhara, Samarkand, Urgench, Khotan, Kashgar, Yarkand (?), and Kucha.

61. Juvainī/Qazvīnī, vol. I, p. 33; and Juvainī/Boyle, vol, I, p. 46.

62. *Hsi-yu chi*, in *Meng-ku shih-liao ssu-chung*, ed. Wang Kuo-wei, pp. 294–295; see *SWCCL* for bibliographic details; Arthur Waley, trans., *The Travels of an Alchemist* (London, 1931), pp. 80–81; and Barthold, *Turkestan*, p. 401. Barchukh was still campaigning in the west at this time.

63. *Hsi-yu chi*, p. 299; and Waley, *Travels*, p. 83.

64. *Hsi-yu chi*, pp. 301–302; and Waley, *Travels*, pp. 85–86. The ruler was Sughnakh Tegin, whose father, Ozar or Buzar, had previously submitted to Chinggis Khan. See Juvainī/Boyle, vol. I, pp. 75–77.

65. The earliest mention of the term *darughachi* in the Chinese sources is from 1215, although in its Chinese dress (*hsing-sheng*, etc.), the office of *darughachi* goes back to 1212–1213. In Central Asia, the *darughachi* at Almalikh, mentioned in Ch'ang-ch'un's travels, is the first to be recorded. See Igor de Rachewiltz, "Personnel and Personalities in North China in the Early Mongol Period," *Journal of the Economic and Social History of the Orient* 9 (1966): 136, n. 1.

66. Soviet scholars, Kutlukov in *TMAE*, p. 90; and Tikhonov, *Khoziaistvo*, p. 58–59, are inclined to place this event in the reign of Möngke.

67. W. Radloff, *Uigurische Sprachdenkmaler* (Leningrad, 1928), p. 30–31. My understanding of this and other Uighur documents is based solely on the accompanying translations.

68. S. E. Malov, "Uigurskie rukopisnye dokumenty ekspeditsii S. F. Ol'denburga," *Zapiski instituta vostokovedeniia Akademiia Nauk* 1 (1932): 136; and Nobuo Yamada, "Uiɣur Documents of Slaves and Adopted Sons," *Memoirs of the Faculty of Letters, Osaka University* 16 (March 1972): 242–243.

69. Jamāl Qarshī, *Mulhaqāt al-surah*, printed in V. V. Barthold, *Turkestan v epokhu mongol'skogo nashestviia, Teksty* (hereafter *Teksty*) (St. Petersburg, 1898), p. 139.

70. Rashīd/Boyle, pp. 177, 183, 218; and Juvainī/Boyle, vol. I, p. 597.

71. *YS*, 3, p. 45.

72. Bar Hebraeus, *The Chronography of Gregory Abu'l Faraj* (London, 1932), p. 411; and Juvainī/Boyle, vol. II, p. 515.

73. V. V. Barthold, *Four Studies on the History of Central Asia*, vol. I (Leiden, 1962), p. 121. See also Juvainī/Boyle, vol. I, p. 246, and vol. II, p. 585; Rashīd/Boyle, pp. 179, 214; and *YS*, p. 44. The latter source does not state the destination of *Burilgitei and his troops, but it appears to refer to the same deployment mentioned in the Persian accounts.

74. *YS*, 180, pp. 4159–61; and Bretschneider, vol. I, pp. 157–63.

75. Rashīd/Boyle, pp. 27–28, 254; and Shao Yüan-p'ing, *Yüan-shih lei-pien* (Kuang-wen shu-chü ed.), 30, 11a. As was mentioned above, in 1252 Khadan had been assigned Besh Balikh as an appanage by Möngke.

76. Khochkhar means "ram" in Turkish. See *DTS*, p. 451.

77. For a brief account of Khubilai's temporary and tenuous restoration of his authority in the regional khanates, see Peter Jackson, "The Accession of Qubilai Qa'an: A Re-examination," *Journal of the Anglo-Mongolian Society* 2, 1 (June 1975): 1–10.

78. Barthold, *Four Studies*, pp. 124–128. On the economic revival, see E. A. Davidovich, "Denezhnoe khoziaistvo i chastichnoe vosstanovlenie torgovli v Srednei Azii posle mongol'skogo nashestviia, xii v," *Narody Azii i Afriki*, no. 6 (1970), pp. 64–67.

79. *YS*, 63, p. 1569. I follow Abe Takeo, "Where Was the Capital of the West Uighurs?" p. 437, in his belief that the Mongol capital was intended in this passage. See also Paul Pelliot, *Notes on Marco Polo*, vol. I (Paris, 1959), pp. 127–128.

80. Cleaves, "Sino-Mongolian Inscription of 1362," pp. 32, 186.

81. Certain Chaghadai princes surrendered to the Yüan authorities there in the 1270s. See Rashīd al-Dīn, *Tārīkh-i Mubārak-i Ghāzānī*, ed. Karl Jahn (The Hague, 1957), pp. 23–27.

82. *YS*, 122, pp. 3001. See also Cleaves, "Sino-Mongolian Inscription of 1362," pp. 91–92, where the Mongol inscription alludes to a move to Khamil.

83. *YS*, 122, pp. 3001–2; and Cleaves, "Sino-Mongolian Inscription of 1326," pp. 33, 87. In the dating of the moves of the Uighur court from Besh Balikh to Khara Khocho to Khamil to Yung-ch'ang I have followed Abe Takeo, "Where Was the Capital of the West Uighurs?" pp. 437–438.

84. *YS*, 165, 3884; 16, p. 33; and Rashīd/Boyle, p. 314.

85. For details, see John W. Dardess, "From Mongol Empire to Yüan Dynasty: Changing Forms of Imperial Rule in Mongolia and Central Asia," *Monumenta Serica* 30 (1972–3): 135–139, and Hsiao Ch'i-ch'ing, *The Military Establishment of the Yüan Dynasty* (Cambridge, 1978), pp. 57–60.

86. *YS*, 11, pp. 221, 232; 12, pp. 240, 244, 251; 14, p. 289; 63, p. 1569; 154, p. 3640; and 165, p. 3889.

87. *YS*, 14, pp. 292–293; 63, p. 1569; 100, p. 2560; and 132, p. 3180. Dardess, "From Mongol Empire to Yüan Dynasty," pp. 139, 142, n. 94, also gives an account of these military measures.

88. Khubilai directed the Uighurs to suppress an uprising along the Kansu-Tibetan border; this seems to be the extent of their military activity in this period. *YS*, 122, p. 3002.

89. See Abe Takeo, "Uigur History," in *Research in Japan in [the] History of Eastern and Western Cultural Contacts* (Japanese National Commission for UNESCO, 1957), pp. 52–53.

90. Mas'ūd Beg and his sons continued to serve the Chaghadai khans and later Khaidu and his successor, Chabar.

91. *YS*, 10, p. 204; and 89, p. 2273. The office of *tuan-shih-kuan, jarghuchi* in Mongol, had much broader administrative responsibilities than the title would suggest.

92. *YS*, 11, pp. 228, 230; 12, p. 253; and 63, p. 1569. Ch'i Kung-chih apparently headed this office. He was the Pacification Officer (*hsüan-wei shih*) of Besh Balikh in 1281 and was the dominant figure in Uighuristan after 1283. See his biography, *YS*, 165, pp. 3883–4.

93. Dardess, "From Mongol Empire to Yüan Dynasty," p. 139, suggests that the Pacification Office replaced the Surveillance Office and complemented the duties of the Pei-t'ing Protectorate.

94. *YS*, 8, p. 161; and 14, p. 295. See also Erich Haenisch, "Die Jagdgesetze im mongolischen Ostreich," in *Ostasiatische Studien: Festschrift für Martin Ramming*, ed. I. L. Kluge (Berlin, 1959), pp. 85–93.

95. *T'ung-chih t'iao-ko* (Peking, 1930), 4, pp. 22b–23b.

96. *YS*, 11, p. 223; 12, p. 252; and 63, p. 1507. The bureau was established in 1280 and the treasury in 1283.

97. In the account of Ch'ang Te's embassy to Iran in 1259, it is stated that "Going west from Po-lo [i.e., Pūlād, a town south of Lake Balkash], gold, silver and copper are used as money; [the coins] have inscriptions but do not have square holes." Wang Yun, *Ch'iu-chien hsien-sheng ta ch'üan wen-chi*, 94, 5a; and

Bretschneider, vol. I, p. 128. This may indicate that the dividing line between the paper currency of China and the metal coinage of the Islamic world was well to the west of the Uighur territories. On Chaghadai coinage of the last half of the thirteenth century, see V. D. Zhukov, "Dukentskii klad monet," *Istoriia material'noi kultury Uzbekistana* 1 (1959): 176–207. These coins, dating from 1273 to 1312, were all minted in West Turkestan, with the exception of a few produced in Kashgar.

98. Mori Masao, "A Study on Uygur Documents of Loans of Consumption," *Memoirs of the Research Department of the Toyo Bunko* 20 (1961): 115, 127–30; Gabain, *Das Leben*, pp. 63–64; F. W. K. Muller, "Uigurische Glossen," in *Festschrift für Friedrich Hirth zu seinem 75. Geburtstag* (Berlin, 1920), pp. 319–322; and *DTS*, pp. 82, 139, 245, 491. In the Persian sources, the word for "pillow" (*bālish*) is also used as an enumerator for paper money (which was called *chaw*).

99. *Uigurische Sprachdenkmaler*, p. 20; and *DTS*, p. 157.

100. See, for example, Fen Tszia-shen (Feng Chia-sheng) and E. Tenishev, "Tri novykh Uigurskikh dokumenta iz Turfana," *Problemy Vostokovedeniia*, no. 3 (1960), pp. 141–149; and Nobuo Yamada, "Uighur Documents of Slaves and Adopted Sons," pp. 217–218, 226–227. According to Feng and Tenishev, these documents are dated September 21, 1280.

101. See for example, *YS*, 124, p. 3047; and the remarks of Maliavkin, "Uigurskoe Turfanskoe kniazhestvo v XIII veke," p. 65.

102. *YS*, 122, p. 3001.

103. *YS*, 16, p. 353; and 19, p. 5031.

104. *YS*, 135, p. 3281, refers to an outbreak of banditry in Besh Balakhasun, i.e., Besh Balikh. This Turkic-Mongolian hybrid form also is used in a Mongol document studied by Herbert Franke. See his "Zwei mongolische Textfragmente aus Zentralasien," in *Mongolian Studies*, ed. Louis Ligeti (Amsterdam, 1970), pp. 143–144.

105. Rashīd al-Dīn, *Tārīkh-i Mubārak-i Ghāzānī: Dāstān-i Ghāzān-khān* (London, 1940), p. 350.

106. *YS*, 10, p. 205; 12, p. 243; 13, pp. 265, 280; 14, p. 292; 15, pp. 320–321; and 21, p. 448.

107. To the best of my knowledge, the document of 1295 translated by Paul Ratchnevsky, *Un code des Yüan* (Paris, 1937), p. 211, concerning taxes on religious personages within the Yüan realm is the last one addressed to affairs within the Uighur lands. After this date, documents addressed to the Uighurs refer only to Uighurs in the areas of Khamil and Kansu. See, for example, the edict of 1313 in the *Yüan Tien-chang* (Taipei, 1964), 53, 36a-b.

108. Published in the *Yüan ching-shih ta-tien*. On the publication date of this work, see Paul Pelliot, "Note sur la carte des pays du Nord-Ouest dans le *King-che ta-tien*," *TP* 25 (1928): 98–100. A reproduction of this map is available in Sven Hedin, *Southern Tibet*, vol. 8 (Stockholm, 1922), plate 8, facing p. 278. For a schematic representation of this map, see Bretschneider, vol. II, facing the title page.

109. Rashīd/Boyle, p. 286.

110. Rashīd/Boyle, pp. 299, 300, 322.

111. Rashīd/Boyle, pp. 23–24, 142, 326–329.

112. Mu'īn al-Dīn Naṭanzī, *Muntakhab al-tavārīkh-i Mu'īnī*, ed. Jean Aubin (Tehran, 1957), p. 106.

113. Abū al-Qāsim ibn 'Alī ibn Muḥammad al-Qāshānī, *Tarikh-i Uljaytu*, ed. Mahin Hambly (hereafter Qāshānī/Hambly) (Tehran, 1969), p. 34.

114. In this struggle the Chaghadai khans were successful. Chabar, Khaidu's son, was forced to seek sanctuary in China. The Chaghadaids, now free of Ögödeid domination, established amicable relations with China, sending tribute to the Yüan court up to 1313. *YS*, 24, pp. 550, 551, 555.

115. Qāshānī/Hambly, pp. 202–203. As an example of his familiarity with the situation, Qāshānī is able to name the commander of each garrison and give its numerical strength in terms of *tümen*!

116. The Persian text has Fūtāq, in place of Qūbāq, an obvious misreading on the part of the editor.

117. Qāshānī/Hambly, pp. 205–208. Naṭanzī, *Muntakhab*, p. 107, notes that the Yüan attack in this area was toward Khara Khocho.

118. See Henry Yule, *Cathay and the Way Thither*, vol. 4 (Taiwan reprint, 1966), p. 234; and Hafiz Abru (Hafiẓ-i Abrū), *A Persian Embassy to China*, trans. K. M. Maitra (New York: Paragon, 1970), pp. 13–14.

119. *YS*, 122, p. 302.

120. This is the reason given by Naṭanzī, *Muntakhab*, pp. 107–108.

121. Qāshānī/Hambly, pp. 208–209.

122. *YS*, 34, p. 755; the tribute was a quantity of wine. Both Rashīd al-Dīn, Rashīd/Boyle, p. 286, and Marco Polo, *The Description of the World*, ed. and trans. A. C. Moule and Paul Pelliot (London, 1938), p. 156, remark on the quality of the wines of Khara Khocho.

123. See Barthold, "Narodnoe dvizhenie v Samarkande v 1365 g.," in his *Sochineniia*, vol. II, ch. 2, p. 363, on the autonomy of towns in the Chaghadai khanate.

124. Transcriptions of these documents, along with bibliographical references to available translations and commentaries, are available in Louis Ligeti, *Monuments Préclassiques, XIIIe et XIVe Siècles*, vol. I (Budapest, 1972), doc. 1, pp. 208–209; doc. 3, pp. 212–213; doc. 7, pp. 220–221; doc. 8, pp. 222–223; doc. 11, pp. 227–228. One of Yisün Temür's predecessors, Jenkshi (r. 1334–ca. 1338), seems to have exercised some authority in Uighuristan, but the extent is uncertain. It is known only that this ruler, under the influence of Uighur Buddhists (*bakshi*), desecrated many mosques in Uighuristan. See Naṭanzī, *Muntakhab*, p. 112.

125. The document of 1338 (Ligeti, doc. 1) has been translated by Michael Weiers, "Mongolische Reisebegleitschreiben aus Čaγatai," *Zentralasiatische Studien* 1 (1967): 16–33; and the document of 1339 (Ligeti, doc. 8) by D. [Gyorgy] Kara, *Knigi mongol'skikh kochevnikov* (Moscow, 1972), pp. 170–171. For the dating of this latter document, see Larry Clark, "On a Mongol Decree of Yisün Temür (1339)," *Central Asiatic Journal* 19 (1975): 194–198. The basic work on the chronology of these documents is Herbert Franke, "Zur Datierung der mongolischen Schreiben aus Turfan," *Oriens* 15 (1962): 399–410.

126. *YS*, 108, p. 2745; 122, p. 3002. Ne'üril had functioned as de facto head of the Uighur government-in-exile prior to his investiture. See Hambis, *Le Chapitre CVIII*, pp. 130–134, for information on the princes of Kao-ch'ang in the fourteenth century.

127. *YS*, 20, p. 437.

128. Dardess, "From Mongol Empire to Yüan Dynasty," pp. 132, 142, 143, 164–165.

129. *YS*, 209, p. 4635.

130. This order is embedded in the *Koryŏ-sa* (Tokyo, 1908–1909), 25, 26a–27b, and translated by Henthorn, *Korea*, p. 194. For another example of instructions issued to a surrendered state, see Gari Ledyard, "Two Mongol Documents from the *Koryŏ-sa*," *Journal of the American Oriental Society* 83 (1963): 225–238.

131. Henthorn, *Korea*, p. 194.

132. While Uighur hostages are not mentioned specifically in the sources, those Uighur princes described as serving at the court were, in reality, hostages. I want to thank Herbert Franke for pointing this out to me.

133. These matters, together with the legal decisions, were recorded in the "blue book" *Kökö debter*, by order of Chinggis Khan. See Paul Pelliot, "Les *Kökö-däbtär* et les *hou-k'eou ts'ing-ts'eu*" *T'oung Pao* 27 (1930): 194–198.

134. Juvainī/Boyle, vol. I, pp. 597–598, and Rashīd/Boyle, pp. 218–219. Tikhonov, *Khoziaistvo*, pp. 100–101, also suggests that the Uighurs were counted in the 1250s.

135. See *YS*, 15, p. 321; 19, p. 503, and above, n. 102. For an account of the census in Tibet, taken in the 1270s, see Giuseppe Tucci, *Tibetan Painted Scrolls* (Rome, 1949), vol. I, pp. 13–14, 251–252, n. 35.

136. The decimal system as a principle of military organization was in use among the Turks before the rise of Chinggis Khan. For examples of the use of these terms in Uighur documents, see S. E. Malov, "Dva uigurskikh dokumenta," in V. V. Barthold, *Turkestanskie druz'ia ucheniki i pochitateli* (Tashkent, 1927), p. 393; and Gabain, *Das Leben*, pp. 55–57, with references to *Uighurische Sprachdenkmaler*. *DTS*, p. 624, gives *ulchi tümen* as a personal name, but this is contradicted by other authorities.

137. From Rashīd al-Dīn's account, Rashīd/Karīmī, vol. I, p. 310, it appears that the total value of the goods sent, as well as the precise items selected, was left up to Barchukh. The *SH*, para. 238, lists gold, silver, gems, and textiles as the items presented.

138. Sayf ibn Muhammad, *Tarīkh namah-i Harāt*, ed. Muḥammad Zubayr al-Siddīqī (Calcutta, 1944), p. 107.

139. *YS*, 3, p. 50.

140. On the evolution of the revenue system, see H. F. Schurmann, "Mongolian Tributary Practices in the 13th Century," *HJAS* 19 (1956): 304–389; and John Masson Smith, "Mongol and Nomadic Taxation," *HJAS* 30 (1970): 48–85.

141. See D. I. Tikhonov, "K voprosu o nekotorykh terminiakh," *Strany i narody Vostoka*, vyp. XI (Moscow, 1971), pp. 78–84, for the dating of the documents containing references to *khubchir* (the Uighur form) and *khalan*. If he is correct, then the terms are Turkic in origin and are a further example of the Mongols' indebtedness to Uighur institutions.

142. *Uigurische Sprachdenkmaler*, pp. 30–32, 57, 93, 121. See also Tikhonov, *Khoziaistvo*, pp. 101–106.

143. S. E. Malov, *Pamiatniki drevnetiurskoi pismennosti; Teksty i issledovaniia* (Moscow and Leningrad, 1951), pp. 204–207. Malov does not precisely date this document, only referring to it as one from the period of the tenth to the thirteenth centuries, but Tikhonov, *Khoziaistvo*, pp. 104–105, 113–114, associates it with the Mongol era.

144. Rashīd/Boyle, p. 94; and n. 76, above.

145. Peter Olbricht, *Das Postwesen in China unter der Mongolenherrschaft* (Wiesbaden, 1954), pp. 40–41. For information on the postal system in other subordinate states, see Tucci, *Tibetan Painted Scrolls*, pp. 12–13; and Henthorn, *Korea*, p. 210.

146. *YS*, 63, pp. 1569–70; Jan Balikh is directly west of Besh Balikh. On the name Basa Chaghri, see *DTS*, pp. 85, 136.

147. *YS*, 11, p. 231; 12, p. 252; 13, p. 271; 63, p. 1569. On the location of T'ai-ho ling, see T'u Chi, *Meng-wu-erh shih-chi* (Taipei: Shih-chieh shu-chü, 1962), 8, 5b.

148. Rashīd/Boyle, p. 326.

149. Rashīd/Ali-zade, p. 345. On the Bekrin, see Paul Pelliot, *Recherches sur les chrétiens d'Asie centrale et d'extrême-orient* (Paris, 1973), pp. 31–33.

150. On the importance of sedentary auxiliaries in the Mongol military establishment, see John Masson Smith, "Mongol Manpower and Persian Population," *Journal of the Social and Economic History of the Orient* 18 (1975): 270–299.

151. Skelton, *Tartar Relation*, p. 56.

152. Muhammad 'Awfī, who wrote in the first decades of the thirteenth century, reports that the Uighurs were a peace-loving nation not noted for their valor, *Jāmi' al-hikāyāt va lāmi' al-rivāyāt*, printed in Barthold, *Teksty*, p. 95.

153. Bar Hebraeus, *Chronography*, p. 368. On Uighur military practices, see Gabain, *Das Leben*, pp. 41–44, 141–149.

154. Rashīd/Ali-zade, pp. 340–341.

155. *YS*, 123, p. 3026; and 134, p. 3262.

156. *YS*, 122, pp. 3001–2. This unit is called a *tamma* (*t'an-ma*). These contingents were mobilized from various privileged tribes and clans (e.g., the imperial consort clans). Most *tammachi* were composed of Mongols, but other privileged ethnic groups, like the Uighurs, also seem to have been allowed to form such units. See Hsiao, *Military Establishment*, p. 16.

157. *YS*, 13, p. 280; 22, p. 506. On *Sösö[k] Tegin, see Hambis, *Chapitre CVIII*, tableau II, facing p. 130.

158. Rashīd/Karimi, vol. I, pp. 55; and Muhammad Haidar, *A History of the Moghuls of Central Asia*, trans. E. Denison Ross and ed. Ney Elias (New York, 1970 reprint), p. 311.

159. Rashīd/Ali-zade, p. 343.

160. On the role of the Naiman as transmitters of Uighur culture to the Mongols, see S. Murayama, "Sind die Naiman Türken oder Mongolen?" *Central Asiatic Journal* 4 (1959): 188-198; and L. L. Viktorova, "K voprosu o naimanskoi teorii proiskhozhdeniia mongol'skogo literaturnogo iazyka i pis'mennosti (xii–xiii vv.)" *Uchenye zapiski Leningradskogo gosudarstvennogo universiteta*, no. 305, vyp. 12 (1961), pp. 137-155.

161. See Kara, *Knigi mongol'skikh kochevnikov*, pp. 15–20; and A. Róna-Tas, "Some Notes on the Terminology of Mongolian Writing," *Acta Orientalia* 18 (1965): 114–147.

162. Juvainī/Boyle, vol. I, p. 7. By the latter half of the thirteenth century, the Uighur script, which is written vertically, had become so well known in Iran that it could be used as a poetic image for hanging tresses of hair. See V. Minorsky, "Pūr-i Bahā's 'Mongol Ode'," in his *Iranica* (Tehran, 1964), pp. 277–281.

163. *YS*, 124, p. 3048. Previously, the Uighur Khara Ighach Buirukh served in a similar capacity at the court of the last Karakhitay *gurkhan*. *YS*, 124, p. 3046.

164. *Yüan Tien-chang*, 31, 1a–1b.

165. Naṭanzī, *Muntakhab*, p. 112.

166. Chao Meng-fu, *Sung hsüeh chai wen-chi*, 7, p. 12a. Uighurs also frequently served in the household establishments of major Mongol princes—e.g., Tolui and Temüge-Otchigin. See *YS*, 134, pp. 3243, 3262.

167. Voegelin, "Mongol Orders," pp. 402–445. Their pretensions to world conquest were noted by the early Western travelers. See, for example, Skelton, *Tartar Relations*, p. 90, and the parallel passage in Carpini, Dawson, *Mongol Mission*, p. 38.

168. See Igor de Rachewiltz, "Some Remarks on the Ideological Foundations of Chinggis Khan's Empire," *Papers on Far Eastern History* 7 (1973): 21–36. On the circulation of the concept of empire building as a heaven-sanctioned activity among the pre-Chinggisid Turks, see Osman Turan, "The Ideal of World Domination among the Medieval Turks," *Studia Islamica* 4 (1955): 70–90.

169. Cf. Wang Gungwu's remarks on differences between the Sung and Yüan attitudes toward vassals in his "Early Ming Relations with Southeast Asia," in *The Chinese World Order*, ed. John K. Fairbank (Cambridge, 1968), pp. 47–49.

TEN

Turks in China under the Mongols: A Preliminary Investigation of Turco-Mongol Relations in the 13th and 14th Centuries

IGOR DE RACHEWILTZ

One of the facts that immediately strikes the student of Chinese history is the international and pluri-national character of the Yüan period—broadly from 1215 (the date of the capture of Peking by the Mongols) to 1368. International because of the political ties and exchanges of the Yüan state with other states, or domains (*ulus*) within the Mongol empire (*yeke mongghol ulus*), as well as with the rest of the world that had not submitted to Mongol rule (*bulgha irgen*). Pluri-national because of the various ethnic groups (*se-mu-jen*) that had settled in China in the wake of the Mongol conquest and gained their living largely by serving their masters in military and administrative capacities.

Among these foreign settlers—Turks from different parts of Asia, Alans from the Caucasus, Armenians, Tibetans, Persians, and Arabs, and a sprinkling of "Franks" (i.e., Europeans)—it is the Turks who stand out conspicuously and command our attention. They were unquestionably the most influential group, both culturally and politically; at times they even played a vital role in the internal affairs of the Mongol court, directly affecting the course of the dynasty.

Although we cannot properly speak of the Turks in Yüan China as forming a state within the state, for this was certainly not the case, there is no doubt that they represented a different and distinctive culture in the society of the time. They retained a sense of identity, even though a number of prominent Turkish families exposed to Chinese culture eventually became sinicized.

Thus, the activity of the Turks in China must be studied within the framework of the intercultural relations of the pluri-national Yüan society rather than within the framework of multi-state relations in contemporary East Asia. Even in the case of political relations between the Uighur *iduq qut* or the Öngüt Turks of North China and the Mongol court, it is a moot point whether one can properly speak of multi-state relations, since the Uighur kingdom was a Mongol protectorate, and the Öngüt kingdom the appanage of the ruling prince (who was the imperial son-in-law), and later became a frontier district incorporated into the metropolitan province administration.

For the purpose of our investigation we must, therefore, retain a somewhat flexible approach to the evaluation of the nature of the relationship between the Mongols, representing the major alien ruling group, and the lesser alien groups, such as the Turks, which though forming part of the management, were, in purely social terms, an artificially established infrastructure between the thin Mongol layer at the top and the broad mass of Chinese subjects at the bottom.

The First Phase (ca. 1200–1259)

Before we start our investigation, we must clarify one important point: what do we mean by Turks? By Turks I mean individuals who identified themselves, or were so identified by the Chinese historian, as belonging to one of several known and well-established Turkish peoples or tribes of the time, such as the Uighur and Kipchak, and whose original language and family background were unequivocally Turkish.

The Turkish peoples that I have surveyed for the present investigation are the following: Uighur, Kharlukh, Khangli, Kipchak, Öngüt, Kereyid, Naiman.

The information that I have collected comes from many Chinese historical, literary, and epigraphical sources.[1] However, since this is a preliminary investigation, additional information, especially from Persian sources, may enlarge the final picture considerably.

The Kereyid and Naiman are included in this survey with serious reservations, as the degree of Turkishness of these tribes is still a debatable point.[2] I have not included the Baya'ut and the Khwārazmian Turks. The Baya'ut tribe poses a problem because the Baya'uts were divided into various branches that had developed independently, and in the thirteenth century they lived in different parts of Asia. Some inhabited northern Mongolia and were definitely Mongols. Others lived among the Khangli and Kipchak peoples in western Asia and seem to have been Turks—at any rate they were thoroughly turkized already in Chinggis Khan's time. it seems, however, that the Western Baya'ut had migrated from Mongolia in the middle of the eleventh century and must, therefore, be regarded also as a basically Mongol people.[3]

As for the natives of Khwārazm, they have not been included because those who are mentioned in the Chinese sources are not necessarily Turks.

In the second half of the twelfth century when Temüjin, the later Chinggis Khan, was struggling to achieve leadership in Mongolia, these Turkish people were distributed as follows:

The Uighurs occupied the region of East Turkestan, modern Sinkiang, that lay just southwest of Mongolia. Their two main centers were Besh Balikh near Guchen, and Khocho near Turfan. They had settled there in the ninth century, and during the following three hundred years they had developed a sophisticated and cosmopolitan civilization. At first they adopted Manicheism as their religion, which they later discarded in favor of Nestorian Christianity and Buddhism. In the period we are concerned with, the Christians represented a minority.[4]

The Kharlukhs lived in the Ili River valley south of Lake Balkash in East Kazakhstan, where they had apparently migrated from the valley of the Chu after the arrival of the Kharakhanids in the tenth century. They had been largely influenced by Islam, and so also had the Khanglis, who had settled in the area of Turgai north of the Aral Sea, and the Kipchaks, who were scattered over the vast steppeland north of the Caspian and Black seas.[5]

The Öngüts lived on the northernmost border of China, in the Ordos region of Inner Mongolia. They were the descendants of Turkish tribes that had been settled outside the Great Wall by the T'ang court in the ninth century. They too had been converted to Nestorianism; at the same time they were very much influenced by Chinese culture.[6]

In Mongolia itself lived two powerful tribes, the Kereyid and the Naiman of northern and western Mongolia respectively, whose ethnic origin is still obscure, but whose ruling clansmen and aristocracy apparently consisted of mongolized Turks. They had benefited from contacts with the Uighurs, and they practiced a mixture of Nestorianism and Shamanism. Of these two, the Kereyid tribe was, historically speaking, the most important, and its leader, in Chinggis Khan's time, was one of the men who unwittingly perpetuated the medieval legend of Prester John.[7]

At the beginning of the thirteenth century, after twenty years of warfare and steppe diplomacy, Temüjin eventually unified the major tribes of Mongolia under his leadership, and in 1206 he had himself elected supreme chief with the title of Chinggis Khan.

Although he was an illiterate Mongol warrior, he had in his immediate entourage a number of advisers and secretaries who were educated men of Chinese and Turkish cultural background. We must not forget also that, as a young man and for many years, Chinggis Khan had been a client and an ally of the Kereyid court, and that he must inevitably have been exposed to Turkish culture through this close association. It is perhaps not fortuitous that the very title he assumed, Chinggis Khan, is of Turkish origin.[8]

In the year 1204, or thereabouts, an Uighur official called in Chinese phonetic transcription T'a-t'a T'ung-a (Tatar-Tonga?), who had formerly been the seal-bearer and chief administrator at the Naiman court, passed into the service of the Mongol conqueror. He is traditionally credited with the introduction of the Turkish Uighur vertical script among the Mongols, a script used with minor modifications until thirty years ago in the Mongolian People's Republic and still used today in Inner Mongolia. Chinggis Khan appointed him his personal assistant and ordered him to teach his sons to write Mongolian using this script.[9] Subsequently, another Uighur Turk called Ha-la I-ha-ch'ih Pei-lu (Khara Ighach Buirukh) was appointed tutor to the Mongol princes.[10] He had previously served in this capacity at the court of the *gurkhan* of the Karakhitay, and had defected to Chinggis Khan soon after the submission of the *iduq qut* Barchukh Art Tegin to the Mongols (i.e., in 1209 or 1210).[11] At that time (1210) the conqueror's four sons were aged about twenty-six, twenty-five, twenty-four, and twenty,[12] and one may well wonder what the Uighur preceptor taught them. However, the point here is that the period 1205–1210 was a crucial one in Chinggis's career, for it marked his consolidation of power in Mongolia, his election as supreme tribal leader, and the reshaping of his army and social organization. Whereas the immediate model for the restructuring of the Guard, which was to form the backbone of his military power, was the Kereyid army organization,[13] the main "outside" cultural influence in the court entourage and administration in this period came undoubtedly from his Uighur Turkish advisers.[14]

Within the following decade, the Kereyid Chen-hai (Chinkhai, 1168/9–1251/2) was put in charge of the newly established Uighur-Mongol Chancellery or Secretariat, subsequently sharing with one or two colleagues the direction of Central Asian affairs at court—a key position which he held on and off until 1251. Chinkhai was an early companion of Chinggis Khan's and took part in all his major campaigns. At various times he wielded immense power, and he is known to us not only through the Chinese and Persian sources but also through John of Pian di Carpine's account of his mission to the Great Khan Güyüg. Chinkhai was a literate man of Nestorian Christian faith, a fact from which we can surmise that his cultural roots were almost certainly Turkish.[15]

Now, by 1225, Chinggis Khan's generals had conquered, or overrun, most of the territories where lived the Turkish peoples I mentioned. The Uighurs and the Öngüts had wisely submitted of their own accord to Chinggis Khan and had given him military support.[16] They were, therefore, in a privileged position, and from then on their ties with the Mongol court, first at Karakorum, then at Daidu (Peking), became very close through adoption and intermarriage, and service in the Guard. As for the Kharlukhs, Khanglis, and Kipchaks, many of their tribesmen were recruited into the Mongol army in the 1220s and 1230s, and gave loyal service to their new masters.[17]

Turkish influence at the Mongol court in Karakorum must have been very strong in the first half of the thirteenth century (i.e., under the first two successors of Chinggis Khan). When Ögödei was enthroned in 1229, he

Table 10.1 Turks in Service of Mongols

	ca. 1200–1259	1260–1294	? (1280–1330)	1295–1368	TOTAL	NO DATA	TOTAL
UIGHUR	37 (12)	73 (21)	32 (9)	169 (47)	311 (89)	158	469
KHARLUKH	7 (1)	10 (3)	5 (1)	19 (3)	41 (8)	20	61
KHANGLI	7	12 (3)	11 (2)	36 (8)	66 (13)	26	92
KIPCHAK	4 (1)	12 (3)	13 (4)	15 (8)	44 (16)	16	60
ÖNGÜT	12	30 (6)	3 (2)	43 (6)	88 (14)	42	130
KEREYID	13 (2)	14 (2)	3 (2)	22 (3)	52 (9)	11	63
NAIMAN	5 (1)	12 (5)	2	25 (8)	44 (14)	26	70
Totals	85 (17)	163 (43)	69 (20)	329 (83)	646 (163)	299	945

NOTE: Figures in parentheses = *darughachis*.

assumed the old Turkish title of *khaghan*, or emperor; and it was during his reign that, through the influence of Chinkhai, the Uighur–Central Asian faction at court took the upper hand. As a result, people from the Western Regions were brought in, in increasing numbers as administrators and advisers. It was in this period, between 1235 and 1250, that the commercial associations known as *ortakh* (a Turkish word meaning "partner") began their operations in the Mongol empire, which by then included also most of the northern half of China. Other Central and Western Asians—chiefly Muslims, judging by their names—were granted the privilege of farming taxes in China.[18]

Although among the members of the *ortakh* associations there were undoubtedly many Turks from different parts of Asia (this would also apply to the foreign tax-farmers), we have only the scantiest information about individuals.[19] However, besides the largely autonomous tax-farmers, the Mongol court also made use of specially appointed commissars, called *darughachi*, for the purpose of tax collection. They were usually placed in charge of a district administration in the conquered territories, and in this early period often combined civil with military functions.[20]

From the beginning of the thirteenth century to 1260, when Khubilai became emperor—a period which, incidentally, is very poorly covered by the Chinese sources—thirty-seven Uighurs are mentioned with the offices they held and other biographical data. They represent, of course, an elite by the mere fact of being so recorded in history.

Of these 37 individuals, 7 held positions as advisers-secretaries and imperial tutors; 9 were military men (i.e., army leaders and officers of the Guard); 16 were local officals, administrators, and judges (*darughachis*, *jarghuchis*, etc.); and 2 were religious (Buddhist) personalities.

The seven Uighurs of the first group included the already mentioned Tatar Tonga and Khara Ighach Buirukh. The other five were the following: (1) Su-lo-hai (Sologhai), Tatar Tonga's son who inherited his office.[21] (2) Yeh-li-chu, or "Elîshû," a Nestorian Christian from Khocho who became a secretary (*bichigechi*) and after the annexation of Chin assisted Shigi Khutukhu in taking the census of North China (1235–1236).[22] (3) To-lo-chu (died before 1260), also from Khocho, who taught the Uighur script to Mongol nobles and also to Khubilai.[23] (4) Hsi-pan, or Shiban (died ca. 1295), another Nestorian and the son of an Uighur officer who had served under Chinggis Khan in the Western Campaign. He also became a tutor to the Mongol princes and taught Uighur script to Khashi (the son of Ögödei), then he served Khubilai as senior secretary before 1260. He had a brilliant career under Khubilai, holding in succession the posts of *darughachi* of the Chen-ting district, Minister of Revenue (*hu-pu shang-shu*), special envoy to Khaidu, Assistant of the Right in the Secretarial Council (*chung-shu yu-ch'eng*), and executive Hanlin academician (*ch'eng-chih*).[24] (5) K'u-erh-ku-ssu—Körgüz, or George (?–1243?), a Nestorian from Besh Balikh and a protégé of Chinkhai's. He was an expert in Uighur and in Central Asian affairs.[25]

The nine military men were mostly leaders of prominent Uighur families and relatives of Barchukh who served in the Mongol armies after the *iduq qut* pledged his support to Chinggis Khan. They fought in western Asia and in China, where several of their descendants settled and became prominent figures in their own right.[26]

As for the local officials, the majority were *darughachis* (12 out of 16), some of them controlling large areas of North China.[27]

Of the two Buddhist personalities, one, An-tsang (?–1293) from Besh Balikh, was a great scholar and leading translator of Chinese classics, histories, and works on government into Mongolian under Möngke and Khubilai.[28]

Among the Uighurs we must include A-li Hai-ya (Arigh Khaya, 1227–1286), Yeh-hsien Nai (Esen Nai, ?–1304), and Ai-ch'üan. The first two came into Khubilai's service when the latter was still a prince (i.e., before 1260), but their duties in this early phase of their careers are not clearly specified in our sources. Both became eminent personalities in the following decades. Ai-ch'üan was an Uighur who entered the service of Tolui (Khubilai's father) and was employed in Tolui's wife's fief in Chen-ting.[29]

But Uighurs were not the only Turks in the Mongol service at this time. For the same period, our sources record the activity of 7 Kharlukh, 7 Khangli, 4 Kipchak, and 12 Öngüt officials. As we might expect, most of them were army chiefs, members of the Guard, and regional (military) commanders, but two of them were *darughachis* (1 Kharlukh and 1 Kipchak).[30]

To the above, we must add 13 Kereyid and 5 Naiman officials. The Kereyid comprise chancellor Chinkhai,[31] his colleague and fellow Christian Bolghai (?–1264),[32] 2 great *darughachis* of Shan-hsi,[33] 1 senior secretary and 1 official in the heir apparent's administration,[34] and 8 military leaders.

Of the 5 Naimans, 1 was Batu's teacher Pai Pu-hua (Beg Bukha),[35] another was Yüeh-li-ma-ssu (? Yörmez, ?–1276), a *darughachi* and special envoy,[36] and the other 3 were military men.

Thus we know of over eighty Turkish personalities who, in various degrees, held power and influence in the early phase of Mongol rule. To be sure, many more Turks are actually mentioned in our sources, but I have not taken them into account. The information about them is far too scanty; often only their names are given with the statement that they "followed" this or that Mongol leader in this or that campaign.[37]

It goes without saying that the lives of many of these Turkish personalities spanned the reign of Khubilai; in fact, several of them reached the peak of their careers under this emperor.[38]

The Second Phase (1260–1294)

The first or early phase ends with the election of Khubilai in 1260 and the transfer of the court from Karakorum in northern Mongolia to Shang-tu and, subsequently, Peking (Yen-ching, Chung-tu, Ta-tu/Daidu).

With regard to the appointment of Turkish officials, Khubilai's attitude was, if anything, even more favorable than that of his predecessors. We must not forget that Khubilai's mother was the Kereyid Nestorian princess Sorghakhtani Beki, the wife, then (after 1231/32) widow, of Tolui.[39] It was Sorghakhtani, by all accounts a most remarkable woman, who personally took care of the education of her famous sons (Möngke, Khubilai, Hülegü, and Arigh Böke).[40]

As was mentioned earlier, Khubilai was instructed in Uighur script by To-lo-chu. While still a prince he had as senior secretary Shiban, and among the people who, in one capacity or another, served him in these formative years were Uighurs like Lien Hsi-hsien, Esen Nai, Arigh Khaya, and Meng-su-ssu (Mungsuz).

Sorghakhtani held great authority and power at court during Ögödei's reign and until Möngke's enthronement (she died soon after, probably in 1252). Both she and Güyüg favored Christianity; therefore, members of the educated Turkish elite, many of whom were Christians, thrived in this period. Under Güyüg, state affairs were virtually in the hands of Chinkhai and Khadakh, and although both of them perished in the purges following the election of Möngke (they had backed another candidate), we know that Möngke continued to show favor to the Christians, that he was surrounded by Uighur monks, and that he appointed Chinkhai's former colleague, the Kereyid Bolghai—also a Christian—as his chief secretary or chancellor.[41]

Möngke died while fighting the Sung in Szechwan in August 1259. When the news of his death and of his younger brother's claims to the succession reached Khubilai, who was also fighting in China at the time, some of his high officials, close advisers, and princes of the blood, as well as his supporters in Karakorum urged him to accept the imperial dignity and set him on the throne in K'ai-p'ing fu on 5 May 1260.[42] Among the officials who played a role in convincing Khubilai to become *khaghan* was the Uighur Mungsuz.[43]

Khubilai completed the unification of China under Mongol rule with the conquest of Southern Sung in 1279. He was, for a Mongol, a liberal and enlightened monarch, and on the whole well disposed toward Chinese culture: witness the Chinese scholars he patronized while still a prince.[44] However, he was not prepared to entrust the management of the country to Chinese officials and therefore continued his predecessor's policy of employing "sundry aliens" (*se-mu-jen*) at the top level of the central and local administration.[45]

Khubilai inherited some of the Turkish officials from the previous administrations and gave offices—which in the Mongol system were normally hereditary—to their sons. He appointed many more Turks than his predecessors did. It is no surprise that these privileged foreign officials, having formed by now powerful cliques and pressure groups, tended to recommend and appoint their own relatives, countrymen, and protégés. This phenomenon is reflected in the breakdown of figures obtained from Chinese sources for the period of Khubilai (1260–1294).

We have records of seventy-three Uighur personalities, more than half of whom continued in office after 1294. Only seven of the seventy-three were military men.[46] One of the leading generals in Khubilai's time was Arigh Khaya (whom I have included among the Uighurs of the First Phase). Of the others, fifty-nine held positions at court and in the central and the provincial adminstrations (twenty-one of them were *darughachis*). Among the high officials some deserve special mention: A-lu-hun Sa-li (Arghun Sali, 1245–1307), A-shih T'ieh-mu-erh (Ashigh Temür, 1250–1309), and the notorious Sang-ko (Sengge), who in 1287 became the head of the Presidential Council (*shang-shu sheng*) and was in charge of government finances until his death in 1291.[47]

With the restoration of the Hanlin Academy (1264) and other learned institutions, several Uighurs were appointed as academicians. Besides the great An-tsang, nine are recorded, one of whom held a concurrent position in the central administration.[48] Among these civil officials we find also several imperial advisers and tutors to the princes,[49] as well as multilingual scholars, who did valuable work as translators, particularly of Buddhist texts.[50] The role played by the Uighurs in the script reform and the creation of the new national script (the so-called square script devised by 'Phags-pa) cannot be overlooked.[51] The translation work of these foreign scholars in China prepared the ground, as it were, for the intense literary activity of the great Buddhist translators of the first decades of the fourteenth century, about whom more will be said later.

Other Turkish groups are also well represented: 10 Kharlukhs, 12 Khanglis, 12 Kipchaks, 13 Öngüts, 14 Kereyid, and 12 Naimans. Out of a total of 90 individuals, 34 were military men and 53 were officials in the central and provincial administrations.[52] The scholars—including translators—in these groups were very few, three in all; however, we can add to them perhaps two who were appointed academicians *after* 1294. All of them were Önguts. Only one, the sinicized Öngüt Chao Shih-yen (1260–1336), deserves mention.[53]

On the other hand, the other ethnic groups produced a number of leading political and military personalities, such as the Kharlukh Ta-shih-man (Dashman, 1258–1317) and his son Mai-nu (Mainu), the Khanglis A-sha Pu-hua (Asha Bukha, 1263–1309) and I-na T'o-t'o (Inal Toghto, 1271–1327), the Kipchak T'u T'u-ha (Tugh Tugha, 1237–1297) and his son Ch'uang-wu-erh (Chong'ur, 1260–1322), the Kereyid Ta-shih-man (Dashman, 1248–1304) and Yeh-hsien Pu-hua (Esen Bukha, ?–1309), and the Naiman Nang-chia-tai (Nanggiadai).[54]

One of the most important figures among them is Tugh Tugha, the Kipchak general under whose command were placed the ethnic armies created between 1284 and 1286.[55] These armies were composed of Kharlukh, Khangli, and Kipchak troops, and their creation had the immediate effect of enhancing the prestige of these groups through the appointment of many of their leaders to high military ranks. It had also a long-range effect, as the security of the throne in the following reigns rested largely on these elite troops and on the Guard.

Before passing to the Third Phase, I should mention that there are a number of Turkish officials whose activity must be placed from the end of thirteenth to the beginning of the fourteenth century, but not later than 1330. Unfortunately, the texts concerning them do not provide specific clues as to the dates for the beginning of their careers; there is no doubt, however, that some of them, perhaps the majority, were already holding office under Khubilai, but this cannot be definitely established. They are 59 in all, distributed as follows: 32 Uighurs, 5 Kharlukhs, 11 Khanglis, 13 Kipchaks, three Öngüts, three Kereyid, and two Naimans. Of these, forty were local officials and *darughachis* and the rest chiefly military men.[56]

The Third Phase (1295–1368)

From the death of Khubilai in 1294 to the expulsion of Toghon Temür from China in 1368, we have seventy-five years of Mongol rule during which the Turks became a key factor in policy making.

For this period, not counting the Turks who had been appointed under Khubilai and who continued in office after his reign, we have the following figures: Uighur officials and scholars, 169, Kharlukhs, 19, Khanglis, 36, Kipchaks, 15, Öngüts, 43, Kereyid, 22, and Naimans, 25.

As usual, the Uighurs are by far the largest group, more than all the other groups together. Sixty percent of them are found in the local administration (among them 47 *darughachis*) and about 20 percent in the central administration. Out of 169 individuals, only 5 were military men—mostly (hereditary) members of the Guard; 46 were scholars and academicians (26 holding *chin-shih* degrees), 28 of whom also held office either in the central or the local administration.

Kharlukhs were mainly appointed to central and provincial posts (3 of them were *darughachis*); only the name of one military man is recorded. An interesting fact is that out of 19 Kharlukhs, 8 were scholars and academicians (6 of them concurrently holding other official posts), 4 of whom had *chin-shih* degrees. Of the 36 Khanglis, 7 were military men, 22 were officials in the central and local administrations (including 8 *darughachis*), and 7 were scholars and academicians of whom only one had a *chin-shih* degree. Of the 15 Kipchaks, 3 were army leaders and 9 were central government and local officials, including 8 *darughachis*. The other 3 held minor posts. Of the Öngüts, 5 were military men, 2 were in the central and 20 in the local administration, including 6 *darughachis*, 11 were scholars and academicians (6 of them concurrently holding administrative posts), 9 of whom had *chin-shih* degrees. Of the Kereyid officials, only 5 were army leaders or military men, fifteen were in the local and central administrations (including 3 *darughachis*), and 6 were scholars and academicians (only 1 a *chin-shih*), all of them concurrently holding other official posts. As for the Naimans, the same trend is discernible: out of twenty-five officials, only three were military men, eighteen were in the central and local administrations (including eight *darughachis*), and six were scholars and academicians—all *chin-shih*—4 of whom concurrently held other official posts.

These are the figures which show the continuous involvement of Turks in government affairs. But, in the Third Phase, more important than the figures is the actual role played by a number of individual Turks in these affairs and in the cultural life of the period.

Among the leading personalities of the post-Khubilai era is Yen T'ieh-mu-erh (El Temür, d.1333),[57] a Kipchak who, as a young officer, had assisted Prince Khaishan in the war against the anti-khan Khaidu and the Ögödeids in 1299. El Temür and his father, together with the Khangli official Inal Toghto[58] and his brother Asha Bukha[59]—all members of the Khaishan faction at court—played a leading part in the successful enthronement of Khaishan (Wu-tsung, 1308–1311) in 1308 against the other pretenders to the throne. In reward for their services, they were all given high-ranking posts in the government and the army.[60]

After Khaishan's death in 1311, the throne passed to his brother Ayurbarwada (Jen-tsung, 1312–1320), then in 1321 to Ayurbarwada's son Shidebala (Ying-tsung, 1321–1323), and in 1324 to Shidebala's cousin Yisün Temür (T'ai-ting 1324–1327). When Yisun Temür died in 1328, the rivalry between the lines of Ayurbarwada and Khaishan started again. The son of Khaishan, Khoshila, was backed by the Kipchak officers led by El Temür, who also had the support of Uighur, Khangli, and Öngüt officials and scholars. El Temür felt strong enough to stage a coup, which was successful. As Khoshila had died in the meantime, his brother Tugh Temür was elected emperor (Wen-tsung, 1330–1332).[61]

The outcome of this operation was that by 1330 El Temür became, as sole chancellor, the most powerful man in China after the emperor. Most of the Guard units were under his direct control. He married his sisters to imperial princes, and his daughter became the wife of Toghon Temür (Shun-ti, 1333–1368) and, therefore, empress in 1333.[62]

Thus, for a few years, the Kipchak clique dominated the court, the government, and the administration until it was suprressed by Bayan and his faction in 1335.[63]

Bayan, a Mongol of the Merkid tribe, was not only a rabid anti-Confucian but was also anti-Turk. After his dismissal in 1340, the Turks came to the fore again, and among the chief ministers in 1341 we find two Khanglis: T'ieh-mu-erh Ta-shih (Temür Tash, 1302–1347)[64] and Ting-chu (d. 1358).[65] Temür Tash was Left Chancellor until 1347. Ting-chu was director of political affairs under the Mongol chancellor T'o-t'o (Toghto, 1314/15–1356).[66] Another Khangli, Yü-shu Hu-erh-t'u-hua (Uch Khurtkha)[67] was assistant of the Right in the Secretarial Council. Soon after, another Khangli Turk, called Ha-ma (Khama),[68] was appointed director of political affairs. It was Khama who, in 1354, brought about the dismissal of Chancellor Toghto, the last great Mongol minister. The chancellorship then passed again into Khangli hands for two years. The last Turk to play an important part in Mongol politics was the famous Naiman Ch'a-han T'ieh-mu-erh (Chaghan Temür, fl. 1352–1362),[69] who was warlord of Shen-hsi and Ho-nan from 1358 to 1362. This was the swan song of Turkish power in China: the Yüan dynasty was fast nearing its end.[70]

It is clear from all this, I think, that among the Turkish groups in China the Kipchaks and the Khanglis played the leading political role, no doubt because they controlled many of the key army units and elite corps in the capital and in strategic areas. The Restoration of 1328 and the dismissal of Toghto in 1354—two major events in Yüan history—were largely the work of the Turkish faction at court. Yet Kharlukhs, Khanglis, and Öngüts became known also as scholars and patrons of letters. For the whole Yüan period (1260–1368), ten men from these groups distinguished themselves for their literary accomplishments in Chinese, their calligraphic skill, and their active support of Confucianism: men like Nai-hsien (a Kharlukh), Nao-nao (a Khangli), and Ma Tsu-ch'ang (an Öngüt).[71]

The Uighurs, as a single group, contributed more to scholarship and culture under the Mongols than any other. Most of the *se-mu* holding *chin-shih* degrees were of Uighur extraction, and from early in the dynasty, Uighur literati knowledgeable in Chinese had been translating Chinese works into Mongolian. One of the most active translators from Chinese in the first half of the fourteenth century was the Uighur academician Hu-tu-lu Tu-erh-mi-shih (Khutlugh Törmish).[72] Moreover, from the time of Khubilai onwards, the Mongol court and nobility favored Buddhism as a religion, and under their patronage translations of important Buddhist texts were carried out by learned Uighur and Tibetan monks. The names of some of them, like that of the famous Biratnashiri, are recorded in both Chinese and Mongolian sources.[73] The most celebrated translator of all, Čhos-kyi 'od-zer, who was active in the first quarter of the fourteenth century, was in all probability an Uighur, although this point is still disputed.[74] Peking was the main translation and printing center in China, and beautifully executed block prints in Uighur-Mongol and 'Phags-pa scripts were produced there.[75]

The Uighur cultural influence is also reflected in the Mongolian language, where most of the terminology relating to culture and scholarship is borrowed from Uighur Turkish; but many of these terms were no doubt borrowed by the Mongols well before Khubilai.[76] Tibetan influence was felt not only in the religious and spiritual field, and in the national script, but probably also in such fields as medicine and art.[77]

It is noteworthy that whereas the Mongol ruling class was on the whole not greatly influenced by Chinese culture, this being too sophisticated for them to appreciate, a considerable number of Uighurs became sinicized, and several of them acquired fame as scholars and literateurs in Chinese. The late Professor Ch'en Yüan (1880–1971) has dealt competently with them in his well-known study on the sinicization of people from the Western Regions in the Yüan period. In his monograph Ch'en discusses the lives and works of about thirty Turkish personalities.[78]

Conclusion

This survey shows that the Chinese sources of the Yüan period investigated so far can supply us with information, sometimes scanty, but often quite detailed, on the lives of 646 Turks from various tribes, the Uighurs being by far the largest single group (311 individuals). Of these 646 individuals, between 10 percent and 20 percent were either top-ranking officials, such as imperial advisers, heads and acting heads of the Secretarial and Presidential Councils, ministers and vice-ministers, grand judges, regional commanders, leading generals, and outstanding scholars. From this figure are excluded (1) eminent Turkish women, who are also occasionally mentioned in Chinese sources (princesses, Buddhist nuns, etc.);[79] (2) Turks whose names have been preserved, but who were neither scholars nor officials;[80] (3) individuals mentioned in the Persian sources and in the Chinese sources that I have not yet tackled, in particular a number of *wen-chi* and gazetteers.[81]

My tentative total estimate of Turks with individual records (which in many cases may be little more than their name) is between 1,000 and 1,500. This, as I said earlier, is only a fraction of the total number of Turks from different parts of Asia who lived and worked in China in the thirteenth and fourteenth centuries. Indeed, there must have been many thousands of Turks in various walks of life: soldiers, tradesmen, couriers, clerks and scribes, interpreters, teachers, minor officials and scholars, craftsmen, monks, and adventurers. The existence of this sizable body of Turks can be inferred, somewhat indirectly, from the edicts and ordinances found in the administrative codes of the period.[82]

Pending a full investigation of other "alien" groups that were active in China in the Yüan period, such as Persians and Arabs, Alans and Russians, Baya'uts, Tanguts, and (sinicized) Khitans and Jurchens, we can say, I think, that the Turks formed the backbone of the *se-mu* people in whose hands the Mongol court entrusted much of the actual management of the country. The trend to delegate the business of the court administration to Turks had already started, as we have seen, in the time of Chinggis Khan and Ögödei. It may be opportune to elaborate this point further so as to place the phenomenon in its correct historical perspective.

It is known that toward the end of Chinggis Khan's life there grew a profound dissension among his sons and heirs and the Mongol aristocracy on such important issues as the succession to the throne and the court's policy toward the conquered territories. The rivalry between Chinggis's sons and, in particular, between the lines of Ögödei and Tolui, accounted for the delay in electing the new khan after Chinggis's death in 1227, and again after Ögödei's and Güyüg's deaths in 1241 and 1248. The Toluid line eventually won, but the ensuing conflict between Khubilai and his younger brother Arigh Böke (and, later on, his cousin Khaidu) highlighted a different kind of polarization in which ideological forces played no small part.

At the core of this conflict there was, in fact, a basic opposition between two antithetic views or tendencies. One tendency was centripetal, or Mongolocentric, and attracted followers among all those elements in society that staunchly upheld the *jasagh* and Mongolian traditional values. The other was centrifugal, as it were, and favored the adoption of religious and political ideas, as well as administrative models from some of the more advanced subject countries, advocating the employment of foreigners (i.e., non-Mongols), to run the business of the administration.

These two tendencies are very evident and in open conflict during

Ögödei's reign, the conservative element (largely but not exclusively represented by the military) eager to carry out the destruction or, at any rate, the ruthless exploitation and parceling of the sedentary population of conquered territories, while at the same time the more enlightened group, composed mainly of non-Mongol officials led by bureaucrats like Yeh-lü Ch'u-ts'ai, was trying to introduce formal rules and regulations in order to rationalize the administration of the growing empire.[83]

However, there was no agreement even among the followers of these two political currents. In the course of the great Mongol campaigns in Central and Western Asia and in China, the Mongol army had been swelled by the steady incorporation of non-Mongol troops into its ranks, so that before the middle of the thirteenth century there were Turkish and Chinese generals commanding authority and respect fighting alongside Mongol generals. Now, these alien military commanders (Kipchak, Khangli, Jurchens, Chinese, etc.) and their troops did not have the world view and attitudes of the Mongol "Old Guard," that is, of men like Sübötei, and naturally tended to lean toward the side of the foreign elements at court and of the Mongol princes who supported them.[84] These foreign advisers and officials were, unfortunately , also divided and, by the end of Ögödei's reign, in open disagreement over administrative and other policies. There was a Chinese faction led by sinicized Khitans and Jurchens and closely linked with Chinese generals, scholars, and influential religious leaders in North China, and a Kereyid–Central Asian faction comprising Muslims and Nestorian Christians. Both factions were, in turn, split by internal rivalries and jealousies (Nestorian Uighurs versus Central Asian Muslims, Chinese Taoists versus Chinese Buddhists), all vying at the same time for the Mongol princes' favors.[85]

Representatives of both the Chinese and the Central Asian (largely Uighur-Nestorian) factions rallied round the Kereyid Nestorian princess Sorghakhtani and her son Khubilai when the latter was still a young prince. The rise of the Nestorian Turks and the decline of the influence of the Chinese advisers must be viewed in the light of the bitter and many-sided factional struggle that took place at Karakorum from the mid-1230s to the late 1250s and its ramifications and repercussions in North China. Khubilai's enthronement and Arigh Böke's anti-khan stand—with Karakorum (the true Mongol capital) posed against Shang-tu—were the inevitable outcome of this ideological contest in which Turks and Chinese played an important and still imperfectly known part.

The involvement of Turks in Mongol state affairs was certainly very close throughout this period, Turks being employed as chancellors, secretaries, advisers, priests, and preceptors. It was this personal involvement that brought about Chinkhai's and Khadakh's downfall and demise at the time of Möngke's election. In Khubilai's time, and later in the Yüan, the

Uighurs continued to be the cultural mentors of the Mongols although they had now to share this role with Tibetan lamas and, to a lesser extent, Confucian scholars. The Uighurs' relationship with the Mongol rulers was a classical case of symbiosis. They carried out essential politico-administrative, economic, and cultural activities for their masters and received in return protection and material advantages. Culturally more advanced than the Mongols—and more removed from the steppe than the Kipchaks, Khanglis, and Kharlukhs—they felt more keenly the attraction of Chinese mores and civilization, which many of them had already adopted during the Yüan dynasty. A similar phenomenon is noticeable among the Öngüts, who had been in even closer contact with China for a long time before the Mongols appeared on the scene.

In the post-Khubilai period other Turkish groups, the Kipchak in particular, came to the fore and became a key factor in the security of the throne. The so-called Restoration of 1328, which led to the enthronement of Tugh Temür in 1330, has been aptly described by Dardess as "to a degree ... a seizure of power by the foreign, largely Turkish elements in China officially known as *se-mu*."[86] From then on, predominantly Turkish—but other than Uighur—factions played power politics with alternate fortunes until the end of the dynasty. Further research is needed to seek the motivation, in terms of "steppe" history as opposed to "Chinese" history, of Kipchak and Khangli factionalism.[87]

Although much remains to be said, I hope that within the limits of this preliminary investigation I have been able to show that the Turks cannot be ignored when we discuss and write about the political, social, and cultural history of China in two crucial and traumatic centuries of her long history. Moreover, in view of the close interaction between Turkish-speaking people and China in previous centuries, especially during the T'ang dynasty, the "Turkish presence" in China may turn out to be an even more significant factor in Chinese history than is generally acknowledged.

APPENDIX
Mongol and Yüan Emperors

Mongol Emperors

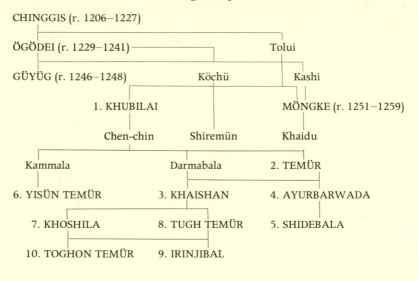

CHINGGIS (r. 1206–1227)

ÖGÖDEI (r. 1229–1241) — Tolui

GÜYÜG (r. 1246–1248)   Köchü   Kashi

1. KHUBILAI   MÖNGKE (r. 1251–1259)

Chen-chin   Shiremün   Khaidu

Kammala   Darmabala   2. TEMÜR

6. YISÜN TEMÜR   3. KHAISHAN   4. AYURBARWADA

7. KHOSHILA   8. TUGH TEMÜR   5. SHIDEBALA

10. TOGHON TEMÜR   9. IRINJIBAL

Yüan Emperors
1. KHUBILAI (r. 1260–1294)
2. TEMÜR (r. 1295–1307)
3. KHAISHAN (r. 1308–1311)
4. AYURBARWADA (r. 1312–1320)
5. SHIDEBALA (r. 1321–1323)
6. YISÜN TEMÜR (r. 1324–1327)
7. KHOSHILA (r. 1329)
8. TUGH TEMÜR (r. 1330–1332)
9. IRINJIBAL (r. 1332)
10. TOGHON TEMÜR (r. 1333–1368)

NOTES

1. These works will be referred to by giving the corresponding number in the Table of Titles, Authors and Editions of the *Index to Biographical Material in Chin and Yüan Literary Works, First Series*, by Igor de Rachewiltz and M. Nakano (Canberra, 1970), preceded by FS; idem, *Second Series*, by Igor de Rachewiltz and M. Wang (Canberra, 1972), preceded by SS; idem *Third Series* by I. de Rachewiltz and M. Wang (Canberra, 1979), preceded by TS.

2. On this controversial problem see Paul Pelliot, *La Haute Asie* [Paris, 1931], p. 25; Paul Pelliot and Louis Hambis, *Histoire des campagnes de Gengis Khan: Cheng-wou ts'in-tcheng lou*, I (Leiden, 1951) (hereafter *Campagnes*), p. 218; Paul Pelliot, *T'oung Pao (TP)* 37 (1943–1944): 36, and by the same author, *Recherches sur les chrétiens d'Asie centrale et d'extrême-orient* (Paris, 1973) (hereafter *Recherches*), pp. 243–244; S. Murayama, "Sind die Naiman Türken oder Mongolen?" *Central Asiatic Journal* 4 (1958–1959): 188–198. See also Louis Ligeti, *A mongolok titkos története* (Budapest, 1962) (hereafter Ligeti), pp. 158–159, 167; A. Róna-Tas in "Some Notes on the Terminology of Mongolian Writing," *Acta Orientalia* 18 (1965), p. 121, n. 7; and William Hung, "Three of Ch'ien Ta-hsin's Poems on Yüan History," *Harvard Journal of Asiatic Studies (HJAS)* 19 (1956): 31, n. 6.

3. See *Campagnes*, pp. 82–95.

4. See *Recherches*, p. 243; cf. J. Dauvillier in *Mélanges Cavallera* (Toulouse, 1948), pp. 307–308. For the Uighurs in the Mongol period, see the information contained in Abe Takeo, *Nishi Uiguru kokushi no kenkyū* (Kyoto, 1955), and *Gendaishi no kenkyū* (Tokyo, 1972), pp. 71–86 of the English text; A. von Gabain, *Das Leben im uigurischen Königreich von Qočo (850–1250)*, 2 vols. (Wiesbaden, 1973), passim; D. I. Tikhonov, *Khoziaistvo i obschestvennyï stroï uigurskogo gosudarstva x–xiv vv.* (Moscow-Leningrad, 1966), passim; M. Kutlukov in *Tataro-mongoly v Azii i Evrope* (Moscow, 1970), pp. 85–99. Cf. P. Pelliot, *Notes on Marco Polo*, I (Paris, 1959) (hereafter *Notes I*), pp. 161–165.

5. The sources on the Kharlukhs, Khanglis, and Kipchaks have not been fully investigated, and there is not yet a comprehensive study of these people. Information about them is scattered in various works, such as E. Bretschneider, *Mediaeval Researches from Eastern Asiatic Sources*, 2 vols. (London, 1888; rep. 1967), esp. I, pp. 301–304; II, 39–41, 68–73; W. Barthold, *Zwölf Vorlesungen über die Geschichte der Türken Mittelasiens*, 2nd ed. (Hildesheim, 1962), see the relevant entries in the Index; by the same author, *Turkestan Down to the Mongol Invasion*, 4th ed. (London, 1977), and *Four Studies on the History of Central Asia*, trans. V. and T. Minorsky, I (Leiden, 1956); *Campagnes*, esp. pp. 109–116; P. Pelliot, "À propos des Comans," *Journal Asiatique* 11, ser. 15 (1920), pp. 133–150; O. Pritsak, "Von den Karluk zu den Karachaniden," *Zeitschrift der Deutschen Morgenlandischen Gesellschaft* 101 (1951): pp. 270–300 (cf. chap. 7 in this book); *Notes I*, p. 402; J. W. Dardess, *Conquerors and Confucians: Aspects of Political Change in Late Yüan China* (New York, 1973) (hereafter *Conquerors*), p. 189, nn. 51 and 53. Cf. also the relevant entries in the *Encyclopaedia of Islam* (both the old and new editions), and in D. Sinor, *Introduction à l'étude de l'Eurasie Centrale* (Wiesbaden, 1963).

6. On the Öngüts (= Önggüts), see provisionally the references given in my translation of the *Secret History of the Mongols*, chapter 6, *Papers on Far Eastern History* 16 (1977): 59, n. 182.

7. See *Notes* I, pp. 303–305. Pelliot's monograph on Prester John which was to be included in his *Notes* s.v. "Uncan" (see ibid., p. 114) has never been found.

8. On the title Chinggis Khan, see *Notes* I, pp. 296–303.

9. On T'a-t'a T'ung-a, see Sung Lien et al., *Yüan shih* (hereafter *YS*) (Peking, 1976), 124, p. 3048; K'o Shao-min, *Hsin Yüan shih* (hereafter *HYS*) (Po-na ed, 1930), 136, 9a; T'u Chi, *Meng-wu-erh shih-chi* (hereafter *MWESC*) (Taipei, 1962 reprint), 45, 1a; P. Pelliot, "Les systèmes d'écriture en usage chez les anciens Mongols," *Asia Major* 2 (1925): 287; and "Notes sur le 'Turkestan' de M. W. Barthold," *TP* 27 (1930), p. 34, n. 1; W. Hung, "The Transmission of the Book Known as *The Secret History of the Mongols*," *HJAS* 14 (1951): 485–486; Ligeti, pp. 207–208; Róna-Tas, loc. cit., and the references contained therein. See also I. de Rachewiltz, "Personnel and Personalities in North China in the Early Mongol Period," *Journal of the Economic and Social History of the Orient* 9 (1966): 100. T'a-t'a T'ung-a has been known in the West for a long time through his biography written by J.-P. Abel Rémusat in *Nouveaux mélanges asiatiques* 2 (1829): 61–63, on the basis of the biography in the Shao Yüan-p'ing, *Yüan-shih lei-pien* (hereafter *YSLP*) (1795 ed.), 28, 2a. His name can be reconstructed as Tatar Tonga (*tonga* means "leopard; hero" in Turkish; but why Tatar?), or Tatar Tungkhagh (*tungkhagh* means "proclamation; order" in Mongolian—it could have been a nickname given to him by the Naimans with reference to his office of seal-bearer or chancellor—still, why Tatar?). In support of the latter reading there are other Chinese texts of the thirteenth and fourteenth centuries in which the name Tung-a alternates with T'ung-ha. See TS, 4/57/30a, 59/2b, and 11/(1916 ed.)/2/12b. However, Tonga was used as a personal name among Turks. There is, in any case, no justification for altering the name T'ung-a into A-t'ung as Yüan Chi has done in his article "Yüan-tai chih Wei-wu-erh" in *Yüan-shih yen-chiu lun-chi* (Taipei, 1974), pp. 192–194. T'a-t'a T'ung-a's dates of birth and death are not known.

10. This personage has a biography in *YS*, 124, 3046; cf. *HYS*, 136, 10a, and *MWESC* 45, 1b. On him, see also *Campagnes*, p. 298. He died before 1224.

11. The *gurkan* or ruler of the Karakhitay/Hsi Liao was then Chih-lu-ku (*Jirgü?; 1178–1211)*, on whom see K. A. Wittfogel and Feng Chia-sheng, *History of Chinese Society. Liao (907–1125)* (Philadelphia, 1949), pp. 621 and n. 26, 646, 652–653. On Barchukh's submission, see Juvainī, *The History of the World Conqueror*, trans. J. A. Boyle (Manchester, 1958) (hereafter Juvainī Boyle), pp. 45–46; Rashīd al-Dīn, *Sbornik letopisei*, I/2, trans. O. I. Smirnova (Moscow-Leningrad, 1952), pp. 152–154; and the *Secret History of the Mongols*, 238 (E. Haenisch, trans., *Die Geheime Geschichte der Mongolen*, 2nd ed. [Leipzig, 1948], pp. 111–112; Ligeti, p. 109). The submission of the Uighurs to the Mongols is discussed in detail by Thomas Allsen in his contribution to the present volume.

12. Jochi was probably born in 1184 (d. 1227), Chaghadai ca. 1185 (d. 1242), Ögödei in 1186 (d. 1241), and Tolui ca. 1190 (d. 1231/32). See *Campagnes*, pp. 266, 375; *Notes* I, pp. 253, 287.

13. See Ligeti, p. 160, n. 170; p. 166, n. 191.

14. A point already made by W. Barthold, *Turkestan*, p. 387. On the adoption of the Uighur script, the origin of the literary culture among the Mongols, and the role of the Naimans, the most recent discussion is found in Ch. Dalai, *Yuan gürnii üeiin Mongol* (Ulan Bator, 1973), pp. 162 ff.

15. There is a considerable literature on Chinkhai (? Chingkhai) and his descendants who held office throughout the Yüan dynasty. His major biographies are in *YS*, 120, 2963, and *HYS*, 1a, both based on material contained in his funerary inscription composed by Hsü Yu-jen (1287–1364). On him, see also Juvainī, p. 737a; Rashīd al-Dīn, *The Successors of Genghis Khan*, trans. J. A. Boyle (New York and London, 1971) (hereafter *Successors*), p. 353b; A. van den Wyngaert, *Sinica Franciscana*, I (Quaracchi-Firenze, 1929) (hereafter *Sinica Franciscana*), pp. 119, 123; C. Dawson, ed., *The Mongol Mission* (New York, 1955), pp. xxiv, 63, 66–67; A. Waley, trans., *The Travels of an Alchemist* (London, 1931), pp. 33–38; (see, however, P. Pelliot in *TP* 28 [1931]: 417–419, and I. de Rachewiltz, "Sino-Mongol Culture Contacts in the XIII Century. A Study on Yeh-lü Ch'u-ts'ai," *Ph.D. dissertation, Australian National University*, Canberra, 1960, pp. 287–291, n. 149); P. Pelliot, "Chrétiens d'Asie centrale et d'extrême-orient," *TP* 15 (1914) (hereafter "Chrétiens"): 628–629; *Recherches*, p. 246; *Notes on Marco Polo*, II (Paris, 1963), p. 825; F. W. Cleaves in *HJAS* 14 (1951): 495, 501 and n. 23; 18 (1955): 397–398 and n. 238, 407–409; W. Hung in *HJAS* 14 (1951): 484–485; Ligeti, p. 208; Róna-Tas, loc. cit.; I. de Rachewiltz, "Personnel and Personalities," pp. 100–101, n. 4. The name Sinkhay or Singhay found in the Uighur document studies by J. Hamilton in *Turcica* 1 (1969): 26–52 (see p. 50), seems to be the Turkish form of Chinkhai. Yüan Chi, op. cit., p. 189, repeats the old error of making Chinkhai an Uighur.

16. The Uighurs were led by Barchukh Art Tegin, as we have already seen. As for the Öngüts, their leader Alakhush Tigit Khuri had pledged his support to Chinggis Khan as early as 1204, and the alliance was sealed with the marriage of Alakhush with Chinggis's daughter Alakhai Begi. The intermarriage between Mongol princesses and Öngüt princes continued under subsequent reigns, so that the Öngüt ruler was regularly called "imperial son-in-law" (Chin. *fu-ma*; Mong. *güregen*). See *YS*, 118, 2924; "Chrétiens," pp. 629–631; *Recherches*, pp. 261–267; and I. de Rachewiltz in *Papers on Far Eastern History* 16 (1977): 59, n. 182, for further references. Barchukh had also married a daughter of Chinggis Khan. See *YS*, 109, 2760; cf., however, *Recherches*, p. 128, and Abe, *Gendaishi*, p. 71. For the relations between the Uighurs and the Mongol court, see also J. W. Dardess, "From Mongol Empire to Yüan Dynasty: Changing Forms of Imperial Rule in Mongolia and Central Asia," *Monumenta Serica* 30 (1972–1973): 128, 132, 139–140; for the Öngüts and the Mongol court, see ibid., pp. 146–147. The article by Yüan Chi cited earlier (nn. 9 and 15) is rather superficial and inaccurate. A useful survey with genealogical tables of Uighur personalities (based largely on those of Ch'ien Ta-hsin and T'u Chi) is Li Fu-t'ung's article "Wei-wu-erh-jen tui-yü Yüan-ch'ao chien-kuo chih kung-hsien" in Sung Hsi (ed.), *Shih-hsüeh lun-chi* (Taipei, 1977), pp. 328–398.

17. See *Conquerors*, pp. 42–43; *Notes* I, p. 304. On the relationship between the first Mongol rulers and the Kipchaks, see the remarks of G. A. Fedorov-Davydov in *Obshchestvennyi stroi Zolotoï Ordy* (Moscow, 1973), pp. 31 ff.

18. On the political and economic changes in Mongolia and North China in the years 1229–1250, there is now a fairly large literature. One should mention in particular the works of Abe Takeo, Hok-lam Chan, E. Haenisch, Hsiao Ch'i-ch'ing, Iwamura Shinobu, S. Jagchid, Meng Ssu-ming, N. C. Munkuev, Murakami Masatsugu, Otagi Matsuo, H. F. Schurmann, Sun K'o-k'uan, Wang Kuo-wei, Yanai Watari, Yao Ts'ung-wu; the unpublished works of Thomas Allsen and Paul Buell,

and my own contributions, in particular my (unpublished) doctoral dissertation. With regard to the organization of the *ortakh*, there is no single comprehensive study of this important institution. See, provisionally, Weng Tu-chien in *Yen-ching hsüeh-pao* 29 (1941): 201–218; Murakami Masatsugu in *Tōhō gakuhō* 13, 1 (1942): 143–196; Sun K'o-k'uan, *Meng-ku Han-chün yü Han wen-hua yen-chiu* (Taipei, 1958), pp. 173–180; Hsiao Ch'i-ch'ing, *Hsi-yü-jen yü Yüan-ch'u cheng-chih* (Taipei, 1966), passim; and Yukio Yamane and Ritsuko Ohshima, *A Classified Bibliography of Articles and Books Concerning the Yüan Period in Japanese and Chinese* (Tokyo, 1971), nos. 595–604, for further references. On the term *ortakh* (Mong. *ortokh* through labialization), see G. Doerfer, *Türkische und mongolische Elemente im Neupersischen*, I–IV (Wiesbaden, 1963–1975) (hereafter Doerfer), no. 446; G. Clauson, *An Etymological Dictionary of Pre-Thirteenth Century Turkish* (Oxford, 1972), pp. 205a-b.

19. References to *ortokhchi* (Chin. *wo-t'o-ch'ih*), i.e., members of the *ortakh*, in Chinese sources are extremely rare. See Tamura Jitsuzō, *Genshi goi shūsei*, I–III (Kyoto, 1961–1963), p. 2247a; TS, 11/1/2b; and the *Indexes to the Yüan-tien-chang* (*Gentenshō sakuin-kō*), published by the Jimbun Kagaku Kenkyūjo, Kyoto University, IV (1961), p. 2b.

20. On the role of the *darughachi*, see the articles by Yao Ts'ung-wu in *Wen shih che hsüeh-pao* 12 (1963): 1–20, and S. Jagchid, ibid., 13 (1964): 293–441; Yang P'ei-kuei, *Yüan-tai ti-fang cheng-fu* (Taipei, 1975), passim; the (unpublished) dissertation of P. D. Buell, "Tribe, *Qan*, and *Ulus* in Early Mongol China: Some Prolegomena to Yüan History" (University of Washington, 1977), pp. 32–34, 87 ff.; I. de Rachewiltz, "Personnel and Personalities," pp. 135–136, 140; and the further references in Yamane and Ohshima, op. cit., nos. 823–828. On the terms *darugha* and *darughachi*, see Doerfer, no. 193; F. W. Cleaves in *Harvard Journal of Asiatic Studies* 16 (1953): 237–255. On the problem of "civil" (*wen*) versus "military" (*wu*) in the Yüan period, see below, n. 46.

21. On Sologhai ("Left-handed"), see YS, 124, 3049; *MWESC*, 45, 1b.

22. On "Elîshû," see YS, 135, 3271; *HYS*, 136, 12b. On his name, see *Recherches*, p. 247. On the connotations of the Mongol term *bichigechi* (*bichēchi*), which derives from Turkish *bitigchi bitikchi*, *bitkechi* "scribe-secretary, minister," see de Rachewiltz, "Personnel and Personalities," pp. 100–102; Doerfer, no. 717; Róna-Tas, ibid., p. 127. In the Chinese sources there are also references to "senior" (*chang*) *bichigechi* (see, e.g., the biographies of Shiban and Ch'ieh-lieh-ko, below, nn. 24 and 34); I wonder whether this title corresponds to Turkish *ulugh bitkechi*, "great secretary."

23. See *HYS*, 192, 8b; *MWESC*, 116, 7a.

24. See YS, 134, 3245; *HYS*, 136, 18a; *MWESC*, 45, 12a. On his name, see *Recherches*, p. 247. His father, Ch'üeh-li-pieh Wo-ch'ih, bacame *darughachi* of K'un-lü ch'eng—one of the earliest such officials appointed by Chinggis Khan in Central Asia.

25. See *HYS*, 150, 7b; *MWESC*, 58, 1a. On his name, see *Recherches*, p. 250, n. 3.

26. One of them was Pa-ssu Hu-tu (? Bars Khut "Tiger Happiness"), the grandfather of T'o-li-shih-kuan, who achieved distinction as military leader under Khubilai. See YS, 133, 3228; *HYS*, 154, 8b; *MWESC*, 47, 4a.

27. Of these local officials one, Hsiao-yün-shih T'o-hu-lien (= lin), Sewinch Toghril, was appointed as *jarghuchi* or judge of Chen-ting; see his biography in YS,

134, 3262; another, Yüeh-chü-lien-ch'ih Hai-ya (Ögrünch Khaya), began his career under Möngke and rose to be associate director of political affairs (*ts'an-chih cheng-shih*) in the Ssu-ch'uan Regional Secretariat (*hsing-chung shu-sheng*) under Khubilai. See *YS*, 135, 3279. Among the *darughachis* four deserve special mention: (1) Pu-lu Hai-ya (? Bu[i]rukh Khaya, 1197–1265), an educated Uighur who under Ögödei became *darughachi* of the important Chen-ting district, then commissioner of all the Surveillance Bureaus (*lien-fang shih*) south of Yen-ching and, soon after, *jarghuchi*. See *YS*, 125, 3070; Su T'ien-chüeh *Kuo-ch'ao ming-ch'en shih-lüeh* (hereafter *KCMCSO*) (1335 ed.), 7, 11b, 12a; *HYS*, 155, 8a; *MWESC*, 79, 1a. (2) Yüeh-lin T'ieh-mu-erh (Eren Temür), who, before his appointment to the key post of general (*tu*) military and civil *darughachi*, i.e., governor general (see below, n. 33), of Ho-nan and other places, had been the tutor of the sons of Chinggis's younger brother Temüge Otchigin. See *YS*, 124, 3049; FS, 7/25/1b, 39/17b, and 16/11/5b, 6a, 8a; *HYS*, 136, 2a; *MWESC*, 45, 3A. (3) Sa-chi-ssu (Sa[r]gis, i.e., Serge), Eren Temür's younger cousin, who began his career as secretary (*bichigechi*) of Temüge Otchigin, then became his principal tutor, eventually rising to be one of the overlords (*hsing-sheng tu-tu*) of Shan-tung and *darughachi* of I-tu. On him, see *YS*, 134, 3243; *HYS*, 136, 5a; *MWESC*, 45, 6a. He had numerous descendants, among them Yüeh-chu (1280–1332), on whom see Ch'en Yüan, *Western and Central Asian in China Under the Mongols: Their Transformation into Chinese*, trans. Ch'ien Hsing-hai and L. C. Goodrich (Los Angeles, 1966) (hereafter Ch'en), pp. 238–239. (4) Meng-su-ssu (transformed into Mo-se-ssu in SS, 40/6/9a). His Turkish name was Mungsuz, "Carefree." He was an educated Uighur from Besh Balikh who became a trusted adviser to Chinggis Khan and administrator of Tolui's fief in Chen-ting; he was appointed *darughachi* under Möngke and *jarghuchi* under Khubilai. He was one of the members of Khubilai's entourage who encouraged him to become emperor in 1260. He died in 1267. We shall return to him later. On him, see *YS*, 124, 3059; *HYS*, 136, 13b; *MWESC*, 45, 11a; 154, 12a; and the *Ch'eng Hsüeh-lou wen-chi* (Ýüan-tai chen-pen wen-chi ed.; Taipei, 1970), 6, 5b, which is a much better edition than *SS*, 40. In the interesting fragments of the Chinese-Uighur block print from Turfan, now in the Museum für Indische Kunst in Berlin-Dahlem, which were recently published by A. von Gabain ("Ein chinesisch-uigurischer Blockdruck," *Tractata Altaica* [Wiesbaden, 1976], pp. 203–210), there is a "Familienbild" of chancellor Meng-su (Mungsu[z]) with the names of 47 members of his family. See H. Franke, "A Sino-Uighur Family Portrait: Notes on a Woodcut from Turfan," *Canada-Mongolia Review* 4 (1978): 33–40. Among the local officials and administrators I have included also Lien Hsi-hsien (1231–1280) from Besh Balikh, son of Buirukh Khaya, who began his career under Khubilai when the latter was still a prince. He was in Khubilai's entourage and in 1254 was appointed by him pacification commissioner (*hsüan-fu shih*) for the region of Peking. He subsequently rose to be assistant of the Right (*yu-ch'eng*) in the Secretarial Council. On him, see *YS*, 126, 3085; FS, 6/65/1a and 20/5/45b; *HYS*, 155, 9b; *MWESC*, 79, 1a; Ch'en, p. 316b.

28. An-tsang, one of the earliest Yüan translators and encyclopaedic men, was appointed by Khubilai as executive Hanlin academician (*hsüeh-shih ch'eng-chih*). Strangely enough, there is no biography of him in the *YS*. See, however, *HYS*, 192, 1a; *MWESC*, 118, 1a; and SS, 40/9/5a. Cf. also W. Fuchs, "Analecta zur mongolis-

chen Uebersetzungsliteratur der Yüan-Zeit" in *Monumenta Serica* 11 (1946) (hereafter Fuchs): 37, 41–43.

29. On Arigh Khaya from Besh Balikh, one of the leading generals in the war against Sung and overlord of Hu-kuang (Hunan and Hupeh), see *YS*, 128, 3124; FS, 5/13/12a, 6/59/1a, and 16/9/37b; *HYS*, 160, 1a; *MWESC*, 92, 1a; Ch'en, pp. 82–83, 179. On Esen Nai, who served in the administrations of Turfan, Yün-nan, Chianghsi, and Shen-hsi, mainly as director of political affairs (*p'ing-chang cheng-shih*), see *YS*, 133, 3227; *HYS*, 154, 7b; *MWESC*, 80, 6b. On Ai-ch'üan, see below, n. 41. On Sorghakhtani Beki, see below, n. 40.

30. Mi-li Huo-che (? Mir Khoja, ?–1260), on whom see *YS*, 133, 3226; *KCMCSL*, 7, 15a–b; *MWESC*, 65, 7a; and Chan-ch'e Pa-tu-erh (? Jangi Bātur), on whom see *YS*, 123, 3031; *HYS*, 152, 4a; *MWESC*, 91, 9b. Both were appointed *darughachi* in myriarch Administrations (*wan-hu fu*), and their role is not clear.

31. See above, n. 15.

32. Bolghai is known in the Chinese sources as Po-lu-ho (Bolgha), Pu-lu-hua (Bulgha), and Pu-lu-huan (Bulghan), as well as in the aberrant form Pu-erh-ha (*Burgha) of the Ch'ien-lung revisors. In the Latin and Persian sources his name alternates Bolgai/Bulghai/Bulgha. On him, see FS, 5/13/7a; *HYS*, 133, 9b; *MWESC*, 50, 4b; *Sinica Franciscana*, p. 584 (cf. Dawson, *The Mongol Mission*, p. 240); Juvainī Boyle, p. 736a; *Successors*, p. 352b. Cf. "Chrétiens," p. 629; *Recherches*, p. 287.

33. They were Su-ko, i.e., Süke (under Ögödei), and his son Hu-lan (Khulan), who inherited Süke's office. See *YS*, 124, 3051–3; *MWESC*, 43, 2b–3b. I think that "great" (*ta*) *darughachi* is synonymous with "general" (*tu*) *darughachi*, corresponding to a governor general of a large district, a term frequently assimilated in this period to *hsing-sheng* "regional commander" and *liu-shou* "vice-regent" (in a district or regional capital). See I. de Rachewiltz, "Personnel and Personalities," pp. 135, n. 3; 137, n. 2. Cf. Buell, "Tribe, *Qan*, and *Ulus*," pp. 126ff.

34. Ch'ieh-lieh-ko (? Keage), on whom see *HYS*, 133, 9b; *MWESC*, 50, 4b; and P'u-lan-hsi (Buralki), on whom see *YS*, 122, 3015; *HYS*, 130, 7a.

35. Beg Bukha was the grandfather of T'ieh-lien (Tering), who has a biography in *YS*, 134, 3247.

36. On him, see *YS*, 123, 3036; *HYS*, 152, 1b; *MWESC*, 84, 11b.

37. Other important personages have not been included in this survey because their ethnic origin is not clear, even though it is almost certain that they were of Turkish origin. The most notable of them is Khadakh, the Nestorian colleague of Chinkhai known to us through the Persian authors and John of Pian di Carpine's account, who was in all likelihood a Kereyid. (A homonymous person, Khadakh Ba'atur, is mentioned in 185 of the *Secret History*; he was the leader of the Jirgins, a subtribe of the Kereyid.) This minister of Güyüg is mentioned only once in the YS (3, 45) among the people who perished in the purges following the election of Möngke in 1251. His name is transcribed as Ha-ta/Ho-ta (Khada[kh]). He is probably the "great judge" (*yeke jarghuchi*) Ho-ta mentioned briefly in *Ch'eng Hsüeh-lou wen-chi*, 25, 17b, and FS, 5/19/10b. On Khadakh, see *Sinica Franciscana*, p. 123 (cf. Dawson, op. cit., pp. 66–67); Juvainī Boyle, p. 751b; *Successors*, p. 364a. Cf. also "Chrétiens," pp. 628–629. In addition to the above, there are Turks holding positions at the Mongol court who are mentioned in the Persian sources, but whom I have not included in this survey, such as the Khangli soothsayer in Ögödei's

service (Juvainī Boyle, p. 193; cf. J. A. Boyle in *Folklore* 83 [1972]: 190).

38. As in the case of Shiban, Ögrünch Khaya, Sargis, Yüeh-erh-ssu-man, An-tsang, Chih-li-hua-t'ai (Jirkhatai), Wang Liang-ch'en, Wang Wei-cheng, Ma Yüeh-ho-nai (Yuhumai), and, in particular, Arigh Khaya, Lien Hsi-hsien, and Esen Nai. In fact, the last three should properly have been listed among the Uighur officials of the Second Phase; however, they did begin their careers under Khubilai's auspices before 1260.

39. The year of Tolui's death is not known with certainty, but it appears that he died in Mongolia in 1232. See F. W. Cleaves in *HJAS* 11 (1948): 318, n. 18.

40. See Juvainī Boyle, p. 550; *Successors*, p. 168. On Sorghakhtani, see Morris Rossabi's "Khubilai Khan and the Women in His Family," in *Sino-Mongolica: Festschrift für Herbert Franke*, ed. W. Bauer (Wiesbaden, 1979), pp. 153–180.

41. On all these questions, see Juvainī Boyle, pp. 550–553, 572 and n. 69, 605; *Successors*, pp. 168–171, 188, 222; *Sinica Franciscana*, pp. 66, 245, 261, 287–289 (cf. Dawson, op. cit., pp. 26, 163, 175, 185–186); "Chrétiens," pp. 628–629; *Recherches*, pp. 66–67. The Chinese sources mention also Turks given by Möngke to his mother, who employed them in various capacities; among them are the Uighur Ai-ch'üan, who was held in great consideration and was transferred to Sorghakhtani's fief in Chen-ting (*HYS*, 192, 9b; *MWESC*, 118, 10b), and the Khangli Ha-shih Po-yao (Khashi Boyo?), who became an official in charge of her herds (*YS*, 134 3263; *HYS*, 199, 6a; *MWESC*, 123, 1a). Both have been included among the Turks of the First Phase. Other Turks in Tolui's service, like Sewinch Toghrïl and Mungsuz, were also employed in the Chen-ting administration. See above, n. 27.

42. See *Successors*, pp. 248–252; *YS*, 4, 61–63; *MWESC*, 7, 2a–3b; *NOTES* I, p. 566.

43. *YS*, 124, 3059. The arguments put forth by Mungsuz were that the throne should not be left vacant for too long and that Khubilai was the senior among the imperial princes and the wisest. From this passage, we can infer that Khubilai had already a reputation for wisdom as early as 1260 and that his epithet of *sechen* probably goes back to this time.

44. See I. de Rachewiltz and H.L. Chan (eds.), *Yüan Personalities* (in preparation).

45. As with other important aspects of Yüan society, a comprehensive investigation of the *se-mu* is long overdue. See, provisionally, Yanai Watari, *Mōkoshi kenkyū* (Tokyo, 1930; rep. 1966), pp. 263–362; Meng Ssu-ming, *Yüan-tai she-hui chieh-chi chih-tu* (Lung-men shu-tien rep., 1967), passim; the relevant articles listed in Yamane and Ohshima, op. cit., nos. 697–724, and Morris Rossabi, "The Muslims in the Early Yüan Dynasty," in John Langlois (ed.), *China Under Mongol Rule* (Princeton, 1981), pp. 257–295.

46. It goes without saying that offices were often cumulative and that in the Yüan it is sometimes difficult to separate a military office from a purely civil one; also, officials could move easily from a civil to a military post and vice versa. This reflects the basic lack of distinction between *wen* and *wu* in the Mongol society of the time, where *wen* was generally in the service of *wu* and, more often than not, a function of it. This phenomenon is well illustrated by the "civil" functions of members of the Guard (*keshig*)—itself the core of the Mongol military organization—and by the institution of *darughachis* in *wan-hu fu* and *ch'ien-hu fu*

(i.e., Myriarch's and Chiliarch's administrations respectively), in the conquered territory. Moreover, some *darughachis* were both "military and civil" (*chün-min*) as, e.g., Eren Temür, on whom see above, n. 27. There are numerous references to this problem and observations by contemporaries in the Chinese sources. This frequent lack of distinction between *wen* and *wu* must constantly be borne in mind when classifying an official. In the present investigation I have defined a person as being a "military man" when his main duties as recorded in our sources were concerned (1) with the actual leadership of troops (as, e.g., a general in one of the Mongol armies); (2) with membership of the Guard *tout court*, i.e., when his duties in the Guard are not specified; (3) with activity of an obvious military nature in the capital or in the provincial administration. Although I have included *darughachis* among local officials, I always mention their number separately in view of the ambiguous character of their functions. On this problem, see Murakami Masatsugu in *Tōhō-gakuhō* 11 (1940): 348–359; Yanai Watari, op. cit., pp. 314–317; Honda Minobu in *Shigaku zasshi* 62 (1953): 701–726; and I. de Rachewiltz, "Personnel and Personalities," pp. 139–140.

47. Arghun Sali (or Sari "Yellow"?) was a native of Besh Balikh who became a multilingual secretary and adviser to the Mongol court, especially on matters concerning the appointment of foreign scholars and education. He eventually rose to director of political affairs in the Secretarial Council. On him, see *YS*, 130, 3174; *FS*, 14/7/12a; *HYS*, 197, 3b; *MWESC*, 118, 2b; Ch'en, pp. 64–67, 81; Louis Ligeti in *Ural-Altaische Jahrbucher* 33 (1961): 235–240. On Ashigh Temür, son of Mungsuz and likewise a native of Besh-Balikh, see SS, 40/7/2b; *HYS*, 136, 14b, 15a; *MWESC*, 45, 12a. He served with distinction as judge in the Department of Military Affairs (*shu-mi yüan*) and as Hanlin academician, and held other important posts. On Sengge (Sang-ko), see *YS*, 205, 4570, et passim; *HYS*, 223, 13a; *Successors*, pp. 293, 297; H. Franke, "Sen-ge: Das Leben eines uigurischen Staatsbeamten zur Zeit Chubilai's dargestellt nach Kap. 205 der Yüan-Annalen" in *Sinica* 17 (1942): 90–113, and in "Ahmed: Ein Beitrag zur Wirtschaftsgeschichte Chinas unter Qubilai," *Oriens* I (1948): 223 and n.; 226; and, by the same author, *Geld und Wirtschaft in China unter der Mongolen-Herrschaft. Beiträge zur Wirtschafts-geschichte der Yüan-Zeit* (Leipzig, 1949), pp. 77 and n. 6. See also P. Demiéville in *Oriente Poliano* (Rome, 1957), pp. 212–214. Sengge has occasionally been referred to as a Tibetan because of his name (Tib. Sen-ge from Skr. *simha* "lion"); however, Uighurs also bore this name; see, e.g., the Sengge mentioned in the Uighur docu-ment studied by P. Zieme in *Altorientalische Forschungen* V, *Schriften zur Geschichte und Kultur des alten Oriens* (Berlin, 1977), p. 161 and n. 53. See L. Petech's essay, chap. 7 in this volume, for another view of Sengge. Sengge is mentioned in many *wen-chi* of the Yüan period, and a biography of this important man is being prepared by the Yüan Biographical Project in Canberra. With regard to the Uighurs' activity in this period it should be noted that as a result of Khaidu's rebellion and his military compaigns in East Turkestan (1275–1290), many Uighur families had left their homeland and settled in China, eventually creating something of a refugee problem.

48. La-chen (Lachin), who was director of political affairs in the Secretarial Council and, concurrently, executive academician. He was proficient in both Uighur and Mongolian. On him, see *YS*, 134, 3263; *MWESC*, 45, 10a. The other eight

were (1) A-shih T'ieh-mu-erh (Ashigh Temür, 1250–1309), teacher of Uighur to Kammala (1263–1302, eldest son of Chen-chin), who was appointed Hanlin academician in 1289. On him, see SS 40/7/4a; *HYS*, 136, 14b; *MWESC*, 45, 12a. (2) Lien Hsi-kung, the brother of Lien Hsi-hsien. See FS, 8/6b. (3) Ta-ch'eng-tu (1228–1299) of Besh Balikh, appointed Hanlin academician in 1295. See SS 40/8/13a; *HYS*, 192, 2b; *MWESC*, 118, 2a. (4) Ta-tz'u-tu, son of Ta-ch'eng-tu. See FS, 7/43/11a; SS, 40/8/20b; *MWESC*, 118, 2a. (5) T'ang Jen-tsu (1249–1301). See *YS*, 134, 3253; *HYS*, 192, 3b; *MWESC*, 118, 7b. (6) Wen-shu-nu. See FS, 9/15/5a; *MWESC*, 154, 30a. (7) Yeh-hsien (Esen), son of Wen-shu-nu. See FS, 9/15/4a. (8) Chia-lu-na-ta-ssu (Karuṇādās[a]; d. 1311). See *YS*, 134, 3260. On An-tsang, see above, n. 28.

49. Chen-chin (1243–1286),Khubilai's second son and heir apparent (1273), had both Chinese and Uighur teachers and assistants. Among the latter were (1) Ta-ch'eng-tu (see above, n. 48), who besides being Chen-chin's assistant was also the teacher of Khubilai's grandson Ananda. (2) Ta-li-tu, the son of Ta-ch'eng-tu, who acted as adviser on literature to Chen-chin; see SS, 40/8/14a. (3) T'ang Chi, T'ang Jen-tsu's father (see n. 48), who was Chen-chin's secretary (*bichigechi*); see *YS*, 134, 3253. and (4) Yeh-li Pu-hua (? El Bukha), Chen-chin's personal attendant, on whom see SS, 6/4/14a. To these Uighur instructors we must add the above-mentioned Ashigh Temür (n. 48), teacher of Kammala.

50. Besides An-tsang, the following Uighur scholars were active as translators in Khubilai's time: (1) Karuṇādāsa (see above, n. 48), who knew Sanskrit and other languages and translated Sanskrit texts into Uighur (or into Mongolian in Uighur script ?). (2) Chieh-shih-mi-erh (1253–1315) from Besh Balikh, on whom see *HYS*, 192, 5a; *MWESC*, 118, 6a; TS, 33/64/4a. (3) Ta-ch'eng-tu, on whom see above, n. 48. There was also Ch'i-t'ai Sa-li (Khitai Sali), the father of Arghun Sali, who was known as a Buddhist scholar and as a religious leader, but not as a translator. On him see *YS*, 130, 3174; L. Ligeti in *Ural-Altaische Jahrbücher* 33 (1961): 235–240.

51. The Uighur Hanlin academician Wen-shu-nu (see above, n. 48), who helped 'Phags-pa Lama (1239–1280) in devising the new script ca. 1269. See FS, 9/15/4a. It is, therefore, tempting to suggest that the adoption of Uighur features for the square script, such as its vertical direction, may have been prompted by Wen-shu-nu, the Tibetan script on which the square script is based being, as is known, written horizontally. On 'Phags-pa's "creation" of the national script, see Ligeti in this volume. As has been noted by other scholars, the role played by 'Phags-pa in devising the script may have been exaggerated. See Louis Ligeti in *Acta Orientalia* 13 (1961): 209.

52. The distribution of personnel is the following: Kharlukhs: 3 military, 7 central and local administration (3 *darughachis*); Khanglis: 3 military, 9 central and local administration (3 *darughachis*); Kipchaks: 8 military, 4 central and local administration (3 *darughachis*); Öngüts: 13 military, 14 central and local administration (6 *darughachis*), 3 scholars and academicians; Kereyid: 3 military, 11 central and local administration (2 *darughachis*); Naimans: 4 military, 8 central and local administration (5 *darughachis*).

53. Chao Shih-yen held various high offices in the central and provincial administration under Khubilai and in the following reigns rose to Hanlin academician and director of political affairs. On him, see *YS*, 180, 4163; SS, 16/95/2a and 40/5/8b; *HYS*, 149, 6a; *MWESC*, 135, 12a; Ch'en, p. 307b; Fuchs, p. 52. The two

post-1294 academicians were the Kharkukh Mainu and the Kereyid Dashman, on whom see below, n. 54.

54. On the Kharlukhs Dashman and Mainu, both high officials in the central and provincial administration respectively, see FS, 7/24/12a, 13b, 18b; HYS, 178, 6b; MWESC, 128, 3a. Mainu was an educated man who began his career under Khubilai as steward (bawurchi) and ended it under Toghon Temür as Hanlin academician. As an example of cultural assimilation he deserves further study. Asha Bukha was a close adviser to Khubilai and director of political affairs in the Secretarial Council. On him, see YS, 136, 3295; SS, 7/no. 45; HYS, 200, 1a; MWESC, 121, 4b; 155, 19a. Inal Toghto, alias K'ang-li (Khangli) Toghto, rose to Left Chancellor (tso ch'eng-hsiang) in the Secretarial Council. On him, see YS, 138, 3321; FS, 7/28/1a; HYS, 200, 3b; MWESC, 121, 4a. On Tugh Tugha and his son, see below, n. 55. The Kereyid Dashman was put in charge of the Bureau of Foreign Trade and Ortakh Administration (ch'üan-fu ssu) and was also Minister of Revenue (hu-pu shang-shu); later (1299) he was appointed executive academician. On him, see FS, 5/13/7a; HYS, 133, 11b; MWESC, 50, 7b. Esen Bukha started his career as preceptor to the heir apparent (Chen-chin) and later became a high official in the Regional Secretarial Councils of Yün-nan and Hu-kuang. On him, see YS, 134, 3266; HYS, 133, 10a; MWESC, 50, 5b. Nanggiadai was one of the leading generals in the final campaign against Sung. On him see YS, 131, 3184; HYS, 161, 11a; MWESC, 116, 5a.

55. On Tugh Tugha, see YS, 128, 3131; FS, 7/31/3b and 12/23/7a–14a; SS, 56/3/17a; KCMCSL, 3, 5b; HYS, 179, 1a; MWESC, 102, 1a; Campagnes, p. 97. His son Chong'ur was director of political affairs and after Tugh Tugha's death in 1297 inherited his rank of chief of the Kipchak Army. On him, see YS, 128, 3135; HYS, 179, 4a; MWESC, 102, 4b. On both these personages, see Conquerors, pp. 244b and 238b. For the establishment of the ethnic armies, see YS, 128, 3133 (s.a. 1286, 1287). On the establishment of the Kipchak Army, already approved by Khubilai in 1284, see YS, 13, 266 (s.a. 1284), and 14, 288 (s.a. 1286). Cf. Campagnes, p. 109, where Pelliot gives the date of 1284 for the establishment of both the Khangli and Kipchak armies. The Kipchak Army was enlarged in 1291. The Khangli Army is mentioned in YS, 23, 511 (s.a. 1309). On these forces, see also Conquerors, pp. 17, 43, 47, 190, n. 61; G. Mangold, Das Militärwesen in China unter der Mongolen-Herrschaft (Bamberg, 1971), pp. 23–25, and Hsiao Ch'i-ch'ing, The Military Establishment of the Yuan Dynasty (Cambridge, Mass., 1978), pp. 46–47, 99–100.

56. The following is a more detailed breakdown of figures: Uighurs: 3 military, 24 central and local administration (9 darughachis), 3 academicians, 2 others; Kharlukhs: 4 military, 1 darughachi; Khanglis: 2 military, 7 central and local administration (2 darughachis), 1 academician, 2 others; Kipchaks: 6 military, 7 central and local administration (4 darughachis); Öngüts: 3 local administration (2 darughachis); Kereyid: 3 local administration (2 darughachis); Naimans: 2 military. The total number of local officials in the above groups was 40, of whom 20 were darughachis.

57. On El Temür, see YS, 138, 3326; FS, 6/26/7a, 18b; SS, 36/14/6b; TS, 113/19/27a; HYS, 179, 7a; MWESC, 126, 1a; Ch'en, p. 189 and n. 19; Fuchs, pp. 52, 61.

58. On Inal Toghto, see above, n. 54.

59. On Asha Bukha, see above, n. 54.

60. See *Conquerors*, pp. 10–11, 16–17.

61. See *Conquerors*, pp. 26–27, 39–46, and 189–190, n. 54.

62. See *Conquerors*, pp. 46–50.

63. On Bayan, see *YS*, 138, 3335; *HYS*, 224, 8a; *MWESC*, 126, 9a.

64. On Temür Tash, see *YS*, 140, 3372; FS, 7/8/10b, 28/1a; *HYS*, 200, 7a; *MWESC*, 121, 11a; 127, 2b.

65. On Ting-chu, see *HYS*, 210, 6a; *MWESC*, 155, 24a.

66. On Chancellor Toghto, see *YS*, 138, 3341; FS, 7/26/20a and 16/13/1a, 14/4a; Chang Chu, *Shui-an chi* (Ssu-k'u ch'üan-shu chen-pen ed., 5th ser.), 4, 3a; *HYS*, 209, 1a; *MWESC*, 125, 1a.

67. On Üch Khurtkha, see *MWESC*, 121, 12a.

68. On Khama, see *YS*, 205, 4851; *YSLP*, 16, 19b; T'ao Tsung-i, *Nan-ts'un Cho-keng lu* (Ssu-pu ts'ung-k'an ed.), 15, 4a; *HYS*, 224, 11a; *MWESC*, 155, 23b; H. Schulte-Uffelage, *Das Keng-shen wai-shih. Eine Quelle zur späten Mongolenzeit* (Berlin, 1963), p. 128 (s.v. Ha-ma).

69. On Chaghan Temür, see *YS*, 141, 3384; *HYS*, 220, 1a; *MWESC*, 129, 4a.

70. On all these events and their background, see Dardess's lucid exposition in *Conquerors*, especially pp. 56, 70, 76, 84, 96, 120–121, 147, and 203, n. 39.

71. On Nai-hsien, see Ch'en, p. 318b; by the same author, "Shih-ssu shih-chi Nan-E-jen chih Han-wen-hsüeh," in *Chung-kuo wen-hsüeh yen-chiu* (1927, 2), Chung-kuo wen-hsüeh yen-chiu she rep. (ed. Cheng Chen-to, Hong Kong, 1963), pp. 667–671. On Nao-nao (1295–1345), see Ch'en, p. 319a; "Shih-ssu . . . ," pp. 672–674; F. W. Cleaves in *HJAS* 10 (1947): 1–12. On Ma Tsu-ch'ang (1279–1338), see Ch'en, p. 318a; Fuchs, p. 52. The other seven were the Kharlukh Pai-yen (Bayan) Shih-sheng (1295–1348), on whom see Ch'en, p. 320a; the Khanglis Pu-hu-mu (1255–1300), on whom see Ch'en, p. 320a, and "Shih-ssu . . . ," pp. 671–672; Hui-hui (1283–1333), on whom see Ch'en, p. 314a, and "Shih-ssu . . . ," p. 672; Chin Yüan-su, alias Chin Ha-la (Khara), on whom see Ch'en, p. 309b; and Ch'ing-t'ung (d. 1368), on whom see Ch'en, p. 310; and the Öngüts Chao Shih-yen, on whom see above, n. 53; and Ma Jun (1255–1313), on whom see Ch'en, p. 317b. (Yüan Chi, "Yüan-tai chih Wei-wu-erh," p. 200, following K'o Shao-min's erroneous identification of the Öngüts with the Hui-hu [see *HYS*, 149, 15a], lists Ma Tsu-ch'ang among the Uighurs.) A notable omission from the above list is T'ai Pu-hua (Tai Bukha, 1304–1352), a *chin-shih* of 1321, well known for both scholarship and courage. However, he was a Baya'ut, and I have, therefore, excluded him from the present survey. On him see Ch'en, p. 322b, and "Shih ssu . . . ," pp. 674–675; H. Franke, "Chinese Historiography under Mongol Rule: The Role of History in Acculturation," *Mongolian Studies* 1 (1974): 16–17.

72. On Khutlugh Törmish ("Happy Born"), see *YS*, 25, 565; *HYS*, 192, 10b; *MWESC*, 118, 11a; Fuchs, pp. 36, 46, 49, 52. See also P. Ratchnevsky, *Un code des Yüan*, II (Paris, 1972), p. 33, n. 7, where his name is reconstructed as Khutlugh-Durmish. Another important translator of Chinese classics into Mongolian and a contemporary of Khutlugh Törmish was the Uighur academician A-lien T'ieh-mu-erh (Eren Temür). He became a close adviser to Shidebala. On him, see *YS*, 124, 3047; *HYS*, 136, 11b; *MWESC*, 45, 2b; Fuchs, pp. 49, 51. As was already noted by Franke," Chinese Historiography," pp. 22–24, and "A Transmitter of Chinese Values: Wang Yün (1227–1304)" (unpublished paper read at the Conference on

Yüan Thought, Issaquah, Wash., January 2–8, 1978), pp. 1–2, not many Chinese works were translated into Mongolian, and the majority of the translations remained in manuscript. On the Uighur *chin-shih* graduates, see H. Franke, "Chinese Historiography," p. 19.

73. On Biratnashiri or Birannashiri (Skr. Prajñāsrī; d. 1332) and other famous Buddhist translators, see *YS*, 202, 4519; *HYS*, 243, 7b; Louis Ligeti in *Acta Orientalia* 20 (1967): 59–62, and *Ural-Altaische Jahrbucher* 33 (1961): 235–244, esp. 242–243; and Fuchs, p. 36. Cf. also G. Kara, *Knigi mongol' skikh kochevnikov* (Moscow, 1972), English Summary, p. 191.

74. On Čhos-kyi 'od-zer, see Pelliot, "Les systemes d'écriture ...," pp. 286–289; and F. W. Cleaves in *Harvard Journal of Asiatic Studies* 17 (1954): 13–18. Cleaves is of the opinion that he was a Tibetan; see, however, Ligeti's remarks in *Acta Orientalia* 20 (1967): 59–60, and D. Cerensodnom, *XIV zuuny üeiin yaruu nairagč Čoiži-odser* (Ulan Bator, 1969). Cf. Kara, loc. cit.

75. Such as the block print of Čhos-kyi 'od-zer's translation and commentary of the Bodhicaryāvatāra printed in Daidu in 1312. See Cleaves, op. cit., pp. 1–129. For the printing of Uighur texts in Peking, see P. Zieme in *Acta Orientalia* 29 (1975): 197–198. The fact that Uighur scholars were to a large extent responsible for translations from other languages into Mongolian accounts for the considerable number of "uighurisms" that we find in these early works. See, e.g., L. Ligeti in *Acta Orientalia* 23 (1970): 274. On the Uighur and Tibetan translations, see also Ligeti, op. cit., pp. 59–64.

76. See Róna-Tas in *Acta Orientalia* 18 (1965): 119–147, esp. pp. 145–146. Cf. also Kara, op. cit., pp. 190–191. Incidentally, in the *Secret History* too the Turkish content, both linguistic and cultural, is far greater than is usually assumed. This is another important problem deserving close investigation. In this context one should perhaps mention that the lingua franca of the Mongol empire, at least in its eastern portion, was almost certainly not Persian, as it is sometimes assumed, but Turkish. As has been pointed out by Pelliot, *Recherches*, p. 90, the nomenclature of Pian di Carpine, Rubruck, and Juvainī: "est beaucoup plus turque que mongole." On the Uighur influence on the Mongols, see also V. V. Barthold's remarks in *Zivaya starina* XVIII, 2–3 (1909), 42–46, rep. in V. V. Barthold's *Sochineniia*, V (Moscow, 1968), pp. 365–368; Dalai, loc. cit. (see above, n. 14), and the recent contribution of A. A. Semenov, *Materialy po istorii i kul'ture uigurskogo naroda* (Alma-Ata, 1978), pp. 22–48.

77. The cultural influence of Tibet on the thirteenth- and fourteenth-century Mongols has so far not received adequate attention on the part of scholars. See, provisionally, Demiéville, op. cit., pp. 205–216; G. Tucci and W. Heissig, *Les religions du Tibet et de la Mongolie* (trans R. Sailley) (Paris, 1973), pp. 373–375; G. Tucci, *Tibetan Painted Scrolls* (Rome, 1949), I, pp. 9–17, 31–39; the articles listed in Yamane and Ohshima, op. cit., nos. 118–122 (on the *ti-shih* or Imperial Teachers) and 956–968; and the recent contribution on the Imperial Teachers by Cha-ch'i Ssuch'in (S. Jagchid) in *Shih-hsüeh lun-chi*, pp. 308–327. Cf. also G. N. Roerich in *Sino-Indian Studies. Liebenthal Festschrift*, vol. V, 3 and 4, ed. K. Roy (Visvabharati, Santiniketan, 1957), p. 174. H. Franke, "From Tribal Chieftain to Universal Emperor and God: The Legitimation of the Yüan Dynasty" (Munich, 1978), pp. 58–63. Some interesting data can be found in the Tibetan sources: see Sh. Bira in *Acta Orientalia*

17 (1964): 80–81; and in the Mongolian *White History* or *Chaghan teüke*: see Klaus Sagaster, *Die weisse Geschichte* (Wiesbaden, 1976), pp. 29–41 et passim. On the Mongol conquest of Tibet and the political contacts between Tibet and the Mongols in the 13th–14th centuries, chapter 7 in this volume and T. V. Wylie's article, "The First Mongol Conquest of Tibet Reinterpreted," *HJAS* 37 (1977): 103–133.

78. See Ch'en, esp. pp. 63–64, 77–80, 82–85, 129, 180, 185, 190–192, 250. One of the leading figures among sinicized Uighurs was Hsiao-yün-shih Hai-ya (Sewinch Khaya), alias Kuan Yün-shih (1286–1324), on whom see Ch'en, p. 315b; Yang Tsung-han in *Monumenta Serica* 9 (1944): 92–100; Tamori Noboru, "Kansansei-kō," *Saitama Daigaku kiyō* 10 (1961): 1–10; R. J. Lynn, "A Poet and His Poems: Kuan Yün-shih (1286–1324)," *Papers on Far Eastern History* 18 (1978): 81–121.

79. So far I have collected data on fifteen distinguished Turkish ladies and Buddhist nuns, but I am certain that a complete survey of Yüan sources would increase that figure. One should also investigate all cases of Turkish ladies married to Mongol emperors, princes, and noblemen recorded in both the Chinese and the Persian sources.

80. I have included in this category also Turks enfeoffed by the Mongols or holding honorary ranks and titles conferred upon them posthumously in recognition of their descendants' achievements, and some members of the *iduq qut*'s and the Öngüts' princely houses. They total 299 individuals distributed as follows: 158 Uighurs, 20 Kharlukhs, 26 Khanglis, 16 Kipchaks, 42 Öngüts, 11 Kereyid and 26 Naimans.

81. Local gazetteers in particular may contain the texts of tomb inscriptions (*mu-chih ming* and *shen-tao pei*) in honor of Turkish personalities which are not preserved in any other sources. Although I have checked all the epigraphical material available to me in literary and other collections, I have not yet carried out a systematic survey of gazetteers.

82. I refer, in particular, to edicts concerning the activity of the *ortakh* associations and the Nestorian Christians (*erke'üt*; on this term see J. Hamilton in *Journal Asiatique*, 1972, pp. 163–164), the majority of whom were Turkish.

83. See N. Ts. Munkuev, *Kitaiskii istochnik o pervykh mongol'skikh khanakh* (Moscow, 1965), pp. 25–29.

84. Cf. L. N. Gumilyov, "The Secret and Official History of the Mongols in the Twelfth and Thirteenth Centuries (As They Themselves Wrote It)," in *The Countries and Peoples of the East. Selected Articles* (Moscow, 1974) (trans. from *Tataro-mongoly v Azii i Evrope*, pp. 484–502), esp. pp. 202–205. Gumilyov's thesis seems to me acceptable only in its general lines, and I do not agree with the inferences he makes on the assumption that the *Secret History* was written in 1240. On the dating of the *Secret History*, see my article "Some Remarks on the Dating of the *Secret History of the Mongols*," *Monumenta Serica* 24 (1965): 185–206.

85. Rashīd al-Dīn says (*Successors*, p. 188) that when Khadakh and Chinkhai were in power and the cause of the Christians flourished, "no Muslim dared to raise his voice to them." Previously, Chinkhai had been forced to flee Karakorum when Ögödei's widow, Töregene, under the influence of her attendant Fāṭima, began persecuting the old ministers, appointing in their place "a crowd of fools," chief among them the Muslim 'Abd al-Raḥmān (whom Chinkhai had earlier introduced to court). See *Successors*, pp. 176–177. On the disagreement between Chinkhai and

Yeh-lü Ch'u-ts'ai, and between the latter and 'Abd al-Raḥmān, see my dissertation "Sino-Mongol Culture Contacts," pp. 458–463, nn. 305–310. See also I. de Rachewiltz, "Yeh-lü Ch'u-ts'ai (1189–1243), Buddhist Idealist and Confucian Statesman," in A. F. Wright and D. Twitchett, eds., *Confucian Personalities* (Stanford, 1962), pp. 207–208. On the Taoist-Buddhist controversy there is a vast literature in several languages, but a good comprehensive study is still lacking. For the origin of the controversy in the early Mongol period, see I. de Rachewiltz, "The *Hsi-yu lu* by Yeh-lü Ch'u-ts'ai," *Monumenta Serica* 21 (1962): 3 et passim.

86. *Conquerors*, p. 45.

87. See G. L. Penrose's remarks in his review of Dardess's work in *Mongolian Studies* 2 (1975): 154.

PART VI

China's Foreign Relations in Historical Context

ELEVEN

Yin and Yang in the China–Manchuria–Korea Triangle

GARI LEDYARD

The triangular relationship between the states in China, Manchuria, and Korea occupies a position of special importance in the general matrix of East Asian international relations during the long period from the tenth through the fourteenth century. Two of the main antagonists of the Sung dynasty, the Khitans and the Jurchens, were Manchurian powers; and even the Mongols, though originating in the northern steppe area, made their first impact on Chinese territory in the northeastern region in and adjacent to Manchuria. The Khitans, Jurchens, and Mongols also exerted an intense, often destructive influence on Korea, which during this period was ruled by the Koryŏ dynasty (918–1392). The relationship between Sung and Koryŏ, unlike that between Chinese and Korean dynasties in both earlier and later times, was suspended for long periods of time, and even when diplomatic relations between the two countries were active, they were often marked by distrust and suspicion. The Khitans and Jurchens generally enforced a break in Sung-Koryŏ relations, and when the Mongols became the successors of Sung in China and the overlords of Koryŏ, international relations in any meaningful sense ceased to exist.

The identification and analysis of the features of international relations peculiar to this period implies a comparison with those of other periods, and the approach in this essay will therefore be to look at the China–Manchuria–Korea triangle in broad historical terms. The first part of this study will consist of a general survey of the relationships in this particular sector from China's first unification under the Ch'in dynasty to the very recent past. In this stretch of time, one can identify three major cycles, each of which has parallel but by no means identical patterns of foreign relations activity. Each cycle begins with the launching of a major Chinese dynasty accompanied by a significant burst of Chinese expansion. The general rationale for this scheme will become clear as the survey proceeds; here I will simply identify the cycles as I, from the Ch'in unification in 221 B.C. to the end of the southern dynasties in 589; II, from the Sui unification in 589 to the fall of the Yüan dynasty in 1368; and III, from the rise of Ming in 1368 to a date in our own century (precisely when is a problem to be examined later).

Within each of these major cycles, two distinct phases can be discerned. In the first, the general direction of movement is from south to north, with China expanding at the expense of the frontier people; in the second, the general direction of movement is from north to south, and the northern frontier peoples expand at the expense of China. I call these phases "Yang" and "Yin," respectively (and arbitrarily, since from the point of view of the northern peoples, their own expansion would be "Yang" and not "Yin"). In this scheme, Chinese frontier history can be divided into six distinct periods which can be identified with the shorthand tags "Yang I," "Yin I," "Yang II," and so forth. The general outline of events in each period will be given in the survey.

The second part of the essay will be concerned with a comparative analysis of the data presented in the survey, first in terms of the general differences between the Yang and Yin phases and the criteria for identifying the dividing point between them, then in terms of the historical development that occurs as one cycle gives way to another. Finally, a special examination will be made of the period which is the focus of this volume, in my scheme to be called "Yin II."

If the chronological coverage of this survey is broad, the geographical coverage is generally limited to the China–Manchuria–Korea triangle. Yet "Manchuria" needs some defining. It was not a term or a concept used in traditional Chinese historiography. Chinese administration generally dealt, on the one hand, with the Chinese communities along the northern coast of the Gulf of Po-hai and in the lower basin of the Liao River, and, on the other hand, with the non-Chinese peoples beyond the pale. The size and extent, and in the earlier periods, even the existence of the Chinese area depend very much on whether the dominant mode is Yin or Yang. But even at its greatest extent, it would not go beyond the area of the present Liao-ning province. As for the non-Chinese peoples, they were divided on general geographical and ethnic grounds into peoples either east or west of the Liao. The term "western Manchuria" will here be defined generally as the territory east of the Hsing-an Mountains and west of a north-south line roughly traced by the Nonni River (Nun chiang) in the north and the lower Liao in the south. This corresponds for the most part with the present-day Inner Mongolian Autonomous Region of the People's Republic of China (except that this entity includes large spaces of land west of the Hsing-an Range as well). In historical times, as in the present day, the peoples in this area were related culturally and probably also ethnically to those living in the pure steppe regions to the west. Some of the major inhabitants have been the Tung-hu, the Hsien-pei, the Khitans, and the Mongols. The second frontier region, here called eastern Manchuria, covered the rest of Manchuria and the present Maritime Province of the Soviet Union and, at times, some of the northern parts of Korea—in general the drainage basins of the Sungari, Ussuri, and Yalu rivers. In the earlier periods this area was dominated by Korean peoples (e.g., Puyŏ, Koguryŏ), although as time went on Eastern Manchuria became more purely Tungusic (e.g., Moho or Malgal, Jurchens, Manchus), and the Koreans eventually ended up mostly south of the Yalu and Tumen rivers. In my view, as ethnic or linguistic labels, "Korean" and "Tungusic" are mutually exclusive terms. Although there have been some cases of mixing between the two peoples, the more significant historical fact is the degree to which they have remained separate from each other.

Historical Development of the China–Manchuria–Korea Triangle

Aside from a few references to the quasi-mythical Sushen and their legendary poisoned arrows,[1] or to the better-known Mo (Korean Maek) peoples,[2] there are very few references in the classical literature of the pre-Han era to the Manchurian or Korean areas. Even the kingdom of Yen, in the area of the present Ho-pei Province, does not enter history in any clear view until the Warring States period. Vast areas of Ho-pei were marshy bogs drained by the numerous channels of the mouth of the Yellow River, which ranged much further north than the diked and bordered mouth of the river today. The northeast was a region to which Chinese of the classical era paid remarkably little attention.[3] However, the people of Yen had devoted much effort to strengthening their northern frontier, and by the end of the Warring States period had already built some of the eastern sections to the Great Wall and had pushed their control into the Liao River area. These defensive installations were taken over by Ch'in after Yen fell to the Ch'in juggernaut. Unified China, indeed, begins with the capture of the northeastern defenses.

Yang I (221 B.C. – A.D. 220)

China: Ch'in, Former Han, Later Han
Manchuria: Tung-hu, Wu-huan, Hsien-pei (west); Chosŏn,
  Yemaek, Koguryŏ, Sushen or Ilou (east)
Korea: Chosŏn, Yemaek (north); Han peoples (south)

During the early years of the Han dynasty, the main frontier threat came from the Hsiung-nu, and the difficulties of this situation prevented any concentrated attention on the northeast. On the other hand, the northeast-

ern part of the frontier was a crucial link in the defense line. In about
195 B.C., the Prince of Yen, a Han vassal, defected to the Hsiung-nu,[4] while
another band of Yen adventurers fled eastward and seized power in the
Korean state of Chosŏn.[5] (The location of Chosŏn's capital is not wholly
clear; some evidence suggests it may have been in the Liao-tung area.)
Thus, not only did Hsiung-nu power reach to Chosŏn in the east, but Yen
collaborators in both areas formed a dangerous link against China. Already
in the 170s B.C., it seemed to some Chinese strategists that an invasion of
Chosŏn was in order, but the dovish Emperor Wen held back and nothing
was done.[6]

Only in the reign of the vigorous Emperor Wu (141–87 B.C.) did Chinese
attention to this area become active. This was the period in which China
made its epochal response to the threat posed by the Hsiung-nu. Emperor
Wu realized that the piecemeal measures of his predecessors—fixed frontier posts, direct military responses, treaties, luxury goods, diplomacy—
would not bring a general solution to the Hsiung-nu problem and resolved
to face them on a frontier-wide basis. This resulted in a policy of truly
continental scope, for it was required that the frontier be pinned down not
only in the middle (the part most accessible to the Chinese capital), but also
at its eastern and western ends. Thus, it was during Emperor Wu's time
that the Chinese first reached the natural ends of their frontier—in the
west through the famous mission of Chang Ch'ien and the military colonization and alliances that developed from it; in the east through the conquest of Chosŏn (Chao-hsien) and the establishment there of permanent
military bases. The work of building this defense line took a generation:
from the departure of Chang Ch'ien in 138 B.C. to the establishment of Lo-
lang Commandery in 108 B.C.

Judging from the account in the *Shih-chi*, the conquest of Chosŏn was no
easy matter, and the difficulties of the campaign must have borne out
Chinese estimates of its military significance. Of the four commanderies
established in the eastern areas following Chosŏn's conquest, two, Lo-lang
and Hsüan-t'u remained in existence for several hundred years. The
original site of Lo-lang was perhaps in Liao-tung and not in the vicinity of
modern P'yŏngyang, but it was certainly located in P'yŏngyang from
around the last half of the first century B.C.[7] Lo-lang had a distinctly
peninsular orientation and even kept tabs, however dimly, on affairs in the
Japanese islands far to the southeast. Hsüan-t'u also moved several times
before settling down in the uplands east of the Liao. In effect, it was the
eastern buffer for Liao-tung, and its principal task was to control the
frontier vis-à-vis the Puyŏ and the Koguryŏ. On all but a few occasions, the
Puyŏ were allies of the Chinese, but the Koguryŏ, from beginning to end,
were unremitting enemies. These two commanderies were prosperous out-
posts of Chinese civilization; Lo-lang in particular was the headquarters for

many rich and powerful merchants. Yet the raison d'être for these commanderies was very likely more military and strategic than economic. The Chinese garrisons in Lo-lang and Hsüan-t'u, together with the manipulation of the surrounding peoples that was possible from these bases, greatly added to the security of the Chinese settlements in Liao-tung and Liao-hsi and thus of the entire northeastern frontier.

Lo-lang and Hsüan-t'u had a checkered history, owing to the fact that political changes in China itself often had the effect of leaving these commanderies adrift and at the mercy of either the surrounding native peoples or Chinese adventurers. Thus, during the domestic strife at the time of Wang Mang, the eastern colonies were unable to keep Koguryŏ under control (much less enlist their support, as Wang Mang found out when they refused to attack the Hsiung-nu on his order),[8] whereas during the last decades of Han the government was unable even to control the Chinese settlements. In this period, the Korean commanderies became almost the private preserve of Kung-sun Tu and his immediate descendants. The Kung-sun family even founded a commandery of its own—Tai-fang, set up as a buffer to protect Lo-lang from the south.[9] The Kung-sun held on to their position and even strengthened it in 207, when Ts'ao Ts'ao struck north to clean out the Wu-huan in the western uplands of Liao-hsi.[10] They cooperated with Ts'ao Ts'ao, and thus not only shook off a potential enemy in the Wu-huan, but earned (for a time) a friend in the Central Plain.

After the fall of Han, the authority of the central Chinese government was temporarily reestablished with the spectacular Wei campaigns against the Kung-sun in 237–238,[11] and against Koguryŏ in 244–245.[12] These brought Lo-lang, Hsüan-t'u and Tai-fang also back into Chinese hands, and Tai-fang became the base for Wei's active campaign, unique in Chinese history, to secure an alliance with the Wa people in Japan.[13] But by about 290, Chinese contact with these areas was decisively lost.

During the period Yang I, there was little that, strictly speaking, could be called diplomacy insofar as the northeast was concerned. The Chinese commanderies in Manchuria and Korea (*chün*) were organized and administered no differently than commanderies elsewhere in China, and some might say that at this time the lower Liao valley and northern Korea could even be considered part of "China proper." With the non-Chinese peoples beyond the pale, such diplomacy as there was, was carried out by frontier commissioners who were also military commanders. Occasionally, tribesmen would show up in Lo-yang to present their tribute and demonstrate their exotic customs, but for the most part, the day-to-day contact between Chinese and foreign peoples was a military man's affair, and the Chinese had the upper hand. The most important exception to this pattern occurred at the very end of Yang I (or, according to an interpretation to be presented later, at the beginning of Yin I), when the Wei envoys made their energetic attempt to establish good relations with the Wa people in the Japanese islands: here there was no military presence, and the essence of the activity was diplomatic. The object seems to have been to make sure that the Wa would not be tempted to give aid to Wei's major enemy, Wu (It was noted at that time that the southwestern territories of the Wa shared the same latitudes with Wu, and in fact there may have been maritime contact of a degree now unsuspected.)

These energetic frontier policies represented a Chinese attempt to continue the Han dynasty's assertive, Yang mode in dealing with alien peoples. But the Yang was already waning, and these policies could not survive the crisis of Chìn in the fourth century, when the northern frontier broke and a flood of foreign peoples washed over northern China, sending the Chìn dynasty south and ushering in the age of "barbarian" states in the north. (The tonal mark on Chìn distinguishes this dynasty from the Jurchen Chin dynasty of the twelfth century.) China's defense line simply ceased to exist. Liao-hsi, Liao-tung, Hsüan-t'u, Lo-lang, and Tai-fang disappeared along with the vanished frontier. Lo-lang's fall in 313, under the combined pressure of the Hsien-pei and the Koguryŏ, occurred fittingly between the sack of the Chinese capital at Lo-yang by the Hsiung-nu (311) and the final southward flight of Chìn (317). The Yin period was actively under way.

Yin I (220–589)

China: Three Kingdoms: Wei, Shu and Wu (north and south); Western Chin, "Five Barbarians," "Sixteen States" (north); "Northern Wei" and successors Chou, Ch'i, and Sui (north); Eastern Chin, Sung, Ch'i, Liang, Ch'en (south)
Manchuria: Various Yen states (Hsien-pei) (west); Koguryŏ (east)
Korea: Koguryŏ (north); Paekche, Silla, Kaya/Mimana (south)

In this period, the tables are turned. The Chinese suffer unmanageable disturbances in their internal political order and can no longer keep the trans-frontier peoples under control. They suffer invasion and occupation from the enemies that up to now they have kept at bay. The Chìn dynasty flees southward and reconstitutes its society in refuge, and then is followed by a succession of "southern dynasties." In the north, following the chaotic century known as the age of the "Five Barbarians and Sixteen States," we have the T'o-pa (or Northern) Wei and several more "northern" dynasties, ending with Sui, which once again brings China under a single rule. For most of this period there is no effective frontier between the various foreign rulers of the north China plain and other foreign antagonists farther north.

As far as Manchuria and Korea are concerned, a reduced Chinese population remains but there is no Chinese political authority. Western Manchuria is taken over by the Hsien-pei, established as the Former Yen dynasty, which also comes to control much of northeastern China and which ultimately goes on to contend for the entire north China plain with the "Tibetan" peoples dynastically established as Former Ch'in (in which attempt, however, they fail). In eastern Manchuria, there is a parallel movement of the northern peoples southward: the Puyŏ, former Chinese allies now defeated by the Hsien-pei, sweep down into the peninsula and take over the southwestern region, which they develop into the state of Paekche, and from which, I have argued, they even sweep across the sea and bring the age of the "horseriders" to Japan.[14] The Koguryŏ people, having evicted the Chinese commissioners, develop a powerful state, which at the height of its strength in the fifth and sixth centuries holds sway from the Liao to the sea, and from the central Korean peninsula to the middle course of the Sungari River. In the southern part of the peninsula, in addition to Paekche, are the states of Silla and Kaya. All three southern states have a basic Han population, but only Silla seems to have had a clearly homogeneous society. Paekche had its Puyŏ overlords, and Kaya (known in Japanese sources as Mimana) seems to have had Wa peoples (the main constituent of the later Japanese nation) among its population. Both Kaya and the main Wa population in the Japanese islands probably had, during the fourth and fifth centuries, some degree of Puyŏ influence, if not control, although in the absence of clear evidence this must remain speculative.[15]

The whole question of the founding of the Japanese state is still very controversial, as is the relationship, if any, of that state to Kaya/Mimana. Although the complexities of the origins of these Korean and Japanese states are too great to permit exploration here, it is worthwhile to stress one point: their development occurred at a time when China was out of the picture. There was, of course, Chinese influence, but it came in alien clothing: on the one hand, through the so-called Sino-Barbarian Culture (*Hu-Han wen-hua*), developed on the frontier areas by mixed societies, and on the other hand, through Buddhism, which in addition to Buddhist teaching per se also introduced many aspects of Chinese civilization. Rootless Chinese survivors of the chaos also made some cultural contributions.

In Manchuria there was naturally strife between Koguryŏ and Yen; indeed, in 342, Yen carried on a particularly destructive campaign against its eastern adversary. But Koguryŏ survived this debacle, helped to some extent by its alliance with Yen's enemy, the Former Ch'in. In the end, Koguryŏ outlasted the Hsien-pei and the various successor Yen dynasties established by them. As the Hsien-pei weakened and fell under Northern

Wei and Koguryŏ pressure, their understudy in the drama, the Khitans, were already on the rise. Although the Khitans did not come to full strength until the period Yin II, they were already a threat to Koguryŏ, which, however, kept them at a distance by means of a strategic alliance with the Juan-juan (ephemeral predecessors of the Türks on the northern steppes), effected in 479.[16] Koguryŏ also maintained friendly relations, for the most part, with the Northern Wei. But with the southern Korean states of Paekche and Silla, Koguryŏ was almost constantly at war.

During the period Yin I, diplomacy came into its own as an important aspect of statecraft. Militarily, there was a stalemate between the Northern and Southern regimes in China, and this situation was also reflected in the Korean peninsula, where Koguryŏ, though it made some gains at the expense of Silla and Paekche, was still kept in its place as a purely northern power. Silla was rather late in developing its diplomatic activities, but Koguryŏ and Paekche were both aggressive in maintaining good relations with the Chinese states. Koguryŏ naturally emphasized those in the north (Former Ch'in, Wei, Ch'i, Chou), while Paekche stressed those in the south (Chin, Sung, Ch'i, Liang, Ch'en); but both courted the opposite Chinese power from time to time in order to minimize each other's influence on the continent. For their part, the states in both North and South China were happy to see the largest possible number of foreign envoys arriving, since visits were prestige chips that each could play in its legitimacy battle with the other. Although the rhetoric that accompanied this diplomatic activity in Chinese sources reflects the superior-inferior relationship so typical of Chinese international relations, in fact it was pretty much an evenhanded game. Obviously, the Korean states were weaker politically and culturally than the Chinese states, but the Chinese were in no position to dominate Korean affairs, and one can see in general a balance of interests.

As the Yin I period went on, the "barbarian" regimes in northern China became more and more acculturated to their subject Chinese populations, and Chinese leaders came to the fore; on the steppe, new nomadic powers replaced the old. The sixth century saw the spectacular rise of a new super-confederacy in the form of the T'u-chüeh, or Türks. As China was pulling itself together under the Sui, the Türks were putting pressure along their entire northern frontier. Almost every sign suggests that with the close of this scene, we have now come full circle and up against a situation parallel to that between Han and the Hsiung-nu.

Yang II (589–907)

China: Sui, T'ang
Manchuria: Khitans, Hsi, Shih-wei (west); Koguryŏ, Moho or
           Malgal, Po-hai or Parhae (east)
Korea: Silla

The men who ruled during the Sui and early T'ang periods, facing a trans-frontier threat of continental magnitude, adopted the continental strategy of their predecessor, Emperor Wu. That is, they sought to tie down China's defense line on the east and west while they kept up the pressure across the middle. On the west, the constant aim was to keep the western Türks detached from their eastern brothers (the split had developed in 583) and ultimately to bring both to heel, a policy that was generally successful. On the east, there was again a split situation: in western Manchuria, corresponding to the Tung-hu and Wu-huan of Han times, there were now the Khitans and several lesser related peoples; in eastern Manchuria and northern Korea, corresponding to the Han-time Chosŏn, were the Koguryŏ. Here too the policy was divide and conquer, or at least divide. The Khitans were brought under general control through the traditional methods of the frontier commissioners (pacification, an occasional full-scale campaign, clever diplomacy, bribery), while the Koguryŏ were the object of several costly and initially abortive invasions, though they were ultimately destroyed. Chinese population reoccupied the Po-hai coast and the lower Liao valley.

The Koguryŏ campaigns carried out by the Sui Emperors Wen and Yang are almost legendary. These began with Emperor Wen's in 598: his armies were destroyed by weather, hunger, and dissension in the ranks.[17] Emperor Yang's campaigns of 612 to 614 were much greater debacles, for which it was harder to find meteorological excuses.[18] No doubt the T'ang historians inflated the size of his armies so as to maximize his defeats and minimize his own personal virtue, thereby to enhance T'ang's own righteous role in replacing Sui; but they were still total defeats. The second bout of anti-Koguryŏ expeditions took place under T'ai-tsung of T'ang (645—648), but his armies found Koguryŏ no easier to crack than had those of Emperor Yang.[19]

It was only when T'ang decided to enlist an ally against Koguryŏ that victory became possible. Koguryŏ's peninsular competitors, Silla and Paekche, were both plausible players for this role, but Silla had a tougher society and probably greater military strength, and it had its own special goal for which it needed an ally, the destruction of Paekche. So it was the T'ang-Silla combination that took the field for the last bout with Koguryŏ. First, Paekche had to be disposed of: this was accomplished between 660 and 663, T'ang invading by sea and Silla attacking over the hills in the rear.[20] With that obstacle out of their way, the two powers went on to obliterate Koguryŏ (668).[21] Here we can observe a combination not possible—or necessary—in Han times: an alliance between the Chinese power and a peninsular state against a Manchurian power. Such combinations were also evoked on other occasions in Sino-Korean history, but this is the only one that got off the ground and succeeded.

T'ang's military solution now attained, it remained to effect the political settlement. T'ang appears to have envisioned military superintendencies for the conquered Korean areas, and even for its ally, Silla. Silla, however, did not appreciate the T'ang offer to confirm its king as "Commander of Kyerim" (the old name for Silla's capital area) and place him under the authority of a Chinese frontier commissioner.[22] Nor did it have any intention of being deprived of its share of the spoils in Paekche and Koguryŏ. The two victors, therefore, became antagonists, and after eight years T'ang's armies were forced to evacuate the peninsula for good.[23] Silla's victory, which was accomplished by a combination of diplomatic and military efforts, was aided by its own lack of ambition for the old Koguryŏ territory north of P'yŏngyang. The strategic import of this was that T'ang kept full control of southern Manchuria, while Silla remained strictly a peninsular power. In eastern Manchuria, Koguryŏ survivors and other eastern Manchurian peoples (mainly Moho or Malgal) established the state of Po-hai (or Parhae). Although on the east coast Parhae and Silla had a short contiguous border in the vicinity of the modern Wŏnsan, in the more important northwest coast region of the peninsula, T'ang effectively kept its two mutually hostile tributaries separate from each other.[24] Thus, T'ang effected for the first time in history a separation of the Manchurian and peninsular powers, an arrangement that in the course of time became typical, even if it introduced new tensions of its own. In spite of some rocky periods, both Silla and Parhae settled down to their respective peaceful tributary/trade relationships with T'ang, and as T'ang began to decline, so too did Silla and Parhae.

Yin II (907–1368)

China: The Five Dynasties (north) and Ten Kingdoms (south); Sung (north and south) (to 1127); Chin or Jurchens (north) and Sung (south); Yüan or Mongols (north and south)
Manchuria: Liao or Khitans; Chin or Jurchens; Yüan or Mongols (all both east and west)
Korea: Koryŏ

The situation after the fall of T'ang in 907 in many ways recalls that following the southward flight of Chin in 317. In both instances there ceased to be any viable frontier between northern China and the traditionally "barbarian" areas. T'ang broke up into nearly a dozen successor states as the great cosmopolis became a collection of regional kingdoms. Three of the "Five Dynasties" in the Central Plain were founded by sinicized Turks, and most were under some kind of control from the Khitans. Even Sung, which found itself the eventual winner in the struggle for the Central Plain, was hemmed in on the northwest by the Tanguts (Hsi Hsia) and on the northeast by the Khitans (Liao): it was, in effect, a state without a frontier.

In the northeast, on this occasion, as on the earlier one in the fourth century, there was conflict between the two Manchurian powers. However, unlike the earlier case, in which the various Yen states and Koguryŏ had ended up in a standoff, the Khitans now quickly disposed of their eastern Manchurian rival, Parhae (926).[25] Thus, for the first time in history, all of Manchuria, east and west, was controlled by a single state.

Finally, in Korea, the collapse of the frontier and the resulting eclipse of Chinese power provided the opportunity for profound political changes. Anti-Silla forces arose in both the north and south. First there was Later Paekche in the southwest, a regional state recalling the memory of original Paekche. Then, in the central and northern portions of the peninsula, another group of anti-Silla forces gradually coalesced into the state of Koryŏ, evoking in name and sentiment the ghost of Koguryŏ. Proclaimed in 918, it defeated Later Paekche in 935 and in the same year accepted the peaceful submission of Silla.[26] Political power in the peninsula swung from the south and the north. The new Koryŏ kingdom consolidated its southern holdings and developed the territory between P'yŏngyang and the Yalu as its frontier area. In the process it absorbed many refugees from Parhae and came into its own inevitable conflict with the Khitans. Koryŏ's mistrust of the Khitans was deep, and the founder of the dynasty, in his instructions to his successors, had enjoined constant hostility against them.[27] As the self-proclaimed successor to Koguryŏ and the protector of Parhae refugees, many of them of Koguryŏ origin, Koryŏ considered the northern territories in Manchuria its rightful legacy. The Khitans, as conquerors of Parhae and the actual holders of the territory, obviously had other ideas. Koryŏ was ultimately successful in laying claim to and holding the old Parhae lands south of the lower Yalu, which were the bone of contention in a series of Koryŏ–Liao wars lasting from 993 to 1018. Peace came after the especially convincing Koryŏ victory in 1018, with Koryŏ keeping its cis-Yalu territory but breaking its relations with Sung and accepting Liao suzerainty (1022).[28] As a result of these developments, the Yalu became Korea's definitive northern frontier, and in spite of the dreams of Korean irredentists ever since, so it has remained.

Geopolitically, Liao's unification of all Manchuria made it the dominant state in East Asia. Sung's embodiment of the Chinese polity was by no means weak, and culturally it was to be one of the great Chinese dynasties. But it was effectively checked by Liao and, indeed, had to pay dearly (in self-esteem as well as in cash) to keep Liao out of the Central Plain. Yet, if Liao was now the only state in Manchuria, it still was not immune from the tensions that had always plagued that ethnically complex place. Thus, it was unable to prevent the rise of the Jurchens, and ultimately went down to defeat before them (1125). But the Jurchens, having established their own Chin dynasty and replaced the Liao, were not content to be a merely

Manchurian power and went on to seize the whole Central Plain from Sung (1127). And still worse disasters were to occur: unlike period Yin I, when the Chinese had been able to maintain their political vitality in the south until the eventual north-south reunification, Yin II saw the Chinese state wiped out entirely when still another northern power, the Mongols, erupted from the steppes to conquer Chin, Koryŏ, Hsi Hsia, Sung, and nearly everything else in their path. Thus occurred one more first in East Asian history: the first complete conquest of all the territory of the Chinese state by an outside force.

So much in this long period of 462 years was new, in fact, that the statesmen of both Sung and Koryŏ found little in the way of precedents to guide their policies. Both states were forced into humiliating concessions to the Khitans and later to Chin, and this situation profoundly affected their relationship with each other. Sung relations were indeed a risky luxury for Koryŏ, which in 1022 had to break them at Liao insistence. Sung, for its part, often suspected that Koryŏ was up to Liao's bidding, and except for a few occasions when it nursed the chimerical hope that Koryŏ might "rise up in arms and act in concert with us so that we might smite the Khitans jointly from outside and in,"[29] it was aloof, if not hostile, when envoys from the peninsula appeared in the capital. After Sung was driven south by Chin, relations with Koryŏ were cut off entirely; Chin, for its part, inherited from Liao Koryŏ's vassalage.[30]

Difficult as Koryŏ's relations with Liao and Chin were, she did not fare badly in comparison with the fate of Sung. While Sung never did inherit the Manchurian territories of T'ang, and actually lost some Ho-pei territory within the Great Wall, Koryŏ managed to hold on to what it had and still add the cis-Yalu area. And while Sung lost all of northern China to the Jurchens, Koryŏ—with some difficulty, to be sure—managed to settle its affairs diplomatically and thus warded off a Jurchen invasion. Although either Liao or Chin could have conquered Korea if it had deployed all its military power, this could have left its Sung front exposed and endangered. Forcing Koryŏ into a tributary relationship as the price of its territorial integrity, Liao and Chin not only pursued a less costly policy but gained the legitimacy that went with the transfer of Koryŏ's allegiance from Sung to them. In the constant pressure that each exerted on Sung, this was not an insignificant advantage.

However "barbarous" were Liao and Chin from a Chinese point of view, their diplomatic and political institutions were of a basically Chinese mold. They founded dynasties, established their own calendars, exchanged ambassadors, and followed ceremonial and protocol procedures of acknowledged Chinese origin. Above all, their territorial sights were aimed only at the well-known landscape of the Chinese ecumene, either China itself or former Chinese tributaries such as Parhae and Koryŏ. In all this they differed substantially from the patterns followed by the Mongols in the early and formative decades of their conquests.

The Mongols were the last power to surge out of the north during the Yin II period. Their first raid on Chin territory occurred in 1210, but since their armies were engaged in attacks not just on China but on all of the major sedentary civilizations of Eurasia, and since their campaigns had to be interrupted from time to time to resolve the succession and other issues, it was to take nearly seventy more years before the Chinese world fell before them. The time spans of their attacks on areas of concern here— defined by the earliest and latest military action in each case—were 1210–1234 against Chin, 1219–1259 against Koryŏ,[31] and 1235–1279 against Sung.

The territory of the Yüan dynasty founded by the Mongols in effect combined that of Chin and Sung, so that Manchuria was wholly joined with China and placed under the same administration. Koryŏ's territory was treated differently, however. By its submission and by the dispatch of the crown prince as a hostage in 1259, Koryŏ was able to preserve its dynastic existence.[32] Koryŏ kings continued to rule the land, although, of course, under the eyes of Mongol resident commissioners (*darughachi*). Koryŏ's northern territory, however, was removed and placed under direct Mongol administration. The northeastern frontier area, in the vicinity of modern Wŏnsan, was incorporated by the Mongols as Shuang-ch'eng fu in 1258;[33] all of modern P'yŏngan Province and part of Hwanghae province were removed from Koryŏ administration in 1269, and incorporated as Yüan's Tung-ning lu.[34] With these expropriations, Koryŏ's territory shrunk to an area somewhat smaller than Silla's had been. The losses, however, proved temporary: Tung-ning lu was returned to Koryŏ control in 1290,[35] and the northeastern frontier area was forcefully recovered by Koryŏ in 1356,[36] although it became a bone of contention between Koryŏ and Ming several decades later, as we shall see. The constant struggle to assert Korean sovereignty over this cis-Yalu region points up the geographical character of the area. The Yalu River unites rather than divides this eastern territory, and a strong power on either side of the river has always tried to control the land on the other bank.

Since the Mongols tended to take a unitary view of all their possessions and conquests, there was really no such thing as diplomacy or international relations in any real sense. But the unified rule of most of continental East Asia did promote relatively free travel and a high degree of cultural and commercial interchange. Tens of thousands of Koreans moved, or were abducted, into the Liao-tung area. Korean officials and scholars mixed in Peking society with people from all parts of the Mongol empire. With the exception of the last, all recognized Koryŏ kings after Wŏnjong (r. 1259– 1274) had Mongol mothers and were raised in Peking. The daughters of

Korean aristocrats married into Mongol ruling familes; one of the most
influential of Emperor Shun's wives was the daughter of a prominent
Korean aristocrat much favored by the Mongols.

The Mongol rulers of China showed greater tolerance for alien cultures
than the Chinese; on the other hand, they did not allow themselves to be
sinicized to the degree that the Khitans and Jurchens had been. Thus, while
most Khitan and Jurchen residents of Chinese areas simply blended into the
landscape when their regimes came to an end, the Mongols were still very
much Mongols when the Yüan dynasty's days ran out, and they continued
and still continue today to maintain a most un-Chinese existence in areas
within and adjacent to China. I will return to some of these unique aspects
of the Yüan period in the more detailed analysis of Yin II below.

Yang III (1368–1644)

China: Ming
Manchuria: Mongols (west); Ming commanderies (Liao-tung);
                 Jurchens/Manchus (east)
Korea: Chosŏn (Yi dynasty)

After Khubilai's reign, Mongol rule in China gradually lost its vitality
and the inevitable Chinese reaction began. From the middle of the 1350s,
Chinese rebel movements became uncontrollable, and in due course one led
by Chu Yüan-chang succeeded and came to power as the Ming dynasty in
1368. Mongol rule in Korea had already collapsed in 1356.

Chinese resurgence along the northern frontier under the Ming resembled the earlier expansions of Han and T'ang in Cycles I and II. As in
the earlier cases, there was a general thrust northward along the whole
frontier, in the west, the center, and the east. Most of this activity (including the last historical rebuilding of the Great Wall) occurred under the
vigorous Yung-lo emperor. Although Ming suffered some embarrassments,
in particular the capture of Emperor Ying-tsung by the Oirat Mongols in
1449 (which itself recalled the Hsiung-nu encirclement of the Han emperor
Kao-tsu in 200 B.C.), the system of frontier bases that had been established
by the end of the Yung-lo reign was generally successful in protecting the
Central Plain from northern enemies until the later years of the sixteenth
century. Ming likewise invested heavily in military activities in the south
and in defense against Japanese pirates all along the coast.

The Ming presence in Manchuria was consolidated only gradually. The
Mongol rulers, though driven from China proper, maintained themselves
as "Northern Yüan" for several decades after 1368 and were not definitively driven from the Liao area until 1387.[37] The lingering of the northern
Yüan presented the rulers of Koryŏ with extensive problems. Some con-

servative forces in Korea, whose interests and background favored the maintenance of ties with the Mongols, managed to promote at various times a shaky diplomatic relationship with them; for their part, the Northern Yüan forces kept on the best terms they could manage with Koryŏ as a support for their position in Manchuria. Newly rising forces in Koryŏ, however, favored the development of close relations with the Ming, and their arguments too carried the day on various occasions. But no consistent diplomatic posture emerged; on the contrary, the continuation of the Ming-Yüan struggle exacerbated Koryŏ's political instability. The resulting vacillation in turn fed Ming suspicion, and even when Koryŏ's openings to Ming were sincere and hopeful, Ming's response was often chilly and hostile. When the Ming armies finally took over the Liaoyang area in 1387, a resolution became possible.

But first the severe Koryŏ-Ming crisis of 1388 had to be resolved. Ming insisted on taking over all former Yüan territories, and these included the northeastern frontier area of Korea that Yüan had administered as part of its K'ai-yüan lu.[38] As we have seen, Koryŏ had already seized this territory in 1356. When Ming presented an ultimatum on this issue in 1388, Koryŏ decided to go to war, and mounted a force to invade Manchuria. But when Yi Sŏnggye, one of the Korean commanders, reached an island in the middle of the Yalu, he dramatically turned his army around, announced the folly and futility of attacking Ming, and headed back instead to overthrow the regime in Kaegyŏng. After four years of indirect control through the Koryŏ kings, he finally deposed them entirely in 1392 and set up the new Chosŏn or Yi dynasty. The bold movements of Yi Sŏnggye reflected the strategy of a true statesman. On the one hand, his initial acquiescence with the war policy of the Koryŏ rulers demonstrated the depth of the Korean determination to retain the cis-Yalu territory that Koryŏ had won in the tenth and eleventh centuries; on the other hand, the abandonment of the invasion policy and his overthrow of Koryŏ showed his fundamentally friendly posture toward Ming. This foundation made possible the Ming-Chosŏn rapprochement that developed during the 1390s. The resulting tributary relationship proved to be very satisfactory to both Ming and Chosŏn, and Chinese aid to Korea in 1592 was certainly the decisive element in saving the country from conquest by Japan.[39]

The sequence of events just outlined demonstrates the centrality of Manchuria in any Chinese-Korean relationship. As long as Manchuria was contested, stable Sino-Korean relations were impossible, and even internal Korean stability could not be maintained. With the resolution of the problem after 1388, good relations followed. Korea's Yalu frontier was reconfirmed; its friendly posture contributed to the stability of China's position in Manchuria, and this position in turn anchored the eastern end of China's long northern frontier.

Unlike the situation in Han and T'ang during Yang I and II, however, Ming's national security was not assured by mere control of the northern frontier. The ensuing centuries had seen a vast and permanent development of the south, and these rich lands, though safe from nomadic plundering, were vulnerable to Japanese depredations from the sea. These lasted for nearly the entire Ming period, coming to a peak in the mid-sixteenth century. The Ming war against the Japanese was thus no passing thing, and its rescue of Korea from Japanese clutches was surely more than mere gratitude for two centuries of Korean loyalty. The campaigns in Korea between 1592 and 1598 were the final and the decisive battles in what could be called the "First Sino-Japanese War." The defeat of Japan in this war was, of course, related to Japan's abandonment of its overseas ambitions for the entire Tokugawa period.

The Japanese attack from the sea during the Ming dynasty was the first episode in what was eventually to become China's most pressing security problem: the maritime thrusts of the newly expansive European powers. It was not for nothing that these people came to be labeled "Ocean Devils" by the Chinese. But in the Yang III period, the ocean men were still a trickle that Ming was able to handle. What it could not handle was the next major threat from the traditionally dangerous northern frontier, the Manchus. The years of Ming despotism, the exhaustion of the armies after decades of wars north, south, and east, the incompetence of the government during the Wan-li years (1573–1619), and the alienation of many of Ming's suffering people, together with the vigor and intelligence of their Manchu adversaries, led ultimately to the loss of China once more to non-Chinese rule from the north.

Yin III (1644–1911)

China: Ch'ing (Manchus)
Manchuria: Ch'ing (Manchus)
Korea: Chosŏn (Yi dynasty)

In classical fashion, the Manchus subdued Korea on the east and the Mongols on the west in the course of their successful campaign against Ming. They captured Peking in 1644 and overcame Ming loyalist resistance in the south within the next four decades (capture of Taiwan, 1683). Although the Manchus maintained the northern frontier and took a Chinese view of security threats from the north, their attitude and policy toward the Mongols was much more comradely, at least after the initial military campaigns. Rather than merely "controlling" the Mongols, the Manchus enlisted them as active supporters and friends. In this sense, there was a blurring of the frontier similar to that in the regimes of earlier northern conquerors. In the western regions, Manchu control was more militaristic, but "Chinese Turkestan," as it came to be called, came no less firmly under control.

For Korea, the rise of the Manchus brought the complications usual for periods of radical change in Manchuria. Reflecting the Yin situations in Cycles I and II, when the Hsien-pei and the Khitans, respectively, put strong pressure on the Korean states as they advanced toward the Central Plain, the Manchus too were unyielding in their insistence on Korean acceptance of their position. If the contests between the Manchurian power and the Central Plain had been quick affairs, Korea would not have had so many difficulties. But inevitably these struggles took time to work out, even if, in these Yin situations, the victory of the north was inevitable. In the course of the battle, Korea was unable to make both sides happy; nor was neutrality a possibility, since the Manchurian power always demanded active compliance.

Korea's vacillation between Ming and the Manchus from 1601, when Nurhaci first requested Korean office and rank,[40] to 1644, when his six-year-old grandson Fu-lin was carried victoriously into Peking, was a measure of the difficult choices involved. The Koreans, having had direct and intimate connections with Ming as a result of the Japanese wars, knew very well the weak and troubled condition of the Chinese state. On the other hand, it was clear that Korea was deeply indebted to Ming for its own survival, and feelings of obligation and gratitude ran deep, especially in the Confucian ruling class. Yet looking north, they knew from their own experience that the Manchus were formidable and dangerous, and while most Koreans looked down on them as unlettered "barbarians," there were significant numbers of statesmen who took a realistic attitude toward their strength. The troubled reign of Prince Kwanghae (1608–1623) was a period of clever shifting on the part of the Koreans. An instructive example is the major Ming campaign, designed to wipe out the Manchu threat once and for all, which was launched in 1619. Ming demanded Korean participation, and the heavily obligated Koreans were in no position to refuse. Yet they had few illusions over the likely outcome. The Koreans in the end marched into battle alongside the Ming troops, but at the first opportunity surrendered to the Manchus, thereby acknowledging at the same time both their obligations and the realities of their position.[41] (The estimated Chinese losses in this battle were nearly 46,000 men in only four days of fighting.)[42] From this time on, many in Korea were inclined to take the Manchu side, but Ming loyalist forces prevailed. Deposing the too realistic (but also dynastically vulnerable) Prince Kwanghae, the pro-Ming hard-liners put their own candidate on the throne (1623) and began taking more positive anti-Manchu measures. These included support for the Chinese general Mao Wen-lung, who operated against the Manchus from Korean bases. The new policy provoked both internal rebellion—that of the pro-Manchu Yi Kwal in 1624,[43] which was defeated—and Manchu invasions. Yet after the first Manchu incursion in 1627, which was not particularly destructive and seems to have been designed more to scare than to destroy, the Korean hardliners continued their pro-Ming efforts, and in 1636 were visited with a much stronger and angrier attack. After a humiliating treaty and the departure of all the royal princes and some leading pro-Ming politicians to their captivity in Shen-yang, the Koreans finally now capitulated to the Manchus and cut off all relations with Ming. Eight years later, when Peking in its turn had fallen, the Korean hostages were allowed to return, and a normal, if icy, tributary relationship began with the Manchus' Ch'ing dynasty. Even so, pro-Ming sentiments and even an official pro-Ming cult continued in Korea well into the nineteenth century, though all of this was kept well away from the eyes of the Manchus.

Of all the northern conquest-dynasties in China, that of the Manchus lasted the longest. During their long rule there were two major new developments for Chinese foreign relations. The first was the virtual end of the possibility of major, unified nomadic confederations arising in the steppe region. This came about with the disappearance of steppe power as the result of successful policies of conquest from both the Manchu and the Russian side. Looked at in another way, the Russians had moved into position to replace the nomads as China's main northern antagonist. The second major development was, of course, the growth of the maritime Western powers and their steady (and after the 1830s, acute) penetration of China. Looked at in terms of internal forces, the overthrow of the Manchu regime was a classical case of Chinese resurgence. But on this occasion there was also the external maritime pressure, which arguably had at least as much to do with the decline and fall of the Manchus as the internal forces. When we contemplate the role of the maritime powers in the fall of Ch'ing, and recall that they had already been having an impact on China for most of the length of the Ming dynasty (major Japanese pirate attacks on the Chinese coast began early in the fifteenth century, and Western merchants and missionaries—with guns on the decks of their ships—began to appear already in the second decade of the sixteenth century), we can then see with the benefit of hindsight that the alien pressures that contributed to Ming's downfall were not just from the north but also from the sea (the human and material costs of the anti-Japanese campaigns both along the southern coast and in Korea were heavy). From the standpoint of this essay, which examines East Asian history from the viewpoint of the north-south rhythms along the Manchurian frontiers of China and Korea, we are justified in bringing the Yin III period to a close with the fall of the Manchus in 1911. But from another viewpoint, which would probably be shared by the statesmen of the People's Republic of China, it could be argued that the major intruders on Chinese civilization in Yin III were not the Manchus but the Western merchants, missionaries, and gunboats, and that Yin III did not come to an end until their expulsion in 1949.

When Does Yang Turn to Yin?

In the classical formulation, Yin and Yang are correlative and not absolute forces. Each implies the other in correlative degree; as one waxes, the other wanes. In the discussion of northeastern frontier relationships above, I have arbitrarily marked the dividing point between the Yang and Yin phases at the end of the major dynasties—Han (220), T'ang (907), and Ming (1644). But like the changes of Yin and Yang, the forces that brought their fall obviously did not rise in an instant, nor did the influence of their institutions and achievements count for nothing after they were gone. Moreover, as may be recalled from the discussion of the end of the period Yang I, there were vigorous Chinese thrusts into Manchuria even after the fall of Han; many of the gains made by these Wei dynasty campaigns were held by Western Chìn until late in the third century, and China was not decisively overcome until 317, when the intensifying Hsiung-nu incursions in the Central Plain finally forced the Chìn dynasty to move its capital to the south. The year 317 marks not only one of the most important social and political divisions in Chinese history, but also one in which a major part—better, *the* major part—of China's land is taken over by non-Chinese aliens. A division of comparable significance is that of 1127, when Sung was chased from the Central Plain by the Jurchens and forced to move its capital to Hang-chou. A good argument could be made for identifying these dates of north-south division as the dividing point between the Yang and Yin phases. In any case, the effort to establish a precise date may increase our understanding of the problems involved, and this is what is important, not the date itself.

In the following two tables, both schemes are laid out. Table 11.1 separates Yang and Yin at the fall of the three major Chinese dynasties; Table 11.2, at the dates of north-south division.

No clear lesson leaps from these figures. The length of Cycles I and II is in the range of 800 years, while Cycle III is noticeably shorter. Although the Yang phase gets shorter with each cycle, the length of the Yin phase shows no particular pattern. The length of Yin II, of special interest to us in this volume, is the longest of any of the phases. In Table 11.2 where there is no north-south division in Cycle III, I continue to date the division in that cycle by the fall of Ming.

In this showing, the Yang-Yin profiles of Cycles I and II are strikingly similar. The Yin phases of all three cycles are of nearly comparable length—about 260 years, while the Yang phase of Cycle III is just about half

TABLE 11.1

CYCLE	YANG PHASE		YIN PHASE		TOTAL
I	221 B.C. – A.D. 220	441 years	220–589	369 years	810 years
II	589–907	318 years	907–1368	461 years	779 years
III	1368–1644	276 years	1644–1911	267 years	543 years
Total		1,035 years		1,097 years	2,132 years

TABLE 11.2

CYCLE	YANG PHASE		YIN PHASE		TOTAL
I	221 B.C. – A.D. 317	538 years	317–589	272 years	810 years
II	589–1127	538 years	1127–1368	241 years	779 years
III	1368–1644	276 years	1644–1911	267 years	543 years
Total		1,352 years		780 years	2,132 years

the length of the Yang phase in Cycles I and II. The fact that both of the earlier cycles had a north-south division seems to coincide with a significantly greater length of the period preceding the division. When we look at the actual dynastic pattern in Cycles I and II, further similarities emerge. In each case, following the major Chinese dynasty (I, Han; II, T'ang), there is a breakup of the cosmopolis into regional states (I, "Three Kingdoms" following Han; II, "Five Dynasties" and "Ten Kingdoms" following T'ang). Then, again in each case, there is a reconstituted, unified Chinese state (I, Chìn; II, Sung), which after a while loses the Central Plain to northern invaders and finishes out its days in refuge in the south.

Although the inclusion of the northern or pre-division years of Chìn and Sung in the Yang phase of Table 11.2 makes for neater figures, it does not square well with the fact that significant pressure from the north is already pronounced by the time the major dynasties had ended, if not even earlier. The heroics of Three Kingdoms Wei in clipping the wings of the Kung-sun satraps in the 230s and of Koguryŏ in the 240s only point up the fact that the challenge from those areas was already intense; besides, Koguryŏ, though severely stung, had over 400 years before it, while the Wei dynasty had just a few more than 20. In Cycle II, the northern pressure on the Central Plain was even more immediate and palpable following the fall of the major Chinese dynasty. The Khitans were already king-makers in the Five Dynasties period and had encroached on northern Chinese territory. There were vast northern tracts of T'ang territory that Sung never saw. Another striking similarity in Cycles I and II is the internal division and strife that follows the fall of the major dynasties.

All of the signs suggest that the fundamental character of the epochs in which Chìn and Sung came to power was introverted and defensive—in the present analysis, a Yin phase. Both states are to be characterized as successor states attempting to restore the Chinese ecumene on the model of their powerful predecessors Han and T'ang. While both states saw the beginnings of much that was new, important, and durable in Chinese culture, in fact they themselves consciously strove to re-establish something that had been lost. In broad East Asian perspective, they were Chinese holdouts in a general age of dominance by northern peoples. Though the residual vitality of Chinese culture and the stored-up inertia of Chinese administration and governance were sufficient to maintain unified Chinese successor states for a time, Chìn and Sung were themselves too weak and too hemmed-in to be able to carry out the frontier-wide strategy that was necessary to drive the invaders out and protect China's heartland in the Central Plain, and in the end they had to flee for their lives to the south.

Yet there is one striking difference between Chìn and Sung. Chìn was relatively unstable politically and rather short-lived, while Sung had remarkable political stability and was one of the most durable of Chinese dynasties. Its unified phase lasted for 167 years (960–1127) and its southern phase 152 years (1127–1279) for a total of 319 years, the longest dynasty in Chinese history if one excludes the three dynasties of the pre-unification era and counts Former and Later Han as two dynasties. The parallel numbers for Chìn are 52 years unified (265–317) and 103 years in the south (317–420) for a total of 155 years.

Observations on the Yang Phase

The most obvious generalization to be made about the Yang phase, in any of the cycles, is that the Chinese have the initiative. The mode of action is expansive. In terms of the Central Plain and the development of the northern frontier, the direction of action is northward, although as southern China becomes more developed, the expansive mode also operates southward and out to sea. On the northern frontier, the Chinese presence is military and aggressive. It is also far-reaching: the strategists are concerned with the entire frontier, all the way from Korea to Sinkiang. It is this comprehensive and strategically unified management of the frontier which gives the Chinese the edge over the much more mobile and warlike nomads. The maintenance of such a system, of course, depends on the general political and social health of the state, and when this begins to decline we can see props and actors being moved into position for the Yin phase.

Diplomatically, Yang periods are the heyday of the "tribute system." China is dominant, demands and receives submission and tribute from newly subject peoples, and reclaims the allegiance of former tributaries. In the other direction, Chinese culture spreads far and wide and arguably exerts more influence and wins more respect for China than its armies do. In Yang I, the culture-bearers are mainly merchants and soldiers, and the emphasis is on material culture: we see plenty of Chinese weapons, metal, money, and manufactures. These items are certainly not absent in T'ang's Yang II, but we see in addition much more representation of the higher culture: Chinese monks and teachers, Chinese books and writing, Buddhism and (more weakly) Confucianism. In Yang III, the peripheral states are already so accustomed to Chinese culture that it is harder to see new things, but one especially significant cultural export is Neo-Confucianism (it is symptomatic of Sung's Yin character that although it develops Neo-Confucianism, it does not export it).

In Manchuria and Korea, the Yang phase always brings an aggressive Chinese army. Emperor Wu conquers Chosŏn and establishes Lo-lang; T'ang's T'ai-tsung and Kao-tsung wear down Koguryŏ; Ming's Hung-wu emperor intimidates the Koreans and threatens invasion over the T'ieh-ling issue. In Yang I, the aggression results in new territory for China, in the form of new commanderies with Chinese governors, officials, soldiers, and even a sizable Chinese population. In Yang II and III, the final arrangement is more satisfactory to the victims: a tributary arrangement that, though it costs them some face and pride, does connect them directly to the Chinese cosmopolis and promotes a significant degree of internal political stability, which lasts as long as T'ang and Ming last. (T'ang's demise is followed quickly by Parhae's and Silla's, while Ming's disappearance radically affects the life and politics of the Yi dynasty in Chosŏn.) One can observe a progressive weakening of the Chinese presence in Korea as the cycles progress. In Yang I there are occupying armies and Chinese administrators. In Yang II the armies invade but they soon go away. In Yang III they do not even invade, though they threaten to do so. Corresponding to the decreasing Chinese military pressure is an increasing political and military sophistication in Korea; the steadily growing strength of its own culture and political order makes it progressively less vulnerable to Chinese aggression. In Manchuria, on the other hand, Chinese administrators and frontier commissioners are solidly in control in all three Yang phases.

It might be instructive, if somewhat risky, to conclude this set of generalizations on Yang situations by observing the opening scenes of Yang IV. One must enter all the caveats: this period as yet has little historical depth, and its trends are perhaps not clear. On the other hand, this survey of the situations of Yang I, II, and III has yielded enough parallels and similarities that it will be at least interesting to see if we can find evidence of corresponding phenomena in the beginning of Yang IV.

The process by which the Chinese have again become dominant in their own political order has been a two-stage one. The revolution of 1911 overthrew the alien Manchus but did not touch the Western maritime powers whose penetration of China during the nineteenth century had done so much to undermine the Ch'ing dynasty. The removal of this second inhibitant to the development of autonomous Chinese authority was accomplished by the communist revolution of 1949. There is room for argument in the assignment of the starting role in this Yang phase. One could see the Republic of China as the forerunner in the reassertion of Chinese control. It overthrew the Manchus and did much to introduce and develop a framework for the future growth of the Chinese state in the modern world. Yet the task was difficult and complex and can now be seen to have been beyond the resources of the Republic, which aside from its own weaknesses had to contend with further depredations from the maritime powers, principally Japan. It never had solid control of the whole country; in addition to having to cope with all the regional satrapies headed by the "warlords" and with the Japanese invasion, it was also involved in a civil war with the communist forces, who had a different design for the future. In the end it could not withstand the communists and had to flee and leave the mainland to them. Some aspects of this short history remind one of the Sui dynasty, an indubitably Chinese dynasty, which played a major role in bringing the period Yin I to an end, but which did not have the energy necessary to launch Yang II. This role went to T'ang.

The People's Republic, on the other hand, already has performed a fair proportion of the traditional Yang role. It has unified China, established centralized institutions whose force carries to the edges of the state, and now devotes its major foreign policy energies to the protection of its northern frontier. It identifies the "barbarians" as the Russians, and it confronts them across the entire northern frontier, from the Ussuri River in the east, through the pro-Soviet Mongolian People's Republic in the center, on to Sinkiang in the west. It is also striking that the first foreign excursion of the Chinese army after the consolidation of its political victory in 1949 was an invasion of Korea, as if Han Wu-ti, T'ang T'ai-tsung, and Ming's Hung-wu emperor were all together down in the prompter's box voicing out the script. The object of this attack was not the Koreans, nor even the Russians, but the Americans, in 1950 the leaders of the Western maritime group of nations that the communists had just expelled from China itself. Their object in this campaign, which they were successful in achieving, was to keep the Americans at a safe distance from their Manchurian frontier and to make sure that the state that bordered "Northeast" (Tung-pei: the term "Manchuria" was no longer used) was friendly and supportive of its goals. Now, thirty years later, the Democratic People's Republic of Korea, which was thus saved from becoming an American base, is seen by China as the support for the eastern anchor of its frontier against the Russians—a role that the North Koreans cannot welcome and which gives them difficulties evocative of those borne at the end of Yin II and the beginning of Yang III by Koryŏ and Chosŏn. The dexterity of today's Koreans compares favorably with that of their ancestors.

The present division of the Korean state into two contending halves is not without parallels to the ending in Yin I, just prior to the peninsular unification that developed in Yang II with the cooperation of T'ang, or to that at the end of Yin II, when Korea was fighting to keep its northern half from being sundered from its southern half as Ming was already advancing into Yang III. All of this suggests a Korean lag that is operative in these modern days as well. The outcome of the present peninsular split cannot be predicted. Both states are strong, and both have powerful supporters who will not be uninvolved in the final solution. For Korea, the end of Yin III has not yet come, but it watches the unfolding of Yang IV in China with great interest.

Observations on the Yin Phase

The end of the Yang phase comes with the progressive decline in the vitality of Chinese political, military, and social institutions. We need not go into the often-cited "end-of-the-dynasty" syndrome here; its features are well enough known. Yet it is worth observing that the terms in which this phenomenon is usually described are more relevant to the Chinese dynasties of Yang phases than to the dynasties of Yin phases, either Chinese or non-Chinese. In any case, as the decline proceeds, the "barbarians" in the north begin to see opportunities, and then to seize them. Ultimately, the Chinese position becomes untenable and the northern invaders sweep in, establishing their own dynasties as they do. The articulation of their political dominance into these states, all with Chinese names and staffed with Chinese officials, is a tribute to the power of the influence of these Chinese institutions over the invaders, as well as a testimonial to the now obvious Chinese inability to command these institutions themselves.

The process by which these alien states are established is not a rapid one. In Cycles I and II, at least, the unified Chinese state falls, but its administrative structure continues to have its influence in fragmented and regional form. This period of regional division lasts for sixty years following the fall of Han in 220 (the "Three Kingdoms") and seventy-one years following the fall of T'ang in 907 (though the "Five Dynasties" come to an end in 960, the last of the "Ten Kingdoms" is not defeated by Sung until 978). A Chinese successor state, Chin or Sung, then arises in the manner we have already described and attempts to reunite China but ultimately fails. At this point the northern invaders move in and establish their states in the Chinese heartland. The whole process of fragmentation, reconstitution, and redivision is seen to take a considerable amount of time. In Yin I, this period covers 97 years (220–317); in Yin II it lasts for 219 years (907–1126). The time element is easily appreciated when we notice that Cycle III, which lacks such a period, is much shorter than Cycles I and II. The absence of the fragmentation—reconstitution—redivision sequence in Cycle III makes it quite different from the first two cycles and has a great deal to do with the general continuity of institutions from Ming to Ch'ing.

It need hardly be repeated that Yin periods always feature the establishment of "barbarian" states in the Central Plain, but there is a progression of this theme from one cycle to another that makes each repetition of the process quite different. In Yin I the "barbarian" inflow is really barbarian: no quotation marks are necessary. The sequence climaxes with chaos in 317 and continues in that mode for the rest of the fourth century. This is the period of the "Sixteen Kingdoms," a term which adequately hints at the political and social dislocations. One general feature that can be seen through all the smoke is that northern China itself tends to be divided between eastern and western blocs. Former Ch'in, the strongest of these northern states, for a decade or so managed to unify both blocs, but the split reemerged after Ch'in burned itself out attacking the south. The T'o-pa (Northern) Wei finally brought some stability and in the process created one of the longest-lasting (385–534) of the northern dynasties, but even this rather successful state ended its existence in eastern and western halves. The final bout of struggle involving these two Weis, the Northern Ch'i and Chou, and the Sui, finally brought this long period to an end. Northern China had not seen its last alien state, but it never again had to suffer the intensity of intrusion that occurred in the Yin I period.

Sung's exceptionally long and successful maintenance of the Chinese polity in the north during Yin II undoubtedly contributed to the strikingly different character of the alien presence in this period. The Khitans, despite their epochal unification of all of the Manchurian area, were successfully prevented from taking over the Central Plain. There is a widespread tendency in the conventional wisdom of sinology to pity poor Sung for having to endure the Khitan humiliation, but given the events of Yin I and II, perhaps we ought rather to sigh in admiration as Sung keeps the Khitans bottled up in Manchuria and northern Ho-pei for 165 years (960–1125). Moreover, this defense is accomplished with the right hand, as it were, for with the left Sung fends off the Tangut Hsi Hsia on its northwest. It is only a new and more vigorous force in the Jurchens that manages to break through and, while replacing the Khitans in the northeast, fulfills the true Yin mission of ousting the Chinese rulers from their heartland. But this routine accomplishment only sets the stage for the Mongols, who go on to displace the Jurchens and take over all the Chinese south as well. This modification in the script remains in Yin III, but the Manchus combine the roles of the Khitans, Jurchens, and Mongols and accomplish the conquest of all of Manchuria and China in a relatively short period with much less fuss and bother.

If there is a progressive simplification from Yin I to Yin III in the mode of alien takeover, there is also a progressive sinicization in the institutions and culture of these states. In Yin I, despite their impressive efforts, Chinese advisers were unable to redeem some of the earlier intruders from their barbarism, although with the Northern Wei they had considerable success. By Yin II, Chinese institutions were so widely known and admired that the Khitans successfully adapted them even without moving from Manchuria into the Central Plain, and this early adaptation assured the similar acculturation of the Jurchens. The large numbers of sophisticated Khitans and Jurchens, in addition to the equally numerous purely Chinese advisers and officials, assured a basic continuum of Chinese life and style under the Mongols, although the Mongols themselves seem to have been markedly less susceptible to this acculturation than most of the other alien intruders in China. In Yin III, the Manchus superbly and rapidly absorbed Chinese culture and institutions, so much so that it is actually difficult, as time goes by, to see their actual alien identity. One might generalize that as China's soldiers fall back, China's culture steps forward and continues the struggle. In most cases, the alien regimes are so sinicized as the Yin phase comes to an end that they only have to be defeated, not literally ousted from China. Only at the end of Yin II are the alien peoples, the Mongols, still alien enough that they must be physically and militarily driven out. It is a common cliché that China does not conquer its enemies but absorbs them. What needs to be pointed out here is that this is for the most part a Yin-phase phenomenon.

One of the crucial areas in acculturation is diplomacy. The alien regimes seem especially receptive to the guidance of Chinese diplomatic practices, even though the rhetoric and orientation of these practices are classically related to Yang and not Yin phases. In effect, the occupiers of the Central Plain assume the position that tributary obligations due the former Chinese occupant are now due them. This introduces a certain strain and contradiction into the process. On the one hand, unlike the clear Chinese dominance of the Yang periods, the Yin eras are more often characterized by a balance and sometimes an equality of forces. On the other hand, acceptance by the tributary of Chinese diplomatic rhetoric is part and parcel of its general acceptance and respect for Chinese civilization itself. When non-Chinese regimes demand no less than the Chinese do, the submitting party may experience strain and tension, not to speak of resentment that it should have to be deferential to people that it may regard as inferiors.[44] This tension can be seen in the diplomatic documents of Yin periods, which though cast in the standard Chinese rhetoric of Yang phases, often present between the lines, and even in the lines, the more complex international problems of the Yin phases.

Looking at the specifically Manchurian aspects of the Yin situations, we can see that the Manchurian power becomes a more important actor as we progress from Yin I to Yin III. In Yin I, the Hsien-pei make an impact on the Central Plain but cannot durably occupy it. In Yin II, the Jurchens occupy the Central Plain. In Yin III, the Manchus go on to occupy all of China. There is a special situation in Yin I, since Manchuria is not unified as it is in Yin II and III. The Hsien-pei contend with Koguryŏ but have their sights set on China. The Koguryŏ and the Puyŏ, however, keep their eyes pointed straight to the south, into the Korean peninsula, and in the end, both peoples, though they have a Manchurian origin, become Korean peoples. The Puyŏ create their own state in Paekche and push their influence deeply into Japan, but the few who remain in Manchuria are either eliminated by the Hsien-pei or absorbed by their Koguryŏ cousins. Koguryŏ involves itself principally in Korean, not Chinese affairs, and in the end develops a peninsular outllook, which continues into Yin II as its descendants in northern Korea create in Koryŏ a state that henceforth accepts its confinement to the lands south of the Yalu.

In their relationship to the Manchurian and Chinese states, the Korean states have a special problem not found in the other East Asian theaters. While the northern peoples are invaded by the Chinese only in the course of the Yang phases, and the Chinese are invaded by the northern peoples only during the Yin phases, the Koreans are invaded in the course of both phases. (Of all the contestants along the North China—Manchuria axis, only the Jurchens did not invade Korea. This was because Koryŏ accommodated the Jurchens' demands and bought off an invasion—though not without considerable internal political turmoil over the issue.)[45] Thus, while China has suffered only three waves of alien assault from the north, Korea has suffered six waves, three from Chinese and three from non-Chinese invaders. Korea is not in either case the prime object of action, but only a secondary object. The primary battle is between Manchuria and the Central Plain. Whichever power has the momentum expects Korea's compliance in its designs. Aside from the period Yang I, in which the Korean peoples' political development is inadequate and they suffer Chinese occupation and administration, Korea is not usually governed by its conquerors. (Again, the Mongols are somewhat exceptional, but even they put only the northern part of Korea adjacent to Manchuria under their direct administration.) In spite of their seeming advantage over the Chinese of the Central Plain in not having to suffer direct alien administration, the Koreans suffer a clear disadvantage in being *everybody's* object of wrath. They are only half a plum, but twice a bone.

A Korean "Lag" and "Jump" in the Timing of Yang and Yin

Another special Korean feature of the Yang-Yin cycle lies in the timing of the two phases. Vis-à-vis China and Manchuria, the rhythm of Yin and

Yang is determined by possession of the Central Plain. But for Korea, the metronome beats in Manchuria. It is axiomatic that in Yang phases the Chinese possess the Central Plain before they possess Manchuria, and history shows that the Korean accommodation to the new Yang phase always comes later still. In Yang I, the definitive pacification of Liao-tung and Korea occurred in 108 B.C., or 113 years after the Ch'in unification in 221 B.C. In Yang II, the T'ang defeat of Koguryŏ did not occur until 668, 79 years after Sui's unification of China, while the successful launching of Silla's peninsular role—accommodation with China but independent control of her own territory—did not occur until the departure of the Chinese military administration in 676, or 87 years after the Sui unification that began Yang II in China. In Yang III, the Ming dynasty was established in the Central Plain in 1368, but the defeat of the Mongol forces in eastern Manchuria did not occur until 1387, and the Korean accommodation was sealed only with the founding of the Yi dynasty in 1392, for a total lag of 24 years. This analysis shows no Korean counterpart for China's Yang I. In that particular instance, Han China destroyed the Korean state of Chosŏn and stayed to administer the conquered territory for some four centuries. There was no Korean accommodation, and the political development of the surrounding Korean peoples, hostile or friendly to the Chinese in varying degrees, was not sufficient for the founding of durable, independent states. For the rest, it is noted that as the cycles progress, the Yang lag in Korea becomes progressively shorter: it would seem that the historical process reflected in the Yang-Yin phasing becomes sharper as time goes on. But this is probably a coincidence, since, as we shall see, the corresponding "Yin jump" is nowhere near so clear; moreover, if my rule is correct—that Korean Yang phases are marked by the appearance of independent, unified Korean states in accommodation with China—then the Korean Yang IV has not yet begun, even though 67 (or 29) years have passed since the beginning of Chinese Yang IV in 1911 (or 1949). Table 11.3 sums up the Yang lag in Manchuria and Korea.

If the Yang beginnings in Manchuria and Korea lag behind those of the Central Plain, the Yin beginnings are usually a jump ahead of them. The rise of the Manchurian states is both a result and a cause of the decline of Chinese control in Manchuria. And by the time that these states are ready to move into the Central Plain, they have already disrupted, if not severed, Korea's relationship with China, so that Korea's Yin period too begins earlier than China's.

The chronological facts of this Yin "jump" are, however, not quite as sharp as those of the Yang "lag." Because the histories are seldom as informative on the process of Chinese decline as they are on the great victories at the beginning of the major dynasties, the actual dates of the loss of Chinese control in Manchuria are less easy to pinpoint, even if the general course of events is clear enough.

Table 11.3

CYCLE	YANG BEGINNING CENTRAL PLAIN	MANCHURIA		KOREA	
		DATE	LAG	DATE	LAG
I	221 B.C.	108 B.C.	113 years	(none)	(none)
II	589	668	79 years	676	87 years
III	1368	1387	19 years	1392	24 years

The loss of Han control in Manchuria began around the 160s and 170s. In 189 the authority of the central government, which in the Central Plain itself was crumbling in the face of rebellion and civil war, was permanently eclipsed when the Chinese governor of Liao-tung, Kung-sun Tu, dissociated himself from the regime in the capital and purged the local pro-Han gentry. From then on until the defeat of Kung-sun Tu's grandson in 238, Manchuria was independent. The Kung-sun family inherited the Chinese military and administrative machinery for frontier control and exercised it with some effectiveness, but the rise of the Manchurian and Korean peoples was under way. The Puyŏ and Koguryŏ kings already presided over moderately developed states, which now, removed from Chinese manipulation and control, began to gather their own momentum. From the point of view of these two states, a date around 200 would be appropriate for marking their emergence as independent forces controlling their own destiny. The southern Korean peoples were still over a century away from this stage, but even they had developed into a force that caused serious Chinese concern; it was to fend off this southern pressure that the Kung-sun satraps established the commandery of Tai-fang, in western central Korea, in about 204. The definitive beginnings of the southern states came as a result of the dramatic Puyŏ and Koguryŏ interventions in the south after the middle of the fourth century.

Fixing the beginning of the Yin phase in Cycle II is no easier than in Cycle I. T'ang's An-tung Military Command, with its headquarters in Liao-tung after 676, lasted only eighty years before its abolition in 756. But firm and generally friendly tributary relations with Parhae and Silla continued almost to the end of the ninth century, even though this activity was limited and perfunctory after the Huang Ch'ao Rebellion of the 870s. In western Manchuria, T'ang's military headquarters at Ying-chou, which administered the frontier with the Khitans, was still active in the last decade of the dynasty. But by 901, Yeh-lü A-pao-chi's unification of the Khitans, Hsi, and Shih-wei peoples was well advanced, and the establishment of his Liao dynasty in 907 preceded T'ang's formal fall, if only by a few months. In this picture, it is not possible to find a single crucial date, but an approximation of about 890 for purposes of calculation would not be wide of the general truth. As for Korea, Silla, like T'ang, came to an end in a swirl of rebellions and secession movements. "Later Paekche" proclaimed its independence of Silla in 891, and "Later Koguryŏ" began in 901. Since it was the latter state that proved to be durable (despite changes in name to Majin in 904 and to T'aebong in 911, culminating in Wang Kŏn's coup and the final change to "Koryŏ" in 918) and inherited the peninsula for the whole of the Yin II period, we could arbitrarily fix the beginning of Korea's Yin II period in that year.

The beginning of Ming's end in Manchuria, and thus the beginning of the period Yin II, is somewhat easier to pinpoint, although a choice of dates could be advanced. Some might argue that Ming was already losing hold during the Wan-li period, but the successful campaigns in the Ordos and in Korea in the 1590s show the Chinese, though beleaguered, still carrying out their Yang mission. But in 1619 the Manchus decimated the Chinese expedition sent against them, and when they captured Shen-yang and Liao-yang in 1621 it was virtually all over for Ming north of the Wall. Korea's Yin III presents an interesting problem, since there was no change of dynasty. The Yi state of Chosŏn continued right up until 1910 (despite a cosmetic name change in 1897), giving it an extraordinary longevity of 518 years. But Korean historiography has always treated the dynasty in two halves and with considerable justification. Yet while Korean historians customarily make the division during the Hideyoshi invasions (known as the Imjin Wars), I would place it in the period of difficulties with the Manchus. Not only was the Korean-Chinese alliance against the Japanese a successful manifestation of Yang achievement, but it was really the Manchus and not the Japanese who were the Yin III force. Korean accommodation to the Manchus, bitter and reluctant as it was, came in 1636 when all hope of further relations with Ming was lost as a result of a militarily and psychologically devastating Manchu campaign. It was this event that began Yin III in Korea.

We can sum up the above discussion in table 11.4, observing only that though the general pattern is clear, the dates are not as sharp as those for the Yang phase.

Although this table attempts only to pinpoint beginnings, the pattern it reveals is also borne out at major nodal points within the complicated Yin II phase. This period saw not one but three northern contenders for the Central Plain—the Khitans, the Jurchens, and the Mongols. Although only the last two actually succeeded in occupying northern China, all three put pressure, often very destructive, on Korea. The Khitan settlement with Sung, represented by the 1005 treaty of Shan-yüan, has an analogue in the settlement with Korea in 993, for a jump of twelve years. (The disruption of relations with Sung, which was one of the stipulations of the 993 agreement, proved to be ephemeral, however, and the more durable Koryŏ-Sung break did not occur until 1022.) The Jurchens defeated the Khitan Liao in 1125, but had already disrupted Koryŏ-Liao relations in 1116, for a Korean jump of nine years. The Mongols destroyed the Jurchen Chin dynasty in

Table 11.4

CYCLE	YIN BEGINNING CENTRAL PLAIN	MANCHURIA		KOREA	
		DATE	JUMP	DATE	JUMP
I	220	189	31 years	200	20 years
II	907	890	17 years	901	6 years
III	1644	1621	23 years	1636	6 years

1234, but had already disrupted Koryŏ-Chin relations by about 1214, a jump of twenty years.

One final aspect of the Korean Yin phases is worth noting. Culturally and politically, these periods reveal relatively greater Korean creativity and independence. Everyone always talks of how important Chinese influence is in the development of Korean civilization, and obviously it is tremendous, but a case could be made for the more interesting and crucial Korean developments taking place when China's influence is weak and removed in the Yin periods. The Korean state itself is a product of Yin I. Korean cultural and political development was more intense and spectacular in a few decades of fourth-century chaos than in 421 years of Chinese rule from Lo-lang. This is not to say that the development itself does not reflect Chinese influence, only that Chinese influence appears much more attractive when Chinese armies and commissioners are far away. And the matrix into which this Chinese influence was introduced was distinctively Korean. The period Yin II vibrates with Korean tremors of independence and assertiveness. The Koryŏ state comes into existence when China is utterly unable to have any say in what happens in the peninsula. Its founder's instructions emphasize Korea's unique culture and values. Although ecumenical Confucianism has its role in Koryŏ, it is Buddhism, with its Korean syncretic elements and its striking appeals to Korean national feeling, that dominates Koryŏ's intellectual and religious life. In Yin III, Korea's virulent (but often hidden) hostility to the Manchus is the other side of the coin of Korean pride and self-esteem, and this period is generally acknowledged to be the most creative half of the Yi dynasty as far as art, literature, and intellectual life are concerned. I do not at all wish to slight the very substantial achievements of Korean Yang periods; it is impossible not to admire the political, cultural, and literary achievements made by Korea in ages when the Chinese model was bright and vibrant in its own right. But most Korean critics nowadays would regard these achievements as more Chinese and less Korean in character and feeling and therefore, in today's nationalist atmosphere, less interesting. The Yin periods, I suspect, give them more to be cheerful about. (Parenthetically, one could observe that it is not just Korea where creativity thrives during the Yin periods. For intrinsic interest and depth, many might argue that Chinese philosophy and intellectual life were much more spectacular and fertile in the Yin periods of the Warring

States, Six Dynasties, Sung, and Ch'ing than in the Yang dynasties of Han, T'ang, and Ming.)

Some Special Features of the Period Yin II

In the foregoing discussion and analysis, various references have been made to the special features of the period I have designated Yin II, which corresponds to the period of East Asian history from the tenth through the fourteenth century, which is under particular scrutiny in this volume. It seems worthwhile to conclude with a summary of these special Yin II features, touching first on China, then on Manchuria and Korea, and finally adding some thoughts on various unique factors associated with the Mongols.

A major conclusion of this essay is that the Sung dynasty was a special dynasty in the long flow of Chinese history. The common tendency is to regard Sung as one of the great Chinese dynasties, ranking with Han, T'ang, Ming, and Ch'ing. Surely there is much to support such a view. Sung ranked with these others in durability and in cultural and social creativity; indeed, many might say that it surpassed them. Its statesmen, thinkers, soldiers, and craftsmen bequeathed an immense assortment of achievements to their posterity and to the world. But Sung was not "just another dynasty." It played an almost unique role in the continuity of Chinese political tradition. Whereas the Yang states of Han, T'ang, and Ming dominated their ages and vigorously extended their power and influence beyond China's borders, Sung was a beleaguered state, under constant pressure from powerful northern neighbors, unable to reassert Chinese control over many regions in the south which under T'ang had been full-fledged constituents of the Chinese state (Ta-li and Vietnam), and unable even to maintain Chinese rule in China's very heartland in the Central Plain. But rather than considering Sung for these reasons to have been a dynasty *manqué*, it would be more pertinent to accept Sung's troubles as an indicator of the overwhelming forces arrayed against it, and therefore as a measure of the genuine success that Sung did have in resisting these outside forces.

Sung spent its entire long life of 319 years in struggle against the alien regimes of the north. The military phases of this struggle were, relative to the entire length of the dynasty, fairly short, but there was no doubt in the minds of most Sung statesmen that, whatever the limits on their action at any given time, the dynastic mission was to hold out against these aliens and, if possible, to prevail over them. The issue was simple: the aliens did not deserve to govern China, and Sung did. A crucial difference between the Yin II period and Yin III is that the latter had no dynasty corresponding to Sung. Sung had picked up the pieces of the shattered T'ang state and put most of them back together again, cohesively enough so that it could hold out against the various Yin forces for an impressive length of time. No such state rose up in Yin III to save the legacy of Ming and weather the icy Yin blasts from the north; rather, Ming simply collapsed and was replaced, virtually overnight, by the alien Manchu regime. Sung did share this particular Yin defensive role with the Chin dynasty in Yin I, as has already been pointed out. Yet in spite of their similar profiles, Chin cannot compare with Sung in achievement. Not only was it much shorter and less stable than Sung, but it suffered a much more severe challenge from the north. After Chin's flight southward, it lasted barely a century before it had to pass its mission on to a series of four more short-lived Chinese dynasties whose rulers never saw the Central Plain.

Sung, in sum, has no close analogue in Chinese history. Not only did it successfully defend Chinese civilization for over three centuries of continuous assault, but it added immeasurably to the luster of that civilization. Ultimately, of course, it fell; it could not last out the Yin II storm. But Sung supporters might take heart that it was no ordinary northern enemy that had prevailed, but a most unusual enemy, the likes of which cannot be found in any other Yin phase: the Mongols. I shall return to them in a moment.

Moving up to Manchuria, we may recall that the Yin II period saw an epochal unification in this region. When the Khitans conquered the extensive state of Parhae (Po-hai) in 926, and launched their sway over a territory that stretched from the western slopes of the Hsing-an Mountains to the shores of the Eastern Sea, they harnessed populations and resources which no mere Yin-phase Chinese state, even a strong one like Sung, could overcome. Combining these resources with the social and political cement of borrowed Chinese culture and administration, they formed a state, in the Liao dynasty, which was able to hold the balance of power in East Asia for nearly two centuries. It was Liao that dictated the terms of survival to Sung, Hsi Hsia, and Koryŏ. These states were strong enough to hold out, but they did not and could not control the action and set the conditions as Liao did. Liao's achievement has no analogue in Yin I, when Manchuria was divided into eastern and western halves often in competition with each other. On the other hand, Manchurian unification became the rule for the rest of Yin II and for all of Yin III. It was a new mode in the Yin phases of East Asian history which was to become permanent.

Another unique feature of Yin II in Manchuria is the establishment of not one but three successive states in that area. Evidently, the unification of Manchuria was such an inspiring achievment to the surrounding peoples that many aspired to the same goal: following the Liao period of Manchurian unification (926–1115) came the Chin unified period of 90 years (1125–1215) and the Mongol unified period of 172 years (1215–1387).[46] It would seem that the rise of a brand-new geopolitical entity, which almost operates with its own rhythm, is one of the reasons why the northern forces of Yin II lasted so long, compared with those of Yin I and Yin III (see Table 11.1, above). But part of this great length must be charged to the special factors introduced by the Mongols, as we shall see.

Finally, the defeat of Parhae in 926 was the final blow to Korean pretensions to the territory north of the Yalu. Some might argue that Parhae was not, strictly speaking, a Korean state in the first place; but at the very least its mixed population certainly had a dominant Koguryŏ element, and it used the name "Koryŏ" in its foreign relations with Japan. Some modern Korean historians consider Parhae Korea's "Northern dynasty" and Silla its "Southern dynasty" in the period from the eighth to the tenth century. Although I do not consider this kind of analysis particularly useful, a case can be made for Parhae as a Korean entity, and to that extent its defeat takes Korea out of Manchuria for the rest of history up to the present time.[47] T'ang had begun this process by promoting separate but equal client relationships with Silla and Parhae early in the eighth century. Since Silla and Parhae had virtually no relations with each other and certainly no regard for each other, one can surely not make any case for a Manchurian-Korean polity after the fall of Koguryŏ in 668. But even a Korean presence in Manchuria ends in 926. This simplifies the ethnic situation in eastern Manchuria; from that point on this is almost exclusively the Tungusic land of the Jurchens and the Manchus. This factor no doubt also contributed to the simpler, unified mode for Manchuria in the subsequent Yin periods.

Turning to Korea, the Yin II situation that calls for comment is Koryŏ's special mission as a bulwark of Korean civilization in a forbidding Yin age of northern conquest and pressure. In this it was quite similar to Sung in China. Koryŏ people themselves debated the historical nature of their dynasty: some considered it to have inherited the tradition and legitimacy of Koguryŏ, others believed that it was the true successor of Silla.[48] Koryŏ's founders doubtless took the former view, as is suggested most directly by their choice of the name of their state. But socially and politically, Koguryŏ's fortunes were subverted by the host of Silla officials that swarmed north to Kaegyŏng, and after the confrontation between the two polar views in the first half of the twelfth century, there was no question but that the Silla tradition had won. This view of Koryŏ fits perfectly with the role played by Sung in China's Yin II phase. Koryŏ is the successor state to Silla in the same way that Sung is the successor state to T'ang. Like Sung, Koryŏ pulls together the fragmented members of a collapsed Yang entity. Also like Sung, it defends the peninsula against northern invaders, and in fact, against the same invaders—the Khitans, the Jurchens, and the Mongols. Like Sung, it presides over significant cultural growth and achievement, although Koryŏ's lesser resources and greater insecurity certainly inhibit this growth relative to Sung's. Unlike Sung, Koryŏ weathered the entire Yin phase, which, as we have seen, is longer than China's because of the Korean lag and jump: Koryŏ worked at its Yin mission for a full 491 years (901–1392). Also unlike Sung, it did not lose but rather gained northern territory over that which its Yang predecessor had controlled. And finally, unlike Sung, it managed to preserve its dynasty and its state in spite of a Mongol conquest.

Given all that they had in common, it is curious that Sung and Koryŏ had such uneven and irregular relations with each other. Koryŏ clearly wished to have good relations with Sung, but was unable to effect them on a durable basis because of Khitan and Jurchen intervention. It was the Sung statesmen who were not completely clear on the matter. It would appear that a substantial body of Sung opinion, led by Su Tung-p'o, still considered Koryŏ tainted with a "Manchurian" character that in their view utterly impaired its usefulness as an ally. But another Sung group, for which Fu Pi can serve as the spokesman, seems to have grasped the reality that Koryŏ was a valid and credible enemy of the Manchurian forces—in other words, that it was now a peninsular power defending a Chinese style of civilization against northern enemies (although they did not put the argument in quite those terms).[49] But Su's views largely prevailed.

Some Problems Presented by the Mongols

Looking over the whole Yin II period, one sees a striking structural similarity with Yin I—up to a point. The actors in the two periods are quite different in character: Chinese civilization is much more developed and mature in Yin II than in Yin I; Korea is represented by a single dynasty and not by a cluster of competing states; the "barbarians" in the north are much less barbarous and correspondingly more sinified, and therefore much more neatly articulated in groups and states. Yet the fundamental stages of action in the two periods have much in common. The Yang states disintegrate into collections of smaller, regional states; these are reunified by a Chinese successor state, which for a period restores Chinese order and fends off the northerners; ultimately, however, the Chinese successor state is pushed out of the Central Plain in the north and is forced to preserve its social and political order in the different environment of the south. Given the Yin I model, one might have expected that in Yin II a new Chinese state would then arise, along the lines of Sui-T'ang, reunify Chinese society, and launch a new Yang phase of Chinese expansion and assertiveness. But that did not happen. Instead, a new and different kind of northern power, the Mongols, erupted out of the steppes, conquered everything in its path, and ultimately occupied all of China. Up until this time, China had always been big enough to find room somewhere for a Chinese state, no matter how severe the "barbarian" inroads, but with the coming of the Mongols, Chinese civilization completely lost control of its own political fortunes. In this sense alone, Yin II was a more distressing period for the Chinese than Yin I. Moreover, as has already been noted, the Mongols were much more resistant to Chinese assimilation than earlier alien invaders and had to be physically chased out of China instead of being merely absorbed by the Ming restorers when their turn came.

Mongol conquests were not limited to China and Korea, but reached far into areas not touched by earlier northern invaders. They conquered the state of Ta-li, which Sung itself had been unable to reincorporate; their armies reached into Tibet and Burma; they attempted to conquer Vietnam and Champa; they sailed across the seas in ambitious but abortive attacks on Japan and on several states in southeast Asia; they incorporated in their domains the oasis states of Islamic Central Asia; they conquered Persia and southern Russia; they pushed into Central Europe and nearly reached the Adriatic. Their ambition was truly universal, limited only by their reach.

In view of the nearly worldwide scope of their conquests, it can be asked whether the Mongols can be accommodated in the Yin and Yang cycles of East Asian history suggested here. It would seem that, especially in the beginning of their conquests, the Mongols were quite extrinsic to any scheme based merely on the traditional landscape of the Chinese and their immediate neighbors. Unlike their predecessors, the Khitans and the Jurchens, in the beginning they armed themselves not with Chinese experts and advisers, but rather with the Uighur culture of the oasis states in Turkestan. It may have been simply a historical accident that Uighur literary influence, Central Asian administrative and governing techniques, and Christian and Islamic religious currents penetrated Mongol life before Chinese practices did, but the effect was to provide the Mongols with many services and techniques that insulated them from the need to seek similar things from China. And when the Mongols did become closely associated with Chinese life, it was not the only form of higher civilization they had encountered, and they were therefore less susceptible to its lure.

Thus, judged either from the extent of the territories they seized or by the style of life they adopted, the Mongols were initially outside and beyond the age-old rhythm of Yin and Yang and the geopolitical conditions of the traditional East Asian territory. They were truly an intrusion on this world in a sense that the Khitans and the Jurchens were not. In smashing into the magnetic field of the Yin-Yang pulse, they distorted and disrupted it. The balances and relationships that tied together such regions as the China–Manchuria–Korea triangle together were destroyed. Multi-state relations of the type peculiar to the Yin I and Yin III periods were rendered useless as the whole world turned into the single camp of Mongol domination. The regular Yin and Yang forces were scattered by the hurricane of a much bigger force.

Yet China is so big, and the historical rhythm of the Yin-Yang beat so well established, that no force, not even one like the Mongols, could permanently disrupt it. Hurricanes and typhoons do develop and expend terrifying energy, but in the end they peter out and yield to the normal flow of the southwesterly winds. When the Mongol asterism lost its push, it was captured in orbit by the Chinese planet and became a mere moon that had to obey the regular laws of the East Asian world. By the end of the reign of Khubilai Khan (1294), the Mongol world was no longer susceptible to unitary rule, and the Mongol conquests in China and Korea began to separate themselves from Mongol conquests elsewhere. The Mongol Yüan dynasty became just one more Chinese dynasty, acting in much the same way as any dynasty of conquest in a Yin phase.

But the Yüan dynasty still had a unique impact on the regular Yin-Yang cycle. It provided China with a territorial unification of even greater extent than those achieved by Han and T'ang, and this was the first Yin-phase unification in Chinese history. China now being already unified, the mission of the succeeding Ming dynasty, which became the agent of the Yang III phase, was not unification, as it had been for Ch'in-Han and Sui-T'ang in Yang I and II, but Chinese restoration and consolidation. Thus there was considerable continuity in administrative institutions and temperament from Yüan to Ming, and along with it a degree of despotism that had been unknown during T'ang and Sung. And perhaps the ordeal of a Yin-phase unification hardened the political cement of China and made subsequent division and fragmentation less likely, or, if it came about, less durable. No such fragmentation followed the fall of Ming in Yang III, as it had the falls of Han and T'ang in Yang I and II, and no north-south split accompanied the onset of Yin III, as it had in Yin I and II. The fragmentation and division that occurred at the end of Yin III was not on the scale of that in earlier Yin periods. The Yüan dynasty seems to stand at a point in Chinese history between an age where fragmentation, though not the rule is a frequent occurrence, and an age where a continuously unified Chinese polity becomes the unvarying pattern.

Conclusion

I am aware that the foregoing Yin-Yang scheme is heavily leavened with speculation and generalities and much in need of detailed studies on various points. Yet I feel confident that the basic framework is valid and provides a point of departure for new and interesting analyses of East Asian history. The Manchurian and Korean aspects of the basic Yin-Yang rhythm, which have been emphasized in this essay, show how useful and important it is for historians of China to look from time to time at the bigger East Asian world. Obviously, China constitutes the critical mass of that world, but China however big, is still just a part of East Asia. Particularly in

Yin periods, which can be confidently presented as a recurring phenomenon, China is deeply susceptible to outside forces and influences, and the rest of East Asia is revealed as a sector of decisive importance. The conventional wisdom on China is heavily in thrall to classical Chinese rhetoric, which—human nature being what it is—emphasizes the Yang far more than the Yin. One could argue, for instance, that the traditional theory of the "dynastic cycle" fits Yang dynasties moderately well (though even here not without serious problems), but hardly ever fits Yin dynasties, whether of northern alien origin or of southern Chinese defensive character. Reorganizing the twenty-odd Chinese dynasties into three cycles, each with an expansive or Yang phase and a defensive or Yin phase, reveals a pattern much more verifiable than the "dynastic cycle" in any given dynasty, and much more useful as a tool of historical analysis, since it transcends dynasties and even transcends China. This pattern operates even in places like Vietnam and Japan, although the force of its impact is obviously less than in areas closer to the Chinese heartland. (The Vietnamese dynastic pattern, though complex, can still be examined with profit in Yin-Yang terms, and Japanese history, particularly cultural history, also shows signs of the Yin-Yang rhythm. The heyday of Chinese cultural influence in Japan, the Nara period, coincides with the most blazing period of Chinese Yang II; during the preceding period, Chinese influence, mixed heavily with non-Chinese influence of Korean and other continental origin and passed to Japan through a non-Chinese medium, is in character with the Yin I period on the continent. The periods when Japan is relatively dissociated from Chinese influence, and when its own culture takes some of its most distinctive turns, correspond mainly to Yin periods.)

The time has come for the establishment of East Asian history as a field in itself, with East Asian history by definition reckoned as something greater than the sum of the histories of its constituent parts.

NOTES

1. *Tso chuan* (Chao 9), 45, 3b (Shih-san ching chu-su); *Kuo-yü* (Lu 2), 5, 11b (Ssu-pu pei-yao); *Shan-hai ching*, 7, 4b–5a, 17, 1b–2a (Ssu-pu pei-yao).

2. *Shih ching* (Mao 261), 18d, 10a (Shih-san ching chu-su).

3. "Not only do we hear nothing (of the Yen area) during Hsia or Yin, even in the Spring and Autumn period one never hears of anything important happening in this region." Fu Ssu-nien, "I Hsia tung hsi shuo," in *Fu Meng-chen hsien-sheng chi* (Taipei, 1952), vol. 4, p. 93.

4. Ssu-ma Ch'ien, *Shih chi*, 8, 392; *Han shu*, 1B, 77–79. All dynastic histories are cited according to the Chung-hua shu-chü ed., Peking, 1959–1976.

5. *Shih chi*, 115, 2985; *Han shu*, 95, 3863.

6. *Shih chi*, 25, 1242.

7. According to Later Han commentator Ying Shao's note in *Han shu*, 28B, 1626, and to the commentary in *Hou Han shu*, Monograph ch. 23 (Geog. sect. 5), p. 3530, the capital of Wei Man, who seized Chŏson's throne in about 195 B.C., was in Liaotung at a place called Hsien-tu. The earliest datable artifacts from the Lo-lang site do not seem to be earlier than the last decades of Former Han.

8. *Han shu*, 99B, 4130.

9. *San-kuo chih*, 30, 851.

10. *Hou Han shu*, 90, 2984.

11. *San-kuo chih*, 3, 111 ff.; 8, 253 ff.

12. *San-kuo chih*, 4, 121; 28, 762. *Tzu-chih t'ung-chien*, vol. 3, pp. 2365–2366, sub 246 : 2.

13. *San-kuo chih*, 30, 857 ff.

14. Gari Ledyard, "Galloping Along With the Horseriders: Looking for the Founders of Japan," *Journal of Japanese Studies* 1, 2 (1975): 217–254. Opinions differ on how and when the Puyŏ element in Paekche arrived; I think it was generally in the first half of the fourth century.

15. Whatever the degree of Puyŏ presence in the Japanese islands, from the very beginning it would have been more or less independent of the Paekche Puyŏ.

16. *Wei shu*, 100, 2223.

17. *Sui shu*, 81, 1816 ff. *Tzu-chih t'ung-chien* vol. 6, pp. 5560 ff., sub 598 : 2; v. 6, pp. 5561–5562, sub 598 : 4.

18. *Sui shu*, 4, 79 ff., 81, 1817. *Tzu-chih t'ung-chien*, vol. 6, pp. 5659 ff., sub 612 : 3.

19. *Tzu-chih t'ung-chien*, vol. 7, pp. 6216–6233 passim.

20. *Chiu T'ang shu*, 199A, 5330 ff. *Hsin T'ang shu*, 220, 6199 ff.

21. *Chiu T'ang shu*, 199A, 5327ff. *Hsin T'ang shu*, 220, 6195 ff.

22. *Chiu T'ang shu*, 199A, 5336. *Hsin T'ang shu*, 220, 6204. These notes on the Sui and T'ang campaigns refer to but a sample of the more important source material. Many more references could be given.

23. For the arguments supporting this conclusion, which is not at all obvious in Chinese sources, see John Jamieson, "The Samguk Sagi and the Unification Wars," Ph.D. dissertation, University of California at Berkeley, 1969, pp. 63–78, and his article "Nadang tongmaeng ŭi wahae," *Yŏksa hakpo* 44 (1969): 1–10.

24. It is not likely that T'ang maintained direct administration over the northwestern part of Korea, as indicated on the map "Sui-T'ang" accompanying *Manshū rekishi chiri* (ed. Shiratori Kurakichi, South Manchurian Railway), Tokyo, 1913; no arguments that would support the map indication can be found in the relevant discussion, vol. 1, pp. 402–406, 422–426.

25. *Liao shih*, 2, 21.

26. Koryŏ, though founded by Wang Kŏn in 918, had inherited the territory and mission of the anti-Silla rebel Kung Ye, who had declared himself king of "Later Koguryŏ" in 901. This state was known as Majin between 904 and 911, and as T'ae-bong from 911 to 918.

27. *Koryŏ-sa*, 2, 15b. (Yŏnse University photolith. reprint of 1451 edition, Seoul, 1955, 3 vols.).

28. On various aspects of Koryŏ-Liao relations, see Michael Rogers, "Sung-

Koryŏ Relations: Some Inhibiting Factors," *Oriens* 11, 1–2 (1958): 194–202; "Sukchong of Koryŏ: His Accession and His Relations with Liao," *T'oung Pao*, 47, 1–2 (1959): 30–42; "Factionalism and Koryŏ Policy under the Northern Sung," *Journal of the American Oriental Society* 79, 1 (1959): 16–25; "Some Kings of Koryŏ as Registered in Chinese Works," ibid., 81, 4 (1961): 415–421; see also chap. 6 in this volume.

29. Paraphrased from Rogers, "Factionalism and Koryŏ Policy," p. 20.

30. Michael Rogers, "The Regularization of Koryŏ-Chin Relations," *Central Asiatic Journal* 6, 1 (1961): 51–84; also his "Koryŏ's Military Dictatorship and Its Relations with Chin," *T'oung Pao* 47, 1–2 (1959): 43–62; also chap. 6 in this volume.

31. Nominally the Mongols came in 1219 as rescuers of Koryŏ, which was suffering from the depredations of a large force of anti-Mongol Khitans, but a "senior and junior fraternal treaty" was agreed to on this occasion. The alleged breaking of this agreement became the pretext for the Mongol invasion of 1231, which was, strictly speaking, the first invasion.

32. W. E. Henthorn, *Korea: The Mongol Invasions* (Leiden, 1963), pp. 150 ff.

33. Henthorn, pp. 137–138, 195–196.

34. Henthorn, pp. 160–161, 196.

35. Henthorn, p. 196.

36. Henthorn, pp. 195–196.

37. Chang T'ing-yü et al., *Ming shih*, 3, 44; L. C. Goodrich, and C. Y. Fang (eds.), *Dictionary of Ming Biography* (New York, 1975), vol. 2, pp. 1083–1084.

38. *Koryŏ sa*, 137, 5a ff.

39. Korean historians, in their treatment of these wars, often emphasize popular resistance movements and the heroics of naval genius Yi Sunsin (1545–1598), but without Chinese aid, these factors, important as they are, would not have been enough to expel the Japanese.

40. *Sŏnjo sillok*, 142, 13a (Sŏnjo 34, 10, chŏnghae).

41. For general mongraphic coverage of Ming-Korean-Manchu relations in the early seventeenth century, see Inaba Iwakichi, *Kōkaikun jidai no Mansen kankei* (Keijo, 1933).

42. Arthur Hummel ed., *Eminent Chinese of the Ch'ing Period* (Washington, D.C., 1943–1944), p. 886.

43. Chindan Hakhoe (ed.), *Han'guk sa* (Kŭunse hugi p'yŏn), pp. 12–14.

44. Observe the Korean chancellery, in a letter to the Mongol court, applying the customary rhetoric of Yang-period foreign relations with China to a northern invader of the Yin period: "We humbly hope that His Majesty the August Emperor will extend to us the affection of Heaven and Earth . . . and, considering our small country not to be of seditious intent, order his great army to turn round its chariot shafts and draw back its battle flags, and to forever protect our small state. Then once more your servants would exert their strength and exhaust their sincerity in annually sending their local products, therewith to manifest their incarnadine devotion, and increase their prayers for a thousand myriad years of longevity for the August Emperor." (Korean letter to Mongol court, December 1232–January 1233, *Koryŏ sa*, 23, 22b). Compare the following lines, from a letter to the Eastern Jurchens, of about the same date: "Now, as to these people you term Mongols, no people are more sinister and cruel. Even being on peaceful terms with them does not

make it possible to trust them. Thus the good terms that our Court has with them do not necessarily spring from our inner feelings'' (Korean letter to Eastern Jurchen court, January–February 1233, *Koryŏ sa*, 23, 25b).

45. See Rogers, ''Regularization.''

46. Between 1115 and 1125, Liao and Chin were in contention, and Manchuria was not unified. The Mongol unified rule in Manchuria is reckoned from the submission of all local Khitan forces there in about 1215 to the defeat of the Mongol general Naɣachu by Ming in 1387.

47. One certainly cannot say (yet) that the Koreans are out of Manchuria forever. Heavy Korean immigration during the late nineteenth and early twentieth centuries has left a sizable Korean population there. In the Yen-pien Korean Autonomous Region alone there are over 600,000 Koreans, and these constitute a solid majority there. They are also quite numerous in other parts of Manchuria. The present North Korean regime has its political and military origins in Manchuria, and its historiography and cartography emphasize this heavily. In North Korean propaganda, Paektu Mountain (known in China as Ch'ang-pai Mountain), which gives birth to the Yalu, Tumen, and Sungari rivers, is given almost mystical significance.

48. See chap. 6 in this volume.

49. See Rogers, ''Factionalism and Koryŏ Policy'' and ''Sung-Koryŏ Relations.''

Glossary of Chinese Characters

A-li Hai-ya	阿里海涯
A-li-ku	阿立骨
A-lien T'ieh-mu-erh	阿憐帖木兒
A-lu-hun Sa-li	阿魯渾薩理
A-sha Pu-hua	阿沙不華
A-shih T'ieh-mu-erh	阿失帖木兒
A-ssu-lan	阿思蘭
A-yü-tan	阿喻丹
Ai-ch'üan	愛全
Ai-tsung	哀宗
an-ch'a ssu	按察司
An Ch'ung-hui	安重誨
An-hsi	安西
An Lu-shan	安祿山
an-min	安民
An-su	安肅
An-tsang	安藏
An-tung	安東
Ch'a-han T'ieh-mu-erh	察罕帖木兒
Chan-ch'e Pa-tu-erh	苫徹拔都兒
Chang Ch'ien	張騫
Chang Chih-pai	張知白
Chang Fang-p'ing	張方平
Chang Lin	張林
Chang Pa-li	章八里

Chang Tsung-i	張宗益
Ch'ang-an	長安
Ch'ang-chou	常州
chao	詔
Chao-chia A-chiu	趙家阿舅
Chao-chia T'ien-tzu	趙家天子
Chao-chih	詔旨
Chao Fan	趙范
Chao Fang	趙昉
Chao Ju-yü	趙汝愚
Chao K'uei	趙葵
Chao Kung	趙珙
Chao P'u	趙普
Chao Shih-yen	趙世延
chao-t'ao shih	招討使
ch'ao-shih	朝事
che-pu	折逋
Chegwan	諦觀
Chen-hai	鎮海
Chen Te-hsiu	眞德秀
Chen-ting	眞定
ch'en	臣
Ch'en Hung-chin	陳洪進
Ch'en Kung-fu	陳公輔
Ch'en Po-chen	陳伯震
Ch'en Yüan	陳垣
Cheng Ch'ing-chih	鄭淸之
Cheng Ssu-ch'ang	鄭嗣昌
Cheng Ssu-tsung	鄭嗣宗
Cheng-t'ung lun	正統論
ch'eng	稱
ch'eng-chih	丞旨
Ch'eng Shih-meng	程師孟
Ch'eng-tu	成都
chi	妓
Chi	薊
chi-erh	羈餌

chi-mi	羈縻
ch'i-ch'ing shih	祈請使
Ch'i-ko	溪哥
Ch'i Kung-chih	綦公直
Ch'i Nan-lu-Wen ch'ien-pu	欺南陸溫錢逋
Ch'i-t'ai Sa-li	乞台薩理
Chia-lu-na-ta-ssu	迦魯納答思
Chia She	賈涉
Chiang-chou	蔣州
Ch'iang	羌
chiao-ch'ao-k'u	交鈔庫
chiao-ch'ao t'i-chü-ssu	交鈔提舉司
Chiao-chih	交趾
Chiao-hsi	膠西
Ch'iao Hsing-chien	僑行簡
Chien-shih-mi-erh	潔實彌爾
chieh-tu shih	節度使
Ch'ieh-lieh-ko	怯烈哥
chieh-chiao ta-pao	檢校大保
Chien-chou	建州
chien-kuo	建國
Chien-ou	建甌
chien-tu	建都
ch'ien	錢
Ch'ien-chou	虔州
ch'ien-hu	千戶
Ch'ien Liu	錢鏐
Ch'ien Shu	錢俶
Ch'ien Tso	錢佐
Ch'ien Tsung	錢倧
Ch'ien Yüan-kuan	錢元瓘
chih	制
Chih-li-hua-t'ai	質理花台
Chih-lu-ku	直魯古
ch'ih-shu	勅書
chin	斤
Later Chin	後晉

chin-shih	進士
Chin Yüan-su (Chin Ha-la)	金元素（金哈剌）
ch'in-cheng	親政
Ch'in K'uei	秦檜
Ching-jung	靜戎
Ching-nan	荊南
Ching Ssu-hui	敬嗣暉
Ch'ing-chou	青州
Ch'ing-ho	清河
Ch'ing-t'ang	青堂
Ch'ing-t'ung	慶通
Cho-chou	涿州
Ch'oe Ch'iwŏn	崔致遠
Chong Chungbu	鄭仲夫
Ch'ŏnsu	天授
chou	州
Chou	周
Chou Shih-tsung	周世宗
ch'ou-lu	醜虜
chu-fan	諸蕃
Chu Mong	朱蒙
Chu Wen	朱文
Chu Yu-kuei	朱友珪
Chu Yüan-chang	朱元章
ch'u	處
Ch'u	楚
Ch'u-chou	楚州
ch'ü-yen	曲宴
chuan-yün	轉運
Ch'uang-wu-erh	牀兀兒
chüan	絹
Ch'üan-chou	泉州
ch'üan-fu ssu	泉府司
Chüeh-ssu-lo	唃厮囉
Ch'üeh-li-pieh Wo-ch'ih	闕里別斡赤
chün	軍
chün-wang	郡王

chung-chieh	中節
Chung-i chün	忠義軍
Chung-shu men-hsia	中書門下
chung-shu yu-ch'eng	中書右丞
Chung-t'ung pao-ch'ao	中統寶鈔
Ch'unp'ung	峻豐
erh-kuo	二國
fa	法
fan-chieh	蕃界
fan-chün ma	蕃軍馬
Fan Chung-yen	范仲淹
fan-shih	泛使
Fan Tsu-yü	范祖禹
fang	方
Fang Hsiao-ju	方孝儒
fei	婔
fei	妃
feng-shan	刲禪
feng-shih	奉使
Fu-i chen	繡辰箴
Fu Pi	富弼
fu-shih	副使
Fujiwara Morosuke	藤原師輔
Fujiwara Saneyori	藤原実頼
Fujiwara Tadahira	藤原忠平
Ha-la I-ha-ch'ih Pei-lu	哈剌亦哈赤北魯
Ha-ma	哈麻
Ha-shih Po-yao	哈失伯要
Ha-ta Ho-ta	哈達合荅
Han Ch'i	韓琦
Han-chia a-chiu ta-kuan chia	漢家阿舅大官家
Han Chia-fang	韓家昉
Han Kuo-hua	韓國華
Han T'o-chou	韓侂胄
Han Yü	韓愈
Hang-chou	杭州
Hao-ching	鎬京

Hao-ho-shang pa-tu	郝和尚拔都
Hei-ta shih-lüeh	黑韃事略
Hizen	肥前
ho-ch'in	和親
Ho-chou	河州
Ho Ch'ü-ping	霍去病
Ho-hsi fan-pu	河西蕃部
Ho Liang	何亮
Hoju	鎬州
Hsi	奚
Hsi-fan	西蕃
Hsi Hsia	西夏
Hsi-liang fu	西涼府
Hsi-pan	昔班
Hsi-p'ing	西平
Hsia-cheng	睛征
hsia-chieh	下節
hsia-kuo	下國
Hsiang-yang	襄陽
hsiao-ch'ih	梟鴟
hsiao-jen	小人
Hsiao Sun-ning	蕭孫寧
hsiao-t'uan ch'a	小團茶
Hsiao-yün-shih Hai-ya	小雲石海涯
Hsiao-yün-shih T'o-hu-lien	小雲石脫忽憐
hsien	縣
hsien	獻
Hsien-pei	鮮卑
hsin-fu kuo	親附國
hsing-shang-shu sheng-shih	行尚書省事
hsing-sheng	行省
hsing-sheng tu-tu	行省都督
hsing-ying ping-ma tu-chien	行營兵馬都監
Hsiung-nu	匈奴
hsiung-ti chih kuo	兄弟之國
Hsü Chih-kao	徐知誥
Hsü Hsi-chi	徐晞稷

Hsü Kuo	許國
Hsü T'ing	徐霆
Hsü Wen	徐溫
Hsüan	宣
hsüan-cheng-yüan	宣政院
Hsüan-ch'eng	宣城
Hsüan-chou	宣州
hsüan-fu-shih	宣撫使
hsüan-hui yüan	宣徽院
Hsüan-tsung	宣宗
Hsüan-t'u	玄菟
hsüan-wei shih	宣慰使
hsüan-wei ssu	宣慰司
Hsüeh-yen-t'o	薛延陀
Hsün-yün	獯狁
hu	戶
Hu Chin-ssu	胡進思
Hu-chou	湖州
Hu-Han wen-hua	胡漢文化
Hu-lan	忽蘭
Hu Meng	扈蒙
hu-pu shang-shu	戶部尚書
Hu-tu-lu Tu-erh-mi-shih	忽都魯都兒迷失
hua-yen	花宴
Huang Ch'ao	黃巢
Huai-hai kuo-wang	淮海國王
huai-jou	懷柔
Huai-nan	淮南
huai-yüan i	懷遠驛
huang-shu	黃鼠
Hui-ho	回紇
Hui-hui	回回
Hui-t'ung kuan	會同館
Hung Hao	洪浩
hung-lu ssu	鴻臚寺
Hŭngwi kwan	興威館
hwarang	花郎

hwat'ongsa	和通使
I-na T'o-t'o	亦納脫脫
i-tu-hu	亦都護
Inŭn kwan	仁思館
Ju-nei nei-shih sheng	入內內侍省
Juan-juan	蠕蠕
jung	戎
jung-lu	戎虜
kai-yüan	改元
K'ai-feng	開封
K'ai-p'ing fu	開平府
Kan-chiang	贛江
Kan-chou	贛州
Kang Kamch'an	姜邯贊
Kao-ch'ang	高昌
Kao-ch'ang Mo-yü	高昌磨榆
Kim Kwanŭi	金寬毅
Kim Pusik	金富軾
k'o-sheng chü	客省局
Koguryŏ chan'ŏl yuch'wi	高句麗殘孽類聚
Kong Ye	弓裔
Kou Meng-yü	苟夢玉
K'u-erh-ku-ssu	庫爾古司
kuan	官
kuan-jen	官人
kuan-kan so	管幹所
kuan-pan shih	館伴使
Kuang-chou	光州
kuang-ch'u	廣初
Kuang-hsin	廣信
Kuang-hua	光化
Kuei-lin	桂林
Kuei-te	歸德
K'un-lü ch'eng	坤閭城
kung	貢
k'ung-lu	狂虜
Kung-shui	貢水

Kung-sun Tu	公孫度
kung-te-shih-ssu	功德使司
K'ung Yen-chou	孔彥舟
kuo chu	國主
kuo-hsiang	國相
Kuo-hsin shih	國信使
Kuo-hsin so	國信所
Kuo-hsin ssu	國信司
Kuo-shih	國師
kuo-su	國俗
kuo-wang	國王
Kwangdŏk	光德
Kyŏn Hwon	甄萱
La-chen	臘眞
Lai-chou	萊州
lai-kung	來貢
li	里
li	禮
li	吏
Li Ch'ang-kuo	李昌國
Li Chi-ch'ien	李繼遷
Li Ch'üan	李全
Li Fu	李福
Li Jen-ta	李仁達
Li K'o-yung	李克用
Li Li-tsun	李立遵
li-pin yüan	禮賓院
Li T'an	李璮
Li-tsung	理宗
Li Ts'ung-k'o	李從珂
Li Tsung-mien	李宗勉
Li Yüan-hao	李元昊
liang	兩
Liang-chou	涼州
Liang Ping	梁丙
liang-te	涼德
Liao Ching-tsung	遼景宗

Liao Mu-tsung	遼穆宗
lien-fang shih	廉訪使
Lien Hsi-hsien	廉希賢
Lien Hsi-kung	廉希貢
Lien-shui	連水
Liu Cho	劉卓
Liu-ku	六谷
liu-shou	留守
Liu Yen	劉巖
Liu Yüeh	劉燏
Lo-lang	樂浪
Lo-tu hsien	樂都縣
Lo-yang	洛陽
lu	虜
lu	賂
Lu Chih	陸贄
lu-chu	虜主
lun-pu	論逋
Lung-pu	隴逋
Ma Chih-chieh	馬知節
Ma Jun	馬潤
Ma Tsu-ch'ang	馬祖常
Ma Yüeh-ho-nai	馬月合乃
Mai-nu	買奴
Mao Wen-lung	毛文龍
meng	盟
meng-shih	盟誓
Meng-su-ssu	孟速思
Mi-li Huo-che	密立火者
Miao-ch'uan	邈川
mien	綿
Min	閩
ming	命
Ming-su	明肅
mo	脉
mo	末
Mo-se-ssu	默色斯

mou-kuan chih-shih	某官執事
mu-chih ming	墓誌銘
mu-hua er-lai	慕化而來
Myoch'ŏng	妙淸
Nai-hsien	迺賢
nan-ch'ao	南朝
nan-chiao	南郊
Nan P'ing wang	南平王
Nan Yüeh wang	南越王
Nang-chia-tai	囊加歹
Nao-nao	嶩嶩
nei-luan wai-huan	內亂外患
nien-hao	年號
Ning-tsung	寧宗
nu	奴
Ou-yang Hsiu	歐陽修
Pa-ssu Hu-tu	八思忽都
pai-hsing	百姓
Pai Pu-hua	伯不花
Pai-yen Shih-sheng	伯顏師聖
P'an-lo-chih	潘羅支
pao-cheng	寶正
pei-ch'ao	北朝
pei-chieh	北界
pei-hsin	北信
pei-jen	北人
pei-kuo	北國
pei-lu	北虜
pei-shu	北書
Pei-ti lai-ch'ao sung	北敵來朝頌
Pei-t'ing	北庭
pen	本
P'eng I-pin	彭義斌
P'eng-lai	蓬萊
P'eng Ta-ya	彭大雅
pi-chi	筆記
p'i	匹

Pieh-shih Pa-la-ha-sun	別失八剌哈孫
Pieh-shih Pa-li	別失八里
p'ing-chang cheng-shih	平章政事
p'ing-li	聘禮
Po-hai	渤海
po-kuan chih	百官志
Po-lo	孛羅
Po-lu-ho	孛魯合
P'o-yang Lake	鄱陽
Pu-erh-ha	布爾哈
Pu-hu-mu	不忽木
Pu-lu Hai-ya	布魯海牙
Pu-lu-hua	不魯花
Pu-lu-huan	不魯歡
Puyŏ	夫餘
P'u-lan-hsi	普蘭奚
Sa-chi-ssu	撒吉思
sadaijin	左大臣
san-chieh	三節
san-lu chün-min wan-hu	三路軍民萬戶
Sang-ko	桑哥
sayŏk wŏn	司譯院
se-mu-jen	色目人
Sha-chou	沙州
Sha-t'o	沙陀
shan-chia ch'ien	贍家錢
Shan-yü	單于
Shan-yüan	澶淵
shang	尚
shang-chieh	上節
shang-fu	尚父
shang-shu sheng	尚書省
Shang-tu	上都
shao-chien	少監
Shao-hsing	紹興
shao-pao	少保
Shen Kua	沈括

shen-tao pei	神道碑
sheng-hsi	生餼
shih	使
shih-chiao tsung-chih yüan	釋教總制院
shih-ch'ien	食錢
Shih Chin Hui-t'ung	石晉會同
Shih Ching-t'ang	石敬瑭
Shih Ch'ing	時青
shih-hsi	世系
Shih Kuei	石圭
Shih Mi-yüan	史彌遠
Shih-pei lu	使北錄
shih-piao	誓表
shih-shu	誓書
Shih Sung-chih	央嵩之
shih-te	失德
Shih-wei	室韋
shih-yün	時運
Shu	蜀
shu-mi yüan	樞密院
Shuang-ch'eng-fu	雙成府
Shuo-fang chieh-tu shih	朔方節度使
Sŏgyŏng	西京
Sŏ Hŭi	徐熙
ssu-fang	四方
Ssu Ku-te	司古德
Ssu-ma Kuang	司馬光
Ssu-to-tu	廝鐸督
Su Ch'e	蘇轍
Su-chou	蘇州
Su-ko	速哥
Su-lo-hai	速羅海
Su-pu-han	速不罕
Su Shih	蘇軾
Su Sung	蘇頌
Su Tung-p'o	蘇東坡
Sun Ch'üan-hsing	孫全興

Sunch'ŏn kwan	順天館
Sun Ju	孫儒
sung	頌
Sung Ch'i	宋祁
Sung sung	宋頌
Ta-ch'eng-tu	大乘都
Ta-li-tu	大理都
ta-lu-hua-ch'ih	達魯花赤
Ta-shih	大食
Ta-shih-man	荅失蠻
Ta-tz'u-tu	大慈都
Ta Yüeh	大越
T'a-t'a T'ung-a	塔塔統阿
Tai-chou	代州
Tai-fang	帶方
T'ai-chou	台州
T'ai-ho ling	大和嶺
T'ai-p'ing yü-lan	太平御覽
T'ai Pu-hua	泰不花
tan	石
t'an-ma	探馬
T'ang Chi	唐驥
T'ang Jen-tsu	唐仁祖
T'ang Su-tsung	唐肅宗
T'ang Te-tsung	唐德宗
te	德
Teng-chou	登州
T'eng Mao-shih	滕茂實
ti-kuo	敵國
Ti-shih	帝師
T'ieh-lien	鐵連
T'ieh-ling	鐵嶺
T'ieh-mu-erh Ta-shih	鐵木兒達識
t'ien-hsia ping-ma tu-yüan-shuai	天下兵馬都元帥
t'ien-pao	天寶
T'ien-t'ai	天台
ting	錠

Ting-chu	定住
To-lo-chu	朵羅朮
T'o-li-shih-kuan	脫力世官
T'o-ssu-ma	脫思麻
T'o-t'o	脫脫
T'ongmun kwan	通文館
T'ongye mun	通禮門
tsa	雜
Ts'ai-chou	蔡州
Ts'ai Hsiang	蔡襄
ts'an-chih cheng-shih	參知政事
Tsao-yang	棗陽
Ts'ao Li-yung	曹利用
Ts'ao Ts'ao	曹操
Ts'ao Yen-yüeh	曹彥約
tso ch'eng-hsiang	左丞相
Ts'ui Yü-chih	崔與之
Tsou Shen-chih	芻伸之
tsung-chih yüan	總制院
Tsung-ko	宗哥
Tu Cheng	度正
tu-hu-fu	都護府
Tu Kao	杜杲
tu kung-te-shih ssu	都貫德使司
tu-t'ing hsi-i	都亭西驛
tu-yüan-shuai	都元帥
t'u	徒
T'u-chüeh	突厥
T'u-fan	吐蕃
T'u T'u-ha	土土哈
tuan-shih-kuan	斷事官
Tun-huang	敦煌
Tung-chan	董氈
Tung-hu	東胡
Tung-ning lu	東寧跟
tung-ti	東帝
t'ung-chih	同知

T'ung-hua	通化
T'ung-kuan	童貫
t'ung-wen kuan	同文館
t'ung-wen shih	通問使
tz'u	賜
wai-ch'en	外臣
wai-kuo	外國
wan-hu	萬戶
Wan-yen Kuang-ying	完顏光英
Wan-yen Tsung-yao	完顏宗堯
Wan-yen Yün-chung	完顏允中
Wang An-shih	王安石
Wang Chi	王楫
Wang Chi-tsung	王繼宗
Wang Ch'i	王治
Wang Cho	王昭
Wang Hae	王楷
Wang Hyŏn	王晛
Wang Kŏn	王建
Wang-lai kuo-hsin so	往來國信所
Wang Liang-ch'en	王良弼
Wang Lun	王倫
Wang Mai	王邁
Wang Mang	王莽
Wang Sun	王詢
Wang Tan	王旦
Wang Wei-cheng	汪惟正
Wei Cheng	委徵
Wei Liao-weng	魏了翁
Wei-lu	威虜
Wei-wu-erh	畏吾兒
wen-chi	文集
Wen-chou	溫州
wen-ling	紋綾
Wen-pu-ch'i	溫逋奇
Wen-shu-nu	文書奴
Wu	吳

Wu-chin	武進
Wu Ch'ien	吳潛
Wu-huan	烏桓
Wu-mo	嗢末
Wu-ssu-tsang	烏思藏
Wu Yüeh	吳越
Yang Hsing-mi	楊行密
Yang Wo	楊渥
Yeh	掖
Yeh-hsien	野先
Yeh-hsien-nai	葉仙鼐
Yeh-hsien Pu-hua	也先不花
Yeh-li-chu	野里尤
Yeh-li Pu-hua	也里不華
Yeh-lü A-pao-chi	耶律阿保機
Yeh-lü Ch'u-ts'ai	耶律楚材
Yeh-lü Ts'ung	耶律琮
Yeh Meng-te	葉夢得
Yeh-te-sha	也的沙
Yen	燕
Yen-Chi	燕薊
Yen-ching	燕京
Yen Shih	嚴實
Yen T'ieh-mu-erh	燕帖木兒
Yen-yün	燕雲
Yepin sa	禮賓寺
Yi Chehyŏn	李齊賢
Yi Chibaek	李知白
Yi Hŭng'u	李興祐
Yi Kyubo	李奎報
Yi Son'ge	李宣古
Yi Sŭnghiu	李承休
yin-chin	引進
Ying-ch'eng Lin-pu-chih	郢成蘭逋叱
Ying-chou	潁州
Ying Ch'un-chih	應純之
Yŏngsŏn kwan	迎仙館

yu-ch'eng	右丞
Yu-chou	幽州
Yü Ching	余靖
Yü hai	玉海
yü-kuo	與國
Yü-lung-po	喩龍波
Yü-shu Hu-erh-t'u-hua	玉樞虎兒吐華
yü-ts'e	玉册
Yü-wen Hsü-chung	宇文虛中
Yüan Hsieh	袁韶
Yüan Shao	袁燮
yüan-shih	院使
yüan-shuai	元帥
Yüeh-chou	越州
Yüeh-chu	約著
Yüeh-chü-lien-ch'ih Hai-ya	月舉連赤海牙
Yüeh-li-ma-ssu	月里麻思
Yüeh-lin T'ieh-mu-erh	岳璘帖穆爾
Yung-ch'ang	永昌

Abbreviations

BA	*The Blue Annals* (trans. G. N. Roerich)
Bretschneider	E. Bretschneider, trans., *Mediaeval Researches from East Asiatic Sources*
Campagnes	*Histoire des campagnes de Gengis Khan* (trans. P. Pelliot and L. Hambis)
ch.	*chüan*
Ch'en	Ch'en Yüan, *Western and Central Asians in China Under the Mongols: Their Transformation into Chinese*
"Chrétiens"	"Chrétiens d'Asie centrale et d'extrême-orient" (P. Pelliot)
Conquerors	*Conquerors and Confucians: Aspects of Political Change in Late Yüan China*, by J. W. Dardess
CP	*Hsü Tzu-chih t'ung-chien ch'ang-pien* (Li T'ao)
CPSL	*Li T'ao Hsü Tzu-chih t'ung-chien ch'ang-pien Sung-Liao kuan-hsi shih-liao chi-lu* (ed. T'ao Chin-sheng and Wang Min-hsin)
CPTC	*Ch'ing-po tsa-chih* (Chou Hui)
CS	*Chin shih*, Po-na ed.
CWTS	*Chiu Wu-tai shih* (Hsüeh Chü-cheng et al.)
CYL	*Ch'eng-yao lu* (Lu Chen)
CYTFSL	*Ch'ing-yüan t'iao-fa shih-lei*
DMSM	*Deb-ther dmar-po gsar-ma* (G. Tucci)
Doerfer	G. Doerfer, *Türkische und mongolische Elemente im Neupersischen*
DTMP	*Deb-ther dmar-po*
DTS	*Drevnetiurkskii slovar*

FS	First Series (*Index to Biographical Material in Chin and Yüan Literary Works*)
Fuchs	W. Fuchs, "Analecta zur mongolischen Uebersetzungliteratur der Yüan-Zeit"
GBYT	*rGya Bod yig-tshang*
HCP	*Hsü Tzu-chih t'ung-chien ch'ang-pien* (Li T'ao)
HJAS	*Harvard Journal of Asiatic Studies*
HKT	Hsü K'ang-tsung, *Hsuan-ho i-ssu feng-shih hsing-ch'eng lu*
HML	*Hua-man lu* (Chang Shun-min)
HTCTC	*Sung-shih ch'üan-wen hsü Tzu-chih t'ung-chien*
HWTS	*Hsin Wu-tai shih* (Ou-yang Hsiu et al.)
HYS	*Hsin Yüan shih* (K'o Shao-min)
JA	*Journal Asiatique*
Juvainī/Boyle	*The History of the World Conqueror* (trans. J. A. Boyle)
Juvainī/Qazvīnī	'Ata Malik-i-Juwaynī, *Ta'rīkh-i-Jahān-gushā* (ed. Muhammad Qazvīnī)
KCMCSL	*Kuo-ch'ao ming-ch'en shih-lüeh*
Khoziastvo	*Khoziaistvo i obshchestvennyi stroi Uigurskogo gosudarstva* (D. I. Tikhonov)
KLTC	*Hsüan-ho feng-shih Kao-li t'u-ching* (by Hsü Ching)
KPGT	*mKhas-pa'i-dga'-ston*
KRS	*Koryŏ-sa*
Ligeti	Ligeti, *A mongolok titkos története*
LS	*Liao shih*, Po-na ed.
MTPL	*Meng-ta pei-lu*, in Wang Kuo-wei, ed., *Wang Kuan-t'ang ch'üan-chi*
MWESC	*Meng-wu-erh shih-chi* (T'u Chi)
Notes I	*Notes on Marco Polo*, I (P. Pelliot)
PHJL	*Pei-hsing jih-lu* (Lou Yüeh)
PSCL	"Pei-Sung Ch'ing-li shih-ch'i te wai-chiao cheng-ts'e" (T'ao Chin-sheng)
PYL	*Pei-yüan lu* (Chou Hui)
Qāshānī/Hambly	Abū al-Qāsim ibn 'Alī ibn Muḥammad al-Qāshānī, *Tarikh-i Uljaytu* (ed. Mahin Hambly)
Rashīd/Ali-zade	Rashīd al-Dīn, *Jāmi' al-tavārīkh* (ed. A. A. Ali-zade et al.)

Rashīd/Boyle	Rashīd al-Dīn, *The Successors of Genghis Khan* (trans. J. Boyle)
Rashīd/Karīmī	Rashīd al-Din, *Jāmi' al-tavārīkh* (ed. B. Karīmī)
Recherches	*Recherches sur les chrétiens d'Asie centrale et d'extrême-orient* (P. Pelliot)
SB	*Sung Biographies* (ed. H. Franke)
SH	*Secret History*
SHY	*Sung Hui-yao chi-kao*
Shiba/Elvin	Shiba Yoshinobu, *Sōdai shōgyō-shi kenkyū* (trans. M. Elvin)
Sinica Franciscana	*Sinica Franciscana* (trans. A. van den Wyngaert)
SKCC	*Shih-kuo ch'un-ch'iu* (Wu Jen-ch'en)
SKCS	*Ssu-k'u ch'üan-shu chen-pen* ed.
SLPT	"Sung-Liao chien te p'ing-teng wai-chiao kuan-hsi" (T'ao Chin-sheng)
SPPY	*Ssu-pu pei-yao* ed.
SPTK	*Ssu-pu ts'ung-k'an* ed.
SS	Second Series (*Index to Biographical Material in Chin and Yüan Literary Works*)
SS	*Sung shih*, Po-na ed.
SSCSPM	*Sung-shih chi-shih pen-mo*
STCL	*Sung ta chao-ling chi*
Successors	*The Successors of Genghis Khan* (Rashīd al-Dīn, trans. J. A. Boyle)
SWCCL	*Sheng-wu ch'in-cheng lu* (ed. Wang Kuo-wei)
TCTC	*Tzu-chih t'ung-chien* (Ssu-ma Kuang)
TFYK	*Ts'e-fu yüan-kuei* (Wang Ch'in-jo)
TMAE	*Tataro-Mongoly v Azii i Evrope*
TP	*T'oung Pao*
TPS	*Tibetan Painted Scrolls* (G. Tucci)
TS	Third Series (*Index to Biographical Material in Chin and Yüan Literary Works*)
Turkestan	*Turkestan v epokhu mongol'skogo nashestviia chast pervaia Teksty* (V. V. Bartol'd)
WHTK	*Wen-hsien t'ung-kao*
WTHY	*Wu-tai hui-yao* (Wang P'u)
WYPS	*Wu Yüeh pei-shih* (Ch'ien Yen)
YS	*Yüan shih*
YSLP	*Yüan-shih lei-pien* (Shao Yüan-p'ing)

Bibliography

Works in Western Languages

Abe Takeo. "Where Was the Capital of the West Uighurs?" In *Silver Jubilee Volume of the Zinbun Kagaku Kenkyusyo, Kyoto University*. Kyoto: Zinbun Kagaku Kenkyusyo, Kyoto University, 1954.

—————. "Uighur History." In *Research in Japan in the History of Eastern and Western Cultural Contacts*. Tokyo: Japanese National Commission for UNESCO, 1957.

Ali-zade, A. A.; Khetagurov, A. A.; and Romaskevich, A. S., eds. Rashīd al-Dīn, *Jāmi' al-tavārīkh*. Vol. I, pt. 1. Moscow: Nauka, 1968.

Amipa, Sherab Gyaltsen. *Historical Facts on the Religion of the Sa-skya-pa Sect*. Zurich: Tibetan Institute Rikon, 1970.

Arts of China, Painting I. Taipei: National Palace Museum, 1955.

Bacot, J. *Introduction à l'histoire du Tibet*. Paris: Société asiatique, 1962.

Bar Hebraeus. *The Chronography of Gregory Abu'l Faraj*. London: Oxford University Press, 1932.

Barthold, V. V. *Four Studies on the History of Central Asia*. Vol. I. Leiden: E. J. Brill, 1956.

—————. *Sochineniia. Vol. 5*. Moscow: Nauka, 1968.

—————. *Turkestan v epokhu mongol'skogo nashestviia chast pervaia, Teksty*. St. Petersburg, 1898.

—————. *Turkestan down to the Mongol Invasion*. 4th ed. London: Luzac and Co., 1977.

Bira, Sh. "Some Remarks on the *Hu-lan deb-ther* of Kun-dga' rdo-rje." *Acta Orientalia* 17 (1964): 69–81.

Bodrogligeti, A "Early Turkish Terms Connected with Books and Writing." *Acta Orientalia* 18 (1965): 93–117.

Boyle, J. A. "Turkish and Mongol Shamanism in the Middle Ages." *Folklore* 83 (1972): 177–193.

Boyle, J. A. trans. *The History of the World Conqueror*. 2 vols. Manchester: University Press, 1958.

———. *The Successors of Genghis Khan*. New York: Columbia University Press, 1971.

Bretschneider, E. *Mediaeval Researches from East Asiatic Sources*. 2 vols. London: Routledge and Kegan Paul. 1967 reprint.

Buell, P. D. "Mongolian Social and Political Organization and the Mongolian State in China." *Yüan Workshop*, Princeton, June 1975. Unpublished paper.

———. "Tribe, *Qan*, and *Ulus* in Early Mongol China: Some Prolegomena to Yüan History." *Ph. D. dissertation*, University of Washington, 1977.

Cerensodnom, D. *XIV zuuny üeiin yaruu nairagč Čoiži-odser*. Ulan Bator 1969.

Cha Kipyok. "Political Thought behind Korean Nationalism." *Korean Journal* 16 (April 1976): 4–20.

Chan Hok-lam. *The Historiography of the Chin Dynasty: Three Studies*. Wiesbaden: Franz Steiner, 1970.

———. *Eminent Chinese of the Reign of Qubilai Qan* (Canberra, forthcoming).

———. "Prolegomena to the *Ju-nan i-shih*: A Memoir on the Last Chin Court under the Mongol Siege of 1234." *Sung Studies Newsletter* 10 (December 1974): 2–19.

Chavannes, Édouard. "Voyageurs chinois chez les Khitan et les Joutchen." *Journal Asiatique* (1897), pp. 390–442; (1898), pp. 361–439.

———. "Pei Yuan Lou. Récit d'un voyage dans le Nord. Écrit sous les Song par Tcheou Chan." *T'oung Pao* 5 (1904): 163–192.

———. "Inscriptions et pièces de chancellerie chinoises de l'époque mongole." *T'oung Pao* 5 (1904): 357–447.

———. "L'instruction d'un futur empereur de Chine en l'an 1193." *Mémoires concernant L'Asie Orientale* 1 (1913): 19–64.

Ch'en Yüan. *Western and Central Asians in China Under the Mongols: Their Transformation into Chinese*. Translated by Ch'ien Hsing-hai and L. C. Goodrich. Los Angeles: Monumenta Serica Monographs, 1966.

Cheng Te-k'un. "The Study of Ceramic Wares in Southeast Asia." *Chung-wen Ta-hsüeh Chung-kuo wen-hua yen-chiu-so hsüeh-pao*. Hong Kong, 1972.

Chi Ch'ao-ting. *Key Economic Areas in Chinese History*. London: Allen and Unwin, 1936.

Clark, Larry. "On a Mongol Decree of Yisün Temür (1339)." *Central Asiatic Journal* 19 (1975): 194–198.

Clauson, G. *An Etymological Dictionary of Pre-Thirteenth Century Turkish*. Oxford: Clarendon Press, 1972.

Cleaves, Francis W. "K'uei-k'uei or Nao-nao?" *Harvard Journal of Asiatic Studies* 10 (1947): 1–12.

————. "The Expression *Jöb Ese Bol* in the *Secret History of the Mongols*." *Harvard Journal of Asiatic Studies* 11 (1948): 311–320.

————. "The Sino-Mongolian Inscription of 1362 in Memory of Prince Hindu." *Harvard Journal of Asiatic Studies* 12 (1949): 1–133.

————. "The Sino-Mongolian Inscription of 1228 in Memory of Jigüntei." *Harvard Journal of Asiatic Studies* 14 (1951): 1–104.

————. "A Chancellery Practice of the Mongols in the Thirteenth and Fourteenth Centuries." *Harvard Journal of Asiatic Studies* 14 (1951): 493–526.

————. "The Sino-Mongol Inscription of 1246." *Harvard Journal of Asiatic Studies* 15 (1952): 1–123.

————. "Daruγa and Gerege." *Harvard Journal of Asiatic Studies* 16 (1953): 237–259.

————. "The *Bodistw-a Čari-a Awatarun Tayilbur* of 1312 by Čosgi Odsir." *Harvard Journal of Asiatic Studies* 17 (1954): 1–129.

————. "The Historicity of the Baljuna Covenant." *Harvard Journal of Asiatic Studies* 18 (1955): 357–421.

Dalai, Ch. *Yuan gürnii üeiin Mongol*. Ulan Bator, 1973.

Dardess, John. *Conquerors and Confucians: Aspects of Political Change in Late Yüan China*. New York: Columbia University Press, 1973.

————. "From Mongol Empire to Yüan Dynasty: Changing Forms of Imperial Rule in Mongolia and Central Asia." *Monumenta Serica* 30 (1972–75): 117–165.

Das, S. Ch. "Tibet under the Tartar Emperor of China." *Journal of the Asiatic Society of Bengal*. Extra Number (1905).

Dauvillier, J. "Les Provinces Chaldéennes de l'Extérieur au Moyen Age." *Mélanges offerts au R. P. Ferdinand Cavallera*. Toulouse, 1948: Pp. 261–316.

Davidovich, E. A. "Denezhoe khoziaistvo i chastichnoe vosstanovlenie torgovli v Srednei Azii posle mongol'skogo nashestviia, xii v." *Narody Azii i Afriki*, n. 6 (1970), pp. 60–67.

Dawson, Christopher, ed. *The Mongol Mission*. New York: Sheed and Ward, 1955.

Defremery, Charles, and Sanguinetti, B., eds. and trans. *Voyages d'Ibn Batoutah*. 4 vols. Paris: Imprimerie nationale, 1877–1927.

Demiéville, Paul. *Le concile de Lhasa*. Paris: Imprimerie nationale de France, 1952.

————. "La situation religieuse en Chine au temps de Marco Polo." *Oriente Poliano*. Rome, 1957. Pp. 193–236.

de Rachewiltz, Igor. "Sino-Mongol Culture Contacts in the XIII Century. A Study on Yeh-lü Ch'u-ts'ai." Ph. D. dissertation Australian National University, Canberra, 1960.

————. "Yeh-lü Ch'u-ts'ai (1189–1243): Buddhist Idealist and Confucian Statesman." In *Confucian Personalities*, edited by A. F. Wright and D. C. Twitchett. Stanford: Stanford University Press, 1962.

————. "The *Hsi-yu lu* by Yeh-lu Ch'ü-ts'ai." *Monumenta Serica* 21 (1962): 1–128.

————. "Some Remarks on the Dating of the *Secret History of the Mongols*." *Monumenta Serica* 24 (1965): 185–206.

————. "Personnel and Personalities in North China in the Early Mongol Period." *Journal of the Economic and Social History of the Orient* 9 (1966): 88–144.

————. "Some Remarks on the Ideological Foundations of Chinggis Khan's Empire." *Papers on Far Eastern History* 7 (1973): 21–36

————. "Muqali, Bōl, Tas, and An-t'ung." *Papers on Far Eastern History* 15 (March 1977): 45–62.

————. "Secret History of the Mongols." *Papers on Far Eastern History* 16 (September 1977): 27–65.

de Rachewiltz, Igor, and Nakano, M. *Index to Biographical Material in Chin and Yüan Literary Works, First Series*. Canberra: Australian National University Press, 1970.

de Rachewiltz, Igor, and Wang, M. *Index to Biographical Material in Chin and Yüan Literary Works, Second Series*. Canberra: Australian National University Press, 1972.

————. *Index to Biographical Material in Chin and Yüan Literary Works, Third Series*. Canberra: Australian National University Press, 1979.

Devandra, D. H. *Guide to Yapahuva*. Colombo, 1951.

Dobson, W. A. C. H. "Some Legal Instruments of Ancient China: The Ming and the Meng." *Wen-lin, Studies in the Chinese Humanities*. Edited by Chow Tse-tung. Madison: University of Wisconsin Press, 1968.

Doerfer, G. *Türkische und mongolische Elemente im Neupersischen*. 4 vols. Wiesbaden: Franz Steiner, 1963–1975.

D'Ohsson, C. *Histoire des Mongols*. Vol. I. La Haye et Amsterdam: Les Frères Van Cleef, 1834.

Drevnetiurkskii slovar. Leningrad, 1969.

Eberhard, Wolfram. *Conquerors and Rulers*. Leiden: E. J. Brill, 1970. 2nd. ed.

Eichhorn, Werner. "Bestimmungen für Tributgesandtschaften zur Sung-Zeit." *Zeitschrift der Deutschen Morgenländischen Gesellschaft* 114 (1964): 382–390.

————. "Notiz betreffend Audienzen am Sung-Hofe." *Zeitschrift der Deutschen Morgenländischen Gesellschaft* 108 (1958): 164–169.

Elvin, Mark. *The Pattern of the Chinese Past*. Stanford: Stanford University Press, 1973.

Fairbank, John K. *Trade and Diplomacy on the China Coast: The Opening of the Treaty Ports, 1842–1854.* Cambridge, Mass.: Harvard University Press, 1953.

Fairbank, John K., ed. *The Chinese World Order: Traditional China's Foreign Relations.* Cambridge, Mass.: Harvard University Press, 1968.

Fedorov-Davydov, G. A. *Obshchestvennyi stroi Zolotoi Ordy.* Moscow: Nauka, 1973.

Feng Chia-sheng and Tenishev, E. "Tri novykh Uigurskikh dokumenta iz Turfana." *Problemy Vostokovedeniia*, no. 3 (1960), pp. 141–149.

Fincher, John. "China as Race, Culture, and Nation: Notes on Fang Hsiao-ju's Discussion of Dynastic Legitimacy." In *Transition and Permanence: Chinese History and Culture. A Festschrift in Honor of Dr. Hsiao Kung-ch'uan* edited by D. Buxbaum and F. Mote. Hong Kong: Cathay Press, Ltd., 1972. Pp. 59–69.

Franke, Herbert. "Sen-ge, das Leben eines uigurischen Staatsbeamten zur Zeit Chubilai's, dargestellt nach Kap. 205 der Yüan Annalen." *Sinica* 17 (1942): 90–113.

———. "Ahmed: Ein Beitrag zur Wirtschaftsgeschichte Chinas unter Qubilai." *Oriens* 1 (1948): 222–236.

———. *Geld und Wirtschaft in China unter der Mongolen-Herrschaft.* Beiträge zur Wirtschaftsgeschichte der Yüan-Zeit. Leipzig: Otto Harrassowitz, 1949.

———. "Zur Datierung der mongolischen Schreiben aus Turfan." *Oriens* 15 (1962): 399–410.

———. "Treaties between Sung and Chin." *Études Song in Memoriam Étienne Balázs.* Sér, I, 1. Edited by Françoise Aubin. Paris: 1970. Pp. 55–84.

———. "Zwei mongolische Textfragmente aus Zentralasien." In *Mongolian Studies*, edited by Louis Ligeti. Amsterdam: Grüner, 1970. Pp. 137–147.

———. "Chinese Historiography Under Mongol Rule: The Role of History in Acculturation." *Mongolian Studies* 1 (1974): 15–26.

———. "A Note on Wine." *Zentralasiatische Studien* 8 (1974): 241–246.

———. "Chinese Texts on the Jurchen." *Zentralasiatische Studien* 9 (1975): 119–186.

———. "A Transmitter of Chinese Values: Wang Yün (1227–1304)." Unpublished paper read at Conference on Yüan Thought, Issaquah, Wash., January 1978.

———. "From Tribal Chieftain to Universal Emperor and God: The Legitimation of the Yüan Dynasty." Unpublished paper, München, 1978.

———. "A Sino-Uighur Family Portrait: Notes on a Woodcut from Turfan." *Canada Mongolia Review* 4 (1978): 33–40.

———. "Einige Bemerkungen zu Gesandschaftsreisen in der Sung-

Zeit." *Nachrichten der Gesellschaft für Natur-und Völkerkunde Ostasiens* 125 (1979): 20–26.

Franke, Herbert, ed. *Sung Biographies*. 4 vols. Wiesbaden: Franz Steiner, 1976.

Franke, Otto. *Geschichte des chinesischen Reiches*, IV. Berlin: W. deGruyter, 1948.

Fuchs, W. "Analecta zur mongolischen Uebersetzungsliteratur der Yüan-Zeit." *Monumenta Serica* 11 (1946): 33–46.

———. "Ein chinesisch-uigurischer Blockdruck." In *Tractata Altaica*, edited by W. Heissig. Wiesbaden: Otto Harrassowitz, 1976.

Gabain, A. von. *Das Leben im uigurischen Königreich von Qočo, 850–1250*. Wiesbaden: Otto Harrassowitz, 1973.

Galstian, A. G., trans, and ed. *Armianskie istochniki o Mongolakh*. Moscow: Nauka, 1962.

Gibb, H. A. R., et al., eds. *Encyclopaedia of Islam*. New ed. Leiden: E. J. Brill, 1960.

Glaubitz, Joachim. "Japanische Arbeiten über Zentralasien." *Der Islam* 35 (1960): 129–139.

Golas, Peter H. "The Courier-Transport System of the Northern Sung." *Harvard University Papers on China* 20 (1966): 1–22.

Goodrich, L. C., and Fang Chaoying, eds. *Dictionary of Ming Biography*. 2 vols. New York: Columbia University Press, 1976.

Granet, Marcel. *Danses et Légendes de la Chine Ancienne*. Paris: F. Alcan, 1926.

Gumilyov, L. N. "The Secret and Official History of the Mongols in the Twelfth and Thirteenth Centuries (As They Themselves Wrote It)." In *The Countries and Peoples of the East*. Reprinted from *Tataro-mongoly v Azii i Evrope*. Moscow: Nauka, 1974.

Haeger, John W. ed. *Crisis and Prosperity in Sung China*. Tucson: University of Arizona Press, 1974.

Haenisch, Erich. "Die Ehreninschrift für den Rebellengeneral Ts'ui Lih." *Abhandlungen der Deutschen Akademie der Wissenschaften: Philoso-phischhistorische Klasse*, no. 4 (1944), p. 79.

———. *Die Geheime Geschichte der Mongolen*. Leipzig: Otto Harrasso-witz, 1948. 2nd. ed.

———. "Die Jagdgesetze im mongolischen Ostreich." In *Ostasiatische Studien: Festschrift für Martin Ramming*, edited by I. L. Kluge. Berlin: Akademie Verlag, 1959.

———. "Zum Untergang zweier Reiche: Berichte von Augenzeugen aus den Jahren 1232–33 und 1368–70." In *Abhandlungen für die Kunde des Morgenlandes* 38, 4 (1969).

Haidar, Muhammad. *A History of the Moghuls of Central Asia*. Translated by E. Denison Ross and edited by Ney Elias. New York: Praeger

Publishers, 1970 reprint.

Hambis, Louis. *Le Chapitre CVII du Yuan-che*. Leiden: E. J. Brill, 1945.

———. "Notes sur l'histoire de Corée a l'époque mongole." *T'oung Pao* 45 (1957): 151–218.

———. "Autour du manuscript Stael-Holstein." *T'oung Pao* 46 (1958): 142–150.

Hamilton, James. "Un acte ouigour de vente de terrain provenant de Yarkhoto." *Turcica* 1 (1968): 26–52.

———. *Les Ouighours à l'époque des Cinq Dynasties d'après les documents chinois*. Paris: Presses Universitaires de France, 1955.

———. "Le texte turc en caractères syriaques du grand sceau cruciforme de Mar Yahballāhā III" *Journal Asiatique* 260 (1972): 155–170.

Hana, Corina. *Bericht über die Verteidigung der Stadt Te-an*. Wiesbaden: Franz Steiner, 1970.

Harlez, C. de. *Histoire de l'Empire de Kin: Aisin gurun-i-suduri bithe*. Louvain: Charles Peeters, 1887.

Harrison, T. "Trade Porcelain and Stoneware in South-east Asia." *Sarawak Museum Journal* 10 (1961): 222–226.

Hedin, Sven. *Southern Tibet*. Vol. 8. Stockholm: Lithographic Institute of the General Staff of the Swedish Army, 1922.

Heissig, W. *Die Familien-und Geschichtsschreibung der Mongolen* I. Wiesbaden: Otto Harrassowitz, 1959.

Henthorn, W. E. *Korea: The Mongol Invasions*. Leiden: E. J. Brill, 1963.

Herrmann, Albert. *An Historical Atlas of China*. Edited by N. Ginsburg. Chicago: Aldine Publishing Company, 1966.

Hirth, F., and Rockhill, W. W., trans. *Chau Ju-kua*. St. Petersburg: Printing Office of the Imperial Academy of Sciences, 1911.

Hsiao Ch'i-ch'ing. *The Military Establishment of the Yuan Dynasty*. Cambridge: Harvard University Press, 1978.

Hummel, Arthur, ed. *Eminent Chinese of the Ch'ing Period*. Washington, D. C.: U. S. Government Printing Office, 1943–1944.

Hung, W. "The Transmission of the Book Known as the *Secret History of the Mongols*." *Harvard Journal of Asiatic Studies* 14 (1951): 433–492.

———. "Three of Ch'ien Ta-hsin's Poems on Yüan History." *Harvard Journal of Asiatic Studies* 19 (1956): 1–32.

Huth, G. *Geschichte des Buddhismus in der Mongolei*. Strassburg: Trübner, 1892–1896.

Inaba Shoju. "The Lineage of the Sa-skya-pa: A Chapter of the Red Annals." *Memoirs of the Research Department of the Toyo Bunko* 22 (1963): 107–123.

———. "An Introductory Study on the Degeneration of Lamas: A Genealogical and Chronological Note on the Imperial Preceptors in the Yüan Dynasty." In *A Study of Klésa: A Study of Impurity and Its Purification in the Oriental Religions*, edited by G. H. Sasaki. Tokyo, 1975.

Jackson, Peter. "The Accession of Qubilai Qa'an: A Re-examination." *Journal of the Anglo-Mongolian Society* 2, 1 (June 1975): 1–10.

Jamieson, John. *The Samguk Sagi and the Unification Wars*. Ph. D. dissertation, University of California at Berkeley, 1969.

———. "The Manchurian Kingdom of Pohai." Paper read at Regional Conference on Korean Studies, University of British Columbia, February 17–19, 1978.

Jūzjānī. *Tabakat-i Nāsārī*. 2 vols. Translated by H. G. Raverty. New Delhi: Oriental Books Reprint Corporation, 1970 reprint.

Kang, H. W. "The First Succession Struggle of Koryŏ, in 945: A Reinterpretation." *Journal of Asian Studies* 36, 3 (May 1977): 411–428.

Kaplan, Morton A. *System and Process in International Relations*. New York: Wiley, 1957.

Kara, G. *Knigi mongol'skikh kochevnikov*. Moscow: Nauka, 1972.

Kim Tai-jin, ed. and trans. *A Bibliographical Guide to Traditional Korean Sources*. Seoul: Asiatic Research Center, Korea University, 1976.

Kotwicz, W. "Les termes concernant le service des relais postaux." *Rocznik Orientalistyczny* 16 (1950): 327–355.

Krompart, Robert J. *The Southern Restoration of T'ang: Counsel, Policy, and Parahistory in the Stabilization of the Chiang-Huai Region, 887–943*. Ph. D. dissertation, University of California, Berkeley, 1973.

Kuchera, S. "Mongoly v. Azii i Evrope: Sbornik statei." In *Tataro-Mongoly v Azii i Evrope: Sbornik statei*, edited by S. L. Tikvinskii. Moscow: Nauka, 1977.

Kwanten, Luc. "Chingis Khan's Conquest of Tibet: Myth or Reality?" *Journal of Asian History* 8 (1974): 1–20.

———. "Chio-ssu-lo (997–1068). A Tibetan Ally of the Northern Sung." *Rocznik Orientalistyczny* 39 (1977): 92–106.

———. "The Career of Muqali: A Reassessment." *Bulletin of Sung and Yüan Studies* 14 (1978): 31–38.

———. *Imperial Nomads: A History of Central Asia, 500–1500*. Philadelphia: University of Pennsylvania Press, 1979.

Kychanov, E. I. "Nekotorye suzhdeniia ob istoricheskikh sud'bakh tangutov posle nashestviia Chingiskhana." *Kratkie soobshcheniia Instituta narodov Azii* 76 (1965): 154–165.

———. *Ocherk Istorii Tangutskogo Gosudarstva*. Moscow: Nauka, 1968.

———. "Les guerres entre les Sung du Nord et le Hsi Hsia." *Études Song in Memoriam Étienne Balázs*. Sér. I, no. 2. The Hague, 1971. Pp. 102–118.

Ledyard, Gari. "Two Mongol Documents from the *Koryŏ-sa*." *Journal of the American Oriental Society* 83 (1963): 225–238.

———. "Galloping Along with the Horseriders: Looking for the

Founders of Japan." *Journal of Japanese Studies* 1, no. 2 (1975): 217–254.

Lee, Thomas H. C. "A Report on the Recently Excavated Song Ship at Quanzhou and a Consideration of Its True Capacity." *Sung Studies Newletter* 11–12 (1976): 4–9.

Legge, James, trans. *The Chinese Classics. Volume Two: The Works of Mencius.* Oxford: Clarendon Press, 1895.

Li Fang-kuei. "The Inscription of the Sino-Tibetan Trety of 821–822." *T'oung Pao* 44 (1956): 1–99.

Ligeti, Louis. "Review of L. Hambis, *Le chapitre CVIII du Yuan-che.*" *Acta Orientalia* 5 (1955).

———. "Trois notes sur l'écriture 'Phags-pa." *Acta Orientalia* 13 (1961): 201–237.

———. "Sur quelques transcriptions sino-ouigoures des Yüan." *Ural-Altaische Jahrbucher* 33 (1961): 235–244.

———. *A mongolok titkos története.* Budapest: Akadémiai Kiadó, 1962.

———. "À propos de la version mongole des 'Douze actes du Bouddha.'" *Acta Orientalia* 20 (1967): 59–73.

———. *Monuments Préclassiques, XIIIe et XIVe Siècles.* Vol. 1. Budapest: Akadémiai Kiadó, 1972.

Lin, T. C. "Manchuria Trade and Tribute in the Ming Dynasty: A Study of Chinese Theories and Methods of Control Over Border Peoples." *Nankai Social and Economic Quarterly* 9 (1937): 855–892.

Liu, James T. C. *Ou-yang Hsiu: An Eleventh-Century Neo-Confucianist.* Stanford: Stanford University Press, 1967.

———. "Yüeh Fei (1107–1141) and China's Image of Loyalty." *Journal of Asian Studies* 30, 2 (1972): 291–297.

Lo Jung-pang. "The Emergence of Chinese Sea Power during the Late Sung and Early Yüan Periods." *Far Eastern Quarterly* 14 (1954–55): 489–503.

Lo, Winston W. *The Life and Thought of Yeh Shih.* Hong Kong: Chinese University of Hong Kong Press, 1974.

Locsin, C., and Locsin, L. *Oriental Ceramics Discovered in the Philippines.* Tokyo: Charles Tuttle, Inc., 1967.

Lynn, Richard. "A Poet and His Poems: Kuan Yüan-shih." *Papers on Far Eastern History* 18 (1978): 81–121.

Mackerras, Colin. *The Uighur Empire (744–840) According to the T'ang Dynastic Histories.* Canberra: Centre of Oriental Studies, Australian National University, 1968.

Maillard, Monique. "Essai sur la vie matérielle dans l'oasis de Tourfan pendant le haut moyen âge." *Arts Asiatique* 29 (1973): 3–185.

Maitra, K. M., trans. *A Persian Embassy to China.* New York: Paragon Books Reprint Corporation, 1970.

Maliavkin, A. G. *Materialy po istorii Uigurov v ix-xii vv.* Novosibirsk: Nauka, 1974.

Malov, S. E. "Dva uigurskikh dokumenta." In V. V. Barthold, *Turkestanskie druz'ia ucheniki i pochitateli.* Tashkent, 1927. Pp. 387–394.

————. "Uigurskie rukopisnye dokumenty ekspeditsii S. F. Ol'denburga." *Zapiski instituta vostokovedeniia Akademiia Nauk* 1 (1932): 129–149.

————. *Pamiatniki drevnetiurskoi pismennosti: Teksty i issledovaniia.* Moscow and Leningrad: Nauka, 1951.

Mangold, G. *Das Militärwesen in China unter der Mongolen-Herrschaft.* Bamberg, 1971.

Martin, H. Desmond. *The Rise of Chingis Khan and His Conquest of North China.* Baltimore: Johns Hopkins Press, 1950.

Masson, V. M. and Romodin, V. A. *Istoriia Afganistana.* Vol. I. Moscow: Nauka, 1964.

Mathew, G. "Chinese Porcelain in East Africa on the Coast of South Arabia." *Oriental Art,* new series, II, no. 2 (1956).

Mauss, Marcel. *Essai sur le don.* Paris: Félix Alcan, 1925. (English translation: *The Gift: Forms and Functions of Exchange in Archaic Societies.* Glencoe: Free Press, 1954.)

Mills, J. V. G., trans. *Ma Huan: Ying-yai Sheng-lan, The Overall Survey of the Ocean's Shores.* Cambridge: Cambridge University Press, 1970.

Minorsky, V. *Iranica.* Tehran, 1964.

Monneret, U. de Villard. *Il Libro della Peregrinazione nelle Parti d'Oriente di Ricoldo da Montecroce.* Rome ad S. Sabinea: Institutum Historicum F. F. Praedicatorum, 1948.

Mori Masao. "A Study on Uygur Documents of Loans for Consumption." *Memoirs of the Research Department of the Toyo Bunko* 20 (1961): 111–148.

Mostaert, A., and Cleaves, F. W. "Trois documents mongols des archives secrètes vaticanes." *Harvard Journal of Asiatic Studies* 15 (1952): 419–506.

Moule, A. C., and Pelliot, Paul, trans. *Marco Polo: The Description of the World.* London: George Routledge and Sons, 1938.

Muller, F. W. K. "Uigurische Glossen." In *Festschrift für Friedrich Hirth zu seinem 75. Geburtstag.* Berlin: Oefterheld and Co., 1920.

Mullie, Joseph. "Tch'eng Yao lou. Relation de Voyage de Lou Tchen." *Geografiska Annaler* 17 (Stockholm, 1935): 413–433.

Munkuev, N. Ts. *Kitaiskii istochnik o pervykh mongol'skikh khanakh.* Moscow: Nauka, 1965.

————. "Zametki o drevnikh mongolakh." In *Tataro-Mongoly v Azii i Evrope,* edited by S. L. Tikhvinskii. Moscow: Nauka, 1970.

————. *Men-da bei-lu "Polnoe Opisanie Mongolo-Tatar."* Moscow: Nauka, 1975.

Murayama, S. "Sind die Naiman Türken oder Mongolen?" *Central Asiatic Journal* 4 (1959): 188–198.

Nakano, M. "An Annotation on the *Ti-shih Pa-pa hsing-chuang.*" *Hsin-A hsüeh-pao* 9, 1 (1969): 93–119.

Needham, Joseph. *Science and Civilisation in China* Vol. IV, no 3. Cambridge: Cambridge University Press, 1971.

Netolitzky, Almut. *Das Ling-waj tai-ta von Chou Ch'ü fei: Eine Landeskunde Südchinas aus dem 12. Jahrhundert.* Wiesbaden: Franz Steiner, 1977.

Nikitina, M. I. *Ocherki Istorii Koreiskoi Literaturyi do XIV v.* Moscow: Nauka, 1969.

Olbricht, P. *Das Postwesen in China unter der Mongolenherrschaft.* Wiesbaden: Otto Harrassowitz, 1954.

Önnerfors, A., ed. *Historia Tartarorum C. de Bridia monachi.* Berlin: W. de Gruyter, 1967.

Pelliot, Paul. "Chrétiens d'Asie centrale et d'extrême-orient." *T'oung Pao* 15 (1914): 623–644.

———. "À propos des Comans." *Journal Asiatique* 15 (1920): 125–185.

———. "Les systèmes d'écriture en usage chez les anciens Mongols." *Asia Major* 2 (1925): 284–289.

———. "Note sur la carte des pays du Nord-Quest dans le *King-che ta-tien.*" *T'oung Pao* 25 (1928): 98–100.

———. "Notes sur le 'Turkestan' de M. W. Barthold." *T'oung Pao* 27 (1930): 12–56.

———. "Les *Kökö-däbtär* el les *hou-k'eou ts'ing-ts'eu.*" *T'oung Pao* 27 (1930): 194–198.

———. "Review of *The Travels of an Alchemist* by Arthur Waley,." *T'oung Pao* 28 (1931): 413–428.

———. *La Haute Asie.* Paris: J. Goudard, 1931.

———. "Une tribu méconnue des Naiman: Les Bätäkin." *T'oung Pao* 37 (1943–44): 35–71.

———. "Le Hōja et le Sayyid Ḥusain de l'histoire des Ming." *T'oung Pao* 38 (1947): 81–292.

———. *Notes on Marco Polo.* Paris: Librairie Adrien-Maisonneuve, 1959–63.

———. *Recherches sur les chrétiens d'Asie centrale et d'extrême-orient.* Paris: Imprimerie nationale, 1973.

Pelliot, Paul, and Hambis, Louis, trans. *Histoire des campagnes de Gengis Khan.* Leiden: E. J. Brill, 1951.

Petech, L. "The Mongol Census in Tibet." In M. Aris, ed., *Tibetan Studies in honour of Hugh Richardson.* Warminster, 1980: 233–238.

———. "Sang-ko: A Tibetan Statesman in Yüan China." *Acta Orientalia* 34 (1980): 193–208.

Pinks, Elisabeth. *Die Uiguren von Kan-chou in der frühen Sung-Zeit (960–*

1028). Wiesbaden: Otto Harrassowitz, 1968.

Pope, John. *Fourteenth-Century Blue and White: A Group of Chinese Porcelains in the Topkapu Sarayi Müzesi, Istanbul.* Washington: Freer Gallery of Art, Occasional Papers, 1952.

Pritsak, O. "Von der Karluk zu den Karachaniden." *Zeitschrift der Morgenländischen Gesellschaft* 101 (1951): 270–300.

Radloff, W. *Uigurische Sprachdenkmaler.* Leningrad: Wirtschafts-und die Sozialverfassung des Staates, 1928.

Rahmet, R. "Der Herrschentitel Iduq-qut." *Ural-Altaische Jahrbucher* 35 (1964): 150–157.

Rashīd al-Dīn. *Sbornik letopisei* I/2. Translated by O. I. Smirnova. Moscow-Leningrad: Nauka, 1952.

Ratchnevsky, Paul. *Un code des Yüan*, I. Paris: Ernest Leroux, 1937.

————. *Un code des Yüan* II. Paris: Presses universitaires de France, 1972.

Rémusat, J. P. Abel. *Nouveaux mélanges asiatiques* 2 (1829): 61–63.

Richardson, H. "The Karma-pa Sect: A Historical Note." *Journal of the Royal Asiatic Society* (1958).

Roerich, G. N. "Mun-mkhyen Chos-kyi-'od-zer and the Origin of the Mongol Alphabet." *Journal of the Asiatic Society of Bengal* 11 (1954).

————. "Tibetan Loan-Words in Mongolian." In *Sino-Indian Studies: Liebenthal Festschrift* (vol. V, pts. 3–4), edited by K. Roy Visvabharati: Santiniketan, 1957. Pp. 174–180.

Roerich, G. N., trans. *The Blue Annals.* Calcutta: Asiatic Society of Bengal, 1949–1953.

————. *Biography of Dharmasvamin.* Patha, 1959.

Rogers, Michael C. "Sung-Koryŏ Relations: Some Inhibiting Factors." *Oriens* 11 (1958): 194–202.

————. "Sukchong of Koryŏ: His Accession and His Relations with Liao." *T'oung Pao* 47 (1959): 30–42.

————. "Factionalism and Koryŏ Policy under the Northern Sung." *Journal of the American Oriental Society* 79 (1959): 16–25.

————. "Koryŏ's Military Dictatorship and Its Relations with Chin." *T'oung Pao* 47 (1959): 43–62.

————. "The Regularization of Koryŏ-Chin Relations (1116–1131)." *Central Asiatic Journal* 6 (1961): 51–84.

————. "Some Kings of Koryŏ as Registered in Chinese Works." *Journal of the American Oriental Society* 81 (1961): 415–421.

Róna-Tas, A. "Some Notes on the Terminology of Mongolian Writing." *Acta Orientalia* 18 (1965): 114–147.

Rossabi, Morris. "The Tea and Horse Trade with Inner Asia during the Ming." *Journal of Asian History* 4 (1970): 136–168.

————. *China and Inner Asia From 1368 to the Present Day.* London:

Thames and Hudson, 1975.

———. "Khubilai Khan and the Women in His Family." In *Sino-Mongolica: Festschrift für Herbert Franke,* edited by W. Bauer. Wiesbaden: Franz Steiner, 1979. Pp. 153–180.

———. "The Muslims in the Early Yüan Dynasty." In *China Under Mongol Rule,* edited by John Langlois. Princeton: Princeton University Press, 1981. Pp. 257–295.

Rotours, Robert des. *Traité des fonctionnaires et Traité de l'armée.* 2 vols. Leiden: E. J. Brill, 1947–48.

Rutt, R. "A Lay of King Tongmyŏng." *Korea Journal* 13, 7 (July 1973): 48–54.

Sagaster, Klaus. "Herrschaftsideologie und Friedensgedanke bei den Mongolen." *Central Asiatic Journal* 17 (1973): 223–242.

———. *Die weisse Geschichte.* Wiesbaden: Otto Harrassowitz, 1976.

Sansom, George. *A History of Japan to 1334.* Stanford: Stanford University Press, 1974.

Sarre, Friedrich. *Die Keramik von Samarra.* Berlin: D. Reimer, 1925.

Schafer, Edward H. "The History of the Empire of Southern Han." In *Silver Jubilee Volume of the Zinbun-Kagaku-Kenkyusyo.* Kyoto: Kyoto University, 1954. Pp. 339–369.

———. *The Empire of Min.* Rutland and Tokyo: Charles E. Tuttle Company, 1964.

Schmidt, I. J. *Geschichte der Ost-Mongolen und ihres Fürstenhauses.* St. Petersburg: N. Gretsch, 1829.

Schuh, D. "Wie ist die Einladung des fünften Karma-pa an den chinesischen Kaiserhof als Fortführung der Tibet-Politik der Mongolen-Khane zu verstehen?" In *Altaica Collecta,* edited by W. Heissig. Wiesbaden: Otto Harrassowitz, 1976. Pp. 209–244.

———. *Erlasse und Sendschreiben mongolischer Herrscher für Tibetische Geistliche.* St. Augustin: VGH Wissenschaftsverlag, 1977.

Schulte-Uffelage, H. *Das Keng-shen wai-shih: Eine Quelle zur späten Mongolenzeit.* Berlin: Akademie-Verlag, 1963.

Schurmann, H. F. *Economic Structure of the Yüan Dynasty.* Cambridge, Mass.: Harvard University Press, 1956.

———. "Mongolian Tributary Practices in the 13th Century." *Harvard Journal of Asiatic Studies* 19 (1956): 304–389.

Schwarz-Schilling, C. *Der Friede von Shan-yüan (1005 n. Chr.)* Wiesbaden: Otto Harrassowitz, 1959.

Semenov, A. A. *Materialy po istorii i kul'ture uigurskogo naroda.* Alma-Ata, 1978.

Serruys, Henry. *Sino-Mongol Relations during the Ming, II: The Tribute System and Diplomatic Missions (1400–1600).* Brussels: Institut Belge des Hautes Études Chinoises, 1967.

Shakabpa, W. D. *Tibet: A Political History*. New Haven and London: Yale University Press, 1967.

Shastina, N. P., trans. *Shara Tudzhi, mongol'skaja letopish' XVII veka*. Moscow-Leningrad: Nauka, 1957.

Shiba Yoshinobu. *Commerce and Society in Sung China*. Translated by Mark Elvin. Ann Arbor: Center for Chinese Studies, University of Michigan, 1970.

Shimazaki Akira. "On Pei-t'ing (Bišbaliq) and K'o-han Fu-t'u-ch'eng." *Memoirs of the Research Department of the Toyo Bunko* 32 (1974): 99–114.

Sinor, Denis. *Introduction à l'étude de l'Eurasie Centrale*. Wiesbaden: Otto Harrassowitz, 1963.

Skelton, R. A., et al. *The Vinland Map and the Tartar Relation*. New Haven: Yale University Press, 1965.

Skinner, G. William, ed. *The City in Late Imperial China*. Stanford: Stanford University Press, 1977.

Smith, John Masson. "Mongol and Nomadic Taxation." *Harvard Journal of Asiatic Studies* 30 (1970): 48–85.

———. "Mongol Manpower and Persian Population." *Journal of the Social and Economic History of the Orient* 18 (1975): 270–299.

Spuler, B. *Die Mongolen in Iran*. Berlin: Akademie-Verlag, 1955.

Steele, John, trans. *The I-li or Book of Etiquette and Ceremonial*. 2 vols. London: Probsthain, 1917.

Stein, A. *Archaeological Reconnaissances in North-Western India and South-Eastern Iran*. London: Macmillan and Co., Ltd., 1937.

Stein, Rolf. *Recherches sur l'épopée et le barde au Tibet*. Paris: Imprimerie nationale, 1959.

———. *Les tribus anciennes des marches sino-tibétaines*. Paris: Imprimerie nationale, 1959.

Tao Jing-shen. "Yü Ching and Sung Policies toward Liao and Hsia, 1042–1044." *Journal of Asian History* 6, 2 (1972): 114–122.

———. "Peace with the Barbarians: Wang An-shih's Policy towards the Khitan." American Oriental Society meeting (Tucson, 1977).

Teng Ssu-yü and Fairbank, John, trans. *China's Response to the West: A Documentary Survey, 1839–1923*. Cambridge, Masss.: Harvard University Press, 1954.

Theophrastus. *Enquiry into Plants*. 2 vols. Translated by A. Hort. London: W. Heinemann, 1916.

Thiel, J. "Der Streit der Buddhisten und Taoisten zur Mongolenzeit." *Monumenta Serica* 20 (1961): 1–81.

Thiele, Dagmar. *Der Abschluss eines Vertrages: Diplomatie zwischen Sung- und-Chin Dynastie 1117–1123*. Wiesbaden: Franz Steiner, 1971.

Tikhonov, D. I. *Khoziaistvo i obshchestvennyi stroi Uigurskogo gosudarstva x-xiv vv*. Moscow-Leningrad: Nauka, 1966.

————. "K voprosu o nekotorykh terminiakh." *Strany i narody Vostoka vyp. XI*. Moscow: Nauka, 1974.

Till, Barry. "A Sung Embassy to the Liao Nation (1067)." *Canada-Mongolia Review* 1, 1 (1975): 57–66.

Tillman, Hoyt C. "Values in History and Ethics in Politics: Issues Debated Between Chu Hsi and Ch'en Liang." Ph.D. dissertation, Harvard University, 1977.

Trauzettel, R. "Ou-yang Hsius Essays über die legitime Thronnachfolge." *Sinologica* 9 (1967): 226–249.

Tsering, Pema. "'rNying-ma-pa Lamas am Yüan Kaiserhof." In *Proceedings of the Csoma de Körös Memorial Symposium*, edited by L. Ligeti. Budapest, 1978.

Tucci, G. *Indo-Tibetica*. Vol. IV, no. 1. Rome: Reale accademia d'Italia, 1941.

————. *Tibetan Painted Scrolls*. 2 vols. Rome: Libreria dello stato, 1949.

————. *Deb-ther dmar-po gsar-ma*. Rome, 1971.

Tucci, G., and Heissig, W. *Les religions du Tibet et de la Mongolie*. Translated by R. Sailley. Paris: Payot, 1973.

Turan, Osman. "The Ideal of World Domination among the Medieval Turks." *Studia Islamica* 4 (1955): 70–90.

Twitchett, Denis. *Financial Administration Under the T'ang Dynasty*. Cambridge: Cambridge University Press, 1963.

————. "Merchant, Trade, and Government in Late T'ang." *Asia Major* n.s. 14, part 1 (1968): 63–95.

————. "The T'ang Market System." *Asia Major* n.s. 12, Part 2 (1966): 202–224.

Unruh, Ellen S. "Reflections on the Fall of Silla." *Korea Journal* 15, 5 (May 1975): 54–62.

van den Wyngaert, A., ed., *Sinica Franciscana*, I. Quaracchi: Collegio di S. Bonaventura, 1929.

Vanin, I. V. *Feodal'naia Koreia v XIII–XVI Vekakh*. Moscow: Nauka, 1962.

Viktorova, L. L. "K voprosu o naimanskoi teorii proiskhozhdeniia mongol'skogo literaturnogo iazyka i pis'mennosti (xii–xiii vv.)." *Uchenye zapiski Leningradskogo gosudarstvennogo universiteta*, no. 305 (1961). Pp. 137–155.

Voegelin, E. "The Mongol Orders of Submission to the European Powers." *Byzantion* 15 (1941): 378–413.

Waley, Arthur, trans. *The Travels of An Alchemist*. London: Routledge and Kegan Paul, 1931.

Walker, Richard L. *The Multi-State System of Ancient China*. Westport, Conn.: Greenwood, 1971 reprint.

Wang Gungwu. *The Structure of Power in North China during the Five Dynasties*. Kuala Lumpur: University of Malaya Press, 1963.

Weiers, Michael. "Mongolische Reisebegleitschreiben aus Čaγatai." *Zentralasiatische Studien* 1 (1967): 16–33.

Wiens, Herold. *China's March Toward the Tropics*. Hamden, Conn.: Shoe String Press, 1954.

Wilhelm, Richard. *Li Gi. Das Buch der Sitte*. Jena: E. Diederichs, 1930.

Wittfogel, Karl, and Feng Chia-sheng. *History of Chinese Society: The Liao (907–1125)*. Philadelphia: American Philosophical Society, 1949.

Wright, Arthur F., and Twitchett, Denis, eds. *Perspectives on the T'ang*. New Haven: Yale University Press, 1973.

Wylie, T. V. *The Geography of Tibet according to the 'dZam-gling rgyas-bShad*. Rome: Istituto italiano per il Medio ed Estremo Oriente, 1962.

———. "The First Mongol Conquest of Tibet Reinterpreted." *Harvard Journal of Asiatic Studies* 37 (1977): 103–133.

Yamane Yukio and Ohshima Ritsuke. *A Classified Bibliography of Articles and Books Concerning the Yüan Period in Japanese and Chinese*. Tokyo, 1971.

Yang Lien-sheng. *Money and Credit in China: A Short History*. Cambridge, Mass.: Harvard University Press, 1962; 2nd ed., 1971.

Yang Tsung-han. "Hsiao-yün-shih khaya (1286–1324)." *Monumenta Serica* 9 (1944): 92–100.

Yi Usŏng. "A Study of the Period of the Northern and Southern States." *Korea Journal* 17, 1 (January 1977): 28–33.

Yü Ying-shih. *Trade and Expansion in Han China: A Study in the Structure of Sino-Barbarian Economic Relations*. Berkeley and Los Angeles: University of California Press, 1967.

Yule, Henry. *The Book of Ser Marco Polo*. 3rd ed. revised by Henri Cordier. 2 vols. London: John Murray, 1929 reprint.

———. *Cathay and the Way Thither*. Vol. 4. Taipei: Ch'eng-wen Publishing Company, 1966 reprint.

———. *Altorientalische Forschungen V, Schriften zur Geschichte und Kultur des alten Oriens*. Berlin: Akademie-Verlag, 1977.

Zhukov, V. D. "Dukentskii klad monet." *Istoriia material'noi kultury Uzbekistana* 1 (1959): 176–207.

Zieme, Peter. "Zur buddhistischen Stabreimdichtung der alten Uiguren." *Acta Orientalia* 29 (1975): 187–211.

Works in Oriental Languages

Abe Takeo 安部健夫.*Nishi Uiguru kokushi no kenkyū* 西ウイグル国史の研究. Kyoto, 1955.

———. *Gendaishi no kenkyū* 元代史の研究. Tokyo, 1972.

Akiura Hideo 秋浦秀雄. "Korai Koso-cho ni okeru Kokusai jijo wo Ken-kaku su" 高麗光宗朝に於ける国際事情を検覈す. *Seikyū Gakusō* 青丘学叢 12 (1933): 108–147.

Akiyama Kenzō 秋山謙蔵. "Sō-dai no Nankai bōeki to Nissō bōeki to no renkei 宋代の南海貿易と日僧貿易との連繋 *Shigaku zasshi* 史学雑誌 44, 12 (1933).

Andō Tomonobu 安藤智信. "Goetsu Bushuku-ō Sen Ryu to Bukkyō-shimpi-e no heikōshō to ōkō-e no yabō" 呉越武粛王銭鏐と仏教—神秘への傾向性と王候人の野望. *Ōtani gakuhō* 大谷学報 50, 4 (March 1971): 28–46.

Ao-shan ta-ch'üan wen-chi 鶴山大全文集. Ssu-pu ts'ung-k'an 四部叢刊 edition.

Aoyama Sadao 青山定雄. "Zui, Tō, Sō sandai ni okeru kōsu no chiiki teki kōsatsu" 隋唐宋三代に於ける戸婁の地域的考察. *Rekishigaku kenkyū* 歴史学研究 6, 4 (1936): 441–446; 6, 5 (1936): 529–554.

———. *Tō-Sō jidai no kōtsū to chishi chizu no kenkyū* 唐宋時代の交通と地誌地図の研究 Tokyo, 1963.

bKa'-brgyud gser-phreng chen-mo. Dehra Dun, 1970 reprint.

bKa'-brgyud yid-bzhin nor-bu-yi 'phreng-ba. Leh, 1972 reprint.

Cha-ch'i Ssu-ch'in 札奇斯欽. "Shuo chiu *Yüan-shih* chung-te ta-lu hua-ch'ih" 說舊元史中的達魯花赤. *Wen-shih-che hsüeh-pao* 文史哲學報 12 (1964): 293–441.

———. "Yüan-tai te hsi-yü" 元代的西域. *Hsin-ch'iang yen-chiu* 新疆研究. Taipei, 1965.

———. "Shuo Yüan-chao te ti-shih" 說元朝的帝師. In *Shih-hsüeh lun-chi* 史學論集, pp. 308–327. Taipei, 1976.

Chang Chia-chü 張家駒. *Shen Kua* 沈括. Shanghai: Shanghai jen-min ch'u-pan she, 1962.

Chang Chu 張翥. *Shui-an chi* 蛻菴集. Ssu-k'u ch'üan-shu chen-pen 四庫全書珍本 edition.

Chang Fang-p'ing 張方平. *Lo-ch'üan chi* 樂全集. In Ssu-k'u ch'üan-shu chen-pen 四庫全書珍本 edition.

Chang Huan-feng 張皖峯. "Sung ku Ssu-ch'uan ... P'eng Chung-lieh kung shih chi" 宋故四川—彭忠烈公事輯. *Sung-shih yen-chiu chi* 5 宋史研究. Taipei: Chung-hua Ts'ung-shu Pien-shen Wei-yüan hui, 1970.

Chang Lei 張耒. *K'o-shan chi* 柯山集. In Ssu-k'u ch'üan-shu chen-pen 四庫全書珍本 edition.

Chang Liang-ts'ai 張亮采. *Pu Liao-shih chiao-p'ing piao* 補遼史交聘表. Peking, 1958.

Chang Shun-min 張舜民. *Hua-man lu* 畫墁錄. In Pai-pu ts'ung-shu chi-ch'eng. Taipei, n.d.

Chang T'ing-yü 張廷玉 et al. *Ming shih* 明史. In *Erh-shih wu-shih* 二十

五十. Taipei, 1965–1966 reprint.

Chang Ya-ch'in 張雅琴. "Shen Kua yü Sung Liao hua-chieh chiao-she"
沈括與宋遼畫界交涉. *Shih-i* 史繹, no. 12 (1975), pp. 10–25.

Ch'ang Pi-te 昌彼得 et al., *Sung-jen chuan-chi tzu-liao so-yin* 宋人傳記.
資料索引. 6 vols. Taipei: Ting-wen, 1975.

Chao Ju-t'eng 趙汝騰. *Yung-ch'i chi* 庸齊集. In Ssu-k'u ch'üan-shu chen-
pen 四庫全書珍本 edition.

Chao Ju-yü 趙汝愚. *Sung ming-ch'en tsou-i* 宋名臣奏議. In Ssu-k'u
ch'üan-shu chen-pen 四庫全書珍本 edition.

Chao Meng-fu 趙孟頫. *Sung-hsüeh chai-wen chi* 松雪齊文集. In Ssu-pu
ts'ung-k'an 四部叢刊 edition.

Chen Te-hsiu 眞德秀. *Hsi-shan hsien-sheng Chen Wen-chung kung wen-chi*
西山先生眞文忠公文集. In Ssu-pu ts'ung-k'an 四部叢刊 edition.

Ch'en Fang-ming 陳芳明. "Sung-tai cheng-t'ung-lun te hsing-ch'eng
chi-ch'i nei-jung" 宋代正統論的形成及其內容. *Shih-huo yüeh-k'an*
食貨月刊 1, 8 (1971): 418–430.

Ch'en Hsiang 陳襄. *Ku-ling chi* 古靈集. In Ssu-k'u ch'üan-shu chen-pen
四庫全書珍本 edition.

Ch'en Pang-chan 陳邦瞻. *Sung shih chi-shih pen-mo* 宋史紀事本末.
Peking, 1977.

Ch'en Shou 陳壽. *San-kuo chih* 三國志. Peking: Chung-hua shu-chü
中華書局, 1960.

Ch'en Shun-yü 陳舜兪. *Tu-kuan chi* 都官集. In Ssu-k'u ch'üan-shu
chen-pen 四庫全書珍本 edition.

Ch'eng Hao 程顥. *Ming-tao hsien-sheng wen-chi* 明道先生文集.

Ch'eng Hsüeh-lou wen-chi 程雪樓文集. Taipei: Yüan-tai chen-pen wen-
chi 元代珍本文集 edition, 1970.

Ch'eng I 程頤. *I-ch'uan hsien-sheng wen-chi* 伊川先生文集.

Ch'iang Chih 强至. *Tz'u-pu chi* 祠部集. In Ssu-k'u ch'üan-shu chen-pen
四庫全書珍本 edition.

Ch'en Ch'ing-hsin 陳慶新. "Sung-ju ch'un-ch'iu tsun-wang yao-i te fa-
wei yü ch'i cheng-chih ssu-hsiang" 宋儒春秋尊王要義的發微與其
政治思想. *New Asia Journal*, vol. 10, no. 1, pt. 1 (1971), pp. 269–368.

Ch'en Yüan 陳垣. "Shih-ssu shih-chi Nan-E-jen chih Han-wen-hsüeh"
十四世紀南俄人之漢文學. *Chung-kuo wen-hsüeh yen-chiu* 中國文學
研究, edited by Cheng Chen-to. Hong Kong: Chung-kuo wen-hsüeh
yen-chiu she, 1963 reprint.

Chin Yü-fu 金毓黻. *Sung-Liao-Chin shih* 宋遼金史. Shanghai: Commercial Press, 1946.

Ch'ing-yüan t'iao-fa shih-lei 慶元條法事類. Tokyo, 1968.

Ch'ien Ta-hsin 錢大昕. *Shih-chia-chai yang-hsin lu* 十駕齊養新錄.
Peking, 1957.

Ch'ien Yen 錢儼. *Wu Yüeh pei shih* 吳越備史. In Ssu-pu pei-yao 四部
備要 edition.

Ch'in Kuan 秦觀. *Huai-hai chi* 淮海集. Shanghai: Commercial Press, n.d.

Chindan Hakpo 震檀學報 38 (October 1974): 203–227.

Ch'oe Pyŏnghŏn, 崔柄憲. "Tosŏn-ŭi Saeng'ae-wa Namal Yŏch'o-ŭi P'ungsu Chiri Sŏl" 道詵의生涯의羅末麗初의風水地理說. *Han'guk-sa Yŏngu* 韓國史研究 11 (1975): 101–146.

Chŏn Haejong 全海宗. *Han-Chung Kwankye-sa Yŏngu* 韓中關係史研究. Seoul, 1970.

Chou Ch'ü-fei 周去非. *Ling-wai tai-ta* 嶺外代答. Taipei, 1975 reprint.

Chou Hui 周輝. *Ch'ing-po tsa-chih* 清波雜志. In Pi-chi hsiao-shuo ta-kuan edition.

———. *Pei-yüan lu* 北轅錄. In *Shuo-fu* 說郛. Taipei, 1963 reprint.

Chou Mi 周密. *Ch'i-tung yeh-yü* 齊東野語. In Ts'ung-shu chi-ch'eng 叢書集成 edition.

Chu Wen-kung chiao Ch'ang-li wen-chi 朱文公校昌黎文集. In Ssu-pu ts'ung-k'an. 四部叢刊 edition.

"Ch'üan-chou Wan Sung-tai Hai-ch'uan Fa-chüeh chien-pao" 泉州灣宋代海船發掘簡報. *Wen-wu* 文物 10 (1975): 28–35.

Ch'üan Han-sheng 全漢昇. "Sung Chin chien te ssu-tsou mao-i" 宋金間的私走貿易. *Bulletin of the Institute of History and Philology, Academia Sinica* 11 (1947).

———. "T'ang-Sung cheng-fu sui-ju yü huo-pi ching-chi te kuan-hsi" 唐宋政府藏入與貨幣經濟的關係. *Chung-kuo ching-chi-shih yen-chiu* 中國經濟史研究. Vol. 1. Hong Kong, 1976.

Ch'un-ch'iu Kung-yang Ch'uan Chu-su 春秋公羊傳注疏. Taipei: I-wen, 1972.

Chung-kuo li-tai chan-cheng-shih pien-tsuan wei-yüan-hui 中國歷代戰爭史編纂委員會. *Chung-kuo li-tai chan-cheng-shih* 中國歷代戰爭史. Taipei, 1976 revised edition.

Chung Yüan-ying 鐘淵映. *Li-tai chien-yüan k'ao* 歷代建元考. In *Shou-shan-ko ts'ung-shu*. Shanghai, 1889.

Dai Nihon shi 大日本史. 1851 woodblock edition.

De-bzhin-gshegs-pa thams-cad kyi bgrod-pa gcig-pa'i lam-chen gsung-ngag rin-po-che'i bla-ma brgyud-pa rnam-thar.

Deb-ther dmar-po. Gangtok, 1961.

'Dzam-gling byang-phyogs kyi thub-pa'i rgyal-tshab chen-po dpal-ldan Sa-skya-pa'i gdung-rabs rin-po-che ji-ltar byon-pa'i tshul gyi rnam-par thar-pa ngo-mtshar rin-po-che'i bang-mdzod kun-'byung.

Erh-Ch'eng i-shu 二程遺書. In Ssu-pu pei-yao 四部備要 edition.

Fan Ch'eng-ta 范成大. *Shih-hu chü-shih shih-chi* 石湖居士詩集. In Ssu-pu ts'ung-k'an 四部叢刊 edition.

Fan Tsu-yü 范祖禹. *Fan T'ai-shih chi* 范太史集. In Ssu-k'u ch'üan-shu chen-pen edition 四庫全書珍本.

———. *T'ang chien* 唐鑑. Shanghai: Commercial Press, n.d.

Fan Yeh 范曄. *Hou Han shu* 後漢書. In *Erh-shih wu-shih* 二十五史.

Taipei, 1955–1956 reprint.

Feng Chia-sheng 馮家昇. "Ch'i-tan ming hao k'ao-shih" 契丹名號考釋. *Yenching Journal of Chinese Studies*, no. 13 (1933), pp. 1–48.

Feng Chia-sheng et al., *Wei-wu-erh tsu shih-liao chien-pien* 維吾爾族史料簡編. Vol. 1. Peking, 1958.

Fu Lo-huan 傅樂煥. "Sung-jen shih-Liao yü-lu hsing-ch'eng k'ao" 宋人使遼語錄行程攷. *Kuo-hsüeh chi-k'an* 國學季刊 5, 4 (1935): 165–194.

———. "Sung-Liao p'ing-shih piao-kao" 宋遼聘使表稿. *Bulletin of the Institute of History and Philology, Academia Sinica* 14 (1949): 57–136.

Fu Ssu-nien 傅斯年. "I Hsia tung hsi shuo" 夷夏東西說. In *Fu Meng-chen hsien-sheng chi*. Taipei, 1952.

Fujii Hiroshi 藤井宏. "Shin-an shōnin no kenkyū" 新安商人の研究. *Tōyō gakuhō* 東洋学報 36, 1 (1957): 2–7.

Fujimoto Hikaru 藤本光. "Nansō Kōba kō," 南宋広馬考. *Tōyōshigaku rōnshū* 東洋史学論集 (1953).

———. "Zoku Nansō Kōba kō," 續南宋廣馬考. *Shichō* 史潮 57 (1955).

Fujishima Tateki 藤島建樹. "Genchō senseiin kō, sono nimenteki seikaku o chūshin to shite" 元朝宣政院考―その二面的性格を中心として. *Ōtani gakukō* 大谷学報 46, 4 (1967): 60–72.

———. "Genchō ni okeru kenshon to senseiin" 元朝に於はる権臣と宣政院. *Ōtani gakuhō* 52, 4 (1973): 17–31.

Fujita Toyohachi 藤田豊八. "Sō-dai no Shihaku-shi oyobi Shihaku jōrei," 宋代の市舶司及び市舶条令. *Tō-zai kōshō-shi no kenkyū* 東西交渉史の研究. Tokyo, 1943.

Gentenshō sakuin-kō 元典章索引稿. Kyoto: Jimbun Kagaku Kenkyujo, Kyoto University, 1961.

Ha Hyŏn'gang 何炫網. "Koryŏ-sidae-ŭi Yŏksa Ŭisik" 高麗時代의歷史意識. *Yihwa Sahak Yŏngu* 梨花史學研究 8 (1975).

Han Ch'i 韓琦. *An-yang chi* 安陽集. In Ssu-k'u ch'üan-shu chen-pen 四庫全書珍本 edition.

Han'guk-sa 韓國史. Vol. 4 by Chindan Hakhoe 震檀學會. Seoul, 1964.

Han Wei 韓維. *Nan-yang chi* 南陽集. In Ssu-k'u ch'üan-shu chen-pen 四庫全書珍本 edition.

Hatachi Masanori 畑地正憲. "Hokusō Ryō kan no bōeki to saizō to ni tsuite" 北宋遼間の貿易と蔵贈とについて. *Shien* 史淵 111 (1974).

Ibn Hauqal, *Kitab surat al-ard*. Edited by T. H. Kramers. Leiden: E. J. Brill, 1938.

Hino Kaisaburō 日野開三郎. "Hoku-Sō jidai ni okeru dō, tetsu-sen no chūzō-gaku ni tsuite" 北宋時代に於はる銅鉄銭の鋳造額に就いて. *Shigaku zasshi* 史学雑誌 46, 1 (1935).

———. "Godai hanchin no kyoshiken to Hokosōchō no yobaiken" 五代蕃鎮の挙絹と北宋朝の預買絹. *Shien* 史淵 15 (March 1937): 114–124.

———. "Godai no namboku Shina rikujō kōtsurō ni tsuite" 五代の南

北支那陸上交通路に就いて. *Rekishigaku kenkyū* 歴史学研究 11, no. 6 (June 1941): 372–402.

———. "Godai jidai ni okeru Kittan to Shina to no kaijō bōeki" 五代時代に於はる契丹と支那との海土貿易. *Shigaku zasshi* 史学雑誌 52, 7 (July 1941): 1–47; 52, 8 (August 1941): 60–85; 52, 9 (September 1941): 55–82.

———. "Godai no ba-sei to tōji no uma-bōeki" 五代の馬政と當時の馬貿易. *Tōyō gakuhō* 東洋学報 29, 1 (1942).

———. "Gin ken no jukyū jō yori mita Godai Hokusō no Sai-hei Sai-shi" 銀絹の需給上より見た五代北宋の蔵幣蔵貝. *Tōyō gakuhō* 東洋学報 35, 1 (1952); 35, 2 (1952).

———. "Ryōzei-hō no kihonteki yongensoku" 両税法の基本的四原則. *Hōsei-shi kenkyū* 法制史研究, no. 11 (1960), pp. 40–77.

———. "Sō-sho Joshin no santō raikō no taise to sono yurai" 宋初女真の山東来航の太勢とその由来. *Chōsen gakuhō* 朝鮮学報 33 (1964): 1–47.

———. "Sō-sho Joshin no santō raikō to bōeki" 宋初女真の山東来航と貿易. *Chōsen gakuhō* 朝鮮学報 37 and 38 (1966).

Hirashima Kiyoshi 平島貴義. "Kittan no bokkō-ki ni okeru Chūgoku to no kankei" 契丹の孛力興期におはる中国との関係. *Shien* 史淵 53 (1952).

Honchō bunsui 本朝文粋. Tokyo, 1648 woodblock edition.

Honchō seki 本朝世紀, vol. 5, *Kokushi taikei* 国史大系. Tokyo, 1896.

Honda Minobu 本田実信. "Chingisu Han no senko" チンギス・ハソのチ戸. *Shigaku zasshi* 史学雑誌 62 (1953): 701–726.

Hsia Shu 夏竦. *Wen-chuang chi* 文莊集. In Ssu-pu pei-yao 四部備要 edition.

Hsiao Ch'i-ch'ing 蕭啓慶. *Hsi-yü-jen yü Yüan-ch'u cheng-chih* 西域人與元初政治. Taipei, 1966.

Hsin-pien Hsüan-ho i-shih 新編宣和遺事. In Ssu-pu pei-yao 四部備要 edition.

Hsü Ching 徐競. *Hsüan-ho feng-shih Kao-li t'u-ching* 宣和奉使高麗圖經.

Hsü K'ang-tsung 許亢宗. *Hsüan-ho i-ssu feng-shih hsing-ch'eng lu* 宣和乙巳奉使行程錄. In *San-chao pei-meng hui-pien* 三朝北盟會編. Taipei, 1962.

Hsü Meng-hsin 徐夢莘. *San-ch'ao pei-meng hui pien* 三朝北盟會編. Taipei: Commercial Press, 1976.

Hsü Tzu-chih t'ung-chien ch'ang-pien 續資治通鑑長編. Taipei: Shih-chieh shu-chü 世界書局, 1961 reprint.

Hsüeh Chü-cheng 薛居正 et al. *Chiu Wu-tai shih* 舊五代史. Peking, 1976 edition.

Hu Su 胡宿. *Wen-kung chi* 文恭集. In Ssu-k'u chüan-shu chen-pen 四庫全書珍本 edition.

Hua Chen 華鎮. *Yün-ch'i-chü-shih chi* 雲溪居士集. In Ssu-k'u ch'üan-shu
    chen-pen 四庫全書珍本 edition.

Huang K'uan-ch'ung 黃寬重. "Pien 'Tuan-p'ing' ju-lo pai-meng" 辨端平
    入洛敗盟. *Shih-i* 史繹 (September 1973), pp. 54–65.

Hung Hao 洪浩. *Sung-mo chi-wen* 松漠紀聞. Nan-ch'ang: Yü-chang
    ts'ung-shu edition, 1915.

Hung Mai 洪邁. *Jung-chai sui-pi* 容齋隨筆. Peking, 1959 reprint.

I-li 儀禮. In *Shih-san ching chu-shu* 十三經注疏. Shanghai: Shih-chieh
    shu-chü, 1935.

Imaeda Yoshirō 今枝由郎. "Pa-ku-pa 'Phags-pa zō Dōshi chō-fukuketsu
    ni tsuite" パクパ 'Phags-pa' 造道土調伏偈について. *Tōyō gakuhō*
    東洋学報 56 (1974): 41–48.

Imanishi Ryū 今西龍. *Kōrai-shi Kenkyū* 高麗史研究. Keijō, 1944.

Inaba Iwakichi 稲葉岩吉. "Kōri zukei wo yomishite" 高麗図経
    ヲ読シテ. *Ichimura Hakase kohi kinen tōyōshi ronsō* 市村博士古稀
    記念東洋史論叢. Tokyo, 1933. Pp. 149–168.

Inaba Shōju 稲葉正就. "Gen no teishi ni tsuite, Oran-shi wo shiryō
    toshite" 元の帝師についてオラーン史を史料として. *Indogaku Buk-
    kyōgaku kenkyū* 印度学仏教学研究 8 (1960): 26–32.

———. "Gen no teishi ni kansuru kenkyū" 元の帝師に関する研究.
    Ōtani daigaku kenkyū nenpō 大谷大学研究年報 19 (1964).

Iwasaki Tsutomu 岩崎力. "Seiryōfu Hanrashi seiken shimatsu kō" 西涼
    府潘羅支政権始末考. *Tōhōgaku* 東方学 47 (1974): 25–41.

Jamieson, John "Nadang tongmaeng ŭi wahae" 羅唐同盟의瓦解. *Yŏksa
    hakpo* 歷史學報 44 (1969): 1–10.

'Ata-Malik-i Juwaynī, *Ta'rīkh-i-Jahān-gushā* 3 vols. Edited by Muḥam-
    mad Qazvīnī. London. Luzac and Co., 1912–37.

Kamei Akinori 亀井明徳. "Sō-dai no yushutsu tōji—Nippon" 宋代の輸
    出陶磁―日本. *Sekai Tōji Zenshū* 世界当時全集. Vol. 12. Tokyo,
    1978.

"Kao-ch'ang Hsieh shih-chia chuan" 高昌偰氏家傳. In *Yüan wen-lei*
    元文類. Shanghai: Shang-wu yin-shu, 1958.

Katō Shigeshi 加藤繁. *Kin-koku ni okeru gin* 金国に於はる銀. Tokyo,
    1926.

———. *Shina Keizai-shi gaisetsu* 支那経済史概説. Tokyo, 1944.

———. "Kōshi no kigen ni tsuite" 交子の起源に就いて. *Shina keizai-
    shi kōshō* 支那経済史考証. Tokyo, 1953.

———. "Sō-Kin bōeki ni okeru cha sen oyobi kinu ni tsuite" 宋金貿易
    に於はる茶銭及び絹に就いて. *Shina Keizaishi Kōshō* 支那経済史
    考証 II. Tokyo, 1953.

———. "Sō to Kin-koku to no bōeki ni tsuite" 宋と金国との貿易
    に就いて. *Shina Keizaishi Kōshō* 支那経済史考証 II. Tokyo, 1953.

Kawahara Masahiro 河原正博. "Ri-chō to Sō to kankei (1009–1225)"

李朝と宋と関係. In Yamamoto Tatsurō 山本達郎, *Betonam Chūgoku Kankei shi* ブトヤム中国関係史. Tokyo, 1975.

Kha-rag gNyos kyi rgyud-pa byon-tshul mdor-bsdus. Tokyo: Toyo Bunko ms.

Kim Ch'ŏltchun 金哲埈. "Koryŏ Chunggi-ŭi Munhwa Ŭisikgwa Sahak-ŭi Sŏnggyŏk" In Yi Ŭsong and Kang Man'gil 李佑成, 姜萬吉 (eds.), *Han'guk-ŭi Yŏksa Insik* 韓國의 歷史認識. Vol. 1. Seoul, 1976.

Kim Pu-sik 金富軾. *Samguk sagi* 三國史記. Seoul, 1972 edition.

Kim Sanggi 金祥基. *Koryŏ Sidae-sa* 高麗時代史. Seoul, 1961.

Koh Pyŏng'ik 高柄翊. "Samguk Sagi-e issŏso-ŭi Yŏksa Sŏsul" In *Hangukŭi Yŏksa Insik* 韓國의 歷史認識 Vol. 1.

Koryŏ-sa 高麗史. Seoul, 1955.

Koryŏ-sa 高麗史. Seoul: Asae munhwasa, 1972 edition.

K'o Shao-min 柯劭忞. *Hsin Yüan shih* 新元史. Po-na 百衲 edition, 1930.

Kungnip chungang pang mulgwan 國立中央博物館. *Sinan haejŏ munmul* 新安海底文物. Seoul, 1978.

Kuo Po-kung 郭伯荼. *Ts'e-fu yüan-kuei* 册府元龜. Taipei, 1967 reprint.

Kuo-yü 國語. In Ssu-pu pei-yao 四部備要 edition.

Kuwabara Jitsuzō 桑原隲蔵. *Hojukō no Jiseki* 蒲寿庚の事蹟. Tokyo, 1935.

Li Fu-t'ung 李符桐. "Wei-wu-erh-jen tui-yü Yüan-ch'ao chien-kuo chih kung-hsien" 畏兀兒人對於元朝建國之貢獻. In Sung Hsi 宋晞 (ed.), *Shih-hsüeh lun-chi* 史學論集. Taipei, 1977.

Li Hsin-ch'üan 李心傳. *Chien-yen i-lai ch'ao-yeh tsa-chi chia-chi* 建炎以來朝野雜記甲集.

Li Jo-shui 李若水 et al, *T'ai-tsung huang-ti shih-lu* 太宗皇帝實錄. In Ssu-pu ts'ung-k'an 四部叢刊 edition.

Li Kou 李覯. *Chih-chiang Li-hsien-sheng wen-chi* 直講李先生文集. In Ssu-pu ts'ung-k'an 四部叢刊 edition.

Li T'ao 李燾. *Hsü Tzu-chih t'ung-chien ch'ang-pien* 續資治通鑑長編. Taipei: Shih-chieh shu-chü edition, 1964.

Liang T'ing-nan 梁廷枏. *Nan Han shu* 南漢書. Hong Kong, 1967 reprint of woodblock edition.

———. *Nan Han-shu k'ao-i* 南漢書考異. Hong Kong, 1967 reprint of 1830 woodblock edition.

Liao Lung-sheng 廖隆盛. "Pei Sung tui T'u-fan te cheng-ts'e" 北宋對吐蕃的政策. *Sung-shih yen-chiu* 宋史研究. Vol. 10. Taipei: Chung-hua ts'ung-shu pien-shen wei-yüan-hui, 1978.

Liao-shih hui-pien 遼史彙編. Vol. 6. Taipei: Ting-wen shu-chü 1973.

Lin Shui-han 林瑞翰. "Sung-tai pien-chün chih ma-shih ma-chih kang-yün" 宋代邊郡之馬市馬之綱運. *Ta-lu tsa-chih* 大陸雜誌 31, 9 (1965).

Lin T'ien-wei 林天蔚. *Sung-tai hsiang-yao mao-i shih-kao* 宋代香藥貿易

史稿. Hong Kong, 1960.

Liu Ch'ang 劉敞. *Kung-shih chi* 公時集. In Ssu-k'u ch'üan-shu chen-pen 四庫全書珍本 edition.

Liu Chih 劉摯. *Chung-su chi* 忠肅集. In Ssu-k'u ch'üan-shu chen-pen 四庫全書珍本 edition.

Liu Po-chi 劉伯驥. *Sung-tai cheng-chiao shih* 宋代政教史. Taipei: Chung-hua, 1971.

Lo Ts'ung-yen 羅從彥. *Lo Yü-chang chi* 羅豫章集. Shanghai: Commercial Press, n.d.

Lou Yüeh 樓鑰. *Pei-hsing jih-lu* 北行日錄. In Pai-pu ts'ung-shu chi-ch'eng. Taipei, n.d.

Lu Chen 路振. *Ch'eng-yao lu* 乘軺錄. In Pai-pu ts'ung-shu chi-ch'eng. Taipei, 1965.

——. *Chiu-kuo chih* 九國志. Pi-chi hsiao-shuo ta-kuan edition.

Lu Chih 陸贄. *Lu Hsüan-kung tsou-i ch'üan-chi* 陸宣公奏議全集. Shanghai: Commercial Press, n.d.

Lu Tai-tseng 盧逮曾. "Wu-tai shih-kuo tui Liao te wai-chiao" 五代十國對遼的外交. *Hsüeh-shu chi-k'an* 學術季刊 3, 1 (August 1954): 25–51.

Lü T'ao 呂陶. *Ching-te chi* 淨德集. Taipei, 1975 reprint.

Lu Tien 陸佃. *T'ao-shan chi* 陶山集. In Ssu-k'u ch'üan-shu chen-pen 四庫全書珍本 edition.

Lu Yao-tung 逯耀東. "Pei-Wei yü Nan-ch'ao tui-chih ch'i-chien te wai-chiao kuan-hsi" 北魏與南朝對崎期間的外交關係. *Hsin-ya shu-yüan hsüeh-shu nien-k'an* 新亞書院學書年刊, no. 8 (1966), pp. 31–61.

Lu Yu 陸游. *Nan T'ang shu* 南唐書. In Ssu-pu pei-yao 四部備要 edition.

Luan-ch'eng hou-chi 欒城後集. In Ssu-pu ts'ung-k'an 四部叢刊 edition.

Luan-ch'eng ying-chao chi 欒城應詔集. In Ssu-pu ts'ung-k'an 四部叢刊 edition.

Ma Tuan-lin 馬端臨. *Wen-hsien t'ung-k'ao* 文獻通考. Shanghai: Commercial Press, 1936 reprint.

——. *Wen-hsien t'ung-k'ao* 文獻通考. Taipei, 1959.

Maeda Masana 前田正名. "Godai oyobi Sō-sho ni okeru Rokkoku no chiiki kōzō kansuru ronkō" 五代及び宋初における六谷の地域構造に関する論考. *Tōyō gakuhō* 東洋学報 41 (1958–59): 439–472.

——. *Kasei no rekishi-chirigaku teki kenkyū* 河西の歴史地理学的研究. Tokyo, 1969.

Marugame Kinsaku 丸亀金作. "Korai to Sō to no tsuko mondai," 高麗と宋の通交問題. *Chōsen Gakuhō* 朝鮮学報 17 (October 1960): 1–50.

Matsuda Hisao 松田寿男. *Kodai Tenzan no rekishi chirigakuteki kenkyū* 古代天山の歴史地理学的研究. Tokyo, 1956.

Meng Ssu-ming 蒙思明. *Yüan-tai she-hui chieh-chi chih-tu* 元代社會階級制度. Peking, 1938.

Mikami Tsugio 三上次男. *Kin-shi Kenkyū III: Kindai Joshin Shakai no*

Kenkyū 金史研究—金代女真社会の研究. Tokyo, 1973.

Miyashita Saburō 宮下三郎. "Sō-Gen no iryō" 宋元の医療. *Sō-Gen jidai no kagaku-gijutsu-shi* 宋元時代の科学技術史. Kyoto, 1967.

Miyazaki Ishisada. *Ajiashi no Kenkyū* アジア史の研究. Kyoto: Tōyōshi Kenkyūkai, 1959.

Miyazaki Ichisada 宮崎市定. *Godai Sōshō no tsūka mondai* 五代宋初の通貨問題. Tokyo, 1943.

Mōko ramakyō-shi 蒙古喇嘛教史. Tokyo, 1940.

Mori Katsumi 森克己. *Nissō Bōeki no Kenkyū* 日宋貿易の研究. Tokyo, 1958.

Murakami Masatsugu 村上正二. "Gensho ni okeru kansen banko setchi no igi ni tsuite" 元初に於はる監戦万戸設置の意義に就いて. *Tōhō gakuhō* 東洋学報 II (1940): 348–359.

———. "Genchō ni okeru senfushi to kandatsu" 元朝に於はる泉府司と斡脱. *Tōhō gakuhō* 東方学報 13, 1 (1942): 143–196.

Nagasawa Kazutoshi 長沢和俊. "Saika no Kasai shinshutsu to Tō-sai kōtsū". *Tōhōgaku* 東方学 26 (1963).

———. "Godai Sō-sho ni okeru Kasei chihō no chukei-kōeki ni tsuite" 五代宋初におはる河西地方の中継交易について. In *Tōzai bunka kōryū-shi*. Tokyo, 1975, pp. 109–119.

Nakajima Satoshi 中山鳥敏. "Seika ni okeru dō Tetsu-sen no chūzō ni tsuite" 西夏に於はる銅鉄銭の鋳造について. *Tōhō gakuhō* 東方学報 7 (1936).

Muḥammad al-Nasawī. *Sirah Jalāl al-Dīn Mankabirtī*. (Edited by Ḥafīz Ḥamdī). Cairo, 1953.

Mu'īn al-Dīn Naṭanzī, *Muntakhab al-tavārīkh-i Mu'īnī*. Edited by Jean Aubin. Tehran: Khayyam, 1957.

Nieh Ch'ung-ch'i 聶崇岐. "Sung-Liao chiao-p'ing k'ao" 宋遼交聘考. *Yen-ching hsüeh-pao* 燕京學報 27 (1940): 1–51.

Nien-ch'ang 念常. *Fo-tsu li-tai t'ung-tsai* 佛祖歷代通載. Taishō Daizoku edition.

Nihon kiryaku 日本紀略. In vol. 8, *Kokushi taikei kōhen* 国史大系後篇. Tokyo, 1895.

Nishijima Sadao 西山鳥定生. *Chūgoku keizai-shi kenkyū* 中国経済史研究. Tokyo, 1966.

Nishioka Toranosuke 西岡虎之助. "Nihon to Goetsu to no kōtsū" 日本と呉越との交通. *Rekishi chiri* 歴史地理 42, 1 (July 1923): 32–62.

Nogami Shunsei 野上俊静. "Gen no senseiin ni tsuite" 元の宣政院に就いて. In *Asiatic Studies in Honour of Tōru Haneda*. Kyoto, 1950. Pp. 779–795.

Nogami Shunsei 野上俊静 and Inaba Shōju 稲葉正就. "Gen no teishi ni tsuite" 元の帝師について. In *Oriental Studies in Honor of Juntarō Ishihama*. Osaka, 1958.

————. "Gen no kudokushishi ni tsuite" 元の功徳使司に就いて.
  Shina-bukkyō shigaku 支那仏教史学 6, 2 (December 1942): 1–11.
Okada Hidehiro 岡田英弘. "Mōko shiryō ni mieru shoki Mō-Zō kankei"
  蒙古史料に見える初期の蒙蔵関係. *Tōhōgaku* 東方学 23 (1962).
Okazaki Seirō 岡崎精郎. *Tangūto Kodai-shi kenkyū* タングート古代史
  研究. Kyoto, 1972.
Ono Gemmyō 小野玄妙. *Bukkyō no bijutsu oyobi rekishi* 仏教の美術
  及歴史. Tokyo, 1916.
Ōsaki Fujio 大崎富士夫. "Sō-Kin bōeki no keitai," 宋金貿易の型態.
  Hiroshima Daigaku Bungakubu Kiyō 広島大学文学部紀要 5 (1954).
Ou-yang Hsiu 歐陽修 et al. *Hsin Wu-tai shih* 新五代史. Peking, 1974
  edition.
Pan Ku 班固. *Han shu* 漢書. Peking: Chung-hua shu-chü, 1962.
P'eng Hsin-wei 彭信威. *Chung-kuo huo-pi shih* 中國貨幣史. Shanghai,
  1965.
P'eng Ju-li 彭汝礪. *Po-yang chi* 番陽集. In Ssu-k'u ch'üan-shu chen-pen
  四庫全書珍本 edition.
Pien-wei-lu 辯僞錄. Taishō Daizoku edition.
Abū al-Qāsim ibn 'Alī ibn Muḥammad al-Qāshānī. *Tarikh-i Uljaytu*.
  Edited by Mahin Hambly. Tehran, 1969.
Ḥamd Allāh Mustawfī Qazvīnī. *Tarikh-i guzīdah*. Tehran, 1960.
Rashīd al-Dīn. *Jāmi' al-tavārīkh*. Edited by B. Karīmī. Tehran, 1959.
————. *Tarīkh-i Mubārak-i Ghāzānī*. Edited by Karl Jahn. The Hague
  Mouton, 1957.
————. *Tarīkh-i Mubārak-i Ghāzānī: Dāstān-i Ghazan-khān*. London:
  Luzac and Co., 1940.
rGya Bod yig-tshang. University of Washington ms.
Sakurai Haruko 桜井ハル子. "Godai jūkoku no Goetsu ni tsuite" 五代
  十国の呉越について. *Nara shien* 寧楽史苑 15 (February 1967):
  11–24.
Sakurai Kiyohiko 櫻井清彦. "Perusha Wan Minabu fukin no Chūgoku
  tōji" プルシヤ湾シナブ付近の中国陶磁. *Matsuda-hakushi Koki-
  kinen Tōzai Bunka Koryū-shi* 松田博士古稀記念東西文化交流史.
  Tokyo, 1975.
Satō Keishirō 佐藤圭四郎. "Hokusō jidai ni okeru Kaikitsu shōnin no
  tōzen" 北宋時代におはる回骨乞商人の東漸. *Chūgoku-shi Ronsō*
  中国史論争, 1978.
————. "Nan-Sō jidai ni okeru Nankai bōeki ni tsuite" 南宋時代に
  おはる南海貿易について. *Isurāmu shōgyō-shi no kenkyū* イスラム
  教商史研究. Kyoto, 1981.
Sayf ibn Muḥammad. *Tarīkh namah-i Harāt*. (Edited by Muḥammad
  Zubayr al-Siddīqī). Calcutta, 1944.
Shan-hai ching 山海經. In Ssu-pu pei-yao 四部備要 edition.

Shao Yüan-p'ing 邵遠平. *Yüan-shih lei-pien* 元史類編. In Kuang-wen
    shu-chü 廣文書局 edition.

Shao Yung 邵雍. *I-ch'uan chi-jang chi* 伊川擊壤集. In Ssu-pu ts'ung-k'an
    四部叢刊 edition.

Shen Ch'i-wei 沈起煒. *Sung-Chin chan-cheng shih-lüeh* 宋金戰爭史略.
    Wuhan: Jen-min, 1958.

Sheng-wu ch'in-cheng lu 聖武親征錄. Edited by Wang Kuo-wei 王國維.
    In *Meng-ku shih-liao ssu-chung* 蒙古史料四種. Taipei, 1975.

Shiba Yoshinobu 斯波義信. *Sōdai shōgyō-shi ronsō* 宋代商業史論叢.
    Tokyo, 1974.

Shih-ching 詩經. In *Shih-san ching shu-su* 十三經注疏 edition.

Shih Wen-chi 石文濟. "Sung-tai Shih-po-ssu te she-chih" 宋代市舶司
的設置. *Sung-shih yen-chiu chi* 宋史研究集. Taipei, 1970.

Shimada Masao 島田正郎. *Ryō-dai shakai-shi kenkyū* 遼代社会研究.
    Kyoto, 1952.

Shiratori Kurakichi 白鳥芳郎. *Manshū rekishi chiri* 満州歴史地理.
    Tokyo, 1913.

Sin Ch'ae-ho 申采浩. *Tanjae Sin Ch'ae-ho chōnjip* 丹齊申采浩全集.
    2 vols, Seoul, 1972.

Sogabe Shizuo 曾我部静雄. *Nichi Sō Kin Kahei Koryū-shi* 日宋金貨幣
交流史. Tokyo, 1949.

Ssu-ma Ch'ien 司馬遷. *Shih chi* 史記. Peking: Chung-hua shu-chü, 1959.

Ssu-ma Kuang 司馬光. *Tzu-chih t'ung-chien* 資治通鑑. Peking, 1956
    edition.

————. *Wen-kuo wen-cheng Ssu-Ma-kung chi* 溫國文正司馬公集. In Ssu-
pu ts'ung-k'an 四部叢刊 edition.

sTag-lung Ngag-dbang-rnam-rgyal. *Chos-'byung ngo-mtshar rgya-mtsho.*
    Tashigong, 1972 reprint.

Su Ch'e 蘇車. *Luan-ch'eng chi* 欒城集. In Ssu-pu ts'ung-k'an 四部叢刊
    edition.

Su Shun-ch'in 蘇舜欽. *Su Shun-ch'in chi* 蘇舜欽集. Shanghai: Chung-
    hua shu-chü, 中華書局 1961 edition.

Su T'ien-chüeh 蘇天舜. *Kuo-ch'ao ming-ch'en shih-lüeh* 國朝名臣事略.
    1335 edition.

Su Wei-kung wen-chi 蘇魏公文集. In Ssu-k'u ch'üan-shu chen-pen
    四庫全書珍本 edition. Taipei, n.d.

Sudō Yoshiyuki 周藤吉之. *Sōdai keizaishi kenkyū* 宋代経済史研究.
    Tokyo, 1962.

Suematsu Yasukazu 末松保和. "Kyu-Sangoku-shi to Sangoku-Shiki"
旧三国史と三国史記. *Seikyū Shisō* 青丘史草. Tokyo, 1966.

Sum-pa mKhan-po *dPag-bsam-ljon-bzang* III. Edited by Lokesh Chandra.
    New Delhi, 1959.

Sun K'o-k'uan 孫克寬 *Meng-ku Han-chün yü Han wen-hua yen-chiu* 蒙古

漢軍與漢文化研究. Taipei: Wen-hsing, 1958.

————. *Yüan-tai Han-wen-hua chih huo-tung* 元代漢文化之活動. Taipei: Chung-hua 中華, 1968.

Sung-chi san-ch'ao cheng-yao 宋季三朝政要. In Ts'ung-shu chi-ch'eng 叢書集成 edition.

Sung Ch'i 宋祁. *Ching-wen chi* 景文集. In Ssu-k'u ch'üan-shu chen-pen 四庫全書珍本 edition.

Sung Hsiang 宋庠. *Yüan hsien-chi* 元憲集. In Ssu-k'u ch'üan-shu chen-pen 四庫全書珍本 edition.

Sung Hui-yao chi-kao 宋會要輯稿. Peking, 1957 edition.

Sung Lien 宋濂 et al. *Yüan shih* 元史. Shanghai: Po-na 百衲 edition, 1935.

Sung Min-ch'iu 宋敏求. *T'ang ta chao-ling chi* 唐大詔令集. Peking, 1959.

Sung-shih ch'üan-wen Hsü Tzu-chih t'ung-chien 宋史全文續資治通鑑. Taipei: Wen-hai, 1969 reprint.

Sung Shou 宋綬. *Sung ta chao-ling chi* 宋大詔令集. Peking: Chung-hua shu-chü 中華書局 edition, 1962.

————. *Sung ta chao-ling chi* 宋大詔令集. Taipei, 1972 reprint.

Ta-Chin kuo-chih 大金國志. Shanghai: Commercial Press, 1936.

Ta-Tai li-chi pu-chu 大戴禮記補注. Basic Sinological Series. Shanghai: Commercial Press, 1941.

Tamori Noboru 田森襄. "Kansansei-kō" 貫雲石考. *Saitama Daigaku kiyō* 埼玉大学紀要 10 (1961).

Tamura Jitsuzō 田村実造. *Genshi goi shūsei* 元史語彙集成. 3 vols. Kyoto, 1961–63.

————. "Ryō-Sō no kōtsū to Ryō kokunai ni okeru keizai teki hattatsu" 遼宋の交通と遼国内に於はる経済的発達. *Seifuku ōchō no kenkyū* 征服王朝の研究. Kyoto, 1964.

Tanaka Seiji 田中幣治. "Goetsu to Bin to no kankei, Binkoku no nairan o chūsin toshite" 呉越と閩との関係—属国の内乱を中心として. *Tōyōshi kenkyū* 東洋史研究 28, 1 (June 1969): 28–51.

————. "Nantō to Goetsu to no kankei" 南唐と呉越との関係. *Shiryū* 史流 16 (March 1975): 1–18.

T'ao Chin-sheng 陶晉生. "Pei-Sung Ch'ing-li shih-ch'i te wai-chiao cheng-ts'e" 北宋慶曆時期的外交政策. *Bulletin of the Institute of History and Philology, Academia Sinica*, vol. 47, no. 1 (1975), pp. 54–56.

————. "Sung-Liao chien te p'ing-teng wai-chiao kuan-hsi" 宋遼間的平等外交關係. *Shen Kang-po hsien-sheng pa-shih jung-ch'ing lun-wen chi* 沈剛伯先生八秩榮慶論文集. Taipei: Lien-ching, 1975.

————. "Wang An-shih te tui Liao wai-chiao cheng-ts'e" 王安石的對遼外交政策. *Bulletin of the Institute of History and Philology, Academia Sinica*, vol. 50, pt. 4 (1979), pp. 657–677.

T'ao Chin-sheng 陶晉生 and Wang Min-hsin 王民信, eds. *Li T'ao Hsü Tzu-chih t'ung-chien ch'ang-pien Sung-Liao kuan-hsi shih-liao chi-lu* 李燾續資治通鑑長編宋遼關係史料輯錄. 3 vols. Taipei: Institute of History and Philology, Academia Sinica, 1974.

T'ao Tsung-i 陶宗儀. *Nan-ts'un Cho-keng lu* 南村啜耕錄. In Ssu-pu ts'ung-k'an 四部叢刊 edition.

T'ien Hsi 田錫. *Hsien-p'ing chi* 咸平集. In Ssu-k'u ch'üan-shu chen-pen 四庫全書珍本 edition.

T'o T'o 脫脫 et al. *Chin shih* 金史. Wan-chen edition, 1929.

———. *Chin shih* 金史. Shanghai: Po-na edition, 1931.

———. *Liao shih* 遼史. Peking, 1974 edition.

———. *Liao shih* 遼史. Shanghai: Po-na edition, 1931.

———. *Sung shih* 宋史. Peking, 1977.

———. *Sung shih* 宋史. Po-na edition. Shanghai, 1937.

Toyama Gunji 外山軍治. *Kinchō-shi Kenkyū* 金朝史研究. Kyoto: Tōyōshi kenkyukai, 1970.

Ts'ai Hsiang 蔡襄. *Tuan-ming chi* 端明集. In Ssu-k'u ch'üan-shu chen-pen 四庫全書珍本 edition.

Ts'ao Yen-yüeh 曹彥約. *Ch'ang-ku chi* 昌谷集. In Ssu-k'u ch'üan-shu chen-pen 四庫全書珍本 edition.

Tso chuan 左傳. Shih-san ching chu-su 十三經注疏 edition.

T'u Chi 屠寄. *Meng-wu-erh shih-chi* 蒙兀兒史記. Taipei: Shih-chieh shu-chü, 1962 reprint.

Tu Yu 杜佑. *T'ung-tien* 通典. Taipei, 1959 reprint.

T'ung-chih t'iao-ko 通制條格. Peking, 1930 edition.

Umehara Kaoru 梅原郁. "Seitō no uma to Shisen no cha" 青唐の馬と四川の茶. *Tōhō gakuhō* 東方学報 (Kyoto) 45 (1973): 195–244.

Vaṣṣāf. *Kitāb-i mustatāb-i Vassaf al-hazrat*. Bombay, 1852–53.

Wada Hisanori 和田久徳. "Tōnan Ajia ni okeru shoki kakyō shakai 東南アジアにおはる初期華僑社会. (960–1279)." *Tōyō gakuhō* 東洋学報 42, 1 (1959): 76–106.

———. "Tōnan Ajia ni okeru Kakyō shakai no seiritsu" 東南アジアにおはる華僑社会の成立. *Sekai no Rekishi* 世界の歴史. Tokyo, 1961.

Wang An-shih 王安石. *Chou-kuan hsin-i* 周官新義. In Yüeh-ya t'ang ts'ung-shu

Wang Ch'eng 王稱. *Tung-tu shih-lüeh* 東都事略. Taipei, 1967 reprint.

Wang Chi-lin 王吉林. "Ch'i-tan yü Nan T'ang wai-chiao kuan-hsi chih t'an-t'ao 契丹與南唐外交關係之探討. *Yu-shih hsüeh-chih* 幼獅學誌 5. 2 (December 1966): 1–15.

Wang Ch'in-jo 王欽若. *Ts'e-fu yüan-kuei* 册府元龜. Hong Kong, 1960 edition.

Wang Kuei 王珪. *Hua-yang chi* 華陽集. In Ssu-k'u ch'üan-shu chen-pen

四庫全書珍本 edition.

Wang Kuo-wei, ed. 王國維. *Meng-ta pei-lu* 蒙韃備錄. In *Wang Kuan-t'ang ch'üan-chi* 王觀堂先生全集. Taipei, 1968.

Wang Mai 王邁. *Ch'ü-hsüan chi* 臞軒集. In Ssu-k'u ch'üan-shu chen-pen 四庫全書珍本 edition.

Wang Ming-sheng 王鳴盛. *Shih-ch'i-shih shang-ch'üeh* 十七史商榷. Ts'ung-shu chi-ch'eng 叢書集成 edition.

Wang P'u 王溥. *Wu-tai hui-yao* 五代會要. Taipei, 1963.

Wang Shih-lun 王士倫. "Wu-tai Wu Yüeh te liang-chien wen-shu" 五代吳越的兩件文書. *Wen wu* 文物 (January 1960), pp. 65–66.

Wang Yü-ch'eng 王禹偁. *Hsiao-hsü wai-chi* 小畜外集. Shanghai: Commercial Press, n.d.

Watanabe Michio 渡辺道夫. "Goetsu koku no kenkoku katei" 吳越国の建国過程. *Shikan* 史観 56 (September 1959): 93–104.

————. "Goetsu koku no shihai kōzō" 吳越国の支配構造. *Shikan* 史観 76 (October 1967): 33–51.

Wei Cheng 魏徵 et al. *Sui shu* 隋書. Peking, 1973 edition.

Wei Hsiang 韋驤. *Ch'ien-t'ang chi* 錢塘集. In Ssu-k'u ch'üan-shu chen-pen 四庫全書珍本 edition.

Wei Shou 魏收. *Wei-shu* 魏書. In *Erh-shih wu-shih* 二十五史. Taipei, 1955–1956 reprint.

Weng Tu-chien 翁獨健. "Wo-t'o tsa-k'ao" 斡脫雜考. *Yen-ching hsüeh-pao* 燕京學報 29 (1941): 201–218.

Wu Ch'ien 吳潛. *Hsü-kuo kung tsou-i* 許國公奏議. Ts'ung-shu chi-ch'eng 叢書集成 edition.

————. *Lü-chai i-chi* 履齊遺集. In Ssu-k'u chüan-shu chen-pen 四庫全書珍本 edition.

Wu Jen-ch'en 吳任臣. *Shih-kuo ch'un-ch'iu* 十國春秋. Taipei, 1962.

Yamada Kentarō 山田憲太郎. *Tō-zai kōyaku-shi* 東西香藥史. Tokyo, 1956.

————. *Kōryō no michi* 香料の道. Tokyo, 1977.

Yamaguchi Zuihō 山口瑞鳳. "Hakuran to Sumpa no Rlangs shi" 白蘭と'Sumpa の Rlangs' 氏. *Tōyō gakuhō* 東洋学報 52 (1969–70): 1–61.

Yamauchi Masahiro 山内正博. "Nan-Sō seiken no sui-i" 南宋政權の推移. *Sekai rekishi* 世界歷史. Tokyo: Iwanami Shoten, 1970.

Yanai Watari 箭内亙. *Mōkoshi Kenkyū* 蒙古史研究. Tokyo, 1930.

Yang Chieh 楊傑. *Wu-wei chi* 無爲集. In Ssu-k'u ch'üan-shu chen-pen 四庫全書珍本 edition.

Yang P'ei-kuei 楊培桂. *Yüan-tai ti-fang cheng-fu* 元代地方正府. Taipei, 1975.

Yao Ssu-lien 姚思廉. *Liang shu* 梁書. Peking, 1973 reprint.

Yao Ts'ung-wu 姚從吾. "Meng-ku mieh-Chin chan-cheng-te fen-hsi" 蒙古滅金戰爭的分析. In Chang Ch'i-yün 張其昀, *Chung-kuo chan-*

shih lun-chi 中國戰史論集. Taipei: Chung-hua wen-hua, 1954.

————. "Chiu *Yüan-shih* chung Ta-lu hua-ch'ih ch'u-ch'i te pen-i wei
'hsüan-ch'a' shuo" 舊元史中達魯花赤初期的本義爲宣差說. *Wen
shih che hsüeh-pao* 文史哲學報 12 (1963): 1–20.

————. "*Hei-Ta shih-lüeh*-chung so-shuo Wo-k'uo-t'ai han shih-tai Hu
ch'eng-hsiang shih-chi k'ao" 黑韃事略中所說窩闊台汗時代胡丞相
事蹟考. *Sung-shih yen chiu chi 5* 宋史研究集. Taipei: Chung-hua
Ts'ung-shu Pien-shen Wei-yüan hui, 1970.

Yeh Shih 葉適. *Yeh Shih chi* 葉適集. In *Shui-hsin pieh-chi* 水心別集.
Peking: Chung-hua, 1961.

Yen Shu 晏殊. *Yüan-hsien i-wen* 元獻遺文. In Ssu-k'u ch'üan-shu chen-
pen 四庫全書珍本 edition.

Yi Kibaek 李其白. *Han'guk-sa Sillon* 韓國史新論. Seoul, 1976 Rev. ed.

Yi Kyubo 李奎報. *Koryŏ Myŏnghyŏn Chip* 高麗明賢集. Vol. 1. Seoul,
1973.

Yi Pyŏngdo 李丙燾. *Koryŏ Sidae-ŭi Yŏngu* 高麗時代의研究. Seoul, 1958.

————. *Hanguk-sa* 韓國史. Seoul, 1961.

Yi Usŏng 李佑成. "Koryŏ Chunggi-ŭi Minjok Sŏsasi," 高麗中期의民族
敍事詩. *Sŏnggyun-gwan Taehakkyo Nonmun chip* 成均館大學校
論文集 7 (1962): 84–117.

Yü Chi 虞集. *Tao-yüan hsüeh-ku lu* 道園學古錄. Taipei, 1968.

Yüan Chi 袁冀. "Yüan-tai chih Wei-wu-erh" 元代文畏兀兒. In *Yüan-
shih yen-chiu lun-chi* 元史研究論集. Taipei, 1974.

Yüan Hsieh 袁燮. *Chieh-chai chi* 絜齋集. In Ssu-k'u ch'üan-shu chen pen
四庫全書珍本 edition.

Yüan Tien-chang 元典章. Taipei: Wen-hai ch'u-pan she, 1964.

Index

Designer: Randall Goodall
Compositor: Asco Trade Typesetting Ltd.
Printer: Braun-Brumfield, Inc.
Binder: Braun-Brumfield, Inc.
Text: 10/12 Apollo
Display: Apollo